MY
DIARIES
Part
Two

BOOKS BY WILFRID SCAWEN BLUNT

PROSE

THE FUTURE OF ISLAM 1882
IDEAS ABOUT INDIA 1885
THE SECRET HISTORY SERIES
  I THE SECRET HISTORY OF THE ENGLISH OCCU-
     PATION OF EGYPT 1907
  II INDIA UNDER RIPON 1909
  III GORDON AT KHARTOUM 1911
  IV THE LAND WAR IN IRELAND 1912
  V MY DIARIES PART I. [THE SCRAMBLE FOR
     AFRICA] 1919
  VI MY DIARIES PART II. [THE COALITION
     AGAINST GERMANY] 1920

POETRY

LOVE SONNETS OF PROTEUS 1880
THE WIND AND THE WHIRLWIND 1883
IN VINCULIS 1889
A NEW PILGRIMAGE 1889
ESTHER AND LOVE LYRICS 1892
GRISELDA 1893
SATAN ABSOLVED 1899
SEVEN GOLDEN ODES OF ARABIA 1903
POETICAL WORKS. A COMPLETE EDITION 1914
POEMS [SELECTION BY FLOYD DELL] 1923

MY DIARIES

Being a Personal Narrative of Events 1888-1914

By
WILFRID SCAWEN BLUNT

With a Foreword by Lady Gregory

PART TWO
[1900-1914]

NEW YORK   ALFRED A. KNOPF   MCMXXIII

FOREWORD TO PART II

No further preface is needed for the present volume more than that prefixed to Part I of these "Diaries," except a brief one of apology for the short period which has been allowed to elapse between the latest of the events recorded in it and their appearance to-day in print. This has seemed a political necessity forced upon the Diarist by the ungenerous terms imposed by the allied Governments at Paris on their opponents vanquished in the war, terms which are still not definitely settled and against which it may be yet possible to appeal on grounds of truth and honour.

For the benefit of those who would follow the logic of events leading to the Great War of 1914, and especially to the war with Turkey and the declaration of a British Protectorate in Egypt, readers are invited to take notice of the Chronology printed as No. VIII of the Appendix. It has been carefully drawn up, and will be found of use to them in forming a correct historic judgment.

W. S. B.

NEWBUILDINGS PLACE, SUSSEX.
Christmas, 1919.

CONTENTS

PART II

1900 TO 1914

APPENDICES

PART TWO

THE COALITION AGAINST GERMANY

PART II

1900 TO 1914

CHAPTER I

DEATH OF QUEEN VICTORIA, 1901

" *23 Jan.*, 1901. *Sheykh Obeyd.*
The Queen is dead of an apoplectic stroke and the great Victorian age is at an end."

Such is almost the first entry in my diary of the new year and the new century. I was in Egypt when the tidings reached me. It was the second day of the Bairam festival, and all our country folk at Sheykh Obeyd were keeping holiday, a glorious morning of sunshine, and I had been watching the foxes in the garden at play among the beans which were coming into flower. It was thus the news reached me. The entry goes on:

" This is notable news. It will mean great changes in the world, for the long understanding amongst the Emperors that England is not to be quarrelled with during the Queen's lifetime will now give place to freer action. The Emperor William does not love his uncle, our new king. On the other hand, it may possibly lead to a less bloody régime in South Africa; not that the Prince of Wales very likely is any more humane than his mother, who had a craze for painting the map Imperial red, but because he knows European opinion better and the limitations of England's power and the necessity of moderating English arrogance. The Queen it was easy to flatter and mislead, the only paper she read was the ' Morning Post,' and the people about her did not dare tell her the real truth of things, but the Prince of Wales hears and knows everything that goes on abroad far more than does Lord Salisbury. All this is to the good. I suppose there must be a new dissolution of Parliament — this also is for the good. As to Her Majesty personally, one does not like to say all one thinks even in one's journal. By all I have ever heard of her she was in her old age a dignified but rather commonplace

1

good soul, like how many of our dowagers, narrow-minded in her
view of things, without taste in art or literature, fond of money, having
a certain industry and business capacity in politics, but easily flattered
and expecting to be flattered, quite convinced of her own providential
position in the world and always ready to do anything to extend
and augment it. She has been so long accustomed to success that
she seems to have imagined that everything she did was wise and
right, and I should not be surprised if the discreditable failure in
South Africa had hastened her end. I see that Roberts went down
to Osborne just before the seizure took place, and perhaps she may
have insisted upon hearing the whole truth from him and, realizing
it for the first time, have had the stroke of which she died. We
shall probably be kept in the dark about this for a long while, for
the public has got to look upon the old lady as a kind of fetish or
idol, and nobody, even now she is dead, will dare print a word not
to her glorification.

"*3rd Feb.*— The Prince of Wales has been proclaimed as Edward
VII and begins his reign with the usual acclamations of the vulgar,
the vulgar in this instance including everybody, all his little failings
forgotten or hidden well out of sight. He has certain good qualities
of amiability and a Philistine tolerance for other people's sins which
endear him to rich and poor, from archbishops down to turf book-
makers, and the man in the street. He will make an excellent
king for twentieth century England. His nephew, the Emperor
William, has come forward to stand his sponsor in face of the world,
an evil conjunction, for William is the Apostle of European violence.
All the same I should not be surprised to see German influence
brought to bear upon the Boer war. Our people are pretty nearly
at their wits' end what to do in South Africa. The war is costing
them a million and a half a week and the financial gamblers are
losing money. There is a reaction against the war now that it looks
like a losing concern, and perhaps they may be glad of a pretext,
such as the Queen's death affords, to try and bring about an arrangement with the Boers. William would be flattered to be the
Deus ex machina and so recover his popularity in Germany which has
been much compromised by his refusal to receive old Kruger. I am
not sure, however, that the Boers will accept anything short of entire
independence. There is talk of the Queen having expressed a strong
wish for peace on her death-bed. What I hear through a very
confidential channel is that Her Majesty's last wish was a very human
one, that her little dog should be allowed to jump up on her bed
and that it was with her till she died.

"*6th Feb.*— We are preparing for another desert expedition.
Things go on in South Africa without change, the Boers having

overrun the British colonies and cut the railway lines and Kitchener
and the army are at a deadlock, unable to move, the soldiers tired
of it and pinched for supplies. There is a report, however, that
the arrangement entered into with Portugal is to come into effect
and that English troops are to be landed in Delagoa Bay. It is
very doubtful, however, whether this will affect the issue much.

"The new hero in England just now is the Emperor William,
whom all abused and laughed at four years ago and whose boots
our people are now licking. There is nothing so mean in the world
as the British mob, unless it be the British aristocracy, but now our
fine lords and ladies, though they adulate royalty, do so with their
tongues in their cheeks, and this saves to some extent their self-
respect. Wilhelm, however, has been made a Field Marshal of the
British army! and I verily believe our people would offer him the
crown of England if he expressed a wish for it. I suppose all this
means that Edward VII has joined the Triple Alliance.

"The Duke of Aosta is attending the old Queen's funeral as a
persona grata on account of Princess Hélène and her sister the
Queen of Portugal, to whose good will very likely the Delagoa Bay
job is due. These things are managed nowadays between Kings and
Princes far more than between Ministers and Ambassadors, and royalty
was never in such high feather as now. The Queen has left an
unknown number of millions, it is said, to her family, but the heir
to the Crown is to have his debts paid by the nation at a time when
not a single million has been spared for the famine in India — truly
we deserve to follow Spain and Rome and the other Empires into
the gulf. There is an article in the ' Fortnightly' signed ' Calchas'
closely on the lines of George's conversation with me eighteen months
ago about the coming struggle of the Empires to eat each other up.
I wonder what George thinks now of his precious policy of forcing
on the war and getting a leader for his government who would allow
him and the other young bloods of the Tory party their ' occasional
amusements,' I think that was his phrase the day we went up
Chanclebury Ring together and he foreshadowed to me the policy of
world-grabbing Chamberlain was to inaugurate.

"13*th Feb.*— Charlie Adeane spent yesterday with us and we
took him for a gallop round the Birkeh. Hampden writes that the
war must go on until every Boer has been killed or wounded or
made prisoner, but he says nothing now about deporting the Boer
women, perhaps because that part of the work has been already done.
His *saugrenu* opinions are of value because he gets them direct from
Chamberlain.

"14*th Feb.*— To-day, while we were waiting for luncheon, we heard
screams from the kitchen, and running to the window, I saw an

old woman rush out brandishing a log of wood. I supposed at first it was a domestic quarrel of the cook's, but as everybody in the house was taking part in the fray, I went down into the yard to see what the case really was, and found them hauling a wolf out of the kitchen by a rope, which they had got round its neck, belabouring it the while with staves. The cook's boy was following them with his hand badly bitten. It appears that the boy had been left in charge of the stewpans, and, while he was watching them, what he thought was a dog, but which was really a wolf, looked in at the door. The boy turned to drive it out, when it sprang up at him and bit him on the hands. He caught it, however, by the throat (or rather, he afterwards explained, by the ears, which he said he could not let go, thus illustrating the proverb) and fell on it, while an old woman who was also there beat it with a log of wood. Then others came, and the boy still holding fast, they got the rope round its neck. When laid on the ground in the yard, the wolf pretended to be dead, though he did not look much hurt, but all declared he was mad and begged me to shoot him, and so reluctantly I did. He died without a groan, and from first to last did not make a sound. He was a fine dog-wolf, about the size of a collie dog, with reddish legs. and altogether a good deal redder than European wolves are, and a fine set of teeth. The boy was rather badly bitten, and after having his wounds washed, we sent him straight to Cairo to the Hydrophobic hospital. I cannot think the wolf was mad, as he was fat and in fine condition. He had no foam at the mouth, nor a haggard eye, nor any appearance of disease. I think rather, this being their breeding time, when they are bolder than usual, he simply followed his nose to a meal. We have often heard him lately howling in the garden, and once at night in the yard, so he probably knew his way about. The old woman, whose clothes had been torn and her legs bitten, but not badly, at once when the wolf was dead took some hairs from him to dress her wound with, and the heart was kept for the boy to eat. I had the wolf skinned; he was a powerful beast, with immense muscles in the throat and great depth of chest. There is at least one other in the garden; indeed, I hear one howling as I write."

N.B. Naturalists affirm that there are no true wolves in Egypt, and the red colour of this one seems to show him to have been a jackal of the large kind which frequents Egyptian gardens. I am, however, certain that the true wolf is also found in the desert east of the Nile, for I have several times seen them at close quarters. The true wolf is a desert animal, and like other wolves, attacks sheep, hovering round the Bedouin encampments for the purpose. Suliman has sometimes suffered from their depredations just outside our garden wall, and in the hot weather they come inside it for the sake of the shade and the water. They breed, however, far away in the desert, whereas the jackal seldom leaves the cultivated district. I have measured wolf tracks in the desert sand as large as my hand.

This incident, which had a tragic sequel, as will be seen later, occurred while we were in full preparation for a desert journey of exploration in the Kalala mountains, and we left Sheykh Obeyd the following morning (15th February), and remained absent till 2nd March, during which time we had no communication whatever with the outer world. It was a very interesting expedition, covering a good deal of unexplored and difficult mountain land, following the romantic Wady Dem Dem to its source at the extreme ridge of the mountain overlooking the Red Sea and the Sinai Peninsula.

On our return after sixteen days' absence we found the tragedy of the wolf already far advanced, and ten days later my diary contains the following:

" 13th March.— The poor boy Mohammed Sueylim, who was bitten by the wolf, is dead. He had been treated in Cairo on the Pasteur system and returned to us from the hospital on the 7th, having finished, they said, his cure. He was in good health and spirits and was at work on Friday in the kitchen as usual, but in the evening he complained that his arm hurt him, and we sent him to sleep at home with his family, intending that he should go back next day to see his doctor at Cairo, but his father, old Sueylim, objected to this, and he did not go. On the 9th he came with his father to the house, looking much frightened, and saying that he had a swelling in his throat and could neither eat nor drink, but still the father would not consent to his going back to the hospital. In the afternoon he was reported to be better, but it was followed by a bad night, and early on the 10th he was taken to Cairo. There the Italian Doctor Simon saw him and sent a note back with him to say he certainly had hydrophobia. He would have detained the boy, but the father would not allow him to remain in the hospital for fear they would dissect the boy if he should die there. However, on the morning of the 11th Sueylim took him in again, but again would not leave him, and the next night the boy, having gone raving mad, died.

" This is a horrible thing for which there seems no accounting according to any theory of Providence, for it is not even a case of our miserable civilization being in fault. It seems as if it might have happened in a pure state of nature, for here at Sheykh Obeyd the wild beasts have been allowed to come and go as they please without interference, nor have they ever before given trouble. Or is hydrophobia an effect of the unnatural condition of the tame dog,

communicated to him by the wolf? Anyhow, it is a pitiful event.
The boy was his father's only son and support, who was doing his
work quietly and well in the kitchen. The wolf, too, they tell me,
leaves a widow and cubs in the garden. The old man complained
pathetically of his loss. ' I have seven daughters,' he said, ' anyone
of which the wolf would have been welcome to, and he has taken my
only son!' "

As to hydrophobia being perhaps an effect of civilization, there is
more to be said in favour of its being so than I first imagined. I
find that all the old travellers in Egypt, or at any rate many of them,
make the remark as a noticeable circumstance that the dogs in Egypt,
though there are so many of them, do not go mad. Hydrophobia
seems to have been introduced with other Western diseases from
Europe during the nineteenth century.

" 16th *March.*— Left Sheykh Obeyd with my nurse for Europe,
leaving Anne and Judith to follow later, and slept at Alexandria,
especially to see Dr. Ruffer, on whom I called in the morning at
his villa at Ramleh. I went on purpose to consult him as a pupil
of Pasteur on our kitchen tragedy. What he told me is briefly this.
He tells me that, whereas only 13 per cent. of bites inflicted by dogs
proved by dissection to have been mad are followed by hydrophobia,
it is more serious in the case of wolf bites, 60 or 70 per cent. being
the proportion of the bites followed by the disease. On the other
hand, he tells me that the Pasteur treatment itself kills a proportion
of 2 per cent. of the cases where it is used. It would therefore, he
considers, be most rash to have oneself treated on the Pasteur system
in the case of a simple dog bite and unless the dog had been ascertained
by dissection to be mad. In the case of wolves or jackals, however,
the advantage of the treatment would be far greater, though it would
not be at all certain. In the case of being bitten Dr. Ruffer recommends nitric acid as the best immediate treatment of the wound.
Burning, he says, is quite insufficient, but he is not very encouraging
as to any cure."

Ruffer's opinion is of value as coming from so distinguished a
disciple of Pasteur. I remember asking him at the end of our talk
whether in his own case he would submit himself to the Pasteur treatment if bitten by a dog ascertained to be mad. He said: " I think
so, but I should first make my will." My impression is that he
believed in the Pasteur treatment as of practical utility only in the
case of wolf and jackal bites, while there was a certain risk of 2 per
cent. in all cases subjected to the treatment whether the dog was
mad or not.

This was the end of our stay in Egypt that winter of 1900-1901.
I had a pleasant voyage from Alexandria to Marseilles in company

with Lord and Lady Chelsea, Hedworth Lambton, Lady Wolverton,
and Lady St. Oswald. With Lambton, who was then in command
of the Royal yacht, I had much conversation about Arabi, whom
he had been to see three years before in Ceylon, a conversation which I
think had much to do, seeing his position with the new King, with
Arabi's release later. He is a good fellow and a gallant officer, and
we made friends.

After spending a week at Hyères on our way homewards with the
Wyndhams, who were established there for the winter, and where I
found George with his son Percy, I went on to England, arriving at
Newbuildings on the 10th of April, where I take up my diary.

" 19th April.— Parliament met yesterday and Hicks-Beach's budget
has produced a sensation. He avows a deficit of 55 millions, and
that the South African War has already cost 152 millions, which means
that it will cost fully the 200 millions I predicted when the war
began. He also had the courage to say that the working class which
made the war ought to be taxed for it, and has clapped a duty on
sugar and coals as well as an extra twopence on the income tax. This
is better than I had dared hope from the Tories, though by rights
the whole deficit should have been raised at once by a 20/- in the £
income tax if necessary.

"I went to Park Lane and found George Wyndham rather crest-
fallen over the narrow majorities the Government got last night and
the show up of his preposterous war 'amusement.' He said he was
all against the sugar and coal taxes as they would make the voters
'tired of the Empire.' Doubtless, too, he is angry with Hicks-Beach
for his plain speaking, for George has always been a member of the
intrigue which, as he told me two years ago, had for its object to get
rid of the old Conservative leaders, especially of Hicks-Beach, who
stood in the way of their little war amusements. George, however,
will not take it too much to heart. His theory of politics is that a
politician should 'play the game,' and that he owes no duty except
to his party. All the same he is more responsible for the war than
anybody else not actually in the Cabinet, for he was one of those
who under Rhodes' inspiration worked to bring it about. It is amusing to see that Rhodes, whose prime object in making the war was to
slip out of his personal responsibility for the raid indemnity, a matter
of a million sterling, has succeeded in getting the Government to wipe
that matter publicly off the financial slate.

"After my talk with George, Sibell took me with her to Grosvenor
House where we found the young Duke, her son, resplendent in
uniform, having just come back from seeing Roberts of whom he has
been begging a transference from the army to the Yeomanry. The

morning sun was streaming through the windows, which made the rooms very beautiful, the 'Blue Boy' being especially splendid.

" 21*st April* (*Sunday*).— To see Meynell, who was as usual full of gossip. It appears that the King's debts have been paid off privately by his friends, one of whom is said to have lent £100,000, and satisfies himself with £25,000 in repayment plus a Knighthood.

" 22*nd April*.— Hampden dined with me in Chapel Street. As to South Africa he is quite converted now to ideas of peace and economy, the effect of the extra twopence on the income tax. He has two sons still at the war.

" 15*th May*.— As I was walking in Rotten Row this morning I was accosted by an imposing personage with the face and figure of a Roman Emperor, seated on a huge drayhorse, and I recognized in him John Redmond. I had not seen him since 1888 when I knew him in Ireland, and he has since become head of the Irish parliamentary party. He was very cordial in his greeting, and I was able most truthfully to congratulate him on the position of Irish affairs, which have never been so hopeful since Parnell died. We talked about George Wyndham. ' He is a nice fellow,' said Redmond, ' and I like him much personally, as we all do.'

" 25*th May*.— Arabi has been pardoned. A fortnight ago I had a letter from him from Ceylon, telling me that the Duke of Cornwall had given him his royal promise to do what he could to obtain his release, and this is the result. If he had been recalled sixteen years ago, as Gladstone intended, he might have been of great use in reforming Egypt, but as it is the pardon has come too late. Arabi will find that the world has marched far during his absence, and the National Party has followed new lines which are not altogether his.

" 11*th June*.— To Sotheby's where the Ashburnham MSS. are being sold. They are very splendid, but quite beyond my reach as a collector. I intend to confine my purchasing to Oriental MSS., where the field is open to a moderate purse, as for some inexplicable reason no one cares for them. Being in Quaritch's shop a few days ago I heard the Librarian of the Bodleian declare that he was inundated with offers of these, for which there were no buyers. With Cockerell's help I have got together about twenty illuminated ones at prices ranging from £4 to £10, though I gave £50 for one, a very fine 'Shah Nameh,' which had belonged to Morris. Some day these Oriental MSS. will be worth much larger sums, analogous to those given for European ones of equally fine execution.

" 14*th June*.— Hampden, whose son has just returned from South Africa, leaving another son still fighting there, and a nephew Campion dead, is now loud in denouncing the war. He would like to have Kruger and Rhodes and Chamberlain tied in a bag together and droppeᴄ into the sea. This from the ex-Liberal Unionist whip is a pretty good conversion.

"The Ashburnham MSS. have sold for £33,000, the finest of them a French version of *Lancelot du Lac* for £1,800, a cheap price for perhaps the most beautiful book in the world.

"*27th June.*— I have been going over old letters. Of men's letters George Wyndham's are by far the best, and I have a good series of them written at the most interesting period of his life, that of his literary interlude between the days when he was Arthur Balfour's private Secretary, and his taking office as Under Secretary of State. They are all a man's letters to a man can be, in some ways better even than Lytton's, wonderful as those are.

"*29th June.*— Hedworth Lambton came over from Portsmouth, where he is in command of the King's yacht. He tells me the Duke of Cornwall's intervention in favour of Arabi's must certainly have been prearranged, probably before he left England, with the King. I took him over to Crabbet where he greatly admired our horses, regretting that his Majesty did not breed Arabs instead of Hackneys.

"*6th July.*— Our annual Arab sale. A great concourse of people from London, including not a few notabilities. We sold twelve lots at an average of over 120 guineas, four (stallions) were bought for the Indian Government, three for New South Wales, two for Java, and one for Germany.

"*25th July.*— News has come of a conflict at Sheykh Obeyd between some English officers fox hunting, and Mutlak, and our Arab guards. Our people have been arrested, and I went up to London to the Foreign Office for information and to protest. Old Giglamps (Sir Thomas Sanderson) received me with a little official manner, and talked of its being necessary to leave the matter to be settled by law, but I overbore him with a torrent of indignation, which is the best way to break down the official fence, and he became amiable, discussed the question with me, promised to speak about it at once to Cromer and advised me to address Lord Lansdowne formally, stating my view of the case. We parted the best of friends." [This was the beginning of a long correspondence between me and the Foreign Office, which as it is embalmed in a Blue Book of forty-seven pages, I need not here relate in detail. The Blue Book is one of the most amusing ever issued by the Foreign Office.]

"*26th July.*— Lunched with Frank Lascelles at the Travellers Club, and we talked of old days and of present days too. His success as Ambassador at Berlin, where he has captured the friendship of the Emperor William, is the greatest diplomatic achievement of our day, which he attributes modestly to his talent for making small jokes of the kind which royal personages like. He would not hear of Wilhelm's being called ' a clever ass.' ' No,' he said, ' not at all. He knows everything and does everything, including painting and fiddling, and most things he knows well. In shipbuilding and engineering he surprises all the experts who have to do with him. Also he is a man. He really commands his army, and really governs his Empire.' ' A second Frederick the Great,' I suggested. ' Just so,' he said. ' That is what he would like to be thought.'

" *27th July.*— With Cockerell to Parkstone to see Alfred Russel Wallace, the Grand Old Man of Science. Cockerell, who knew him already, had asked him to have a talk with me about the prehistoric horse, and an excellent talk it was. He lives in an uninteresting little red villa near the station, but the old man himself is a treasure. Though not able to give me much information on the subject I had come to him about, the early domestication of animals and especially of the horse, he was most instructive about the primitive races of mankind. He divides mankind into three great families, the White, the Black and the Yellow. Among the first he classes not only Semites and the lighter coloured Hindoos, but also the Dravidians, the Hairy Ainus and the Australians. He classes them by their features, and by the quality of their hair, which is long and wavy. The black races are the negroes, the negritos and all others who have crisped hair. The yellow race is characterized by comparatively hairless faces, and the absence of wave in their hair. The Aryans, he says, are a mere linguistic division of the white family, the distinction has nothing to do with the race. He holds it probable that civilization had only one birthplace, and from it had spread everywhere. The taming of animals was imitated from a first example of success by tribes communicating with the successful tribe. His socialistic talk was also interesting, and he displayed wonderful vigour of intellect for so old a man. He complimented me on my pamphlet, ' The Shame of the XIXth Century ' and expressed strong views on the pauperization of India. There was a number of the paper ' Light ' lying on his table, and I asked him if he still adhered to his belief in spiritualism, and he said very positively that he had not receded from it in the smallest degree."

The month of August was occupied with a driving tour I made to Clouds and the West of England. While at Clouds I saw a good deal of one of our Royal Princesses, who was staying there, and whom it fell to my lot to entertain on a number of drives seated by me on the box seat, for I had my four in hand there. This was Princess Louise, daughter of Princess Christian and granddaughter of Queen Victoria. My conversations with this royal lady were a revelation to me of the political atmosphere in which our royal personages move.

"*20th Sept.*— In London. A day of disaster for His Majesty's arms by land and sea. Two defeats in South Africa, three guns lost to Botha in Natal, the 17th Lancers cut to pieces in Cape Colony, and His Majesty's ship 'Cobra' totally wrecked off the Yorkshire coast. I called on George Wyndham and talked the situation over with him. The whole army, he says, is overdone and stale, the 17th Lancers have been on the run since the 10th of May, trying to catch the Boers, without a day's rest, and it is the same with them all, horses and men can do no more. He thinks now the winter is over and the grass up on the veldt, our army will have to mark time and stay on the defensive till next year. He is beginning to think we shall have to make terms with the Boers. I suggested a 'Reservation' for them such as the Basutos have where they could be free and govern themselves and live in their own way. He told me in confidence he had long ago proposed exactly this solution as the only one to end the war. The Boers ought to be allowed a 'blow hole.' What they wanted was to lead a patriarchal life according to their own ideas. He thought that if this was allowed they would be eventually amalgamated with the rest of South Africa by the natural processes of progress. George is much pleased with his work in Ireland, and is glad now he did not get the War Office as he had wished. He is taking my advice of doing nothing, and waiting instead of forcing the situation, as people were urging him to do. He described a yachting tour he has made in very stormy weather with his son Percy. We also talked over the Fox-hunting case at Cairo; he has been staying with Lord Lansdowne.

"*21st Sept.*— There is another defeat this morning, two more guns taken. Hampden is now all for ending the war.

"*25th Sept.*— Rennell Rodd is gazetted our Ambassador to Rome.

"*28th Sept.*— Cromer's marriage with Lady Katharine Thynne announced.

"*3rd Oct.*— Captain H—— came to shoot with me and Neville. He has just come from the war. He thinks the fault lies in not hanging the Boers, man, woman, and child.

"*4th Oct.*— To London. Met Austin Lee at the Club. He tells me Cromer's engagement was a very sudden affair. Cromer had been down to lay a wreath on his late wife's grave at Bournemouth, and had taken his place in the steamer for Cairo with Gorst. Gorst had gone on to Paris, and he was to meet him there, but this engagement has intervened.

"*11th Oct.*— At Gros Bois on my way to Egypt, and find here a large party of French people come over from Paris for the day, the Duchesse de Trévise and her daughters, and her son-in-law, de Brissac, and with them Lady Windsor and Lady Paget. In the afternoon I was taken out shooting by Wagram, the other two guns being country neighbours, de Kergoulet and Lagrange, in the Forêt de Notre Dame. Berthe's two girls are growing up charming, with the prettiest possible manners, and quite unspoilt.

"*13th Oct.* (*Sunday*).— The ladies all went off in Berthe's new automoblie to Vaux, and I with Wagram to Paris. There we were met by Alexandre, and after breakfasting at Durand's we went to see a new play at the Theâtre Antoine, 'L'honneur,' a piece translated from the German of an exaggerated Ibsen kind, which interested me not a little. Alexandre acted the cicerone there to his father and me, explaining the play to us learnedly as it went on.

"*14th Oct.*— Shooting again with Wagram. All his ground here is beautiful and of great extent, and he has pride in every inch of it. Some 7,000 acres, if I understand him rightly, in a ring fence, for France a very large estate, and only surpassed anywhere near Paris by those of the Rothschilds, who have between them about 30,000 acres.

"*15th Oct.*— After a last day's shooting I left in the evening for Marseilles and Egypt with Anne, who had joined me in Paris.

"*24th Oct.*— *At Sheykh Obeyd.* Mohammed Abdu came to spend the morning. He tells me he has incurred the Khedive's displeasure by having performed the marriage ceremony for one of the Khedivial Princes in Switzerland this summer. The Khedive had given his permission, but had intended to back out of it. We discussed the Fox-hunting case. This, he assures me, contains not merely strainings of the law, but positive illegalities on the part of the English authorities. Then we talked of Arabi's return to Egypt. Mohammed Abdu blames him for having held communications with the newspapers, and without waiting to ascertain the true state of things, having proclaimed that everything done by the English in Egypt was good. This has got him into trouble with the native official world, which has given him the cold shoulder, though he is much run after by the common herd. Boys follow him in the street shouting '*Allah yensurak ya Arabi!*' (God give you the victory O Arabi!), and in the mosque when he goes to pray the poorer sort kiss his hands. He, Abdu, disapproves of this, and has not called on him, but I think I have persuaded him that it will be best to make the most of the popularity, and he has promised to meet Arabi at my house when he comes. I am of opinion that a deal might be profitably made of Arabi in the cause of Egyptian freedom, but Arabi's popularity with the vulgar was always a source of jealousy with the well-to-do.

"Later Raffiuddin Ahmed, a leader of the Mohammedan community in London, called on me, and I had with him also a long and interesting conversation. He told me things that were interesting of the influence over the late Queen Victoria exercised by her Indian Munshi, with whom he was intimate. Her Majesty allowed the Munshi to have the key of her despatch boxes and to read all their contents, even during the Cretan difficulty and the Sultan's war with Greece. He read the despatches every morning, and told the Queen which were the most important. The Prime Minister knew this and did not object, as the Munshi was really discreet. As soon, however, as the Queen was dead he was packed off back to India. Raffiuddin seems to have read everything I have ever written, and has a surprising memory of dates and facts. He tells me that through his friend the Munshi, he got the Queen to read my protest published in the 'Times' against the massacre of Omdurman. He was to have been put forward by Lord Salisbury for a seat in Parliament, but happened to be away in Constantinople at the time of the general elections. Now, poor man, I fear he is in very ill-health, and is on his way back to India to recover, or, as to me seems more probable, to die.

"*26th Oct.*— To-day Arabi came to lunch with us in company with Ali Fehmy and their friend the doctor. Arabi is still a hale and hearty man, and his white beard becomes him well. I found him simple and affectionate, and very grateful to me. It appears that my telegram of congratulation received by him on the 23rd of May was the first news he had of his release and pardon. It was not officially communicated to him till the 26th. I had a long talk with him about the attitude he was to observe on political affairs, and was pleased to find him with definite opinions. He is too trustful, to my mind, of English good intentions, having experienced only kind treatment during his exile, and it is right he should be grateful, otherwise his view does not differ much from mine or Abdu's. I advised him to be content with what he had already said publicly, to call on the Khedive, if the Khedive would receive him, and on Lord Cromer. He has so much dignity, frankness and honesty that his personal presence must do good. Then Mohammed Abdu came in and they embraced, and talked till luncheon, and through it and afterwards for an hour and more, recounting old experiences and discussing modern men. The meeting was eminently a success, and was really a touching one for us all in many ways. I had, however, fever on me, and was glad to get to bed as soon as they were gone."

Arabi's return to Egypt was robbed of the success it ought to have been by his initial mistake of having allowed himself to be interviewed

on his landing at Suez by one of the staff of the " Mokattam," a newspaper carried on by certain Syrians in the interest of the British
occupation, who gave a garbled account of what he had said in praise
of the reforms introduced under the English régime so as to make
it appear like a recantation of his patriotism.   The Khedive, too, never
really forgave him nor did Lord Cromer.   Arabi was too simple-
minded a man not to give opportunities to those ill disposed towards
him, and he made the mistake when calling upon Cromer of concealing the fact that he had first called on me, and this was used
against him.   On the 19th Nov. I called on Lord Cromer and spoke of
this with him, who made me a history of the pressure he had put
on the Khedive to get him to consent to the exile's return, the line
taken by him being that Arabi was no longer of any political consequence.   He had received him but they had had little conversation
together.

The history of Arabi's recall from exile is without doubt that King
Edward thought it would be politic and insisted on it with the Foreign
Office.   I have always suspected that Admiral Lambton's visit to me
at Newbuildings, though ostensibly to look at my horses, was really
in connection with this matter as during it we had talked much of
Arabi.   Lambton had been a believer in Arabi from the time of Arabi's
trial in 1882, when he had given useful evidence in his favour.   Lambton was also with the Duke of York (now King George V) when he
visited Colombo and had the talk there already referred to with Arabi.
The exile's recall had been in consequence imposed on Lord Cromer,
who was conscious that the whole case for intervention by England
in 1882 rested on the logic of Arabi's being a rebel and his patriotism
unreal.   While therefore Cromer submitted to the pressure put upon
him by the Foreign Office he was determined to neutralize the good
effect of it as an act of tardy reparation for a wrong done by managing to get the pardoned exile put in coventry by Mustapha Fehmy
and the rest of the Khedivial Ministers.   In that way Arabi's initial
popularity was neutralized and robbed of any political effect.

" *23rd Nov.*— To-day I went to see the Khedive who was as cordial
and affectionate as usual.   He began by making me an elaborate
apology for not having paid me his promised visit at Crabbet when
he was in England in June 1900 (I had not been to see him since)
and how he had several times asked Rennell Rodd, who had been
appointed by the Foreign Office to look after him, to arrange the visit,
and how Rodd had always said there was no time.   Then I thanked
him for having pardoned Arabi, and he told me that Arabi had displeased him by his political pronouncements on arrival and by his
always being with Ali Fehmy who had behaved so badly to his father
Tewfik, and how he had also heard of Mohammed Abdu's having been

to lunch with me when Arabi came to Sheykh Obeyd, and how wrong
it was of Abdu. But I told him I was the only person to blame in
the matter as I had entrapped Abdu who had been most unwilling,
and he laughed and said he would make it all right with Abdu when
he saw him. Then we talked about the Fox-hunting case and he told
me of the *peur bleue* he had been in for years past lest the English
soldiers should break in on him at Koubbah where his garden was so
little protected; also of the Omdeh of Waila having been stopped on
the road by a party of Lancers on his way home as he was riding
with two servants, and how they had struck him on the head and
how he had died a fortnight after it. He is off to Khartoum next
week and he went with me to the door shaking hands and assuring
me of his great affection and that I was the only true friend they
had in Egypt.

"*28th Nov.*— Our yearly *mowled* of Sheykh Obeyd, a festival
attended by about a thousand people and all the Arabs and Sheykhs
of the villages round, and we had horse races and *jerid* play the
whole day long in the bit of desert outside, and not a European
showed his nose from dawn to dusk.

"*19th Dec.*— Rosebery has made a speech which is causing much
excitement at home, offering himself as alternative Prime Minister
to Salisbury on equally jingo lines. Salisbury is bad enough, but
Rosebery would mean merely Government by the Stock Exchange.

"*30th Dec.*— Left Sheykh Obeyd for England, having hurried my
departure principally on account of the fox-hunting case which was
being brought forward in Parliament. We went by way of Port
Said and Brindisi. Rhodes, Jameson and other of the South African
gang were to have taken the same steamer but I believe missed it.
They had come to Egypt with the intention of going up the Nile to
Khartoum, but Cromer, who hates Rhodes, put a veto on that and
stopped the party at Assouan.

"*16th Jan.* 1902.— London. Hampden dined last night with Rosebery, where he was more or less solicited to join Rosebery's party,
and we talked over the prospects of Liberalism. My advice to him
was that if he wanted office or further employment of any kind,
Rosebery was as likely to give it him as any other, though he would
never come into office as head of the Radical party. Apart from this,
however, there were only two policies on which party lines could
run, the first of Imperialism, which meant a bid for the Empire of
the world, a gambling venture which would entail the sacrifice of
everything we have of value at home, personal liberty, freedom from
conscription and financial prosperity; the other Anti-imperialism, which
meant letting the world alone and leaving the colonies to work out

their own destinies without our interference, and the same for Ireland.

"*22nd Jan.*— Lunched with Labouchere, who was as usual very amusing, describing the intrigues and dissensions of the Liberal leaders. 'If you were to take them all together,' he said, 'and boil them in a pot, Campbell Bannerman, Asquith, Morley, Rosebery, and Grey, you would not get the worth of a mouse out of them.' Of the Liberal Imperialists none had any following in the country except Rosebery. He told, too, some interesting stories about his own past adventures, how he had ridden once from Cairo to Suez in company with Shepheard, the founder of the hotel, sleeping one night on the road, also from Damascus to Palmyra with Lady Ellenborough and her Bedouin husband Mijuel some time in the fifties, when she was still almost a young woman. And again in Mexico with a notorious robber. He was in every way most pleasant. I have known Labby now for forty years and feel a real affection for him.

"*24th Jan.*— Called on Redmond at St. Ermin's Club. He holds a high position now in the House of Commons and in the world. He was in America last autumn and tells me everyone there is pro-Boer including Roosevelt, the President.

"*28th Jan.*— I have been, since Saturday, at Hewell and have seen much of Rowton who is staying here. He has been most agreeable. I have had him pretty nearly to myself and we have made great friends. He still delights to talk of his old master Dizzy and described how they first met at Raby in 1865. There was a large party in the castle, and Rowton, a young fellow then of five-and-twenty, was asked by the ladies one evening to play the fool for their amusement, and he had sung a comic song and was in the middle of a breakdown when he caught the eye of the old man fixed on him and was filled with shame at being detected in such absurdity, but in the course of the evening a hand was laid upon his shoulder and a lugubrious voice said, 'Mr. Corry, I shall ask you some day to be my impressario.' This led to a talk on serious subjects, and eventually to Rowton's being taken on as assistant private secretary. Ralph Earle was then the first private secretary, but he threw up his position with Disraeli to take an appointment in the City soon after, and made use of his former position to look in at Downing Street and read the confidential papers for his profit on the Stock Exchange. Rowton was given his succession, but had the disagreeable task assigned him of telling Earle he was to come there no longer. Earle revenged himself by making a bitter speech against his former master at a critical moment in the House of Commons. The thing affected Dizzy deeply, less from the ingratitude shown by Earle than from shame at having been taken in and trusted his secrets to such

a man. Rowton is full of such anecdotes, and when I pressed him
to write them, even if he did not publish, confessed that the real
reason was that he lacked the literary gift and could not do it well.
He told me, too, of the story current that Dufferin was really Disraeli's
son, but he had found evidence in the papers left him that Disraeli
had only made Lady Dufferin's acquaintance six years after Dufferin
was born. Dufferin, who had heard the story, was most grateful to
Rowton for letting him have the memorandum proving this, and had
inserted it in his mother's life. Another story was of how Disraeli
came to be Christianized. Isaac Disraeli, the father, had given offence
to the Jews by his unorthodox writings and was fined £50 by his
synagogue. This angered him and he went straight away and joined
the Church of England and had his children christened, Dizzy being
then about ten years old. But for this quarrel the son never could
have got into Parliament or made even the beginning of a political
career.

" *3rd Feb.*— Lunched with Mark Napier who is just back from
India where he has been settling a legal claim for a native prince.
It had been hung up for thirteen years, but he got it pushed through
by George Curzon in ten days. (Such is the virtue of the Crabbet
Club.) He gave a good account of George and of his surprising
energy and power of work, which leaves him no time for amusement. He is master of everybody, Mark says, and so is not altogether popular with the high officials, but seemed to be so with everybody else.

" *4th Feb.*— Called on George Wyndham and had a long talk with
him about Ireland, which wholly occupies him. He is far more in
sympathy with the Nationalists than with the Castle party which he
despises for its sycophancy or the Ulster Protestants whom he dislikes for their sour bigotry. His own people, however, are constantly worrying him to coerce, and he has been obliged to make a
show of doing something in that way though most unwillingly. He
told me he had quite come to agree with me that there was no possibility of doing anything of real good in Ireland under present conditions and the less done by a Chief Secretary, the less the harm.
He thinks, however, that if Ireland could be governed as a Crown
Colony for five years things might come right. This is a curious
remedy which would need fifty, not five years to have any effect. He
was delighted when I repeated what Redmond said about him and that
the Irish members still regarded him with a friendly eye.

" Then he read me a long letter from his brother Guy written at
the end of the year, describing a fight he had been engaged in in Cape
Colony against Smuts in which he took credit that he had held his
ground. I remarked that I had thought the Boers had long ago been

cleared out of Cape Colony, at which George laughed aloud. Guy in another letter said that to try to prevent Boers going where they chose to go was like trying with a single squadron to prevent two squadrons passing a line between Bath and Salisbury. It is clear the war is far from over.

"*14th Feb.*— Found George Wyndham at breakfast and walked with him across Green Park to his Irish Office. I congratulated him on the new Japanese Alliance (the Convention of Alliance with England had been signed on 30th Jan.) which is the best thing the Government has done for a long while, but George is quite disillusioned about politics or the possibility of much affecting the course of the world's events. Chamberlain is the hero of the day in spite of his absurd blunders in South Africa, because he talks big and defies European opinion.

"There is a funny story current:

Master to Boy: "Who was it made the world?"

Boy: "Mr. Chamberlain."

Master: "Think again. Wasn't it God made the world?"

Boy: "Oh, go on! You are a pro-Boer."

"*22nd Feb.*— Rosebery has cut the Liberal painter and has passed out into the wilderness.

"*23rd Feb.*— Lord Dufferin's death is in the papers. His end was tragic, but carelessness in money matters was the weak point in his character. When he came of age, I remember hearing, he had a quite unencumbered estate of £20,000 a year, but he muddled it away, Heaven knows on what, for he was not a gambler nor a runner after women, only he kept no accounts and liked to do things on a grand scale. For the last thirty years he has lived on his pay as a Government servant, always in the highest posts. Then when his time of service was over he found himself with a large family of children and a pension of less than £3,000 a year. He took Whitaker Wright's £6,000 a year to enable him to live. In all things else he was singularly high-minded, with a chivalrous devotion to his mother, the one passion of his life. He trifled with women rather than made love to them, and when his mother died, his chief affections went to his children. He was a faithful friend, retentive of old memories and was rightly beloved by all. I knew him when he was only thirty-three, a good-looking and attractive young man travelling in the East with his mother. His marriage was arranged for him by his mother, a year or two later, and he accepted it as he would have accepted anything else from her hands.

"*28th Feb.*— Yesterday I went to see poor Peploe Brown (the painter), and found him strangely altered. He has been paralysed for some years and is now a little wizened old man, quite helpless

in his chair, but preserving all his old powers of talk. He sits there
a pathetic figure in his studio in York Place surrounded by canvases
of gigantic size, the monuments of ancient failures in his art, blind
and alone but for the devotion of a man servant who waits always
within call. This man, Fred, deserves a medal of gold if ever a
servant did, for he puts his whole soul into his service, and I fancy
even without wages, for Brown is almost penniless. Poor Brown,
what a terrible life! yet he does not complain because he can still
see light out of the corner of one eye, also he suffers no pain, and he
sleeps well.

" *2nd March (Sunday).*— Walked across the Park and lunched
with Frederic Harrison. I sat next to Miss Hobhouse, recently come
back from South Africa where she was prevented by our authorities
from landing. She is an amiable middle-aged woman, much persecuted on account of her action in the concentration camps. People are
rude to her, refuse to shake hands, and they get up to go when she
enters a drawing-room. Others of the party were Henry Arthur
Jones the playwright, young Trevelyan the poet, and Lady Gregory.

" In the evening with Lady Gregory to Newton Hall to hear
Harrison deliver his farewell address on retiring from the leadership of the Positivists. The beginning of it was rather tame and I
was dosing off when I was awakened by an allusion to my work in
Egypt and hearing my name cheered. After this Harrison gave a
really fine address, saying many hard things and true things of
modern England, touching, too, from the fact of its being his last
spoken word.

" *11th March.*— Learned last night of the defeat and capture of
Methuen by Delarey. The news of the capture was heartily cheered
by the Irish in the House. It was the King's wedding-day.

" *12th March.*— Called on Father John Gerard, S. J., in Farm Street,
whom I had last seen fifty years ago at Stonyhurst where he was
my special boy friend. He had written to me, and hence my visit.
I found him a worthy matter-of-fact Jesuit advanced in years but
preserving just the little touch of romance which had prompted his
letter to me about our childish school friendship when we were both
twelve years old. He reminded me that we used to keep caterpillars
in paper boxes and that I had insisted upon pricking holes in the
lids in the form of the constellations so that the caterpillars inside
might think they were still out of doors and could see the stars.

" *14th March.*— Methuen has been released and the newspapers
are full of praise of Delarey, the first time they have had a word of
civility for any Boer since the war began.

" *15th March.*— To the Zoölogical Gardens to look at Prevalsky's
wild horses, just arrived. They are miserable specimens, like the

poorest and weediest of the New Forest ponies, coarse-headed, knock-kneed, cat-hammed and with drooping donkey tails, yet distinctly horses.

"*17th March* (*St. Patrick's Day*).— To George Wyndham, who explained to me the difficult position he was in with the Tory Press on account of his Irish policy. 'They are all waiting,' he said, 'to pounce on me because I won't go their way in Ireland.' He promised to tell me some day the whole history of the last fortnight, as to which I gather from him that he was obliged to threaten resignation rather than go in for a policy of extreme coercion, which has always failed and will fail again. Then to John Redmond in Wynnstay Gardens. I found him just arrived by the night train from Manchester, where he spoke on Saturday, but alert and smiling. It being St. Patrick's Day, somebody had sent him a little box full of shamrock and he opened it and gave me a bunch which I shall try and grow at Newbuildings as it has a root, but he warned me it would never grow out of Ireland. We talked about George. He was perfectly aware how matters stood with him. 'I am obliged,' he said 'to be fierce with him in public, but I know he is with us in his heart, and we all know it.' I like Redmond, he is a thoroughly straightforward good fellow, strong and practical and self-reliant but not self-assertive, a worthy successor of Parnell. I was surprised to hear him regretting Rhodes' illness and saying that he would be a great loss if he died. I asked him why, and he said that Rhodes has always been a Home Ruler about Ireland as part of his Imperial Federation scheme, and also because he thought the Irish quarrel ought to be settled in the interest of the Empire. Redmond had seen a great deal of Rhodes when he was in South Africa, and believed he still held to his Home Rule opinions. My own opinion of Rhodes, on this as on other points, is that he is a rogue and a humbug. The King and Queen are sending him their royal condolences about his illness.

"*21st March.*— John Dillon was suspended last night in the House of Commons for calling Chamberlain 'a damned liar.'

"*22nd March.*— Dined in Park Lane and met there Lady Ormond and the Berkeley Pagets. George explained to me his new Irish Land Bill after dinner, which he does not profess to regard as anything but a makeshift. As far as I understand it, it is a scheme devised to buy up the quite small holdings in the West and group them into farms of fifteen and twenty acres. He again said that he was very averse from Coercion, but added that the Government might be driven into it, and it would then mean something much more than what had hitherto been done, and would involve the imprisonment of all the leaders of the League, and government by force in

Ireland after the manner of a Crown Colony. He would do what
he could to make things go quietly, but there were strong forces at
work pushing to extremities, witness the 'Times' articles. I told him
I was inviting Redmond to dinner, and asked him whether he would
come. He said there was nothing he should like better, but it would
be too dangerous in his present position, and as long as he was Chief
Secretary.

"*24th March.*— Took my niece Mary Milbanke, it being Lent,
to a mediæval morality play, 'Everyman,' being just now revived,
a terribly dreary business, which more than half reconciled me to
having been born in the nineteenth century. These ancient plays have
only an archæological interest and are impossible on our modern stage.
They are worse than the worst comic parts of Shakespeare, which is
saying a great deal, crude, childish, long-winded. The mediæval
idea of life in Christian Europe with death and hell as a perpetual
background of all pleasure, is repellent, when put nakedly before us
in action. There is a brutality in the view of all pleasure being sin-
ful, which is only tolerable when mixed with a large dose of sceptic-
ism, as in Boccaccio. These north of Europe plays with their serious intention are like having a bucket of cold and very dirty water
poured over one for a joke.

"In the evening to hear an excellent lecture by Sir William Butler
on Cromwell in Ireland, a most able and brilliant performance. I
was asked to say a few words afterwards, and did so lamely enough.

"*25th March.*— George has made a brilliant speech introducing
his Irish Land Bill, and I see Redmond and his men are very civil
to him. I pride myself on having contributed to this good feeling.

"*30th March (Easter Sunday).*— Rhodes is dead. I did the rogue
an injustice when I thought he might be shamming as a pretext for
getting away from the Cape and the prosecution of Princess Radziwill,
in which he is implicated, but Rhodes was one of those of whom
one always had to ask oneself, '*Quel interêt peut-il avoir en mourant?*'
The capitalist newspapers are, of course, full of his praises. He is
supposed to have bequeathed a part of his millions for Imperial purposes. I look on him only as a lucky speculator, a gambler on rather
wider lines than the rest, shrewd, or rather lucky, in his calculations for a long while, and then, having made a series of gross
blunders, unscrupulous enough to save most of his own money at the
expense of a war and ruin for everybody else. I suppose he will live
in history as he has given his name to Rhodesia, and has engineered
the Boer War. If the British Empire recovers from this and as-
serts itself permanently in South Africa he may count for something
more, but it is quite certain that he miscalculated the whole Transvaal
business. His pronouncements from time to time during the last

five years have been always contradicted by events. Some people
say this was only an excess of roguery. I think he really blundered
and blustered and pretended to be wise to people who looked upon
him, on account of his first successes, as an oracle. I have seen just
the same thing at Homburg in the old gambling days, when a man
who had broken the bank once was followed by admiring crowds,
who credited him with supernatural intelligence, and went on believing in him till the day he lost all and disappeared. Rhodes had
the intelligence to go away with a large share of his winnings in his
pocket, but his friends have been ruined following his lead.

"My niece Mary Milbanke is with me. I am very fond of her;
there is something soothing in her phlegmatic nature and absence
of all ambition, personal or otherwise.

"*11th April.*— 37 Chapel Street. I entertained Miss Hobhouse at
lunch with Meynell and Margaret Sackville, and we discussed Rhodes'
will, the topic of everybody's talk. It is astonishing the general adula-
tion bestowed on the man. People do not see that the £4,000,000 he
leaves to public purposes are £4,000,000 robbed from the public and
bequeathed to the ends of new robberies. Meynell was amusing and
pleasant as he always is.

"*17th April.*— St. George Lane Fox brought his cousin Lord Russell
with him to lunch with me to-day. We talked over matters connected
with Egypt and the attack I am making on Cromer as having tampered
with the Criminal Courts at Cairo. Russell, though wrong-headed,
is a very able man, and has legal experience and much practice in
speaking as alderman of the London County Council and in Committees of the House of Lords. He is also quite fearless of Governments. I should not be surprised to see him some day Opposition
leaders in the Lords. He has a good presence, a good voice, and a
wonderful memory. Our luncheon was amusing.

"*19th April.*— Hunted from Fernycroft with the Foxhounds.
Young Bron Herbert was out and rode with me very pluckily,
poor fellow, with his cork leg replacing the one lost in the Boer
War. He is a very clever and very nice young man, but has been
captured for service on the 'Times'— a bad education. His sister,
he tells me, has joined the Theosophists and gone off to live in
California.

"*26th April.*— Lady Gregory called and took me off to dinner with
her and Yeats and afterwards to a meeting of the Irish Literary
Society, where the Cuchulain Saga was discussed. I spoke on it and so
did O'Donnell, he partly in Irish, partly in English — an interesting
man. Yeats also spoke well. He is a pleasant talker on his own
subjects, and in appearance is of that most interesting dark Irish
type with pale face and lank hair.

" 5th May.— Anne writes from Egypt announcing somewhat enig-
matically that Cromer has had a final quarrel with the Khedive
and is trying to depose him. I think this not unlikely, but it would
be difficult for him to do unless the Great Powers were to decide
to divide the Mohammedan States between them. This is nearly certain to happen some day. I suppose France will be given Morocco;
Italy, Tripoli; England, Egypt; Germany, Syria and Asia Minor;
Austria, Constantinople; and Russia, Persia. [Compare Secret
Treaties of 1916.]

" 6th May.— Lunched with Ralph. He has decided at last to publish the great Byron Secret, and has drawn up the case against Byron
and Mrs. Leigh in the form of a book called 'Astarte.' This is
very ably done, but to my mind is marred by an introduction violently
attacking Murray, the publisher, with whom he has quarrelled over
Murray's recent edition of Byron's Works. I shall endeavour to get
him to modify this; indeed, I think the whole thing might without
much injustice to Lady Byron's memory be let sleep. It is an ugly
story, however told.

" 10th May.— Anne has returned from Egypt. I met her at Charing Cross and gave her breakfast here in Chapel Street and saw her
off to Newbuildings, I being obliged to go to Ockham for Sunday
with Cockerell, where Ralph is to consult us about 'Astarte' and its
form of publication.

" 11th May (Sunday).— At Ockham. Cockerell and I have spent
the day trying to persuade Lovelace to omit his attacks on Murray,
which are really undignified, and also, we think, unjust in so far as
they concern the present representative of the firm.

" 18th May (Sunday).— I have sent in my letter to Lord Salisbury. It went last night to Hatfield with a private note inside to
Schomberg McDonnell explaining that I hoped Lord Salisbury would
read it himself. It is a big venture as I am attacking Cromer personally, but in big game shooting it is safest to leave the antelopes
alone and go straight for the rhinoceros. It being holiday time makes
it a favourable moment.

" 21st May.— My bomb against Cromer has exploded with a real
bang. The 'Daily News' gives it a leading article, the 'Standard' a
whole column, the 'Morning Post' printed my letter to the Editor
and a *résumé,* the 'Chronicle' and 'Daily Mail' are also good, only
the 'Times' and 'Telegraph' fail us. It could hardly have made a
bigger noise."

The great publicity obtained on this occasion in the Press made
it unnecessary for me to pursue it further, and it was agreed not to
bring it forward in Parliament. There was, of course, not the smallest chance of obliging the Foreign Office to publish the correspondence,

and the publicity was already obtained. Moreover, before the Foreign Office Vote came on for discussion the King's illness had occurred, and nobody had any attention to pay elsewhere. The case was of importance, not so much in itself as from the demonstration it gave of the unscrupulous methods resorted to by our diplomacy at Cairo to hide its tampering with the Law Courts and whitewash the misdeeds of the Army of Occupation; the publicity made it possible for me later to fix on Cromer the responsibility of the scandalous Denshawai case.

"*29th May.*— An early luncheon with George Wyndham and sat talking with him for a couple of hours, mostly on his Irish policy. I am amused to find him more and more of a Home Ruler, though he does not quite avow it. He seems to have found out that it is a choice between that and Government as a Crown Colony. I asked him whether he did not think the Local Self Government Bill in Ireland had played entirely into the Nationalists' hands, and he admitted that perhaps it had, but it had been a necessary part of the general Unionist policy of treating Ireland precisely on the same lines as England. It might lead indirectly to a sort of Home Rule, that is to say it might come to a union of the local councils under one general council at Dublin which would practically settle all Irish affairs. In the meanwhile the law had to be carried out. There was hardly any real crime in Ireland; but where the law was very clearly broken the Crimes Act must be put in force. He believed the Irish leaders would secretly quite approve of this, for they did not want crime any more than the Government did. What had always been resented was the blundering in the choice of cases to be dealt with. On the whole, the thing as far as he was concerned was to get his Land Bill passed and his Catholic University Bill, both of which he meant to carry through, and get through his term of office as peaceably as was possible. He did not expect the Government to last out longer than October 1903.

"We talked also on the larger aspects of Imperialism, and he agreed with me that the violences done in connection with South Africa, necessary as perhaps they were, had had an ill effect on our national character, and that it might well happen that personal freedom and strict legality would both suffer here in England in consequence. I have been reading Stowe's Chronicle of the reign of Henry VIII, and I reminded George of the destruction in a very few years of both freedom and legality, and how it had ruined the character of Englishmen to the extent that at the close of the reign each nobleman was ready to betray his fellow-conspirator, and each Bishop to recant his heresies, and each gentleman condemned to death to beg abject pardon of his King for having opposed him as if for a crime.

"*2nd June.*— Peace has been signed at Pretoria. The country is thoroughly war sick, and I hope will so remain during my lifetime. King Edward was determined to have an end put to the fighting before his coronation, and I fancy the Boers have had better terms given them than people are aware of, and that the peace has been arrived at over Chamberlain's head and Milner's. Talking of Chamberlain on Thursday, George said of him that his character was completely misunderstood by the public, who, judging by his face, thought him a cool, unimpassioned calculator. He was just the reverse, being rash and impulsive in his decisions, to a great extent a political gambler, anything but a safe man to be at the head of affairs. George is beginning to learn things now he is in office.

"*3rd June.*— Madeline Wyndham took me to tea at Apsley House with her son Guy and his wife and stepdaughter, a pretty child just out. The Duke and Duchess showed us all over the house from garret to cellar, or rather to the underground chamber, where the plate is displayed in huge glass cases. The old Duke must have had a passion for silver plate, for every crowned head seems to have presented him with some, the most magnificent being the gift of the Portuguese Government. This last includes thirty-two dozen silver dinner plates. It is unfortunately all of a date which leaves its value something less than the weight of the metal, though the Portuguese is better than the rest, enormous pieces of preposterous design of the time of George IV, practically unusable. There is something melancholy in such a vast display for every one except the head butler, who has the proud charge of it. The Duke and Duchess, however, take a full interest in it all, and explained everything in detail to us very amiably. They are excellent people, he rather stiff and formal as becomes the representative of his great ancestor, whose half whisker he imitates; she a good-natured soul, and both without pretension. They have only succeeded to their kingdom within this last year. Upstairs the great ballroom is a really fine thing, hung with a few good pictures and many bad ones, the best the ' Velasquez ' obtained in Spain, and a sweet little religious picture of two panels, I know not by whom; it is called an Albert Dürer. We had tea in the garden under the old thorn trees just in full blossom. An interesting visit.

"*4th June.*— To bid good-bye to Rowton at his house in Berkeley Square. He has been very ill, and is going away on a sea-voyage to the Cape and back, which he thinks will set him right. I hope, indeed, it may, for I have a considerable affection for him. His rooms, which had been newly cleaned and decorated, looked bare and uncomfortable. He complained of having no one to look after him or hang his pictures, or arrange his furniture — the misery of never having married. 'You see me,' he said, 'in my sixty-fourth year, and I have never proposed to any woman in the way of marriage, and there is no one who will care whether I live or die.' He has been through a terrible time, having one of his ribs cut out by Bennett at St. George's Hospital. 'It was a question of life or death in twenty-four hours, and I said "Do it."' He asked me what I had myself felt when at the point of death, and I told him, 'A great indifference.' 'It was the same with me,' he said, 'I did not care which way it might go.' It is strange to see a man with so many friends yet apparently so little loved. There is nobody who looks after him, no woman who spends her time with him, not even a nurse, nobody he thinks that loves him. This must be terrible. Neither has he any religion to give him a false hope, nor even a belief in his own philanthropic work. His nearest thing to a creed is his worship of his old master, Disraeli.

"Then I went on to see John Dillon, and had a long talk about Ireland. He is rather sceptical of George Wyndham's Nationalist sympathies, and says that he is putting the Coercion Act in force more vigorously in some ways than Arthur Balfour did formerly. He gives hard labour now as well as imprisonment, with a view to disqualifying men from serving on County Councils. Dillon also talked much about the peace in South Africa, as to which his views are much the same as mine. He was pleased at my calculation that each Boer, man, woman, and child annexed will have cost the British Government just £1,000. He talked strongly of the ineptitude of the Liberal leaders in the House of Commons.

"Had tea with Princess Louise of Schleswig-Holstein, whom I had met at Clouds in the autumn. She is living in a very small house in Queensbury Place, which she has decorated with an enormous Union Jack in honour of the peace. With her I found an old friend, Mary Hughes, her lady-in-waiting, and a visitor, one Landon, who has been 'Times' correspondent for the last five years in South Africa. Landon gave us a long acount of the origin and rise of the war, which was extremely interesting. Inspired by the Princess's sympathy, who interjected at every mention of a Boer or of a pro-Boer, 'He ought to have been shot — he ought to have been hanged,' he unfolded all his budget, and let us into many secrets. 'I am perhaps,' he said, 'the only man who has ever ventured to ask Mr. Chamberlain directly, whether he knew of the Jameson Raid before it happened. I had myself known it was intended nearly a year before,

as it was talked of quite openly at Johannesburg as due to take place
at the end of the year, and it did in fact take place on the 31st of
December. Mr. Chamberlain, in answer to my question, said. 'Well,
I was consulted as to what would be the attitude of the Government in the case of a *bona fide* popular rising at Johannesburg, and
my answer was that if it was *bona fide* the High Commissioner would
be instructed to intervene to restore order, and of course that would
have meant by the forces of the Crown.' 'As a matter of fact,'
Landon explained, 'the raid as nearly as possible succeeded. What
hindered its success was that the Johannesburgers could not make up
their minds what flag they should hoist, the Union Jack or the flag of a
Republic, and they had agreed to send a Commissioner to Cape Town
to settle this question, and while they were awaiting the answer Jameson grew impatient, for his men got tired of doing nothing, and were
drifting away from him, and he resolved to risk the coup. Jameson
was always a gambler. When he was making £2,000 a year as a Doctor, he used to lose £1,000 and £1,500 a night at cards, and he treated
the raid in the same gambler's spirit. He had 500 men still with him,
in another week he would have had only fifty, and he played his stake.
If the Johannesburgers could have made up their minds, they could
have got possession of the fort and with it of the whole situation, for
all the ammunition, artillery, and supplies of the Transvaal were there,
and there were only seven men to guard it. The thing might have been
done quite easily. As it was it failed through Jameson's folly. He
ordered the advance in spite of seventeen telegrams he received ordering him to stop, including one from the Queen. 'Yes,' said the Princess, 'Grandmama has several times told me long before it happened,
that she only hoped to be spared living to see another war in South
Africa.'

"Landon also told us about the part Schreiner had played in what
he called 'the black week.' Schreiner had up to that time been the
trusted leader under Hofmeyr, of the Bond, but he had the wit, Landon said, to see that the defeat of the British armies would oblige England to destroy the Dutch Republic, and he came over secretly to Milner.
It was this that prevented a general rising in Cape Colony, for all
trusted Schreiner, and when he advised against it the Dutch followed
him. He spoke of the Orange State as a model of good Government,
honest in all branches of its administration, and on good terms with
the English Government. I pushed him to say what reason there was
for the war, which he avowed was forced on by our side. He said it
was one entirely of racial ascendancy, and that if matters had been left
alone for a few years more, the Dutch would have become predominant
in South Africa. When I further asked what harm there would have

been in that, his reply was that a Dutch Government would have been a corrupt one, after the fashion of the South American Republics. I walked back with him as far as Hyde Park Corner.

" 10*th June*.— A lecture by Yeats at the Clifford's Inn Hall in explanation of his theory of recitation. As an entertainment it was excellent, as he had got three ladies who recited admirably to the accompaniment of the psaltery invented by Dolmetsch, who himself took the chair at the meeting and explained everything musically. Yeats, however, was far from convincing me that the method was either new or good as a way of reading poetry, indeed it reduced the verse to the position it holds in an opera libretto. It was impossible to distinguish whether the words were sense or only sound, and the whole effect depended on the reciter.

" 11*th June*.— With Neville to another lecture to hear Bernard Shaw defend his position as a Socialist (especially as to the part he had taken against the Boers in the late war). It was a very clever performance, for he is a brilliant and ready speaker full of paradox and ingenious jesting, but it was clear his socialist audience was not much with him, and it was impossible to take his doctrines seriously. To me the Fabian position has nothing to recommend it. It is socialism without the few humanitarian virtues which commonly go with it, without romance and without honesty of principle, only opportunism.

" 15*th June (Sunday)*.— Newbuildings. Yeats is here with others, and we had an afternoon of poetry, but all agreed that Yeats' theories of recitation were wrong, useful only for concealing indifferent verse. When he recites it is impossible to follow the meaning, or judge whether the verse is good or bad. All the same he is a true poet, more than his work reveals him to be, and he is full of ideas, original and true, with wit into the bargain. We all like him.

" I am trying to dramatize one of the Cuchulain episodes for Yeats to bring out next year in his Cuchulain cycle of plays at Dublin [' Fand '].

" 23*rd June*.— The whole of London is decorated for the Coronation, the line of the processions being barricaded with stands for spectators, covered with red cloth. Though the decorations are not generally in the best taste, the general effect is gay, and the grime of London is clothed and put out of sight. Very few modern buildings are not improved by being faced with scaffolding. Immense crowds parade the streets, and traffic is blocked.

" 24*th June*.— A bolt has fallen from the blue. The King is ill, has undergone an operation, and the Coronation is postponed." [So little was the misfortune expected that the King and Queen had been photographed, robed and crowned in anticipation. I have one of these photographs by me still. There never was so dramatic a misfortune.]

"*25th June.*— Called at Dorchester House to write my name down for Princess Hélène, who with her husband represents the King of Italy at the Coronation, and at 35 Park Lane to give Lettice her wedding gift and the Sonnet I have written her. I found her with Lord Beauchamp, her fiancé, a good looking, smooth faced young man, who complained much of the deception that had been practised on the public in regard to the King's illness. Passing through the Park I found Rotten Row crowded, not a trace of trouble on any face, though the newspapers talk of general gloom. On the contrary, streets are full of gay sightseers, satisfied to look at the decorations since there will be nothing more. Returning after dark I found the Park still crowded, but almost exclusively by lovers who occupied each bench in pairs reposing, according to the naïve London custom, in each other's arms.

"*5th July.*— The day of our horse sale. I am camped at Caxtons very pleasantly. As a social function all went off most prosperously. Five hundred and ninety people had accepted invitations, and some five hundred sat down to luncheon. Also the quality of the guests was exalted — Princess Louise, the Sultan of Perak with a turbaned suite, Pertab Singh, Maharajah of Idar with the same, some twenty Colonial big wigs, including Barton, Prime Minister of the new Australian commonwealth, and a fair show of our own Lords and Ladies. My health was proposed by Lord Egerton, and I made a rather longer speech than usual in reply. There was no hitch in any of the arrangements, and all the world was pleased. The sole thing wanting was the presence of buyers for the horses. It was the worst sale we have had in all our twenty years, as last year's was the best.

"*10th July.*— Newbuildings. Hilaire Belloc came to see me and stayed to dinner. He is a very clever fellow, a good talker, and a powerful wine drinker, as his book, 'The Path to Rome,' indicates. (I had not met him since sometime in the eighties, when he came as an Oxford undergraduate to consult me on a plan he had of bringing out a Catholic magazine.) We had an amusing evening trotting out paradoxes." [This entry records Belloc's arrival to take up his residence in Shipley, who was afterwards to prove so good and interesting a neighbour to me for so many years.]

"*13th July (Sunday).*— Labouchere and his wife and daughter, Bill Gordon and Sibyl Queensberry are here (Newbuildings) for a Sunday visit. Labouchere in the highest possible form, brimming over with wit and good stories, the most brilliant talker in England, now Oscar Wilde is gone. Gordon, too, is no bad talker on his own subjects. Labouchere is to retire from Parliament at the dissolution, and has bought Michael Angelo's Villa at Florence, where he means to live. He is busy pulling the Villa about 'to suit it,' he says, 'to modern requirements,' uprooting old trees in the *podere* and planting new ones.

About this vandalism, as about all else, he is shamelessly amusing. ' Old Michael,' he explained, ' didn't understand how to make a house comfortable, it's time we should teach him.' His daughter tells me he is a model father, always in good humour, and never scolding her. Indeed he is full of private kindnesses in spite of his public ferocity, and they are a very happy family. I like them all. We sat up till half-past one last night, and he must have told quite a hundred stories and nearly all new. To-day Belloc joined us at dinner, and proved too talkative for Labouchere, who would not compete with him."

" The Duke of Norfolk's undeveloped son is dead, and Meynell, whom I saw on Friday was full of anecdotes about him, tragical enough, from his birth, which when it happened was considered an event of the extremest significance in all the English Catholic world, down to this drear conclusion. Perhaps the most pathetic incident was when he was on pilgrimage at Lourdes to which place they repeatedly went in search of a miracle for him. As the ducal party approached the shrine they found themselves face to face with a crowd of joyous French peasants chaunting in honour of a cure which had just been wrought, and the verse of the psalm they were singing was ' He hath filled the hungry with good things, but the rich he hath sent empty away.' ' We shall have no miracle,' said the Duke, and the Duchess burst into tears. The boy as he grew up had a beautiful face, but he had no mind, and he never learnt to speak. The only words he knew were ' Pretty boy, pretty boy,' which he had heard strangers say who came to see him, and he repeated these when he became excited mechanically. His father spent several hours every day with him, but he did not know his father, except as a playfellow, and when the Duke came back from his campaign in South Africa the boy had clean forgotten him. This was a sad wound to the Duke. The Duke, some think, will never remarry. He considers that he resisted a vocation when he did not become an Oratorian, and that he was accursed for this in his son by Heaven. He is more likely to end his days as a priest. The little Lord Arundel is to be buried to-day.

" *14th July.*— Lord Salisbury has resigned, and is succeeded as Prime Minister by Arthur Balfour. This has disappointed the extreme Imperialists who have been intriguing for the last four years for Chamberlain, but I think Balfour will be found just as uncompromising a Jingo as the other; however, it makes for morality in England, and so on the whole I am glad.

" The Tower of St. Mark's at Venice has fallen, its foundation probably undermined by the wash of the steamers and the dredging of the canals.

" *21st July.*— There are to be changes in the new Cabinet, Hicks

Beach has resigned and Lord Cadogan, so George Wyndham will get his step whether he stays in Ireland or not."

The first fortnight of August was spent by me in making my annual driving tour, this time through East Sussex, and afterwards for a month at Fernycroft, writing my play, " Fand," with other poetry. I find nothing of political importance in my diary for many weeks. In November I was for a week at Gros Bois and Paris, where I found everything in a state of political quiescence, all that was being talked of being a certain growth of Socialism. On the 22nd, being about to start finally for Egypt, I went to see George Wyndham in Park Lane, and he gave me a full account of his plans for Ireland. Next session he is to bring in a bill to deal finally with the land question on the basis of compulsory purchase, aided with English credit. He has got a majority, and more than a majority of the Irish landlords to agree to it, and thinks he can carry it through at a cost, if I understand him rightly, of about seventy millions. The extreme cost he put at £120,000,000, the security for which from the English taxpayer is to be got out of the Public Aids given to the local rates, which will be stopped if the tenants of the County aided fail to pay their yearly rent. He intends to deal very liberally with the readjustment of the financial relations of England with Ireland, and the money thus paid annually to Ireland will be the security of the Land Purchase settlement. Lastly, he will endow a Catholic University. I asked him what he thought would be the outcome of all this if it was, effected. Home Rule or a closer Union. He admitted that it would probably lead to Home Rule, but said it was not his business to look so far ahead. Indeed if he carries out all he talked of he will have done enough for one man. As to coercion, he said his revival of it was the price he had had to pay for obtaining a free hand from his colleagues in the Cabinet. He had made large use of the London press, and the support of the " Times " could only be bought by coercion. George was in his most sanguine and optimist vein, and felt certain of success. We were interrupted at this point, and he promised to look in on me at Chapel Street in the afternoon. This he did, but we were no longer alone, and the Irish talk was not renewed.

CHAPTER II

GEORGE WYNDHAM'S IRISH LAND BILL, 1902

King Edward VII's reign began with a fair promise for the world, or at least for the British Empire, of peace; and there was good reason to hope that a more reasonable foreign policy would be pursued than that which had so violently disturbed the last years of Queen Victoria's reign. King Edward was by nature and habit a peacemaker, and one of his chief occupations as Prince of Wales had been to use his social influence in composing his friends' quarrels. It was disagreeable to him that persons of his Court with whom he came in contact, and in whom he felt an interest, should be on ill terms with each other, and he had long felt a pride in bringing them together. His own life had not been altogether free from domestic storms, but these had not been due to faults of temper on his part, rather of conduct, for he was a lover of pleasure and allowed himself wide latitude in its indulgence. This had involved him in more than one scandal out of which he had always managed to emerge without serious injury to his reputation. These irregularities had indeed rather added to his popularity for they showed him to have a kindly heart and he had always proved faithful to his friends. His experience, too, had made him a good judge of character both with men and women, and gave him a certain facility in his intercourse with both which was not without it diplomatic uses. Thus when for the first time he found himself in a position to influence the conduct of foreign affairs (for Queen Victoria had been always jealous of his being entrusted with state secrets) his natural instinct was to use it in the interests of peace, especially with France, where the chief friction was found, and from the first days of his accession he busied himself in bringing about a settlement of the international differences.

As Prince of Wales he had been in the habit of spending a certain number of weeks every year on the continent, and especially in Paris, where he had become personally popular, through his somewhat Bohemian tastes and love of the French stage. In Germany he was almost equally at home, though not on the best of terms with his nephew the Emperor William, and he was on pleasant terms, too, with the Russian Court, and indeed all the Courts, having a family connection with most of them. I knew much of his private life, more than I can relate here, through certain common friends entirely in his confidence, and my feeling towards him has always been for this reason, that of a well-wisher as well as a loyal subject.

The very first object which he set himself to bring about as King was to put an end to the Boer War, not so much perhaps on any humane principle as ending what he was well aware had become the cause of vast discredit to England throughout Europe, and in this he succeeded notwithstanding the Tory obstinacy of those in power. A second scandal which he would have willingly seen ended was that of Ireland. He was aware, as very few Englishmen had discovered, how grave a scandal the long disloyalty of the Irish race was in the eyes of the outside world, and how seriously it affected the dignity of the British Empire and of himself personally as Ireland's king. Thus the title bestowed on him, not quite seriously at first, of "Edward the Peacemaker" was in my opinion well deserved, though, through the diplomatic blunders of our Foreign Office and the incurable cupidities of our advanced imperialists, the seeds of peace sown during his reign were so perversely misapplied as to bring about the cataclysm of the general European War which ten years later overwhelmed his successor. Lord Salisbury's retirement from office immediately after King Edward's coronation and Mr. Balfour's succession as Prime Minister marks the true end of the Victorian era, and the beginning of another, better let us admit in its intentions, but disastrous beyond all possible foresight on King Edward's part, in its results of ruin for the European world.

I spent the first winter of the new reign, 1902–1903, once more in Egypt. On leaving London, I wrote " 28th Nov., I had met Frank Lascelles at my Club and had had a long talk with him about old times and new. He had been staying at Sandringham with the King and the Emperor William and told me much about them both. It is pleasant to find him still affectionate as in old days and unspoilt by the dignities of his position. The truth is these diplomatic dignities seen close are small things and do not turn their possessors' heads unless they come very suddenly and unexpectedly. An ambassador in the regular service blossoms gradually and has plenty of time to remember that he was once an attaché and is still a mortal. On my way through France I had travelled with Sir John Gorst (the elder) on his way to attend the opening of the great Assouan dam and to visit his son Eldon at Cairo. Talking about past events in Egypt he told me that in 1886 it had been intended by Lord Salisbury to supersede Cromer and appoint Drummond Wolff in his place and as he, Gorst, was in Cairo at the time, Stafford Northcote had commissioned him to find out how the change would be regarded in native quarters, and he had gone to Nubar, then in office, and consulted him. Nubar had told him that if Cromer went he and his colleagues in office would go too, and it was in consequence of Gorst's report in this sense that Cromer was allowed to stay on. It is curious that it should have been Gorst, Wolff's intimate friend, who did him this ill turn, though doubtless Gorst was only fulfilling the commission given him by his superiors. It was a decision of critical importance, for on it really rested the question of the alternative policies in Egypt, Cromer's which was a policy of remaining and anglicizing the Nile Valley, Wolff's of restoring National self government."

On our voyage from Marseilles to Alexandria "I have been reading the Documents connected with the trial of Joan of Arc which have just been published. Her death is perhaps the most stupendous political crime ever perpetuated in Western Europe, certainly the blackest in English history, and this, remembering Cromwell in Ireland, the suppression of the Indian Mutiny and the desecration of the Mahdi's tomb, is saying much. At the same time there was undeniably a certain legal case against Jeanne in the Ecclesiastical Court which condemned her. The position she took up and persisted in with regard to her visions and her mission from God, made it impossible for the Inquisition to hold a middle course concerning her. Either she had been inspired by God or she had been inspired by the devil, for in those days the idea of mental hallucination was unknown, and if not by God she was necessarily a sorceress worthy of death. In reality Jeanne was a pious, good girl, persuaded of the truth of her ' visions ' and acting single-mindedly in obedience to them. A claim is made for her by the editor of the book that her answers to her judges have a character of supernatural wisdom. This seems to me to be exaggerated; she was often at fault, and to some very simple questions gave answers by no means wise, as when she refused to repeat the Pater Noster or to say who counselled her to put on male attire. So much for the ecclesiastics. The conduct of the English commanders Bedford, Warwick, and the rest, was infamous to the last degree and without a shadow of excuse. They burned her and scattered her ashes in the Seine for precisely the same reason that Kitchener and his scoundrel officers blew up the Mahdi's tomb and threw his body into the Nile. It was the dastard spirit of revenge against one who had beaten English armies in the field, and of whom they had all been afraid.

" *4th Dec.*— We arrived off Alexandria at daybreak, the city looming out of a bank of smoke and black cloud for all the world like Liverpool. It was only a local effect, however, and we were soon in the sunshine and on our way across the Delta, and are now at Sheykh Obeyd. Between Damanhur and Cairo I counted seven pied kingfishers, three hoopoes, two spur-winged plovers, one snipe, one false snipe, and fifty-two little white herons, a thing to note in view of the rapid extermination of birds in Egypt. We arrived at home a full hour before sunset, having found Hamouda Abdu, now made a Bey, expecting us at the Cairo station. His brother the Mufti had just left for Assouan for the opening of the great Nile dam.

"The building scheme at Kafr el Jamus has been going on apace, the whole area north of the village has been laid out in streets and squares, though these have not yet been built over, indicating the rise of the tide which will one day join us in continuous houses with Cairo. Our neighbour Selim Bey Faraj, the Christian judge of Benha, is dead, a poor unmanly creature who had managed to get on bad terms with all the Moslems round. He had got possession of forty acres of land to which he clung pertinaciously in spite of some persecution by the Arabs provoked by his own covetousness. He had a passion for litigation and was memorable for a record series of actions at law brought against his wife which he carried before every tribunal in Egypt, native and foreign, and then on appeal before the Sultan at Constantinople, and as a last resort before the Pope at Rome, and lost them all.

"*19th Dec.*— The Grand Mufti (Sheykh Mohammed Abdu) came and sat with me this morning for a couple of hours talking. He had sent me Butler's 'Conquest of Egypt by the Arabs' of which he had received a presentation copy and I explained its contents to him, for he does not read English. He treats Butler's theory of the Makawkas being identical with Cyrus the Melchite Patriarch of Alexandria as rubbish. He says that it is certain the Makawkas was a Copt, the Governor of Memphis, and that he and the mass of the Copts favoured the Arab invasion which relieved them of the Roman tyranny. If it had not been so, how could the Copts have obtained such very favourable terms from Amru and enjoyed the liberty and self government they did for so many centuries after? It was only the crusades and especially the attack made on Egypt by St. Louis that caused the Copts to begin to be persecuted, they having declared for the invaders. We talked also about contemporary affairs at Constantinople. The Khedive is now on bad terms with the Sultan, having been ill-received by him this summer. Abdul Hamid refused to receive him at all until he had promised not to mention the affair of Thasos. The affair of Thasos is this: the Khedive, who is owner of the island though it forms no part of Egypt, has managed matters there so badly, raising the taxes and imposing import duties that the people of the island complained of it to the Sultan who made it a pretext for sending his own troops there as garrison. The Khedive wanted these removed, but could not get a hearing at the Palace.

"Abbas is now much under the influence of a Hungarian lady

who has become his mistress. She was with him at the time of his motor car mishap, some weeks ago, when he missed his way coming back at night from Dar el Beyda and stuck fast in the sand. The *ghaffirs* who refused to help him he put to forced labour for a week, a thing reported to the British agency and made a cause of quarrel there against him. We talked also of Midhat Pasha and the death of the Sultan Abdul Aziz. Abdu confirms the account of this given me by Dr. Dickson in 1884 as one certainly of suicide.[1] He tells me also how Midhat was starved to death at Taif. They gave him bread so hard that the old man broke his teeth over it and they allowed him no convenience of any kind in his cell for his natural wants till he died of ill treatment, and his head was then cut off and sent to Constantinople. Of Abdul Hamid, Abdu spoke as the greatest scoundrel living, a strong word for a Grand Mufti to use of his Caliph.

" *22nd Dec.*— An Arabic newspaper has published a fantastic account of my life and doings. I am by birth, it says, an Irishman, born with an hereditary hatred of England, originally without fortune of my own, I espoused the daughter of a great English lord under the following condition. The lord, many years before, while travelling in the Ottoman dominions, had been assassinated, and died leaving £4,000,000 sterling to his daughter, with an injunction that she should avenge him. She consequently imposed upon her suitors that they should take oath of vengeance, and as I was the only one with sufficient courage, I had been accepted, and had since devoted my life to an attempt to ruin the Ottoman Empire. This I had sought to accomplish by stirring up the Arabs to proclaim an Arabian Caliphate. It attributes the present coolness between the Khedive and the Sultan to my machinations, as also the war now going on in Arabia between Ibn Rashid and Mubarrak of Koweit, whom I had supplied with arms, and a great deal more nonsense of the same kind. I talked the thing over with Mohammed Abdu, who suggested that I might make use of this as an opportunity for publishing in Arabic a full account of my connection with the affairs in Egypt of 1881–82." [Out of this grew the work which occupied me all that winter in conjunction with the Mufti, and which was published five years afterwards as my " Secret History of the English Occupation of Egypt."]

" *1st Jan.* 1903.— We celebrated the New Year (the second day of Shaban), by dining with the Mufti, and talked over the old political days of 1882."

5th January to 14th January were occupied in a desert journey by Tel el Kebir, Salahieh, Ismaïlia and back by Kassassin and Om Kamr home. Our party consisted of Anne and me and Miss Law-

[1] See my " Secret History."

rence, with eleven camels, four mares, and a donkey, Suliman
Howeyti, Mutlak, and servants. I give a few extracts:

"*6th Jan.*— A short day, but an amusing one. Soon after starting we crossed the track in the sand of two wolves, and followed
them to a high tell. There we sat looking out over the desert, and
I presently caught sight of the wolves cantering across a piece of
open sand about a mile away. Then I sent Mutlak back for Suliman,
and we went down with him to the place and after some search hit
off the tracks, and he followed them with us for an hour back to
the Kittaban, where we had camped last night. As we were going
up wind, we got close to them before they saw us. Then they
were away both together over the high sand ridge, and we after them
full gallop. They were immense big wolves, one darker than the
other — it looked quite black against the sand. When we reached the
top of the ridge they were already a quarter of a mile away, with
Mutlak close behind them, for he was riding Manokta, who has great
speed. Anne and I did not follow beyond the ridge, but watched them
going as straight as a line for Kafr Abusir, till they disappeared in
the great distance. Mutlak, after following a couple of miles, had
to give it up. It was a fine sight, and the genlemen of the 11th
Hussars would have had their work cut out for them if they had
got upon the line. The track of the larger of the two wolves in the
damp sand was as big as the palm of my hand, with immense sharp
claws. After this we had a long canter to catch up our camels. We
have camped about five miles from Belbeys.

"*7th Jan.*— We are camped on the field of battle of Tel el Kebir,
inside Arabi's line of earthworks. These are of immense extent,
though for the most part a mere ditch and bank, which any cavalry
regiment would cross almost without checking speed. As we arrived we sighted a jackal running along the embankment, and in another direction half-a-dozen British soldiers in their red coats out for
a day's holiday to look at the scene of their country's glory.

"*8th Jan.*— We rode all along the front line of entrenchments,
in the ditch of which are still numerous human bones and a few
skulls of the 'poor patriots, partly purchased, partly pressed,' who
died there twenty years ago. The embrasures of the half dozen forts,
where the artillery was posted, are built in part of the rushes of the
Wady put in to strengthen the gravel. The lines, though broken
through in places by the passage of camels, are still mostly intact, and
in this dry climate will last for several thousand years, and I fear
outlast the fame of the peasants that built them, in their one assertion
of manhood, to defend their country. The outlying fort in front of
the lines was visible eastwards. It was there that Ali Rouby was
stationed in command of the cavalry, Ali Rouby who betrayed his

trust and allowed the English to march past him without giving warning.

"*9th Jan.*—To-night we are encamped near a high sand dune, from the top of which there is a fine view of the line of the Suez Canal with the low sandhills beyond it, and far away southwards Jebel Attaka and the line of hills to Hamum; close at hand Abu Tufaïleh, where there are some palms, not far from Ismaïlia, which is also distinctly in sight. There are shepherds and camelherds of the Maaze near, some in tents, some squatted under bushes, all very happy. We saw a fox, a hare, an eagle owl and the track of two wolves. An immense spider of a light sand colour, with brown bars, was found in my tent in the morning about three inches across. I never saw the like in any of my journeys.

"*13th Jan.*—Travelling all day across the great gravel plain south of the Wady in a straight line to Om Kamr. On the way we met Abdallah Ibn Majelli, of the Hannadi Arabs, out on a hawking expedition, with four dependents, two hawks, and five greyhounds. These last, as it turned out, were all descendants of our old English greyhound bitch Fly, a daughter of whose, Jerboa, we gave some fifteen years ago to Prince Ahmed. In spite of many crosses with Arab greyhounds the English type is well preserved, though the dogs are smaller and lighter. Their master told us they were quite acclimatised, and stood the heat and the hard ground as well as their own greyhounds, retaining something of their English speed. We saw them kill a hare after a rather long course among the small bushes with which the plain was sprinkled. The hare must have doubled forty times before the greyhounds got her. One of the hawks waited overhead, but did not pursue the hare after the first minute. The party had got a hubhara also in the morning. They were suspicious of us when we first rode up to them. I fancy that, being away from their own *dira,* they were afraid.

"*14th Jan.*—Rode in to Sheykh Obeyd.

"*22nd Jan.*—Professor Browne from Cambridge came to luncheon, bringing a letter to me from Alfred Lyall. He is most intelligent about Eastern things, not merely as an Orientalist, but also politically. He has lived some time in Persia, and has written a couple of books about it, and knows Persian and Turkish and Arabic, but having little colloquial knowledge of the last, has come here to practise it. With this view he has been attending Mohammed Abdu's lectures on the Koran at the Azhar, and already understands them fairly well, but his accent in talking is peculiar. We took him to see Mutlak and Suliman in their tents, the first 'houses of hair' he has ever sat under. He has been seeing something of our English officials here, and tells amusing stories about them, especially about

Dunlop, the Adviser of the Ministry of Instruction, who told him
roundly that he would not have any Englishman under him who came
to Egypt knowing a word of Arabic. It only gave them romantic
ideas about the natives, and they would waste their time explaining
what they taught to the natives in Arabic instead of making these
learn English. For this reason he would not hear of accepting young
men from Cambridge who had passed an examination in Arabic.
He prefers to go to England, and pick up young men himself for
the places vacant in his department.

" 28th *Jan.*— An interesting man has been here, one of Ibn Rashid's
slaves from Haïl, a half-bred Arab negro born in Nejd, by name
Eïd. He is here on a political mission of some kind to find out what
is going on in the world, and possibly to seek alliances for the new
Emir Abd el Aziz Ibn Rashid. His master is just now in rather bad
luck, having lost a considerable battle to Ibn Saoud, and been driven
out of Aáred. He gave us a graphic account of the battle, and how
Ibn Rashid's standard had been passed on from hand to hand by
his *khayal* (horsemen) as one after the other was slain, he himself
taking it at last, though Mutlak declares it fell into the hands of
Ibn Saoud. According to Eïd, Ibn Saoud has now gained possession of Aáred, and is living at Derayyeh, but Kassim is still under
Ibn Rashid, who has his Wakil at Bereydah. I asked him what part
the Dowlah (the Ottoman Government) had played in the matter,
and he protested that it had played none, except that the Sultan had
sent a present of Martini rifles and cannons to Abdul Aziz on his
accession. Of the English he said that Koweit was full of them.
Mohammed Abdu, who came in while we were talking, helped to
cross-question him, and there is no doubt the man is what he states
he is, for he knows all the politics of Nejd past and present; he is
quite new to the outside world, having travelled by way of Jof to
Damascus, where he left his *delûl* and came on by steamer from
Beyrout, a strange experience for him. He has stopped the night
with us, and this morning he is to go back straight to Haïl. I gave
him a piece of parting advice, and a message to his master and to
Hamoud and Majid, and the rest of them there. 'Listen,' I said,
' to my word, and let these listen. There is danger to the Arabs
from the Dowlah, and there is danger also from the English; have
nothing to do with either of them. Make peace at once with Ibn
Saoud and remain quietly in your own country; leave Mubarrak alone
at Koweit and leave Ibn Saoud alone in Aáred, otherwise the Government of the Ibn Rashids at Haïl will perish. You have seen here
what comes of English intervention, how the Khedive's Government
has been undermined and destroyed, and so it will be with you in
Arabia if you do not mind your own affairs. Have nothing to do

with either our Government or the Sultan's, your own is better than
either. You have liberty at Haïl and you are happy under it, and may
it last a hundred years.' I enforced this advice with a present of
five pounds as a proof of my sincerity, and he seemed much impressed. I feel sure that he will deliver my message to Abdul Aziz,
whether his master follows my advice or not." [This incident is
of interest as fixing the date of the beginning of the rival intrigues
on the one hand of the Ottoman Government, and on the other of
the Government of India in Peninsula Arabia with large distribu-
tions of firearms to the rival tribes, and the stirring up of strife, leading to the larger results we have seen within the last years in the
Hedjaz.]

"*30th Jan.*— To-day Mahmud Pasha Sami came to see me with
the Mufti. I had not seen him since we were in Ceylon nineteen
years ago, a very distinguished gentleman now in his old age, a poet
and a man of letters, nearly blind, who has to be led by the hand.

"Also later one Abdul Kerim Murad of Medina, whose brother
had given Anne her first Arabic lessons in 1880. He has since
been travelling round a large part of the Mohammedan world during the last few years, including Nigeria and Senegal, of which he
gave a most interesting account. [Especially of Sokoto in Nigeria,
describing the great wealth and industry of that city and its honourable government since overthrown by the English.]

"*8th Feb.*— Hamouda Bey, the Mufti's brother, was here to-day,
He has been seriously ill of late through overwork at his legal business. He has been recently given the rank of Bey, and in virtue
of his new title was invited the other night to the Khedive's ball, as
to which he gave us a naïve and amusing account. ' I went,' he
said, ' with two friends, men like myself in the legal profession, and
we arived among the first, none of us having ever been at such an
entertainment before. As we were depositing our coats and um-
brellas, for it had rained, at the vestiary, suddenly I saw in a mirror
a sight reflected such as I had never in my life beheld, two women
who were standing behind me, naked nearly to the waist. I thought
it must have been some illusion connected with my illness and I
was very much frightened. Their faces and arms and everything
were displayed without any covering, and I thought I should have
fallen to the ground. I asked what it meant and whether perhaps
we had not come to the right house, but my friends took me on
into the ball-room, where they showed me a number more women in
the like condition. "Who are they?" I inquired, and they told me,
"These are the wives of some of our English officials." "And
their husbands," I asked, "do they permit them to go out at night
like this?" "Their husbands," they answered, "are here," and they

pointed out to me Mr. Royle, the Judge of Appeal, before whom I
had often pleaded, a serious man and very stern, as the husband of
one of them. This judge I saw dancing with one of these naked
ladies, gay and smiling and shameless, like a young man. "And he
is here," I said, "to see his wife thus unclothed? and he dances
with her publicly." "That," they answered, "is not his wife, it is
the wife of another." I was dumbfounded with shame for our profession. Just then I saw Lord Cromer pass by. His coat was unbuttoned and showed his shirt down to here (pointing to his stomach).
I did not see Lord Cromer dance, because as I was looking the
Khedive entered the room leading another of these ladies, and there
was a crush of those near me to look at him. I found myself jammed
close to two of the naked ones, their shoulders and bosoms pressed
against me. I was terribly ashamed. As soon as I could free myself,
I called to my companions, "Come away, my dear friends, this is no
proper place for us," and I took them with me home. We would
not stop for the refreshments which were being served and where
wine was being poured. The Khedive calls himself a good Moslem.
He says he never drinks wine and leads a respectable life, but this
entertainment of his was not respectable, and he himself was there,
and they tell me that the ladies of his household are allowed by
him to look from behind a screen at all these abominations.' Such
was Hamouda's naïve account of his adventure. 'My dear fellow,'
I said, 'you do not understand that this is our work of civilizing
the East, wait another twenty years and you will see all the Cadi's
of Egypt with your brother the Mufti among them, dancing with
ladies even more naked than these, and who knows, going with their
own heads bare.' 'I can understand everything,' he said, 'except
this, that the husbands of these ladies were there, actually there, in
the dancing room, and did not send them home.'

"*19th Feb.*— Mr. Bourke Cockran called, having been introduced
to me by John Redmond as the most prominent Irishman in America.
I found him an intelligent, old-fashioned Irishman, and altogether
worthy. He told me he had been one of the strongest opponents
of the Philippine policy of the American Government, and that he
hoped yet the Philippines would get their Home Rule. He had seen
George Wyndham in Ireland, and had talked to him, and was confident he meant well with his Irish Land Bill.

"*25th Feb.*— To Cairo for the first time this winter to see the
Khedive. I found him grown older and less fat and gay, with a
rather harassed look, like a man who had been worried and bullied,
but whether by Cromer or by his new Hungarian mistress I do not
know, but a new lady he certainly has, for we met him out camel
riding last week with her, attended by an eunuch and with a soldier

riding behind them. The lady was in European dress, with a gay hat, as if for a garden party, and they were all mounted on handsome white camels. It was in the desert near Kafr el Jamus.

" To-day he began at once to me about the different troubles he had had in the Waïli and other affairs, and he went on to complain of Mohammed Abdu's ingratitude, in having continued to be friends with a certain Reshid who had sinned against him. I defended the Mufti on this point and exhorted the Khedive to make up the quarrel. I cannot help liking Abbas in spite of his many vacillations and inconstancies. He has this merit, that he always speaks out his mind, and is never offended at one's speaking one's own. I fancy Cromer must hold some secret rod over him and make him feel it from time to time.

" There is a scandal at Cairo which is grieving English society, Lady R. having gone to a ball with her legs bare and dressed as a *saïs*. This is considered a terrible impropriety, not so much for the thing itself as because ' she had just been dining with Lady Cromer,' and ' natives were present.' There has been a case of assault by two Bedouins on Englishmen at Mariut about which the Khedive also told me, the matter concerning him personally as he has property at Mariut.

" *26th Feb.*— Lunched at the Mufti's, Professor Browne being also there. It is surprising with what fluency Browne now speaks Arabic, which he only knew as a scholar without having ever spoken it when he came here two months ago. He has been attending the Mufti's lectures at the Azhar, and tells me they are admirable and very fearless, and that he has a ready facility in answering objections made to him by the old-fashioned interpreters of the Koran. I talked to the Mufti about the Khedive's complaint against him and he will write to His Highness and explain the mistake. A reconciliation between them is most necessary in public interests. Acting together they are able to effect much, apart they neutralize each other and are powerless.

" *6th March.*— Mohammed Abdu brought Sheykh Reshid, the cause of the Khedive's wrath, to see me, who seems a worthy man, and with him Hafiz Ibrahim, a Fellah poet, with whom we discussed the Moallakat. They all three maintained that the best Arabic poetry was not that of the Ignorance but of the second century of the Hejrah. This is quite contrary to our English ideas, but for Eastern ears the standard of merit is different from ours. What the learned here admire in poetry is the prosody, not the meaning of the verse. They care very little for the naïvetés of the pre-Islamic poets, regarding them only as blemishes, and they cannot understand that

there is any merit at all in the Abu Zeyd cycle. I could see that these
gentlemen despised me for admiring it.

" *14th March*.— There has been a very large wolf in the garden
for the last week or ten days, which has been hanging about the
tents at night, where the sheep are folded just outside our wall.
There are several flocks here just now as there is no pasture in the
hills, and the wolf has come in with them probably. We have seen
him more than once by daylight, and at night he has howled near the
house. Two nights ago, however, a dozen new tents were pitched
just outside with a quantity more sheep belonging to the Howeytat
on their way back from the Riff, where they have been at bersim.
The wolf came upon them about midnight. There was a terrible
noise of dogs barking and men shouting and shots fired. In the morning I went out to see what had happened, and old Eid came to me
from the Assara and told me they had shot the wolf, and a little
further off I saw a group of Arabs digging a grave, as I thought
for the dead wolf. On coming close, however, I found it was no
wolf but a large dog, very old and very lean and covered with blood.
They told me that it was a mad dog which had rushed in among
the sheep and which they had killed. The singular part of the story,
however, is that they have not only buried the dog, but have made
up a regular grave for it exactly like a Moslem grave with tall bones
set up at either end and neatly trenched. It is a new thing for me
that a dog should be thus honoured, one I should have thought impossible in a Mohammedan country. Suliman, whom I set to find out
the truth about it, says they buried the dog for fear that their own dogs
should eat it and so go mad, but it does not explain the grave.

" *15th March*.— Our Mowled of Sheykh Obeyd. There were present the four chief Sheykhs of the villages round as well as Yusuf
Abu Shenab, Hassan Musa el Akkad, and a number more important
neighbours in addition to the Arabs. Professor Browne, who had
lunched with us, came on for the festival. The feast was a general
one, the poor of all our four parishes being fed. One incident only
marred it in the display of horsemanship. Hamdan, an Agheyli from
Bereyda, got his arm hurt with a *jerid* to which a point had been
maliciously given with a nail, and he accused Mutlak of the treachery,
but though Mutlak had given the blow it had been given with one of
a number of *jerids* got ready for the occasion, and it was probable
a trick was played on him through jealousy. The wound, though only
a scratch, has produced much ill-feeling.

" I have finished my Moallakat translation with Anne, and an introduction to the volume. We hope to get it published during the summer.

" *16th March*.— Arabi lunched with us and remained talking the
whole afternoon. He gave me a full account of the events of 1881–82,

more especially of his relations with Khedive Tewfik in 1881, the Circassian conspiracy of the following year, the riot of Alexandria, and the battle of Tel el Kebir, a very plain-spoken narrative as to which I cross-questioned him closely. It impressed both Anne and me, and confirmed our high opinion of him morally and intellectually. His present circumstances, poor man, are to be pitied. He has returned to Egypt after twenty years' exile and finds a cold shoulder from every one in authority, from the Khedive, who has not forgiven him his rebellion, from Cromer, who considers him a nuisance, and from his fellow countrymen at Cairo, who, misled by the fanciful tales invented by the French Press of his having sold his country to the English, regard him with unmerited suspicion. We are sorry for him, but I fear it is too late to set things right.

"*23rd March.*— On Saturday John Dillon and his wife, who are in Egypt, came to spend the day. He gave us much Irish news and spoke of the danger George's land bill is running through the growing weakness of the Government. He fears they will never get it through the House. He expressed a high opinion of Winston Churchill's ability, but says he is even more unscrupulous than his father was. He thinks also that the abstention of the Irish party this session from its long opposition will have done harm by making people suspect a secret understanding between Wyndham and Redmond. Nevertheless, he says, Irish prospects were never higher than now, and Home Rule in some form must come soon. We talked, too, about Egyptian affairs, which he knows pretty well, having always taken an interest in them, and I have given him letters to Hafiz Effendi Awwad and Carton de Wiart to help him in my absence to a right understanding of the situation, for we leave for England to-day."

We left Egypt for England on 24th March and arrived there on the 28th.

The next two months, which I spent principally in London, were mainly occupied by me in using what influence I possessed with the Irish Party to carry through George Wyndham's Land Bill, as to which he had appealed to me for help. The negotiations, of which I have a complete record in my diary, are extremely interesting, and though they have no direct concern with the main subject of this volume, namely, Egypt and our foreign policy, I give them in their entirety here.

"*28th March.*— Arrived in London and glad to be back. On issuing from the Mont Cenis tunnel yesterday I found an English newspaper with a report of the introduction of George's Land Bill in Parliament. I had hoped to be in time for it, for it is the biggest piece of legislation that has been attempted for Ireland since Catholic Emancipation.

George seems to have presented his case splendidly, and so far has met with no opposition. It is a very daring scheme, and follows closely all he told me about it last autumn. I never thought he would be allowed to have it so much his own way — for it involved a hundred millions sterling — especially after Brodrick's antics at the War Office and the reaction for economy.

" *29th March (Sunday.)*— Lunched in Mount Street. Windsor and Lady Windsor — nobody else — our talk mostly about George and the Irish Land Bill, all in high praise. Then to Wentworth House, where Judith is staying, and all there too in high good humour about Ireland. Lastly to Belgrave Square where new raptures about George and his bill — how could it be otherwise? George wants to see me.

" *30th March.*—Lady Windsor came this morning. She has seen George since yesterday, and brings me a message from him to the effect that I could help him with the Irish members about the bill. Of course I shall be delighted to do this, and it is all the easier because Redmond wrote some weeks ago asking me to let him know as soon as I returned to England. I must see George however first.

" *31st March.*— Found George at his breakfast in Park Lane at the hour appointed yesterday and he began at once about his Irish Land Bill. He told me what a desperate fight he had had to get it adopted by the Cabinet and how nearly it had more than once been wrecked. Even within forty-eight hours of his bringing it forward in the House all had seemed lost, and it was only the splendid support given him by Arthur Balfour that had carried the day, as I understand him, by a single vote against Chamberlain's opposition — he did not mention Chamberlain by name. Ritchie too had supported him, and the silent vote of Akers Douglas and the Tory phalanx.

" Then he gave me a brief historical account of how he had engineered the whole affair during the autumn and winter. The first thing had been to secure the ' Times,' without which nothing could have been effected. He would not say exactly how this had been done, though he promised to tell me that and every detail some day, but I imagine Arthur Balfour must have promised Walter his long expected peerage. Then George had used his personal influence on the landlords, had gone to stay with Dunraven, had encouraged Mayo, and had expostulated privately with the leaders of the Landlords' Convention when they proved obdurate. The result had been the agreement come to at the Land Conference. He spoke in high praise of the Nationalist leaders and said O'Brien had behaved splendidly, quite justifying the character of patriotism I had given him when we had last talked about him. It was to help O'Brien to get out of his difficult position towards the evicted tenants that he had inserted the clause in his Bill providing for their reinstatement.

" I told him how at a critical moment I had written to Redmond, and he highly approved. Everything had worked out most fortunately till Parliament met in the Spring. Then the financial difficulties had begun. I asked him who had suggested the finance of his scheme, and he assured me he had done the whole thing entirely himself, which is also what his mother told me on Sunday when she described to me how he had always had a mathematical head at school and how at an examination he had drawn without a mistake the whole of the figures of the second 'Book of Euclid' from memory. Since the meeting of Parliament, however, he had been in most tempestuous waters. Brodrick's Army Bill had frightened everybody by its extravagance, and when the Funds fell to 90 he had thought all was lost. Only Ritchie encouraged him then, and he quoted a word of Ritchie's that had been repeated to him. Ritchie had said, ' Brodrick asks for millions, but he can't explain what he wants them for. But Wyndham explained everything and *convinced* one — or (correcting himself after a pause) the contrary.' But for Ritchie, the whole thing would have had to be abandoned as involving the Government in ruin. Then came the loss of the two by-elections, Woolwich and Rye, and the Cabinet meeting on Chamberlain's return (from South Africa). What I gather from George is that the Liberal Unionists opposed the Bill. The Duke of Devonshire, Lords Lansdowne and Londonderry, and probably also Brodrick and Lord George Hamilton, all these being Irish absentee landlords or representing them.

" I asked him about Chamberlain, but he was reticent. ' I will tell you now,' he said, ' exactly what the present situation is. When I got up in the House of Commons last week, I felt that I had my back against a wall and was fighting for my life; and, as often happens in such circumstances, I was able to do my very best. The question was so complicated a one that I knew I could not hope to make it clear to everybody, but I knew that on each section of it there was a group that would understand on one side or other of the House. So I turned to each in turn and got into a condition of magnetic touch with each, so that they leaned forward towards me and I could see that they understood. So much was this the case that, as I approached the City financial part of my argument, I felt, though I could not see, that there was somebody behind me in close sympathy, and I turned round and asked " Am I right? " " Quite right," was the answer. It was from Edgar Vincent. Thus I was able to get through the whole speech without wearying my audience, and at the end had succeeded in gaining the sympathy in turn of every section. This for the moment. Since the first reading, however, and the publication of the Bill, one of the most representative members of the old Tory phalanx has been to Arthur Balfour and has represented to him that much of the Bill is hard to swallow, and that the only thing that makes it possible for them is the idea that the settlement is a *final* one of the whole land quarrel, and that unless the Irish members will declare in this sense there will be a revolt.   The situation, therefore, is very critical, and if you can do anything to make the Irish leaders understand how not only I but the whole cause of Irish land legislation may be wrecked by a lack of discretion on this particular head you will be doing a good service, and you may use your discretion about our talk.   I have twice thought of my own resignation and political ruin a certainty, and it may be so yet.   But if it happens it will equally ruin Irish hopes, for they will never again find an Irish Secretary who, with my example before him, will dare to risk so much or go so far.   Of course I quite understand that the present vote may really not be quite final.   The millions may not prove quite enough, and perhaps in a few years three or four millions may be necessary.   But when the time comes and the thing has proved a success nobody will then grudge a supplement.   Only, to declare now that it is only an instalment and not final would ruin everything and we could not pass the Bill.'

" We then went on to talk about possible Home Rule in some form as an ultimate result of the peace to be established in Ireland between landlords and tenants, and he admitted that, if all united in demanding it, it could not be refused.   Indeed, George admits himself to be theoretically a Home Ruler, though he does not consider Home Rule as yet within the range of practical politics.   The less said about it just now the better.

" Lastly, he told me how he had captured certain Irish millionaires, and induced them to put their capital into Irish concerns.   Lord Iveagh had promised to finance a motor company for the sale of agricultural produce, and an Irish American publisher had offered him £100,000 for any enterprise he liked, suggesting a paper mill on the Shannon. This done, I went home and tried to find Redmond, and made an arrangement with his wife to lunch with them to-morrow, and I am to report progress to Sibell and George at breakfast on Friday.

" 1st April.— Oliver Howard called on me this morning to talk over his plan of going to Nigeria.   Being tired of London and domestic happiness, and being Chamberlain's private secretary at the Colonial Office, he has volunteered for service under Lugard.   Lugard has just made a raid on Kano and Sokoto, mopping up both kingdoms ' in Imperial interests.'   Nothing with less excuse has been perpetrated in the history of British aggression.   The two States, say with twenty millions of inhabitants, were happy and prosperous, and peaceable, carrying on industries established and flourishing for a thousand years, and now, to gratify Lugard's ambition, they are to be annexed to the pitiful British Empire, and all the English world is pleased.   Oliver tells me Lady Lugard (ex Flora Shaw) has come home very angry with the Nigerian climate, which has laid her on her back. I would have tried to deter Oliver from going, as he is too good for such bad work, but he is already engaged, and all I could do was to advise him to make it a condition he should be employed inland, and not on the river. Still, it is about an even chance that he leaves his bones in the country. [Which he did.]

"Lunched with John Redmond and his wife. I told him in all possible confidence what George's difficulty was, and the precarious position of the Bill. He said, 'I quite understand Wyndham's difficulties, but you must believe me when I say mine are quite as great. There is a party in Ireland headed by Davitt and Archbishop Walsh that is determined to go against the Bill, and there is sure to be wild talk at the Convention. I saw Wyndham yesterday evening, and he told me something about the necessity of accepting the Bill as final, not as an instalment, and I am entirely in accordance with all he said. Of course the Bill will require amending, but I will do my best to get it through, and let the English imagine if they like that they are doing a fine and generous thing. But we can't stop the talk. I can depend thoroughly on William O'Brien who thinks exactly as I do about it, and all our Parliamentary party, even John Dillon, who I know does not like the Bill. He would be quite loyal to us. The difficulty is outside. Davitt is a land nationaliser, and is altogether opposed, and so is Archbishop Walsh. If it would make matters easier I shall be happy to communicate with Wyndham through you, and arrange what amendments it would be possible for him to accept. It would be easier to do it through you than directly, for it is difficult for him to talk quite frankly to me, and I have to go openly and knock at his door in the House of Commons when I want to speak to him, without knowing who there may be there with him. It would be very dangerous for it to get about that there was an understanding between us. But if he will do it through you it will be safe. So you must let me keep in touch with you. I go to Ireland to-morrow till after the Convention, which will be on the 16th. The critical time lies between this and then, and there may be things to communicate.'

"And so it was arranged between us. I asked him what his view was about a Catholic University. He said, 'You must not be shocked with me if I say I don't care twopence about it. Of course it would be a good thing, but it is not essential, and it is no good weighting ourselves with it till we have got the other job through.' This was almost word for word the answer I gave George yesterday to the same question.

"*2nd April.*— Breakfast again with George and told him of Redmond's proposal in regard to the amendments and of communicating

through me.   To this George readily assented, and it is agreed between
us that after the Easter recess he shall meet Redmond at my house
and discuss all things amicably there.   He had already met Redmond
once at Dunraven's, but it will be much more confidential here in Chapel
Street.   George has to speak tomorrow at Manchester, and will at
my suggestion say something in the direction of still further relieving
the evicted tenants.   I hope it may all turn out well.

"*4th April.*—A letter has come from Redmond of so important a
kind that I dare not send it on to George, but shall wait till I see him
on Monday.   In it Redmond gives a list of the amendments which
will probably be adopted at the Dublin Convention, and he expresses a
special hope in regard to the King's visit just announced for Ireland,
that the King will not receive any addresses while there.   Redmond
says that, while the Irish are quite prepared to receive the King in a
friendly way, they cannot officially show loyalty.

"*6th April.*— Arriving in London I went to Park Lane, where I
found George waiting for me.   I showed him Redmond's letter, and we
went through the various points of it together, and he then went into
his inner room to write an answer, leaving me to talk to Sibell meanwhile.   At the end of about three-quarters of an hour he came back
with the paper he had written, which, considering the difficulty and
importance of the questions dealt with, I hold to be a considerable feat.
In it he treats each of Redmond's suggested amendments, agreeing to
modifications of his bill as to most of them, but putting his foot down
on all demand of increasing the bonus of twelve millions.   In regard
to that he says:

"' I fear that any attempt, and above all any attempt *now,* to increase
the £12,000,000 would give a *dangerous* advantage to those in England
who are hostile to the whole plan.   *I think this is a great danger.*'

" This memorandum I am to copy out and send in my own handwriting to Redmond, and in such a way as not to compromise George
more than is necessary on account of the great risk.   ' Chamberlain,'
he said, ' is sure to cross-question me as to my having had any direct
communications with the Irish Party, or come to terms with them.   It
must be kept absolutely secret.'   I told him how dangerous a man I
knew Chamberlain to be, and how he had ruined all his rivals and
opponents at Birmingham in times past.   It is certain that the great
danger for the bill lies in him.   Yet Michael Davitt is publishing in
Dublin the tale that Chamberlain is the author of the whole Land
policy, and that he means to go on and give some sort of Home Rule
in the autumn.   This, no doubt, was once Chamberlain's policy in 1885,
and he will find it difficult to oppose it openly now, but his jealousy of
George's success may make him oppose it secretly, and he will be without
scruple.   The truth of the matter is that the Land Bill is supported

now in the Cabinet by Arthur Balfour and the Tories. It is opposed
by the Liberal Unionists. Chamberlain has held an ominous silence
since his return from South Africa. I should not be surprised if at the
last moment he should join Rosebery in betraying the bill. I was congratulating George on his having so far conciliated everybody. 'Wait
a little,' he said, 'there will be opposition enough presently.'

"I went home at once and sent off a copy of George's memorandum to
Redmond, changing only George's 'I's' into 'We's,' as if by any chance
it should fall into wrong hands it would be less personally compromising. I could not get any answer from George about the King's visit.

"*7th April.*— Lunched with Victor and Pamela Lytton in their new
house in Queen Anne's Gate. They have made it very pretty, and are
expecting very shortly a son and heir. Victor goes almost daily to
listen to the debates in the House of Commons, feeling cut off from a
political career by being in the Lords. He is looking older and his
face has grown longer. I see in him a certain likeness now to his
grandfather, the novelist.

"*9th April.*— To 'Homewood' to see Edith Lytton in her new
cottage. She took me over Knebworth, which is not at all changed
since last I was there some fifteen years ago — in the autumn of 1887,
when I had been campaigning in Ireland, and went down there to introduce George Wyndham to Lytton. The house is a perplexing combination of good and bad taste — true *bric-à-brac* and sham — I am afraid
mostly sham. What it wants is whitewash and white paint. But
Edith was shocked at my saying so. Her own cottage is nice, the work
of her son-in-law Lutyens.

"*20th April.*— I have been in bed with influenza, my fever taking
the form of my puzzling myself with the clauses of George's Bill and
the Dublin Convention.

"*25th April.*— On Thursday, 23rd, John Redmond came to see me
and gave me an account of how he had managed the Convention at
Dublin. Davitt had given much trouble at first, but had come to
terms when he found the Convention so much against him. Sexton
was still a considerable danger, as he was clean against the bill, and
if he insisted on returning to Parliament might make things very
difficult, as he was the only financier they had among them. But when
the question of his re-entering Parliament was moved at the Convention there was such strong opposition that it had been with difficulty
Redmond had been able to prevent an open quarrel. Sexton was 'a
queer fellow,' but of immense ability. He and the Archbishop, and
Davitt and, if they could get him, John Dillon, when he returned from
Egypt, would make a very strong combination. He thought I should
do well to see Dillon on his arrival in London, and tell him what the
dangers were. 'Dillon,' he said, 'has great confidence in your opinion.'

" About George, Redmond said, the great thing was for him to show a conciliatory attitude at the Second Reading in regard to amendments generally, and not to put his foot down on particular ones, whatever he might do in Committee afterwards. He also urged that Kilbride should be released from prison before the second reading, as his case was one that would be made the ground of a strong attack.

" Yesterday George came to see me. I told him about Kilbride, and he will release him on the plea of ill-health. He will also adopt as conciliatory a tone as he dares about the amendments. But he said the danger from his own friends was by no means over; Chamberlain was cunning and unscrupulous, and would trip him up if he could get an opportunity. If he gave him any opening he would wreck the bill, getting at Arthur Balfour and telling him it was impossible the thing should go on.

" There has been a ' disaster ' in Somaliland, which I hope may satisfy our people — a dozen of our young blood-letters who made the war for their amusement cut up, with the wretched natives they commanded. There never was less reason for any war than this, not even a reason of possible gold, only the lust of a rampage. If the whole of our military staff could be made to bite the dust, the world would be a happier place. But they won't be satisfied. War is the new form of sport all are wild to enjoy.

" *28th April.*— George has sent me a confidential note with a new message for Redmond. He has got a ' touch of influenza,' which Sibell tells me is really nothing but a cold, an excuse for his staying indoors and keeping himself quiet for next week, when the second reading of his Bill comes on. Redmond, under the circumstances of his illness, had proposed to call on him in Park Lane, but he can't see him there, and he wants me to be his medium of communication in discussing the amendments with Redmond. I have sent Redmond word that it is important I should see him at once, but so far have received no answer, and time presses.

" *30th April.*— Redmond came to-day. He tells me John Dillon is back from Egypt, very much opposed to the Bill. He does not want a reconciliation with the landlords, or anything less than their being driven out of Ireland. He will not, however, do anything ' shabby ' in opposing the Bill. But it makes the situation more difficult. Sexton is ' bitterly opposed,' and has the ' Freeman ' to back him and Archbishop Walsh. ' O'Brien and I,' he said, laughing, ' have risked a great deal in taking the attitude we did at the Convention.' I asked him what view American opinion took. He said ' They don't understand the Land Question there, nor the Bill, and they will take the view we take.' Such being the case, there are certain points Redmond *must* press at the Second Reading, the chief of which is the withdrawal of the 30 and 40 per cent. limit of reductions; but he will not insist upon an augmentation of the bonus, though in reality the twelve millions will not prove enough. He is to send me a memorandum, however, this afternoon from the House of Commons, for he is not himself well enough up in the Land Bill to put it down on paper without consultation. He will also be happy to see George here either to-morrow or Saturday.

"*1st May.*—Redmond's memorandum has come. In sending it he says, after asking for Kilbride's release from gaol:

"'Yesterday the matter was raised at the meeting of the Irish party, and I feel sure that some very decisive action must be taken if his imprisonment continues much longer, and I cannot conceive why his continued imprisonment should be apparently deliberately placed in our path by the Government. I hope you will be able to send me good news on this point, and should our friend desire to see me I can keep any appointment you may make for to-morrow or Saturday.'"

The memorandum itself is long and technical, and though interesting at the moment, I omit it here. It concludes: "I confine myself to the points I consider vital to the success of the Bill. If there was a certainty of satisfaction on these particulars (even though it should not be considered advisable to make a declaration publicly on the second reading debate), it would make it possible for us to avoid a contentious attitude towards the Bill, and allay a growing apprehension in Ireland (30th April, 1903)."

"To-day I went to see George. Dermot (Lord Mayo) was in the house with him, so I was shown upstairs to the drawing-room, and there we talked. He told me there had been a new Cabinet Council, at which his enemies, Chamberlain and the rest, had raged, and he had been obliged to give a promise that he would give no pledges whatever to the Irish Party before the Second Reading, nor hold any communication with them, so I was to consider what he told me as casual talk, and if I repeated it to Redmond it must be merely my impression of his views — no message."

"N.B. This is almost identical with old Gladstone's reservation when I asked him for a message of sympathy with Arabi in 1882. Nevertheless George gave me pencil and paper, and I wrote notes at his dictation, though he made me also many explanations, which I did not write. The long and the short of the thing is that he will concede a number of points in Committee, though he can make no pledge to do so on the second reading. We were more than an hour over this.

"On my return home I sent at once for Redmond, who came to Chapel Street in the course of the afternoon; and I read over my notes to him, and told him all I could remember of George's talk. On the

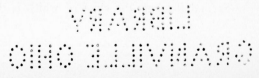

whole he is satisfied with it, and I am convinced all will go well. It has been a great satisfaction to me to manage this matter.

"*2nd May.*— Spent the morning writing a letter to the 'Times' about Somaliland. This exhausted me, as I am still very weak, so weak that I could not sit out the Irish play, to which I went in the afternoon. The first piece was a terrible infliction, called 'The Hour Glass,' by Yeats — a stupid imitation of that dull old morality, 'Everyman,' which bored me so much last year. What Yeats can mean by putting such thin stuff on the stage I can't imagine. It was not even well acted, for Yeats had drilled his actors to imitate Irving and other English mediocrities. They talked pompous stage English, and were not allowed their natural Irish accent. I felt inclined to get up and protest that we had not come to the Irish Literary Society for that. I was indignant, too, but it exhausted my little strength. I was determined, however, to hear Lady Gregory's piece, 'Twenty-five,' and was rewarded, for it is quite the most perfect little work of art and the most touching play I have ever seen acted. Only it made me weep in my weak state. I could not stay on for the final piece, 'Kathleen na Houlihan.' So I went home. I expect to see unbounded praise of the 'Hour Glass' in the London papers.

"*May 3rd (Sunday).*— William O'Brien came unexpectedly to see me and I talked the Land Bill over with him. I hope he will be prudent in what he says on the second reading, but he seems determined to press for an all round reduction of 15 per cent., which George told me was one of the most dangerous points, as Chamberlain is lying in wait to demand a withdrawal of the Bill if the twelve million limit is threatened, also, George believes, Hicks-Beach. While we were talking and I was impressing on O'Brien George's conversion on the Irish question, who should come in but Percy Wyndham. 'I see the world is very small,' said O'Brien, 'and perhaps I had better be off,' and off he went. He was to have sent Dillon to me, but this morning I have had a note from him saying he thinks it might have an awkward effect if the suggestion of his calling came from him. (They had quarrelled.) Percy had been told that O'Brien was with me and was much *intrigué* about him. Percy, though immensely interested in George's success, is too old a Tory to like the Bill, and prophesies all kinds of trouble for Ireland in the future. As to myself I have written as follows to Redmond:

"'I see you are asking subscriptions for the Irish Parliamentary Fund. I have much pleasure in sending you £50. You have done such admirable service during the past year as Leader of the Opposition, in place of the half-hearted and unintelligent gentlemen who sit on the Liberal Front Bench, that all lovers of Liberty here have come to look upon the Irish Party as its sole reliable support. Also I need not say how warmly I sympathize with your triumph in having brought our Government to the position where it stands to-day, of having abandoned its secular policy of governing Ireland in the interests of the English " garrison."

" ' I look upon the new Land Bill, if as I hope it passes the second reading, as the first piece of quite honest legislation for Ireland which will have been carried through Parliament in my recollection, and the certain prelude, however little the Government may have it in their minds, some day of Home Rule. In a few years you will have the present Landlords, who will be still considerable Land-owners in their demesnes, all with you as enthusiastic Irishmen; and then, with the country united for Home Rule, Home Rule must come.

" ' Therefore I wish, as always, more power to your elbow.'

" *5th May.*— John Dillon came to see me early and gave me his views of the situation very frankly. He spoke last night in support of the Bill, but he tells me that but for loyalty to his party he should be inclined to oppose it in Committee and vote against it on the third reading. His view is that it is useless trying to get the landlord class on the side of Nationalism, that they would always betray it when the pinch came, that the land trouble is a weapon in Nationalist hands, and that to settle it finally would be to risk Home Rule, which otherwise *must* come. For this reason he was opposed to the Conference with the landlords, and was opposed now in principle to the Bill. He should, however, of course, support it, since it had been decided to do so, for the one thing for Ireland was union in the Parliamentary Party. As long as that was maintained they commanded the situation in the House of Commons, and no matter what party was in power it would have to be their servant. We then discussed the prospects of a change of Government. He said that Rosebery would certainly be in the next Cabinet, probably at the head of it; that though he was thoroughly contemptible as a politician, he held them all through social influences. Harcourt was sick, perhaps dying; Campbell-Bannerman was weak; Morley had no power of leadership. Rosebery quite recently had made advances to Lloyd George, the most able of the Radicals, and Lloyd George had responded. To him, Dillon, it was a matter of indifference which of them was leader, or who became Prime Minister. The Liberal Party could not help itself and would be obliged to give Home Rule. All that was wanted in Ireland was patience and to keep the Parliamentary party together. United they had nothing to fear, even from their worst enemy, Chamberlain. I told him I thought there was a chance of Chamberlain heading a new Unionist schism, and that if he came into power on these lines with the popularity he had acquired by his imperialistic antics he would disfranchize Ireland and perhaps govern her as a Crown Colony. He did not think there was any fear of this, but I still think there is a remote danger.

" We also discussed Somaliland, on which Dillon also spoke a day or two ago in the House. Dillon has more statesmanship, I think, than any of them, having a wider experience and a better knowledge of history. His cynical view of the English parliament is fully justified. All the same, I think he is wrong about the Land Bill, as I believe it will prove a great step to Home Rule. But I agree with him that, whether or not it passes, the next Government that comes into power must do the Irish bidding. O'Brien is to speak to-day.

" *6th May.*— The debate is going capitally. O'Brien spoke with moderation and on the lines I pressed on him, especially as to the finality of the Bill as a land settlement. He was followed by Grey, who to our surprise has supported the Bill warmly. On Monday Arthur Balfour made an admirable speech in support of it, and Grey's was on the same lines. The Tory opposition has cooled down. I look upon the second reading as assured. George will, I think, be obliged to agree to the Irish demands on most of the amendments in Committee, and barring accidents, the thing is safe. Chamberlain seems to have made up his mind to a glum silence. He had his own Transvaal fish to fry to-day.

" *10th May.*— George's Bill has passed the second reading triumphantly by 417 to 26. I believe the biggest vote on record.

" *14th May.*— Chapel Street. Margaret Sackville came to lunch with me and talk over her plan of an Irish magazine to be called ' The Celt ' she is trying to start. I have given her some verses for it, and have promised some prose.

" *16th May.*— To the Academy, where the most remarkable thing is Sargent's portrait of Cromer. Sargent has a genius for seeing and reproducing the base passions of his sitters; and here is Cromer with bloated cheeks, dull eyes, ruby nose, and gouty hands, half torpid, having lunched heavily. Truly my quarrel with him is avenged. The newspapers complain that, instead of our "glorious Pro-Consul,' Sargent has given them nothing but a full-fed obstinate Indian official.

" Found Lady Z. at home. She has enjoyed her German visits and a lunch with the Emperor William. She found him an enormous talker without being exactly a good talker. He talks about everything, sometimes well, sometimes stupidly in a random, ill-balanced way. She says the Germans — I suppose she means the German officials and aristocracy — laugh at him for his wild utterances and constant mistakes; but he gives them no time to complain, passing with extraordinary energy from one thing to another, so that his blunders are forgotten;

and they like him, and are in a sort of way proud of him, as a remarkable personality who fixes the attention of the world.

"17th May.— A letter from Redmond about the maximum reductions, asking that the Government should declare its intention about it. He writes:

"15 *May* 1903.

"'My dear Blunt.— I duly received your letter. I am handing it and the proposed question to my brother, and asking him to look after the matter. I cannot do so myself as I am going to Ireland on Sunday for a few days.

"'About the Land Bill. The crux still is the question of the maximum reduction, and I have very great misapprehensions on this matter. If the Government persists in keeping in the maximum reductions there will undoubtedly be a very bitter conflict on the very first clause of the Bill in Committee with possible recriminations between the representatives of the landlords and the tenants.

"'This would undoubtedly spread to Ireland, and the present unanimity of opinion, which in my view alone makes it possible to carry the Bill, may entirely disappear. The retention of this maximum reduction is really a small matter, and the Government ought in my opinion seriously to consider the responsibility of again raising a conflict between classes in Ireland threatening the whole future as well as the passage of this Bill. The Ulster members are all of our way of thinking, and I cannot conceive any valid reason why the Government should stand by this maximum. I take the very gravest possible view of the situation, and I do hope that before it is too late the Government will make a concession on this matter which will enable the Bill to be passed without conflict, and which will preserve the good feeling which at present exists in Ireland.

"'I hope you will be able to press these views with vigour.

"'Very truly yours,
"'J. Redmond.'

"20th May.— I have been at Newbuildings since Saturday enjoying the new oak leaves, and the bluebells. This morning I came up to London and went at once to see George, to whom I showed Redmond's letter. In return he read me one he had received from Dunraven in precisely the opposite sense, declaring the resolve of the Conference of Landlords to fight any attempt to withdraw the maximum clause, and to get it reinserted by the Lords if the Commons amended it. He told me the situation. On Saturday Chamberlain went to Birmingham, and made a speech about the corn duty, contradicting all that Arthur Balfour had just said. I feared that this meant a revolt on Chamberlain's part, and a bid for leadership. But George assured me it was

not so. ' Chamberlain,' he said, ' is an impulsive fellow, and, now he
has blown his steam off, he has come back pleased with himself
and in a better temper. I am not afraid any longer of his wrecking
my bill. He will leave it alone. It is quite impossible, however, that
we should give up the maximum limit. The landlords won't stand it,
and the Lords would put it back if we did.' He then wrote me a
memorandum to show Redmond as an answer to his letter. ' He is
getting fussy,' he said. Armed with this I went on at once to Redmond, and caught him at home before he went out to the House. The
result is shown in the following letter :

"37, CHAPEL STREET, *May* 20, 1903.

" ' DEAR GEORGE.— I saw Redmond at twelve, and explained to him
the situation, with the help of the notes you gave me. Also I expressed
my personal view that the maximum was not worth fighting about.
He said that he also personally thought its importance had been exaggerated. But such was not the view taken in Ireland, where it had
been much worked up in the press, or by most of his colleagues ; public
opinion had gone too far for him to be able to control it. It was
largely the fault of the Conference landlords, Dunraven and Mayo,
who till the other day had agreed with him to a withdrawal of the
limit, and then for some unexplained reason had suddenly turned
round. The difference between them would now have to be fought out
on the floor of the House. It would be so, as far as he personally was
concerned, without acrimony, but by others, he feared, with bitterness.
He did not seem to think much of the reference to the House of Lords.
Within the last fortnight I have talked with others of the Irish members,
and I fear there is no doubt of there being a growing section among
them indifferent, if not hostile to the Bill. It seems to be the general
opinion that unless the tenants specially affected are given easier terms
than the Bill provides there will be new combinations against purchase.

" ' Such is my impression of the situation. It will be a pity, having
got so far, if the concordat ends in a new quarrel, but, if what Redmond tells me of Dunraven's sudden change from agreement to disagreement is accurate, it is hardly Redmond's fault.

" ' W. S. B.'

"To this I got a brief note from George. ' I am not pessimistic.'
Neither for that matter am I. I don't believe the maximum point
is a very serious one, and, even if there should be a new quarrel
between the Nationalists and the Dunraven Landlords, it won't stop the
bill, which has gone too far now to be upset. Chamberlain was the
only real danger.

" *3rd June.*— Newbuildings. Prince Scherbátoff came down to see the horses, and I went over with him to Crabbet. He is an extremely well informed man, and gave me an excellent account of the way the emancipation of the Russian peasantry is working out. He is himself a very large landowner, and cultivates 30,000 acres of land with 4,000 yoke of oxen. The peasants work their own land mostly on the communal system, preferring it. This the officials have been trying to alter, but the Emperor has just issued a decree confirming the peasants in their rights. There is a rule that they are unable to sell, or mortgage their land, which protects them against the usurers. All this is very analogous to what is proposed for Ireland, and I have promised to take him to see George who will be pleased to hear his account.

"*5th June.*— Margaret Sackville came to Chapel Street with her friend Katharine Horner to talk about 'The Celt.' I urged her to put her own name to the little venture as its only possible chance of success.

"*11th June.*— The great Ministerial crisis is over for the moment, and Chamberlain has been reduced to silence. The Government got a vote last night of 425 against 28, the whole Opposition and the Irish Party voting with them, against Chaplin and the Protectionists.

"*13th to 15th June.*— At Newbuildings — a very delightful party. Margaret Sackville, Katharine Horner,[1] who is a very pretty and clever girl of sixteen, and a writer of poetry, and is quite charming, the Poet Laureate and Meynell. The P. L. was in his best form, and Meynell amused us all with his anecdotes of Dizzy and other heroes.

"*17th June.*— Looked in at Belgrave Square where I found Madeline just back from the House of Commons, much excited about the Irish debate in Committee. This was stormy, and things are ticklish for the Bill. She was enthusiastic about the speaking of the Irish members, especially Redmond's. George had looked up twice to the Ladies' Gallery when it was over. She takes it as a sign he is satisfied.

"*18th June.*— To George in Belgrave Square where he is staying, and we walked together to the Irish Office. He told me the situation, and the danger there was from Chamberlain and from the landlords — and complained that the Nationalists had not kept to their agreement at the Landlords' Conference. However, he considers the worst risks over now. 'My position,' he said, 'is that of peace-maker in the Cabinet, of trying to persuade everybody that they all have really the same opinion — at any rate until my Bill is through. I take no side on the Preferential Tariff question till this is safe, being a practical politician.' All the same, he says, it will be very necessary for him to have a talk soon with Redmond, and he says it had better be at my house. He will let me know more in a day or two.

"*19th June.*— A letter from Redmond saying that affairs are very critical for the Bill, and that, unless George Wyndham adopts a more

---

[1] Afterwards Mrs. Raymond Asquith.

conciliatory attitude, the Bill will be wrecked. I went at once to Belgrave Square and found George preparing a speech he had to make in the evening. I explained to him the danger, especially of Dillon's attitude towards the Bill, and he agreed to meet Redmond at my house on Tuesday morning at 11.15. I hope they may patch up their difference, as it would be ruinous now for all concerned if the Bill falls through.

" *21st June (Sunday)*.— Mesaoud is sold to the Kleniewsky Stud in Poland for £240, a small price. But his going there will be an advantage to him and an advertisement to us. I have been calculating the price at which we have sold his stock, sons and daughters, and it amounts to over 5,000 guineas for 40 animals. We purchased him as a yearling colt for £50.

" *22nd June*.— Messrs. Boyes and Collier, English farmers from Basutoland, came to see the Stud. They are much impressed with our mares, and in raptures over the four stallions, especially Seyal and Nejran. Boyes has a commission to buy two for the Basutoland Government. They are violent anti-Boers, and spoke with contempt of the natives. They complained that the English colonists everywhere were being starved out, while the Boers lived on, on rubbish, and prospered.

" *23rd June*.— On coming up to London this morning I found George already established in Chapel Street with his red official despatch box arranging his papers. He told me he had had a regular Irish Parliament, consisting of Lords and Commons, debating Clause I of his Land Bill for the last day or two, which was a begining of Home Rule. Redmond joined us in five minutes, and they set to work at once on Clause I, George expounding his views of a possible compromise. He had drafted an amendment which he thought would obviate delay in the sales, but Redmond preferred Duke's amendment, and to something of this George in the end agreed. I was much struck with the lawyer-like ability both showed in seizing points as they rose, and developing them. The discussion was carried on in all possible good humour, and much personal sympathy. The contrast between the men was striking, though both were in their way good Irish types — for George is far more Irish than English — George gesticulating a good deal with his hands, and very eager, Redmond sitting with his hands nursing his great double chin seriously, but expanding from time to time in genial smiles when the points of agreement were reached. Both were intensely anxious to come to an understanding and carry the Bill, the real difficulty lying in the vacillation of the landlords, who are most of them too stupid to understand the Bill, and whose only firmness is obstinacy.

" The final agreement was that George should adopt the Duke amendment, or something like it, as his own; that Redmond should express his satisfaction with it, and his belief that it would be accepted as satisfactory in Ireland; and that no other amendment should be pressed to a division. Redmond next brought up the evicted tenants question, and here, too, they came, after some fencing, to an amicable agreement. Both talked of the political situation with the greatest frankness. George announced the release of McHugh, which Redmond already knew of, and he complimented George on having saved Kilbride's life by arresting him, inasmuch as Kilbride was drinking himself to death, and had now come out of gaol a sober and serious character. And so, at the end of about three quarters of an hour, they shook hands, and Redmond departed. George stopped a few minutes to talk it over with me in great delight, and then was off to his Cabinet Council at twelve. This I felt was an historic event, as I saw George into his hansom at the door with his red box — a great day for Chapel Street! We consider the Bill safe.

" Later I went to Belgrave Square, where Madeline made me stop and dine alone with her and George. It was one of the most amusing dinners I ever remember, just us three, George in tearing spirits, having spent the day in a series of encounters of a hair's-breadth kind. He described the Cabinet Council as *très accidenté,* and then he had had a tussle with the Duke of Abercorn and a number of the most violent landlord extremists, and then one with Dunraven, Mayo, and the rest,— and had succeeded in persuading them all round. As the dinner proceeded he became more and more eloquent, romancing almost like a schoolboy about his political career, describing the dexterities with which he had piloted his ship in the past, and what was to be his future. To us it was all delightful, and we hope it may all turn out true. George has in him the fire of genius, and whether as leader of the Conservative party, or of Irish Home Rule he will be equally conspicuous, and as superior to any English party leader as Disraeli was in his day. Then he rushed off back to the House to finish drafting his plans for to-morrow.

" *24th June.*— I lunched in Mount Street, and having met there the Poet Laureate went later to his box at His Majesty's Theatre to see his play, ' Flooden Field '— a piece of melodrama absurdly acted, which was followed by an adaptation of Kipling's story, ' The man who was.' This last was painful, too painful, in my view, for the stage, though the acting was good. Margaret Sackville was with us.

" *25th June.*— The papers announced George's safe passage of the Irish Land Bill Clause I through the House; and there are amusing comments about ' secret arrangements ' of the quarrel. Anyhow it seems to have been a great Irish triumph, and all Irish parties have been embracing each other.

" Frank Lascelles came to lunch with me in order to meet George, and we had a pleasant talk with Lady Windsor as fourth.

" Gorst is being married this afternoon to an heiress named Rudd. I did not go to it, though I sent a wedding gift. The Khedive arrived in London yesterday, and is staying with the King's millionaire, Cassel, in Grosvenor Square.

" *27th June.*— A letter has come from Brewster Bey, saying that the Khedive would like to visit the stud at Crabbet to-morrow. Sunday is an inconvenient day to have chosen, as there are next to no trains. So I have had to order a special one, and telegraph all over the place in preparation. Caffin fortunately was here to-day, and I was able to arrange a programme with him.

" *28th June (Sunday).*— A piping hot day, so we drove over to Crabbet early to make the necessary arangements. We had all the horses dressed and got ready. The house was looking lovely, and, the tenants being away, we had it all to ourselves. Then Judith and Neville arrived from Rake, and with them Marsh, and we lunched at Caxtons, and were lying out to cool in the little lane behind when a telegram arrived. Before I read it I guessed what it must be about. The Khedive in consequence of ' unforeseen circumstances ' could not come, professes his ' profound regret,' etc. It is quite clear that the King has prevented him. My only wonder is that he was allowed to propose it. So we have had our trouble for nothing.

" *29th June.*— A letter has come from Brewster confirming his yes- terday's telegram. The Khedive wishes to impress on me the fact that ' the circumstances which *prevent* his coming *are* altogether beyond his control,' and reiterates his ' profound regret,' and assures me that if it had been possible to come His Highness would surely have come. The absence of all definite reason given, either of indisposition or other engagement, together with the use of the present tense, ' prevent his coming,' quite clearly indicates a permanent prohibition, and my only doubt is whether it is the Foreign Office or the King that has interfered. I feel pretty certain, however, that it cannot have been a lesser per- sonage than the King himself, acting through Cassel — for the Khedive would hardly be such a goose as to be frightened by Lord Lansdowne, and he is under Cassel's charge, and Cassel is the King's man. How- ever, I am determined to get at the truth of it, and am writing to Brewster to say that ' knowing as I do the kindly feeling His High- ness has for so many years entertained towards me, and remembering the distressing circumstances of his political position, I hold him in no way responsible for the slight offered me, that I thank him for the honour intended, and cordially accept the expression of his regret for an act of discourtesy foreign to his nature, and which only pressure from the very highest quarter could have forced upon him, a quarter to which I, too, owe obedience."

" This will, I think, draw the whole truth from him, for he cannot leave my letter unanswered without admitting that it is in reality the King who forbade him. If it is not the King, he will make haste to explain what other personage it was. In either case I shall arrive at the facts.

" *30th June.*— There is an account in to-day's papers of a banquet given last night by the King to the Khedive, with a long list of the guests. Here are all the officials who for the last ten years have been worrying the Khedive's life out of him at Cairo, thirty or forty of them, Rodd, Lane, Talbot, and the rest. Also an uncle of Lord Lansdowne's with Rodd again. This is intended to impose upon the world, and persuade the British public that the Khedive is England's devoted servant.

" *1st July.*— That other high and mighty prince, Athrobold Charles Stuart de Modena, *alias* William Brown, the coachman's son at Frimley and ex-footman, has been brought before the Winchester Assizes. The charges of felony, which would have necessitated a public inquiry into his past life, were at the last moment withdrawn by the Crown, and he was allowed to plead guilty to a misdemeanour only, that of marrying Lady Russell under a feigned name. This looks as if there had been a desire to screen the other noble ladies he befooled.

" *4th July.*— Our annual Crabbet Sale, but most of the fine ladies from London failed to come, only 300 persons sitting down to luncheon in the tent. The speeches were good, Cunninghame Graham proposing my health. Redmond and Dillon were both there, and I sat between Mrs. Redmond and Caroline Grosvenor."

[N. B. This was our last public sale at Crabbet.]

" *8th July.*— To London and lunched with Ameer Ali, who talked to me about a scheme of a Mohammedan University for India as an original idea of his own. We also discussed George Curzon. George Wyndham told me the other day that it is settled that Curzon comes back to England at the end of the year. He will cease to be Viceroy, for a Viceroy may not leave India. But if the Tories are still in office six months later, he will be reappointed for a new term.

" *9th July.*— Saw George this morning in Belgrave Square, where he was still in bed, having been up late getting the last clauses of his Land Bill through Committee. He was very triumphant.

" *11th July.*— George writes me confidentially (9th July, 1903):

' The sections interested in the Sugar Convention, Education, and the Tariff proposals seek to " blackmail " the Government over the Land Bill by delaying it to extract time for *their* favourite questions. Unfortunately, some whose advice may be taken, want Education to go to the Lords before the Land Bill. The only way to defeat this accidental chance combination of *opposite* interests is to press on not only Report, but also the Third Reading of the Land Bill. . . . The question resolves itself into this — can Report be finished on Friday, 17th, to Monday, 20th? If so, by a *coup de main* we might get Tuesday, 21st, afternoon sitting, for the Third Reading. . . . If this plan succeeds I *know* that the Land Bill will be driven over at least to the 27th-31st, with the result that it will not reach the Lords before Monday, 3rd August.

'All the above is no doubt gibberish to you. But as you have taken so deep an interest in the fortunes of the Land Bill, I *wish* you to know exactly how the matter stands. You might like to see me on Tuesday morning with anyone else who takes a deep interest in the fortunes of the Bill. At any rate I felt impelled to acquaint you with the situation, etc.'

"13th July.— Henley is dead. I got a note from George on Saturday telling me he was very ill, but the end has been sudden. About Henley's relations with Stevenson, Meynell, who was with me to-day, was again eloquent. He knew the Henleys well, having been godfather to the daughter that died, and he says that Henley's anger against Stevenson was of old date, from at least the time of Stevenson's marriage. He could not forgive him for having forsaken the Bohemian convivial ways Henley delighted in, and, though he constantly received money help from Stevenson afterwards, always resented his conversion to respectability. He considers Henley's attack upon his friend an unpardonable offence. I confess I do not like Henley, though I have tried to like him for George's sake. But he is both physically and intellectually repugnant to me. He has the bodily horror of the dwarf, with the dwarf's huge bust and head and shrunken nether limbs, and he has also the dwarf malignity of tongue and defiant attitude towards the world at large. Moreover, I am quite out of sympathy with Henley's deification of brute strength and courage, things I wholly despise. Thus I could never feel at my ease with him, and George's affection for him has always seemed to me a puzzle.

"14th July.— To London early, and found notes in Chapel Street from both George and Redmond, who have met elsewhere and arranged about the Third Reading of the Bill. George and Sibell at Belgrave Square were just starting in black for Henley's funeral. They wanted me to go with them, but I excused myself. I never go to funerals or wish anyone to go to mine.

"At four Miss Cornelia Sorabje called to talk about some Indian affair which interested her. She came clad in an orange garment after the fashion of ladies in her own country, which became her well. She has been a very pretty woman, though now I imagine thirty, with an exceedingly sweet voice, and I gave her tea.

" *20th July.*— George goes to-night to Ireland with the King, leaving Arthur Balfour to pilot his Land Bill through its Third Reading to-morrow. I asked his mother whether the King had had anything to do, as the Irish believe, with the bringing in of the Land Bill, and she said, ' Nobody at all, I believe, except George.'

" It is probably an exaggeration that the King bears the Nationalists any great goodwill, though he is less bitter than was the late Queen.

" *30th July.*— A note from George; he is just back from Ireland, where he has been with the King, and says that all has gone off excellently well so far. There is no chance now of the Lords amending the Bill, and it is certain to become law.

" Afterwards for a walk with Percy in the Park. We found Philip Currie there in a bath chair, unable to use his legs, and so being wheeled about. Later I lunched with him and Angelina in Princes Gate. [This was the last time to my sorrow I saw either of them.]

" At my club to-day I found myself faced at a little distance by an old fogey whose features I seemed to know, and by degrees made out that he was Victor Drummond, my fellow *attaché* once at Athens. I had not seen him since we said good-bye at the Piræus in 1860, yet I recognized him and he me. Another ancient, too, there, was Horace Rumbold. All these I remember young and gay, and all are tottering to their graves.

" *4th Aug.*— It has been announced that a new Pope has been elected, Cardinal Sarto, from Venice, who has taken the name of Pius X. Pope Leo died a fortnight ago after a prolonged agony, which was made more horrible for us by the daily accounts of the surgical experiments used to prolong his life, so that at last the poor old man became like a nightmare on the public mind, and all rejoiced that he was dead.

" Of Pope Leo my recollection is a very intimate one, and still extremely vivid. It was in the Spring of 1886 when, after my failure at the Camberwell election, I was sick alike of the affairs of the world and of the vain pursuit of happiness. I went to Rome as on a pilgrimage, with the vague hope that perhaps I might there recover my lost faith in supernatural things and end my days in piety. I had many friends among the resident clergy, including Monsignor Stonor and Cardinal Howard, among the Pope's household, and Father Lockhart, head of the Rosminians, to whom I had been introduced by Cardinal Manning, Prior Glyn, and other of the Irish hierarchy; and a little programme of holy pleasures had been sketched out for me, and I was determined to open my mind wide to the influences of the place, that my soul might have its full chance. It was thus predisposed that I arrived at Rome. I made a general confession of my sins, and if I had been unmarried, I should have attempted to join some religious order as a desperate protection against my own unbelief. As it was I indulged dreams of living as *custode* to some church of the many churches in and about Rome. It was in this mood that Monsignor Stonor suggested that I should have an audience with the Pope, and he without difficulty procured me one. I had brought my old diplomatic uniform with me, I know not with what prevision, and it was in that dress that I went to the Vatican, where I was received by the Papal household with marked distinction. They thought, I believe, that I had some diplomatic mission, for Pope Leo was highly interested in the idea of a renewal of diplomatic relations with our Foreign Office, and so I was admitted to the most private of private audiences. Be this as it may, my reception by His Holiness was of a kind which surprised and touched me almost to bewilderment when I heard the door shut behind me, and I found myself absolutely alone with one so nearly divine, if there was divinity anywhere to be found on Earth. The vision that I saw before me was that of a little old man of wonderful dignity, clad in white and seated on a low throne, his face pale, but lit with luminous dark eyes, which seemed to hold all knowledge of this world and the other, the figure of a Saint, and at the same time of one who knew the world, and, strange to say, reminding me of that wonderful figure of Voltaire seated in his chair at the Theatre Français, for the attitude was the same, bending towards me with a look of inquiring kindliness. When I had kissed his feet he raised me up, though I continued kneeling, and on his invitation spoke to him about Ireland. What he then said has been already related (see my 'Land War in Ireland'), but what I have not said and what I cannot here altogether say is, that the personal interest he seemed to take in me, for he continued to hold my left hand with his own right hand and to press it to his knee, gave me the courage to speak of my own spiritual affairs as in a confessional, and to ask his help. He could not give me all I asked, but when I left him it was in tears. I had been with him for over twenty minutes, and the chamberlains, when I found myself outside the audience chamber, cast on me eyes of reproval for having been so long, and they seemed to guess to such little public purpose.

"*6th Aug.*— Newbuildings. Mohammed Abdu arrived from Egypt yesterday with his brother Hamouda, and I drove them to-day to Crabbet and back, calling at Forest Cottage on our way, where I found Button with his mother and his wife, and his beautiful little daughter Daphne. He told me much that was interesting of the new Pope, Cardinal Sarto, while he was Patriarch at Venice, where Button has been for some time living. He spoke also of our King Edward, who has come to be looked upon abroad as the greatest diplomatist of the

day, and how French opinion has been quite converted by him to
friendliness with England. At his Paris club, Button, who had previously been treated coldly as an Englishman, was received the other day
as he passed through almost with demonstrations.

"Mohammed Abdu sat with me during our drive on the coach-
box, I driving my four Arabs, and we had much conversation on
Egyptian affairs.

"*9th Aug. (Sunday)*.—I have had an interesting time these last
few days with the Mufti, and to-day, walking in Newbuildings Wood,
we had a long talk about religion. I asked him especially as to his
belief in angels and spirits. About these, though not denying their
existence, he said ' No one has seen them, nor is it possible to know
anything about them. About God, too, it is impossible to know.' I
asked him about a future life. In this he believes, and that there will
be a happy and an unhappy state, but in what way he does not know.
He does not believe in *eternal* punishment.

"We have talked also about the events of 1882, and he has
read through the papers I have here connected with Arabi's trial,
and urges me strongly to publish a history of that time. My difficulty,
however, is that my most important documents are letters written by
persons still living who might and probably would object, while without them it would be impossible to put forward an irrefutable exposure
of our English intrigues. There is nothing personal in these letters,
and they are quite fair historical documents, and must some day
see the light, and it ought to be soon. Lastly, we have discussed the
actual state of justice in Egypt, as to which the Editor of the ' Manchester Guardian ' has asked me to give him information. This I
shall now be able with the Mufti's help to supply.

"*10th Aug.*—With Mohammed Abdu to Brighton to see Herbert
Spencer. (It was especially to see Spencer that he had come to England, as he held him to be a great philosopher, and had translated
his volume on education into Arabic. I had written to Spencer to
explain this and propose a visit.) Spencer sent his carriage, and his
secretary, Mr. Troughton, to meet us at the Brighton station. We
found the old man in bed in his back drawing-room at Percival
Terrace, where he has been bedridden since April. The stroke he had
then has not affected his mind, and we found him quite lucid in his
ideas as well as strong in voice, but he is terribly thin, and his hand
is a mere skeleton's. He received us for a short time before luncheon, and again at three o'clock. At first he tried talking French, but
very deliberately and looking for his words, and soon dropped into
English, which I translated to Abdu. He lamented the disappearance
of ' right' from the range of modern politics in Europe, and denounced the Transvaal war as an outrage on humanity. 'There is

coming,' he said, ' a reign of *force* in the world, and there will be again
a general war for mastery, when every kind of brutality will be practised.'

"For the afternoon visit he turned to philosophy, and asked the
Mufti whether it was true that thought in the East was developing
on the same lines as the thought of Europe. Mohammed Abdu
told him that what the East was learning from the West was the
evil rather than the good, but that still the best and most enlightened
thought of both was the same. ' To go to the bottom of things,' said
Spencer, ' I suppose that the conception of the underlying force of
the world, what you call Allah and we call God, is not very different?'
In his reply the Mufti made a distinction which struck Spencer as
new. ' We believe,' said Abdu, ' that God is a *Being,* not a *Person.*'
Spencer was pleased at this, but said the distinction was rather difficult
to grasp. ' At any rate,' he said, ' it is clear that you are Agnostics
of the same kind as our agnosticism in Europe.' We had not time
to develop this train of thought, as Spencer is only allowed a few
minutes' talk at a time, but later, on our way back to the station, I
questioned the Mufti more closely on the point. *I.* ' Do you believe
that God has consciousness, that he knows that you exist and that
I exist, and is not such knowledge personality?' *The Mufti.* ' He
knows.' *I.* ' If he knows, he knows that you are good and I am bad.'
He agreed. *I.* ' And he is pleased with you and displeased with me?'
The Mufti. ' He approves and disapproves.' *I.* ' And he approves
to-day because your actions are good, and he disapproves to-morrow
because your actions have become bad. Is not this change from
approval to disapproval characteristic of personality? How then has
God no person?' *The Mufti.* ' God knows all things at all times; to
him there is no to-day and no to-morrow, and therefore in him is no
change; His is an eternal unchanging consciousness of all things.
This I call Being, not Personality.' *I.* ' And Matter? Is not Matter
eternal, too, or did God create it? If he created it he made a change?'
The Mufti. ' Matter, too, is eternal as God is eternal.' Here evidently
is the foundation of Abdu's thought, and we agreed that our ideas are
the same.

"With Spencer, however, we could not argue all this out, and
we took leave of him only half satisfied, but glad that we had had
the privilege of even this small glimpse of his mind. The young
ladies whose acquaintance I had made four years ago are still living
with him, and they gave us an interesting account of the old philosopher's way of life. He takes a certain pleasure in their company,
having no relations of his own except one deaf old woman and hardly
any friends. He has seen only three or four people since his illness
in April. Last year, however, he was in comparatively good health, and

spent the summer near Leith Hill, and went out sometimes with them to picnics, which he enjoyed, taking an interest in the flowers and birds, and now he has them to sit with him every evening and makes them play chess or drafts or cribbage in his presence, ' and he always wishes to know,' they said, ' which of us has won.' [1]

" We went on to London, and Professor Browne and Cockerell joined us at dinner in Chapel Street. Abdu is to go to Oxford to-morrow and to Cambridge on Wednesday. It has been lovely weather during all their visit at Newbuildings.

" *22nd Aug.*— To Hatfield for Lady Galloway's funeral. Her death came upon me as a sudden shock, for I had not heard of her illness, a very short one. She was taken with a severe pneumonia on Friday, and only yesterday I had had a letter from Wagram telling me that his son Alexandre was going to stay with her in the New Forest, and I had been looking forward to seeing her there. She died at Cuffnells, which she had rented for the autumn. I remember her first as a girl not yet out in 1866, the year of Sadowa, with her mother, who was then Lady Salisbury, at Homburg, but I did not meet her again till one evening, when I sat next to her at a dinner at the Admiralty, and later when we were both staying at the Paris Embassy the year before Lytton died. Then we finally made friends. She had led a sad life, but her later years were happier. Now all is over suddenly and for ever.

" To-day was a lovely day after several of heavy rain. At King's Cross I found Pom McDonnell, and we travelled down to Hatfield together, having also with us Eddy Stanley, whom I had not before seen. At the church there were not a dozen mourners, besides the few house servants and retainers, with Lord Arthur Cecil, her brother, and one of Lord Galloway's brothers as chief mourners, Arthur Balfour, who though four years older, was her nephew, Lady Hayter, and Miss Mildred Hope, her two chief women friends, George Leveson Gower, and me. Of all her society friends there was not one, and none of Lord Salisbury's sons, while Lord Salisbury himself, her ' big brother ' (as she used to call him) lay dying in the great house hard by. It was pitiful, tragic, touching, with the sunlight streaming in through the windows on the Cecil monuments. I took a place away from the official mourners, for it was a very private funeral in the Cecil family burial ground, and I was not one of them, but I went with the rest to the grave which they had made in a sunny corner under the wall. The churchyard is a very pretty one and is the place where she had chosen to be laid. She always had a passionate love for Hatfield, her early home. When all was finished I went on into the park, meaning to spend an hour or two there before going

---

[1] Compare "Home Life with Herbert Spencer," by Two.

back to London, but as I was passing by the house one of them asked
me in and we all sat down in the great hall to a luncheon which stood
ready, but the lord of the palace lay dying in a room upstairs, as we
all knew, and the funeral baked meats stuck in our throats. I doubt
whether any one of us had the courage to eat more than a few mouth-
fuls. Then I went on for my walk alone and wandered an hour
in the park, where children were playing and shouting as if nothing
momentous were taking place in the great house. The deer were lying out in a cool place in the open, and rabbits were busy nibbling under
the great oaks, and the ownership of it all was passing from one
Cecil to another, for Robert Lord Salisbury died at sunset.

"*31st Aug.*— At Clouds. Lord Salisbury is being buried, I believe
to-day, quietly at Hatfield, the offer of a grave in Westminster Abbey
having been rejected. This is in keeping with his life, which has
always scorned honours and hated publicity. He has been certainly
in his way a great man, and without much pomp or parade, one who
has achieved great things. People only half recognized these as yet
because he has never talked much about them, but they are very
real, and will some day be recognized for what they are; not that I
am in sympathy with his doings, only in the manner of their doing.
By far the largest of his achievements has been the partition of Africa.
This was imagined in secret and developed silently. It may be said
to have begun at Berlin in 1878, when the joint financial intervention in
Egypt was arranged with France and Tunis was given her in return
for Cyprus, a scandalous beginning, followed by the retention of Egypt
and the various deals with Italy, Germany, Belgium, Portugal, and
France, which have mapped out the whole Continent between the four
Powers, England getting the most valuable if not quite the largest
share. The reconquest of the Soudan was a policy wholly Lord Salisbury's, and I believe he had his full share in the intrigues which brought
on the reconquest of the Transvaal, though perhaps less directly responsible than Chamberlain. At the Foreign Office he re-established in
large measure England's influence on the Continent. He engineered
the Entente Cordiale with America at the time of the Spanish War
and got round the Emperor William in anticipation of the Boer War.
All these were notable triumphs. Hardly less so at home has been
his rehabilitation of the monarchy as an effective force in politics,
the resurrection under his guidance of the House of Lords, and
the reducton of the House of Commons to impotence except as a
machine to support the Government. His anti-Home Rule policy in
Ireland alone has been a failure. It seems now to be breaking down
at all points, especially his idea that twenty years *resolute* government
would destroy opposition. I think, too, that he has sacrificed the real
interests of rural England, with which Conservatism is bound up on

not a few vital points. Under his guidance the Jew capitalists have flourished while the agricultural community has decayed. This he certainly did not intend, and here have been his failures. Nevertheless, he was head and shoulders taller as a statesman than the other statesmen of his day, including Gladstone and Disraeli, I mean judged by results, for he was neither an orator like Gladstone, nor a writer like Disraeli. Personally in my few dealings with him I always found him kind and courteous. I met him first, if I remember rightly, in 1880, when I travelled down with him and Lytton by train to Lewes. It was an accidental meeting. Then I had an interview with him about the same time at the Foreign Office to talk over the affairs of Arabia, Syria, and Egypt, but this I think must have been before the other meeting, as he left office in June 1880 and Lytton did not return to England till August. Later, in 1883, I had a curious talk with him at the House of Lords about the Palmer business, and since then have had from time to time bits of correspondence with him about Egyptian matters. In all these he took the trouble of writing to me himself and always with great courtesy. As long as Lady Salisbury lived her influence with him was, I think, favourable to me. I was rather friends with Lady Gwendolen, and Lady Galloway was his half-sister. His retirement from the Foreign Office was a loss to me in every way. Peace be with his ashes.

"*1st Sept.*— To-day George arrived from Ireland. This is George's holiday time, and he has no red office boxes following him about, but I found him full of talk about his political plans. He considers things will go smoothly now in Ireland, and that the large majority of estates will change hands under the new Act which comes into operation in October. About preferential tariffs (Tariff Reform), he took me into his confidence. He considers that Chamberlain has absurdly exaggerated the importance of the Colonies, especially Australia. 'For all practical politics,' he said, 'they are negligible quantities, that is to say for the next thirty years, though they may become of importance later. We need take no count of them at all now, only Canada needs to be considered, and whatever we do in the way of preference must be for her alone. This is what will be decided at the next Cabinet, and we shall develop in our speeches in October. Canada's position must be taken in connection with the United States, which again is the only world power likely to rival our own. Germany and France we need not worry about as rivals.' Of his own position and prospects he talked with his usual naïve self-confidence. 'I am just forty,' he said, 'and find myself with the balance of power in my hands. I mean of power in the Cabinet. We shall go out of office next year, then I shall take a long holiday. I shall go travelling all the world over, and not trouble myself in opposition, at least for a while. In fifteen years' time I shall leave politics for good, the more one sees of them, the more futile they appear, and I shall have had enough of them by the time I am fifty-five. Of course I must be Prime Minister first, I am sure of that. I am constantly approached already to lead the Party, and I can do so when I please. I don't see who is to be my rival in it, George Curzon will be in the House of Lords, and I am younger than all the rest. It is surprising how little ability there is, but I don't mean to go on for ever with it. I have other things to do.'

"*3rd Sept.*— I asked George to-day about the King, and what impression he had made on him during the visit to Ireland. He said, 'The King is intelligent about political matters, and quick to seize ideas, almost too quick. He is really interested in Ireland, and the Irish have found out he is favourable to them. I don't know how they knew about it, but they know.'

"*7th Sept. to 11th Sept.*— I paid a visit with Anne to Ashley Coombe where the Lovelaces are settled for the autumn. He very busy cutting trees and attending to other improvements much needed. I had not been there to stay since my honeymoon. We had a pleasant time now riding every day through the oak woods, which are very beautiful, and extend from the shore of the Bristol Channel to the edge of Exmoor, with its open heaths a thousand feet above us.

"Ralph has given me his 'Astarte' revised to read. It is much improved, though it still retains his attack on Murray.

"*30th Sept.*— Austin Lee writes from Paris that Berthe Wagram who has long been ill is not expected to live many days. She has received the last sacrament. Poor Wagram, he says, is in a terrible state of despondency and nervous excitement. [Lee telegraphed again two days later to tell me she was dead.]

"Meynell has dedicated his new book on Disraeli, for whom he has a great *culte,* to me. I have written to him as follows:

"'I have now read the whole of your two volumes, and am only sorry there are not two more. Your Dizzy is indeed a creature of loveable qualities, and the human part of him you have brought admirably out, his affection, his lightness in hand, his wit. This last I place next in the world to Voltaire's, his intellectual father. Tancred, Coningsby, Ixion, these have more wit in them than anything in literature since Candide. So far I go with you.

"'You must not, however, call me a "Dizzy-*worshipper,*" as you do in your dedication. I am a hundred miles away from that. Æsthetically our good Jew was a terrible Philistine; and politically (I say it with some timidity to you his apologist) a very complete *farceur.* I don't like to call him anything worse than that. "Mountebank" and *charlatan* are abusive terms which imply deception for an

ignoble end, and of this there is no sign, for his ambition was pure
of all money calculations. Only you cannot persuade me that he ever
for an instant took himself seriously as a *British* statesman, or expected any but the stolid among his contemporaries to accept him so.
His *Semitic* politics of course were genuine enough. For his fearless-
ness in avowing these I hold him in esteem — for a Jew ought to be a
Jew — and I enjoy as a *tour de force,* his smashing of those solemn
rogues the Whigs, and his bamboozling of the Tories. Our dull English
nation deserved what it got, and there is nothing funnier in history
than the way in which he cajoled our square-toed aristocratic Party
to put off its respectable broad-cloth, and robe itself in his suit of
Imperial spangles, and our fine ladies after his death to worship their
old world-weary Hebrew beguiler under the innocent form of a primrose. All this was excellent fooling, but the joke has been rather
a poor one for the world at large, and has saddled us at home with
what we see, a bragging pirate democracy.

"'So don't call *me* a worshipper. I will laugh as much as you like,
and I will even love the brother of Sara — but I will not take the
member for Maidstone seriously, or the Creator of the British Empire,
even on his way home to his Queen-Empress from Berlin.

"'P.S. I am not sure I ought not to ask you to add this letter
to the dedication in your next Edition.'

"*5th Oct.*— I hear on extremely good authority that an arrangement
has been come to between Cromer and Gorst to the effect that Gorst
is to have Cromer's place at Cairo on condition that later he is to
give way to Cromer's son, Cromer having the ambition to found a sort
of dynasty in Egypt. This is to take place next year, I mean the
first step of it, Cromer's retirement. His new wife has just presented
him with another son.

"*6th Oct.*— The great political excitement of the last three weeks,
consequent on Chamberlain's resignation of the Colonial Office ended
yesterday, with the resignation of the Duke of Devonshire and the
publication of the names of the new ministers. Chamberlain's resignation was at first taken as indicating a collapse of his plans, but it
almost at once transpired that it was only an intrigue between Arthur
Balfour and himself for the better execution of their programme, and
to rid themselves of certain colleagues who were declared free traders,
while keeping the Duke whose influence in the country, as a safe if slow
man typical of the old Whigs, is great. In my opinion however, the
whole fiscal agitation has been got up by Chamberlain in order to
divert public attention from his own blundering in South Africa, which
it was almost incredible the British public could condone if it had had
time to examine it fairly. Chamberlain is not a man of sufficient
intellect to get any real grasp of large questions even of trade. All

his career proves this, and the only wonder is to find him in·friendly partnership with a man of honour like Arthur Balfour. Arthur, I see, has just put Alfred Lyttelton into the Colonial Office, continuing thus the tradition of what I call the ' Soul's Cabinet,' Milner having refused. The appointment is amusing to those who know the feminine side of things. St. John Brodrick, another of the set, goes to the India Office in spite of his incapacity; the two, with George at the Irish Office and Arthur, make up a Soul quartet at which one smiles. And to think of all these fine gentlemen being hustled and browbeaten by that great . . . Joe of Birmingham. What a comedy!

" *14th Oct.*— Shot the Woodgaters beat with Dormer, Robert Gregory, and Caffin, getting seventy-two pheasants. Young Gregory is a distinctly good shot, and an extremely nice fellow.

" *21st Oct.*— With Dorothy to Annunzio's Italian play, Francesca da Rimini, the chief part played by Duse. We found the play intensely interesting, quite admirably acted, especially by the men; the fourth act is I consider the finest dramatic conception, and was the most finely executed of any I have ever seen on any stage. As a rule I hate mediæval plays, but this one has all the reality of a thing of to-day, while it sacrifices nothing of the atrocity inseparable from mediæval Italy. It is the work of a great genius comparable to that of Victor Hugo at his best, Corneille, Racine, and even Shakespeare. We were both deeply moved, and the impression was sustained to the end.

" *22nd Oct.*— George tells me he had great difficulty in evading the War Office, which was thrust upon him in the recent Ministerial changes. ' But,' he said, ' I go on the Cromer principle of sticking to one thing until it is done thoroughly, and I mean to stick to Ireland. I could have had any place I liked, but I would not move. He is now going to take up the Catholic University, not that it is urgent, but as part of the programme, and because the present will be a capital moment to start it when everyone is busy with the preferential tariffs. ' I like,' he said, ' fishing in troubled waters, but I shall not force the thing on. I must get my colleagues to go with me.' I asked him how he was going to endow it, whether he was going to take funds from Trinity College or how? He said, ' No, I never take anything from anybody, my plan is always to give. I shall endow a Catholic University and a Presbyterian University out of the public Funds, the money admittedly due to Ireland. It will be a great thing to do both at once, because then I shall split the religious interests into three, instead of as now into only two, and shall always be able to get two with me against the third. I asked him whether he is going to announce his scheme at Dover where he is to speak to-morrow, and showed him the article

in the ' Times ' of this morning, which he had not read. He read it,
and was rather put out by it. ' It is too stupid of Buckle,' he said.
' I must write him a strong letter at once, and put a stop to this.'

" 31*st Oct.*— Here I close this year's journal as far as my life in
England is concerned. The part I was able to play in Irish affairs
this summer has given me confidence my life has been not quite
wasted. I await the future calmly, feeling that I have almost completed my life's work.

" Victor Lytton, who has been staying at Whittinghame and other
headquarters of information, has given me a true and particular account of the recent Ministerial crisis. Chamberlain's first shot, fired
in the Spring at Birmingham, was in consequence of the refusal of
the Exchequer to grant a preference in favour of the Colonies on the
Corn Tax or to continue the duty. The refusal was quite unexpected
by the rest of the Cabinet and was not taken seriously by them at
first; later Arthur Balfour's whole effort has been to keep the Cabinet
together, but as he has been gradually converted by Chamberlain to
retaliation, and as Ritchie is an out and out free-trader it became impossible to do so, and the free-traders in the Cabinet had to go.
Ritchie and Hamilton and the Duke of Devonshire resolved together
on this course the day before the Cabinet meeting, and the two first sent
in their written resignations, but the Duke, who was always behind-
hand through slowness of thought, delayed writing his. So Arthur was
able to persuade him to stay on. Arthur is furious now with the
Duke, because in his own slow time he has got to understand the
drift of what was going on, and has now resigned and left them in
the lurch. It is like keeping on a cook after she has given warning.
She gives you nothing but cold mutton, and chucks up altogether
the day of your dinner party. Victor gave some amusing stories
of the Duke's slowness and forgetfulness. Lord Dudley had been
invited to dinner one day at Devonshire House, and as he was
driving up to the door saw a royal carriage entering the court-
yard in front of them, and began to trouble himself because he
had not put on his orders. When the carriage stopped at the front
door the King stepped out, but nobody seemed prepared for their
coming, and it transpired that the Duke had told no one of having
invited the King, and had forgotten about it himself. He was found
playing bridge at the Turf Club.

" I stopped to luncheon with Victor and Pamela and met there
for the first time young Winston Churchill. He is a little, square-
headed fellow of no very striking appearance, but of wit, intelligence, and originality. In mind and manner he is a strange replica
of his father, with all his father's suddenness and assurance, and I
should say more than his father's ability. There is just the same

gaminerie and contempt of the conventional and the same engaging
plain spokenness and readiness to understand. As I listened to him
recounting conversations he had had with Chamberlain I seemed once
more to be listening to Randolph on the subject of Northcote and
Salisbury. About Chamberlain he was especially amusing, his attitude
being one of mingled contempt and admiration, contempt for the man
and admiration for his astuteness and audacity. In opposition Winston
I expect to see playing precisely his father's game, and I should
not be surprised if he had his father's success. He has a power of
writing Randolph never had, who was a schoolboy with his pen,
and he has education and a political tradition. He interested me immensely. He is writing his father's life and told me he had found a
number of my letters and asked me for any I might have of his
father's, which I was glad to promise him for his book. There was
also there a young man Murray of the same political set.

"Now I must stop, being overwhelmed with work before starting for Egypt."

CHAPTER III

My visit to Gros Bois that autumn on my way Eastwards was a sad one, Princesse Berthe having died in the course of the summer, and there were no visitors and none of the bright talk I had so long enjoyed there.

"We arrived at Shekh Obeyd on the 12th of November. That same evening Sheykh Mohammed Abdu called and gave us a full history of his adventures after leaving Newbuildings. At Oxford he had found a number of Arabic manuscripts known by name only at the Azhar, and among them the correspondence of a certain Arab philosopher, El Sebaïn, with Frederick the Great. He is going to have a number of them copied with funds supplied by the Awkaf (the Ministry of Endowments). He then went to Switzerland and on to Algeria and Tunis. He drew a black picture of the state of things in French North Africa, compared to which he said the sufferings of native Egypt at the hands of the English were as light to darkness. In Algeria the whole administration is directed in the interests of the European Colonists at the expense of the natives. For these there is hardly any legal protection, and absolutely no liberty. There is neither freedom of the press nor even of speech, espionage is worse than at Constantinople, nor is the state of things better in Tunis than in Algeria. It had been proposed to him at Tunis to ask an audience of the Bey, but he had been informed by the Austrian Consul General that permission would have to be first asked of the French Resident, who would have sent a Frenchman to be present at it. The Mohammedans of Tunis had said to him, 'Your journals in Egypt complain of their lot under the English, but all we ask of Providence is to be given five years of your régime as a respite from the hell of our own.' The Mufti told me these details because I had seen it published in the 'Figaro' that he had expressed himself as entirely pleased with the condition of things for his fellow-Moslems under French rule. His account accords with all I have heard from other quarters about Tunis, and with what I remember of Algeria in 1873. There is no doubt that the English régime in Egypt is exceptional in the history of such régimes, which are in their essence tyrannies and oppressions, and

I think I may take some credit to myself for having made it exceptional by forcing Egyptian rights upon English public attention in 1882, and by keeping up the publicity whenever these rights have been freshly attacked.   In France and Tunis no single voice is raised by any Frenchman against his countrymen's iniquities in North Africa, and crime is heaped upon crime, and so it would be here in Egypt if the European colony were allowed to have its way.   Fortunately for Egypt there is practically no English colony, and our officials live under fear of criticism in the London press and parliament, otherwise we should have a purely military government at Cairo. Already, in answer to what I published in the ' Manchester Guardian ' last summer about the abuses prevalent in the Ministry of Justice at Cairo, a move is being made by Cromer to get the Kourbash reintroduced, but I think we shall be able to prevent this, or at least to make it impossible for Cromer to do it on the sly.

"Finally the Mufti told us the latest doings of the Khedive. He has now gone in wholly for money making and speculation. He has got Cassel (the King's friend) to lend him half a million sterling for various schemes without interest, and he is projecting a building venture at Ghizeh, for which purpose an exchange of land is being proposed with the Awkaf, all to the Khedive's advantage.   Abdu, however, as Mufti, has a veto on such transactions, and he will not allow any swindling of the public purse.   He has seen the Khedive lately, who is ostentatiously friendly, but Mohammed Abdu knows he is intriguing to get him deprived of his Muftiship.   The Khedive will not tolerate anyone who does not fear him. The unfortunate Minshawi was, it seems, basely sacrificed by Abbas, who had commissioned him to find the stealers of his cattle, but who denied it when questioned by Cromer.[1]   There is also a quarrel, in which the Khedive is concerned, about some emerald mines on the Red Sea coast.   Cromer, to his credit, stoutly discountenances all speculative mining.

" *22nd Nov.*— Rowton, poor fellow, is dead at his house in Berkeley Square.

" *23rd Nov.*— Yesterday I sent the French edition of our ' Pilgrimage to Nejd ' to Mohammed Abdu to amuse him during Ramadan, and later he came to see me.   Speaking of Midhat Pasha, of whom an account is given in the book, he told me Midhat was a man he had never liked in spite of his sympathy with the constitutional cause at Constantinople which Midhat had championed.   Midhat, he said, was a hot head, and very imprudent, especially in his cups, for he had a habit of drinking, and this was the cause of his ruin.

[1] For an account of this episode see my pamphlet, " The Atrocities of Justice in Egypt."

While Wali at Damascus Midhat had attended a large dinner given at Tarablus, and had made a speech, in which he had described himself as the destroyer of two Kings (alluding to Abd el Aziz and Murad). This was reported to the Sultan, and was the cause of Midhat's disgrace. As a reformer he was shallow and Europeanized in the worst sense, nevertheless his fall had been a real misfortune, and his end a real tragedy.

" Mohammed Abdu has had another talk with the Khedive, who told him the whole history of his not having kept his appointment with us at Crabbet in the summer. The reason was precisely what I suspected. When the visit was first proposed no objection had been made by the Englishmen appointed to dry nurse the Khedive during his stay in England, but the very morning of the Sunday when he was getting ready to start for Crabbet, Cassel, whose guest he was, on behalf of the King in London, spoke to him about it, and told him that his going to see me would offend the King, that it would be interpreted at Court as meaning that he had not been satisfied with the King's reception of him. Cassel's words had been, ' I do not say that you ought not to go, but if you do it will be understood in this sense.' The Khedive sent the explanation as a message to me through the Mufti, but not for publication; he wishes me to see him as usual, but I shall not go, and have told Abdu to say that since the King has commanded the Khedive not to see me, and the Khedive has thought fit to obey, I, as the King's subject, am still more bound to obedience.

" 24th Nov.— The papers give an account of Dora Labouchere's marriage at Florence to a son of the Minister Rudini. I am glad she has made a good alliance, it will please her old father who deserves to be pleased.

" 2nd Dec.— The Mufti called to-day and gave me an account of what is going on at headquarters in the matter of judicial reform. He had an interview with Cromer yesterday, having been sent for to talk the various projects over. Cromer asked him his opinion of the plan of perambulating judges, and the Mufti said its value would all depend upon whether these were appointed by the Government or by the Court of Appeal. If the latter good men would be chosen, if the former not. McIlwraith was then sent for, and in the Mufti's presence received a lecture from Cromer on the necessity of consulting the best native opinion, and especially the Mufti's. He is satisfied now that they will adopt a reasonable scheme. He expostulated also against additional power being put into the hands of the police in its present corrupt condition. He tells me the Khedive is very angry with him for having insisted on his paying the full price, £20,000, in his deal with the Awkaf, and that he is doing what he can to get

him deprived of his position of Mufti. Abdu, however, is so firmly
established now that it is of little importance what the Khedive
intrigues against him, and it seems really as if at last his influence
would become what it ought to have been from the first, the supreme
one in Egypt. He is in high spirits, and I congratulated him on becoming Grand Vizier. Cromer supports the Mufti now. The Khedive is very foolish, for he allows real evils to go on unchecked and
intervenes only in trifles.

"*7th to 9th Dec.*— A short outing in the desert, in the hills behind Cairo, exploring the cleft of Wadi Dijleh, where vultures still
have their roosting place, both the great vulture and the Egyptian.
They are getting rare now in Egypt, owing to our sanitary arrangement which forbids the leaving of carcases, which were their food.
The black and white Egyptian vultures used to be as plentiful as
domestic fowls; ' Pharaoh's chickens ' Frank travellers called them.
When the French in 1801 had Suliman el Halabi impaled for the
assassination of General Kléber, the sentence passed on him by their
Court Martial was that he was to remain impaled until the vultures had devoured him. I have been reading Jabarti's Chronicle,
which is intensely interesting. It shows the French invasion of Egypt
to have been a wanton and most criminal proceeding, absolutely
ruinous to the still prosperous country. Cairo was almost completely
destroyed by them, and when they evacuated, it was left as a prey
to the Bedouins to its complete destruction. Yet the French are at
this moment raising a monument at Cairo to Kléber and the rest
of them, inscribed: ' To the heroic Martyrs of Civilization who died
during the campaigns of Egypt and Syria.'

" On our way back to Sheykh Obeyd we followed the Mokattam
range to its extreme edge overlooking Cairo. The view of the vast
city, half Oriental, half European, approached thus as we approached
it suddenly from the desert, is, I think, the most astonishing in the
world. We arrived after several days' wandering in an absolute
waste, the last mile of the way being waster than all the rest, and
difficult for camels to cross, for the heights have been blasted with
dynamite, and all is a labyrinth of holes and heaps, I suppose to
prevent a surprise by artillery, the whole plateau being uninhabited
and unvisited, except by kites and vultures, a sheer naked wilderness of stones, nor could one possibly guess the existence of life
anywhere within miles of it, until gradually one began to hear the
roar of the city below. It is not until one is actually within twenty
yards of the cliff's edge that one gets the slightest hint of the living
world spread out close beneath one's feet, the immense city of Cairo,
with its citadels and towers, and walls, and minarets stretching away
for miles, the splendid ancient city, and beyond it modern Cairo,

with its turmoil of tramways, railroads, and other modernities, and yet
further still the Nile and the Nile Valley, seven miles across and
green as a spinach bowl, with the yellow desert, far away in Africa
with its Pyramids.   The immediate foreground is dazzlingly white, a
huge stone quarry, where men in gangs are at work like ants,
quarrying the white limestone of which modern Cairo is being built.
The sudden contrast brought tears into my eyes as sudden wonders
are apt to do.

"*11th Dec.*— More interesting talk with Abdu.   The Khedive is
still very angry with him about the £20,000 of Wakf property, and
is revenging himself upon the Mufti by trying to get up a new quarrel
with him on religious grounds connected with the proposed savings'
bank, which gives offence to old-fashioned Moslems, as allowing de-
positors to receive interest on their money, a thing forbidden by their
religious law.   Abdu, as Mufti, has issued a *fetwa* on the subject,
recommending a change in the wording of the decree which institutes
the Bank, but the Khedive has taken up a high religious line against
him, condemning the thing altogether, this, although the Khedive puts
his own money unscrupulously out at interest everywhere, and makes
no secret of it.   Cromer, however, supports Abdu, so that he is in no
actual danger from the intrigue.   In all this, as in much else, the
Khedive acts absurdly, allowing real evils to go on without protest,
and intervening only in trifles.

"*20th Dec.*— The Ramadan fast is over to-day, a thing for which
I am always thankful.   How much more comfortable the world
would be without its feasts and fasts.   As I lie here on the roof
watching the birds, who care for none of these things, I realize what
a long way humanity has wandered out of the region of common
·sense.   Three quarters of our man's miseries come from pretending
to be what we are not, a separate creation superior to that of the
beasts and birds, while in reality these are wiser than we are, and
infinitely happier.

"*20th Dec.*— Herbert Spencer is dead, poor old man, at the
age of eighty-three, and another death announced is that of Henry
Stanley (Lord Stanley of Alderley) at seventy-six.   About Stanley,
Blanche Hozier sends me an excellent account of his character,
written by her mother, who was his sister.   'I do not think,' she
writes, 'that he has been a sad man, for he has had joys of his
own, being at one with his God, from whom he takes all willingly
without repining, and in this submission there is great content, and
he loved nature and real sport, and Oriental learning, and order
and obedience, and he had a fair estate to rule over, and he enjoyed
improving it in his own way.   No, I think he had been a happy
man.   He is dying in his small, frugal room he had from a boy,

when I was so much with him before I married. Alderley has been a beloved place for many generations. God bless those who go out and those who come in.' I consider that a most touching account and most true. He was one of the best and least selfish of men, a sincere Moslem without parade. The last time I saw him I remember he was rather hurt with me because I said something implying a disbelief in the divine ordering of things in the world. In his domestic life he was unfortunate, his Spanish wife, Fabia, being socially impossible and mad. Yet he was kind to her, though she weighed like a mill-stone round his neck, and he spent half of his time with her at Alderley. He told me once that he had consulted the Grand Mufti at Constantinople as to whether he might avail himself of his Moslem right and put Fabia away, but he never had the heart to do so, nor would he do anything which might cause a scandal to his religious profession. He did an enormous deal of good to those about him whatever their beliefs, and helped to the best of his power in Parliament all Orientals who were suffering wrong. For this he got scant thanks and no credit. His deafness made public life almost an impossibility, and his many eccentricities and strange manner and appearance caused him to be more laughed at in the House of Lords than listened to. Yet he achieved from time to time success by his insistence for the causes he took up. Personally I had a great regard for him, indeed affection, and we remained for forty-three years firm allies.

"*23rd Dec.*— I have finished Jabarti, whose Chronicle is as good as Stowe's, and written much in the same style, and with certain characters of men he had known as good as Plutarch's."

Jabarti was by birth a Somali and by position an Alem of the Azhar at Cairo, who, finding himself there from the middle of the eighteenth century till well into the nineteenth, in a position of knowledge, though he took no part in public affairs, kept an accurate Chronicle of Egyptian events, relating all with strict impartiality. His history includes the episode of Bonaparte's invasion, as seen through Egyptian eyes, and is of the utmost value. He continued keeping it till the year 1820, when he was waylaid as he was riding home one evening on his ass from Shubra and murdered — it has been asserted — by Mohammed Ali's order.

"*25th Dec.*— I am glad to see that Stanley was buried according to the Mussulman rite, in his Park at Alderley, in presence of the Imam of the Turkish Embassy and one of the Secretaries, as well as of members of his own family.

"The Mufti came in the afternoon with Minshawi Pasha, the same who played an honourable part at the time of the bombardment of Alexandria, saving many Christian lives at Tantah, near

which he lives. The English Government gave him a decoration
after the war for his humanity, but Cromer has since persecuted
him as a partisan of the Khedive. He is very rich, and has recently
given a large sum of money, £14,000, to the Mufti for various
Mohammedan purposes. The Mufti is still being worried by the
Khedive, who has been putting pressure on a number of the Sheykhs
of the Azhar to denounce him on grounds of impiety in the form
of an *ardahal* (petition) precisely as Mohammed Ali did against
the Sheykh El Saadat of Jabarti's time. He tells me that in spite of
all he has gone through in his life, he has never lost but two friends,
having made it a principle always to forgive.

"*8th Jan.*, 1904.— Greville, manager of the Bank of Egypt, came
to luncheon and brought news that war between Japan and Russia
is nearly certain. I have not myself seen how it could be avoided.
The occupation of Manchuria by Russia with her seizure of Port
Arthur makes the position of Japan in those waters too dangerous
for her to acquiesce without fighting, and it became a question between trying conclusions now, and waiting to be swallowed up at
leisure. The present moment is favourable to Japan because the
English Government has promised to help Japan if a third power
intervenes to help Russia. Of course, it is a great risk but of the
two Japan seems to be choosing the lesser, if not the less imminent
danger. I wish her all possible success, she being the representative of Oriental independence against the European Powers. If she
succeeds in beating the Russians at sea, she may be able to get the
hegemony of China and so frustrate altogether the Western invasion.
Neither China nor Korea has the least chance of being able to stand
alone against Russia and would be gradually absorbed, as would Japan
too if she fails in the war."

It had been part of our plan for the winter that Auberon Herbert
should spend it with us at Sheykh Obeyd, but for one reason and
another though he came to Egypt he had established himself the
other side of Cairo, at Helouan, and it had been a matter of much
correspondence between us how we were to meet, as neither of us
liked going through the town, and it was at last decided that we
were to have a rendezvous in the Mokattam Hills behind Cairo some
ten miles away, at a certain hour on a certain day, a plan which
was attended with an almost certain risk of our not meeting at all, for,
though we knew the hills well, he had no knowledge of them, nor was
there any definite landmark. The result was as follows:

"*9th Jan.*— To Wady Abensur, which Europeans call Wady Hof,
and encamped just above the great Sudd at noon, having left Sheykh
Obeyd at 6.30. I then sent Mutlak down in the direction of Helouan
to meet Auberon and Salem Aweymer on my *delûl* to look for him

in the valleys, as he had proposed to walk from Helouan and the
valleys are so intricate here that I was sure he would not find us.
At half past two I also went in search of him on my mare and rode
almost to Helouan and then back up the main valley and I was
just on the point of giving it up when I heard a shout behind me.
Auberon had been found, having wandered away up another valley,
Wady Melag, and presently he appeared with Salem, as extraordinary a figure as one well could see. He was clad in grey
flannels, without a coat, and was carrying a lantern in one hand and
a staff in the other, with a wallet full of stones strapped to his
back, like the pictures of Christian with his bundle of sins in the
' Pilgrim's Progress.' I had the greatest difficulty in getting him to
mount the camel, though it was already late and the road along the
edge of the valley is a dangerous one to be in after dark and I was
anxious to be back at the tent. However, at last he mounted and we
arrived just at nightfall, and he stopped to dine with us and set to
like a famished man, which he was, for he had been wandering in
the valleys since eleven and had brought nothing with him but some
coffee and milk in a bottle. He stayed on with us talking afterwards, interestingly on many subjects, including that of Herbert
Spencer, whose influence over him as a young man he described as
immense. Spencer had given him for the first time solid ground on
which to stand, though he had since gone further than Spencer in
certain directions. On one subject, however, he talked as it seemed
to me not quite sanely, namely the stones he was carrying in his
wallet. He turned these out for us to examine. They were quite
common bits of limestone, flakes from the cliffs with which all the
valleys about here are strewn, but he insisted in seeing in them carved
faces of grotesque personages, with big noses and helmets, and declared them to be the work of primitive men who had formerly inhabited the valleys. He chose me out a few of the smaller ones
and made them over to me with much earnestness to examine at my
leisure, handing me also the small sum of five piastres as a present
to those who had found him in the valley. Then taking up his
wallet and his stick and lighting his lantern he set out, in spite of
all remonstrances, in the direction he had come. I sent Suliman with
him as far as the Sudd, but he would not allow him to go a yard
further, saying it would spoil his night's walk. It appears to be his
habit to spend his nights in the neighbourhood of Helouan with his
lantern looking for these stones, and he told me he had been accosted
in the dark on one occasion and nearly attacked by a man with a
nabut. I think he runs great risks, for the hills are frequented by
convicts escaped from the prison at Toura, and I told him so, and as
he nevertheless persisted in his midnight tramp, I made him write on

a scrap of paper that he absolved me from all responsibility in case of accidents."

This proved to be the last time we met. Two days later I heard from him, that having wandered all night he had found himself at daybreak in an unknown country but had made his way down to the Nile and so got back to his hotel. He died the following year.

"*17th Jan. (Sunday).*— The Mufti has been to Alexandria where he has seen the Khedive, who received him, as his way is, with smiles and jokes, though he had been doing his best to get Cromer's consent to depose him. The Khedive has a new grief against him, his having issued fetwas to certain Mohammedans from the Transvaal in answer to these three questions:

" 1. May a Moslem in a foreign country eat meat not killed according to rule?

" 2. May a Moslem in a foreign country wear a hat?

" 3. May a Shafeite at prayer range himself in the same line with a Hanafite?

To all these three questions Mohammed Abdu had answered in the affirmative, and the Khedive, though he himself eats and wears a hat and says no prayers when in Europe, affects to regard the decision as atheism. Cromer, however, supports the Mufti; it is a queer position.

"*22nd Jan.*— The Mufti was here to-day for his usual Friday's luncheon in the garden under the bamboos. He has a new worry in the death of one of the chief Azhar Sheykhs, which will be the cause of fresh trouble with the Khedive as to his successor. Fortunately, His Highness, ' our young man,' the Mufti calls him, is to start on a journey in the direction of the Tripoli frontier, which will give everybody about him a little holiday and the Mufti hopes himself to be off then to Khartoum, where he promises me to find out what the real state of feeling in the Soudan is towards the present *régime.* We had a long and interesting talk about the Mameluke days in Egypt, as also about the condition of the Jews in Arabia before the coming of Mohammed, and other matters of Eastern history in which he is very learned. I know no society so pleasant as his or so improving, it is all the society we have here as we see nothing of Europeans. We are in a kind of Coventry now with the English officials, but no matter, as long as Egypt is not annexed to the British Crown I shall go on with my opposition.

" He talked, too, about the Khedive's commercial propensities which he indulges without regard for his political position. He has taken to hiring and reletting the ferries over the canals, and he has been trying to get a concession of the fishing rights in various places at the expense of poorer people. Cromer has taken him to task for this and has told him that he must choose between being a Khedive and being a tradesman, in which Cromer is in the right. All the family of Mohammed Ali have been keen traders and Abbas cares for nothing now, Abdu says, but money making.

" *23rd Jan.*— The reason of Gorst's return to Europe is explained. He went to try and get the French Government to agree to an abolition of the Caisse de la Dette, and has been at Paris seeing M. Delcassé with that object. I have written to the Editor of the ' Manchester Guardian ' about it, explaining how very necessary it is to preserve the Caisse de la Dette as a check upon financial extravagance here. What our people specially want just now is liberty to spend all the Egyptian money they can get on the Soudan, which is an English, not an Egyptian interest. There is a scheme of railway making between Souakim and Gerber, and also between Khartoum and Abyssinia, the Cape to Cairo line, and there is an ultimate plan of great irrigation reservoirs to supply Manchester with Soudanese cotton. It is only the Caisse de la Dette which stands in the way of Egypt's being made the milch cow of our African Empire. I hear, however, that the French Government has refused to consent to the abolition."

[N.B. These were the first negotiations with the French Government, which resulted some months later in the Agreement known as the *Entente Cordiale,* whereby France gave England a completely free hand in Egypt in return for a free hand given her in Morocco.]

" *4th Feb.*— My letter to the ' Manchester Guardian ' is published, and comes in pretty opportunely, though I understand the French Government has definitely refused to waive its rights on the Caisse de la Dette. It appears that there was really a proposal into which Gorst entered of some gigantic operation in the Soudan, a concession of Government lands on a vast scale for twenty millions to Cassel, with irrigation works, and a Government guarantee which required the consent of the Caisse; also it was said an attempt was made to abolish the Caisse altogether, a huge scheme of developing the Soudan at the expense of Egypt. Fortunately this has been put a stop to by the French Government, and the whole thing has fallen into the water. The Khedive was certainly mixed up in it, and from what I can understand Cromer did not altogether approve. Mohammed Abdu says that Gorst has been playing into the Khedive's hands of late financially, and there is talk of his leaving the Egyptian service.

" *11th Feb.*— The Russo-Japanese War has begun, and some Russian ironclads have been sunk in Port Arthur.

" There is a split between George Wyndham and Redmond over the Catholic University. As far as my politics are concerned I should be sorry to see entire harmony between Ireland and England, for then we should have the Irish as Imperialist as the worst of us.

" 14th Feb. (Sunday).— The Mufti lunched with us and talked about Egyptian history.   He said that the Circassian Mameluke system in its later development had an immoral foundation, but such had not been the case with the earlier Mamelukes, who were principally those slaves brought into Egypt by Salah ed Din (Saladin) Nothing had ever exceeded the crimes of the later Mamelukes, Ottoman and French alike.   It was common with these to try the sharpness of their swords at the armourers' shops on the passers by, by cutting off their heads or cutting them in two at the waist.   Good Mohammed Abdu sitting here on my sofa in his turban telling these tales looked for a moment like a very terrible Turk making passes as he spoke with an imaginary sword.   He also cited a good saying of Seyyid Jemal ed Din, ' Justice is found where equal forces meet,' meaning thereby that unless the strength of the ruler is opposed by the resisting strength of the ruled, there will always be tyranny. This in allusion to the passivity of the Egyptians under wrong.

" There has been a new scandal at Cairo, the Khedive having invited his Hungarian mistress to a Court Ball.   The wives of the Consuls were offended at this, and would have made a public matter of it, but Cromer appeased them.

" 24th Feb.— Cockerell has arrived from England to spend some weeks with us.

" 26th Feb.— Everything is going splendidly in Manchuria, and there really seems to be a chance of the Russians being driven finally back into Siberia.   Their sea power seems broken, and there is a good chance of the Japanese being able to cut their railway line, and so starve them out at Port Arthur.   It is not likely there will be much sympathy with the Russian Government, though they are trying to get up a cry of ' Christian civilization in danger.'   Apart from all special knowledge of the rights and wrongs of an international quarrel between nations, I think it a wise rule to give one's good wishes to the power which is fighting nearest home, that is to say, nearest its own capital and seat of Government.   It is preposterous that a Government should claim rights of any kind a thousand miles away from home.

" 29th Feb.— Took Cockerell to call on the Mufti, whom we found in bed with influenza, but he conversed with his usual wisdom.   Talking about a proposal made by Ali Yusuf at the General Assembly to create Parliamentary Government in Egypt, I objected to the word creation, seeing that parliamentary Government had been won in Egypt twenty-two years ago, but Abdu says its revival now is only an intrigue, and that he had opposed it, though ineffectually, for it was put to the vote and carried by a majority. In this I think he was wrong, for, intrigue or not, a parliament is the best chance there is in Egypt of getting rid of English dictation. Cromer has declared such a proposal to be beyond the competence of the Assembly. Abdu tells me that Gorst has been certainly helping the Khedive in his commercial speculations, and there has been a quarrel between him and Cromer on the subject. It is not expected that he will retain his post here of Financial Adviser.

"*4th March.*— There has been a good debate about the Somaliland war, more or less in accordance with my programme, published on the 10th February in the 'Daily Chronicle.' Ritchie reproduced some of my arguments, and Willy Redmond rubbed them in. The campaign will now be allowed to drop.

"*10th March.*— The following is a story current about Gorst's quarrel with Cromer. It appears that last winter, or rather the winter before, a lady, a friend of the King's, came to Egypt and received what she considered scanty attention at Lady Cromer's hands, whereas Gorst made himself agreeable to her, and an intrigue was started between them favoured by the King, to whom the lady had complained, according to which Cromer at the end of the year was to be retired, and Gorst to have his place at the Cairo Agency. It was supposed that Cromer would be willing either to join the Government at home, or perhaps take the Paris Embassy. The King was dissatisfied at the time with Monson the actual Ambassador at Paris, because, being poor, Monson did not, in the King's opinion, represent him with sufficient dignity. At any rate Gorst was promised Cromer's succession, and counted on it (an arrangement which I had already heard of) as also that eventually Cromer's son Errington was to have the place in reversion. Cromer, however, himself does not seem to have been told about it, and when the time came for the change refused all offers inducing him to budge, and was very angry when he learned what had been going on. Matters, moreover, have been further complicated by money transactions with Cassel. Cassel had lent His Highness half a million at 2½ per cent. to speculate with, while Gorst as Financial Adviser granted Cassel concessions. All this made up an elaborate intrigue, but it has been upset by Cromer who has put his foot down, and now declares he means to stay on indefinitely in Egypt. The Khedive, so Mohammed Abdu says, has been lectured, and told to choose between being a Khedive and being a tradesman. Gorst has had to leave Egypt, and is now through the King's influence being provided with a post at the Foreign Office, as Assistant Under-Secretary, with the promise of an Embassy some day. Errington has been packed off to the Legation at Teheran, and the lady is to come no more to Cairo. I must say that I think old

Cromer is to be sympathized with, and I am glad the intrigue failed, though Gorst has been personally friendly with us here, but these money speculations at the Finance Office are intolerable, and Gorst deserves his disappointment. Yesterday Dormer (who is in the Finance Office), came to luncheon, and added his share of information. Gigantic financial operations are in progress. A concession of all the Egyptian State railways is being given to a company of which Rivers Wilson is head. For this the Company is to pay forty-two millions sterling down. The present income from the railroads is sixteen hundred millions, so that the company at actual rates will get three per cent. for its capital, with prospect of indefinite extension. Cassel, too, has been in treaty for a concession of all the Government lands in Upper Egypt for some other prodigious sum. We suppose the idea is to convert and pay off the whole public debt, and so get the Caisse de la Dette and all other restrictions abolished. For the present, however, the French Government holds out against all changes.

" In the evening I looked in on the Mufti and recounted to him the whole story of the Gorst-Cromer quarrel. I always tell him everything, and he tells me everything, and so between us we know everything. He said that the account fitted in with all that he had himself heard and noticed during the past year. The Khedive, when he was in London, had attempted to open the question of Cromer's retirement at the Foreign Office, but had been stopped, and Cromer this winter had spoken to him (the Mufti) impatiently of Gorst, so that he was quite prepared for what I had to tell him, and he knew all about the financial intrigues which Gorst had encouraged the Khedive in. Gorst had allowed the Khedive, for instance, to purchase the large Mariout property of the Government for a very trifling sum, and had helped him in other ways to make money, more or less at the Government's expense. He was much amused at the lady's part in the intrigue. It had come round to him through a friend who happened to be on board the ship that took the Khedive last summer to Constantinople, that His Highness had boasted to his fellow travellers that a certain high English personage had promised to get rid of Sheykh Mohammed Abdu for him. Abdu had talked the incident over with his friend, Mustapha Pasha Fehmy.

" *15th March.*— It is now decided we are all to go to Damascus on Thursday. Anne and I, Cockerell and Miss Lawrence and Mutlak, to look for horses. To-day the Mufti called. He had talked of going with us to Damascus, but has reflected that it would not do. ' If you and I,' he said, ' were to go together to Damascus the Sultan would go mad. He would think that we had come to proclaim the Arabian Caliphate.

" *17th March.*— I have written to George Wyndham to get him to stop the Somali campaign, and to provide for the safety of the ' friendly tribes,' on the Arab principle of paying blood money so as to end the feud between them and the Mullah. ' The British forces should then retire to the seaports and leave the interior strictly alone. If there are any friendly chiefs who feel themselves too much compromised they should be given handsome pensions and invited to live at Berbera under English protection. The rest of the tribes will very soon come to terms with the others, *only don't leave British garrisons anywhere in the interior,* and forbid all travelling and sporting expeditions by our officers for some years to come. You should consult Zoheir's Ode in the Moallakat as to peacemaking by payment.' "

We left the same day for Damascus and arrived at Beyrout on the 20th by sea from Port Said.

" *21st March (Sunday).—* By train to Baalbek, a slow business, the pace being but little, if at all faster than formerly by diligence, which used to run between Beyrout and Damascus, and was so capitally horsed. We travelled from Zahleh with a respectable man and his wife, Christians of the place who, finding we talked Arabic, gave us a good deal of information. The country of the Lebanon is very prosperous now, entirely, so he told us, through the emigration there has been to America, the emigrants coming back with money made there in trade. Every cultivable acre of land is taken up and prices have gone up prodigiously. He pointed out to me a property in the Bekaa which had been bought as derelict forty years ago by Dervish Pasha for £6,000 and which is now worth £60,000 or £70,000. The taxation is not excessive, certainly not as compared with Egypt. There is a yearly tax of 4 per mil. on the capital value of all land, and 12½ per cent. is taken on the gross produce besides being paid in kind. Certainly, the people look prosperous, new houses and new plantations of mulberry trees everywhere, children with rosy cheeks, and men and women well dressed. He puts the population of the Lebanon at 150,000 Christians, 100,000 Moslems, and 40,000 Druses, with as many more Druses in the Hauran. I had no idea of such prosperity.

" At Baalbek we went to the ruins which I had never seen. They are, I think, the most splendid in the world. They have been to a certain extent *remis à neuf* for the Emperor William when he was here, and there is an absurd tablet commemorating the event of his visit, evidently of Constantinople origin, with the names of the Emperor and the Sultan side by side. Otherwise the repairs have been sensibly done. There are the usual American tourists here, fortunately not more than half-a-dozen, the most senseless type of human nature, being quite insensible to beauty or decorum and with the manners of shop-boys, who ramble through the gardens of the ancient world with as little knowledge of their value as beasts have, defiling all and tramp-

ling all.   Yet I noticed that one of them, a thick-set porker with pend-
ant chaps, little cunning eyes, and a bullet head, after discussing the
East in the language of Wall Street, and with comparisons drawn from
the gutter of his financial mind, was able to give a sensible account to
a neighbour who questioned him on the subject of the licensing laws
of his own New England State.   A proof that in its own environment
there is no race entirely without value.   They should be kept at home,
for they have no business in these ancient lands.

" *22nd March.*— On to Damascus by the new railway which is carried
down the wooded valley of the Baradah, very beautiful and very unlike any other.   The railway twists and twirls dangerously in and out
among the villages, and rounds sharp corners with no outlook 50 yards
ahead; there have been many accidents, a single line, and the trains
rock prodigiously.   Here we are at a hotel, the Hotel d'Orient, a
quiet place where few tourists go, but hotels are novelties still at
Damascus.

" *23rd March.*— To the Consulate.   Richards, who is in charge of it,
confirms the prosperity of the Lebanon and says that most of the
emigrants return with money from America, some few are Mohammedans, the greater number Christian.   The country is quite undisturbed and safe.   He sent a *kavás* with us to visit our house in the
Kassab quarter, which we bought in 1881, and certainly never should
have found without help.   (I had forgotten even the name of the
street where it was.)   When we came to the door I recognized it so
little that I was sure the *kavás* was mistaken.   The little low door
into the street had a chink opened when we knocked, but there were
only women inside, the man, our tenant, having gone to market to
sell his wheat.   The *kavás,* however, got hold of a watchman and so
we were admitted.   A funny little place it was, but nice inside with
an inclosure of about an acre walled round and planted with lucerne,
and a fine old stone wall, shutting us in from surrounding gardens.
Lady Ellenborough used to live next door, and the house belongs now
to her stepson, a son of her husband Mijwel, who lets it, and on
the other two sides lies the great garden, called Bostan el Basha, belonging to Sheykh Hassan el Attar, a chief of the Damascus Ulema.
Ours is almost the last house at the extreme north-eastern end of
Damascus on the road to Palmyra.   The name of the street is Shariah
Musjid el Kassab.   In the afternoon we went there again and this
time found the whole family of our tenant assembled, Sheykh Saleh
Tillo and his three sons.   They are well-off people and the rooms are
richly furnished with good carpets and pillows, and one or two really
handsome inlaid chests, besides china and glass, some old, some new.
We are pleased with our little house and feel inclined to make a part
of it habitable for ourselves and spend six weeks in it every year,

but there would be a difficulty about getting possession. The rent they pay is only eleven pounds a year.

" From there we went to the Maidan quarter and drank coffee with Ahmed Ibn Jamil, a horse dealer, whom we had known in Egypt, but he showed us no good horses.

" I find very little change in the town since I was here last except on the north-western side, where the railroad has caused some building, and a big barracks has been put up. The rest of the city is much what I remember it in 1880, not at all Europeanized. The bazaars which were burnt down in Midhat Pasha's time have been rebuilt and are as busy as ever. There are no modern shops or Frank innovations, or by-laws, or other Christian tomfooleries; things are made too uncomfortable for Europeans for there to be any resident foreign merchants. Newspapers of all kinds are forbidden, the post is unsafe and irregular, and at the Central telegraph office there are no printed forms. We were given with difficulty a sheet of notepaper to write a message on.

" *24th March.*— Visited the Ottoman Bank and reopened my account there, finding £12 still to my name, which had been lying there for 23 years. The house has been all these years in the care of the British Consul, who has been changed many times in the interval, the consular dragoman having been put in charge of it who, through lapse of time, had come to consider the property his own. There has been a wonderful flight of storks over the city, travelling in front of a storm from the south-west, many hundreds of them on their annual migration.

" *26th March.*— A night of tempest and a day of rain, but in the evening, the weather having cleared, I walked with Cockerell to Salahieh, the new quarter of the town where houses are being built, we were glad to see on good Turkish models with overhanging stories made of wooden frames filled in with plaster, cheap, practical, and pretty. Richards gives an excellent character of the present Turkish Waly Nazim Pasha as honest, sensible, and pacific, but he is building a huge Government house in European taste which must disfigure that quarter of the town. The view from Salahieh is among the first half-dozen great views of the world, the others being perhaps the view over Cairo from the top of Mokattam, (2) the harbour of Rio Janeiro seen from Corcovado, (3) the Lake of Geneva from the hills above Lausanne (4) Constantinople, from the Tower of Galata and (5) the Red Sea with Mount Sinai from the summit of Kalala. All these will stop one's breath for wonder and bring tears to one's eyes.

" *27th March.*— We spent the day in the bazaars, which are the best and cheapest in the world. It is a pleasure buying in them because the sellers are so amiable and do not worry travellers to

buy.   Everything is astonishingly cheap and one might live comfortably
with one's family in Damascus on £100 a year. A man can dress
himself well for £1 from head to foot, a woman for 10 s., a child for
2s. 6d., house rent is one tenth what it is at Cairo.

"I am becoming converted to the Sultan's mode of government;
though it is a wearisome tyranny for the rich, the poor are happy
under it and are more fortunate in the circumstances of their lives
than any population in Europe, and there is less discontent. The
people in the streets here are all well dressed and fat and healthy,
many of them have beasts to ride and there are very few beggars,
food is plentiful, and all the small industries flourish. Our European
factory system is unknown. Except for military conscription, an evil
which they share with all the peasantries of Europe, they have nothing
to complain of, and do not complain. I find an immense practical advance since twenty-five years ago. On the other hand the educated
and wealthy classes are treated like children. No man may travel
as far as Beyrout without a passport, or to Europe without special
leave or leaving a deposit behind him of £100, or if he takes his wife
with him, £200 more. No newspapers are allowed to enter the country, or any to be published of more value than a childish sheet of
local news. What is extraordinary is that nearly all the Government
offices in Syria are filled with political exiles from Constantinople.
Nazim Pasha, the Governor, is the same person I remember head of
the police at Constantinople during the Armenian massacres, and who
was made a scapegoat of to save the Sultan's face. The military
commandant is a young Turk, and so are nearly all the functionaries,
that is to say, they were Young Turks, but now dare not express any
opinions. Constantinople has been emptied of late years of its political
notabilities, and as the Sultan will not allow them to go to Europe they
are sent in exile to the various provinces, the more dangerous of them
being provided with Government appointments to keep them quiet.
The wonder is that they do not combine and rebel, but in fact the
population is not with them, and except sporadically, there is no discontent. Such is the impression I have formed of the present *régime*
at Damascus. Peace has been made with the Druses and with all disaffected communities." [This state of things helps to explain the
rapidity with which the revolution, four years later, of 1908, spread
through the Ottoman provinces, when it had once declared itself at
Constantinople. Nazim was Commander-in-Chief against the Bulgarians later and was assassinated in 1913 at Constantinople.]

"After luncheon I went with Cockerell to see the great Mosque,
which is being rebuilt, and in better taste than any rebuilding on a
large scale we have seen in Europe. It is a splendid piece of archi-
tecture, and the view from its minaret is superb; only the tomb of

Saladin has been badly restored, it is said by a Russian Prince in Constantinopolitan taste, the ancient wooden sarcophagus having been removed by him; also it is still adorned with ribbons placed there by the irrepressible Emperor William. We are to leave for Egypt again to-morrow morning.

" *28th March.*— By train to Beyrout. We had for travelling companion, Ali Pasha Abd el Kader, the old Algerian Emir's second son, with whom we had much talk. He is more of a Circassian in appearance than an Arab, and is not unlike the late Sultan Abdul Aziz. He is a great personage in Syria, and at all the stations where we stopped he was greeted by acquaintances, who kissed his hand, for he holds a semi-religious position here. He would not agree to my proposition that the people of Damascus were prosperous or contented, but did not give his reasons. He is a fat and heavy man, without great intelligence, but possessed of a certain dignity. His elder brother, Mohammed, whom we knew in 1880, lives now in Constantinople; another brother, he told me, was in Morocco, taking part in the war there, but none of them are allowed to go to Algeria. He has had news, he said, of an arrangement which had been come to between France and England for the partition of Morocco. He had travelled in France and England, but speaks no European language." [This news, casually given me by Ali Pasha Abd el Kader, was the first I received of the Anglo-French Convention, afterwards known as the Entente, whereby the two Governments agreed to divide Egypt and Morocco between them, the first step of the coalition between England, France, and Russia against Germany, the initial cause of the Great War of 1914.]

" *31st March.*— Returned to Sheykh Obeyd yesterday. The Somali War has been stopped, but whether through my letter to George Wyndham or otherwise, I do not know.

" *3rd April (Easter Sunday).*— Dined with the Mufti, and discussed the affairs of Islam. He told an amusing story of an episode which had happened to him while an exile at Damascus. There was in London at that time (1883) a certain Rev. Isaac Taylor, who had conceived the idea of bringing about a union between the English reformed Church and Islam upon a basis of their common monotheistic creed. In this he was encouraged by the old Persian, Mirza Bakr, who carried the idea to Syria, and made Propaganda for it, to a certain extent obtaining Mohammed Abdu's sympathy, who, with others, drew up a letter to Taylor, which he signed with two more of the leading men of the Damascus Ulema. Taylor was of course delighted, and had the letter at once published, as being the general opinion of the Mohammedan learned of Damascus, and arguing from it that the union between Christian and Moslem was on the point of accomplishment; and as such it came to the knowledge of the Sultan. No names had been mentioned in the published version, but the Turkish Ambassador in London was at once telegraphed to, and ordered to find out those of the five signatories, and thus, without suspecting the danger, Taylor let the Ambassador know, and all five were expelled from Syria. Abdu, however, before leaving Damascus protested, and had the opportunity of arguing the matter out with the authorities, and it transpired that the reason of the Sultan's alarm had been the idea that if England should be converted to Islam the English Sovereign would *ipso facto* become the most powerful personage in it, and the Caliphate would naturally devolve on Queen Victoria to the Ottoman prejudice.

" *5th April.*— Lunched with Carton de Wiart, who gave me a deal of information about official doings, not much to the credit of the English administration [I do not transcribe them here]. Cromer, according to him, has become very slack and careless since his new marriage, and no longer takes the trouble to master the details. He is largely under the influence of his Secretary, Boyle, who, in his turn, is under the influence of the Nimr brothers, the Syrian editors of the Mokattam newspaper, who provide him with the bulk of his information on native affairs. Cromer at the same time has become very obstinate, and nobody dares contradict him. I asked him about the Khedive, and he confirmed to me all that Abdu had told me about his speculations with Cassel, and he gave me a curious instance of His Highness's lack of the sense of what is due to his position where money matters are concerned. It appears that on the property he bought some time ago from the heirs of Halim Pasha there was a certain disreputable house let at a high rent, the payment of which was much in arrear. It was desirable to close the house, but the Khedive, in his eagerness to get in the money due, kept it open to its frequenters for six months on his own account, putting in a man from his Daira (Estate Office) to receive the profits. Cassel's is a very bad influence for him, as he encourages him in all his irregularities.

" He talked also about Cromer's quarrel with Gorst. Cromer disapproves his intimacy with Cassel, and had been also displeased because the Khedive went to Gorst's wedding. Gorst has left Egypt now, but in Carton's view will return at the end of a year or so, and get Cromer's place. I also went with Cockerell to the Museum, and had an interesting talk with Maspero.

" *10th April.*— We have left Sheykh Obeyd for England. Yesterday I wished Mohammed Abdu good-bye. He has written a letter to Tolstoy which Anne is translating for him into English (see Appendix). News has come of the Anglo-French Agreement about Morocco and Egypt. I have been long expecting it. As to Egypt the terms might have been worse, for the political status is untouched, but it will be a bad day for Morocco. Here there will be a rush of speculators, and Abdu has given me the detail of the 100,000 feddans conceded to Cassel.

"*15th April*.— We landed at Genoa on the 14th, and came on the following day to Turin, where we are staying at the Palazzo della Cisterna with the Duke and Duchess of Aosta. On landing, I found a copy of the 'Times' containing Cromer's annual report with a long despatch from Lansdowne explaining the Anglo-French Convention. Cromer's report is in the usual First Chapter of Genesis style, and nobody would guess from it what wars and rumours of wars there have been at Cairo. Cromer publicly laments Gorst's departure, and no hint is given of the Khedive's misdoings, or of any of the tragi-comic events of the winter. Yet Cromer would doubtless be indignant if it were said of him that he was not a scrupulously truthful official narrator.

"Lansdowne's despatch is a very important document, as it puts all the dots upon the i's of the Convention. It is clear now that the two Governments understand it as a division of spoils, not quite yet complete, but to be so in the near future. The French are to have the same footing in Morocco that we have taken in Egypt, and as certain clauses in the arrangement are to last for thirty years, the final partition of Turkey is evidently foreseen in it, and so the permanent incorporation of Egypt into the British Empire; at least this is how I read the despatch and Convention taken together. One thing is clear, viz., that the Anglo-Egyptian Government will now have a free financial hand for both spending and borrowing, and that the old economy will be abandoned in favour of a forward financial policy on the Indian model. Egypt will be run for the Soudan. The best one can say is that Egypt might have been annexed, or formally protected, and that the chapter of accidents still remains open to prevent this last misfortune. For Morocco it hardly could be worse, seeing what French methods are.

"Poor old Queen Ysabel of Spain is dead at the age of seventy-three, and is to be buried at the Escurial. It is just forty years since I first saw her at Madrid, but the recollection of her and her Court remains a vivid picture in my mind, while so much else is forgotten. It gives me the image of a great, fat, colourless, blue-eyed, good-humoured woman, with arms like rounds of raw beef. Beside her, her husband Don Francisco de Assiz, a little stiff man in a much embroidered coat, and the two royal children, the Ynfanta, a thin anæmic girl of thirteen, and her brother, the little Prince of Asturias, a child of six (he afterwards was King), all four personages sitting on great gilt chairs in a row, having their hands kissed by a

long procession of Spanish Grandees and Officers, the child fast
asleep. We of the Diplomatic Corps had to stand just opposite the
throne and watch the *besa-manos* for an hour or more together, thus
it is all photographed upon my memory.

" 16*th April*.— We are at the Palazzo della Cisterna, which has
been thoroughly furbished up since I was here three or four years
ago, but it is still a somewhat gloomy house, as few of the windows
look out on open spaces, and many are filled with opaque or coloured
glass. We have been given, however, a cheerful apartment of half-
a-dozen small rooms looking out on some chestnut trees in their
first leafage filling the square acre plot which is the Palace Garden.
Here blackbirds are singing gaily, though the day has turned to rain.
We were handed over on arrival by the porter, a splendid apparition
in scarlet, to the Marquese de Torregiani and his wife, Lord and
Lady in waiting. He a Florentine brought up as I was by the Jesuits
at Stonyhurst, she an American who has never been in America.
These have made us very comfortable. The Princess is looking her
best with her two boys, Amadeo and Aymon, charming children, with
pretty manners, and talking already three languages, Italian, English,
and German. French they have not been taught as they are expected
to pick it up naturally later from their parents who talk it *en intimité*.
The Duke was not at luncheon as he is still crippled by a broken leg,
but he was wheeled in afterwards. In appearance he is altered greatly
for the better, as he no longer affects the coiffure of the Emperor William, and he made himself very agreeable talking of horses and travels,
and the Japanese War, as to which I was glad to find we were agreed.

" Another naval smash has befallen the Russians. Admiral Macaroff
blown up in his Flagship the Petropaulowski.

" I have been reading Lafcadio Hearn's books lately which have
increased my interest in the Japanese. His explanation of Buddhism
is I suppose as lucid as is possible, though it passes European wit
to understand it entirely. He makes out the case well between Buddhism and the monotheistic religions, but not I think as between Buddhism
and materialism, the latter occupying far sounder metaphysical grounds.
The weakness of Buddhism lies in this, that while accepting the eternity
of matter it insists also on the eternity of mind. This may or may not
be the truth, but it is a mere theory resting on no evidence or probability. The Buddhist doctrine of the composite nature of the soul
is just as much a fancy as the Christian one of the soul's simplicity.
Both exaggerate the importance of mental phenomena, which as far as
our experience goes are confined to an infinitesimally small fraction
of the material universe, and only seem of importance to us, because
in ourselves they so strongly predominate. The idea of a soul as
something possible, apart from an organized body, is a superstition

like all the rest, and when expounded by the Buddhist teaching, and put to the test of practice becomes equally unthinkable, whether it is complex or simple. To me as a pure materialist the soul cannot be logically distinguished from sensation, and when the organized body ceases finally to feel in death, the soul also ceases. The Buddhist theory of the transmigration of souls, of being born again to a series of new lives, rests on a fallacious reading of what birth is as well as what death is. It is just as much a mistake in physics to suppose the soul enters a new body at birth as to suppose it leaves an old one at death. Birth is simply the continuation of an organic form by its dividing itself into two. In the case of a tree this may occur by a seed growing up, or more simply by a branch bending down and taking root. The seed, however, and the root are in reality portions of the parent body extending and multiplying itself. Peg down a branch of a lemon tree and you will see it sprout; sever the branch and you have two lemon trees. Or again in the case of sexual generation of two bodies prolonging themselves together. There is no real solution of continuity, no real beginning of a new body. Death is simply the wearing out of the original organism, or of such part of the organism as has failed to multiply or extend itself. If there are no offshoots from the parent stem the whole organism perishes. If there are offshoots it continues to be alive in these. The Japanese idea of Mr. So-and-so's child dying, and its soul being recreated in the womb of Mr. What's-his-name's wife is to ignore the physical reality that the new infant is no new organism, but a joint continuation of his two parents. There is no room for Mr. So-and-so's child's soul to creep in. Thus the whole doctrine of transmigration is to my mind absurd. We have had great discussions on these points with the Princess who is interested in Buddhist philosophy.

" 18*th April.*— The Princess has given me a Buddhist catechism to read, and I have been much interested in it, though it seems to be almost as dreary a religion as our Western Christianity. Both take the same dark view of life in this world, that it is an evil thing, and that we are to reject all happiness if we are not to be more miserable, consoled only by the dim prospect at the end of it of an unreal bliss in Heaven or in Nirvana, of which there is no visible certainty. I would rather believe in the Mohammedan heaven if I could, which at least is a tangible possibility of happiness, but annihilation, of which there is much more inherent probability, is, after all, more comforting than either of them to those who have lived; an eternal, dreamless sleep without waking. I have it in my mind to write a short treatise in development of this thought, to be called ' The Religion of Happiness.'

" In the afternoon there was a grand parade of all the Duke's horses in the royal stables, which have been made over to him by the King, and which are kept up as no stables are that I have ever seen. He must have quite forty animals, most of them English weight-carrying hunters in the prime of life, and obtained at high prices, with as many men in livery to look after them. He cannot spend less than £10,000 a year on his hobby. In the morning we had been to see the two children ride in the riding school, which they did wonderfully, considering their age. They are courageous boys, thoroughly well brought up, and with the prettiest manners in the world. The Duke has been most amiable, going the round of the stables with us himself, wheeled in his chair.

"At dinner to-night I was interested to meet the Marchese di Guiccioli, grandson of the husband of the famous Contessa of Byron's days. I should have liked to ask him what view the family took of this episode, but refrained. He told me his family had left Ravenna early in the last century, and had since lived in Venice. He is Prefect here in Turin at the present moment, an intelligent man with much manner of the world, reminding me a little of Sir Henry Layard, and like him, a good talker. After it we discussed French poetry, especially Victor Hugo's, and the Princess quoted several of the best pieces of the 'Legende des Siècles.' In the morning she had taken me to the studio of the sculptor Canonico, to see a bust he has made of her. It is good, better than anything we could get done in England. Canonico is an intelligent young fellow, much absorbed in his work, and talking fluently about it. He has done several excellent busts of children, and two of our gracious King and Queen, rather painful performances, and a terrible Pietà on a gigantic scale for a cemetery, as is the taste just now in Italy.

"*19th April.*— We left for England, and crossing Mont Cenis in floods of rain, reached home on the 20th.

"*21st April.*— The news is that Winston Churchill has just seceded from the Tory party, and has been invited by half-a-dozen constituencies to stand as an independent Free Trader at the elections.

"*23rd April.*— At Park Lane I found both Sibell and George Wyndham, and took George to lunch with me at the St. James's Club. In Ireland he has got into slack water with his Land Purchase, and his Catholic University scheme is tied up. He wants to see Redmond, and I am to arrange a meeting between them in Chapel Street. He has acted on my suggestion about Somaliland, and has got the Prime Minister on his side and also Arnold-Forster, and the war for the time is stopped. They have not, however, yet withdrawn all the troops to the coast, nor made a final settlement on my plan with the tribes, but he is working for both and hopes to manage it. The chief obstacle lies in the Foreign Office, which began the war, and does not

like acknowledging a failure. From this we passed on to India and
George Curzon and the Japanese War, where we are at one. George
is getting sick of office, and longs to be away writing poetry. He
recited to me a sonnet he had just made, a very good one, and told me
as a great secret that he had been asked by Rowton's executors to write
Disraeli's Life, but has been obliged to decline, as he cannot spare
the time. I asked him why his party should wish to stay in office for
another year? He said there were two or three things they had to
finish first, the re-organization of the army and the reconstruction of
South Africa, then they would be glad to go.

" *26th April.*— Saw Redmond at the House of Commons. The
Land Purchase, he says, is going on well, more estates sold than the
Government have money for, but it was lucky they got the Bill through
last year, as this year it would have been impossible. He gave me
the history of O'Brien's secession from the Irish Party. I found him
not very keen about meeting George, though friendly towards him.
' Wyndham,' he said, ' may be quite ready to do everything for us,
but he has no power.' I asked about the King, who has just gone to
Ireland. ' We all think him friendly to us,' Redmond said, ' and perhaps we may get Home Rule through him. But I don't myself believe
that we shall get it except indirectly, and a bit at a time. Meanwhile
all is going well.'

" Elsa Wagram is engaged to marry the Prince de la Tour
d'Auvergne.

" *4th May.*— Saw George and arranged with him about a lunch
with Redmond next week. He tells me he believes he has succeeded
now in getting a final end put to the Somáli Campaign. There has
been a last splutter there, the bombardment of a small seaport, Illig,
but the army is to be withdrawn, and the occupation of the country
to be confined strictly to the Coast towns. This is something accomplished. Strict orders have been sent out to Swain the Consul General,
that he is not to interfere with the tribes.

" The victory of the Japanese at Yalu is now fully confirmed. We
talked also about George Curzon and the Tibet War. My relations
with George Wyndham are very pleasant ones now, as he consults
me on all his political affairs, and as Arthur Balfour consults him I am
beginning to have a practical influence on public events.

" *9th May.*— Yorke Powell is dead, which grieves me. It is only
a day or two since I heard from him. He was the most sympathetic
of men, and my memory of him runs back to 1863, when I first met
him, he being a boy, with his mother in the Pyrenees. They were
friends of Madame Bertrand de Lis at Madrid, hence our acquaintance. He was fond of Spain and France, and the East, and of much
else that I loved. I lose much by his death. I have written to

George in the sense of our conversation of yesterday, urging him to get the Tibetan expedition withdrawn, now that Russia has been so smashed up in Manchuria, proposing also a scheme of settlement for Egypt.

" 10*th May*.— Dined with Lady Gregory, Yeats, Gilbert Murray, and Robert Gregory. Yeats is just back from America, where they have made a great fuss with him, and he takes himself very seriously in consequence. Though doubtless a man of genius, he has a strong touch in him of the charlatan, and his verse is thin stuff, not so good as his prose. Gilbert Murray is worth ten of him as a poet, and is bringing out his ' Hippolytus ' this month at a London theatre. I walked home with Murray as far as Hyde Park Corner. I like him, though he is rather dry in his talk, a sayer of the obvious rather than of the exquisite, the antipodes in this to Yeats, who is brilliant in conversation and full of affectation, while Murray, in spite of his poetic gift, is dull. Yeats talked to me about getting George Wyndham to grant them a patent at Dublin for their new theatre. This I readily agreed to see to.

" 11*th May*.— Lunched in Park Lane. George promised at once to befriend the Abbey Theatre as I was sure he would. Then we got on to Eastern politics. George told me he had been adverse all along to the Tibet expedition, and would be glad to stop it now if he could. On all these matters he declares Arthur Balfour to be quite sound, and he explained to me the standing Committee in the Cabinet on Foreign Affairs, and how well it was working in the way of preventing Departmental extravagances. I told him there was one thing that needed reform more than all, that was that instead of promoting an official who had caused an unnecessary war as they always do, he should be punished. I am glad to see him taking an interest in foreign affairs, and if he could one day be Foreign Secretary, my life's hopes would be fulfilled.

" 18*th May*.— I have been reading Herbert Spencer's autobiography, an astounding document, one of those that console the least of us that he is not a great man, comic too, and reminiscent of Happy Thoughts, and the author of ' Typical developments.' Burnand must have known Spencer to have written it.

" 30*th May*.— To the Lyric Theatre with Cockerell to see Hippolytus. I expected to find it dull, and perhaps vulgar, in spite of the beauty of the poetry as translated by Murray, but it was all the contrary. I have never seen a tragedy like this, not even Salvini's Othello, or Annunzio's Francesca da Rimini. Hippolytus stands upon a higher and nobler plane. It has dramatic effects one does not dream of when reading it, not that the acting was more than moderately good. Most of those on the stage were amateurs, and rather clumsy, but I think this

added to the effect. Even the few professionals were sobered into a
kind of good taste. With the exception of Theseus and a nurse
nobody was vulgar, and the messenger (Granville Barker), who recites
the catastrophe, was admirable. Everybody enunciated well, a thing
more necessary in verse than prose, and the chaunting chorus seemed
to me in its place. The slow movement for the first act is an artistic
preparation for the rest, and throughout it is the piece that enthralls, no
cleverness of the actors. Compared with Shakespeare the superiority
lies in the workmanship quite as much as in the tragic atmosphere.
The piece has an ordered sequence no play of Shakespeare's possesses.
There are none of Shakespeare's vulgarities, his appeals to the gallery,
his wearisome Elizabethan jokes. The rhymed verse, too, I find more
effective than blank verse, at any rate than the very best, and a vast
amount of Shakespeare's is mere wind. The climax of Hippolytus
is tremendous, the catastrophe the most powerful thing in dramatic
literature. At the end of it we were all moved to tears, and I got
up and did what I never did before in a theatre, shouted for the
author, whether for Euripides or Gilbert Murray I hardly knew.
Nobody cared to call for the actors, this I consider the most complete
feature of the triumph. Percy and Madeline were there with Dorothy, also Carlisle, sitting almost next to me, and his son-in-law
Roberts, and Mackail, and his wife. Murray with his family in a
stage box, and a full house behind us. When it was over I went to
tea in Belgrave Square.

"31*st May.*— To Cambridge on a visit to Browne, whom I found
with Sheykh Hassan Towfik, the recently installed Arabic tutor. With
Sheykh Hasson I had a long talk in Browne's rooms at Pembroke, and
found him a most interesting man, who had already gained much
influence with such of the undergraduates as were studying Arabic
for employment in Egypt. (His sudden death a few days afterwards
was a great misfortune.) Then on to Babraham where I dined and
slept.

"6*th June.*— Lunched with George and Sibell, he very full of the
Montem at Eaton, to which he had gone on Saturday, an honoured
guest with George Curzon. The pair are to be given Doctor's degrees
at Oxford. 'I like honours and dignities,' said George. He talked,
too, with enthusiasm about Rodin and Paris, from which he had just
returned.

"7*th June.*— I have it from the same source from which I originally
heard it, that Eldon Gorst is certainly to succeed Cromer at Cairo in
two years' time. I wrote to Mohammed Abdu to tell him this, and of
the probability of a new régime being started at Cairo.

"15*th June.*— Dined with George Wyndham, and among others
Dunraven, a pleasant party, with much talk about Ireland. Both

George and Dunraven enthusiastic in their praises to me of William O'Brien. Who would have thought it possible fifteen years ago, and to me, but Time has strange revenges.

"*17th June.*— A large dinner in Park Lane. I had some talk with Lord Percy after dinner about Arabian matters, he being Under Secretary for Foreign Affairs. He is an intelligent young man, but without genius it seemed to me, or special wit, inferior for instance to Winston Churchill. There were also at dinner Lord Manners, a Dowager of Westminster, Percy and Madeline Wyndham, with Dorothy, Charles Gatty, Paget, a young Mahaffy, and Hugh Lane. George much bored between two dowagers.

"*20th June.*— Madeline Wyndham's birthday dinner, always to me the pleasantest of anniversaries. Each guest's name, there were twenty-two of them, was written on a card with a heart and wings. I had some talk after dinner with Bendor about South Africa and the land he bought there three years ago. It consists of 60,000 acres close to the Basuto frontier, and he is letting it in 300 acre lots to farmers he is bringing out from England. He has six thoroughbred stallions there from the Eaton Stud, and spoke in high praise of the Arabs, wanting me to go out and see it all.

"*24th June.*— To see Dr. Andrews, of the Natural History Museum at Kensington, who showed me fossil bones of primaeval horses, and other ancient beasts, also the new Okapi stuffed. It is a miniature Giraffe, striped on the hind quarters like a Zebra. Andrews is a queer, rough little man, but a good fellow, who knows his trade, and mocks at conventionalities. Lunched afterwards with Amir Ali and his English wife. He has retired from the Indian service, and is domiciled now permanently in England, bringing up his children at schools and universities as Englishmen.

"*28th June.*— To Yeats' Irish play, ' Where there is Nothing,' a very poor piece, without either wit or sense.

"*30th June.*— Gave a scientific luncheon to Andrews, Lydekker, Cockerell and his scientific brother from America, to discuss the origin of the horse. This we did pretty thoroughly, deciding that it was quite possible the Arab was a separate wild breed, that there might be aboriginal wild horses in Africa, and also on an island in South America, Chiloe. Lydekker considers both the existing Prevalsky horse and the Tarpan to be wild breeds, though probably crossed with feral stallions. Andrews believes that a heavy horse of the shire type existed once wild in the Thames valley. All agree, I think, that the origin of the wild horse was multiple. Andrews attaches much importance, as indicating a separate wild origin for the Arab, to the depression found in their skulls to receive the tear gland as also to the high setting on of their tails level with the croup.

" *2nd July.*— Good old Watts is dead, full of years and honour. His pictures this year at the New Gallery were almost as good as ever they were, and he was well and in good spirits down to a few days before his end. He was a great painter — on the whole the greatest in England since Reynolds.

" Another death is that of Stanley, the explorer, who has left £135,-000, got by doing dirty work for the King of the Belgians on the Congo, a charlatan, who has had the cheek to express a wish he should be buried in Westminster Abbey.

" *6th July.*— Lunched with Margot, at her house in Cavendish Square. On the doorstep I found myself with Coquelin père, to whom Margot gave an effusive welcome. We had an amusing meal, Margot making her little girl Elizabeth recite some verses of Stevenson's about a butterfly, which the child did prettily, dressed up in a Velasquez costume with stiff hoop and petticoat. Coquelin good-naturedly suggested that ' perhaps Mademoiselle would be shy,' but Margot would not hear of it, ' There is no shyness,' she said, ' in this family,' nor was the child at all embarrassed. Coquelin then gave a little entertainment of his own, imitating an Englishman's account of him, Coquelin, in absurd Anglo-French.

" *13th July.*— Lunched with George. He is dying to be out of office, and live an irresponsible life away from politics, which he declares to be an abomination. He says that I am the only person who has learnt the secret how to live. We are to spend next Saturday to Monday together in Worth Forest, where I have seen deer lately. They seem to have come originally from Buckhurst, where the Park fence had been allowed to get out of repair, and they have spread themselves over the whole Forest district as far west as Shelley's Plain and Leonardslee, a distance of some twenty miles, and are to be found in small herds in all the great woodlands. It is a reoccupation of the Forest by its ancient inhabitants (not by strangers), where they do no harm, and so are preserved by everybody, except the German Count Münster at Maresfield, who complains that they interfere with his *chasse*. This comes of Harvey Pechell's snobbery in bequeathing Maresfield, an old Shelley property left him by his wife, to the Prussian Ambassador, because he had been socially polite to him.

" *16th July.*— George has been with me in Worth Forest occupying a tent we have pitched. He declares he will take five years holiday after the General Election. We have ridden all over the Forest in Tilgate and Smith's Charity, talking always of past days, and the glories of the Crabbet Club, and devising schemes of an ideal life in woods, with a pleasant society of men and women on Boccaccian lines, which we are to call the Fellowship of the Holy Ghosts, but George returns to his parliament to-morrow.

" *9th Aug.*— Went by appointment to see Winston Churchill at his rooms in Mount Street. He is astonishingly like his father in manners and ways, and the whole attitude of his mind. He has just come in from playing polo, a short, sturdy little man with a twinkle in his eye, reminding me especially of the Randolph of twenty years ago. He took out his father's letters which I had left with him six weeks ago, from a tin box, and read them to me aloud while I explained the allusions in them, and gave him a short account of the political adventures of the early eighties in which Randolph and I had been connected. There is something touching about the fidelity with which he continues to espouse his father's cause and his father's quarrels. He has been working double shifts this session in Parliament, and looks, I fancy, to a leadership of the Liberal Party, and an opportunity of full vengeance on those who caused his father's death. I promised to let him see extracts from my diaries of 1884–1885.

" Mary Milbanke is with me at Newbuildings. She is much enlivened and improved by her trip to the West Indies last winter. I am very fond of her, having acted as a parent to her from the time she was a child.

" *14th Aug.*— Fernycroft. I drove here, starting on the 11th, with Miss Lawrence and the two boys, Alfred Kensett and Harry Holman, taking tents and camp equipments with us. We went by Fernhurst and Midhurst, and nearly had an accident going up the steep hill at Holly Coomb, for we were overloaded, and it was only by putting the four horses we had been driving in pairs together with the four in hand harness we had with us that I managed with a rush to get at full gallop to the top. There had been heavy rain and the road was much broken up by it, and it was touch and go whether they could do it. Holly Coomb is a romantic place with great oak woods, where they used to boast in former times that they could kill a woodcock every day of the year.

" I have had a long talk with Meynell, who is staying here, about Roman politics and Catholic prospects. He tells me the true cause of quarrel between the Vatican and France is that Combes has all along intended to do away with the Concordat, and that Merry del Val is young and imprudent. The first quarrel raised by Merry as to the French President's visit was so ill-chosen that it raised protests everywhere in the Catholic world and so had to be abandoned. The other quarrel has been forced upon the Pope. The Bishops of Laval and Dijon had two or three years ago been denounced at Rome, the one for immorality with a Carmelite Abbess, the other for being affiliated to a Freemasons' Lodge. He had been seen in plain clothes coming out of a house where the Masons were holding a meeting, and at Rome his action was connected with the story of there being a secret plot, supported with much money, for the dissemination of Masonic ideas among the French priesthood. Young men had been educated for the purpose in the seminaries, and it was supposed the Bishop was one of them. On being summoned to Rome the Bishop refused to go and declared a higher allegiance to be due to the French Government. He is now excommunicated. As to the other's immorality it has been condoned whether proved or not, and he has been given an archbishopric *in partibus* at Rome and thus made his peace. Meynell thinks it will lead to a rupture of the Concordat. The French Government mean to appropriate the churches in France and lease them back to the Catholic communities, but Meynell doubts whether these will be disposed to pay a rent reckoned at £2,000,000. I am inclined to think that the quarrel will eventually be of advantage to the faith, but Meynell doubts."

Here follows an account of a driving and camping tour ending at Clouds. My arrival there is thus described. We had camped the night before on the down above Wylye.

"*5th Sept.*— We had arranged that I was to wait in camp till nine for George Wyndham who was to ride from Clouds in the early morning; and sure enough at 8:30 I heard the sound of galloping hoofs and presently a view holloa and they arrived, George and his son Percy, both bareheaded, and with them Dorothy, and I gave them tea in my tent. It was a joyous meeting on a joyous morning, for George has cast his official cares to the winds and is in his most expansive mood. Then we all went on to Clouds, my four horses pulling double with the excitement of the galloping outriders. There are two terrible hills on either side of Hindon, and these we raced up at a gallop, the team going gallantly and out-pacing the riders, all except George, who was well mounted and led the way. What a morning! We spent the day discussing the Japanese victories and international questions and building by-laws and religion. The elder Percy was curious as to the exact extent of my beliefs. He asked me whether I believed in nothing at all supernatural. I answered ' Yes, I have a small belief in the evil eye.' This was hailed as a great pronouncement.

"*6th Sept.*— A day of galloping on the downs to Whitesheet Castle, and this afternoon I read them my version of Lebid's ' Ode ' and my play ' Fand.' I am satisfied with ' Fand ' and believe it has even acting capabilities. We had some discussion what to call it, a drama or what, George maintaining that it should be called a tragedy, because it ends in the hero going back to his wife.

" I asked him about Somaliland and what instructions had been given to Swain. He told me he had pressed my views of pacification by blood payment, and had no doubt Swain's instructions for peace had been stringent because all the military men were furious against him. As to Thibet, Lhassa is to be really evacuated, another triumph of our joint influence. We also talked about Egypt. I gave him my views of a new régime there based on Mohammed Abdu's letter. He said they were quite aware that the present state of things at Cairo was unsatisfactory, but the great obstacle to any change was Cromer, who was entirely satisfied with all as it is. George had met the Khedive Abbas at a dinner party in London, where the Khedive had treated him with obsequious politeness. This had given him a contempt for him.

"*8th Sept.*— George has left us, and with him the life of the party. He is egotistical but not, I think, selfish, monopolizing attention to his own talk and his own ideas. Some people resent this, but on me it has a stimulating effect, rousing me to repartee; thus I am always happy in his company, almost as his mother is who adores his self-glorifications, which are a schoolboy's in simplicity.

"*10th Sept.*— Left Clouds. On my way back through Wilton I passed the statue which has been put up there to George Pembroke. It is on a colossal scale but very like him. It feels strange that I should have known him as a boy.

"*17th Sept.*— Chapel Street. To-day I signed the settlement, making over Crabbet to Judith, thus ending my reign there after thirty-two and a half years of it, though I still retain the Lordship of the Manors of Worth and Oram, with Worth Forest, Springfield, and Newbuildings. It is rather a leap in the dark but has not been taken without reflection. George also signed the settlement and also Eddy Marsh, as witnesses. George starts to-morrow, with his son Percy, for Frankfort in order that he may learn German. He is a charming young man and George is immensely proud of his good looks. For himself, his one thought now is to get back to poetry.

"*18th Sept.*— Dined with old Philip Webb at Caxtons and discussed Tolstoy's ideas with him which I quarrel with on two points. (1) His belief that the world is improving in the direction of justice and (2) His view that religion of any kind makes people unselfish.

"*23rd Sept.*— Anne has left for Egypt. I am to follow in six weeks. Herbert Bismarck is dead; his wife, Maggie Hoyos, was a nice, simple girl when I used to go and see them at Paddockhurst, some fourteen years ago. I see in the papers that she threw herself on her husband's coffin at the funeral; their marriage had been a very happy one.

"*28th Sept.*— Dined in Belgrave Square, George being with us, having returned from Germany. He has just published a letter in the 'Times' repudiating a programme put out in his absence by Dunraven of a kind of Home Rule for Ireland. I know this kind of

Home Rule to be in accordance with his views, but he gets out of the difficulty by declaring, that it is absolutely contrary to those of the Unionist Party, a distinction which has so far escaped the criticism of opponents." This was the first mistake made by George Wyndham in his management of his Irish policy and the beginning of great trouble for him, though he did not at the moment foresee it. His short run to Frankfort was the first real holiday he had taken during his three years at the Irish office, and he had given orders not to be disturbed during his absence by having letters forwarded to him. He was consequently unaware until his return that Lord Dunraven, with whom he had been acting in concert, had launched their scheme of ' Devolution ' on the world and without due reflection he had written his letter to the ' Times,' an unfortunate blunder which cost him his political career.

" 1st Oct.— Sir William Harcourt is dead, the last of the great 1880 Liberals. I am sorry he did not live to see the return of his party to power and the revival of the Harcourt earldom in his own person. He lived just long enough to inherit Newnham. The last I saw of him was some three months ago when I found him in his carriage in Green Park and exchanged a few words with him. He was always pleasant and kind to me and allowed me full liberty of laughter and plain speech, though he never, I think, quite forgave me my gibes at ' Paradise Lost.' (I had called Milton once ' a bombastic windbag.') This was touching a sacred subject to him, but perhaps I exaggerate the incident. Politically he was straighter than most of his fellow politicians, and when he condoned the Jameson Raid at the inquiry, I believe it to have been out of loyalty as a Privy Councillor to the Queen. His domestic life was very beautiful, and at home he was adored.

" 10th Oct.— Alexandre de Wagram is here for a day or two's shooting. To-day our last beat was the Sprinks Plantation, where we got seventy-two pheasants, all driven high overhead. The light happened to be favourable and the shooting very good. For myself I got twenty-five birds down at one stand with only thirty cartridges, the best I ever did in my best days.

" 13th Oct.— Oliver Howard and his wife arrived here last night having gone to a wrong station and wandered in flies for several hours. She is a very pretty but rather captious little person, which perhaps accounts for Oliver's going to South Africa.

" I am working out a scheme of small holdings here with a bungalow cottage and ten acres each at moderate rents, in pursuance of an article I published on the by-law tyranny in the last ' Nineteenth Century Review.'

" 24th Oct.— An extraordinary incident has occurred. The Russian fleet issuing from the Baltic, and bound for Japan, has at midnight attacked the English fishing fleet on the Dogger Bank, sunk one or two of their craft, killed two fishermen and wounded others. The newspapers treat the affair as a mistake, or panic on the part of the Russian officer in command. I do not take this view. The Russian aristocracy is immensely irritated just now against us English and is in the condition of mind when a man slaps another's face, without regard to the consequences. I am a man of peace, but under the circumstances were I in Arthur Balfour's place, I would stand on no ceremony, but should order out the Channel fleet, and bring the Russian squadron into Spithead. The commanding officer was in all probability drunk at the time, but that is no excuse. [I wrote in the same sense to George and he answered me briefly thus: 'Many thanks for your letter on the North Sea outrage; it was a shocking affair. We cannot contemplate the high seas of the world becoming a vast imitation of a running camp poker saloon.']

"*29th Oct.*— The Russian Government has given in, thanks to the firmness of our Cabinet. The Russian officers are to be submitted to an International Inquiry, and punished if found guilty, and in the meanwhile our Baltic Fleet is to stay where it is at Vigo. Arthur Balfour has certainly managed things dexterously and well. Whether the punishment will be very real I doubt, but the main object is already accomplished, that of showing it is impossible to do these things with impunity.

"*2nd Nov.*— With Madeline Adeane to see Bernard Shaw's new play, 'John Bull's other Island.' It is a roaring burlesque, the most amusing I ever listened to. I laughed till I cried, sitting in the uppermost tier of the gallery, for we could get no other seats. Shaw has certainly made an epoch on the English stage, using it also as a platform for his political fancies. In this play he hits all round, making all the Parliamentary parties equally ridiculous, including the Irish.

"The arrangement of the Dogger Bank affair turns out less rosy than Arthur Balfour announced it to be. The Czar has declared publicly his belief in the torpedo story told by the Russian officers, and the Russian Fleet, with its Admiral Rojesvenski, has left Vigo for Japan. It will probably end in our having to pocket our slap in the face, and perhaps in having the torpedo story saddled on us in history.

"*11th Nov.*— I leave to-day for Egypt, after having taken all my male servants down to Shipley to vote for Turnour, the Tory candidate."

At Gros Bois from 14th November to 20th November.

"*17th Nov.*— The great talk here at Gros Bois is of General André's resignation, a matter of domestic politics. They take no interest here in the Baltic Fleet outrage, or much in the Russo-Japanese War, Wagram being convinced that Russia must win in the end, otherwise it would mean an invasion of Europe by '*les jaunes.*'

" This was a sad visit. On the 18th I went with Wagram and the rest of the family to a memorial service he has performed monthly at Boissy for poor Berthe, where she lies under her cold pyramid which marks the family vault, though Wagram is preparing for her a less dreary resting place outside in the sun hard by. Wagram had brought his little bunch of violets, and we both prayed for her, but alas, what matter, she does not know. ' Though the Heavens and the Earth be broken, she shall not arise, nor waken out of her sleep.'

" *20th Nov.*— La Tour d'Auvergne is here, and Alexandre came to-day from Saint Cyr, which he has joined for the Army. He was proud of having driven his motor the distance (forty kilometres) in as many minutes, it being the best and straightest road he says in France, and with the fewest villages. We were taken out shooting as in former days, and killed eight or nine *faisans vénérés,* with a number of the common sort. These *vénérés* have been thirty-four years wild at Gros Bois, having escaped from their pens during the Prussian War and multiplied greatly, but Wagram complains that the length of their tails has suffered. Formerly the birds measured as much as 2 metres 10, whereas now they seldom reach 1 metre 80. Otherwise they have flourished exceedingly, we must have seen at least forty on one beat. They are somewhat puzzling to shoot, as they are very sudden and irregular in their movements, coming through the woods with a great noise and flourish, and, when you expect it least, perching on the outer trees and chattering like parrots. Thus many birds are missed.

" *22nd Nov.*— Venice. With Button Bourke, to see the sights, he doing *cicerone* with considerable knowledge. I was pleased to find that the loss of the great tower is really a gain to St. Mark's, which one now sees in its true porportion. The tower dwarfed it, and it is best away. St. Mark's is, I say once more, the most beautiful church in Europe, and the most interesting. By good luck I find Tintoretto's great ' Paradiso ' picture taken down from its place where it was difficult to see, and set in a good light on a gigantic easel, so that one can examine every detail. It is a really splendid thing. Button has been now two years living at Venice, and already has the ways and language of the ' oldest inhabitant. He occupies a little house in San Giacomo dell' Orio, where there is a large garden in which he stows the odds and ends of outdoor sculpture he buys for the London market, a business by which he makes a scanty living and which makes him happy, having found in it a vocation in life. He is, as always, a delightful companion.

" *23rd Nov.*— Lunched with Button and his chief friend here, Horatio Brown, who has taken on old Rawdon Brown's work at the Venetian archives. I remember old Rawdon Brown when I was here with Anne thirty years ago.   Both are interesting men.   I told Button the story of the Gorst intrigue at Cairo, and he gave me in return the latest Egyptian news which he got from a friend in the War Office, namely, that Cromer has been in correspondence as to the withdrawal of the Army of Occupation.   Cromer has declared himself ready to do without any English regiment beyond a Corporal's guard at Alexandria. He says he can rely absolutely on the Egyptian troops, that the English garrison is not wanted, and that he declines to pay for it.   The London War Office, however, insists on keeping it on in Egypt, as they thus make a saving of English expense, the cost of the army being put upon Egypt.

"*28th Nov.*— After a stormy passage I find myself once more at Alexandria and Sheykh Obeyd.   During the voyage I read Frederick Harrison's novel which he has just published, a strange mixture of historic fact of the most interesting kind, and melodrama of the most conventional.   The romantic episodes will not, I think, redound to Harrison's philosophic fame, for it is naïvely unreal, but these take up but a few pages, and might as well have been omitted altogether, while the historic background is vigorous and well told, only, as in every historical novel, the parts that are true ought to be printed in sober type, the parts untrue in red.   As it is we don't know what to make of the cream-coloured Arabs and the coal-black Barbs, which would seem to have been borrowed from Disraeli.   I must write to him about it.   The Creevy Papers is another volume of good gossiping value.

"Here at Sheykh Obeyd things change slowly.   The city creeps gradually nearer us, and the old distant view of Cairo, which was so beautiful, is half shut out by new houses.   The garden remains, as always, an unchanging refuge.

"Mohammed Abdu has given me an account of all that has happened during the summer.   The chief incident has been an escapade of Sheykh Ali Yusuf's, in which the Khedive has been mixed up.   The Khedive, ever since his first visit to London and the acquaintance he made with our King, has taken to a life of amusement with ladies of doubtful character, and has surrounded himself with boon companions.   Sheykh Ali Yusuf, whose connection with the Court was originally a literary one, but who is a pleasant fellow, has been adopted into this set, and, though no longer young, has put on the garments of youth in the Khedive's company.   Among other ladies honoured by His Highness was a daughter of the Sheykh El Saadat, whom her father from mer-cenary motives had not allowed to marry, though she is now twenty-seven, his high position as head of the Moslem nobility putting it into his power to exact rich presents from suitors for her hand, to whom he afterwards refused consent.   The young lady, however, has been furious at the delay, and through the connivance of the Sheykh el

Bekri, who had married an elder sister, the Khedive had made her
acquaintance, and seems to have wished to establish her with Ali
Yusuf. Ali Yusuf was therefore put forward as a suitor, his suit
being supported by Abbas, but the old game of preliminary presents and
then delays was the only result, and Ali Yusuf getting tired of this,
arranged with El Bekri and the young lady that she should elope with
him. Now elopement is a quite unheard of thing in Islam, and bears
the character of a theft, inasmuch as it is stealing a man's daughter
without paying the customary dower, and the scandal caused in Ali
Yusuf's case has been everywhere immense, nor has it been made less
by Lord Cromer's having ultimately settled the dispute by advising
the young person to return to her parents. Mohammed Abdu tells me
that the Khedive's position at Constantinople is that of being made use
of by the Sultan as a spy for him on what goes on in Egypt, and
for this he has lost his popularity.

" *17th Dec.*— I have been a week in bed with a strong fever, a
soul-crushing evil, and now feel twenty years older than when I
left England hardly a month ago. The things of this life seem very
far away, or seemed so till this morning, not merely the things of youth,
love, ambition, vanity, but equally so the things of the spirit, all hope,
all fear, all wish to live or die. In these depths, the problem of a
future life seems foolishness; God, heaven and hell, good and evil, duty
of any kind, responsibility, words without meaning. Above all the
heart is dead. Who is there that can help or heal? The good to us
are as one with the wicked. There is no voice in all the world that
can reach us or console. Only with the dead, those who have passed
through the shadow where we stand, are we able to converse as equal
to ourselves in sorrow. I seemed to grope in blind impotent search for
a dead hand, Cowie's, as she used to be here sixteen years ago, when
we lived like mendicants in the little garden house, and as she had
nursed me in Ceylon. Then I could have howled like a wild beast
in my desolation. Such were the last few days.

" Now I am better, the fever almost gone."

This was the beginning of a long illness which eventually declared
itself as Mediterranean fever, and from which for two years it seemed
unlikely I should recover.

It is with reluctance that I waste space in recording these ups and
downs of health which would be better passed over in entire silence, for
I am sufficiently old-fashioned to be of the opinion of our forefathers,
that bodily infirmities should be hidden as far as possible from public
view, and that self-respect should require us as men to follow the
dignified course of the wild creatures of the forest, who retire out of
sight when suffering, and end by dying of old age in some remote

retreat alone. It is, however, not possible for me, in the present volume, to avoid all reference to those evil hours, seeing that they have covered so large a section of my later years. It has been fortunate for me that, however often pain has incapacitated me physically during the last decade of my life, it has always left my mind its full vigour, and allowed me to continue, with rare interruptions, its long acquired habit of setting down my daily record in these diaries. So far, indeed, has this been the case that during the years 1904 and 1905 I actually got through more literary work than in any other half dozen years of middle life. The necessity of bodily inaction forced me into activities of another sort which, in their turn, enabled me to survive. For this I thank a kindly Providence and the persistent devotion of not a few untiring friends who encouraged me to work, and working to live on.

CHAPTER IV

LITERATURE AND POLITICS

" 2nd Jan., 1905.

" This is the first day I have been able to write. I have had a terrible time of depression, the climax being when news came in from the desert that Suliman's pretty Bedouin wife Aïda had died suddenly of smallpox. This is so miserable a thing that I still cannot bear to think of it. From the time Suliman married her I have had a little sentiment about her. She was old Dahil Allah's daughter, a tall, straight girl with beautiful eyes and a sweet pathetic voice. Suliman was very choice with her and he covered her veil with coins. She was a happy sight, leading out her flocks to pasture, and, later, with her children. She had always a pleasant word of greeting for me, and she used to make me little ornamented head stalls and camel ropes of wool each year for my camels. This year when I came back I was distressed to find that for some reason she had been driven with her sheep out of our enclosure and that she was camped in a wretched place outside among the mounds of Heliopolis. I went with Suliman to see her. Her pretty clothes were soiled and ragged and her youth had faded sadly away from her. Perhaps it is best she should be dead. She kissed my hand and held it awhile and I asked after her children. She was to go away with them two days later, to Wady Hárbelamá, taking the flocks to the new pasture which is plentiful this year after the rain in the hills, and I promised to ride a little way with them on the morning of the *rahala* (flitting) and to pay them a visit later at their new camp, but it was a damp sunrise when they started, and I did not go out till too late. Aïda was taken ill only two days after their arrival at Hárbelamá, and seven days later she was dead. Poor old Suliman is partly paralysed. What now will he do?

" 3rd Jan.— Port Arthur capitulated yesterday after a pretty stubborn defence, 5,000 men of the garrison left. How foolish our stupid English generals must feel when they see the strongest fortress in the world taken, fort after fort, by storm by the Japanese. This will probably end the war, for with all their talk the Russians will know now their case is hopeless.

" 4th Jan.— To-day I insisted upon being put upon my mare, and carried to the outer enclosure, where we have a tent pitched. Miss

113

Lawrence wept and said it would cause her death as well as mine, but it all went off well. I lay all day long enjoying the fresh air and the sun, and paid a little visit on my way back to the tomb of Sheykh Obeyd, where Salem, my Egyptian servant, has been saying prayers ever since I have been ill to the saint, and I stopped at the tomb to recite a *fatha.*

" 10*th Jan.*— I have been taken out every day to the tent and it has done me good. My illness has been very unfortunate. Suliman's three young children have sickened of the smallpox and the youngest has died. If I had been well I should have gone out to him, for he must be in want of provisions, though he has the milk of his goats. Smallpox is the one thing that terrifies the Bedouins, and they fly from it, a visitation in the natural world before which all are powerless. I sat yesterday for an hour with the Mufti in his garden. There was with him one Mohammed Bey Talaat Harb, a very intelligent man who is writing a history of the Arabs from Mohammed to the present day. The fall of Port Arthur is universally rejoiced in here as a triumph of East against West. It appears now that 48,000, not 5,000, Russians surrendered. The Khedive has made overtures of peace lately to Mohammed Abdu.

" 12*th Jan.*— I have been reading FitzGerald's translations from Calderon which are rather poor stuff, more Calderon's fault than FitzGerald's, only two of the plays were worth translating, ' The Mayor of Zalamea' and the merry little comedietta at the end of the volume which reminds me pleasantly if not very closely of the Madrid of my youth, forty years ago. The rest of the plays are dull, with little of wit or passion. FitzGerald's blank verse, too, though good in its way, makes heavy reading; perhaps it would be better on the stage, but why does he misaccentuate the names of his characters, scanning " Álvaro " as " Alváro," " Huán " as " Iúan," " Otañéz " as " Otáñez," " Guillén " as " Guìllen," " San Lúcar " as " San Lucár," and so on. It seems trouble thrown away to translate and be so very slipshod.

" 21*st Jan.*— Mohammed Abdu has gone to the Soudan to look after various matters connected with Mohammedan interests.

" 25*th Jan.*— A short desert journey with Neville to visit Suliman and take him provisions. We found Suliman's other wife watching for us on the hill-top and presently we came upon his two little tents pitched in a hollow near the high gravel ridge three or four miles east of the Nahiadeyn, a nice little spot, the scene of the tragedy of Aïda's death. We found her poor black shirt cast away at some distance from the tent, doubtless on account of the infection, and the camp had a squalid look in the lonely wilderness, the flocks being away at pasture and the rain of two nights ago had run through both tents, round

which a little trench had been dug.   Poor Suliman was sitting like Job
in his sorrow on one of the gravel hillocks, and hobbled feebly to meet
us.   His palsy has grown on him and he can hardly walk, his left
arm powerless.   He smiled a little and said the conventional *hamd ul
illah* (Praised be God!) when he had narrated his sufferings.   The
elder boys are now past the worst of the disease, but nothing can make
up for Aïda.   We left our sack of provisions with him and money
to buy clothes for his children.   One can do nothing really in a case
like this, an accident of desert life and the ' act of God.'

"*27th Jan.*— There has been something in the nature of a revolution
in Russia.   I wish I could think it could succeed, but unless the soldiers
make common cause with the people I do not see how this can be.
The armed power of modern troops is so great that a mob, however
determined, has no chance.   Russia, too, is so immense a country, and
the towns in it are so small and far apart that cohesion between them
is difficult.   The mass of the peasantry has little in common with the
townspeople and cannot and will not help them.   It is all a question of
the army's fidelity to orders.

"*19th Feb.*— Mohammed Abdu has returned from Khartoum.   He
is pleased with what he saw there; says the Government is better
managed than in Egypt, that the people are content, especially in the
matter of the slave trade, and that the education at the College is being
sensibly given.   The Soudanese criminal code is simpler and better than
the Egyptian.   Wingate's rule is mild, and there is good feeling between
the English and the Soudanese.

"Lady Gregory writes that Yeats has read my play ' Fand ' to his
company and that they are anxious to act it, and perhaps it will be put
on the stage in April.   Yeats, she says, has declared that if I had
begun to write plays when I was thirty, I should now have a European
reputation.   I fear it is too late for that now, also Gilbert Murray has
written in praise of it and Mackail.

"George Meredith has been appealing for funds to help the revolution in Russia, and I have subscribed £10, and yesterday came news
that the Grand Duke Serge had been blown up with a bomb, so I
am subscribing again.   Assassination is the only way of fighting a
despotism like that of Russia.   It shows that the revolutionists mean
business.   I have taken my place for Europe by the steamer of the 11th
March.

"*28th Feb.*— I see in the papers that George has got into trouble
with his Irish policy, as I feared he would, over the Dunraven programme.   His defence in the House of Commons reads well, but there
is something behind.   To the best of my knowledge, though I do not
know it from George, the sudden policy of conciliation he adopted two
years ago, was at the suggestion of the King who, when he came to the

throne, was anxious to be able to go to Ireland and have a loyal reception.   Also he has great regard for Continental opinion, which he knows well, and he was ashamed of the disgrace of there being a part of his United Kingdom where he was not welcome, otherwise I cannot account for the sudden accession of official fervour in the matter. George, however it began, certainly became converted to views not very distinguishable from Home Rule, as I have often discussed them with him, only he was not prepared for Dunraven's sudden announcement of the programme.   I believe, too, that he is quite justified in saying that an elected general council was not in his plan.   Where he made the mistake was in his too hasty and not happily worded repudiation of the manifesto by writing to the ' Times.'   He would have done better to have expressed his sympathy with it while saying that in its present form it was not compatible with the Unionist policy.   For his views were so well known that his rather bald pronouncement read both to friends and enemies like a sudden recantation, and it has prejudiced his later explanations.   I fear it will harm his political position, though to me personally his retirement from the Government could only be a gain.   What will probably happen is that he will be shifted later to some other office in the Cabinet.   It is a thousand pities he did not leave Ireland after passing his Land Bill and take the War Office when it was offered him.   It is impossible for any one to win in the long run as Irish Chief Secretary.

" *1st March.*— I hobbled out this evening to the tomb for tea, the garden looking lovely in the perfect light which I suppose I shall never see again after this month.   There is a gigantic scheme of building a garden city over the whole desert round here, which will be the end of Sheykh Obeyd's solitude, with its jackals and its foxes and its doves and kites, and its long-eared owls and its night ravens, but I am consoled by the thought that I shall not see it again.

" *2nd March.*— I see that George has made a second speech in Parliament about his Irish policy, far better than the first.   This time a quite frank statement, reading the letters which passed between him and MacDonnell.   It restores him to the position of an honest statesman, though probably not politically.   He can hardly any longer do much good in Ireland amid the yelping of the Ulster pack, and the counter yelping of Healy and Sexton; even his optimism can scarcely carry him through another year there.

" *9th March.*— I am laid up again with the malarious fever and other troubles, and feel like a hare headed first by one greyhound and then by another.   I was to have left for England to-morrow but Milton, the Cairo doctor, who was called in, declared it impossible, so my journey is put off till the 18th.   George has resigned.   I was afraid they were going to give him Milner's place at the Cape, which would have plunged him deeper than ever in the slough of Imperial politics, but they had already appointed Selborne, so George is free.

"*12th March.*— Mukden has been taken by the Japanese and the Russian army under Kuropatkin seems on the point of capitulation. It is the biggest thing that has happened in war since Sedan, but it is more than this, it is the first great victory of the East over the West since the Ottoman conquests of the sixteenth and seventeenth centuries, and may change the whole face of the world's history for as many centuries to come.

"The inquiry into the attack made on our fishermen at Dogger Bank has turned out pretty much as I expected, the Russian admiral is hardly blamed for his 'mistake,' and nobody will be punished. We have had our ears boxed very prettily and everybody is pleased, including it seems the British public, which has as much sense of its dignity as a clown in a circus; however, the Japanese have done the fighting so effectually for us that the Russians cannot raise much of a crow.

"*15th March.*— Harold Spender of the 'Daily News' has been here, come out to study the Egyptian question. Cromer delights in men of this sort and has been cramming this one with his confidences. He has told him that he wants the whole Army of Occupation withdrawn, that he can depend for order on his native police, that he would like a native administration, but can't find any Egyptians fit for responsibility, etc., all which the good man has swallowed and admits it as an axiom that England has come to Egypt to stay. Mohammed Abdu happened to come in while Spender and his wife were with us, and stopped to dine, and has given Spender another picture of the position, but I fear it has been casting pearls before swine.

"*17th March.*— I left Sheykh Obeyd this morning, as it seems to me for ever. The place is very dear to me with its perpetual sunshine and its wild beasts and birds. Woe is me, who will look after them all when I am gone? Mohammed Abdu came to see me off at the Cairo station and we stayed on talking to the last minute with sad farewells." [I never thought to see him again when we parted, but it was not I, it was he that died within the year.]

"*24th March.*— Venice. The last week has been a terrible experience of fever and pain, and but for some fresh milk found for me at Brindisi, I could hardly have got through, and for being met here by the good Cockerell, who came out from London to see me home, and Van Someren, an English doctor, who has put me to bed, saying that if I go on to England as I am it will mean that I shall die in the train. He allows me no food of any sort, only Vichy water with a tea-spoon of brandy in it twice a day, so here I am stuck fast.

"*1st April.*— The régime of starvation reached its climax yesterday. I was reduced to such a point of weakness that I could hardly turn in my bed and began to have visions, so I rebelled and insisted on a new-laid egg and I am now reviving. Button has returned to Venice, having been away, and has taken charge of me.

" *6th April.*— Still no change, but the doctor is fairly out of his reckoning and I am determined at all risks to move on homewards, convinced that my best chance with the fever is to get away from the Mediterranean. I have been a fortnight here in bed.

" *18th April.*— Chapel Street. On the 8th I made the venture, and, thanks to Button, successfully. I was carried out just as I was, undressed, in bed on a stretcher, and placed in a gondola and from there into the train, where a first-class carriage had been prepared on purpose and so, still all the way in bed, and helped with morphia, to Boulogne and so to Folkestone and London. It is pronounced now that I have Malta fever.

" *13th May.*— Easter has come and gone and I have been a fortnight at Newbuildings in beautiful weather but hardly any better.

" George, who promised to come down here to see me before making his final apologia about Ireland, seems to have been captured by Arthur Balfour at Clouds and brought over to a position of mere party obedience.

" *30th May.*— George writes proposing to come to see me. I am glad of this. There is news to-day of a great naval victory by the Japanese.

" *8th June.*— I have been back in London seeing doctors, but to no profit, as I still suffer continual pain and grow no stronger. George has been several times to see me, and has explained to me all his Irish story. He has sacrificed himself to party necessities and his devotion to Arthur Balfour."

The next month is without record in my Diary. I had hardly got down to Newbuildings when I began to be seized with a pain in the nape of my neck, which gradually increased in violence till it became a perpetual agony, preventing me from taking any rest whatever either day or night. It is no exaggeration to say that for a full six weeks I did not get one minute's sleep, in spite of all the drugs that could be given me. Neither could I lie down nor even rest my head upon a pillow, and if for an instant I lost consciousness it was only to be awakened by the sensation as of a spear transfixing me from shoulder to shoulder through the spine, an indescribable agony. With this, continuous fever and drenching sweats. I had a bed made up for me in the hall, but could not actually lie down on it, and remained day and night propped up, my forehead resting on a band fastened to the bed head against which I leaned it, or I would wander from room to room and from chair to chair on the ground floor, followed by my nurse. I remember one especial night, when a new nurse had come who did not understand my ways.   In my wanderings from room to room I had sunk into the big high-backed chair which stands in the hall, and she, thinking I should rest awhile, had left me there.   After a while I fell as I have described into a momentary unconsciousness, and in the same instant awoke with a pain so great that I howled aloud, and the sweat ran from me in streams.   It was to me then as to a wild beast in a trap, caught by its steel teeth and held a prisoner, which knows that it cannot escape its doom.   I could not move, I could do nothing for myself.   I had an absolute certainty that all for me was over.   " No man," I said to myself, " ever came back from a depth of physical despair so deep as this and lived."   The nurse came to me with some conventional words of inquiry, and anger seized me, and I cursed her for a fool.   The anger gave me strength to stamp my foot and rise. I think it saved my life.

With my nurse Lawrence it was otherwise.   Her handling soothed me.   She would take me sometimes to the room on the ground floor which had been Cowie's, and where she died.   I used to imagine that there my pain was easier.   But I was mad with the pain and the drugs, and the long lack of sleep.   It was accepted by all then that I could not recover, and Dr. Haig, who had been brought to me by Judith for an opinion, gave me not three days to live.   All thought my lungs were affected, and my weakness was such that it seemed to me at times that a single cough would have been my end.   It would have shattered and destroyed me.   Nevertheless I did not die, though emerging as one who had passed through the Valley of the Shadow of Death.

" *8th July.*— I have been again to London to try and get relief from pain by Swedish treatment, and have seen many friends who have come to me in Chapel Street.   George has given me an interesting account of the difficulty the Government finds in keeping George Curzon in order.   He was very near bringing on an Afghan War, but was prevented.   He resents having a nonentity like Brodrick placed over him at the India Office, but Brodrick is backed by the Cabinet."

From this time till the 20th of May the pain I have described continued, and then I went down to Newbuildings.   Almost the only entry is of 28th July.

" The great event transcending all others is that Mohammed Abdu is dead!   A terrible personal loss to me, and a public one quite incalculable for the world of Islam.   We cannot help fearing there has been foul play, as the death was very sudden, and the Mufti had many political enemies."

On the 20th of September I was moved to Brighton, where I gradually recovered the power of sleep, and began to find life tolerable, though still helpless to leave my bed, except for an occasional short drive, propped up with pillows. I find in my Diary, 16th October, a note of the death of Lady Currie, who had been Violet Fane, the best of our living women poets, to whom many of my earlier sonnets had been written. I had been able, too, in spite of my illness, to get the first volume of my Egyptian Memoirs into print, and had been in correspondence with Frederic Harrison about them, who pronounces them " of extraordinary interest and importance, but impossible to publish at present." [1]

" *26th Oct.*— With George I have had much interesting talk, as he has been with me at Newbuildings. He showed me a letter he had received from Chamberlain, saying that he (Chamberlain) had always looked on George as one of his strongest supporters in the Cabinet, and asking him to join him in his Tariff Campaign. On this George consulted me, and I of course advised him to have nothing to do with Chamberlain, and he has answered him that he cannot take any part in the campaign, though in terms that ought not to leave Chamberlain his enemy. Another interesting letter he read me was from Lord Hugh Cecil, which shows him rather at a loss what political line to take, as he may be unable to retain his seat at Greenwich except with the support of Liberal voters, and he hints that he may have to join Rosebery. This would be a great pity. I look on Lord Hugh as one day destined to lead the Conservative Party, and should like to see him and George acting together. This George will probably endeavour to bring about. George considers Arthur Balfour to have been very unwise in not dissolving this autumn, as his chances at the coming election are getting worse and worse. We talked also about George Curzon. The quarrel between him and Kitchener, is, he says, entirely a personal one. He, George, advised Curzon not to go back to India last year, and it is a pity he went. He cannot understand his having been so foolish as to have made the Thibet Campaign, and to have stirred up trouble in Afghanistan. What Curzon will do on his return to England is a problem. He thinks he would do best by taking a peerage with a seat in the Lords. He asked me what I thought ought to be done in India. I told him the practical thing would be to reduce expenditure. With Russia beaten in the field and revolutionized at home, the Indian Army might be greatly reduced.

" *7th Nov.*— To London yesterday for a new consultation and X-rays. It is now pronounced that I am to remain on my back in bed for at least three months, a terrible sentence. Meynell and Cockerell dined with me. Meynell read us 'Modern Love,' and expounded it to us as Meredith had expounded it to Mrs. Meynell. According to this the last two stanzas mean that the wife, 'Madam,' commits suicide so as to

---

[1] The edition privately printed 1915.

leave the poet free to marry ' My Lady.'   Cockerell thinks that to have
been an afterthought, and that the poem really ended before the two
last stanzas, and that the wife eloped with her lover.   Meredith,
Meynell says, seems to have persuaded himself that his wife, in real
life, left him for some such altruistic motive, but this must have been
self-delusion, as she certainly lived with her lover till her death.

" 16*th Nov.*— I have become reconciled to my fate, the more so
because the rest has done me good, the pain is less and I have
lost all inclination to get up.   Numbers of friends have been with me.
Yesterday I saw Ross, Oscar Wilde's friend, who was with him in his
last hours.   I was curious to know about these and he told me everything.   Ross is a good honest fellow as far as I can judge, and stood
by Oscar when all had abandoned him.   He used to go to him in
prison, being admitted on an excuse of legal business, for Ross managed
some of Mrs. Wilde's affairs while her husband was shut up.   He told
me Oscar was very hardly treated during his first year, as he was a
man of prodigious appetite and required more food than the prison
allowance gave him, also he suffered from an outbreak of old symp-
toms and was treated as a malingerer when he complained of it.   Ross's
representation got attention paid to these things, and in the last eight
months of his imprisonment, Wilde had books and writing materials in
abundance and so was able to write his ' De Profundis.'   I asked him
how much of this poem was sincere.   He said, ' As much as possible in a man of Oscar's artificial temperament.   While he was writing
he was probably sincere, but his " style " was always in his mind.   It
was difficult to be sure about him.   Sometimes when I called he was
hysterical, at other times laughing.   When Oscar came out of prison
he had the idea of becoming a Catholic, and he consulted me about it,
for you know I am a Catholic.   I did not believe in his sincerity and
told him if he really meant it, to go to a priest, and I discouraged him
from anything hasty in the matter.   As a fact, he had forgotten all
about it in a week, only from time to time he used to chaff me as one
standing in the way of his salvation.   I would willingly have helped him
if I had thought him in earnest, but I did not fancy religion being
made ridiculous by him.   I used to say that if it came to his dying I
would bring a priest to him, not before.   I am not at all a moral man,
but I had my feeling on this point and so the matter remained between
us.   After he had been nearly a year out of prison he took altogether
to drink, and the last two years of his life were sad to witness.   I was at
Rome when I heard that he was dying and returned at once to Paris
and found him in the last stage of meningitis.   It is a terrible disease
for the bystanders, though they say the sufferer himself is unconscious.
He had only a short time to live, and I remembered my promise and got
a priest to come to him.   I asked him if he would consent to see him,

and he held up his hand, for he could not speak. When the priest, an Englishman, Cuthbert Dunn, came to him he asked him whether he wished to be received and put the usual questions, and again Oscar held up his hand, but he was in no condition to make a confession nor could he say a word. On this sign, however, Dunn allowing him the benefit of the doubt, gave him conditional baptism, and afterwards extreme unction but not communion. He was never able to speak and we do not know whether he was altogether conscious. I did this for the sake of my own conscience and the promise I had made.' Wilde's wife died a year after he left prison. She would have gone to see him at Paris but he had already taken to drink, and Ross did not encourage her to do so. Ross made £800 by the 'De Profundis.' He had intended to pay off Oscar's Paris debts with £400 of it and devote the rest to the use of the boys, but just as he was going to do this the whole sum was claimed by the bankruptcy court and the affair is not yet settled.

"*26th Nov.*— Button Bourke came last night to dine with me. He told me a curious story about the death of the Prince Imperial, Napoleon the Third's son. He, Button, was at that time 'Daily Telegraph' correspondent with Chelmsford's staff in South Africa, to which the Prince was attached. The Prince was bored with the staff duties and got Chelmsford to allow him to go out with the scouting parties. On one of these expeditions to survey the line of march, they fell in with the Zulus, who surprised them while they were having their lunch. Cary, who was in command of the scouts, gave order for a *sauve qui peut* and all rushed to get on their horses. The Prince had a habit of vaulting into his saddle, but the girths having been loosed, the saddle turned round with him and he fell and was speared by the Zulus after running forty or fifty yards. Cary and the rest had meanwhile ridden away and returned to camp with the news. He had met Grenfell on the way and had told him that they had been attacked by a large force of Zulus and that the Prince had been shot. Five other men had lost their lives. The next morning Button had gone out with Grenfell and others to look for the bodies and had found them, first coming upon a Boer, who had been one of the scouts, then they found the Prince's body, pierced with spears through the eye, the heart, and other parts, but with no shot wounds. Upon this Cary was tried by court martial for cowardice in the field, Button acting as his 'friend' on the occasion. His defence was that he had never learnt to ride as a boy, that he had then served in a West Indian regiment where the officers were not mounted, and that until he had come out to South Africa he had never been on horseback, that they had all scrambled on to their horses as they best could and that, he being unable to manage his horse, had been run away with and had not even been able to look behind him, all his thought being how not to fall off. Button told me that this line of defence was strictly true, but that he knew it would not be accepted as an excuse, seeing that the court martial was chiefly composed of Hussars, and so it had resulted, Cary was condemned and would have been shot but for the fact that Chelmsford's rank in South Africa was not that of Commander-in-Chief, but only that of Commanding-in-Chief, which last gave him no power to confirm a death sentence and the case was referred to England. There, the Lord Chief Justice, I think it was, finding that there was no record in the papers submitted to him that the evidence had been given on oath, tore them up, and Cary was sent back a free man to his regiment. Button and Grenfell had heaped up stones on the spot where the body was found, and this enabled the Empress Eugénie afterwards to identify the place and build her monastery there.

" *29th Nov.*— Button again dined with me and with him Philpot, my doctor. Button told us that war with France over this Fashoda affair was narrowly prevented by Monson through one of the old-fashioned diplomatic tricks. Lord Salisbury had drawn up an ultimatum, and instructed Monson as Ambassador in Paris to deliver it. Monson, however, who knew the ultimatum, if formally delivered, would be refused, and who wished to prevent a war, gave Delcassé, the French Minister for Foreign Affairs, warning confidentially through one of the secretaries of the Austrian Embassy of what was impending, and that if Delcassé should see him put his hand into his breast pocket he would know that the limit of English patience was reached, and that the ultimatum would be handed to him. When therefore the next day their discussion had reached the limit Lord Salisbury had laid down, Monson gave the signal, and Delcassé, who also wished to avert war, gave in, and allowed the dispute to remain at the point it had reached, and so between them the thing was arranged." [I received confirmation of this story later as exact from a near relation of Sir Edmund Monson.]

Anne left for Egypt yesterday.

" *10th Dec.*— George tells me that he has received an answer from Chamberlain to what he wrote some weeks ago, to the effect that Chamberlain quite understands his position, and thinks him right not to come forward on any political platform just now. Arthur Balfour resigned office on Monday. He had told George of his intention a week before.

" *31st Dec.*— On Xmas Day Margot had the charity to dine with me. And so the year has gone by. I have ceased to worry about public affairs. Margot is the best and kindest of women.

" My article on Ridgeway and his theory of the origin of the Arabian Horse is out in the ' Nineteenth Century.'

" Looking back on the past year I see it as physically *une année terrible,* but it has brought me many consolations. During the last six weeks in London I have seen more friends, and more of them than in the preceding six years. I have ceased to worry myself about public affairs. I shall never, now the Mufti is dead, go again to Egypt, nor even, I think, across the Channel. If I recover I mean to live out my few remaining years as much as possible with my friends here in England, and enjoy the little things of life at home. My friends, and I have had very many of late to see me, now, I perceive, look on me as wise. It is all old age can reasonably aspire to in the way of happiness.

" *9th Jan.,* 1906.— Parliament was dissolved yesterday, and the new one will be elected by the end of the month.

" I have been reading Winston Churchill's life of his father. It is wonderfully well done, and on the whole a very fair statement of Lord Randolph's career. He under-estimates, however, Randolph's Home Rule dallyings in 1885. To me, Randolph always talked at that time as a Home Ruler, though not prepared to declare himself one as yet. Lord Salisbury was his difficulty, but he hoped to convert him, but all he could get Lord Salisbury to do was to declare against coercion, and when he had been himself a few weeks in office he fell into the way of thought held by his party. Randolph's annexation of Burmah destroyed my confidence in him as an anti-aggressionist, and his Home Rule talk did not survive the General Election of that year.

" *17th Jan.*—' Astarte ' has been published, and I am surprised to find what good literature it is. Since I saw it last, two or three years ago, it has been almost entirely rewritten, and is now really admirable in style. Indeed, Ralph has invented a new form of prose, or rather, perhaps, re-invented it, for it reminds one of Hazlitt and his contemporaries. I have written to congratulate him, but I expect he will come in for plentiful violence of counter-attack in answer to his own violence.

" The excitement of the General Election is not yet over. Arthur Balfour's defeat at Manchester has amused me greatly, and Gerald's at Leeds, and Alfred Lyttelton's at Warwick. With these three front Bench men gone, George Wyndham will remain leader of the Tory opposition, for even Hugh Cecil has been submerged in the general deluge. What a *débâcle!* As to the future, people talk of violent democratic changes. I do not believe in them, the new Cabinet is a Whig Cabinet. The Liberal Party will split up into two camps, Whig and Socialist, and in their wrangles things will continue to drift on much as they are. He who lives longest will see most.

" *29th Jan.*— The elections are over, giving the Liberals a clear majority over all other sections of some 89. This is immense. The Tories keep no more than 156 seats. The Labour Party have got 51.

All the same I don't expect to see any very revolutionary legislation.
They will probably get into difficulties before long over South Africa
or Foreign policy, and Redmond will get his chance of upsetting them
as he upset Balfour. Arthur Balfour is to have a seat in the city.
Anne writes from Sheykh Obeyd that she is selling those acres of land
near the Railway station for £300 an acre. [This was the beginning of
the great land boom in Egypt when extravagant prices were realized,
only to go down as rapidly.]

" 30*th Jan.*— King Christian of Denmark is dead, an old man. I
remember him in 1862 when he came to Frankfort with his two
daughters, Alexandra and Olga, and they had luncheon at the English
Legation. They were very unimportant personages then, the girls badly
dressed, and their father quiet and unobtrusive. I was a little hurt in
my feelings, as the spoiled child of the house, when Lady Malet asked
me to give up my place in her carriage to the Danish Prince when we
were going to some review. Now he dies senior monarch of Europe
and progenitor of our Queen and of half the royal and Imperial
houses.

" 8*th Feb.*— George Wyndham has been to see me and we talked of
' Astarte ' which I had lent him to read. He has done this carefully,
and criticized it with his usual insight. There is no doubt it is a very
original piece of prose, almost a work of genius, but singularly ill-
arranged as an argument. Moreover the diatribe against the Murrays turns out to be entirely without justification. Murray has published in a monthly review a dignified answer in which he shows not
merely that all Ralph says in his preface about his dealings lately with
himself over the new edition of Byron is incorrect, but he also quotes
letters from him acknowledging the kindness of the Murrays for
three generations to his family.

" 9*th Feb.*— Frederic Harrison was here in the afternoon. He still
has hopes of his Byzantine play, ' Theophano,' being acted in London,
but I doubt any manager taking it as it is purely spectacular, and could
not be put on the stage without great expense. The managers tell
him it is superb, but so far have refused it. He talked of ' Astarte,'
refusing still to believe the main fact.

" There are strange tales current of the goings on at C——, where
ladies were invited by the hostess, with express designs upon their
virtue. They were invited without their husbands, and given rooms
near those of their intended lovers, and if they locked their doors at
night the other ladies staying in the house would refuse to speak to
them. I daresay there are pretty free doings at C——, but the boy-
cotting of the virtuous ladies next morning does not sound to me as
according with the ways of society, even in the most advanced set.

" 10*th Feb.*— There is an article in to-day's ' Tribune,' by Principal

Morgan on Haeckel's philosophy, which interests me, because Haeckel's
is precisely the argument I made out for myself forty-five years ago
when I was at Frankfort as a boy of twenty-one, asserting the eternity
of matter and the natural origin of mind as an 'accident' of matter
in the metaphysical sense of the word 'accident,' and the consequent
lack of any necessity of an eternal creative mind. I wrote a paper,
which I have still, dated 1861, giving this argument briefly. I wrote
it in answer to a paper shown me by Count Usedom asserting that
God could be discovered in Nature, and I developed it later in my
correspondence with Dr. Meynell, published anonymously in seventy-
six, under the title, 'Proteus and Amadeus.' In 1861 Haeckel had, I
believe, published nothing. This is curious.

"13th Feb.— George looked in and gave me the latest political
news. On Thursday they are to have a party meeting at Lansdowne
House, where three resolutions will be proposed and voted on, the first
two unimportant, the third to raise the Tariff question in an aggressive
form. George is beginning, he says, to lean towards Protection, which
probably indicates that Balfour also leans that way.

"19th Feb.— George was with me for an hour and a half yesterday,
confiding to me his political secrets. He has been constantly with
Arthur Balfour during the last week, and is not at all satisfied with
Arthur's present attitude. George knows more than Arthur of public
opinion, and sees that his vacillations have done him harm. He
described to me the meeting at Lansdowne House, where Balfour
accepted Chamberlain's programme. Chamberlain spoke first, then
came the Duke of Devonshire, who had read the correspondence with
Chamberlain as he came up to London in the train. He declared
himself in accord with every part of the Unionist creed except Tariff
Reform, remaining a Free Trader. At the end of all Hugh Cecil
spoke, his speech short but excellent, showing great courage. He
asked whether as a Conservative Free Trader he would be allowed
to stand as a Conservative at the elections, without having a Tariff
Reformer started against him. He put the case well and with humour,
and made the meeting laugh, and he was listened to. Arthur gave him
no certain answer. As to Ireland, Arthur has gone right round to
the extremists again, coercion and all the rest, with Walter Long as
his prophet. George's own relations with Long are curious. During
the whole of his tenure of the Irish Office Long was one of his
steadiest supporters, indeed admirers. They were very intimate, and
Long professed to take George as his guide and master in Irish affairs.
They are still quite cordial, calling each other by their Christian names,
but George has told him that during the coming session he means to
take his own line about Ireland, and that Long must answer for himself if the late Government there is attacked. He tells me in great

confidence that he has received indirect overtures recently from O'Brien who, he says, seems more in accord than anyone else with his policy, Redmond and Dillon having coalesced.   Also Dunraven has made him advances, and yesterday he had met Sir Anthony Macdonnell, and talked with him on the most friendly terms.   It was their first meeting since George left the Irish Office.   All this encourages him to take a line of his own about Ireland.   He means to strike in early in the new Parliament, making religious education his special subject.   'I am much mixed up,' he said, 'with High Church people, through Sibell and others, and take an interest in it, though not much myself of a believer.   Opportunities of attacking the Government are sure to come.' He fears Hugh Cecil will not be able to get into this Parliament, and he expects trouble for the party.   Chamberlain is to lead the Opposition till Balfour gets a seat, and he should not be surprised if he got them into difficulties.   Chamberlain, though the public does not know it, is becoming senile, and talks inordinately.   George is looking the picture of health, having put himself on a *régime* of meat and drink. We touched upon old times and my campaign in Ireland, and I told him how nearly I had won the campaign against Balfour in 1888 while I was in prison.   At my trial in the Four Courts, eleven out of the twelve jurymen were for me ; had I secured the twelfth I should have won my case, had I won my case I should have won the Deptford election, and had I won the Deptford election I should have upset Balfour, his coercion policy being so distasteful to his party.   George agreed that it was so, and that it was a touch and go moment.   He and Balfour had always considered the decision in the Four Courts as the first solid foundation of their policy under the Crimes Act.   Everybody connected with it on the Government side had been rewarded.

"*28th Feb.*—I see Dick Fox of Bramham is dead.   I first made acquaintance with him and his brother George on my seventeenth birthday, when, with my own brother Francis, we ascended Monte Rosa.   We were a young party, two of us being eighteen, one seventeen, and one sixteen.   We did the ascent to the top and back to the Riffelburg in twelve hours.   On our way down, while climbing along the narrow snow ridges between the two summits, Dick, who was just in front of me, slipped.   He had hurt his foot the day before, but had concealed the fact from his elder brother that he was lame until we had well started.   We were too young and careless to have ourselves bound together with ropes, which were not so generally used then as now ; and away Dick slid, followed by a guide who, in trying to catch him, lost footing too.   It looked like inevitable death for both of them to me, who was immediately behind them.   It happened, however, that just where the slope down which they were hurried was turning over to a sheer precipice of several thousand feet, the snow beneath them bedded, and they lay there not daring to move till our other guide cut steps in the ice down to them, and so rescued them. It was a wonderful escape. George Fox, the elder of the two, became a Catholic, and was disinherited by his father, the old Squire of Bramham, for his change of religion, and Dick became the heir. He passed his whole life fox-hunting, and died when he could no longer ride.

"*9th March.*—George was again yesterday full of his parliamentary plans. He is taking the lead in Opposition now, which he does well, though I hate most of his public politics. His private ones are very different. I gave him my idea of a policy of education, and he said he would follow it when the question came forward in the House. What I thought he might say is this: ' It is right and proper that education should be compulsory to the extent of the three R's, writing, reading, and arithmetic, for this the State should pay, but no child should be be compelled to go beyond this, or to attend school after twelve years old. The State school should be undenominational, inasmuch as the three R's can be taught without involving any religious question. Beyond the age of twelve each denomination should provide its own education, History, Literature, and Science being unteachable without involving religion. Such secondary schools should not be compulsory.' This would certainly be enough in the country schools, and would help to keep labourers on the land.

"*18th March.*— There has been a new life of Richard Burton published, and much discussion of his character in the papers. I will try and recollect my own impression of him. I knew his wife when she was an unmarried girl, having met her several times at the house of her aunt, Monica Lady Gerard, at Mortlake, in the fifties or early sixties. At that time she was a quiet girl enough, of the convent type — at least so I remember her — fair-haired and rather pretty — very different from my recollection of her in later years. When I next met her it was at Rio Janeiro in the autumn of 1867, where I spent some days in her company on my way to the Legation at Buenos Aires. Her husband was Consul then at Santos in Brazil, and he was travelling somewhere in the interior of Brazil, and had left her at Rio during his absence. She had developed into a sociable and very talkative woman, clever, but at the same time foolish, overflowing with stories of which her husband was always the hero. Her devotion to him was very real, and she was indeed entirely under his domination, an hypnotic domination Burton used to boast of. I have heard him say that at the distance of many hundred miles he could will her to do anything he chose as completely as if he were with her in the same room. Burton's sayings, however, of this kind, were not to be altogether depended upon, and he probably exaggerated his power.

" A few months later Burton himself turned up, but without his wife, at Buenos Aires, the announcement of his arrival having been made beforehand with some parade in the local newspapers. The great traveller, it was stated, had the project of making a new exploration of Patagonia and the western Pampas and of ascending the highest summits of the Andes, including Aconcagua, then a virgin peak, and paragraphs were from time to time printed as to the preparations being made beforehand for so great an adventure. On his arrival, however, it was soon abundantly clear that there was nothing very serious in the plan. Burton, in spite of his naturally iron constitution, was no longer in a physical condition for serious work, and though he talked about it for a while to all who would listen, the expedition was gradually let drop by him and ended by becoming a matter of joke among his friends. I remember what I think was my first meeting with him, at Mrs. Russell's house in the autumn of 1868, where we had both been asked to dinner and with us the notorious Sir Roger Tichborne, in whose company Burton had arrived and with whom he chiefly consorted during his two months' stay at Buenos Aires. They were a strange, disreputable couple. Burton was at that time at the lowest point I fancy of his whole career, and in point of respectability at his very worst. His consular life at Santos, without any interesting work to his hand or proper vent for his energies, had thrown him into a habit of drink he afterwards cured himself of and he seldom went to bed sober. His dress and appearance were those suggesting a released convict, rather than anything of more repute. He wore, habitually, a rusty black coat with a crumpled black silk stock, his throat destitute of collar, a costume which his muscular frame and immense chest made singularly and incongruously hideous, above it a countenance the most sinister I have ever seen, dark, cruel, treacherous, with eyes like a wild beast's. He reminded me by turns of a black leopard, caged, but unforgiving, and again with his close cut poll and iron frame of that wonderful creation of Balzac's, the ex-gallérien Vautrin, hiding his grim identity under an Abbé's cassock. Of the two companions Tichborne was distinctly the less criminal in appearance. I came to know them both well, especially Burton, his connection with the Consular service bringing him to us at the Legation, and I have sat up many nights with him talking of all things in Heaven and Earth, or rather listening while he talked till he grew dangerous in his cups, and revolver in hand would stagger home to bed.

" On the first occasion, however, of our dinner at Mrs. Russell's my curiosity was excited more towards Tichborne than towards him. He had already laid claim to the Tichborne baronetcy and was commonly called by his title, and his business at Buenos Aires was to collect evidence, proving his identity for the lawsuit he was about to bring for the family estates. Burton at that time, it is worth recording, more than half believed in him as being what he pretended, his wife's connection with the Catholic world probably disposing him to take an interest in the result. I too had something of a similar interest. I had been at school, not indeed with the real Roger Tichborne, but with his younger brother, Alfred, who had been a boy of about my own standing and whom I knew well. When, therefore, I was told I was to meet 'The Claimant' at the dinner I brushed up my recollection of Alfred so that I might be prepared to see or not to see a likeness between them. Alfred at the age of sixteen had been a rather nice looking boy with a round, good-humoured face, across which, a very notable feature, his thick eyebrows met. Without being stupid he was a quite unintellectual boy, and had passed by seniority into the highest class of the school without, I think I may safely say, having learned a dozen words of Latin or Greek. It was about all he could do to write in ungrammatical sentences an English letter, and his time was spent in entire idleness and smoking so incurable that he had been allowed at last to indulge it as an alternative to his expulsion. I was consequently not prepared for special intelligence in his pretended brother, but I looked out for the eyebrows and there, without question, they were across Sir Roger's face. I treated him, therefore, as Burton did, in the light of a young man of decent birth gone woefully to seed. His huge frame and coarse manner seemed to conceal reminiscences of aristocratic breeding as authentic perhaps, it was not saying much, as Alfred's.

"With these two men I therefore spent much of my time during the next few weeks but naturally more with Burton. (I unfortunately kept no notes nor journals then.) My talks with Burton were of a most intimate kind, religion, philosophy, travel, politics. I had hardly as yet visited the East, but Eastern travel had interested me from the day I had read Palgrave's 'Journeys in Arabia,' and Burton was fond of reciting his Arabian adventures. In his talk he affected an extreme brutality, and if one could have believed the whole of what he said, he had indulged in every vice and committed every crime. I soon found, however, that most of these recitals were indulged in *pour epâter le bourgeois* and that his inhumanity was more pretended than real. Even the ferocity of his countenance gave place at times to more agreeable expressions, and I can just understand the infatuated fancy of his wife that in spite of his ugliness he was the most beautiful man alive. He had, however, a power of assuming the abominable which cannot be exaggerated. I remember once his insisting that I should allow him to try his mesmeric power on me, and his expression as he gazed into my eyes was nothing less than atrocious. If I had submitted to his gaze for any length of time — and he held me by my thumbs — I have no doubt he would have succeeded in dominating me.

But my will also is strong, and when I had met his eyes of a wild beast for a couple of minutes I broke away and would have no more.

" On matters of religion and philosophy he was fond, too, of discoursing. There I could argue with him and hold my own, for he was not really profound; and always at the bottom of his materialistic professions I found a groundwork of belief in the supernatural which refused to face thought's ultimate conclusions. I came at last to look upon him as less dangerous than he seemed, and even to be in certain aspects of his mind, a ' sheep in wolf's clothing.' The clothing, however, was a very complete disguise, and as I have said he was not a man to play with, sitting alone with him far into the night, especially in such an atmosphere of violence, as Buenos Aires then could boast, when men were shot almost nightly in the streets. Burton was a grim being to be with at the end of his second bottle with a gaucho's navaja handy to his hand.

" His visit to the Pampas ended tamely enough in his crossing it with ' The Claimant,' the two inside the ordinary diligence, to Mendoza and thence on mules to the Pacific. As to Aconcaguá (he always insisted the mountain should be pronounced ·with an accent on the last syllable) we heard no more of it, after the appearance of a final paragraph in the Buenos Aires ' Standard ' making fun of it and him. ' The great traveller Burton, it is said, has just completed his final preparations for his exploration of the Pampas and Andes. Among his latest acquisitions with this object are, we understand, a small fieldpiece to be mounted on the roof of the diligence in which he proposes to travel and a few torpedoes for use in crossing rivers.'

" The Buenos Aires ' Standard ' of those days was the creation of a cheerful and irresponsible Irishman named Mulhall, to whose office I used now and then to go for a quarter of an hour's gossip about local matters, when he would ask me to lend a hand with his ' copy ' and turn a ' paragraph.' I am not sure that the paragraph just quoted was not one of mine. Mulhall afterwards rose to eminence in the world as a statistician, to the surprise, I imagine, of everyone who in 1868 knew him at Buenos Aires.

" Such is my personal recollection of Burton when he must have been forty-eight years old as I was twenty-eight. He seemed to me then already a broken man, physically, nor did he impress me very strongly on his intellectual side. For that reason, perhaps, I have never been able to rate him as highly as have done most of his contemporaries, the friends who knew him. I am aware that I saw him at his worst, but from a literary point of view, too, he seems to me second-rate. His prose style is certainly of a poor order, and his verse as bad. As an oriental linguist he was no doubt great, and in his youth he had great powers of simulating Eastern character in various disguises. His face was one that lent itself to this, for it had in it little of the European, and there must certainly have been a cross in his blood, gipsy or other. At the same time in his talks with me, and also in his books, he showed little true sympathy with the Arabs he had come to know so well. He would at any time, I am sure, have willingly betrayed them to further English, or his own professional interests. His published accounts of Arabia and the Arabs are neither sympathetic nor true. His 'Pilgrimage to Mecca' is largely made up with literary padding, and as a narrative reads to me insincere. It certainly exaggerates the difficulty of the undertaking which in those days was comparatively easy to anyone who would profess Islam, even without possessing any great knowledge of Eastern tongues. At Damascus, when I was there in 1878, he had left a poor reputation, having managed to get into hot water with every native class — Turk, Arab, Syrian, Christian and Moslem alike — though this I believe was greatly his wife's fault. She was indeed a very foolish woman, and did him at least as much harm in his career as good. Her published Life of him, however, which has the ring of a true wife's devotion, redeems her in my eyes, and it is a fine trait in his character that he should have borne with her absurdities for the sake of her love so long."

CHAPTER V

About this date an incident occurred which was to prove the beginning of a series of violent mistakes made by Cromer in Egypt, and endorsed by Sir Edward Grey at the Foreign Office, and which, as will be seen, led to the long quarrel between our Government and the Mohammedan world, as represented by the Sultan at Constantinople. This was what was known as the Akabah incident, which was briefly as follows:

It arose more or less accidentally. A young Englishman, Bramley, had for some time past been making camel journeys in the Libyan Desert, and with such success as to attract Cromer's attention, and, though not in the Government service, had been given a kind of commission by him to make a tour of the desert East of the Suez Canal, and report to him about the Bedouin tribes inhabiting it, a district known generally as the Sinai Peninsula. An ostensible object was to inquire into disputes that had occurred among them, but in reality to find out what truth there might be in reports which had reached Cairo of an intention on the Sultan's part of making a branch line from Maan on the Hedjaz railway to Akabah. During the course of his perambulation Bramley had come across a small detachment of Ottoman troops camped around a well at an uninhabited spot called Tabah, a few miles outside Akabah on the Suez road. With them Bramley had come to loggerheads, and had reported the incident in a serious light, and Cromer had taken it up as seriously, seeing in it a first step on the Ottoman part in the pretended railway scheme, not only to Akabah, but beyond it, towards Egypt, and as such a danger to the British Occupation. On this very slender suspicion, for it was nothing more, a claim had been raised by him in the name of the Khedive to the whole of the Sinai Peninsula as forming part of Khedivial Egypt, which geographically it had never been, for it had always been reckoned part of Arabia, and so of Asia, not yet politically, except in connection with the land pilgrimage between Cairo and Medina, and a very doubtful grant to Mohammed Ali of the fortresses on the pilgrim road. The claim had been pressed with quite unnecessary violence by Cromer, and the evacuation of Tabah demanded of the Sultan in peremptory terms (as to which see later and in the Appendix and my letter to Sir Edward Grey).

133

It was a trifling quarrel pushed to extreme lengths, and most foolishly engaged in by our Government, who ought to have known that its connection with the pilgrim route was sure to rouse Mohammedan feeling against us and place it on the Sultan's side. And so it proved, as will be seen.

" *31st March.*— To-day John Redmond came to see me, and stayed an hour and a half talking. I asked him how they were getting on with the new Parliament, and he said they were doing capitally. All on the Government side except a very few were with him. Bannerman was sound about Home Rule and Reid, and he thought he could count on Bryce and Morley and on the rank and file. The Whig section of the Cabinet, Grey, Haldane, Asquith and Fowler were opposed, but had hardly a handful with them. If he, Redmond, were to propose a resolution in favour of Home Rule of however complete a kind, he should have a large majority for it in the House; he only did not propose one, because he was waiting to see what the Government would bring forward as a measure next session, and he did not wish to embarrass them. Talking about Morley I noticed a kind of hesitation in what he said of him, and I put in ' Yes, Morley is a wretched fellow,' to which he answered, ' You may well say so, he is exactly that. Last year when I was bringing forward my resolution in favour of Home Rule, which I got the whole Liberal party to vote for, I wrote to Morley and asked him to look through the terms of it, and suggest amendments. This he did, and struck out the words " National self-government," and other expressions of the kind. But after the vote, Bannerman told me, " You might just as well have left in the words you struck out, we should have voted for it all the same." Morley has no courage, you can't depend upon him. Yes, he is a wretched fellow.' I then asked about the quarrels there had been in the Irish party, and he said, ' It is entirely a personal matter between O'Brien, and Dillon, and Sexton.' O'Brien and Dillon had been at two ever since the Parnell split, and now they were quite at loggerheads, did not even speak when they met. O'Brien insisted there should be a round table conference about Home Rule as there had been about the Land Bill, but the conditions of the two cases were not the same. About the Land Bill, both sides wanted to come to an agreement. On Home Rule, the Ulster members and the Home Rulers were hopelessly at odds. All they could hope for this Parliament was to get a half-way house as an *instalment*. No half-way house could last, and it must end in Home Rule. About the influence of the priests in Ireland, he said it was quite untrue that it had increased in the last twenty years. On the contrary it had never recovered from the shock it had sustained from the time of the Parnell split. The best proof of their little influence to-day was that the priests could not carry a single constituency against the Parliamentary Party at an election. Archbishop Walsh was a man of little influence, he was too constantly changing his mind. Even on the University question it was impossible to say what his present opinion was.

"From this we went on to South Africa, which is the question of the moment, the Government having first intervened to reprieve twelve Kaffirs sentenced to death in Natal by a court martial, and then having climbed down for fear of Colonial white opinion. He said the Radicals were very angry at Lord Elgin's pusillanimity, and the case was to be debated on Monday. The Radicals were angry, too, at the Whig section of the Cabinet not having voted for the Trades Union Bill. Altogether they had lost much ground already this session. If the opposition had any men of ability they might make an effective attack; as it was, George Wyndham was their only good man. Of George Wyndham he spoke nicely, said he had been sorry for him at the time of his breakdown last year when he resigned, but he had quite recovered his position now. I told him I should not be surprised if George helped them to get Home Rule, and I also repeated to him how Arthur Balfour had told me long ago that if they were to have Home Rule at all he hoped it would be *separation*. On the whole Redmond was most satisfied with the position. The Labour members went solid with the Irish, so that they made a compact party of 120 or 130 members. Redmond is a good-hearted fellow, getting up several times to arrange my invalid pillows for me while we were talking.

"*7th April.*— The interest of the week has been about the Zulu rising in Natal. Our wretched Whig Government, after intervening to reprieve the twelve men sentenced to be shot, gave in to the Natal colonists, whose Ministry had resigned, and on Monday the unfortunate Zulus were executed. This is a dastardly business, and has disgusted the Radicals with Lord Elgin, and there has since been a serious Kaffir rising. How it will end no one knows, but the Government has now committed itself to the general principle of protecting the natives.

"*8th April.*— Sir Wilfrid Lawson called, much broken with age, I am sorry to see, but still full of interest in the things that interested us both twenty-five years ago. I think that with his help we have put a spoke in Cromer's wheel, and prevented a bombardment at Akabah."

This was the last time I saw Sir Wilfrid, whose death, a few weeks later, was an immense misfortune to the cause of liberty, and the rights of backward races and small nationalities oppressed by British Imperialism. He was fearless, unselfish, and absolutely honest, with an inexhaustible fund of wit and rough eloquence, an old-fashioned Cumberland squire of the best possible type.

"*10th April.*— Neville sent me word this morning that Bernard Shaw was sitting to him for his portrait, and I looked in (his house is next to mine), and spent an hour with him. Shaw was in the papal robes in which Neville is painting him, seated in an ancient cinque-cento chair, a grotesque figure, with his trousered legs showing through the lace cotta transparent to his knees. He is an ugly fellow, too, his face a pasty white, with a red nose and a rusty red beard, and little slatey-blue eyes. Neville's portrait is wonderfully like. Shaw's appearance, however, matters little when he begins to talk, if he can ever be said to begin, for he talks always in his fine Irish brogue. His talk is like his plays, a string of paradoxes, and he is ready to be switched on to any subject one pleases, and to talk brilliantly on all. He was talking about his marriage when I entered. ' I should never have married at all,' he said, ' if I had not been dead at the time. I tumbled off my bicycle, and the surgeons made a hole in my foot which they kept open for a year, and me in bed. I thought I was dead, for it would not heal, and Charlotte had me at her mercy. I should never have married if I had thought I should get well. Then I tumbled again, this time downstairs from top to bottom. When I found myself on the floor in the hall with every bone broken I felt satisfied. I could not do more and I took to my bed again.' These particulars were *à propos* of my having said that there were two quite happy moments in one's life, the first when one took to one's deathbed, and the other when one got up from it. He told us next his experiences in public speaking, and how shy he had been, and described his first open-air speech in Hyde Park when he had practised on three loafers lying on their backs on the grass, and how one of them without getting up had called out '' ear! ' ear! ' He said the great art of speaking was to get somebody to interrupt you with a question, and for you to misunderstand it, and he gave us some funny instances. I then got him to give his views on land reform, which he said was a very simple matter. You had only to get all the agricultural labourers to migrate into the towns, where they would make themselves useful by loafing in the streets and attending music halls, the only thing they understood, and by sending the townspeople down into the country to cultivate it by electricity and explosives. If he had a farm he thought he would plough it by firing cannon up and down it — amusing rubbish, which I fancy concealed a complete ignorance of the agricultural branch of the socialistic case. Shaw is a capital fellow all the same, and one I should like if I knew him better. He showed himself personally kind and of much practical dexterity when I got him to help me to my feet from the sofa on which I was, when the sitting was over.

"*15th April (Easter Sunday)*.— It being a beautiful day I was taken out for the first time in a kind of invalid chair, where I am able to lie flat, to Rotten Row, and lay there in the sun looking at the hyacinths and tulips by the Serpentine pond head. No smart people to be seen, only shopkeepers and working men of the London variety.

"*21st April*.— To Clouds at last. I thought I should never get there, my journey having been so often put off by my illnesses, but all has gone successfully, and I have travelled up in my wheeled chair from Semley station. There is the usual Easter family party in the house, with Arthur Balfour, Sir Oliver Lodge, and Butcher, M.P.

"*22nd April*.— I was able to get downstairs this afternoon and to lie in the smoking room, where they all came to talk to me, Arthur Balfour with much kindly unction giving me a two-handed greeting. We had not met here since September, 1887. This time we did not talk any politics, but art, poetry, and science, the last especially with Lodge. Lodge, though somewhat pompous, is a good fellow, and talks well on his own subjects, and, as I had just been reading Haeckel's 'Life,' and being engaged on my 'Religion of Happiness,' I was able to discuss materialism with him to some effect. He is really much more of a materialist than his books suggest, and except that he believes in a future life and some kind of God, there is not much difference between us. He admits the probability of a material origin of life through spontaneous generation, and his God is not God the Creator but a very shadowy being devoid of personality.

"*23rd April*.— Lodge has gone back to Birmingham but he came up to my room for a final talk before he left. He is grateful to me for having cured a toothache he had with a small dose of morphia. He has left his book against Haeckel with me to read and invites me to answer it in print.

"Percy tells me he was present at the celebrated conference at Oxford in 1860 when Huxley defended Darwin's theory, and the Bishop of Oxford, Wilberforce, denounced it. He remembers Haeckel being there in support of Huxley, which is curious, seeing that Haeckel's biographer says that Haeckel did not till two years later accept Darwinism.

"Arthur Balfour has been doing a rest cure for some time in London, recovering from his political defeat, and is still an invalid. I find him singularly unaware of current events, as he still refuses to read newspapers, expecting others to supply him with news of what goes on. An odd instance of this took place to-day. He received a telegram by mistake addressed 'Balfour, London,' from San Francisco, telling him that some property had been saved from the earthquake, and he could not make it out. 'What earthquake?' he asked; 'what earthquake?' having heard nothing of what all the newspaper world has been talking about for the last five days, and he was put out at not having been told. 'I told you, at any rate,' one of them said, 'of the eruption of Vesuvius,' an event three weeks old, but he did not seem to know much about that either.

"*24th April.*— Maurice Hewlett was here to-day, a literary man of some standing, and his wife, who talked to me about the Arabs on the strength of a visit to Algiers. Butcher has left us, a man of no importance, and absurdly deferential to Balfour as his party chief, yet member for Cambridge University.

"*28th April.*— Arthur Balfour went away to-day. The last two evenings I have dined with the rest of the company downstairs, and have had a good deal of conversation with him, very little on politics, but much on unimportant things. In conversation he is a pleasant trifler, avoiding serious discussions, and showing, as I have remarked already, a curious ignorance of things of general information. He had no idea, for instance, last night, on what the Duke of Orleans and Don Carlos founded their respective claims to the French and Spanish thrones, and he jumbled up the Soudan with Somaliland. He told us a story which specially amused us. During the North Sea crisis, when there seemed a probability of war with Russia every hour, he happened to be at Panshanger for Sunday, and they wanted a fourth to play bridge. Lady Cowper, knowing the Russian *chargé-d'affaires* was the best bridge player in London, a telegram was sent asking him to come. The Russian, of course, thought that the Prime Minister had some grave news to tell him, and hurried down to Panshanger, and there had been great difficulty in persuading him that he had nothing really to tell. To me Balfour shows a great deference (if I may use the term) and when he wished us all good-bye after luncheon, he came round especially to me where I lay on my couch and addressed me in a little speech which was almost affectionate. I am touched at this and return it, and it is a feeling he very generally inspires. Ego is here, a very charming fellow, a tall intelligent Oxford undergraduate. They talk of putting him into the army, though he does not really fancy it.

"*29th April (Sunday).*— Matters with the Sultan have come to a violent crisis. The Sultan has refused point-blank to evacuate Tabah (just opposite Akabah), and it is universally believed that Kaiser Wilhelm stands behind him. All the papers in London have become truculent, including the 'Tribune,' and I have written a long letter to Redmond suggesting that he and the Labour members and the extreme Radical section should adjourn the House, and debate the situation as one of urgency. This is how I explain the case to him:

"*29th April,* 1906.

"Dear Redmond.— Would it not be possible to adjourn the House so as to get explanations from the Government about this quarrel with the Sultan? Up to the present Grey has refused papers, and everybody is in the dark about it. Then the next step will be to send an ultimatum — and then they will say it is too late and that the honour of England is engaged.

"As far as I can make the matter out, the Egyptian frontier as granted in 1841 to Mohammed Ali was drawn in a straight line from Suez to El Arish on the Mediterranean, El Arish being a village situated near the mouth of a small river or rather stream which was the ancient boundary between Egypt and Palestine, and is mentioned as such under the name of the ' River of Egypt ' in the Bible. I find that in 1840 the boundary of the Pashalik of Acre contiguous to that of Egypt was officially drawn at that time from Suez to El Arish. In the firman granted to Mohammed Ali in the following year the passage occurs: ' I have reintegrated you in the Government of Egypt comprised within the limits drawn on the map which has been sent you.' I think this map should be asked for, as I am convinced that it would show the boundary to be the Suez to El Arish line.

"All the subsequent ' firmans of investiture ' granted to the Viceroys of Egypt have followed much the same lines, the exact frontier not being specified. This was the case with Ishmail Pasha's firman in 1866, and Tewfik's firman in 1879, and, I believe, Abbas' in 1892, though I have not got a copy of it.

"The origin of the claim in the Sinai Peninsula raised now for Egypt is to be found in a permission given to Mohammed Ali, who, it will be remembered, reconquered for the Sultan the province of Hejaz in Arabia, with the holy cities Medina and Mecca, that he should garrison certain stations on the pilgrim road from Egypt. These were Nakhl [a fort half way between Suez and Akabah], Akabah, Moelhe, and Wej, the last two being small ports on the eastern shore of the Red Sea. All these were considered to be in Arabia, and are marked as such on European maps of as late date as after the opening of the Suez Canal in 1869, though the forts remained in the occupation of the Egyptian Government till 1892. Akabah, Moelhe, and Wej were then, if I remember rightly, abandoned by Egypt, the pilgrimage no longer being made by land, the only post on the pilgrim road still occupied with a small garrison of perhaps a dozen men being Nakhl. In 1892, though nothing definite was said about the boundary in the firman, a letter was written by the then Grand Vizier (I believe it has been published but I have not a copy of it) saying that the boundary of Egyptian administration would be a line drawn from El Arish to Akabah, the Egyptian Government holding the former, the Ottoman Government holding the latter. No exact demarcation, however, of the village district of either El Arish or of Akabah was made, and I believe that in fact the Egyptian Government has exercised jurisdiction for a number of miles east of El Arish. The boundary stone spoken of as having been recently removed by the Turks is, I suspect, considerably east of the village and of the Wady of El Arish (the River of Egypt). So that if the Sultan now claims some miles of land west of the Akabah fort and village he is probably doing no more than the Egyptian Government has long been doing at the other end of the frontier line. It is obvious that a frontier line cannot be drawn exactly to the walls of either village.

" As to the exercise of administration in the disputed district, that is to say, the desert between the southern inhabited limit of Palestine and the Suez Canal, there has been practically none by either Government. In 1876, and again in 1881, I travelled through the whole of it, and can affirm that with the exception of the fort of Nakhl there was then no permanently inhabited place, and that the very few Bedouins camped in it owned allegiance to neither Government.

" The Bedouins of the Sinai district, which lies south of Nakhl, are very poor and few in number. Before the Suez Canal was made, they lived by trading their dates and such small curiosities as their district produced, including rough turquoises, at Cairo, and by conducting Russian and Greek pilgrims to the Sinai monastery. The cutting of the canal, however, has made a barrier between them and Egypt, which has practically ruined them, through the imposition at first of tolls for crossing the canal and later by quarantine regulations either for themselves or their animals. I know well their sufferings on this head, as for the last twenty-five years they have made me the confidant of their complaints. Moreover, a concession was given of their turquoise mines to a European company, now I believe abandoned as unworkable, whereby they were much harassed, and the whole peninsula has been treated as an infected district through the establishment of a quarantine station at Tor for the Mecca pilgrimage. Thus they have shared in no way in the material prosperity of Egypt and have been persistently ignored by its government, until apparently for a political reason we find Lord Cromer, in his this year's Report, detailing the benefits he proposes to bestow on them. The scheme he mentions of irrigation for the Peninsula is mere nonsense, as the whole district is dry desert without streams, for the most part an elevated plateau with a very rare rainfall, and no alluvial soil. I mention these matters because it is sure to be put forward that in opposing the Turkish occupation of Tabah we are defending the inhabitants from Ottoman oppression. No such inhabited place as Tabah existed when I was in the country, and there probably exists none now, the whole district being many miles away from any Arab camping ground.

"As to the excitement in Egypt, it is the natural consequence of the system of a 'Veiled Protectorate' which we have been pursuing there for the last twenty years, and of the repression of all political liberty or exercise of self-government. Before we came with an army of occupation to Egypt we were popular with the natives of all classes, and the Sultán was either ignored or despised. Now it is we who, in spite of the material prosperity fostered by Cromer, are hated and despised; and it is the Sultan who is looked upon as the only possible protector against perpetual foreign domination. Cromer, though a very able administrator, is no statesman in any constructive sense. He has allowed nothing in the way of self-government to make even the beginning of a reappearance in Egypt from the day when it was put down at Tel-el-Kebir. He has governed through the weakness not through the strength of the native population, and more and more every year through Englishmen. Whatever patriotism there is left in Egypt is strongly anti-English, and it is just as well that our credulous people here should learn how things stand politically and morally, and should discount Cromer's self-glorifying annual Reports on any point but that of Egypt's material progress. These Reports always remind me (to compare small things with great), of the first chapter of Genesis, where 'the Lord saw all the things that he had made and found that they were very good.' This calling for reinforcements by Cromer, who less than two years ago boasted that he could govern Egypt without any army of occupation at all, would be amusing if it was not likely to lead to a collision. I suspect the Khedive is playing partners with the Sultan in the Akabah affair. Certainly a quarrel on such a question, involving as it does the protection of the pilgrim road, will make a great ferment in the Mohammedan world from China to Senegal and may cost us dear.

"I should be glad if you would show this letter to some of the Labour members and those Radicals who care more about peace and retrenchment than Imperial glory — and get them to try and put a little sense into the Government — or they will go exactly the same way to ruin as Gladstone went after the elections of 1880. I see all the Radical papers are beating the war-drum just as they did in 1882, but perhaps something may be done in the House of Commons.

"It is worth noting that on the 23rd of March, 1886, just twenty years ago, the excellent Campbell Bannerman, as representing the War Office, announced to the House that the evacuation of Egypt would be effected with as little delay as possible.

"You will of course consult Dillon, to whom I wrote about the

matter on Friday, if he is back in London. You will not forget that
Balfour, in one of his speeches in the House three years ago, defined
Egypt as 'a province of the Ottoman Empire in the military occupation of England.' We have of course no legal right there by any rule
of international law, nor by any European instrument except the private
agreement lately made with France. We are sure to be called to
account internationally for our presence there one of these days, as the
position on the Suez Canal is too important in the world for the other
Mediterranean Powers to acknowledge it permanently.

" Yours very truly.
" W. S. B."

" A Cabinet Council sat yesterday, and the King is returning in haste
from the Mediterranean; a pretty kettle of fish it is. Cromer has
called for reinforcements in Egypt, not, I imagine, to attack the Turks
with, but to overawe the Nationalists, and because he cannot depend
upon the Egyptian army in a case where the Sultan is concerned.
The great doubt is about the Khedive's attitude; that he hates the English *régime* is certain, and also that he has of late years been hand in
glove with the Sultan, but the London papers announce that he has just
been entertaining the Prince of Wales at Cairo, and that he has promised to pay him a return visit in England this summer. Abbas, however,
has become such a double dealer that he is probably on the Sultan's
side secretly, and towards Cromer is playing precisely the same old
game played by his father and grandfather of running with the Nationalist hare and hunting with the European hounds. Cromer has just
published a grandiloquent Report of his year's achievements, and he
has shoved into it a plan of reforms and improvements for the Sinai
Peninsula, doubtless in view of the Tabah dispute which began as
long ago as January. If the Sultan stands to his guns I don't see
precisely what our people can do in Egypt. They have not the force
there to turn the Turks out of the disputed territory, and they cannot
bombard Constantinople without a gross breach of the European peace.
A naval demonstration is their only remedy. They will probably
blockade Hodeida and so endeavour to apply pressure, but I doubt if
the Emperor William will allow action at Smyrna of the kind taken by
France a few years ago. In Natal, too, they are in difficulties through
a Zulu revolt, so that it may well happen that our splendid Radical
government, pledged up to the eyes to peace and retrenchment, may find
themselves with two wars on their hands within six weeks of their
coming into office.

" *2nd May.*— As to my letter to Redmond I see that Grey and Fitzmaurice have explained themselves. Also Cromer's Report has come,
and I have written a long article on it of 2,000 words for the ' Man-

chester Guardian,' criticizing Cromer's political as contrasted with his administrative policy in Egypt, explaining his relations with the Khedive and blaming his quarrel with the Sultan.

"*6th May (Sunday)*.— The 'Manchester Guardian' has published my article on Cromer in a prominent way with a leading article adopting my view that the present troubles are largely caused by Cromer's having failed to re-establish the Liberal National Party in 1883, and later by his injudicious brow-beating of Abbas. It says that self-government ought to be begun now in Egypt. On the other hand the ' Tribune ' has gone right round, and is extravagantly jingo, denouncing the Sultan, and printing an aggressive picture of John Bull threatening to demolish him. The 'Daily News' is preaching a crusade. It says, ' it is a maxim of Liberal policy that no foot of land abandoned by the Turk can ever belong to him again,' all this in consequence of the announcement that an ultimatum has been addressed to Constantinople.

"*7th May*.— I have decided to write a public letter to Grey expostulating with him on the ultimatum, and have spent the whole day over it, from half-past two in the earliest morning, but I feel it to be necessary. As far as I can understand the case, our Government is technically in the wrong in asserting a claim for Tabah as *territory* of the Khediviate, or at any time within the ancient boundaries of Egypt, or that it has ever been administered from Cairo, except in connection with the Pilgrim Road.

"*9th May*.— I left Clouds and came up to London. I have sent in my letter to Grey, and Eddy Tennant (who is an intimate friend of Grey's) has promised to speak to him about it. He is to give him a message, too, from me, that my letter is written in no hostile sense to the Government, but that if I receive no answer I shall consider myself at liberty to publish. I have also sent a copy of it through Arthur Ellis to the King. I fear, however, that it is too late to stop warlike operations. [*Note.* For the text of my letter to Grey see Appendix.].

" Meynell dined with me. He talked a good deal about the Education Bill, which is now much discussed. Birrell, he says, repudiates it as his own, saying that it is really Lloyd George's drafting forced on Birrell by a Cabinet majority.

" *11th May*.— Percy Wyndham came to lunch with me, and immediately after John Redmond. They had not met before, but Percy made a polite speech about their having sat together twenty years ago in Parliament, and then left us to our talk. This was principally about Akabah. The Radical members, Redmond says, are so furious against the Sultan that they will none of them join in any protest against the ultimatum, though not one of them understands in the least what the quarrel is about. I explained the matter to him, and he said there would be papers published on the case on Monday, and opportunities of discussion Tuesday and Thursday on the Estimates. He would send Dillon to me.

" There is a report to-day of the quarrel with the Sultan having been arranged, but the British fleet is assembled at the Piræus, and almost anything may happen. The Emperor William has backed out of any encouragement he may have given at Constantinople, and clearly cannot help the Sultan in a material way. I am inclined to think that if it comes to a naval demonstration it would be one of forcing the Dardanelles and threatening the Sultan at Yildiz.

" 12*th May.*— The ' Daily News ' and ' Tribune ' publish epitomes of my letter to Grey, and the ' Manchester Guardian ' gives it in full, with a good leading article in support. John Dillon lunched with me, and we discussed Akabah, of course. He knows more about Egyptian politics than anybody now in the House of Commons, but, like Redmond, he says, the Radicals will do nothing to stop the war.

" 13*th May (Sunday).*— The ' Observer ' announces that the Sultan has yielded to the British demands, these being (1) That all the positions occupied by the Turks should be abandoned; (2) That the Sinaitic frontier should be delimited by a mixed commission. This is hailed as a complete triumph for Sir Edward Grey."

The triumph proved an unfortunate one for our Foreign Office, as it was the beginning of the long quarrel between Sir Edward Grey and Constantinople, which resulted eight years later in the alliance of Turkey with the central European Powers in the Great War, a combination which gave to Germany its victory over Russia. Not a soul in England understood its importance, or cared to understand. For this reason I print the details here at full length.

" Philip Currie is dead after a long illness and a week of unconsciousness, the papers say. In his youth Philip was a merry fellow, one of the smart young men of the Foreign Office, where he had rooms for many years as resident clerk, with his retriever ' Pam,' so named after Palmerston, his first chief. He had wit and a pleasant tongue. He figures as second hero of Violet Fane's poems, ' From Dawn to Noon,' whom he afterwards married, Clare Vyner being her first hero. Philip rose in the Foreign Office to the rank of permanent Under Secretary of State, and then got himself made Ambassador at Constantinople, and later at Rome, retiring on a pension some three years ago, his time being out. We were cousins and good friends always, without being quite bosom friends. He was a good official friend to me while I was in diplomacy, though my incursions into foreign politics in later years estranged us at times. The last time I saw him was two years ago in the Park, being wheeled there in a bath chair in broken health, and I went home to lunch with him in Prince's Gate. Now both he and Violet Fane have disappeared into the eternal nothing.

" *22nd May.*— The Sultan has yielded everything about Akabah. Though Redmond and Dillon promised me to press for papers, they have not done so, and our Foreign Office has explained nothing. I am disgusted with the Irish for playing thus into Grey's hands, politic though they may find it to be for their own purpose of getting a Home Rule Bill out of the Government. Not that I expected much other result, for I have always felt that the Irish, if they once got their own freedom, would join England and the other robber nations of the world in the work of Imperial spoliation. Parnell's declaration in favor of Imperial Federation twenty years ago was an indication of this to me. It was my main reason for retiring from Irish politics, and for the future I shall economize my subscription to their Parliamentary Fund.

" *28th May.*— I have been all last week in Chapel Street, seeing my various friends. To-day Betty Balfour came to lunch with me, having first sent me a new batch of her father's letters to read and advise as to publishing. They deal mostly with his Indian Government, and I have advised her to abridge and cut freely, as the volume is to be one of private, not political letters. We discussed the respective intellectual powers of her husband Gerald, and of Arthur.

" Curiously enough, precisely the same question turned up later in the afternoon, when I had a visit from Margot. She has, of course, known Arthur intimately for the last twenty years before she married. She insisted that Arthur's real mind was metaphysical and religious, that he had a vivid sense of the present life being of very little importance, an ante-chamber to another life. On one occasion he had told her that, in his view death, apart from the physical pain of it —' and I am a coward in regard to pain,' he had said, ' being altogether without that kind of courage '— was an incident no more alarming than the passage ' from this room into that,' the world to come being infinitely more interesting and important. ' It is for that reason,' Margot said, ' that he has no profound convictions about politics, they attract him only as a game which he thinks he plays well, and which amuses him much as a game of chess might do, but he does not really care for the things at stake, or believe that the happiness of mankind depends on events going this way or that.'

" Dillon was to have come to me to-day, but has had to go suddenly to Ireland to see Davitt, who is in a dying state. Betty Balfour, talking of Dillon, was very severe about his ' lying and insincerity,' but I could not get her to give an instance of either. I told her that for my part I had the highest respect for Dillon, and had always found him perfectly honest and straightforward, a far better patriot than others whom she was praising.

"*31st May.*— To Newbuildings for the Whitsuntide holiday, Anne being expected home from Egypt on the 4th.

"*11th June.*— This is the anniversary of the Alexandria riots, a date always memorable to me. On Saturday we made an expedition to Chanclebury Ring, I in my wheeled chair with a donkey, the others in the American trap, and we took luncheon with us. While we were there, a horseman rode up who turned out to be Goring from Wiston, who is owner of the Down, and we renewed acquaintance. He told us, among other things, that his father's and his grandfather's lives together covered 180 years, their tenure between them of the Wiston estate 150 years. The Gorings got Wiston by a marriage with the Fagges, who had bought it of the Shirleys, when these became involved in the civil war troubles. It is the history of more than one Sussex estate, of the Burrels at West Grinstead, and of ourselves at Newbuildings.

"*20th June.*— Anne arrived last night from Egypt. She confirms my view of the political situation there, saying that while nobody wants the Sultan's rule at Cairo, they nevertheless take his side about Akabah. This is the case with even the most advanced of Mohammed Abdu's disciples. As to the Khedive's attitude, it is not known precisely what line he took, as he seems to have held one language to Cromer and another to Mukhtar Pasha. There can, however, be little doubt that he was with the Sultan in the affair, as he has just gone to Constantinople, which certainly would not be the case if he had taken the English side. It has been a year of terrible drought for the Bedouins.

"*21st June.*— To-day the 'Manchester Guardian' has published a protest I have drawn up against the intended execution of certain fellahin, near Tantah, for the so-called 'murder' of a British officer, and the hurting of several more, which took place on the 13th. [This was the notorious Denshawai affair, which led to world-wide results.] It is an abominable case. As far as one could learn from the telegrams and some slight admissions made by Grey in Parliament, the officers were part of an English military force, making a promenade through the Delta, with the object of demonstrating for political purposes the military power of Great Britain. Finding themselves encamped near Tantah, they could think of nothing better to do than to shoot the tame pigeons in a village hard by, and went out, seven of them, in uniform for the purpose. They say they were invited there by an Omdeh of the village, but when they got there the villagers objected, and as none of them knew Arabic they got frightened; a gun then went off in the hands of one of them; a woman and some men were killed or wounded, and the officers were belaboured with *nabuts*. Two of these ran away, it is said to bring help from their camp, seven miles off, and one of them was found dead four miles from the village. This is exactly like all these cases, except that it is the first time an officer has been killed, and Reuter's telegrams are violent for punishment of the natives. I got Dillon to ask some questions in Parliament on Monday, and yesterday there was a special telegram in the ' Daily Chronicle ' saying that Cromer had decided to have the villagers shot. This, be it remarked, before any trial had taken place, and all treat it as a case of murder with prearrangement, not on the part of the officers, but of the fellahin. It is the usual course these affairs take in Egypt, but a more than usually plain demonstration of the kind of justice dealt out between Englishman and native. Fortunately the ' Manchester Guardian ' has taken up the matter strongly, and may perhaps save some lives, but I doubt it. English feeling on these matters has become absolutely callous, and I believe if Cromer ordered a dozen of the villagers to be crucified or impaled, no serious objection would be made to it here, still I have done what I could, and there is a chance. The ' trial ' is to be on Sunday.

" *23rd June.*— I see a telegram in the ' Pall Mall ' which seems to show that Cromer has received a hint to be moderate in his zeal. It is reported that he has ordered Captain Bull's body to be exhumed and examined medically, with the result that it has been discovered that he died not of wounds but of sunstroke.

" *27th June.*— Still writing to Dillon, the ' Manchester Guardian,' and the ' Tribune,' about the abominable Denshawai affair which is to be judged to-day, or rather to be sentenced, for the whole thing has been judged by Cromer already and the so-called ' trial ' will simply record his decision.

" *28th June.*— They have condemned four of the Denshawai villagers to death, four to penal servitude for life, three to fifteen years' imprisonment, six to seven years, three to one year with fifty lashes, and five to fifty lashes, thirty-one acquitted. This is a monstrous sentence and ought, I think, to do more to break up the legend of Cromer's paternal rule in Egypt than anything we have seen since its commencement. Dillon is bringing forward the case in parliament, but nothing is likely to stop the executions.

" *29th June.*— I have worried myself all day about the Egyptian villagers, and I see now that they were hanged yesterday under circumstances of revolting barbarity. All day I have been writing, and the thing is weighing on me like a nightmare still.

" *30th June.*— Terence Bourke came down from London for the day and gave me news of Tunis. The French, he said. have turned over a new leaf there and are trying to reconcile the Arabs to their rule. He thinks they are succeeding. He is now for an Arabian Caliphate under English protection. The Germans, however, are making a vigorous propaganda in their own interests in North Africa. Anne has left for London, and I am alone here.

" *1st July (Sunday)*.— George Wyndham came down by the early train, and Cunninghame Graham a little later, and we spent a pleasant day in talk. The executions in Egypt were our chief topic. I had fortunately finished my letter to the ' Manchester Guardian ' before they came, and I read it out to them. Graham is to get the Labour members to support Dillon, when he proposes a reduction of Grey's salary on the Foreign Office vote on Thursday. George, though he will not help, will look on with ' benevolent interest.' We sat all day under the trees of the Jubilee garden. After lunch Graham went away, and George and I stayed talking poetry. He read me his essay on Ronsard, and some of his translations, which are admirable, and we had much intimate personal as well as literary talk, and I told him the history of my religious opinions. It is odd his championing the cause of High Church Christianity, he who really believes in nothing of these things, altogether a day of extreme beauty and intellectual pleasure.

" *3rd July*.— Chapel Street. Cromer has been given the Order of Merit ! Dillon came to luncheon and stayed for an hour and a half talking over the Denshawai case. He is hopeless of getting a good hearing for it in Parliament, though the Radical feeling is strong of indignation, but every kind of pressure is being put upon members of the Government to get them to be silent, and the press also is being appealed to. What a state of things ! Here we have a judicial crime of the largest dimensions committed by our Representative in Egypt, the thing hardly denied, quite undeniable and defaming the fair face of English justice throughout the world, yet on the very day the hangings take place our Representative is honoured with the supreme reward of the Order of Merit ! Sir Edward Grey, for the Government, when questioned as to the trial and executions, alleges that he cannot give any information, *because he does not know,* and he must wait till a detailed report arrives from Egypt, and this although Cromer is in England and was actually in the Gallery of the House of Commons while the questions were being put, Cromer who knows every detail of the affair and is the sole person responsible. The truth, however, of the situation, Dillon tells me, is this. The Radicals had designed to have a full dress debate in condemnation of the Congo atrocities committed by the King of the Belgians, and are enraged to find that atrocities quite as startling have been committed by our own officials in Egypt. With what face can they now denounce the mote in the Belgian eye, yet we are hypocrites enough to do this even with this Denshawai beam, astounding as it is, in our own eye, but the Radicals are fools and deserve their fate of jackaling their Whig leaders, and I am a fool to fash myself with the abomination of our rule in the world.

" Sir Wilfrid Lawson is dead, the only quite true man on the Radical side in Parliament. Dear good man, we shall not see another like him.

" *4th July.*— To Clifford's Inn, to see Neville's exhibition of pictures, his Bernard Shaw portrait among them.

" *6th July.*— I have had a letter from Keir Hardie, the Labour leader, asking my opinion about Grey's statement, and have answered him. [The peculiarity in Hardie's letter was that it showed him to be entirely ignorant even as to where the atrocities had taken place, imagining it to be somewhere in the Soudan.]

" *8th July (Sunday).*— The new Egyptian Nationalist leader, Mustapha Kamel, writes to me from Paris saying he wishes to see me, and I have telegraphed back proposing that he should come over to England, and offering to lodge him at Chapel Street. There was a sickening account on Friday in the ' Pall Mall ' of the Denshawai executions. I think it *must* smash Cromer. There are a number of French and English papers, too, come from Cairo which make a damning case of abuse of justice in the trial. I intend to write a pamphlet to be called ' Atrocities of Justice under English Rule in Egypt.' [1]

" *11th July.*— Anne and I spent yesterday writing in connection with this, and translating the Egyptian newspapers. I have written as well as telegraphed to Mustapha Kamel urging him to come to England without delay. The moment is most propitious for a National Egyptian demonstration. To-day being the anniversary of the bombardment of Alexandria, I headed my letter ' Anniversaire du bombardement d'Alexandrie. Que Dieu le venge.' He has telegraphed in return that he will come to London on Saturday, and sends in the meantime a manifesto addressed to the English nation and the world at large, which he is having published in the ' Figaro.' Robertson, too, the Radical member for Newcastle, in whose hands Dillon left the case while he is away in Ireland, writes saying he wants to see me. So I went up to London. Robertson tells me that he has seen Grey, and he ' has hopes that Grey will propose reforms in the way of a new edict, which will make the sentences of the special tribunal subject to appeal, and stop *public* executions and *perhaps* all floggings.' This is all rubbish; the Appeal Court is too entirely under Cromer's thumb to be of the least use, except, perhaps, to delay future executions. As to stopping *public* executions, it would only make matters worse for the Egyptians, who would then be hanged and flogged in private, to them a greater punishment, and more beyond the control of English and native opinion. Of course this privacy is exactly what Cromer would like, and I hope Robertson would refuse to accept it as any mitigation.

" *12th July.*— There is a splendid article in the ' Tribune,' thanks to Meynell, who got them to put it in, the best we have yet had in any paper. Robertson came to breakfast, and I had a good two hours with him. He has put down a number of questions for this

[1] See Appendix.

afternoon in the House, and altogether things seem warming up. At least we have gained it that Parliamentary papers have been promised for this day fortnight, and an opportunity of discussion before the session closes.

" 14*th July.*— Back to Newbuildings yesterday, much knocked up by my work, leaving it to Neville to take my place at the luncheon I was to give to Mustapha Kamel and Robertson on Monday.

" 15*th July (Sunday).*— Mustapha Kamel arrived by the early train and we spent the whole day together in the Jubilee garden. He is certainly a very wonderful young man, more like a very clever young Frenchman than an Egyptian, though it is physically quite evident that he is really one, without any taint of northern blood, Circassian or other. He tells me his family have lived for the last three generations at Cairo, though originally from the provinces, and he has the good sense to pride himself on his pure Egyptian birth. He is enthusiastic and eloquent, and has an extraordinary gift of speech, but he is no mere babbler, but a man with perfectly clear ideas — a thing so rare in the East — and a knowledge of men and things really astonishing. I take him, too, to be quite sincere in his patriotism, and I could not detect throughout the whole of his talk to-day a single false note. He also has great courage and decision of judgement, not scrupling to disagree with any opinion expressed in conversation where his own differs. He has given me the information I wanted about himself. First as to his relations with the Sultan, he, like all educated Egyptians, hates and distrusts Abdul Hamid as a tyrant and a dangerous man who at any moment, for some personal interest or through fear, might barter away Egyptian independence to England, and make some *entente* with her, such as the French have made, a thing which would be death to all their hopes. For this reason Egypt cannot afford to quarrel with Abdul Hamid, and the connection of Egypt with the Ottoman Empire is a guarantee to her, while it lasts, against annexation by an European Power. His hope lies in Abdul Hamid's death, and in getting a liberal and reforming successor to the Caliphate.

" Of the Khedive Abbas he tells me precisely what Abdu always said about him of late years, that he had become corrupted. ' I knew him well,' Mustapha said, ' before he came to his present position, as we are exactly the same age within three months, and I saw much of him while we were both being educated in Europe. He was then charming, and full of patriotic ideas, and I was his devoted adherent, absurdly so, but now he has fallen entirely into the hands of rogues, and thinks of nothing but making money, and he is also in the hands of his Hungarian mistress. He has in this way lost all his friends and has ended by having no influence whatever in Egypt.

If he had had any courage he might over and over again have held
his own against Cromer and done incalculable good to his country,
but he cares nothing now for his country, only for money. He puts
up with endless indignities from Cromer, who has a hold over him
through a knowledge of his rascalities; and he clings to his £100,000 a
year, his civil list allowance, and makes himself Cromer's servant.
In the Tabah Akabah affair Abbas was at first altogether with the
Sultan and Mukhtar Pasha, but when it came to the pinch Cromer
took him by the ear, and said, "Look here, my boy, you must leave
off this and come over to us," and he went over. He had promised
Mukhtar to support him throughout, but he betrayed him. This has
cost him what little influence was left him, and we may consider him
now *une quantité negligeable* [it was in French we were talking]; he
could not do anything to interfere with us if we got a Constitution,
and we could run the thing quite well now as we have plenty of
good men. We are quite ready to leave all the finance to the English.'

"Cromer, of course, is the great obstacle. I asked him who could
replace Cromer if he resigned? 'There is only one Englishman,'
he said, 'who could inspire us with any confidence, and that is
Chitty, the Director of Customs at Alexandria. He was born in Egypt,
knows Arabic, and understands us, he is also a good financier, with
him we could easily work a Constitutional Government.' Of Mohammed Abdu, Mustapha talked with modified admiration, sympathiz-
ing with his views but blaming him for having clung to his position
as Mufti instead of resigning when the Khedive publicly insulted
him. 'He cared too much for having official influence. He would
have had more real influence if he had resigned, we should have all
worshipped him as the champion of our liberties.' Mustapha assures
me that Abdu's death was really due to cancer. He knows his doctor,
who announced the nature of his disease three months before he died.
He spoke highly of Mukhtar, and on the Tabah question said that
every word of my letter to Grey was correct. He went back to London
in the afternoon. I am glad to have made his acquaintance and to
know that there is so intelligent a man to lead the Party.

"18th July.— As we were lunching to-day under a tree at Gosbrook,
Belloc and his wife with a boy presented themselves. Belloc, with a
bottle of wine in his pocket, and we had an amusing talk. He had
with him also a friend, Professor Phillimore from Edinburgh. Egypt
was our principal subject of conversation, and the slaughter of the
Zulus, an infamous deed. The two atrocities together ought to shut
English mouths for ever about Russia and the Congo and Abdul
Hamid.

"20th July.— The Blue Book on Akabah has appeared and it fully

confirms what I said of it in my letter to Grey. Cromer's pretensions
on historic grounds rest on an original misunderstanding of a passage in
Abulfeda. It also shows that the Sultan's action in occupying Tabah
was prompted by a belief that Bramley's mission had for its object
to seize and fortify positions commanding Akabah. As to a design,
by the Sultan, against Egypt there is not a trace of it in the correspondence, though Cromer's insistence about Tabah made people in
Egypt believe that some design must exist. It can hardly be claimed
as a diplomatic victory for Cromer, seeing that it was only gained
at the cost of mobilizing the British fleet and rousing the anger of the
whole Moslem world. Cromer has got the Order of Merit but he has
destroyed his own reputation; he will not survive Denshawai.

" *22nd July* (*Sunday*).— Mustapha Kamel came down again for
the day and with him Button. Kamel tells me that Robertson has
had it in so many words from Grey that he does not now believe
in the agitation in Egypt being fanatical in any religious sense, only
in a political sense. This can only be that the Foreign Office repudiates
Cromer's reading of the situation and Button declares he will retire.
The great thing will now be to make it patent to the world that it is
the Egyptian National movement that has driven him to this and to
get a new policy adopted favourable to Nationalism by whoever shall
be Cromer's successor. We talked the matter fully over and have
decided that in default of better, Gorst would be our best man. We
are, therefore, to open a campaign in the autumn against Cromer, and
in favour of re-establishing Constitutional Government in Egypt. In
the evening Mustapha returned to London."

Though I do not put it in my diary, poor Kamel was very unwell
that afternoon, suffering pain and, I think, taking morphia to ease it.
He went up late to London in Button's company and was seriously ill
on their journey. Button was of great assistance to us in our plans
at this time, encouraging us to attack Cromer. He declared that no
case of hanging where the victim was innocent ever failed in England
to ruin the man who did it. " You may commit any injustice you
like," he said, " in English public life so long as you don't hang your
enemy, but to do that is fatal."

" *27th July*.— The last week has gone by quietly. I have not been
up in London but have left Mustapha Kamel to the care of Button
and Neville and Meynell. On Tuesday the Panislamic Society in
London gave him a banquet, and on Wednesday he delivered himself
of a speech at a luncheon party, which has been reported in the
' Tribune ' and other London papers, the ' Manchester Guardian ' having become strangely silent.

" *28th July*.— The Denshawai Blue Book is out. Though all the
arts of evasion are tried in it, even to the complete suppression of

the evidence, it remains a document altogether damning for Cromer. He gives himself away in it completely. It is announced in the 'Westminster Gazette' that the matter of Denshawai will now be allowed to rest in Parliament and that Liberals would support Lord Cromer.

"*9th August.*— Fernycroft. I have been here since the 2nd having gone up to London to see Robertson. He managed at the very last minute in the debate on the adjournment to bring on the Denshawai case and got certain admissions out of Grey, indeed Grey gave Cromer's case away by withdrawing what had been said about *fanatical* unrest in Egypt. This has now become *political* unrest, a very different thing. Grey used wild words, too, about a Crown Colony in connection with Egypt which cannot but add fuel to the fire.

"*18th August.*— At Clouds. George and Guy Wyndham have come from Guy's camp at Bulford where he is commanding the 16th Lancers. Last week there was a party at Tedworth for a sham fight to amuse the King of Spain, the entertainer being Sir Ian Hamilton and one of the party being John Burns. Burns, according to these, has developed and holds advanced Jingo views, his whole mind being wrapped up in army matters. His one idea now is to send a fleet into the Baltic and fight the German Emperor. He knows the history of every regiment and is 'quite a good fellow.' Such is their report. George was very brilliant at dinner with all kinds of theories. 'The true way to be happy,' he said, ' is to be able to say, " I want " and " I won't," ' and after dinner he wrote some blank verse lines on the subject which were good.

"At Fernycroft and Clouds I was much occupied with my ' Atrocity ' pamphlet, and on the 29th my brother-in-law, Lord Lovelace, died, an event which caused many family changes.

"*13th Sept.*— My ' Atrocity ' pamphlet is out and there is a capital leading article on it in yesterday's ' Manchester Guardian,' and to-day the ' Times ' prints a letter about it from Suez by a correspondent who denounces its title as reprehensible and even abominable. Frederic Harrison writes congratulations, he says it is ' a tremendous work.'

"*27th Sept.*— Great events have happened in the last fortnight. First, as to Egypt, my pamphlet has had more effect than I expected, and still more my ' Times ' letters. My old adversary, Moberly Bell, was tempted into the field against me and he published in the ' Times,' of which he is now manager, a violent attack on me in relation to the events of twenty-five years ago, backed up by as ferocious a leading article. This gave me a splendid opening, as Bell had mentioned my poem, ' The Wind and the Whirlwind ' as one of my crimes and I was able to quote ten stanzas from it in very effective reply, which will now spread the fame of it, all the world over. It has brought me congratulations from many quarters and I feel like an *Espada* in the Spanish bull-ring who has planted a blow he knows to be mortal, and who walks away wiping his sword and leaving the dying bull to rage an instant by itself before it falls. ̄ Moberly Bell will leave me alone for the future. Also I have written a formal letter to Grey, sending the pamphlet and begging him to make a personal inquiry into the Denshawai case instead of leaving it to be dealt with by the permanent officials. So all is going well. Mustapha Kamel has entrusted me with the task of finding him an editor for his new Anglo-French paper at Cairo, ' The Egyptian Standard.'

" There have been terrible doings in America, lynchings and massacres of negroes, acts of reprisal against the black community for isolated assaults, understandable but just as brutal and iniquitous as the massacres of Jews in Russia, or of Armenians in Turkey. There is no pretence that any of the negroes murdered by the mob had any connection with the particular assaults, therein lies the abomination of injustice. I am not one who condemns the severest punishment of men found guilty of violent sexual crimes, I am for hanging, flogging, what you will; in such cases it is even right that a man taken *flagrante delicto* should be killed on the spot, but to slay the innocent for the guilty, as was done at Atlanta and by us at Denshawai, moves my indignation.

" On the 24th we had an amateur performance of my Irish play, ' Fand,' at Newbuildings.

" *29th Sept.*— My article in the ' Independent Review ' advocating a change of policy at Cairo has an excellent leading article in support of it in the ' Tribune,' and I look upon our game as won. Cromer will, of course, return to Egypt in November but it will be his last winter there, and he will be found to have something the matter with his liver or his eyes, and he will take his pension and retire. The only question is who will succeed him. Perhaps by that time Abdul Hamid, too, will have disappeared from the scene and the further question may have been put, who will succeed the Sultan?

" *1st Oct.*— Out shooting in my wheeled chair and managed to kill six or seven pheasants.

" *6th Oct.*— Brailsford, the ' Tribune ' leader writer, having written to me privately to ask my advice about his line regarding Egypt three days ago, came down to luncheon and gave me a curious account of the way Cromer has taken with the newspaper editors in London. ' He showed,' he said, ' great emotion and is quite upset about the Denshawai business.' He may well be so. Also of Grey: Brailsford says that he knows absolutely nothing of foreign affairs. Grey has only once been abroad and then only to Paris, and he speaks not a word of French or any foreign language. Haldane manages all that for him. His strength is that he is good-looking, with an imposing manner and an appearance of common sense and honesty which the House of Commons likes. Brailsford knows much of the ins and outs of Eastern affairs, having been in Crete as newspaper correspondent, and is a very clever fellow.

"*15th Oct.*— The article on Egypt which I wrote for the ' Figaro ' has been a great success. I wrote it in French, and intrusted it to Mustapha Kamel to get it published, and to-day I get a letter from Mme. Juliette Adam and Pierre Lôti jointly signed.

JULIETTE ADAM AND PIERRE LÔTI TO WILFRID BLUNT

' En séjour à Hendaye chez Pierre Lôti et Abbaye de Gif. Seine et Oise, 9. 10. 06.
' MONSIEUR,
' Votre article au Figaro est un acte de courage et de loyauté dont il faut que tout ami de l'Egypte vous félicite. Pierre Lôti et moi nous venons de le lire tout haut. Je tiens la plume pour tous deux et pour vous dire que nous ne confondrons plus la politique de Lord Cromer avec la politique *des Anglais*. Une exception, de la haute valeur de la vôtre, oblige à en tenir largement compte.

' Pierre Lôti, à qui le repos est ordonné pour quelques jours, signe avec moi en vous assurant comme moi de sa haute sympathie.
' JULIETTE ADAM.
' PIERRE LÔTI.'

" The substance of the article has been telegraphed to Egypt, and it is sure to be printed there in all the newspapers. I feel that I have done now all I possibly could for the National cause, and must leave the rest of the work to others. I have had several threatening letters from English jingos menacing me with death if there should be a native rising at Cairo. Such letters are I fancy written by idle fellows over their whiskey and water at pot-houses. One fool says to the other, 'Here is that damned fellow Blunt at it again, let's give him one,' and they scribble, but don't sign. One of them, however, signs his missive.

" *18th Oct.*— Betty Balfour's book of her father's letters is out, and very good it is. She has condensed the political part of it, and made it as readable as a book should be. It has been very favourably received, and I look forward now to Lytton's being recognized at last for the man of genius he undoubtedly was.

" *8th Nov.*— Cromer has been obliged already to make changes in his administration. Chitty Bey, the only English official who sympathizes with Nationalism, has been given a high post in the Ministry of Finance, which will give him control of the budget, and Saad Zaghloul, one of Mohammed Abdu's disciples whom I remember in prison as an Arabist in 1883, has been named Minister of Public Instruction."

This mention of Saad Zaghloul has become of especial interest since the first part of this book was published through the leadership he has taken of the Egyptian Nationalist Party. He is an honest and very capable man, the worthiest of all those who have been acknowledged National Leaders during the British Occupation. I am glad to remember that it was due to my intervention with Cromer, and beyond Cromer with Gladstone, that I obtained his release from prison in 1883.

" The Denshawai Case is to be brought forward by Dillon next week in Parliament. I feel that I have gained a notable success, and am master now of native opinion in Egypt, and to a large extent of Mohammedan opinion outside Egypt.

" Auberon Herbert is dead, a man of original thought and high integrity, slightly touched in his later years with eccentricity. I need not describe his character here as I have said so much of it already in these diaries. There was much in common between us in the view we took of public things, but he was more of a doctrinaire than ever I was, and he has had greater belief in the effective power of appealing to principles of right and honour with Englishmen. In appearance he was the most refined of men, an ideal countenance, such as Shelley might have had if he had lived to the age of seventy. His place in politics will not be filled, for he was the last of the uncompromising individualists of the Victorian age, the most consistent and the ablest.

" *9th Nov.*— George Wyndham came down in the evening and Neville, to shoot with me, and we talked far into the night on literature, politics, and art. He is pleased with the success of his Ronsard which is certainly good, though I am of opinion that it ought to have been still better. With his talent of verse translation he might very well have given us a hundred of Ronsard's Sonnets and Odes, instead of only thirty.

" *10th Nov.*— Belloc joined us at dinner, and once more George's tongue was loosed. Both he and Belloc are admirable talkers. Belloc's best story was of an Italian brigand, who had regularly confessed his sins every Saturday from his youth up in his own village, but who was refused absolution at last at the age of eighty, as profaning the sacrament of penance, by going on with his confessions about women. ' E cosa impossibile,' said the priest.

" *11th Nov. (Sunday).*— I have got George to read my ' Atrocity ' pamphlet, and it has formed the text of a discussion which lasted

till midnight on the whole Egyptian question. George was very communicative, and he gave us an account of how the Anglo-French
Entente had been managed by Arthur Balfour, Lansdowne, and himself, and how they had expressly disclaimed all ulterior intention of
making the Occupation of Egypt, a stepping stone to annexation, or
a protectorate. This it is most important for me to know. George
assures me that the permanent retention of Egypt is not part of
English policy, at least of English Tory policy, and that they fully
admit that neither Egypt nor the Mediterranean could be held by us
in time of serious war. The new naval strategy is based on evacuating the Mediterranean in war time, and holding the Cape route to
India. The Occupation of Egypt was prolonged because a withdrawal
of troops would be interpreted as a provocation to Germany to send
in German troops. He had had, however, a talk with the German
Ambassador in London last December, which had convinced him that
Germany would abstain from intermeddling in Egypt if given a free
hand in the Euphrates Valley and the Persian Gulf-head. This he
thought would be the solution. As to Denshawai he admitted that it
was without precedent as an act of folly, and was only explicable on
the supposition that Cromer was failing in mind. George laid down,
as a general rule, that it was always folly to hang a man, unless you
intended to do a very violent deed, and to have that deed remembered.
He hears it commonly said now that Cromer's régime has been a
failure. I pressed him to help us in the House to get a day for
discussion of the case from Grey. He did not quite refuse, and will
leave a copy of my pamphlet in Arthur's way, and take half-a-dozen
more copies for others of his late colleagues. Dillon is to be back
in the House by Monday, and promises to do his best to bring it on.
I go up, therefore, on Tuesday, to help arrange the attack.

" *14th Nov.*— Chapel Street. John Dillon came to luncheon, and
we had a long talk about Egypt. He will bring forward the Denshawai case at once, and with Robertson will ask for a day to discuss
it. If that is refused he will ply the Government every week with
questions till the end of the session, and bring it on again on the
Address in February. He talked well about several of our leading
politicians. He considers the Independent Labour Party to be of no
importance, Keir Hardie, though honest, to have little weight. He
admires John Burns, speaks very highly of Churchill, who is ' cleverer
than his father, a better speaker, and with a sounder political instinct.'
Of Loulou Harcourt he has the highest opinion, a poor one of Herbert
Gladstone. He spoke more kindly of Chamberlain than he deserves,
said that there were only two men in the house who could hold their
own with him in debate, Asquith and Churchill, but Asquith had less
weight from having a lawyer's mind. He considers Haldane's position

at the War Office absurd, 'a Chancery barrister,' he said, 'of twenty years' standing.' He has a great respect for Hugh Cecil, none for Arthur Balfour.

" 15*th Nov.*— Mme. Arcos (the Empress Eugénie's lectrice and lady-in-waiting) came to tea with me. Talking about the memoirs of Dr. Evans, the Paris dentist, she assured me they were in no way due to co-operation with the Empress. There was much exaggeration in Evans' account of his intimacy with Her Majesty. She recommended, as more exact, a book by Miss Stothard, which is just out and very accurate. She took away with her a copy of my pamphlet for the Empress, who, she said, would be delighted with it, as she dislikes Cromer. He was rude to her in Egypt two years ago.

" 21*st Nov.*— A splendid letter has come from Madame Juliette Adam in praise of 'The Wind and the Whirlwind,' worth many rude articles in the 'Times.'

" 23*rd Nov.*— My dear friend, Hampden, is dead, one of my few quite old friends. Politically we found ourselves always in opposite camps. During the Egyptian revolution, he being an under secretary in Gladstone's Government, ranked himself with the financiers for intervention, then when Home Rule came four years later, he and I changed sides, he following Hartington into the Unionist camp, and this went on till the other day when he rejoined the Liberals. He was away for four years in Australia as Colonial Governor, and on his return he shared my rooms with me in Mount Street and Chapel Street. During my illness he was very good to me. Then suddenly, fifteen months ago, old age seemed to take him, and he went away to a house of his own, and last summer to a place he had hired in Westmorland for his health. His death is a great loss to me.

" To see Shaw's play 'The Doctor's Dilemma,' the wittiest ever put upon the stage, and admirably acted, its medical absurdities appealing to me personally, remembering as I did how old Sir Douglas Powell urged me, 'as he would *urge* his own son or *order* a man in a hospital ward, to submit to a slight operation, the merest touch with an instrument,' to relieve an imaginary something on my right lung, an operation which I afterwards learnt would have been almost certainly, in my weak state, fatal, while the lung was sound. When I met Shaw at Neville's last Spring, I told him my experience, and I daresay it has been among the contributory causes of his play. I have written to tell him how much I admired it.

" 24*th Nov.*— To call on Margot at her house in Cavendish Square, who came out to talk to me, bareheaded, where I lay in my wheeled chair at her door. Though she has lost some of her old prettiness, her wit and all her charm have survived it. We stayed on in the street talking for quite twenty minutes, and she is to come to lunch

with me on Monday. On Thursday Horace Rumbold dined with me
and told me a number of interesting political things. Among others
that he had quite recently been shown a confidential report drawn
up by Cromer, detailing a new plan of reforms for Egypt in a
Liberal sense, intended no doubt to do a duty of reparation for past
mistakes. I strongly suspect that Grey has shown it privately to
Robertson and the other Radical members of the Egyptian Committee,
and so has bought their silence for the future about Denshawai.
George Wyndham, whom I saw to-day, does not doubt that such is
the case. 'It is of a piece,' he says, 'with their management lately
of other difficult and disgraceful cases.' Horace, at our dinner, discussed the Egyptian question with me *à fond,* assuring me that the
Government had come to an understanding about Egypt with the Emperor William, and that our occupation of it would certainly be
permanent. Horace's view is no doubt the Foreign Office view, and
he has means, besides his position as ex-ambassador, of knowing, as he
has a son at the Cairo Embassy and has just had Findlay with him,
Cromer's chief subordinate there. He says Cromer means to stay on
at Cairo.

"*25th Nov. (Sunday).*— George came to lunch with me and then
Dillon, with whom I had two hours' good conversation. He tells
me that it is perfectly true that Robertson and the rest of the so-
called Egyptian Committee have been got at by Grey, who has had
them into his private room and has been most amiable to them, and
has persuaded them to hold their tongues about Denshawai. He affected, when with them, not to know that the husband of the woman
shot by the officers had been condemned to penal servitude for life,
and promised to write to Cromer about it, and got them to be satisfied with this. They have behaved like children in the business, and
have even allowed themselves to be made use of by Grey to the extent
of supporting Cromer's proposal for the abolition of the Capitulations
in Egypt, the Capitulations being the only remaining protection there
against Cromer's absolute power, and the only safeguard for the freedom of the native press. Idiots! The London Press, too, Dillon assures me, has been captured, even the 'Tribune,' which in spite of
Brailsford's promise of assistance has refused to answer the questions
asked in the House of Commons about Denshawai. The 'Manchester
Guardian' is equally silent.

"We talked about the announced changes in the Government.
Dillon says that Bannerman is much broken since his wife's death,
and will probably go to the Lords with Fowler, while Ripon will
retire. Of Bryce he talked as of a man learned and excellent, and
historically sympathetic with Ireland, but strangely ignorant of modern
conditions, incapable of taking in a new idea and quite unfit to drive

a satisfactory Irish Bill through the House of Commons. Personally he liked him much, and has taken great pains to instruct him on Irish affairs, but without much effect. I asked him about Anthony Macdonnell. He told me he had never himself believed in him as a Nationalist, and now nobody believed in him. Macdonnell's idea of Nationalism was that he, Macdonnell, should be able, with the help of an Irish Council, a consultative body, to manage Irish affairs without interference from Downing Street, the sort of independence that the Government of Madras has, or of Bombay. 'He would like to treat us like Indians,' he said. 'I have told him frankly that we won't put up with that.' Dillon thinks the present Government will break up in two years' time. Every Liberal member is hunting his own hare, there is no cohesion among them. Then we went on to Fenianism and Devoy, who was a personal friend of Dillon, though they differed on many points, for Devoy is quite opposed to the Parliamentary party. Dillon himself, of course, began by being a Fenian.

" *12th Dec.*— Dillon has put his question to Grey about Denshawai, and has got from him only negative answers. He will not give a day for discussion, he will not give Cromer instructions, he will not say whether any reform in the criminal law in Egypt will be recommended. Robertson and the rest of the Radicals have been mute as fishes. I have no doubt in my mind that Robertson has been secured by some promise of a place in the Government, a junior lordship or even less." [This is precisely what happened some months later.] " The ' Times ' correspondent telegraphed a fortnight ago that the Khedive had supplied the money for Mohammed Kamel's new English paper, 'The Egyptian Standard,' and when this was telegraphed back to Cairo Cromer would not let Reuter publish the telegram. Then Cromer went, so it is said, to the Khedive, and threatened him with deposition; and the Khedive denied, and Kamel denied; now Kamel is on his way back to England and has telegraphed his arrival to me at Brindisi.

" Meanwhile we have the French Government sending a fleet to Tangier for the ' protection of French subjects, a state of anarchy having been shown to exist there,' and a bogus communication has been published by Reuter from Raisuli to the Governor of Tangier announcing ' a Jehad and massacre of Christians.' Just the old story of Tunis in 1881 and Alexandria in 1882, supported once more by the ' Times.' "

This was the first step taken by the French Government in their aggression on Morocco in accordance with the Anglo-French entente of 1904, an act which, as will be seen, entailed on them a renewal of their quarrel with Germany, and for a while with Spain.

" War seems to have been declared at last between the Pope and the French Republic. It will be interesting to watch the result. On the whole I think the Pope is well advised. He will probably lose a large proportion of his nominal spiritual subjects in France, but he will retain a firmer hold over the remainder, and the cause of the Church there will gain by being disendowed. All the same it is incredible that Christianity, as a dogmatic faith, should much longer survive the assaults of science among a people so logical as the French and so little serious. Among our northern peoples it will continue through its connection with morality for a long while yet, till gradually the dogma will disappear and the name alone will be clung to. In France the connection between dogma and morality is less felt.

" 13*th Dec.*— Robertson has written to the ' Times ' repudiating what has been said about his change of opinions, so I hope it is all right, at least as far as his political honesty goes, though he has probably fallen into line with the Government about Denshawai. We shall see as time goes on, and when Cromer's report is published next session. It is clear that Cromer has had orders to nationalize to a certain extent the Egyptian administration, though still of course on despotic lines. Saad Zaghloul has begun well at any rate in his department, but I have no confidence in Cromer.

" Joseph Potocki was here on Saturday to see our horses. He gave me an interesting account of things in Russia. He was a member of the first Duma, and describes it as having been entirely revolutionary. He found himself alone among the members as a Conservative. And when he opposed their motion for the abolition of property in land, it was singly, while they watched ' with eyes as of hyenas.' He is, however, like them all, a Constitutionalist, though not in favour of representative Government. He says that could not be in Russia. He would like Home Rule in Poland under the Crown, that is to say, an independent administration for local affairs. I asked him if the Duma would be allowed to continue, and he said, ' Not if the new Duma is revolutionary like the old; if it is moderate, yes.' I asked also whether the Court Party, if it came to a conflict with the Duma, could count upon the army and he said, ' Yes, at any rate for a few years, though as the young generation grows up with revolutionary ideas these will perhaps affect the army.' Potocki's testimony has this value, that being a Pole, he sees things with more detachment than most members of the Duma can claim to show in their judgements.

" 19*th Dec.*— Went up to London to meet Mustapha Kamel and arrange matters for him connected with his paper ' The Egyptian Standard.' He has come to London with two of his principal supporters, Farid Bey [afterwards leader of the Egyptian National Party in succession to Mustapha Kamel], the lawyer who protested against French Rule at the Conference in Algeria, and Osman Bey Ghaleb,

Professor of Medicine at the Medical School, an old friend of Mohammed Abdu. With these I discussed all the important questions connected with Egyptian Nationalism.

" Kamel gave me a detailed account of the Khedive's attitude in the
Tabah affair. ' The Khedive,' he said, ' was reduced some years ago
by Cromer's having excluded him from all political power, to an attitude of despair. This turned his ambition to money-making — he has
always had a love of money. Then he got under the influence of King
Edward and was persuaded that, if he would be good and give Cromer
no trouble, life would be made easy for him and he would be allowed
to enrich himself. So he let Cromer do what he pleased. This went
on till the present year when Cromer began the Tabah quarrel with the
Sultan, and in the first stage of it the Khedive was docile. But when
it came to the ultimatum sent in by the British Government, and when
he found that all Egypt supported the Sultan and that even the
fellahin in the villages were declaring they would sooner be badly
ruled by the Sultan than any longer endure the English tyranny, then
he began to reflect and think, " I cannot betray my religion and my
country altogether." Cromer was at that moment pressing him to
write a letter authorizing the English Government to represent him
in the boundary dispute, but he finally refused to do this, much to
Cromer's discomfiture. He even went so far as to have a schedule
drawn up of his property so as to know how much money he was
privately worth in case it came to his deposition or resignation of
viceroyalty. Since then he has been completely *brouillé* with Cromer.
Great efforts were made to induce him to go to England before going
to Constantinople last summer, but he said to himself, " The Sultan is
a greater danger to me than the King of England, as he can at
any moment depose me while the other could not." So he went to
Constantinople first. The Sultan by this time had been thoroughly
frightened by the English Government, and by the failure of the Emperor William to support him and he intended to give Abbas a bad
reception. But, when he heard it reported that in Egypt all public
opinion was against Cromer, the Grand Vizier sent a message to
Mukhtar Pasha biding him inquire how this was, and ask the opinions
of all prominent men. On this ground Mukhtar sent for me for my
advice, and said that on the report sent by him would depend how
Abbas would be received at Yildiz. Now, I had had a quarrel with
the Khedive and had not been near the Palace for three years, but
I saw that the Khedive ought to be supported and I said that the
independence of Egypt depended on the Sultan's receiving him well ; and
Mukhtar telegraphed this to Constantinople. The Sultan was in two
minds on the subject when the Khedive arrived, and at first received
him coldly, but in the course of the audience Abbas burst out laugh-

ing and the ice was broken between them, and the Sultan sent him away with presents. Then, while the Khedive was still at Constantinople, the Denshawai executions took place and the Khedive was so angry at his name having been used for the hangings and floggings, and pardon having been refused in his name without his being consulted, that for two hours he was like a man out of his mind walking up and down in absolute silence while his entourage stood bent like this (making a gesture) round him. Since then he would have nothing to do with the English in Egypt. He stayed at Alexandria so as not to be present at the review on the King's birthday. Then Cromer got up the story of his having subscribed £20,000 for the new Egyptian " Standard," or rather Faris Nìmr got up the story and foisted it on Cromer, who was very angry and went to the Palace and charged the Khedive with it. On this the Khedive said, " I will answer you in three ways: first, things have not yet come to such a pass in Egypt that you have a right to ask me what I do with my own private money; secondly, Mustapha Kamel has not set his foot in my house for three years, and, thirdly, he has had no money at all from me for any purpose." So Cromer got no satisfaction from him, and we have taken Abbas back into favour. You must not write any more against him, as he may be useful to the Nationalist Party. All the same he and the whole of his branch of the family of Mohammed Ali are worthless. They ought to be eliminated from the succession. The sons of Halim are respectable and liberal.

" Of the Sultan he, Mustapha Kamel, said he had behaved miserably in the Tabah business. But he spoke highly of the Grand Vizier, Jawdat Pasha; Mukhtar was a *' brave homme dont on respecte le passé militaire, mais naïf, trop naïf.'* I asked about Idris Bey Ragheb, the proprietor of the ' Egyptian Morning News ' and ' l'Egypte,' and the Doctor (Osman Ghaleb) said, ' He tried to go against us but has been obliged to give it up.'

" About Saad Zaghloul, Kamel said he was the antipodes of his brother, the traitor of the Denshawai case, a perfectly honest, good man. He has begun well at the Ministry of Public Instruction, insisting that all papers should be brought to him, not to Dunlop, the English Adviser, that the examiners in Arabic should know Arabic, and that Dunlop should come to him on business, not he to Dunlop. We shall see how long he is able to maintain his command of the situation.

" Of Cromer they all talk as of a lost force in Egypt. He no longer has any native following. The Denshawai case did for him entirely, for every one knows he was solely responsible for the hangings. ' We wish Lord Cromer to remain on now,' Kamel said, ' he does us more good by staying than he could possibly do by going.'

He would like, when the change is made, that it should be Gorst rather than an outsider. Gorst at least would endeavour to conciliate Mohammedan feeling, he hates the Syrians who now have Cromer's ear.

" Back to Newbuildings for Christmas. Belloc dined with me. He will do all he can to help Kamel, but just now is full to the eyes of work.

" *31st Dec.*— Newbuildings. This is the last day of the year, and I make up my account with it. It began with a dark prospect. I was lying more than half paralyzed in bed, unable to use my hands, unable to sit up, unable to walk more than across the room. I did not myself think I could recover, I hardly wished it. I had suffered too much pain to desire to pass through the same experience again. Yet, even so I was light-hearted. My head was clear, quite unaffected by my illness, and I was mentally busy with the Memoirs I was dictating. Also I was lapped in the affection of my friends. Thus the first months of the year passed for me, in Chapel Street in bed. Over a hundred of my acquaintance came to see me there, everybody I think that I had ever loved, a huge consolation. Then I gradually recovered, and my literary work went on. I have finished my two volumes. My play of ' Fand ' has been written, and announced for acting in Dublin. It gives me the consciousness of renewed intellectual power, moreover, and what has been the least expected marvel of my year, my half-dead hopes connected with Egypt have come into political blossom. We have smitten Cromer hip and thigh from Tabah to Denshawai, and from a lost force at Cairo I have become a power again; never since Tel-el-Kebir have the fortunes of Egyptian Nationalism seemed so smiling. Such have been my consolations. The last days of the old year have been spent merrily here at Newbuildings with Cockerell, Mark Napier and Belloc, and his friend Kershaw."

There is little worth copying out of my diary of the first months of 1907. They were mostly spent at Newbuildings, with occasional changes to Chapel Street. I give a few extracts:

" *24th Jan.*— Mustapha Kamel has gone back to Cairo, and I hear of Robertson as touring in the Delta. Bernard Shaw sends me the proof sheets of his preface to ' John Bull's other Island.' It contains a rattling attack on Cromer and the Denshawai business.

" *13th Feb.*— Parliament has met, a great flourish about a quarrel with the House of Lords. I shall believe it when I see it.

" *19th Feb.*— Robertson to breakfast with me in Chapel Street. He gave a full account of his adventures in Egypt. He describes Cromer as very nervous and sensitive about public opinion in England, and Machell, who organized the executions at Denshawai, a blundering fool, quite unfit for his position. Cromer, he says, is in perfect ignorance of native opinion, and imagines he still has adherents, whereas the very people he most confides in talk most strongly against his *régime* in private. Of Mustapha Kamel he had heard none but good reports from native sources, though the English officials talk against him. Robertson will bring forward the Denshawai and other questions whenever possible in Parliament. He has come back a thorough Nationalist."

Notwithstanding all this fine talk, on his return from Egypt Robertson did next to nothing when Parliament met, and soon allowed himself to be secured by Grey. He took the official shilling, a subordinate post in the Government.

" Sir William Wedderburn came to luncheon. He is an excellent man, and if he were only ten years younger would make a good successor to Cromer; as it is he thinks Lord Reay would do for it. He talked a good deal about India, and gave a history of the partition of Bengal, which he describes as a very serious matter. It was all Curzon's doings, devised with a special purpose of weakening the power of the High Court at Calcutta. He would not hear of the Bengal Mohammedans as being otherwise than at one with the Hindoos in the affair. He spoke highly of the Amir of Afghanistan in spite of his Europeanized dress and ways, a hardworking, honest ruler, he said, in every way estimable.

" *20th Feb.*— George Wyndham and his brother Guy dined with me. Guy is appointed military *attaché* at St. Petersburg. George, when his brother was gone home, told me of his disgust with politics, and how he considered the Tory Party had ruined its prospects by forcing on the General Election after the Boer War, the Khaki election. It had been all Chamberlain's doing, he, George, having strongly opposed it in the Cabinet. It was unfair according to the rules of Party politics, and they were suffering from it now.

" *2nd March.*— To London to vote against the Progressives at the London County Council elections. I do this as a protest against the running into debt by public bodies, especially for municipal trading; the Moderates very likely are as bad, but they are not in office and these are.

" *5th March.*— Sheykh Ali Yusuf has demanded a Parliament in the general assembly at Cairo. There is an article about it in the ' Times,' but the Radical press says nothing. What reptiles these party journalists are. They have been preaching the virtues of popular Government for months past in Russia, in Persia, in the Transvaal, and God knows where not else, but the moment it comes to our duty in Egypt they have not a word to say, all dumb dogs.

" *6th March.*— Sir Henry Cotton lunched with me. I had been reading his ' New India,' an excellent book. He spoke of my ' Ideas about India,' published twenty-two years ago, and said it applied very exactly to present conditions. He was surprised I should have been able to foresee these and understand India so well with such short experience as mine had been.

"*7th March.*— To see George Wyndham in Park Lane. He is strategically opposed to a continued occupation of Egypt, but I am not to repeat this. I understand such is Arthur Balfour's opinion, too. George would therefore be in favour of establishing a National Government if one could be secured friendly to English interests. As to Cromer's successor he thinks Gorst inevitable. I walked with him as far as Rotten Row and home by myself, the first time for two years I have ventured alone in the streets. At twelve John Dillon came and arranged questions with me to be asked in Parliament. He is doing all he can, pestering Grey constantly about Egypt.

"*9th March.*— The first number of the ' Egyptian Standard ' is out at last. It mentions me as among its collaborators, in company with Madame Juliette Adam and Pierre Lôti.

"*12th March.*— Staal, our late Russian Ambassador here, died a fortnight ago, one of the very best men I have known in the world, and extremely kind to me, with good advice, when I was a boy at Athens. He has died at the age of eighty-four.

"I have been reading the life of Lafcadio Hearn, an interesting man, whom the accident of his life in Japan has made one of importance in literature. But for this piece of good fortune, he would never have been more than a very superior journalist. Accident, however, drove him into a region of romance which he had the wit to recognize as his proper home, and so has achieved a great work and enduring fame.

"*14th March.*— Lady Gregory dined with me in Chapel Street. She gave me a long account of the row that took place at her Abbey Theatre, over the production of Synge's piece, ' The Playboy of the Western World.' The first night, she said, passed fairly well, with only a few hisses, but on the second night there was an organized opposition, and, fearing mischief, she sent for the police, and afterwards there was a tumult every night of the week till the last performance, when the opponents of the play got tired of their noise. She considers, therefore, that she has won a victory, but fears the incident will have harmed her in the provinces, where the play is resented more than in Dublin. At Gort, her county town, the local council has boycotted her, forbidding the school children to attend her teas and entertainments, lest their morals should be corrupted. She is going abroad for awhile with her son.

"15th *March*.— Fisher Unwin has agreed to publish the first volume of my Egyptian memoirs.

"Rothstein came to see me, the new London correspondent of the 'Egyptian Standard.' That paper seems likely now to make its way. Brailsford who was also here this afternoon has suggested to Mustapha the issue of a weekly edition, as no one can spare time for a foreign daily paper. M., who came to luncheon, told an amusing story about the late Queen Victoria, who when there was talk about the meeting of dead people in another world was huffed at the idea of allowing King David to be presented to her on account of his 'inexcusable conduct to Uriah.'

"23rd *March*.— Mark Napier has returned from Egypt where he has been on business for me. All is quiet there, he says, politically. The Khedive has been frightened into submission by Cromer, and has withdrawn his support from the Nationalists, King Edward having written His Highness an autograph letter enjoining him to have nothing to do with Mustapha Kamel. He had this last from Carton de Wiart, and it was confirmed to him by Reuters' agent, so it was probably true.

"24th *March*.— The 'Pall Mall' reports from Cairo that the press laws are to be put in force against the 'Egyptian Standard.'

"28th *March*.— Mark Napier was here again to-day. He went to see Cromer before leaving Cairo, who spoke to him about my 'Atrocity' pamphlet, regretting that I should have published it, but pretending that he had not read it. Cromer, he says, appeared much broken in health, and he thinks will not stay on long at Cairo, though he intends to stay. He was touchy on the subject of the pamphlet.

"1st *April* (*Easter Monday*).— Ujda has been occupied by French troops, the first military act of the 'pacific penetration' of Morocco.

"11th *April*.— I have been writing an article for the 'Daily News' in answer to Cromer's annual report, and had gone to bed as I usually do before dinner, and was fast asleep when a telegram was brought me signed by Meynell containing the joyous announcement of Cromer's resignation. I was at once full awake and laughing so that the bed shook under me, nor could I stop for several minutes. I sent back in return the single word, Whoo-whoop! I am off to Chapel Street, and Clouds to-morrow, feeling like a huntsman at the end of his day's sport with Cromer's brush in my pocket, and the mask of that ancient red fox dangling from my saddle.

"Whoo-whoop!"

CHAPTER VI

FRANCIS THOMPSON

I have had a pleasant week at Clouds, and am to stay on to the 25th, a house full of children, relations, and friends, busy, too, indexing my " Secret History," and writing a programme of new Egyptian policy for the " Manchester Guardian."

" *19th April.*— Things are going well in Egypt, Cromer's breakdown in health has resolved itself according to the ' Daily Telegraph ' into ' an attack of indigestion, which has prevented his taking his usual nourishment.' It has not prevented his attending a public luncheon party, or accepting an engagement to deliver a farewell speech at the Opera House at Cairo. What rot it all is, and now Fox-Bourne (of the Aborigines Protection Society) writes that the Egyptian Committee has decided not to oppose a parliamentary grant to him of money, or honours. I have suggested his being raised to the dignity of Duke of Denshawai.

" Talking about the Anglo-French Entente with Percy Wyndham he tells me that the agreement was signed here at Clouds, in the East Room, the three signatories being Arthur Balfour, Lansdowne, and his son George. This adds to the interest of what George told me about it last year, viz, that it was agreed upon by a very small inner Cabinet of the Cabinet, and that they understood it as a bar to anything in the way of annexation or permanent retention of Egypt as a British possession. It was signed during the Easter recess of 1904, which Arthur always spends at Clouds.

" Percy is much troubled at Asquith's new Budget, which increases the death duties on fortunes of over £150,000; I don't think myself it much matters. All it means is that the very great houses will have to reduce their scale of domestic expenditure, and live in a smaller way. He feels himself over-housed at Clouds, and I, too, personally find myself much happier at Newbuildings where I can live in a quite small way, than I was at Crabbet.

" *22nd April.*— Pamela Tennant is here with sundry children. Among them is a boy of nine (Bimbo), who has writen some good verses. His mother recited some of these to me, especially a Blakian rhyme addressed to her, which I thought excellent. In the afternoon George arrived. I think I have persuaded him that mine is a wiser view of Egyptian things than Cromer's. We have talked also about Ireland, as to which he talks more and more in a Home Rule sense, not as liking it, but as a necessity. He says it ought to be complete Home Rule on the plan of a self-governing Colony, giving the Irish full command of their finances, their police, and their customs duties, and reserving for England only their army and navy, and their Foreign relations. He would like also to reserve some special privilege as to the enlistment of soldiers. Ireland should take over responsibilities incurred on her behalf by the Imperial Government, especially in regard to land purchase. He scouts all idea of ' a half-way house,' which he said would settle nothing. He approves, or half approves, my publishing my Egyptian memoirs, as they attack the Liberal party, not his own. I have written to Madame Adam about its production in French at Paris.

" To-day I read aloud the whole of the Song of Solomon from a MS. copy Miss Offer has made for me. It is the first of all the love poems in the world, and I would sooner have written it than the whole of the rest of literature. How it got into the Canon of Holy Scripture is a puzzle, for it is pure sexual passion without the least trace of religious sentiment, all the more beautiful for that. George showed me some new verses he has written in the manner of Ronsard. Good, if not quite first rate.

" *23rd April.*— The ' Pall Mall ' of last night contains in the largest type an announcement of my play ' Fand,' having been performed at the Abbey Theatre at Dublin with great success. I never was more astonished, as when I saw Lady Gregory last she told me it was put off *sine die,* and that she would let me know when it would be given. It is only in Ireland, I suppose, that a play could be performed for the first time and the author know nothing about it.

" *24th April.*— Reading poetry all the morning, and in the afternoon to Summerleas, the most beautiful spot imaginable, shut in with thorn trees white with blossom, and May trees coming into leaf, blackbirds singing, and wood pigeons, and yaffles.

" *25th April.*— The ' Manchester Guardian ' has printed my article on a new *régime* for Egypt, with a leading article recommending it strongly. Things look more favourable for liberty on the Nile than has been the case for twenty years.

" *27th April.*— Mustapha Kamel publishes a manifesto in the Paris ' Figaro ' on the lines of mine in the ' Manchester Guardian,' demanding a Parliament and a native administration for Egypt. Among the appointments gazetted in connection with Cromer's resignation is that of young Errington to be Private Secretary to Hardinge at the Foreign Office. It was part of the bargain proposed to Cromer four years ago if he would resign, that Gorst was to succeed him at Cairo, and act there as warming pan to Errington who was to have the reversion of the Cairo Agency when high enough up in the service. This looks like a step in the intrigue.

"*4th May.*— There has been an outburst of agitation at Cairo. The whole Arabic Press refuses to bid Cromer a friendly good-bye. Gorst has arrived in Egypt, but the Nationalists are abstaining from either praise or blame of him till he shows his hand; in this they are wise. There have been riots at Lahore and Rawal Pindi indicating that the Indian question is also coming on.

"*6th May.*— Cromer has given proof of his 'genuine ill health' by making a great speech in the Opera House at Cairo, a farewell speech of self-glorification. The secret of his policy, he said, had always been to 'speak the truth.' Only three Egyptians, however, as far as is reported, were there to support him, among a mass of strangers, Mustapha Fehmy, Riaz, and Saad Zaghloul. He is confident on this showing that the mass of the Egyptians like him, and that if they don't now they will some day.

"*9th May.*— I have been for a week in London. George Wyndham came to dine with me and Mark Napier, and we were very merry. George was in one of his communicative moods, and told us the whole history of how he had financed his Irish Land Bill, and how he had stopped the Somali war, and how it was certain there would be war with Germany, perhaps in five years, perhaps in thirty, and we discussed Egypt and India, and the whole world round, and George Curzon, and a number of other interesting things, past, present, and to come.

"*10th May.*— There have been great doings at Lahore, the town invaded by some hundreds of ryots with bludgeons, Englishmen insulted in the streets, and the military called out. Also native agitators have been arrested by *lettres de cachet,* and deported untried by order of the immaculate Morley. Morley is just the weak-kneed administrator to resort to 'firm measures,' and we shall see him using all 'the resources of civilization,' practiced in Russia. On Monday Cromer is to return home in triumph: I have written to Redmond, calling on him to oppose the vote of thanks the Government is to bring forward, but his answer says neither yes nor no.

"*12th May.*— Rivers Wilson, whom I saw to-day, is open-mouthed about Cromer whom he calls an imposter. Cromer is to arrive from Egypt to-morrow and be met by Campbell Bannerman, Grey, and the Prince of Wales, and to be received by the King.

"*13th May.*— Questions are to be asked about the arrest of Lajpat Rai in India, I shall be interested to see whether Redmond and the Irish members take part in these. The present is a crisis in the affairs of the Empire and the Irish party will have to take sides, with or against liberty in the East. The evening papers give accounts of Cromer's arrival at Victoria Station, a great show of official welcome but no street enthusiasm; the earliest arriver at the station, Moberly Bell!

"14th May.— With Meynell to see the Academy pictures. He is an art critic and also has much to tell about the private life of the painters; Sargent is the especial object of his admiration. The ladies he paints, according to Meynell, generally bore him so that he is obliged to retire every now and then behind a screen and refresh himself by putting his tongue out at them. He has made an exception, however, to this practice in the case of Mrs. Sassoon, of whom there is a really fine portrait by him this year with another almost equally good of a lady in plain white, without jewels, a much prettier woman, but she, too, bored him. He paints nothing but Jews and Jewesses now and says he prefers them, as they have more life and movement than our English women. With the exception of these two portraits I saw little of any great merit in the show, though Meynell tried hard to make me admire some of his favourites. I have an experience now of just fifty years of Royal Academies and find the general level lower than formerly, especially in the matter of colour, but the two Sargents are quite first rate.

"20th May.— Bill Gordon came to see me — dying, I fear, poor fellow, of consumption and will hardly see the year out. We had a long talk about Egyptian affairs. Among other interesting things he told me the story of his uncle's first disagreement with Cromer. This was in '78 or '79 when the Khedive, Ismaïl, had sent for him to Khartoum to confer with Lesseps about his finances. Gordon and Lesseps both advised suspending a half year's coupon which would have enabled Ismaïl to tide over his difficulties, but Baring opposed it and being supported by the Bond-holding interest prevailed. Baring was new then in Egypt and affected to ignore Gordon's experience and they interchanged words in consequence. Cromer was always from this time opposed to Gordon and continued his ill-will to him, Bill, notably on the occasion of his retirement from the Egyptian service. He spoke strongly of the injustice done to Egypt while reconquering the Soudan, through the work of the Egyptian army, and then annexing half the sovereignty of the country to England, while saddling Egypt with the expense. They had even tried when Khartoum was retaken to charge the cost of the English Union Jacks hoisted there on the Egyptian treasury, and he cited several instances of jobbery in the interests of English firms. He is delighted at Cromer's downfall.

"21st May.— Called on Mrs. Belloc in their new house at Shipley, of which they have made quite a habitable place. The principal room had been used as a shop, but is now again the parlour, the little orchard and garden are nice, and the windmill is an attraction with its view of the church and village, a most enjoyable little property.

"*22nd May.*— The Dublin Convention has voted unanimously against Birrell's new Irish Councils Bill. I am doubly glad of it, both because I do not believe in any halfway house to Home Rule, and because the rejection will leave Redmond's hands freer to oppose the Government on Indian and Egyptian affairs.

"*26th May (Sunday).*— The political arrests in India continue. Lajpat Rai has been deported to Burmah, exactly as they deport suspected people to Siberia in Russia. Jemal-ed-Din always used to tell me these arbitrary deportations were an Anglo-Indian practice, but Anglo-Indians denied it. It is grand to see Morley at the work.

"*29th May.*— Chapel Street. Lady Gregory came to luncheon, in terrible trouble about her plays. She had gone to Italy to get away from the worry, with Yeats and her son, and had engaged to bring out 'The Playboy' with other pieces at Oxford and in London but the Censor interfered and she was telegraphed for to come back. Birrell, however, to whom the case was referred, withdrew the Censor's opposition. I am of opinion she would do better to withdraw the play, but she has others to consult and Yeats is obstinate.

"*1st June.*— Newbuildings. Lady Gregory is in worse trouble than ever. The Editor of the 'Freeman' has written threatening her with new displeasure if she persists with 'The Playboy' in England, and I fear her theatre will be altogether boycotted. I advise her to submit to Irish opinion, but though she admits that it was a mistake to produce the play, she says it is too late now to withdraw it. The worst of it is that she is already boycotted personally on account of it at Coole, the Local Council forbidding the school-children to go to her house, or even to accept cakes or presents of any kind from her; it is the Sinn Fein that has done it.

"She told me an interesting fact of past history connected with Layard's life at Constantinople and his secret despatch against the Sultan which Granville published. The Sultan's mind had been set against Layard's by someone and, at an audience, though they had been close friends, Abdul Hamid behaved in such a way as to show that he feared Layard would attack him. This was the occasion of the secret despatch being written. It cost Layard the peerage he aspired to, for Lord Salisbury had promised it, but the Queen refused, saying that no ambassador ought to write in such terms of the sovereign to whom he was accredited. Lady Gregory knows this, as Sir William (her husband) was intermediary in the affair of the peerage.

"*4th June.*— My 'Secret History' is out, I received a first copy this morning. I am sending copies of it to Bannerman, Grey, Churchill,

Gorst, Kaiser Wilhelm, and Roosevelt, as also to Eddy Hamilton and Rivers Wilson.

" 10*th June.*— Called on the Lucases at Thakeham and found Father Tyrrell there, my ex-Jesuit friend, with Miss Petre and Mrs. Urquhart.

" 11*th June.*— Cockerell, who has been in Paris arranging for a French edition of my ' Secret History,' writes an amusing account of a visit he paid Mme. Juliette Adam at her country house, the Abbaye de Gif. He says, 5*th June* :

" ' Madame Juliette proposed an encounter yesterday afternoon and Geoffroy kindly agreed to go as my protector. She lives in a lovely valley, an hour by train from Paris. The house also capable of being made very beautiful, but I grieve to say that her taste in pictures and furniture is execrable. However, she received us with great kindness and promised to do all possible to make the French edition known, but she says you must not expect the sale of it to extend beyond a small circle. Mustapha Kamel wrote a book which nobody would read and which has made Perrin (the publisher) a little shy of books on Egypt. When we had discussed the matter for a quarter of an hour with Juliette and her friend and contemporary La Comtesse X, enter *à gauche* Le Colonel Marchand, his arms full of yellow broom. He is the most stagey Frenchman imaginable, very jerky and jack-in-the-boxey and with a furious military air. He covered me with compliments in a moment, mistaking me for the illustrious author of the " Secret History " and when these had had time to run off me we engaged in an exciting discussion about the politics of the world. Madame Adam and the brave Colonel unite in unbounded admiration and fear of England and English diplomacy. *Le Roi Edward VII* is the subtlest beast of the field that ever was created. He has outwitted everyone and has *dindonné* France into an alliance which will probably cost her another war with Germany. Never was England so strong and unassailable as now, etc., etc., etc., hammer and tongs for an hour and a half. I interjected remarks in my execrable demi-French, most of which were understood without a smile. Geoffroy was very silent as he knows even less of politics than I. We left after tea in a rollicking humour.'

" 15*th June.*— Prince Mohammed Ali, the Khedive's brother, came down to see the horses, bringing with him Saadullah Pasha Yusri, and Yusuf Bey Sadyk, son of the old Mufettish, whom Ismaïl murdered. I found all of them loud against Cromer, especially in connection with the Denshawai case. The Prince is far more intelligent than at first sight appears, and his political views seem quite sound.

" 16*th June.*— Called on Mrs. Belloc with whom I had an interesting talk about Father Tyrrell and Catholic reform. Later wrote the heads of a speech for Willy Redmond to make in opposing the Cromer vote, his brother John having suggested it.

"*21st June.*— A young Indian, a Hindoo, called. He told me that recent events, and especially Morley's violent dealings with Lalla Lajpat Rai had sent the moderate reformers into the extremist camp. They had lost all hope now of converting Englishmen of any party to the cause of Indian Home Rule and were preparing for a revolution which alone could free the country from English officialdom. Their plan was to make Government impossible by strikes and boycotts. The example of the Japanese had given them courage and there were great numbers ready to sacrifice even their lives for the freedom of their country.

"*30th June.*— My book seems making its way. Willy Redmond has announced that he will oppose the Cromer vote, which is to be for £50,000. He has written to tell me this and I have sent him the draft of a speech for the occasion. He 'has talked the matter over,' he says, with our young men here and there will be strong opposition.'

"I hear that my book is beginning to be talked about in London as 'very mischievous.' I expect the opposition to the Cromer vote will about finish me in polite society; however, I was prepared for this.

"*13th July.*— My play ' The Bride of the Nile ' has been acted here, at Newbuildings, with great success. Margaret Sackville took the part of Belkis and did it admirably, far better than her part of Fand last year. She had clothed herself in a lovely light garment of white and gold, deepening in the skirts to Orange, with strings of beads and long gossamer sleeves. Her recitation of the song, ' If I forget,' was perfect, given with the guitar accompaniment of one Allen Booth from London, an excellent little man who had composed it for the occasion. But this was surpassed by her dance, a real Oriental one, quite the most beautiful I ever saw. Dorothy, of course, was Jael, in which part she too was perfect. She looked lovely in a black Egyptian woman's shirt with a blue veil. The most popular of them all, however, proved to be little Nellie Hozier, who did Hatib, a pretty joyous child of nineteen, who having just been condemned by doctors only two days ago as having in her the germs of consumption was determined to enjoy her time to the uttermost before going to a health establishment (Nordrach) in Germany, the only chance for her of cure. I dressed her in my old travelling Arab dress, all in rags as it was, and arranged the *kifiyeh* and *aghal* for her pretty head, and she looked, with a spear in her hand, a splendid Bedouin boy, and spoke her lines with admirable spirit, bringing down the house. The final scene, where Hatib espouses the two ladies, was especially delightful, for she put her arms round both their necks by a spontaueous impulse which we had not designed and which was better than all other possible arrangement. Barix was played by Mark Napier and Alexis by his son Claud, both well, though

Mark had to read his part. Claud was costumed in one of George
Wyndham's old undress Guard's uniforms he had sent us for the occasion. He could not come himself to see the play. Guy Carleton did
Boilas. The other actors were Benjamin by Everard Meynell, a wonderful personation of an Oriental, the Makawkas by Lucas, the Patriarch by Daisy Blunt, with Mrs. Lucas and the youngest Meynell girl
for Coptic women in attendance on Jael and afterwards as Arabs.
Though we had only had three rehearsals the play went off without a
hitch.

"*27th July.*— Lady Paget was here to-day and talked very pleasantly, telling amongst other things the latest spiritualistic story according to which the late Lord Carlingford has re-entered into communication with the living and is carrying on a correspondence in his own
handwriting with one of his friends, principally on Irish politics, of
which he has found a new devolutionary solution. He is in daily intercourse with Gladstone and has converted him to the doctrine of protection!

"*28th July.*— Horace Rumbold has been staying with me, and his
son Horace, now Secretary to the Madrid Embassy, was here for the
day yesterday. Horace is seventy-eight and rather feeble, but still a
good companion. I had a long talk with him last night about European,
Egyptian and Indian politics. He gave me an interesting account of the
King's influence in foreign affairs. His Majesty insists now on making
all important diplomatic appointments himself, and busies himself
much more than ever the old Queen did in the foreign policy adopted.
This works sometimes for good, sometimes for harm. The King and
the Emperor William have been for years on the worst of terms, and
it is only quite recently that the quarrel between them is being made up.
Seckendorff, the confidential adviser of the Empress Frederick, who,
people say, married her after the Emperor's death, had talked to him
about it, and had done his best to bring about a better understanding.
The Emperor of Austria had greatly desired to attend the late Queen's
Diamond Jubilee, as he had never been in England, and the sole
reason why he was not invited was, that he could not be so without
inviting also the Emperor William. Wilhelm was a bitter enemy of
England, and if he lived would some day make Germany a danger to
us. I told him of the old Prussian scheme of uniting with Holland
and reviving the claim to the Dutch Colonies. [I had learned this fact
in 1866 from Count d'Usedom, the Prussian Minister to Italy; while I
was staying with him at the Villa Capponi at Florence. He told me
that this was a settled policy of the Berlin Foreign Office.] Rumbold
said it was news to him, but he quite believed it, and some day this
would come about through a failure of direct heirs to the Dutch
throne. He considers England would be easily invaded from the

Continent. In nearly all of this we are agreed. I told him the history of the intrigue four years ago against Cromer, and of the arrangement then made that Gorst was to have Cromer's succession in Egypt. He had not heard of it, but he knew that Cromer was anything but pleased at Gorst's appointment. He gets his news of the Cairo Agency through his son Horace, who was there till last January, and through Findlay, with whom he is intimate.

" *31st July.*— The Cromer debate has come on more successfully than we could have hoped six weeks ago, as 107 voted against the grant of £50,000, a minority of 147. Willy Redmond made the speech I wrote out for him, or one closely like it, and Kettle, who had also written to consult me, spoke strongly, Grayson, the new Socialist member, making a third. Robertson and his friends of the Egyptian Committee held their foolish tongues.

" Speaking of the King the other day, Horace Rumbold told me that Hardinge, of the Foreign Office, is his special man, going everywhere abroad with him, and fulfilling the functions hitherto appertaining to the Secretary of State as Cabinet Minister. All diplomatic appointments are, in fact, made by the King through him. This makes Hardinge's taking young Errington as his private secretary the more significant.

" *1st Aug.*— To London and saw George Wyndham. He tells me the opposition to the Cromer vote was even more of a victory for us than I imagined. Not only did some sixty or seventy Liberals and Labour members vote against the Government, but a hundred Liberals walked out without voting, while the Government was only saved from defeat by the Tory vote. Willy Redmond's speech was very effective, and he congratulated me on the result, though he himself had of course voted for Cromer.

" *2nd Aug.*— Willy Redmond writes: ' The division was very good on the Cromer grant, and the fact that both front benches could only muster 250 out of 670 members is very striking. I know no better report of *your* speech than the ' Freeman's Journal ' of yesterday. . . . The house was really worked up over Denshawai, and I am sure the prisoners will be released.'

" *5th Aug.*— Father Tyrrell came to lunch with me, and I had some interesting talk with him. His position now is a very difficult one to maintain. As an ex-Jesuit he is debarred from receiving ' faculties ' from any bishop without the Jesuit Provincial's leave, and they imposed on him a promise to submit all private letters he might write to anyone to Jesuit censorship. This he refused, and so is unable to say Mass, hear confessions, or perform any priestly office. His mental attitude is very nearly, if not quite, one of revolt.

" I asked him if he thought it would be possible to keep the Liberal

Catholic party in line with the main body of the old unadvancing Church, and he seemed to think it very doubtful. It was impossible to say whether the new wine could be held in the old bottles. Indeed, his views, judging from his talk with me, seem quite incompatible with any church teaching I have ever heard of. If I understood him rightly even such fundamental doctrines as that of a future life were matters of no certainty, and he spoke as strongly as I could myself have spoken about the absence of any indication of a belief in it in the Old Testament, and the futility of the interpretation by the Fathers of the Church of the Book of Job in a contrary sense. I told him very frankly of my own acceptance of pure materialism, not only as logically certain, but as satisfying to the needs of my soul, though in my younger days it had not been so. He seemed quite willing to agree with the thought that our desire of a future life was like the desire of a child who, if in the middle of his play, is threatened with being put to bed, looks upon it as a terrible punishment, yet comes at the day's end to be quite ready for his nurse to carry him away to it. The repugnance we feel for annihilation is a physical repugnance connected with our bodily strength, and decaying with its decay. I had not time, however, to go into these things fully with him, but we are to meet again at Storrington.

" Later I learnt more of Tyrrell's ideas from Meynell, with whom he is intimate. According to Meynell, Tyrrell holds with the consensus of mankind on matters of moral teaching, rather than with any dogmatic infallibility of the Christian Church. He thinks that the religious intelligence of humanity as it advances will agree upon certain articles of supernatural belief, such as the existence of God, the hope of a future life, and some form of rewards and punishments to come. These will be held by all religions, just as the plain rules of moral conduct. But in this view account is not taken of the views held by Buddhism and other non-Christian religions. Tyrrell told me what is doubtless true, that Judaism no less than Christianity is trying hard to find a *via media* between the ancient and the modern thought, as also is Mohammedanism, but the tendency of all three is, as he readily admitted, towards materialism, and it was no argument that because intellectual men clung closer to-day to religious beliefs than in the days of Voltaire, they were therefore any nearer to a solution favourable to religion. The desire was stronger now because the practical dangers of unbelief were better understood. I feel that I cannot do Tyrrell justice in this recollection of his talk, but the impression it has left on me is clear, that he must end in agnosticism, probably in pure materialism.

" 13th *Aug.*— Hafiz Awwad, Editor of the ' Mimbar ' at Cairo, has been here to dine and sleep. He is an extremely able and interesting man, and we have discussed every phase of the Egyptian question. On this he is thoroughly sound, representing Mohammed Abdu's views more completely than any other I have met. Of the Khedive he gives a hopeful account. 'The experience of the last year,' he says, 'has made His Highness once more serious, and though quite alive to his faults and his hereditary ill tendencies, he thinks he can now be fairly well relied on to work with the National Party. Two years ago the Khedive had despaired of politics, and had given himself up solely to pleasure and money-making, but the events of Akabah and the demonstrations about Denshawai had shown him that he would find support in the country if the hour of resistance to English rule should come. Even if he should fail them, Hafiz is confident the Egyptians could work out their National salvation without him. Talking of Cromer's resignation, he said, as they all do, that the Sultan's popularity in Egypt came as a surprise to Cromer, and entirely upset his calculations. Denshawai was an act of anger, alarm, and disappointment, a supreme folly which had ruined his position in Egypt. Cromer had not quite understood how entirely this was the case till his return to Cairo last autumn. Then he had attributed the sudden unanimity of feeling against him to the Khedive's intrigues, and he had tried to get Abbas deposed. It was the refusal of the English Government to go with him to that extreme extent that had led him to resign. Hafiz does not think the Khedive knew of the resignation before it was announced. His Highness was on the point of making one of his desert journeys from Alexandria when he heard the news, and hastened to Cairo out of politeness, expecting to find Cromer really ill, but when they met it was only to receive a violent scolding on account of an allowance Abbas had made to a certain religious Sheykh, an itinerant preacher whom Cromer accused him of putting forward to foment sedition.

"As to Gorst, Hafiz is very sceptical of his proving any great change for the better. As far as Nationalist hopes are concerned, he might well be in some ways worse. He is anxious I should, if possible, see the Khedive and encourage him to hold fast to his patriotic principles, but Abbas was very weak.

"Of Mustapha Kamel he talked reasonably, said he could be relied on as honest and patriotic, but he was vain and impatient of competition, and jealous of being considered the one National Leader. He had acquired great influence, and his ability was great.

"*15th Aug.*— Drove to Storrington to call on Miss Petre and Father Tyrrell. Her 'Home for the Unhappy' is a charming old eighteenth-century house in the village street opposite the Black Horse Inn, inside and outside perfect, rooms panelled and white painted, all scrupulously clean, with a semi-conventual primness, but prettier than convents are. The door was opened by a demure maid, very neatly dressed, with downcast eyes. Behind the house is a nice square plat of lawn and garden, with a row of low buildings beyond, all adding to the cloistral look.

" Miss Petre is a young woman of about thirty-five, plain, but with a pleasant, ruddy countenance, and a look of extreme honesty. I had twenty minutes' talk with her, before Father Tyrrell appeared, on matters connected with the establishment, a serious, good woman, large minded, but without much humour; that was my impression of her.

" *20th Aug.*— Clouds. My birthday of sixty-seven was spent here. To-day Sir Reginald and Lady Graham came for the afternoon. He is an old friend of the Wyndhams of fifty years standing. He talked to me of my Aunt Leconfield, who died in 1863, with great admiration, as one always charming and kind, who had had a difficult part to play at Petworth at times. Graham, poor man, had been badly crippled by a fall, and suffers much pain.

" I have been reading a collection of very delightful letters written by old Lady Campbell, Madeline's mother, to Miss Emily Eden. These show what a wonderfully attractive woman she was, with a vast fund of life, wit, and broad-mindedness, just such another as is Madeline herself. I remember Lady Campbell forty years ago, very what Madeline now is, with snow-white hair and the same kindly ways. There is a delightful description among the letters of Madeline's birth in 1835.

" *24th Aug.*— Newbuildings. Meynell and his son Everard brought Francis Thompson down by motor to stay a week with Everard at Gosbrook, a cottage close by, belonging to me. The poor poet seemed to be in the last stage of consumption, more like death than anything I have seen since Bill Gordon was here, and he died a fortnight afterwards. He is emaciated beyond credibility, his poor little figure a mere skeleton, under clothes lent him for the occasion by the Meynells. He has the smallest head and face of any grown man I ever saw, colourless, except for his sharp nose, where all light is concentrated, and his bright eyes. It is the face of a Spanish sixteenth-century Saint, almost that of a dying child. When he had rested a bit at Gosbrook, I drove him down to tea at Newbuildings, and he revived there a little and began to talk with Everard and me. I took him a toddle round the garden, but he does not know one flower from another any more than twelve years ago, when he could not distinguish an oak from an elm. The poppy was the only flower he recognized. ' Ah, that's a poppy,' he said, as if greeting a friend. He has not been out of London for a year.

" *26th Aug.*— Thompson is distinctly better to-day. I fetched him down from Gosbrook in the phaeton, and had a long talk with him after luncheon. We first got into touch with each other over a common hatred of European civilization and the destruction wrought by it on all that was beautiful in the world, the destruction of happiness, of the happier races by the less happy, and so gradually to the despair of the intellectual part of mankind with what life gave and the craving for a life after death. I gave him something of my view and asked him abruptly what his own view was. He said, ' Oh, about that I am entirely orthodox; indeed, it is my only consolation.' This led to a question about his Catholic bringing up, and he told me that he was a Catholic born, both his parents having been, however, converts, neither of them Irish, he was without any Irish blood that he knew of. His mother was from Lancashire, his father, I think he said, originally from Rutland, but settled in Manchester. I asked him whether either parent was alive and he said no, his mother had died before he left home. It was a mistake to suppose that his father had treated him harshly. The fault had been his own and a misunderstanding. He had thought that his father insisted on his studying medicine; this was a mistake, it was his mother (meaning his stepmother) and her friends that desired it. If he had spoken openly to his father telling him how repugnant the details of doctoring were to him he would not have insisted, but as he did not speak, his father did not know and he acquiesced in what was arranged for him. His repugnance was a physical one which he could not overcome. The dissection of dead bodies he had partly got over, but the sight of blood flowing he could never endure. I told him how it was with me, and how I still could not look without physical repulsion on a wound. I gathered from what he told me, though he did not say it, that it was his stepmother rather than his father who had been hard to him; however, he blamed no one but himself. ' As a boy of seventeen,' he said, ' I was incredibly vain, it makes me blush now to remember what I thought of myself. Neither my father nor my mother had the least appreciation of literary things or the least suspicion that I had any talent of that kind, but I was devoured with literary ambition, all my medical studies were wasted because I would not work, but ran off from my classes to the libraries to read. If my father had known it he would not have forced me to go on. Then I failed to pass the examinations and I behaved ill in every way and took to drink and the rest. I was in every way an unsatisfactory son.' I asked him whether he had not seen his father before he died and he said, ' Oh yes, three months before, at Pantasaph, and he was entirely kind.'

" We talked next about the Franciscans and his stay of two years with them. He was allowed at that time to go in and out among them, but he said all had been changed now and they were kept to their strict rule. Of his two special friends, Cuthbert and Angelo (the same who had come to me for help to go to Rome), Angelo had broken away, not only from the order, but from the church, and was now a clergyman of the Church of England. The other had modified his views of reform and was working among the hop-pickers in Kent. Their idea in going to Rome had been to found a new order. On the whole I find Thompson much saner and more sensible than I expected. Of his poetry he talked reasonably and said that he took a soberer view of his talents now than he had done as a boy. ' I have written no verse.' he said, ' for ten years past, and shall write no more. If I have at all succeeded it is because I have tried to do my best.'

" Talking with him I am more than ever convinced that there is no essential difference between a man of great talent and what is called a man of genius. Thompson, if any living poet can now be said to be so, is a man of genius, yet one sees precisely how his poetry has come about. If he had lived a happy, easy life at home he would probably have done nothing very noteworthy, but the terrible experiences he has gone through have given him that depth of thought and feeling which is the feature of his poetry, distinguishing him from his fellow poets. His ear, of course, is a very fine one, but a vast amount of the beauty of his verse lies in the underlying tragedy, while the wealth of imagery and the elaboration of his diction have been produced by sheer hard work. Above all it is the essential goodness of his character shining through it that attracts. There is so little of material selfishness, so great a sympathy with all forms of suffering, such thankfulness for the small change of beauty in the world, scattered as alms to the poorest. All this is beautiful and of immense value, but I see nothing supernatural in it, nothing above the nature of many other good people who are without his talent of speaking what he feels in rhythmical words.

" *30th Aug.*— Neville has been over here, having been summoned by me, and has made an admirable drawing of Thompson, a profile in coloured chalks. It is an absolutely exact presentment of what he is, and will be very valuable as a record in the days to come. He, Thompson, is pleased with it himself. To-day the elder Meynell came down for the day and I had a long talk with him making him give me over again the history of his connection with Thompson. What he told me was this:

" ' It was twenty years ago when I was editing " Merrie England," that I received a very dirty crumpled envelope containing some MS. verse and an essay. They looked so uninviting that I did not read them but put them away in a pigeon hole and it was not till six months afterwards, that wanting something for the magazine I took them out and read them. The essay was on —' (I forget what Meynell told me was the title, but something to do with the claims of body and soul) ' a commonplace subject of which I expected nothing new. I soon saw, however, that there was nothing commonplace in the essay. It was full of originality and had a wealth of illustration and quotation quite unlike the essays I generally received. Also the verses were so good that I showed them to Alice (his wife) who said that, unless they were, as sometimes happens, accidental successes, I had discovered a new poet. I at once published one of these and the essay. They were signed " Francis Thompson " with the address " Charing Cross P.O.," but when I addressed him there I found that he no longer called for his letters and so I could not pay him for the MS.

" ' I had, however, published them with his name and I trusted that someone who knew him would call his attention to their having appeared. This is precisely what happened. Some few days later I received a letter from him complaining that I had been wanting in courtesy in not sending him a cheque for the writings published. This time the address was at a house in Drury Lane. As I was now convinced that I had found a true poet, I consequently went at once to the address given and found it to be that of a chemist who told me that the writer did not live there, his only connection with the house being that he occasionally bought drugs there, and was actually owing 4s. 6d. for laudanum which the chemist invited me, as a supposed relation, to pay. Thus informed I wrote to Thompson and invited him to come and visit me, which he presently did. His appearance then was terrible in its destitution. When he came into the room he half opened the door and then retreated and did so twice before he got courage to come inside. He was in rags, his feet, without stockings, showing through his boots, his coat torn, and no shirt. He seemed in the last stage of physical collapse. I asked him how, being in such a condition, he had been able to consult the books out of which he had gathered the quotations for his essay. He answered, " Books I have none, but Blake and the Bible." All the quotations had been made from memory. I gave him a cheque for his work and told him to come and see me again, any evening I would see him.

" ' A few days later he came again and I gave him dinner, and he stopped talking with me till about ten, when he became uneasy and said he must be going. I asked him what obliged him and he explained that he was obliged to earn tenpence every day to live. This he did by waiting at the doors of theatres and calling cabs, and by selling matches in the neighbourhood of Charing Cross. Soon after I took him to a doctor who pronounced his case hopeless; it was one of laudanum slow poisoning. He said all that could be done was to help him to die easily. If he left off drugs it would kill him at once. I have always disbelieved, however, in doctors, and I got him into a hospital from which six weeks later he was discharged practically cured. I had already before this given him a bath and a suit of clothes, and I now took him into my house for awhile, and then arranged for him to live in the Premonstratensian monastery at Storrington. It was here that his best work was done. It was a constant series of beautiful poems. He did not beat about for subjects but wrote on the simplest subjects with unfailing wealth of thought and power of language. He had become devoted to my wife, and many of his poems were addressed to her or her children. Both his first volumes date from this time at Storrington, as was his magnificent " Ode to the Sunset " which for some reason was omitted from these and stands in another volume. He owed much in his style to Coventry Patmore. It was through me that they became acquainted. The bond between them was a common adoration for Alice. Thompson went to stay a week with Patmore in the country and they made friends, talking constantly of her, and afterwards corresponded always about her. He took opium again, after he left Storrington, and went back to his life in the London streets, but not again to the slums. He used, before I know him, to sleep at night under the arches of Covent Garden where every quarter of an hour he was liable to be kicked awake by the police and told to move on. It was in an empty space of ground behind the market where the gardeners throw their rubbish, that, just before, he had resolved on suicide. He then spent all his remaining pence on laudanum, one large dose, and he went there one night to take it. He had swallowed half when he felt an arm laid on his wrist, and looking up he saw Chatterton standing over him and forbidding him to drink the other half. I asked him when he told me of it how he had known that it was Chatterton. He said, " I recognized him from the pictures of him — besides, I knew that it was he before I saw him — and I remembered at once the story of the money which arrived for Chatterton the day after his suicide." Just the same thing happened to Thompson, for a friend having seen the copy of " Merrie England " told him about it the very next morning with the result I told you of.'

" I asked Meynell whether he thought Thompson had ever seriously to do with women. He said, ' I hardly think so. The only thing he ever mentioned on such a subject was about the girl I once told you of. It was when I was proposing to take him into my house, and I was surprised, being as he was then destitute, that he should hesitate to accept my offer. He then explained to me that his reason was that a girl, a street walker, he never told me her name, had made a friendship with him out of her charity. She lived in Brompton, but frequented the streets near the Strand, and when she had failed to secure a companion for the night she used to take him home with her and give him a supper and a shelter. She liked his poetry, not any of it then published, and they were friends in this way. He had told her of my offer, and when she heard it she had said at once that he must give up coming to see her, for it would not do for him with his new respectable friends. But he would not give her up, until one day, soon after, he missed her in the Strand, and when he went to her lodging he found that she was gone, leaving no addresss. It was clear that she had resolved to disappear so as not to injure his better prospects. There was a reminiscence of de Quincy in the unselfish incident.' Meynell, however, feels sure that there was no sexual love between them — though who can know?

" *6th Sept.*— The Radical papers are up in arms at last against Grey, who has just concluded an arrangement with the Russian Government, which seems to amount to a partition of Persia. There is very little doubt that the partition of the whole of Asia is in the programme of our Foreign Office, and would already be a *fait accompli* but for Kaiser Wilhelm. According to the present treaty, or whatever else it may be called, Persia is to be divided into spheres of interest just as North Africa has been divided. The whole thing is, of course, abominable, but what fools the Radical members are to have put up with Grey these two years since the General Election. Meanwhile the aggression on Morocco is going the usual course of such adventures, with all their scoundrel features of lying provocation and bombardment.

" I had a long talk yesterday with Thompson on these things as to which we are in full accord, also about the misery of the poor under the conditions of Western civilization. Of this last he has had a rude experience. During the first years of his being in London, his father allowed him, he tells me, a few shillings a week, but during the last year, until Meynell discovered him, nothing. This was because he had finally failed to retain any permanent employment. It had convinced his father that he would never come to any good, and he cast him off. I asked him whether he had ever had to labour with his hands. He answered, ' I was physically unfit.' I did not like to press him further, but according to Meynell he got his living by fetching cabs, selling matches, and blacking boots (very unsuccessfully). He has been ill, poor fellow, with a bad attack of diarrhœa, so that we have been alarmed about him. I saw him last night at David's and found him brighter. [N.B. I had taken a room for him at one of my cottages called Rascall's Corner, Southwater, where he lodged with my old servant David Roberts, who looked well after him, after Everard Meynell had gone back to London.] He is very comfortable there and is glad to stay on.

" *9th Sept.*— In America six hundred Hindoos have been set upon by a mob and beaten, an act of race fanaticism. If this had happened to Englishmen in Turkey we should have had the whole British Press breathing fire and fury, now not a paper has an article about it, except a feeble one in the ' Times.' Our people are afraid, and though the Hindoos are British subjects, nothing will be done.

" *12th Sept.*— An attack has been made on Japanese in Vancouver

which will bring matters to a crisis.   Our Government is faced at last
with a question which will go far to break up the Empire.   If it proves
anything to Radicals it will prove that their old doctrine is the right
one, namely, that the Colonies are no strength to England, but a weakness.   George III was logical in his day, when he insisted on governing North America as well as holding it under the Crown.   It is quite
illogical to hold it and to be powerless to govern, as our Whigs are
trying to do.   The result will be that we English shall be responsible
for all the evil done in the Colonies, and shall become demoralized by
consenting to it.   We shall have to choose very soon between the
Colonial Empire and our Indian Empire.   We shall try to keep both,
and please God we shall lose both.

"Thompson goes on in a half alive state at David's, apparently
content with his existence purely negative.   He takes laudanum, David
reports, daily, and sleeps at night with a stertorous sound.   At noon
every day I send a vehicle for him, and he joins us here at luncheon,
very feeble and quite silent, except it be on some very trivial subject.
He seems incapable of bringing his mind to bear on any complex
thought, and sits through the afternoon with a volume of Dickens'
'Martin Chuzzlewit,' sometimes held upside down in his hand, which
he does not read, nodding, and three parts asleep, like a very aged man.
He seems happy, however, and I do not disturb him, nor does he ask
that anyone should talk to him."

We lunched at that time always in the Jubilee garden, where he was
much annoyed by the wasps, which were particularly numerous that
summer, even to the extent that on one occasion he cursed them for
the drunken brutes they were.   He used to appeal to me to help him
when they got into his wine.   "Will you please kill this wasp for
me, I cannot do it, I have never killed anything in my life."   At last
one bit him and he had his wrist bound up in lint with a strong solution
of ammonia, and going to sleep soon after it raised a blister which remained an interest to him till he died, wearing the rag, as saints are
represented carrying the instruments of their martyrdom.   It has remained a legend here, but I do not vouch for its authenticity as a
miracle, though it is a fact, that for three years after this there were
no wasps in the garden.   It was on the long wicker sofa, the same
that was my brother's during his last illness, that he was usually laid
out to sleep through the afternoon in the New Room on the ground
floor where his portrait now hangs.

"*21st Sept.*— To London, and lunched with Horace Rumbold, and
he talked again about the Crown Prince Rudolph's death, giving me
new details.   'Rudi Hoyos,' he said, 'was a charming man of about
fifty, very popular in Vienna.   The girl's mother had been a Baltazzi,
married to a diplomatist of the minor nobility almost bourgeois.   The

girl had been driven in his fiacre from Vienna by a well-known character named Bratfisch, who must have known all about it, but whose
mouth remained afterwards for ever absolutely closed.   Bratfisch was
an amusing personage, a cabdriver, who used to be had in by the
young men of fashion to entertain them with his talk, as he knew all
the scandalous stories of Vienna.   Horace supposes that the girl finding
the Prince was dead, and herself so entirely compromised, committed
suicide, but either story might be true.   Nobody would ever know.
The Emperor, Francis Joseph, never allowed the subject to be mentioned before him.   He considered it too mean an affair and too great
a family disgrace.'

" *22nd Sept.*— I am staying for the week end with Rivers Wilson at
his country house, Fox Hills, near Chertsey.   With us has been Sir
Lepel Griffin who has entertained us with many anecdotes of Gladstone
and other personages.   From Rivers I have received a detailed account
of the Mufettish Ismaïl Sadyk's death at the Khedive Ishmaïl's hands
in 1876.   Rivers told how some time before it happened, he (Rivers)
was coming home one night from seeing the Khedive at his palace at
Ghezireh when, passing through the garden, he observed a figure issuing from the shadow of the trees in the moonlight, and a man had
seized his arm, crouching to him, and imploring him not to leave Egypt.
It was the Mufettish, and Sherif Pasha, who was walking with Rivers,
translated what the suppliant said, and explained the situation, for
Rivers knew no word of Arabic, and was alarmed, thinking he might
be an assassin.   The Mufettish's appeal was very pitiful.   When the
old man's arrest became known the American Consul had gone to
Ismaïl, and had threatened him with Consular displeasure if anything
violent should happen, and the Khedive had become alarmed and sent
at once to stop the execution of his orders, but his messenger had been
met on the way by another coming from the steamer, who had thrown
up his arms and given the news that it was too late.   Lepel Griffin,
once my adversary on Indian affairs, is a little white-haired rotund
personage with some humour in conversation, self-indulgent and cynical as Anglo-Indians often are.   An Ulster Irishman by birth he affects
an English lisp and drawl, and talks about himself as an Englishman.
We have had also here Allen, the Canadian head of the Allen line of
steamers, with whom Rivers as head of the Canadian Pacific railroad
has business relations, a highly intelligent man.

" Fox Hills is a very beautiful place of which Rivers has a seven
years' lease.   The domain was formerly a common, which Charles
James Fox planted with Scotch firs, many of which are now splendid
trees.   There are a number, too, of very large birch trees grown from
the stub in a way one seldom sees.   The ground is finely tossed about
and covered with fern and heath, a sanct solitude in which Rivers

lives the life of a rich city man. Several parties of Canadians and Americans arrived from London to spend the afternoon, and talk business with him. Rivers has become emphatically a *beau vieillard,* well dressed, well cared for, alert and pleasant to all. He has what after all is the chief consolation of old age, the sense of having succeeded in life, though he did not succeed in Egypt.

" *28th Sept.*— Thompson remains on at Rascall's Corner, somewhat better in health, but intellectually defunct. His whole interest in the last few days has been his wasp bite, which has been made worse by the ammonia. He has managed, I believe, at last to finish his article for the ' Athenæum.' [It was on Sir Thomas Browne.]

" *3rd Oct.*— I am much interested in two long letters Father Tyrrell has published in the ' Times,' a reply to the Pope's Encyclical, which will probably bring on him a formal excommunication. I have written to him to express my sympathy, and to tell him that if there had been any exponent of views like his forty-five years ago, it might have made all the difference to me in my spiritual life.

" My niece, Mary Wentworth, has been staying here.

" *16th Oct.*— Thompson paid me his farewell visit to-day, Everard Meynell having arrived in the morning to fetch him back to London. We had become alarmed about him latterly, as since the weather began to break up he has remained entirely indoors, shut in David's cottage with a big fire and doors and windows carefully closed, a bottle of laudanum, David tells me, beside him, and ill with diarrhœa. It has reduced him to a skeleton. Meynell has sent a priest to see him, and I felt that any day he might go suddenly. He needs some one with him who can exercise control over him, but I doubt his living over Christmas. As an intellectual force he is already dead, and his poor body is dying, too."

My account of Francis Thompson's visit to Newbuildings needs supplementing on some points. During the first week he lived with Everard Meynell at Gosbrook, a cottage which I had lent to them for the purpose, and they came daily to us for luncheon, and to spend the afternoon at Newbuildings. This was from 24th August until the end of the month. Thompson at that time could walk the distance, a mile there and a mile back, and he spent his afternoons with us as already described out of doors in the Jubilee Garden, and each day, when we had finished luncheon, he would retire to the New Room, carrying with him a glass of wine with which he mixed some white powder, and lying down on the long Madeira sofa, the same which had been my brother's in his last illness, there remained half asleep during the rest of the afternoon, going back to Gosbrook with Everard in the evening. After Everard's return to London he moved to David Robert's cottage, where he was well looked after by David and his wife.

At first he continued coming to Newbuildings every day for luncheon, but as he grew weaker I had to send a carriage for him, and then he gradually ceased coming; the incident of the wasps he took very seriously. The last fortnight he was at Rascall's he gave himself up entirely to taking laudanum, and David and his wife were alarmed at his condition. The drug was sent him by post from London, and I heard that he took as much as six ounces of it daily. The last time he came to see us at Newbuildings he was so weak that he had to be helped back into the carriage.

" Father Tyrrell has written me an interesting letter in answer to mine, in which I had expressed a hope that he would not allow himself to be driven out of his ground, on either side (as a Liberal Catholic or as an obedient member of the Church). He writes: ' As you may imagine, the air is full of missiles directed at my head, and I am busy dodging them. It is not pleasant, yet to my Irish blood not wholly unpleasant.' Also, in allusion to what I had said about the influence such teaching as his might have had on me forty-five years ago, ' Yes, had Knowledge been welcomed earlier, many might have been saved to the Church, but she (Knowledge) has had to force herself in, and the result may be rather destructive for her unwilling hostess, yet the gain of Rome to the cause of reason and humanity would be so great that one is loath to abandon the effort, at all events I can never admit that I am beaten.'

" *20th Oct. (Sunday)*.— Rivers Wilson has been here with Neville and Cunninghame Graham and a friend of his from Morocco, one Fernan, an Anglo-Belgian merchant of Casa Blanca, who was there during the recent bombardment by the French. Fernan tells me the bombardment was without sufficient excuse. Trouble had arisen through the opposition of the native Moors to the new harbour works being constructed by a French company, and especially to the appointment of Frenchmen as revenue officers to the Custom House. This had led to excitement, and four or five Europeans had been killed by roughs; arrests, however, had been made by the local authorities, and there was no real danger in the town when the French man-of-war arrived. The commander of the vessel had promised to give three hours' warning before taking steps, but chose to give it at 2 o'clock in the morning, and began firing at 5, the pretext being that a single rifle shot had been fired on the French landing party. Fernan is a strong partisan of the Moors, or rather against the French. Between the reigning Sultan, Abdul Aziz and Mulai Hafid, he thinks there is not much to choose, but he has only seen the latter once some years ago when he was a provincial Governor. The French, he thinks, are hampered in their projects against Morocco by the difficulty of provid-

ing a sufficient army without denuding either France or Algeria of
troops.

" Rivers is fierce against Cromer, especially because Cromer, having
been his subordinate in Egypt in 1887, has never acknowledged the
fact that the work of financial regeneration there was begun while he,
Wilson, was head of the financial commission. This is true. Cromer
has always ignored every reform in Egypt effected before 1883, the
date of his own arrival there as Consul General. Of Riaz Pasha
Rivers speaks with affection, and of how Riaz had helped him on the
financial commission.

" I have had a correspondence with Malet in the ' Times ' about the
passage in my ' Secret History,' where I record that I went to Downing Street to get him ordered, for his safety's sake, on board ship just
before the bombardment of Alexandria. Malet insists that by this
I meant I had got him ' recalled,' which certainly was not in my mind.
The dispute with Malet was of no importance, but the ' Times ' has
taken occasion to vent its spleen or rather Moberly Bell's spleen against
me in a leading article, to which by Rivers' advice, I have replied,
showing Moberly Bell's part in the affair.

" *30th Oct.*— Cromer has made a speech in the City of the most
rampant bureaucratic kind, and Grey has refused again to release
the Denshawai prisoners.

" *14th Nov.*— Broadly called on me in connection with my ' Times '
pamphlet. Then to Neville's studio in Chelsea, where I am sitting
to him for a portrait in Arab dress, and from that on to lunch with
Button at Fulham. I found Button established there in a delightful
old house in Church Row called ' The Hermitage,' with a large open
hall and a garden behind it adjoining the Bishop of London's garden
which he has filled with his marble vases and well-heads brought from
Italy, among them some really fine things.

" Button leads a solitary life at Fulham as if in the country, never
going into London, and depending chiefly on his clerical neighbours
for his society. He took me out after luncheon for a short walk,
and passing the churchyard he pointed out to me old Lord Ranelagh's
grave there. On it we were surprised to find some newly-cut flowers,
all red ones, laid. This, although the old fellow had been dead for
twenty years.

" As I was leaving Chapel Street in the evening to return to Newbuildings a note reached me from Meynell announcing Francis Thompson's death, and asking me to write a memorial of him in the ' Academy.'
This I did, and it was so arranged that nothing was known of Thompson's death till mine and a number more articles about him were
ready to print. This accounted in some measure for the sudden in-

terest taken by the public in him as a great poet, one fully deserved, for he was our greatest religious poet since Herbert. He died in a private hospital to which Meynell had taken him a fortnight ago. He saw him there on Tuesday and he died on Wednesday the 13th at dawn.

" *17th Nov. (Sunday).*— Terence Bourke is here. He tells me that in Tunis things are going prosperously now, that the French have adopted a more conciliatory policy towards the Moslem inhabitants and that these are accepting the French *régime*. The French are discontinuing their fortification of Bizerta now that the Anglo-French Entente is signed.

" *24th Dec.*— The release of the Denshawai prisoners is announced in the papers, so that episode is over, but it has done more towards shaking the British Empire in the East than anything that has happened for years. It smashed Cromer and it has half smashed Grey. Its sound has gone out into all lands, into India, Persia, and throughout Asia. Egypt it has saved from her long apathy and it will continue to inspire the new Nationalism.

" *1st Jan.,* 1908.— Eversley has written me a very important letter confirming my acount of the Egyptian doings in 1882. As he was a member of the Government at the time it is of great value, in it he says:

" ' Many thanks for your letter and still more for the copy of the second edition of your book. I have read it carefully with the greatest interest. It is the most complete vindication of your own conduct throughout the whole of the Egyptian business.

" ' I think you have been fully justified in quoting from conversations and letters as you have done. There must come a time when such things may be made public and when the convention as to privacy no longer will hold good. It seems to me that after more than 20 years, during which the British policy has prevailed in Egypt almost without question, and when at length a new phase is arising in that country it is quite legitimate to tell the whole story without reserve.

" ' The objection, however, in any case can only come from those who are entitled (if at all) to complain — such as Malet, Colvin, E. Hamilton, etc., but I do not understand that they have made any complaint. Why then Frederic Harrison should do so on their behalf I do not quite understand. I think you hardly do justice to Mr. Gladstone or appreciate the difficulties of his position — how he was fed with lies from the Foreign Office and other quarters. Would he have been justified in breaking up his Government or in resigning himself sooner than give his consent to sending Wolseley to Egypt? What

kind of case could he have made for doing so? All the official information was to the effect that Arabi was at the head of a military insurrection and not of a national movement.

" ' Chamberlain and Dilke were mainly responsible for what was
done. I recollect well them boasting in the Lobby of the House of
Commons that they had cornered the " old man." I have also always
understood that Lord Granville complained that Dilke played him false
in the House of Commons by answering questions in a manner to
suit his own policy and not that of his chief.

" ' John Morley was at that time completely under the influence
of Chamberlain. The passages you quote from the ' P. M. G.' are
very discreditable. They must have been supplied by Dilke and Chamberlain. Judging by what you say of Arabi and especially his want
of physical courage I doubt whether he could have formed a stable
government in Egypt. Sooner or later the question of financial control
would have arisen and would have forced an issue not very different
from that which was arrived at. What occurred was in fact the
logical conclusion of the policy of financial control that was the *fons
et origo mali.*'

" *6th Jan.*— The ' Daily News ' announces what seems to be the
death of the ' Times,' at any rate of the ' Times ' as we have known it.
If true this will be a new scalp for me.

" *7th Jan.*— It is officially announced that the ' Times ' is to be turned
into a Limited Liability Company under the chairmanship of Walter
and that the director manager is to be Pearson. This means that the
old ' Times ' is indeed dead, and Moberly Bell discarded, a swift triumph for my pamphlet. I cannot help, however, regretting the old
Thunderer now he is gone.

> " ' Zeus, thy right hand is unloaded
>   Where the thunder did prevail.
> In the idiocy of Godhead
>   Thou art staring the stars pale;
> And thine eagle blind and old
>   Roughs his feathers in the cold.
> Now Pan is dead! '

[The pamphlet here referred to was one I had just published against
the ' Times ' in connection with certain letters published by their manager, Moberly Bell, containing attacks on me which the ' Times ' had
refused me my right of reply to. The matter is not of sufficient consequence to include in the present volume.]

" *10th Jan.*— I have been reading Miss Petre's book, ' Catholicism
and Independence.' It interests me immensely, and surprises me also,
for I did not at all guess her intellectual gifts. These essays show

her to be the best serious woman writer of her time. She has certain qualities women rarely possess, precision, sense of proportion, accuracy of illustration. Her psychology is original and true.

" 18*th Jan.*— We have had a little festivity arranged for us by my bailiff, Laker. Eight or nine old men and young from the parish who sang Sussex songs, well supplied with beer in the business room, some of the singing very good, and so all the evening till a nine gallon barrel was empty. Though I have lived off and on at Newbuildings for close on forty years I had never before heard these songs.

" 24*th Jan.*— The latest scandal is about the theft of the Crown Jewels in Dublin, one of the same kind that caused so much scandal at Berlin. It is being hushed up, it is said, because a full revelation would make the Government of Ireland impossible.

" 26*th Jan.*— Ouida is dead, poor woman, in great poverty at Villareggio. She had continued her correspondence with Cockerell ever since we saw her at Lucca.

" 28*th Jan.*— In the afternoon I sat to Neville for my portrait. Coming back with him we met his Aunt T. (Mrs. Earle) at her door, and went back with her to tea. She is a most amusing woman, and told us a number of good things. While there, Cambon, the French Ambassador, looked in. We had not met for several years. ' Ah, Voilà l'ami des Arabes,' was his greeting.

" 30*th Jan.*— George Wyndham came to lunch with me. He is hopeful about the political situation from his party point of view. He considers that the Government has got into difficulties all round, in the Transvaal, in India, and at home. He is now an out-and-out Tariff Reformer, and expects to win on it. Campbell Bannerman is seriously ill, and the Government have mismanaged things absurdly in Ireland. He is glad the Irish Nationalists have settled their differences. The scandal about the Crown Jewels is sure to come out, and the Government's position is a quite impossible one. It is Birrell's fault, he says, who is idle about his work, and was away abroad amusing himself when the discovery of the loss of the jewels was made. In his absence Macdonnell had decided that the best way of treating the matter would be to get rid of Vicars on some other pretext, and then Macdonnell also went away. Birrell, however, on his return ordered an inquiry, and this gave Vicars, who had taken good legal advice, his opportunity. The inquiry was to be held in secret, and not on oath, and Vicars refused to give evidence before it, claiming publicity. Macdonnell was very angry about this on his return, hence the rumours of his resignation, and now they don't know at all what to do, for the King is furious at the idea of there being a scandal here like the one at Berlin, and it cannot long be kept secret as everybody at

Dublin knows it. As to who actually took the jewels George does not know. Lord Aberdeen had made himself a laughing stock at Dublin in connection with it. Vicars had gone to him and had bullied him, and had chivied Aberdeen round the room when he had said that he could not give an answer without consulting Birrell, but George does not profess to know the whole facts of the case.

"*2nd Feb.* (*Sunday*).— Lunched at the French Embassy. On my way there I saw placards in the streets announcing the assassination of the King of Portugal and his heir apparent. Cambon was of course full of this sinister event. He told us that he had only yesterday received a letter from Lisbon dated the 29th, warning him of the existence of a conspiracy against the King. It had been written to him by a leader of the constitutional opposition, and Cambon considered the assassination to be the work, not of anarchists, but of political opponents of the King's unconstitutional rule. For some time past Portugal has been governed, not by Parliamentary ministers, but despotically by decree, Franco, the King's minister, having made himself with the King's support Dictator. 'One must not,' Cambon said, 'take a Parliamentary *régime* in Portugal seriously, any more than in Persia or Turkey. The mass of the peasants care nothing for politics, and questions of Constitution only concern a few people. He would not hear of its being the work of anarchists. It was rather the way in which political party strife manifested itself in Portugal, the struggle of one party against another for the loaves of office; there had been great corruption there.

"Mrs. Earle was at the luncheon, and Mrs. Arkwright, and Mrs. Crawshay; the last told me that she had lunched yesterday with Margot, and had learned from her that it was definitely settled that Asquith should have Campbell Bannerman's succession, whenever he retires from the premiership. The only competitor had been Grey, but Grey had said that he was overworked already at the Foreign Office and could not undertake it. Asquith intends as soon as the event happens to dissolve parliament, and go to the country for a new mandate.

"*5th Feb.*— John Dillon came to see me and we had a long and most interesting talk. He told me first about Irish politics, how all the Parliamentary party had come together again, and were working together pleasantly, 'even Healy, though he and I have not spoken for fifteen years.' They have come to terms, too, with the Government, the Government having engaged themselves to pass a resolution in favour of Home Rule this Session. All will vote for it, even Asquith, and Grey, and Haldane. This will bind the Liberal Party once more to a Home Rule policy, and they will ask a mandate for it at the next General Election. He spoke well of Birrell. 'Birrell,' he said, 'has refused to use coercion in Ireland, in spite of tremendous pressure brought to bear upon him.' I told him what I had heard of Asquith's intention of dissolving parliament, and he said he thought it very likely, but it was not improbable the Liberals would be beaten at the election. This brought us to general politics, and the rupture there was sure to be between the Labour Party and the Liberals, with an eventual division of the country into a Conservative party, and a party more or less socialistic of opposition, such as there is in Germany. Dillon is much more of a democrat than I am, though neither of us is at all Socialist. Dillon is for Colonial Federation, and is not without a tinge of Imperialism. He is a believer in the ' Yellow Peril,' and thinks that the Colonies if left to themselves will be sooner or later invaded by Asiatics. Australia and Canada, he says, are rapidly becoming Catholic countries. I asked him the reason of this, and he told me that in both Colonies, and for that matter in the United States, the English colonists had left off breeding children and so were dying out, whereas the Irish, French, and Italian colonists continued to have large families. It was entirely owing to the influence of the Catholic Church which forbade the use of restrictions. Dillon avowed a strong belief in the Italians as ' a thoroughly virile race, physically and intellectually, and that it will survive when others succumb, in spite of Lord Salisbury's ridiculous pronouncement about the Latin races.' The Boers of South Africa are another vigorus race for which he has the greatest admiration. He is for Colonial Federation on their account. They would outlive the other white races in South Africa, and the connection with England would preserve them from trouble with Germany. He is entirely against the Indians in the Transvaal, and has not much sympathy with the blacks ; he would not agree with me when I said there would be recognized slavery in South Africa before another generation was out. This could only be by the extermination of the warlike tribes, but that is just what I think will be done, when the feebler tribes will be reduced to forced labour, perhaps on wages, but still forced.

" As to India, Dillon professed to have no knowledge, but thought that its connection with the British Empire could not long be preserved, in face of the awakening of the East through the successes of Japan. His Imperialism only applies to the white Colonies. He stopped to luncheon, but did not talk much himself as a Mr. Percy Addleshaw had joined us, having come to see me, it so happened, to talk about this very question of India. Addleshaw is an old pupil and friend of York Powell's, in bad health, who has become acquainted with some of the Indian leaders.

" 10*th Feb.*— The Bellocs came to tea bringing with them Bron Herbert, now Lord Lucas, as good and charming a young man as he was ten years ago when I saw him last at Oldhouse. He tells me his sister Nan has made Oldhouse over to the Theosophists, the sect founded by Madame Blavatsky, which she has joined.

"As I was at dinner a telegram from Rothstein was brought me announcing the death of Mustapha Kamel. Though Malony had written me news of his illness only a few days ago, the telegram was to me a great shock.

"*11th Feb.*— The news of Kamel's death is in all the papers.

"Morley has announced in Parliament a punitive expedition in India against the Agha Khels. In this, as in all his policy at the India Office, he follows the permanent official lead, being the weak man he is.

"To London and saw Rothstein who gave me the Egyptian news. Mustapha Kamel had been ailing for some time past and had had a congestion of the lungs from which he was recovering, but going out too soon had a relapse. His, however, has always been a frail life and the first time I saw him, a year and a half ago, I doubted whether he would live long. We had a suspicion then that he took some drug, probably morphia, as a stimulant to enable him to do his excessive work. He always lived at high pressure and seldom took a rest.

"*12th Feb.*— Brailsford called to consult me about a visit he is to pay to Egypt. I explained the situation there as far as I knew it and besought him to do his best to encourage Mustapha Kamel's followers and find a successor for him and bring about a fusion of the various sections of the National Party. Brailsford goes with me in believing that a forward policy of strong opposition to the English occupation is the only one likely to have any effect. A policy of supplication will obtain nothing. Brailsford is a thorough going good fellow, a quite sound Nationalist, with some experience of the East; I am glad he is going to Cairo.

"To see Shaw's play, 'Arms and the Man,' which amused me immensely. I laughed from beginning to end of it. There is not a word in it that is not good, and it is a splendid *reductio ad absurdum* of the romance of war.

"*13th Feb.*— The Paris 'Temps' has a panegyric of Mustapha Kamel. Fifty thousand people followed his funeral at Cairo, so says Reuter, though the 'Times' reduces it to ten thousand. This is a wonderful testimony to so young a man. He was only thirty-four.

"*20th Feb.*— Mohammed Farid has been chosen to take Mustapha Kamel's place in Egypt. It was he who, at the Mohammedan Conference, at Algiers, had the courage to denounce French rule there.

"Morley has begun a new war in India against the Afridis under the direction of Kitchener, whom in 1889 he attacked for his brutalities of warfare in the Soudan. Now he finds it all right and proper.

"There has been talk of intervention by Austria and by Russia

in the Balkans, as to which I have no special knowledge or opinion
except the general one that it is desirable in the interests of the
rest of the Eastern world that the two Empires should quarrel.

"*22nd Feb.*— Belloc came to ride with us and stayed to luncheon
afterwards. He is no great horseman, and came mounted on an ancient mare of his he calls Monster, which he rides in blinkers. He is
very pleased just now with having succeeded in bringing forward in the
House of Commons the case he has had *in petto* for a long time, of
the employment of secret party funds. Talking of Mustapha Kamel's
death he declares that the Jews in France are beginning to think that
a National movement in Egypt may create trouble for them financially
and perhaps it would be better the English occupation was ended. If
that is so we shall not remain there long.

"*27th Feb.*— Cromer's book on Egypt is out. The historical part,
as far as I am concerned, is of small importance, being poorly done,
and without the writer's having taken the trouble to go thoroughly
into any obscure matters. It is interspersed with notes referring to
my book, acid in tone, but with no attempt to deal with the charges
made in it against our diplomacy.

"*5th March.*— Farid Bey writes telling me of his succession to
the Leadership of the National Party in Egypt, and begging me to
continue my support and advice.

"*10th March.*— We have been issuing circulars to friends asking
subscriptions to the Denshawai Memorial School. Evelyn with his
usual generosity has at once sent a cheque of £120. I have answered
Farid's letter in one dated *6th March* as to their line of policy.

"*11th March.*— This afternoon as the hounds were running across
my fields I joined them on my old grey mare, Shiekha. She was excited
and enjoying the sport when I found her beginning to stagger about,
and had just time to get off her when she fell back, gave a gasp
and slight struggle, and was dead. The poor old mare was over
twenty years of age and had become rather infirm, and it is well for
her. She died with as little pain as any creature can suffer. [This
was my last appearance with any hounds.]

"*12th March.*— Chapel Street. Walking in the Park, found John
Redmond riding, and had some talk with him about Egypt and Ireland.
Then Cunninghame Graham joined us. He is just back from Morocco,
and declares himself in favour of Mulai Hafid as Sultan. I am glad
of that, as the French seem tempted to use Abdul Aziz exactly as
we used Tewfik in Egypt. If it had not been for Mulai Hafid's rising
and proclamation of himself as Sultan, the French Government would
have advanced £6,000,000 to Abdul Aziz, and thus committed themselves to the Government of Morocco. I asked his help to get our
Labour members to move in matters of this sort, but he tells me they

are a hopeless lot. When they get into Parliament they are at once bitten with the absurd idea that they are to be no longer working men, but statesmen, and they try to behave as such. ' I tell them,' said Graham, ' that they would do more good if they came to the House in a body drunk and tumbling about on the floor.'

"13th *March*.— Spent an hour with Margot at her house in Cavendish Square. She is talking already about her impending move to 10 Downing Street, for Asquith is to have Campbell Bannerman's succession as Prime Minister and so she will at last gain the object of her ambition. She intends to do things splendidly as Prime Minister's wife; neither Mrs. Gladstone nor Lady Salisbury had taken advantage of the social side of her duties, only she will be terribly hampered for a sufficient income to do it on. Among other things she talked about Cromer, with whom she had been playing bridge yesterday, and how he had told her of his wish to re-enter political life. ' He fancies,' she said, ' that he can make a party with George Curzon and a few other free trade Unionists. His difficulty is that he cannot swallow old age pensions.' This is funny, considering his own old age pension of £50,000 which he swallowed without winking.

" 19th *March*.— John Redmond lunched with me. He says a resolution in favour of Home Rule will certainly be passed this session, binding the Liberal party once more to them, and they will bring in a Catholic University Bill, but he thinks that if Asquith dissolves, the Liberals would be beaten at the new election, mainly on account of the Licensing Bill. He has a small opinion of them. About Morley at the India Office he was very scornful, and repeated what he has more than once told me, that Morley was the weakest and worst Chief Secretary they ever had in Ireland.

" 20th *March*.— Nicholas O'Conor is dead at Constantinople, our Ambassador there, a very worthy fellow, a Catholic Irishman of no great ability, but amiable and good natured. He got shoved on early in his profession by Philip Currie, to whom he had proved *serviable* at the Paris Embassy, paying attention to English ladies there, and helping them to buy their bonnets. He was rather a friend of Sarah Bernhardt's, and I remember meeting him in the green room of whatever the theatre was, when Sarah first came over to England in the seventies. He is said to have done well at Constantinople.

" 26th *March*.— Several new books. Sarah Bernhardt's ' Memoirs,' exceedingly well written and most amusing. Shelley's letters to Miss Hitchener, also most amusing as well as amazing. Gosse's ' Father and Son.' How Gosse can have written so good a book I cannot imagine, but it is altogether admirable.

" 1st *April*.— To see Lady C. who had written after a long interval. She talked about the Duke of Devonshire, just dead, repeating what

I have often heard her say, that he was a thoroughly good fellow, but quite without intellect, who would have done nothing in politics if it had not been for the Duchess, who had insisted on it both before their marriage and afterwards. The old Duke, his father, was a far more distinguished man. She does Lord Hartington injustice, however, for though a slow thinker he was a considerable power in politics, capable of solid reasoning, if not of eloquence.

" *5th April.*— Cromer's son Errington was married yesterday to a daughter of Minto's and there has been a grand *tamasha* over it. He has been working a year past as Hardinge's private secretary at the Foreign Office to fit him for a great career and the King's favour.

" *6th April.*— Campbell Bannerman has at last resigned and Asquith is to go to Biarritz to the King who is away there. I am writing to congratulate Margot.

CHAPTER VII

ASQUITH AT DOWNING STREET

"9th April, 1908.

Anne writes from Egypt telling how the Court *hakim,* the Khedive's chief physician, stopped her the other day to express his gratitude to me for all I had done for the National cause. This I am glad to get, as I have been much in doubt how my 'Secret History' had been taken at the Palace.

"13th April.— The full composition of the new Ministry is announced. Elgin and Portsmouth retire, having both of them somewhat compromised themselves, Elgin by mismanaging South Africa, Portsmouth by a foolish quarrel with one of his country tenants for shooting hares. Winston enters the Cabinet, and Morley becomes Lord Shillyshally.

"15th April.— A good letter·from Brailsford, just back from Egypt. He is rather disappointed with the political organization of the Nationalists and their little hold over the country districts. He calls them terribly urbanized and this is doubtless true, but I believe the same may be said of all movements of the kind, and that to wait till the peasantry of any country is politically educated is to wait till Domesday. He is not yet converted to the English official view, and wants to talk things over with me.

"16th April.— Asquith's new Ministry is fully formed, and one is able to judge more or less what the change means. It is certainly retrograde as far as humanitarian views are concerned, and is now as purely Whig Imperialist as it could well be made. The Colonial Office will be run on lines of pure Imperial Federation. We shall see the colonists in South Africa allowed their way with the native blacks. The Zulus will be harried in Natal, and Dinizulu hanged or deported. I do not trust Crewe, who always had a Colonial twist, and we shall see a hack Under-Secretary answering inconvenient questions in the House of Commons. It will be the same at the India Office with Morley removed to the Lords. The Government was bad before, it will be worse now. The bright spot in the situation is Redmond's declaration against Asquith. It can hardly mean anything else than war with the Whigs, and a strong opposition on imperial questions. Bannerman being a thorough Home Ruler has hitherto been a stumbling block to the Irish, but about Asquith they have no illusions.

"*20th April.*— Passing through Horsham to-day I saw on a poster, ' The Sultan of Turkey defies Italy. Mobilization of the Italian Fleet.' This looks like a beginning of a new partition of the Ottoman Empire, to the extent of allowing Italy to occupy Tripoli. The reason given in the papers is that the Sultan has refused to allow the Italian Government to have a separate post office in Ottoman territory, an absurd pretext for a war, but Asquith's is a Rosebery Cabinet and we may expect any violence in the East with its connivance. I suppose the Emperor William has been squared."

This was the first premonitory thunderclap of what was presently to prove the great storm which, beginning with the aggression by Italy on Turkey, was to involve Eastern Europe in a series of wars, and eventually the whole Western world in the overwhelming catastrophe of 1914. For the moment the storm was averted, as I understand, by the Emperor William *not* having been squared, and his unwillingness at that time to have the peace of Europe broken. The French Government, however, and our own, can hardly have been acquiescent in Italy's ambition of an African Empire. They had already the thought that in this way Italy might be won over and detached from the German-Austrian Alliance. It is significant that the incident here recorded should have synchronized with Campbell Bannerman's retirement, giving as it did a position of sole authority on foreign affairs to Grey in Downing Street.

"*22nd April.*— The Italian Invasion of Tripoli has been staved off by the Emperor William, who has persuaded the Sultan to yield the point about the post office, so the sailing of the fleet is countermanded.

"*23rd April.*— I have had staying here Cecil Sharp, the collector of folk songs. I find him an interesting man, with great knowledge of his own particular subject and enlightened views on others. I took him to-day, after lunch, to see old Jupp at Carpenters, and we made him sing his Bristol song and ' The Fisherman,' of which last I took down the words.

THE FISHERMAN

As I was a-walking one morning in May
  All down by the river side,
There came in a boat a bold Fisherman
  A-rowing down on the tide.

" Who are you, you bold fisherman?
  And what are you doing here? "
" I am a-fishing for your sweet sake
  All on the river so clear."

He has tied his boat fast to a stump
    And to the fair maid he went,
"I have come to kiss your lily white hand
    For so it was my intent."

He has unbuttoned his morning gown
    And laid it gay on the ground,
And she has seen a chain of gold
    On his body three times round.

She has fallen down on her bended knees
    And loud on his mercy called,
"I thought you was a bold fisherman
    And I see you are a lord."

"I will take you home to my father's house,
    And married straight will we be,
And you shall have a bold fisherman
    To row you on the sea."

"Campbell Bannerman is dead, good old man, the last of the Gladstone Liberals of 1880, except Ripon, who is still in the Cabinet under Asquith, but who has given up his leadership of the House of Lords to Crewe. I don't know that there is much to say about Bannerman except that he was a worthy soul and did his best to carry on the better tradition.

"*26th April.*— Winston Churchill has lost his seat at Manchester. It is a bad blow for Asquith, as Winston had just pledged him and the Cabinet to a full Home Rule programme for the next general election, and Redmond had accepted a declaration and had pronounced in Churchill's favour.

"*30th April.*— Chapel Street. Meynell came to dine with me. He is bringing out a new edition of Thompson's poetry, of which he expects much. I think Thompson is secure of a high position now, not only from the excellence of his workmanship, but because he is unique as a religious poet. I know of no good religious poet since George Herbert, or one who can anyway compare with Thompson, for Newman, with the exception of 'Lead, kindly light,' wrote nothing really first rate. His 'Gerontius' has been made much of because of its doctrinal character, but as poetry it is poor stuff. Later George Wyndham came to see me and sat talking for a couple of hours, his discourse more of poetry than politics. He recited two love songs he had made, one of them really beautiful, with triple endings, which he called, 'From the Persian.'

"He was full of his son Percy's adventures abroad with Bendor, how they had steered a motor boat race at Palermo, and other golden deeds, worthy, he said, of one of Ouida's heroes. He talks with disgust of politics; it is a glue he will never get free of. He has had George Curzon to dine with him lately, and has persuaded him not to commit himself against Tariff Reform, as his doing so would prevent him taking any leading part in the Tory party should occasion offer.

"Then came Brailsford with more about his experience in Egypt. He rates the Nationalists very low intellectually; Saad Zaghloul and a few disciples of Mohammed Abdu he considers the best, but they have no influence, while Mustapha Kamel's successors, who have influence, are without force of character or sufficient intelligence to direct the movement. He heard bad accounts of the Khedive, who was gaining influence, but using it for his own purposes. Of the present Cabinet at home he says it is much worse than the last. When Bannerman's Cabinet was being constructed in November, 1905, Grey at first refused to join it unless Bannerman would go to the House of Lords. This little secret was oddly enough betrayed to the ' Times ' by Morley and published, but the very same night Grey was persuaded to withdraw his objection on condition he should be allowed his own way absolutely in foreign affairs, and he had ever since been extremely jealous of Bannerman, a jealousy which had accentuated his obstinacy in pursuing imperialist lines. This would now be at an end, and Grey might be by so much the more amenable to the views of his colleagues. It is a thousand pities Bannerman missed his opportunity of getting rid of Grey altogether when it was offered.

"*5th May.*— There has been a considerable incident in India, a bomb has been thrown which has killed two Englishwomen out driving in their carriage. There is also a rising on the Afghan frontier. There is talk of sending British reinforcements.

"*11th May.*— Newbuildings. Brailsford and his wife have been here for the week end. Mrs. Brailsford is a charming woman, very clever and sympathetic. He is a Fabian. She takes my larger view of things. There is news of a great conspiracy in India, and a great manufacture of bombs with the help of European anarchists. It is being made use of by the reactionaries to get a repeal of the liberty of the native press.

"Churchill, beaten at Manchester, has got back into parliament at Dundee.

"*27th May.*— Farid Bey, who arrived in England a few days ago, came to see me. He is, I think, a pretty good man, not first rate, but sensible and honest. He is anxious to see Grey, and I advised him to get at him through Redmond and to refuse seeing any of the understrappers at the Foreign Office in his place. Then if Grey consented to receive him to put to him one question only, ' Are the English

Government honest in their profession of eventual evacuation?' Unless Grey can give some new public assurance on this head, it is useless discussing details.   The latest pronouncement has been Cromer's, that 'Egypt cannot be made self-governing under three or four generations,' let us say never.   As long as there is a doubt about this, all Egyptians will be banded together against England.   Farid gives much the same account of the Khédive Abbas's attitude toward the National movement as Mustapha Kamel did.   His Highness talks one thing to one man, another to another.   He is friends with Gorst and Cassel, who help him to make money.

"*30th May.*— Grey has refused to see Farid on the ground that he also refused to see Kamel.   Redmond writes to me about it.   In it he says: 'I had an interview with Sir Edward Grey this morning (about his seeing Farid) and he states that when Mustapha Kamel Pasha was over here as the leader of the Nationalist Party he declined to see him, and that under these circumstances he cannot see his way to see his successor.'   This is marked private.

"Cockerell has got the place of Director of the Fitzwilliam Museum at Cambridge.

"*6th June.*— I have been extremely ill for the last three weeks, threatened with I know not what, needing an operation in my throat, which I have refused, preferring to die a natural death.   In the afternoon Meynell arrived, having been all the morning with Archbishop Bourne.   Bourne, he tells me, was at one time curate to Monsignor Denis at West Grinstead, and knew Newbuildings well in John Pollen's time, and he remembers having met me at one of the Capuchin festivals at Crawley.   His (Bourne's) position, in regard to Modernism is, contrary to what I imagined, one of disapproving the Papal Encyclical as unnecessary in England and ill-timed, and this, Meynell says, is the general opinion regarding it, so much so that Wilfrid Ward has been able to persuade the Duke of Norfolk to write in that sense to the Pope.   The Pope, curiously enough, is believed to be himself not so violent against Modernists as might be supposed from the public pronouncements.   Who then is the *causa causans*?

"Meynell has just been to see Francis Thompson's sister, the nun at Manchester.   He describes her as an enthusiastic, impulsive creature, who kissed his hands when she saw him and sat for hours talking about her brother's early life.

"*7th June.*— The crisis of my illness is over.   My doctor, when he arrived, remarked cheerfully, 'Well, we have saved you this time from the surgeon's hands!'   Nature has operated its own cure, but doctors will be doctors.   E. V. Lucas and his wife came for the afternoon, very nice people, he the author of 'Wisdom while you wait.'   I have spent the afternoon talking pleasantly with Meynell about Thompson's fame as a poet. Meynell thinks that I too shall be given a permanent place as a poet twenty years hence, but I am doubtful. Certainly I have no such place of any kind now. It will depend very much, I think, upon how things go with the Eastern Nations. If, as I hope, they achieve their independence of Europe, I shall be acknowledged as a forerunner of their cause; if they fail, I shall fail. Anyhow my work in the world is pretty near over. I shall fight and write no more.

" 14th June (Sunday).— That ' wretched fellow ' Morley has had a new Press Law passed in India giving power to local authorities to seize printing presses and confiscate without trial where sedition has been published. It was this same John Morley of whom Lytton used so bitterly to complain to me as his most violent attacker while in India, notwithstanding their personal friendship, and on these very points, if I remember rightly, of his Afghan campaign and his Press Law, which is identical with this of Morley's to-day. Morley is adopting all the methods used by Russia in its imperial dealings.

" 21st June.— An odd visit this afternoon from a stranger (sent to me by Cockerell), Lord Osborne Beauclerk, who had bicycled from London. He is a pleasant young man who has travelled much in Asia, and has ideas about horses, poetry and ethnology. He professed himself in a great hurry as it was late and he wanted to get on to Wake-hurst for dinner, so he put me at once through a number of questions on all these subjects. It was like being interviewed for the Press. I showed him the stallions and gave him a copy of the ' Golden Odes.' He says he will come again." [This was the beginning of a pleasant and very constant friendship.]

" 27th June.— Brailsford and his wife are here. A good book has been sent me from America called ' Egypt and its Betrayal,' by one Farman, who was Consul General for America in Egypt in Ismaïl's time and till after the bombardment. It quite corroborates my account of the doings of the time. Things are going badly in Egypt. They have been playing the fool and quarrelling with the Copts. The Khedive has been in London the last few days, come over, Mark Napier tells me, to raise money on mortgage.

" Things in Persia also look badly. The Shah with the help of some Russian officers lent him by the Russian Government, who have drilled him a few hundred Cossacks, has effected a reactionary *coup d'état* at Teheran, breaking up the Mejliss, slaughtering the people and hanging newspaper editors. This is the first fruits of Grey's treaty with Russia and the King's visit to the Czar. Brailsford's opinion of Grey is that it is more stupidity and ignorance with him than ill will. He thinks he really believes in Russian promises. All the diplomacy is done by Hardinge and the King, while Grey is their mouthpiece in the House of Commons, having a fine presence and an impressive manner with a wonderfully fine speaking voice. In Russia, in Persia, in Egypt, and in India, the reaction is in full swing. No one will listen to anything but force in dealing with the National movements. Something of the same kind about Hardinge and the King was told me by Beauclerk who again paid me a flying visit. He arrived from Wakehurst where Frank Lascelles is staying, and brought me messages from him. Lascelles is out of favour now with the King, as being too German in his sentiments. He wanted to have the Paris Embassy, but the King refused on the ground that he was not married, so he is to retire. They hold him responsible for the Kaiser Wilhelm's unfriendly attitude. Wilhelm told him lately that he was sick of England and everything to do with it.

"My dear old friend Evelyn is dead at the age of eighty-six. I had been intending to drive over to Wotton to see him as soon as ever I was well enough, as he had asked for me to come some three months ago. He has been my political ally now for twenty-five years, latterly my only ally, we two being the last of the Tory Home Rulers and anti-Imperialists. With certain defects of temper which led him into quarrels with his neighbours, he was the most generous of men, and to me always staunch and true. I remember him first fifty years ago, a shy young man, already M.P. for Surrey, but submitting to be patronized in his bullying way, by my guardian old Henry Currie, at West Horsley. Our friendship came on later in connection with Egypt and Ireland. His domestic life was not altogether happy, his Irish wife, a Chichester, having strong Orange proclivities, which worried him much, while a certain obstinacy of character caused him trouble in his parish, and a long feud with the parson, against whom he waged persistent war through a local newspaper carried on for twenty years. To me his death is a great loss. At one time he had named me guardian of his son John in his will, but John is now of age and succeeds him at Wotton, we all hope worthily.

"*29th June.*— Brailsford tells me of a dinner given lately by Maurice Baring to his uncle, Cromer, at which were also Bernard Shaw, J. M. Robertson, Belloc, and other one or two Radicals, this doubtless to conciliate Shaw in connection with Denshawai. I shall be curious to hear the result. Cromer has always been a past master in dealing with the press.

"*1st July.*— Edward Malet is dead, at the age of seventy, having been long ailing. The papers give him a fair meed of praise. He and Colvin are now both dead within a few months of each other, and all the chief actors in the Egyptian tragedy of 1882 are gone.

"*11th July.*— Rothstein writes about the difficulty of getting assistance from the Radicals in Parliament on Egyptian affairs. I have answered that I consider it does not matter. It is hopeless to attempt the conversion of Radicals more than Tory opinion. Nobody in England wishes for Egypt's independence, and the issue does not depend upon English, but on other influences in East and West. What we have to do is to go on agitating and opposing as they do in Ireland.

"*13th July.*— Percy Wyndham, who has been staying here, went away. At breakfast he gave me some interesting particulars about his family history which I had asked him for. He tells me as to his grandfather, Lord Egremont, and his marriage, that his (Percy's) grandmother was the daughter of a certain Reverend Iliffe, a beneficed clergyman of Surrey, Vicar of Bramley, I think, who made her over to him when quite young. She was very beautiful and very innocent. Lord Egremont practically bought her of her father, and for some years they lived together very happily. There were three sons of the union, George, Hugh, and Charles, and two daughters, Lady Burrell, a very pretty woman, and Mrs. King. Lady Munster was by another woman, a celebrated *demi-mondaine,* Mrs. Fox. George, the eldest son by Miss Iliffe, was born in 1787. Later Lord Egremont married her and had a daughter, Lady Elizabeth Wyndham, but no son. Then they quarrelled, as she found out he was unfaithful to her, and there was a legal separation, and she lived alone for many years at Fulham in the house now the Bishop of London's Palace. She was a well educated woman and affected science as her hobby to the extent that Lord Egremont got the Royal Society to give her a medal for some pamphlet she had written. Her house at Fulham was much frequented by scientific people. She was quite respectable in every way except her connection with Lord Egremont which at the time she began it she probably did not understand the meaning of. ' Her subsequent marriage with him,' Percy said, ' would, if it had been made in Scotland, have legalized us all.' When Lord Egremont died nobody knew how he would leave his property and a great number were disappointed. His nephew, who succeeded him as Lord Egremont, he did not like and used to laugh at. He, the nephew, got the Orchard Wyndham property and the property at Dinton, and he began to build an enormous house intended to rival Petworth, but he never finished it, and it is now a ruin. Hugh got Cockermouth and the Cumberland property which he never knew how to manage, getting no more than £5,000 a year from it when it was worth £30,000, and afterwards, when it reverted to Petworth, became worth perhaps £100,000. Charles got Rogate, and George Petworth and the rest. Lord Egremont had more confidence in George than in the others, and rightly. The persons most disappointed by his will were the Herberts, his sister having married one of the Carnarvon Herberts. When the will had been read they ordered their carriages and went off. This at the outset embittered Percy's father towards these relations. When the quarrel between Lord Egremont and his lady occurred, Percy's father (he was then thirteen) had been told to leave off writing to her, and having disobeyed was flogged by his father —all this is interesting and most of it new to me. Some of the Iliffe family spell their name Ayliffe. Percy is of opinion that his grand-father's political wisdom and ability have been somewhat overrated He, through life, avoided taking part in public affairs or joining a party, and so his talents were never put to the proof. He was a very gen-erous dealer with his wealth, maintaining a number of needy hangers-on at Petworth who had almost permanent lodging and board in the house, and painters and other artists innumerable.

" 14*th July*.— Terence Bourke came for the day, he has bought a farm called Pekes, in East Sussex, and intends to settle there, though without selling his property at Bizerta. Things in Tunis, he tells me, are no longer so interesting as they were for him, the Anglo-French Entente having smoothed down disputes between French and English, and the project of making Bizerta a naval seaport and arsenal has been abandoned. The country is making material progress, the agricultural part, though in the towns the position of the Moslems has not improved. There is a small philo-Arab section of French opinion, but the Moslems are still without anything like a free press, or other means of protesting against injustice.

" 25*th July*.— For a week past there has been talk in the papers of a military revolt in Macedonia, and to-day the great news is published of the Sultan's having dismissed his Grand Vizier, Farid Pasha, recall-ing Kiamil Pasha and Said Pasha Kutshuk, and summoned a Parlia-ment under Midhat's constitution. This is, indeed, good news, only I hope the revolution will not leave Abdul Hamid on the throne, or he will play them false again, as he did in 1879.

" I have been asked to a dinner given by Ismaïl Pasha Abaza and other members of the Egyptian Legislative Council who are in London. Tilak, the head of the Indian revolutionary party in India has just been sentenced to six months' deportation to the Andaman Islands for a ' seditious ' article in his newspaper, the ' Kesari ' of Bombay. Morley is playing the high old Russian game there, and there is not a man in the House of Commons to ask a question about it. It is sickening.

" Belloc has just published a new book, ' Clutterbuck's Election,' very amusing.

" 27*th July*.— Things are going splendidly at Constantinople. There has been universal rejoicing all over Turkey, Moslem and Christian and Jew embracing one another, just as I remember it at Cairo in 1881 when the Constitution was proclaimed there. The revolution has oc-curred in the very nick of time, for it is pretty clear that the Anglo-Russian agreement about Macedonia come to by the King at Reval was intended as a first step towards the dismemberment of the Ottoman

Empire. This will now be prevented indefinitely; it would also immensely strengthen the demand for a restoration of the Constitution ·in Egypt.

"*30th July*.— Hyndman writes asking me to help financially in a campaign he proposed to make in favour of Tilak and other imprisoned Indian patriots. This in answer to a letter of mine. Ismaïl Abaza's deputation of Egyptian Legislative Councillors is, I think, a good move, though repudiated by Farid Bey. Abaza succeeded in getting an interview with Grey, though what passed at it has not been published. The revolution at Constantinople will have greatly strengthened his hands.

"*1st Aug*.— The young swallows in the bathroom have flown, but they still come back to their nest at night. It has been a great pleasure watching them, the old swallows having come in and out of the room by the window while I was in the bath quite undisturbed though the nest was just above it, built on a curtain rod. There were four young ones hatched and all have flown.

"*4th Aug*.— Belloc who was here to-day tells me that it has been communicated to him in confidence that Grey has said that Egypt shall have a Constitution granted to her in two years' time. If true, and I think it likely in view of events in Turkey, it is most important.

"*5th Aug*.— A girl of seventeen, a daughter of Merrick Burrell's wood-reeve, was run over and killed by a motor at Buck Barn cross roads, and to-day I went to the inquest, the first one I have ever attended. It took place on the spot where the thing happened, a dangerous place, but not for a careful driver. At the cross roads I found a score of local people, neighbouring farmers and the like, collected, with the parish policeman, who was showing the exact spot where the collision took place with the marks of the girl's blood still visible on the road. The traces showed that the girl had been dragged thirty-two feet by the motor, which had only been brought to a stand after eighty-two feet. While we were examining the coroner drove up, and then in a smart motor the three young men who had caused the death, and we all went into the barn close by, where the inquest was held.

"The scene inside when the court assembled was a curious one. It was a good old threshing floor with oak timbers, and on each side of the wide floor sat the twelve jurymen on forms, the coroner and one or two others at the far end of the table. The jurors were all local people, farmers and labourers, with the Shipley parson, Sir Merrick's coachman, and Captain Turner, a close neighbour. There was something mediæval about the thing, a fine survival from the days of the Heptarchy, which seemed very real when the coroner explained that we were assembled under authority of the King to inquire into the cause of the death of one of his Majesty's lieges, to wit, Mabel Mary

Denman of this parish. Then the jury having been sworn, they were instructed to cross the road and view the corpse on which they were sitting, and I went to the cottage with them where the girl's body lay. Our proceedings were all the more impressive from the intermittent roar of holiday motors passing in quick succession outside along the Worthing road, joy-riders, without slackening of speed or knowledge of or care for what had happened, or was happening, light-hearted Londoner folk concerned with nothing but their own pleasure and the thought of in how few minutes they could make the run from one point to another of their outing to Worthing.

" Inside the cottage the dead girl, a great, strong, healthy country girl, lay there in her coffin, looking hardly dead, for the brown of the summer sun in the hayfields was on her face, only there were two great wounds on the forehead, and others on cheek and chin, where the motor had dragged her, face downwards, on the road.

" On our return to the barn the proceedings were resumed, the first witness, the girl's brother, a young fellow of eighteen, not unlike her, a tall, well-shaped, ruddy country boy, with a straightforward, honest face. He told very simply how he and his brother had been on their bicycles to West Grinstead station; how, coming back, he had met his sister, who had been sent to her father in the field to carry him his dinner, how she had asked for a ride back to their home half a mile away, how he had taken her on the step behind him, her little sister riding with the brother. It was only a few hundred yards to the cross roads. Arrived there, he had looked up the Horsham road and had seen a motor coming, but as it was thirty yards away and he was already on his own road, he held on his course, but the motor neither slackened speed nor turned aside and before he could get clear across it caught them. All was over in an instant. Another rustic witness corroborated the account, and the police gave details of measurements and distances, and the doctor who had found the girl lying by the roadside bleeding from head and mouth, with other injuries. She never recovered consciousness. I was allowed by the coroner to put several questions, for the motorist had pretended that the girl had fallen off, but both eye-witnesses were clear against this. Such was the main evidence. The defendant, a young bank clerk from Balham, who had been driving the motor, was a respectable youth in every way, but short-sighted, and wearing spectacles. What came out was that if he had kept to the near side instead of along the crown of the road there would have been no accident, for the road was wide and there was ample room, but he had gone on without thought, it being a good piece of the road for speed, slightly downhill, keeping along the crown, and chancing what might be in front. The jury, I am thankful to say, returned a verdict of manslaughter. The thing made me angry, and I intended, if there was no sufficient verdict, to call an indignation meeting in the parish. It will now, however, come before the Horsham magistrates, and at the Assizes.

[N.B.— The motorist eventually got two months. I interested myself for a while in these motor cases, and I think was instrumental in checking the joy-riding. It seemed to me an invasion of the enemy in our peaceful Sussex weald.]

"*7th Aug.*— Chapel Street. To London to see Hudson, who had written to me that he was hopelessly ill. It was a pathetic letter, complaining that he was a man without a creed, unlike me, he said, who had the advantage of being a Catholic. It had been written in answer to one I had sent him about his new book on Cornwall, which is a very good one. But when I arrived at his house in the extreme west of London I found he had gone out. [This was the well-known writer of many admirable books, mostly on birds and on his early life in South America.]

Meynell, who dined with me to-night, professes to know what the King thinks about the danger of a war with Germany, and what the Kaiser Wilhelm's plan is. Wilhelm, as soon as he is ready for it, will throw a *corps d'armée* or two into England, making proclamation that he has come, not as an enemy to the King, but as grandson of Queen Victoria, to deliver him from the socialistic gang which is ruining the country. He will then in conjunction with the King dissolve parliament, and re-establish the King's autocratic rule as feudatory of the German Empire. Such is the programme, and the King believes in it as true.

"*10th Aug.*— Professor Browne has asked my advice about Persia, he being in despair at the counter-revolution there. I have written advising that he should go to Constantinople, and get the new Turkish Government to take the Persian Constitutionalists by the hand, and bring about an end of the Sunni-Shia feud. I am advising Farid to make common cause with the revolution at Constantinople. Belloc repeats that Grey has privately promised Egypt shall have a Constitution in two years' time.

"*14th Aug.*— Blanche Hozier writes from Blenheim that her daughter Clementine is to marry Winston Churchill. She says of him, ' yesterday, he came to London to ask my consent, and we all three came on here. Winston and I spoke of you and of your great friendship with his father. He is so like Lord Randolph, he has some of his faults, and all his qualities. He is gentle and tender, and affectionate to those he loves, much hated by those who have not come under his personal charm.' It is a good marriage for both of them, for Clementine is pretty, clever, and altogether charming, while Winston is what the world knows him, and a good fellow to boot."

I spent my birthday of sixty-eight as usual at Clouds, where I met, amongst others, the Duchess of Wellington with her delightful daughter Lady Eileen Wellesley, who is clever in the way young ladies are clever nowadays, with a great knowledge of poetry and literature, besides being extremely pretty. She read aloud Swinburne to us in a peculiarly sweet voice, and I followed with Mrs. Browning's " Gods of Hellas," a very favourite piece with me.

" *20th Aug.*— At Clouds. George arrived in the afternoon from Elbarrow. With him Shelah, Duchess of Westminster. They had been at the manœuvres all the morning, had then motored over here, some thirty miles, stopped an hour for tea, and were to motor back, and go out to dinner. This is a good example of the life at high pressure of our ladies of fashion. She has with her in camp, a lady's maid, a footman, a chauffeur, and a cook. The Duke in the meanwhile is away motoring in Ireland with another chauffeur, another cook, and more servants, besides a motor boat, the one he races with. The life of both of them is a perpetual gallop. This sort of society cannot last, it will end in Bedlam.

" *22nd Aug.*— To-day old Kipling, Rudyard's father, came to dinner, and I had a long talk with him about India. I wanted to find out from him, who is a typical Anglo-Indian, what remedy he would apply to the present condition of things. Like all the rest, however, he has no remedy to propose beyond ' severe repression ' for the time being, though he does not pretend that this will cure the disease. He puts down as its causes: (1) The Japanese victories, (2) Education, and (3) Official lack of time to be polite; these are the common explanations, but for none of them has he a remedy. The Japanese victories are a fact not to be denied, the education given cannot be withdrawn, the lack of race sympathy cannot be mended. He admits the necessity of a new policy, but can suggest none.

" Looking over old letters from Burne-Jones to Madeline I was glad to find one from Rottingdean, dated 27 December 1882. ' Thank Mr. Wyndham for sending me a poem, by Wilfrid Blunt, about the Egyptian crime. Of course I heartily agree with it, but admired it, too, and felt it in parts a real poem.' This was the ' Wind and the Whirlwind,'

" To-day Percy read out to us an act of one of Bernard Shaw's plays. He reads very well, having an excellent voice, and some skill in dealing with dialects.

" *30th Aug. (Sunday).*— I have been reading Father Tyrrell's new book, ' Mediævalism.' The reasoning of it is forcible, but the tone petulant and undignified; it takes that most difficult of all forms, an open leter addressed to Cardinal Mercier in answer to a Pastoral issued by him to his Belgian Diocese against Modernism. Mercier's Pastoral,

though severe, is not uncharitable, and speaks of Tyrrell politely, even
in a friendly tone, and should have been replied to if at all in the
same polite spirit, but Tyrrell is needlessly aggressive. Thus, while
scoring in argument, he loses in effect, but the truth is both he and
the Cardinal are fighting a battle which neither side can possibly win,
and where the plain unbeliever will remain the *tertium gaudens*. It is
inconceivable that the uncompromising attitude of what Tyrrell calls
Mediævalism, can maintain itself for ever against the logic of science,
and it is equally inconceivable that scientific people will go on trying
to believe in a divine relation on Church lines. In his heart Father
Tyrrell has already lost faith in it, and must be driven into open rejection of *Roman* Catholicism just as Dollinger was, indeed much farther
than Dollinger, for Tyrrell is logically a materialist, no less than I am;
however, the book interests me extremely.

" 31*st Aug.*— Princess Hélène writes telling of her travels in Somaliland, where she has shot a rhinoceros. She says : ' Mon voyage m'a
fait un bien énorme, je n'ai qu'un rêve, retourner dans ces pays là.
Plus je vis, plus j'ai en horreur ce qu'on appelle la civilisation qui n'est
que corruption et méchanceté humaine. Si je n'avais pas un mari et
des enfants j'irai m'établir là-bas.'

" 1*st Sept.*— Mohammed Bedr, Egyptian President of the Islamic
Society of Edinburgh, came here (Newbuildings) on his way to Egypt.
He is a very superior young man, a disciple of Mohammed Abdu, and
a strong Nationalist. I asked him the truth about the Mohammedan
attitude in India, and he assured me that though certain leaders like
Husseyn Bilgrymi and the Agha Khan supported the British régime,
the great mass of Indian Mohammedans were in sympathy with the
Hindoo Nationalists. He believes now in the revival of Asia, and the
maintenance of its independence against Europe. He asked my opinion about the prospects of Constitutionalism in Egypt. I told him
the thing to aim at was not so much *legislative* power as the right of
the Chamber to control the *executive,* that is to say that the choice of
a Ministry should rest with them and not with the Khedive. Unless they
obtained this right, the other would be useless, and the Khedive will
at any moment be able to revoke the Constitution, with the aid of an
army officered by foreigners. He asked what should be their plan of
action? I said, ' You must get together a society of young men of
sufficient means to be independent of Government employment, and
send them round to the country towns and large villages to give lectures, and instruct the fellahin in the duty of patriotism. When you
have accomplished this you will be ready at any time to take advantage
of circumstances to demonstrate effectively against the British Occupation. This had been done in Ireland, where the strength of Nationalism had been found in the peasantry through a propaganda of this kind.

He is himself, he said, member of a wealthy landowning family in the Sherkieh Province, and would try what could be done.

"*4th Sept.*— Eddy Hamilton is dead. This would have meant a great deal to me twenty-five years ago, but he has long been practically defunct, paralysed, and mentally decrepit. Sackville also has dropped out at the ripe age of eighty-one, a thoroughly good fellow, with whom I was never intimate, but always friends. He had a hale old age, a quiet, good man, whom I should regret more were I not myself among the dead.

"*7th Sept.*— E. V. Lucas and his wife were here to-day with Dr. Philpot, and Belloc in the afternoon. Lucas tells me that Harmsworth now controls the whole policy and writing of the ' Times.' A copy of the ' Times ' is annotated by him, with remarks, every morning. His sole object now is to restore its character for respectability. This was just what I recommended six months and more ago, when Eddy Tennant was interested in it.

"*11th Sept.*— The Poet Laureate (Alfred Austin) arrived from Swinford to-day, and we have had much talk about politics and religion. He is sensible enough when one gets him alone. We discussed Modernism and the Eucharistic Congress, his position towards the Church being much the same as mine. He has never renounced Catholicism, he says, though he does not believe in any religion, but he has leanings once more towards it now he is getting old. For me, as I get older I care less. Austin is seventy-five. We first met about the year '58, or it may be a little later, when he was reading law in London. A little cock sparrow of a man, he was already with an ambition of becoming Poet Laureate; it is astonishing he should have won to it. His uncle left him some money, enough to live upon, and he abandoned the Law after making once the Northern Circuit. Then he travelled in Italy, became interested in Garibaldi, and married in 1865. In 1870, being at Berlin during the war, the ' Standard ' took him on as its correspondent, and he followed the German army to Versailles as such. He had a chance interview with Bismarck which made his journalistic fortune, and from that time was kept on as leader writer on the paper for its foreign affairs. This brought him into connection with Lord Salisbury who eventually made him Laureate. So are poets made, *fit non nascitur,* but he takes himself very seriously now, attributes Bismarck's confidences to a poem of his the great man had read in praise of Prussia, and Salisbury's choice of him to his acknowledged position at the head of English literature.

"*12th Sept.*— To London for the Winston-Clementine wedding. It was quite a popular demonstration. Lord Hugh Cecil Winston's best man, and the great crowd of relations, not only the Church [St. Margaret's] full, but all Victoria Street, though that may have partly been for the Eucharistic Congress which began to-day. I went up in the train with Belloc who was to speak at the Congress. At St. Margaret's I arrived late when all the seats were taken, but Blanche Hozier found me one in the family pew, where I sat between her sister, Maud White, and Hugo Wemyss, others in the pew being Lady Airlie, old Maud Stanley and Lady Grove. Little Nellie bridesmaid. The bride was pale, as was the bridegroom. He has gained in appearance since I saw him last, and has a powerful if ugly face. Winston's responses were clearly made in a pleasant voice, Clementine's inaudible.

" *15th Sept.*— The King has sent a telegram to the Sultan congratulating him on having appointed Kiamil Pasha his Grand Vizier, and predicting that he will obtain ' the veneration of future ages.' This is meant evidently for Indian consumption, an astute move. [Less astute, however, in the sequel, as will be seen, for it bound English diplomacy to the fortunes of Kiamil for the eventual ruin of our influence at Constantinople.]

" *24th Sept.*— The first two of my articles on ' The New Situation in Egypt ' are printed in the ' Manchester Guardian,' and the third is promised for to-morrow. The moment is a propitious one, for the King is holding a kind of Council about Egypt at Balmoral, having with him Gorst, Wingate, and Slatin, with Asquith; Cromer being conspicuously absent. This really looks a new policy of some kind, and a policy favourable to Egyptian hopes.

" *25th Sept.*— The Poet Laureate has been here again, very pompous. He is good enough to approve my Egyptian articles, ' every line of them,' and offers to forward them to Grey with a letter to that effect. I said it was very good of him, but I hoped he would not say I had asked him to do so. His patronage is not likely to be much good to me at the Foreign Office.

" *27th Sept.*— Meynell has arrived, and our talk has turned on Francis Thompson on whom the Poet Laureate has been absurd in his pronouncement. Austin's great object now, Meynell tells me, is to get Wilfrid Ward to write an article about him in the ' Dublin Review.' He has confided to Meynell that he has been sounded as to his willingness to be given a title (we suppose a knighthood), but that he has answered that the only title he aspires to is ' one that would give him the right to address his peers in parliament.' He may whistle for that.

" There is a complication in Turkey, the Bulgarian Government having seized the Orient railroad. This may lead to war, but all depends on whether Bulgaria is backed by Austria or by Russia. It is curious how the situation of 1876 is being reproduced, and also the situation which was so near occurring in 1885. The Bellocs dined with us, to the discomfiture of the Poet Laureate, to whom Belloc paid scant deference, and whom he quite extinguished in talk.

" *28th Sept.*— They are all gone at last, I am glad to say, and ' silence like a poultice came to heal the wounds of sound,' for we have had a terribly noisy time.

" Oliver Howard has died, of fever, in Nigeria. What a gratuitous mischance. There was no call whatever for him to go to these malignant countries, no necessity of money or his profession, only a perverse desire for that worst madness which possesses young Englishmen, the sport of arbitrary power in wild countries, with the occasional chance of shooting black men — this is what attracted him.

" *10th Oct.*— I have been laid up all the week by a feverish attack while great events have been taking place in the world.

" On Tuesday Bulgaria declared itself an independent kingdom; on Wednesday Austria annexed Bosnia and Herzegovina; on Thursday Crete annexed itself to Greece; and on Friday came news of Albania having declared its independence. The fat is, therefore, very much in the fire. The European situation, which was very difficult to understand, has gradually become clearer. There has most undoubtedly been a plot, instigated I imagine by Kaiser Wilhelm, betwen Austria, Germany, and Italy, having for its object to bring about the overthrow of the Constitutional party at Constantinople, perhaps a partition of Turkey. What puzzles me is the attitude of Russia in the affair. As things now appear, she is standing with England and France as the upholders of Constitutional Turkey. It is probably in consequence of some agreement of alliance between the three Powers, England, France, and Russia, against Germany, initiated by our King at Reval last summer, suggested by the powerlessness of Russia to advance on Constantinople at present. What probably will happen is that a conference will be proposed which will come to nothing. Then either there will be an acceptance of the *fait accompli,* public opinion in England having got tired of the thing, or there will be a war of coercion. It is clear in all this that if our Government is to take up the high moral line of respect for treaties and declarations, and for the letter of international law, it cannot refuse any longer to keep public faith about Egypt. It will be too absurd, if having strained at the Bosnian gnat it declines to disgorge the Egyptian camel."

This diagnosis of the situation, though not quite accurate, is near the truth. The Balkan conspiracy against Turkey at that moment in which Bulgaria took the lead was undoubtedly encouraged by Austria, which viewed with disfavour the prospect of regeneration for the Ottoman Empire opened by the revolution at Constantinople, which saw in it, should it succeed, a permanent obstacle to its *Drang nach Osten,* while Kaiser Wilhelm still regarded the Sultan Abdul Hamid as his friend and the Constitutionalists as unfriendly to Germany. At the outset of the Turkish revolution public opinion in England had expressed itself strongly in favour of the Constitutionalists, and to the extent that Grey and our Foreign Office had been carried off their legs and obliged unwillingly to a display of sympathy which found its expression in the King's telegram to the Sultan congratulating him on the event, and having appointed Kiamil Pasha his Grand Vizier. Kiamil had long been considered a friend to England and England's Egyptian policy. He had been the Khedive Tewfik's tutor at one time, and had approved of the English intervention in Tewfik's favour at the time of Arabi. For the moment, therefore, the new régime at Constantinople was regarded as a triumph over Austrian and German influence. The friendly feeling, however, did not last long, as England was already bound in the chains of the Franco-Russian Entente, and Russia was at least as opposed to the regeneration of Turkey as was Austria. The situation resulted in an attitude of vacillation and insincerity on the part of our diplomacy, which led to a series of betrayals of the Turkish Government by Grey, as will be seen later. What is a quite correct appreciation of the situation here is that which is said of the agreement come to between England, France, and Russia at Reval, which developed into a coalition between these Powers against the Central Empires, and which was interpreted in Germany as a design of " hemming in," which in fact it was, proved the cause of the Great European War, six years later.

" *11th Oct.*— Father Tyrrell has sent me a wild letter in which, after speaking about Thompson's poetry, he says *à propos* of the doings in Bosnia and Bulgaria, ' Will you join me in a friendly visit to the Emperor Francis Joseph, taking in the Czar and the Kaiser on our way home? I feel it is time to *do* something instead of fizzling like a spent crab. The political rascalities of the last few days has upset my liver.'

" *12th Oct.*— I have finished Nevinson's book about India. It is very well written and interests me greatly, his experiences having a close resemblance to my own of twenty-five years ago. It is disheartening that the Indian reformers should have made so little way since then, for they are hardly any further advanced. Nevinson does not go far enough for me, perhaps he dares not.

" It being a lovely morning I drove over to Storrington and found Father Tyrrell in the annex to Mulberry House, busy, he told me, with a philosopho-theological work of some encyclopædic kind for a publisher. His study is a dark little ground-floor room, and we went out into the sunshine of the garden to talk. I asked him about his relations with Rome, and he told me he feared there was little chance of their improving. He is almost hopeless about the Church ever now putting itself upon progressive lines. They have committed themselves too far at the Vatican. He will not, I think, long retain even what remains of his connection with it. I exhorted him, however, to stay on as long as he can, for though I had myself passed beyond all possibility of belief, I thought it a pity there should be no half-way house anywhere. As regards his personal circumstances he has no need to seek a change, for his life at Storrington is an ideal one for a thinker, retirement in a lovely village with pleasant, intellectual society, male and female, and ample time to write and read. Presently Father Fawkes joined us, a fellow Modernist priest, and then Miss Petre and we sat an hour under the trees. He is to come to Newbuildings for a couple of nights when he can find time.

" 13*th Oct.*— Farid Bey has telegraphed about a rumour current in Egypt that England has declared a protectorate. Though possible it is very unlikely. I have telegraphed back to tell him so.

" 16*th Oct.*— The situation in Bulgaria grows more and more warlike. In my opinion Grey is being taken in by the European diplomatists, who are one and all, except perhaps the French, opposed to reform in Turkey, having their own axes to grind there. These are encouraging Bulgaria to pick a quarrel with Constantinople and bring about a counter-revolution and will probably succeed. It is just the old game of 1876–77. The Turkish army is disorganized (only half mobilized) while the Bulgarian army is on a war footing. Our English support of the Young Turk is clearly platonic, though we may intervene if Constantinople itself is threatened.

" 18*th Oct. (Sunday).*— Malony, the Irish editor of the ' Egyptian Standard,' has arrived from Egypt. He is a sensible and good young man. His account of the situation in Egypt is not encouraging. They suspect the Khedive of having been won over by Gorst to English interests and money interests. Mustapha Kamel's death has disorganized the National party. Malony gives a high character to Farid as an honest patriot and sensible man, but says he lacks initiative and that rapidity of decision so necessary in a leader and so remarkable in Mustapha. Ali Kamel, Mustapha's brother, puts himself forward in rivalry with Farid. There is no one person who commands the obedience of the party.

" Margaret Sackville and Mary Wentworth are here, and we spent a literary evening. Malony went to mass this morning with Mary, while I went out riding with Margaret. In the evening I read them out Margaret's fine lines about Ireland, ' I am the eternal dreamer.' (These are on the highest level of all she has written.)

" Malony goes to Constantinople on Tuesday as correspondent to the ' Manchester Guardian,' as well as to his own Cairo paper.

" 19*th Oct.*— Back to London. The news to-day is better. There is some prospect of the Bulgarians and Turks settling their differences between themselves without waiting for the European conference.

" Meynell, who dined with me, is anxious to get a monument put up to Francis Thompson in St. Paul's, if not in Westminster Abbey.

" *20th Oct.*— Nevinson came to see me just back from India, where he has been in the thick of the revolutionary movement. His book had given me the idea that he was rather hopeless of its continuance, but he assured me that it was not so; the danger was that it would go too fast, there would be riots which would be suppressed with great barbarity, and that would make reform impossible, the hatred of England has become so great. Only if we left India what profit would it be to the Indians, they would fall a prey to some other Empire, German, Russian, who knows what? Nevinson is a remarkable man in appearance, tall, and with a severe manner. He did not smile on entering, and from his expression one might have thought him come with hostile intent, but he warmed to our conversation, and talked pleasantly and freely, and has offered to send some of the Indian Mission which has just arrived in London, Gokhale and Lajpat Rai, to see me. Gokhale he says is now the real leader of the revolutionary movement. We talked about Morley and his projected reforms. He thinks he means to do something of value in the direction of increasing the number and power of the native members of council, even perhaps that he will reverse the partition of Bengal. He agreed with me all the same in my estimate of Morley as a weak-backed politician, quite ignorant of India and the East, swayed by the permanent officials, and principally anxious for general praise and his social position. We were wrong he said in expecting so much of him. On the whole Nevinson pleases me greatly. He has strength, and is as regardless of the conventional attitude as a journalist can well afford to me.

" Next Rothstein came in a pessimistic mood about Egyptian and Turkish things. He wants some action taken at Cairo, but I don't see what can be done there till the Legislative Council meets in December, when a demand for a constitution might be made to the Khedive backed up by popular demonstrations. This seems to me the best programme, with a repetition of it by the General Assembly which is to be convoked in February or March.

" *21st Oct.*— George Wyndham came to lunch, and we discussed the whole Eastern situation. He agrees with me that the trouble in Bulgaria and Bosnia was originally of German-Austrian raising. He also considers Grey to have made a mess of things. His support of the new régime in Turkey was quite right, but he ought to have gone further, and when Austria announced the annexation of Bosnia he ought with France to have declared that England would allow no infringement of the Treaty of Berlin, and stuck to it. He, George, had al-

ways been in favour of the alliance with France, and if they had made
a firm stand Austria would have had to give in, but the Government
is in too great a mess at home to have any courage abroad, and now
they will miss their opportunity of permanent influence at Constantinople.

"Rumbold, whom I called on in the afternoon, thinks with George
and me that the Conference will be dropped, but he is very positive that
the annexation of Bosnia had nothing to do with the Ottoman revolution. It had been decided on to his knowledge as much as three years
ago, and the only thing that had delayed it was the difficulty of settling,
whether Bosnia should belong to Austria or to Hungary. As to Bulgaria, he could not explain how it had come about, that Prince Ferdinand had been so well received by the Emperor of Austria, for the
Emperor had often talked to him, Rumbold, of Ferdinand as an in-
triguer and a scoundrel, who had connived at the murder of Stam-
bouloff.

"Later I met George again, and dined with him and Sibell, and
Pamela Tennant in Park Lane. We had a merry dinner and discussed
once again the Eastern situation. I told him Rumbold's opinion about
Bosnia, but he would not hear of its being a correct one. He declared
it to be certain that the whole trouble was concocted in Berlin, and in
corroboration told how a week before the annexation was announced, he
was staying at Wynyard with the Londonderrys, whose party included
Metternich, the German Ambassador. Metternich, however, had
hardly arrived before a despatch reached him while at dinner of such
urgency as to oblige him to go at once, in Londonderry's motor, to meet
a messenger at a distant railway station, the result of his journey being
that he left for London by the first train in the morning. It must,
George says, have been an affair of the most absolute importance to
require this of him, for he was less than twelve hours at Wynyard, nor
was there any other question in public view at the time. George declares categorically that the crux of the whole situation is that Kaiser
Wilhelm means war with England on the first favourable opportunity,
and in the meanwhile to stir up trouble wherever he can for us. I
think this very likely, and also that there would be no great difficulty
in an invasion of England whenever he is so minded.

"*22nd Oct.*— Gokhale and Lajpat Rai came to see me, sent by
Nevinson, and stayed an hour, and we discussed the situation in India
very thoroughly. I am disappointed with both of them. Gokhale is a
well bred, highly educated and intelligent man, a Maharata Brahmin, I
believe, and according to Nevinson the Leader of the National movement. He expresses himself well in English, and I have no doubt
is an able speaker. But he is clearly no leader of a revolution, and
they will effect nothing without one. He lacks the enthusiasm which

a belief in ultimate success would give, or even the bitterness which is also the force of hatred and despair. He told me that he did not like being called a moderate, but if he represents anything that can be called extreme, there is small chance for India. I asked him what in his view was the end to be aimed at. He said, ' Of course we hope some day for complete independence, but that is far away. Perhaps in ten years' time we may get Provincial self-Government, but for that we must educate ourselves, and the educated class is very small.' I asked him what means he proposed to use in order to obtain it. He disclaimed an appeal to force in any shape. ' What could we do,' he said, ' against Kitchener and the army?' He would not hear even of obstruction. ' It is no use,' he said, ' trying to overthrow the present administration until we have something to put in its place.' Language of this sort may be true, as it certainly is prudent, but it is not the language of revolution. I asked him whether he expected to convert English people, or the English Government by appeals to reason and justice? He said he believed that Morley had a scheme of extending the representative character of the councils, and they would have to be content with that at present. He had been a great believer in Morley, and had read all his writings on liberty, but he feared that Morley was more for *personal* than *national* liberty. I told him Morley was a broken reed. ' In that,' he said, ' my friend here,' pointing to Lajpat Rai, ' will agree with you.' On this I turned to Lajpat and asked him to give me *his* opinion. Lajpat is a different sort of man altogether, much more purely Oriental, but inferior in breeding, and very much in intelligence to Gokhale. He has a poor command of English, and it seemed to me a confused mind, timid too, and deprecatory in manner. It was difficult to see in him anything that the Indian Government could possibly have been afraid of, or that Morley can have thought it necessary to arrest by a *lettre de cachet* and deport him without trial as a danger to India. His views were less pacific than Gokhale's, but all without precision. ' I know nothing,' he said, more than once, ' about India in general, only about my own province, Punjaub.' Perhaps if he had been alone with me he would have had the courage to speak out, but he was afraid of his companion, and I frightened him when I asked him what chance there was of the native army taking the National side. We had a long discussion about the attitude of the Indian Moslems, and I told them how I had tried to influence the last in 1884, to join the Hindoos in the Congress movement, but they assured me the Moslems were all against them now, and Gokhale seemed to think that they would be a danger in any reconstruction of India on a national basis, because, though they were much less numerous, and less rich, they were more united. ' All we hope for is,' he said, ' that the movement of self-government in Turkey and Egypt may spread to

Mohammedan India, and then they may join us. I asked them if I
could do any good by writing my views, especially on this point, but
Gokhale said it would be useless, though if I went to India it might be
of use to them. It was clear that I was much too revolutionary for
either of them. Lajpat in leaving pressed a little book into my hand.
It was a printed account of his arrest and deportation, a naïve, and in
places quite childish narrative, which I hope may not get into the
hands of our Anglo-Indians here to make sport of. It is really preposterous that its author should have been made a national hero. I
augur ill for the success of their mission to England. They would
have done better to send a firebrand like my friend X—— with curses
on his lips to show our Radicals that India has men to be afraid of.
These fair-spoken pleaders for justice and the rights of humanity will
get no profitable hearing, and I told them so.

" *23rd Oct.*— Grey has made a declaration about Egypt, which shows
that the leopard has not changed his spots. In answer to a question put
to him by Robertson, he has declared (1) that he knows nothing of any
demand made in Egypt of being represented in the Ottoman Parliament ; (2) that a scheme of Representative Provincial Councils is being
worked out in Egypt ; and (3) that there is no reason to think that
the new developments in Turkey will create new difficulties in Egypt
against English control. I have written to Farid Bey to warn him
against expecting a Constitution in Egypt, even of the most limited
kind.

" *24th Oct.*— There is a Reuter's telegram in all the papers, giving
what purports to be a declaration by Gorst at Cairo of the Government intentions. It begins by contradicting the rumour of a Protectorate or Annexation. Great Britain, it says, had given solemn
pledges to Turkey and to the European Powers to respect the Sultan's
rights here, and did not desire to go back on that engagement. This
declaration, if official, is of the greatest importance, but its form, that
of an interview with a correspondent of the Mokattam, is unsatisfactory, and I shall try to get a question asked about it in the House
of Commons. The telegram goes on to say that it is also an unfounded
rumour that Sir Eldon Gorst has been instructed to introduce a constitutional *régime* in Egypt, Egypt already having a constitution.

" The papers also announce Frank Lascelles' retirement from the
Diplomatic Service. There was a paragraph in the ' Westminster
Gazette ' headed, ' A Great Diplomat '— how oddly it all reads to me,
whose recollection of him is of an unpaid *attaché* at Madrid, with whom
I played battledore and shuttlecock in the Chancery, and shared many
other pleasures ; official greatness is made up of very small things, as a
mountain is made up of a tumble of small stones.

" *29th Oct.*— The ' Daily Telegraph ' has published a new manifesto

by Kaiser Wilhelm, in the form of an interview with a retired diplomatist. It is most compromising with regard to past history, the most
remarkable thing in it is where he declares that the French and Russian
Governments proposed to him in the winter 1899–1900 to intervene
against England in favour of the Transvaal, which he refused to join
in doing, and that he then supplied the English Government with a
plan of campaign against the Boers, which was the one adopted successfully. As to the first part of the statement, what I heard at the
time was that it was Wilhelm himself who proposed the intervention,
promising to get England out of Egypt if France would waive all claim
to Alsace-Lorraine, and that the French government refused. If authentic, which it has every appearance of being, it is a wonderful document.

"*30th Oct.*— Went picknicking at Storrington on the heath below
the Windmill. Father Tyrrell joined us, and he gave us his interesting
views about monastic life *à propos* of the Premonstratention convent
close by. They are a branch of the Augustinians, and came to England
originally on the invitation of the Emperor Napoleon when in exile,
but they had a quarrel with the Empress, and some twenty years ago
migrated to Storrington, and being very rich, built the huge monastery
outside the village. All went well till the Father in charge of their
finances ran away with the money and disappeared, since when they
have settled down to an indigent and sleepy life. Tyrrell thinks the
monastic orders of that kind are doomed to extinction in the modern
world. As for himself, he is clearly becoming more and more emanci-
pated, and cannot, I think, hold on much longer to his connection, slight
as it is, with the church. I should not be greatly surprised to see him
throw off his cassock altogether, though I should regret it. If he had
a less happy life than he leads at Storrington, I feel sure that this would
happen, for he does not believe enough in ecclesiastical authority to
worry himself about his excommunication. He is an interesting and
charming man, and whatever line he may take I shall approve. He
read us out a part of Thompson's 'Ode to the Setting Sun,' which was
very appropriate to the time and place. He also told us that some
lines he had written in Gwendolen Ryan's autograph book, and which
I was so much taken with, are a translation from the German, the
fourth verse only being an addition to his own. They are these:

> ' Two chambers hath the heart
>   Wherein do dwell
>   Sorrow and joy apart.

> ' When in the one joy wakes
>   Then in the other
>   Sorrow her slumber takes.

'Hush joy! oh hush! refrain,
  Laugh not too loud
  Lest sorrow wake again.

'Let sorrow when she weepeth
  Weep low and know
  Joy is not dead but sleepeth.'

" The whole of Europe is up in arms against the Emperor Wilhelm for his pronouncement, especially his own people in Germany. This will, I hope, simplify matters at Constantinople, but there never was a moment when the complications of European diplomacy were more difficult for an outsider to unravel.

" *31st Oct.*— Belloc dined with us last night, and looked in again to-day, amusing as always, and full of literary projects; amongst others, of publishing a volume of verse, but I think he will not do anything of real value in the way of serious work, looking always for immediate applause in what he does. It is the snare of all brilliant talkers and facile writers, and is Belloc's; witness, as an extreme example, Oscar Wilde. He tells me that he knows, from friends at the Foreign Office, that Grey has made up his mind to allow Constitutional Government in Egypt as a necessary effect of the Constitution in Turkey, the Foreign Office having been converted to that view, and even old Giglamps (Sir Thomas Sanderson) now holds it to be necessary. It is very possible, but there are Constitutions and Constitutions, and it will be a sham one that will be put forward at Cairo. I have intrusted Belloc with the questions I want asked of Grey in Parliament, and he promised to get it done.

" *3rd Nov.*— The chief public event besides the Emperor Wilhelm's interview, has been our Emperor Edward's Proclamation to the Indian people, a bit of verbiage which the Indians are not taking seriously.

" *6th Nov.*— There is a quarrel started between the German and French Governments over the Casa Blanca incident with rumours of possible war. Father Fawkes came to luncheon. He is a Modernist and a pleasant man, a friend of Tyrrell and of Miss Petre.

" *10th Nov.*— Grey, or rather his substitute, has answered my questions put to him by Belloc, about Egypt, notably that relating to Gorst's interview with the 'Mokattam.' The answer is given thus. 'The language used by Sir Eldon Gorst is correctly quoted, and is approved by His Majesty's Government.' It is a declaration of Government policy, and is most important as putting annexation out of the question or a Protectorate, though it leaves things otherwises much as they are.

" *12th Nov.*— In India they seem getting to work. Our King's self-complacent manifesto has been met with ridicule, and in Bengal they have answered its omission of all mention of the Partition by an attempt to assassinate the Lieutenant-Governor, with hootings in the streets, and vengeance taken on 'approvers' of their own race, a repetition of the old Fenian days in Ireland. They have burned the body of the man who slew the informer, Gossain, in prison, and whom our people have just hanged at Calcutta, according him all the honours given to a saint, and have sent fragments of his bones as relics through India.

" 13*th Nov.*— Osborne Beauclerk arrived fresh from Persia, where he has been shooting wild sheep east of the Caspian. He has been staying with Sykes, the British Consul at Meshhed, whose business there is to watch the Russian Consul. All that part of Persia is in great confusion, and Sykes has fortified his house on scientific principles, intending to hold it against all comers with the thirty soldiers he has at his orders. Beauclerk described this in detail, and how the defences included a mine projected under the Vizier's residence, which is close by, 'carrying things rather too far,' Beauclerk thinks. The whole of Persia, he says, might be ridden over by a squadron of European cavalry without hindrance as it lies open and there is no force to oppose it. Tabriz and the North he did not see. In the rest of Persia there is nothing that can be called a nation, only a number of tribes and races, mixed up without any bond of cohesion. Beauclerk's ideas, however, are rather vague, and I had difficulty in persuading him that the Meshhed of Eastern Persia was not the same as Meshhed Ali. The hill country where he was shooting he describes as the extreme limit eastwards of the great Forest of elm and sycamore, which stretches 120 miles from the Caspian, ending in juniper scrub, where the wild sheep are. I asked him whether these ever drank, and he said he thought not, having seen no trace of them near water. This bears out what Suliman Howeyti used to tell me about the *kebsch moyych* between the Nile and the Red Sea, which never drinks. I am immensely taken with Beauclerk, who is quite the most sympathetic young man I have met for many years. Without being quite intellectual he is extremely intelligent, has seen much and thought much, has every good impulse and desire, and is feeling his way how to live up to them. He is hardly at all educated, but has a large experience of men and cities, or rather of wild places which are not cities. He has been at Eton and understands its snobbery; he has been in the Army and understands its futility; he is a landlord and understands its duties; he is without pretention and has a kindly heart.

" 22*nd Nov. (Sunday).*— There is a new interview with Kaiser Wilhelm published, more astonishing than the last. We are promised it in a few days, though £10,000 were paid by the German Ambassador at Washington for its suppression, so says the 'Observer.'

" 2*nd Dec.*— Father Tyrrell writes from Storrington: 'I am occu-

pied with much serving; when things are cleared away and washed up
I will come and sit at your feet and hear your words.' This is giving
me a high position as heresiarch, almost that of Antichrist.

" There is an agreement of importance come to between the American and Japanese Governments for the maintenance of the *status quo*
on the Pacific Coast. It is practically a guarantee of the independence
of China. This is to the good.

" 11*th Dec.*— Newbuildings. Mark Napier is here. He has told
me an interesting story about his life with Asquith twenty and more
years ago. Mark lived for eight years with the present Prime Minister
when they were twenty-two and twenty-three and onwards in chambers
at the Temple. Asquith did not make more than £500 in the whole
of those eight years at the Bar. He was the son of a Nonconformist
in business in the north of England, his mother being also from the
north, and a very clever woman. From the age of eight Asquith had
kept himself and provided his own education at school and at the
University. Then he came up to London and read law. He was a
very industrious fellow and made £200 a year by writing for the Press,
principally in the ' Economist.' When he was twenty-three he married
a nice little woman. She had £500 a year, and they lived in a small
house at Hampstead, with a garden behind the house where they kept
chickens. He went in and out to his chambers daily on the top of an
omnibus, and lunched at an eating-house kept by women at 4*d*. He
was a very ready writer, and could write out his articles without
erasures, articles of a serious kind. One way and another he and his
wife made up £1000 a year.

" 15*th Dec.*— Father Tyrrell came to dine and sleep, bringing with
him a Modernist friend, Bell, who is lame. We had some good talk
about Stonyhurst, the Jesuit system of education, Gifford Palgrave's
career, Eastern politics, and poetry. Both he and Bell are good talkers.
Bell is an Oxford convert, now a Modernist, but still resident at Hert-
ford College. He gives a poor account of the intelligence of the
undergraduates, especially in the matter of poetry. Very few of them,
he said, read any verse.

" 17*th Dec.*— Cromer has made a speech at the Eighty Club about
Egypt. He is certainly the most shameless dealer with facts in our
public life. He has the face now to pretend that he has always been
an ' Oriental Liberal,' that he has never been a partisan of the Occupation, that he has never been an opponent of Nationalist views, and
that if he was ' once shown the prospect of a Constitution ' which
should really represent the views and interests of all the inhabitants
of the Nile Valley which would inspire the confidence of Europe and
maintain the reasonable rights of the Khedive, he would become ' an
ardent Egyptian Constitutionalist.' This is indeed a jest.

" Sabunji writes from Constantinople saying he has received my
' Secret History,' which ' records faithfully all our joint doings in the
land of the Pharaohs.' I am glad to have his testimony to my accuracy.

" 18*th Dec.*— Morley's much expected Indian Reform speech has at
last been made in the House of Lords, amid much Tory applause,
great care having been taken that there should be no hostile criticism
here or in India. Here the speech was put off till the last working
day of the session, and in India the leaders of the opposition, including the chief newspaper editors, had been clapped into prison. These
reforms, if they had been produced three years ago when Morley
first came into office, or if they had been announced now as an avowed
first step towards Home Rule, or again, if they had been accompanied
by an abandonment of the Division of Bengal and a release of the
political prisoners, might have affected a reconciliation with the extremists, but now I feel it is too late. In themselves the reforms are
poor things. There are to be unofficial majorities in the Provincial
Councils, and a single native is to be allowed on the Executive Council
of Calcutta. A great parade is made about this last, but it amounts
to very little, as the native member is to be nominated by the Viceroy,
and he will always be able to choose a tame man, Hindoo, or Mohammedan, or Parsee (Gokhale perhaps), just as they name tame Copts
to be Ministers in Egypt, while in the Provincial Councils the Governor
or Lieut.-Governor is to retain the power of veto. If native India is
satisfied with this, well and good, we shall see. What is certain is that
under cover of the reforms announced the reign of political terror will
be allowed its full way, arrests, deportations, imprisonments, and the
impounding of printing presses. The same would be done in Egypt
if our officials there could get rid of the Capitulations.

" *23rd Dec.*— Tyrrell has written me an interesting letter on my
' Future of Islam,' which he has been reading. He says:

" ' It makes one think furiously. You would have been God the
Father had you foreseen all that has happened since you wrote it;
and I wonder how this attempt at constitutionalism will affect the
hegemony of the Turk in Islam. Should Turkey become politically
strong, she might perhaps become a cynosure for the eyes of re-
nascent Islam everywhere, a sort of mother and mistress of churches,
but she must then keep her Caliph or Pope, and that would bode ill
for a liberal state, giving equal treatment to all religions. Without
the Caliph, or with a mere figure-head Caliph, Turkey would be denounced by the reactionary majority of Islam as Liberal and Apostate,
and the spiritual headship would pass to some other land. Of course
a Constitutional Persia and a Constitutional Turkey, and perhaps the
Mussulmans in India might sympathize and stand together. I think
Islam as less committed to a complex dogmatic system could " modern-

ise " more easily than the Papacy. But they have their infallible *corpus juris* tied round their necks. You would set an infallible Pope above this Bible to whittle it away. That is a double-edged sword. The Isidorian decretals were forged in the interests of episcopal liberty; they issued in episcopal slavery. The Popes freed the people from secular tyranny only to subject them to their own. It would be safer to let theological ingenuity find a way out of the letter of the law. It can do anything under pressure. The " Catholic Times " to-day explains that, in the Bishops' oath, *hereticos persequar et impugnabo* means I will follow up the writings of heretics and refute them. Better still, the inevitable spread of history and criticism will destroy the mechanical conceptions of inspiration and infallibility for Islam as for Christendom.'

" 31*st* *Dec.*— The last day of the year. Politically things have gone better this year in Persia, in Turkey, in India, and in Egypt, the cause of liberty has been making progress and Cromer himself. This time last year Cromerism, if not Cromer, seemed to be having it all his own way, now the self-Government of Asia seems an admitted principle, even at our Foreign Office. Grey and even Morley are being dragged at the heels of Eastern progress. Thus ends the year 1908.

" 1*st Jan.* 1909.— An earthquake in Sicily. Messina destroyed.
" 5*th Jan.*— The Government has certainly managed things cleverly in India. A few days before Morley made his speech announcing his reforms they arrested all the leaders of the Opposition, and impounded the chief organs of the extremists at Calcutta and elsewhere, and in this way silenced hostile criticism. Then they got hold of Gokhale to give them a good word, and also, it would seem, telegraphed the headings of Morley's speech in a more favourable sense than the reality (a common Government trick), just as the Moderate Congress began its sittings, thus getting declarations from it of a ' loyal ' character, which, as the Extremist Congress had been forbidden to meet, has been accepted as the unanimous voice of educated India. I suspect that a good deal of the more recent bomb throwing, which has hurt nobody, has been managed by the police, so as to give the Government an excuse for violent measures. In the meanwhile, here in England, Morley had delayed his speech till the last day of the session, so as to prevent his measures being discussed in Parliament. Now the subject of India is dropped, and we shall hear no more of it till the next crisis comes.
" 6*th Jan.*— I have been reading the ' Love Letters of a Portuguese Nun,' the most beautiful ever written; I wish I could be sure of their authenticity, but it seems to me very doubtful. They are too perfect as literature for any Portuguese nun to have written, and nobody has

ever seen the original Portuguese. They were first printed in French in 1769, and their authenticity seems to rest solely on what St. Simon says about them, namely, that they were addressed to the Comte de Chamilly. I should like to believe in them. (*Traduttore tradittore.*)

"*8th Jan.*— There is an article in to-day's 'Daily Graphic' which amuses me. It is a protest against Russian designs in Persia which have reached the stage of threatening intervention there to put down anarchy and re-establish the deposed Shah, with a Constitutional régime at Teheran. What amuses me is the moral indignation of the 'Daily Graphic,' an extreme jingo journal, at Russian insincerity, entirely forgetful of the history of our own intervention in Egypt which was undertaken on exactly the same excuse. The 'Daily Graphic' says: 'That Great Britain should abet so scandalous a conspiracy against the liberties of the Persian people is incredible. The condition of Persia is not one of aimless anarchy but of revolution, and in such a state of things no foreign Government has a right to interfere. That the movement against the Shah is a national one is proved by the revolt of Ispahan. The pretence that the people are not ripe for a Constitution will be most convincingly answered by the Persians themselves, possession is the best title to popular liberties . . . in any case Great Britain cannot be a party to an intervention aimed at a people struggling for freedom, more especially as this freedom is already theirs by Constitutional right.' Every word of this might have been written against our intervention in Egypt in the Spring of 1882, but our Tories are incredible in their self-blindness.

"*10th Jan.* (*Sunday*).— Malony writes an interesting account of affairs at Constantinople and the probability of there being a line of cleavage between the Turkish-speaking and the Arabic-speaking elements in the Ottoman parliament. This was sure to be, but the immediate danger is of a Balkan war pressed on by Austria which will break out in the Spring. Haymerlé, I remember, used as long ago as 1860, when we were attachés together at Athens, to explain to me that it was a settled part of Austrian policy to shift the centre of the Empire eastwards, and make good the imperial title of Emperor of the Oesterreich. They will never allow the Turks to reform themselves in earnest, and all the more now that Russia, beaten by Japan, is no longer so great a military rival. I am writing to Malony to warn him of this and not to trust too much to English help. If given at all it will be restricted to the defence of Constantinople.

"*12th Jan.*— There is a telegram to-day confirming my fear of Austrian intervention in the Spring and of a secret understanding between Austria and Bulgaria for intervention in Macedonia, it can hardly be otherwise. [Compare Dr. Dillon's 'Eclipse of Russia.']

"*14th Jan.*— An arrangement is said to have been come to between

Austria and Turkey which I hope may prove an end to the danger of war, at least for the present, and so Turkey may get breathing time for its internal affairs. In my letter to Malony I advised that no attempt should be made at coercing the tribes in Arabia, and that the Turks should restrict themselves to holding the seaports so as to prevent European aggression. I am sure this is their wisest policy. Eventually there will have to be some form of administrative autonomy in the Arabic-speaking provinces.

" 16th Jan.— To-day is the centenary of the battle of Corunna, where my father was wounded. He had made the campaign with Sir John Moore as junior ensign of the 1st Grenadier Guards, and was carrying the colours at the final battle when he got his wound. He was carried on board the ' Victory,' and came home in her and was landed at Plymouth where he arrived with little hope of recovery, his wound having been neglected from the multiplicity of cases, the calf of one leg had been shot away and he remained lame through life and was obliged to leave the army on account of it, though able afterwards to ride and even walk, shooting with the best. On landing at Plymouth he was taken charge of by his uncle Glanville at Catchfrench and nursed by his cousins there. The miniature of him in scarlet uniform shows him a pale young man just convalescent. He was only sixteen when he joined the Guards, and was sent out straight from Harrow where he had been a younger contemporary of Byron. The campaign, according to my father's account of it repeated to me as a child, must have been carried on in a curiously amateur way. My father, like the rest of the officers, was allowed to take with him his fowling-piece and a brace of pointers for sport on the campaign, and I have now the heavy mahogany desk and still heavier box for papers which were among his baggage. The officers were mounted, but on the retreat, in order to encourage their men, they walked on foot. The pointers were left behind while fording a river which they could not swim, and thus put an end to the sport. ' The Burial of Sir John Moore ' was amongst the first pieces of poetry I learned, my mother explaining to me that the line originally printed ' The foe was suddenly firing ' ought to have been printed ' sullenly ' as it always now is. My father retained a great devotion to Moore. There is probably not another person in England to-day whose father was in the battle.

" 19th Jan.— The ' Egyptian Standard ' is dead. It has been moribund for six months.

" I have been reading Haeckel's Berlin lectures on evolution. They interest me immensely, first because they are quite clear and easy to understand, and secondly, because I see in them my own reading of the Universe and the ' Matter God,' a philosophy I jumped to in 1861, exactly reproduced in the lectures and laid down and proved. I have a paper of that date which I wrote for Usedom who had given me an article in a Berlin scientific journal of the day, on 'Design in Creation,' of which he thought a great deal, and in this paper I give boldly, but with sufficient clearness, my doctrine of pure materialism which Haeckel claims to have been the first to propound in 1863."

I find among my records of that year, 1861, a short paper showing how rapidly my mind had worked, which is worth mentioning here, for it contains as I think the germ of the Monist philosophy elaborated some years later by Haeckel, and which is still the soundest line of materialistic argument. The paper was written not for publication, but in private answer to an article which Usedom had given me to read, taken from the "Zeit" newspaper, in reviewing Ulrici's work, *Gott und die Natur*. The ground taken by the article had been Paley's old one with the precisely same formula our Jesuit censors had condemned at Stonyhurst, "Through the contemplation of created things, by steps we may ascend to God." The writer in attacking evolution, had referred his readers to the evidence of the *Natur-Forscher,* the Naturalist, who in an infinite variety of living things had found the evidence of a creative Mind. For every effect, he had argued, there must be a cause, and that cause is God. Taking up this point in my reply to the writer, I begin by asking, " What is the God he, the *Natur-Forscher,* finds in Nature, an impersonal or a personal God? If impersonal, why dignify the recognized forces, whose existence none doubts, with so high a name? If personal, including the idea of first causer and planner, why *assume* that Nature is an *effect* when that was the very point to be proved?" Why speak of a Creation unless to postulate a Creator? If we find an order in Nature, is it necessary to assume an Orderer? Why should blind forces be necessarily a chaos? Is not every "Law of Nature" the statement only of a continuous fact? Might we not as well assume a Disorderer, were no order there? Order is but the way of material being.

I went on from this to examine what the *Natur-Forscher* showed us; — with his telescope, a Universe apparently unbounded and so infinitely great; with his microscope, a world infinitely divisible, infinitely small; — a Universe without bound in Time, therefore apparently Eternal, eternal in the past as it shows no sign of beginning, eternal in the future as it shows no sign of decay; nothing is added to the material, nothing taken from it; it remains unchanged in substance, varying in form only. What must we reflect, I ask, upon such news as this? Here are the old attributes we assigned to God, " He who is," the Eternal, the Infinite. Why then not the Self-Existent? Neither in Time nor Space has any fact revealed an external power,

Creation is but a metaphysical idea untested by fact. Again, our *Natur-Forscher* will tell us that Mind is a mere phenomenon of yesterday as compared with Matter, that it sprang therefrom by a gradual and sufficiently marked development, but so gradually that it is impossible to note where it began. Is the actinia a fish or a plant? Where does Mind preponderate over Matter in the brute creation?—in the lower forms of Man himself, *der Gipfel der Natur? Der Mensch ist was er isst.*

The second half of my syllogism was this: "It is a law of human reason (that is to say its universal experience) that the simplest cause is the best. We are bound, as philosophers call it, to aim at unity; two reasons may not be admitted where one suffices; it is useless to search for the law of the law. Arrived at the Universe we have the law, then why go farther? Here is no knot. Then do not bring in a God to solve it. . . . Thus we see that Nature does not lead us necessarily to believe in God, that its order is rather a proof of its self-existence than of its dependence. The *Zusammenhang* shows that it hangs only on itself. Disorder must suppose a Disorderer quite as much as an Arranger, etc."

Such was the argument of my paper, which is headed *Nec Deus intersit nisi vindex judice nodus.* I was but twenty when I framed it, a doctrine of pure Materialism with its Monist formula " Mind an accident of Matter "; and when I wrote the doggerel verse called " Body and Soul." It is an argument I still hold unanswerable in logic, and which, in spite of more than one desperate effort in after life, has ever since dominated my reason. Yet though it satisfied my reason it did not all at once content me. On the contrary, its cruel logic oppressed me with a sense of irreparable loss and I still clung, notwithstanding reason, to an unreasoning belief in God as an inherited instinct of my soul. My last words in this very paper, were " For God's sake and His recognition among men, let us avoid the *Natur-Forscher* and hold fast by our eternal unreasonable consciousness of a Father who is in Heaven." The Matter God I had imagined in place of the personal God was a thought that made me giddy when it presented itself first to me, as a demon by my incantations out of the forbidden books that I was reading; and in the middle of my intellectual debauch I found life unutterably sad. But once evoked I could not evade it or the destruction it involved of that other consoling doctrine of Man's supernatural destiny, his life beyond the grave. I found myself as it were deprived of my soul's birthright, proved to be no lawful heir; no child of God with Heaven for my inheritance and eternal bliss for my reward, but just a common " by-blow " of Nature, undistinguishable from her humblest offspring the thousand and one forms of the brute beasts that perish—a humiliating and demoralizing thought.

" *1st Feb.*— Terence Bourke has been with me for the last two days. He is now quite with me about the reform movement in the East and the Future Independence of Egypt. There is better news from Persia, where it is reported that the Shah's army has been defeated by the Constitutionalists, and the three Russian officers in his service are flying for their lives. Browne is issuing a useful pamphlet about the revolution there.

" *5th Feb.*— I have moved to London for some weeks, to Chapel Street. Cockerell dined with me, very happy, he tells me, at Cambridge, enjoying the life there and acquiring influence with the undergraduates.

" *9th Feb.*— In the afternoon came Brailsford, with whom I discussed Turkey, Persia, Egypt, India, and Somaliland. He thinks Grey is practically selling both Turkey and Bulgaria to Russia, as he sold Persia. Brailsford is making a good fight for them in the ' Daily News.'

" *13th Feb.*— There is another crisis in Constantinople, an attempt by Kiamil Pasha, the Grand Vizier, to bring about a reactionary *coup d'état*. He has dismissed the Ministers of War and Marine, and appointed new ones. If the Parliament does not insist on his dismissal the Constitution will go to ruin, as it went thirty years ago, at least so I read the telegrams.

" *17th Feb.*— The crisis at Constantinople has passed off well, the Committee of Union and Progress, with its great majority in Parliament, having forced Kiamil to give in his resignation. This will be an excellent example, and was absolutely necessary if they are not to lose what had been gained by the revolution. The ' Times,' however, and ' Pall Mall ' and other financial papers are very angry, just as they were angry when Sherif Pasha had to resign at Cairo in 1882. There are finance schemes at the bottom of it all now as then, and precisely the same arguments are used about military pressure having been put upon the Chamber, the *pronunciamento* it is called.

" *25th Feb.*— Morley has produced his Indian Bill in the Lords, a great flourish of trumpets about a very small matter. Morley will not be at the India Office long enough to set the reforms really going, and his successors and the Anglo-Indian officials will take care that these are neutralized in detail, as they easily can be. If Morley had been serious he would have brought in his Bill three years ago when he had an all-powerful Radical House of Commons behind him, but he did absolutely nothing, nor would he have done anything but for the boycottings and assassinations. Then he tried the first sham reform, a council of tame landlords, suggested to him by the Anglo-Indian officials, and now he puts forward this other sham suggested by Gokhale. They will lead to nothing. Still the East is awake and moving.

" Conny Lytton has been arrested with other suffragettes, and is to-night in Holloway gaol. She has led a hermit's life at home for the last fifteen years, seldom going away from her fireside, nor from her mother's wing, now she suddenly takes up this suffrage question in its most violent form.

" I hear from Lady C. that the poor King is really very ill, though they do all they can to hide it. The present attack they say dates from his visit to the Kaiser Wilhelm at Berlin, caused by wearing a Prussian uniform too tight at the throat.

" *1st March.*— I have been reading Newman's ' Loss and Gain,' which I read years ago, but had forgotten. In style I think it quite perfect, having the same sort of quiet humour one finds in Jane Austen's novels, but even more subdued. The characters are admirably drawn, and justify themselves in speech and action in a way so many novelists miss, including Meredith ; thus it continues to interest one in spite of its strangely out-of-date controversial Theology. Newman's mind, at any rate in his Oxford days, seems never to have faced the real issues of belief and unbelief, those which have to be fought out with materialism, yet the book was published less than a dozen years before Darwin's ' Origin of Species.' What a gulf separates us from that time, the epoch of undoubting belief in the literal inspiration of the Holy Scriptures. It seems difficult to realize the time when the best and sanest minds in England were arguing about the Apostolical Succession and the Councils of the early Church, unconscious of the wider issues about to be opened, just as they were at Constantinople about the Procession of the Holy Ghost, while Sultan Mahmud was hammering at the gates.

" *5th March.*— Chapel Street. Frank Lascelles lunched with me, and we had a pleasant talk about old times. He has seen much lately of the King, having been at Sandringham and Windsor, and constantly asked to meet his Majesty at dinner and play bridge with him. He gives the same account of the King's short temper that Lady C. did, and of the language he uses to his partners when the cards go wrong. I asked him whether the King was a good player, and he said, ' Oh no, when he has a good hand with his dummy he knows how to make the best of it, but he has no knowledge of where the unseen cards should be.' The King is off to-day to Biarritz, and I gather that there is something seriously the matter with his throat. Frank talked highly of the King's knowledge of Foreign politics, and of his tact and skill in dealing with them. Cromer was Frank's subordinate in Egypt in 1879, and he told me that meeting Cromer the other day, he had remarked, ' I suppose we shall be having the Emperor William talking again in a few days, it seems impossible to make him hold his tongue.' Frank's reply hit Cromer hard : 'Yes, as impossible as it is to make you

hold yours.' Cromer deserved it, for he has been talking a deal of
nonsense since he returned from Egypt about things he does not understand. Lady Cromer has become a suffragette in opposition to her
lord.

"Next we talked about the Sackville case, which is just now much
in the papers. I asked him what his recollection was about Lionel
West's having ever acknowledged his marriage with Pepita, and he
said that he had never heard him acknowledge it, though, of course,
they were together at the Paris Embassy. If he had acknowledged it
Frank would have taken his own wife to call on her. But there was
never question of it. Lionel was the most secretive of men. Some
years ago he had written to Frank to ask him what his memory was
on the point of such acknowledgment, and Frank had answered him
in the sense just given. On the other hand, there were one or two
curious facts within Frank's recollection. Pepita died at Arcachon
during the Commune, while Lionel was in charge of the Embassy at
Paris, and Frank was with him when he received the telegram announcing her death from Lord Lyons, who was at Bordeaux, which
was as follows: '*Votre pauvre femme vient de mourir. Vos enfants
vous appelent.*' Lionel asked him what he ought to do. Could he
leave Paris? It was agreed that certainly he ought to go. Lionel was
terribly overcome, for he was devoted to her, and Frank saw him
off to the Orleans station in a private brougham they found in the
street, for there were no cabs on hire — as an affair '*de vie et
mort.*' This would seem to show that Lord Lyons recognized the
marriage, but nobody actually knew. John Bidwell once put the
question plainly to Lionel, and his answer was 'the person most
interested in knowing knows the whole facts.' Another curious incident, taken in connection with the present case, which is being tried
at Madrid, of a page in the entries of the marriage register having
been torn out, is this: It happened also while Lionel was in charge at
Paris. Sir Richard Wallace had been married at the Embassy, and
Lionel one day looking through the Register, found the entry recording
it and tore out the page, saying, 'the marriage is an irregular one,
and ought not to be here.' Atlee, who was Librarian in charge of the
Archives, was shocked at this, and insisted that Lionel should restore
the page and write an acknowledgment of its having been torn out.
My own impression from all this is that Lionel wished to make a legal
marriage with Pepita, but knew of her previous marriage, and perhaps
went through some form of marriage with her secretly, wishing to
legitimize the children one day, at least in France — that in order to
secure this he got the page of the Madrid register torn out which
would have been evidence against them, indeed of his own first
marriage. It is certain that he entered his later children as legitimate.

Afterwards, however, when he had become Lord Sackville, the succession to the title and estates became a matter of importance, and as his chief love was for his daughter Victoria, whom his marriage could not legitimize in England, for she was born before the secret marriage, and whom he had married to his nephew, he changed his mind and wished to destroy all trace of it and, to make matters surer for his nephew, Victoria's husband, got him to restore the torn out page recording Pepita's first marriage to its place in the Madrid register. This, I think, is the only possible solution of the puzzle consistent with Lionel's honourable character, the love he bore to Pepita, and the love he bore to Victoria. It would account, too, for his nephew's part in the affair, for there would be nothing dishonourable in *restoring* a missing page to its proper place. The truth about the double marriage was probably told by Lionel to his brother Edward and Edward's son, the present peer, and it was agreed between them to say nothing about it, and trust to chance, as the case could not legally arise during Lionel's lifetime. I expect all this will come out when it is tried in the House of Lords. Meynell, however, whom I saw later in the day, declares that the burden of proof will lie with those who deny Lionel's marriage. I am of opinion that the nephew and Victoria will be able to retain their possession of Knole and the title. But it is a most interesting problem.

"*8th March.*— Called on Margot in Downing Street, and finding her alone stayed on for an hour. We talked among other things of Conny Lytton's imprisonment and the doings of the suffragettes, from whom she gets numerous threatening letters, not all of them anonymous, menacing her with bombs and even the murder of her children. She got one only the other day and has to be guarded by police. There were two at the door as I came in and every caller has to be scrutinized, and I had been kept waiting five minutes for this in the hall before I was allowed upstairs. ' Even my brothers,' Margot said, ' have to submit to this.' I told her of a letter I had received about Conny from her sister Betty, and she expressed great concern and asked what she could do to make her comfortable at Holloway. Could she send her things to eat, or what? I told her there was nothing to be done except to keep her in hospital, where she would be well looked after, but I advised her strongly to cease the war with the suffragettes if she could; there was nothing so demoralizing for a country as to put people in prison for their opinions. This could be seen in Ireland, where nobody felt it any longer a disgrace to be in gaol. She said: ' I suppose they will get what they want in the end, though I don't suppose it will do them any good. Henry says that it all depends on the Cabinet, where there is a majority in favour of the suffrage, but he does not see how women could be kept out of Parliament if they got the vote, and that would never do. From this we went on to Francis Thompson and other pleasanter themes till the hour went by, and her doctor calling, I said good-bye. I am very fond of Margot. Years do not change her nor the deceitfulness of politics.

"*10th March.*— Father Tyrrell and George Wyndham came to luncheon with me, and we had an interesting discussion on poetry, literature, and religion. We talked about the proposed new 'Life of Newman,' which is being brought out by Wilfrid Ward. Tyrrell doubted whether it would be a sincere one as to Newman's attitude towards Papal Infallibility, and he told us how a letter from Newman to Lord Emley, dated 1870, had recently been destroyed, in which Newman had spoken strongly against it. It was untrue to say that Newman had never had a doubt since he joined the Church. Newman, he agreed with me, had never really argued out the fundamentals on which Christianity is based, the existence of God and the reality of a revelation. Newman's attitude is epitomized in his 'History of My Religious Opinions': 'I believe in God because I believe in the existence of myself and in my consciousness of right and wrong, all the rest is a matter of development,' or words to that effect. Tyrell to-day was in his most attractive, least aggressive mood.

"After this I went on to Farm Street, which had been so long Father Tyrrell's home, and sat an hour with his once fellow Jesuits, Fathers Gerard and Pollen. Father Gerard showed me his 'History of Stonyhurst,' where we had been at school together, and gave me a little play, an extravaganza he had written for the centenary of the College. He talked also of Alfred Russel Wallace and his opinions, which he thought illogical, and of W. H. Hudson, and of various matters of natural history, which has always been his hobby.

"*11th March.*— John Dillon came to lunch and we discussed Persian, Turkish, and Egyptian affairs, about which he has been worrying the Government in Parliament. We talked also about old times in Ireland, when we two worked together. 'It is astonishing,' he said, 'how all the doings of that time are forgotten. There is hardly a young man in Ireland now who has any knowledge of what the Land League accomplished, or who Michael Davitt was, or what was the Plan of Campaign. The ten years that followed the Parnell split were a political blank. It has left a gap in our history.' I asked him whether George Wyndham's Land Bill had done good or harm? 'Something of both,' he said, 'the people who have taken advantage of it had become better off, but it has not stopped the decrease of population nor the emigration. One thing it has not changed, the ill-feeling towards England is stronger than it ever was.' 'As long as that is the case,' I said, 'things are going right.'

" 12th March.— I was premature in thinking I had converted Margot in the direction of peace with the Suffragettes. She writes in strong language about them: ' I personally think the women criminal as they threaten people's lives and incite the rotters in the street to storm anything and anybody. They are hysterical, full of vanity, and too idle to promote their cause in an intellectual way. . . . Let them have the vote after a general election approves of it, but let us be in peace till then.' I am answering: ' You must not be angry with me for what I said in favour of the Suffragettes. I have no brief for them, nor do I take much interest one way or another in their cause. I should be against them if I thought there was the smallest chance of woman rule in England, but there is none, no more than there is danger of " the Yellow Peril " in Europe, or the " Negro Peril " in America. Women have never ruled men anywhere and never will except indirectly by being better and kinder and less selfish than we are. You are one of these, and if I talked as I did it was because I was afraid you might focus on yourself the resentment of some foolish women who would do you an injury in anger at having been treated criminally for a political offence. I know how violent ideas work in enthusiastic people's minds. That is my chief interest in the quarrel. So absolve me. The whole woman's movement is not worth a curl of your brown head, which may God protect from evil.'

" An Indian gentleman, Mr. Khaparde, called on me with a letter of introduction from Hyndman. Here is a genuine Nationalist of a very different type from Gokhale and Lajpat Rai. He is in England now for the first time to do what he can in favour of his friend Tilak, who has been deported to Mandalay. He brought Tilak's case before the Privy Council but, of course, without result, and he is now trying to get a petition signed in favour of his friend's release, and present it in Parliament. He spoke very openly in an extreme national sense, saying that everyone in India now was for eventual independence, even the moderates, though people dared not say all they thought. ' Even the Mohammedans? ' I asked, and he said there was no real difference of opinion between them and the Hindoos, ' in a revolt they would all be with us. They hate English rule, perhaps more than we do, because, except in the West, it was they, not we, who had been deprived of power by the English. The Moderates,' he said, ' were swayed by motives of personal interest, but they had no following in the country. Gokhale found it to his advantage to play the English game or he would not be where he is. As for Lajpat Rai, his arrest had been a blunder, for he was a man of no importance, the real leaders of the riots being still at large.' He said he found our people here in England very different to what he had imagined them. He had been brought up with the tradition of their being full of good qualities, liberal hospitable, and kindly, he found them entirely engrossed in money-making, and it was impossible to get them to take any interest in Indian questions. His visit to England had convinced him that it was useless to appeal to any sense of justice, there must be more than talk in India before any change could come about and violence there would be. He was scornful about Morley's reforms, they would be useless except to the few hangers-on to the Government who would get places and pay. They would never have been given at all but for the bombs, and the reforms were not intended now to be effective. The Indian Government had got all it wanted — special powers of arrest and imprisonment and of putting down the freedom of the Press. I asked him whether this would stop the revolutionary movement. He said on the contrary, it would accelerate it, they would work on all the same in secret and more effectively. Khaparde has adopted European dress but still wears his red turban; he has great intelligence and his ideas are precise and strongly expressed. He is to come again.

" 16th March.— Poor Peploe Brown is dead. Yesterday his servant Fred called on me and gave me a long account of his master's illness and death. It was a pathetic story told in that odd cockney language 'Fwed' was famous for. I had never heard exactly about Peploe's early life, for great talker as he was, he never spoke of it to anyone, and Fred had only learned it from a brother who came to him in his last days, for all that he had ever said to Fred was that 'God had been hard to him in his youth.' It appears that forty-six years ago, being a young lieutenant in the army, he had married a girl he loved and who loved him, but almost in their honeymoon she had been taken with a fever and died. This destroyed his life. He left the army, wandered about the world, took up painting and adopted Bohemian ways. For the last twenty years he had occupied a studio in York Place, where he died. He had squandered all his money and lived there in the greatest poverty. I knew him through his fellow-painter, Molony, who had made friends with him many years before at Madrid. He was the kindest of men, and when Molony grew old he nursed him and took great care of him notwithstanding Molony's somewhat scornful protests, who used to swear at him as 'that damned fellow Peploe.' About the time Molony died he himself got a return of malarial fever which attacked his spine (much as my case was), and for the last twelve years he has been practically paralysed and has remained day and night sitting in his armchair, never going to bed or lying down, and often at a loss how to get a meal, for he could not sell his pictures. He could not have lived but for his servant Fred's good care, who for the last fifteen years had done early hour to the studio and staying on till eight or nine at night and never a day off during all those years. There was no bed for him in the studio. Peploe spent his lonely nights reading, sometimes Fred said for thirteen hours at a time, though he was almost blind and had to use microscopic glasses applied to his single valid eye. Being alone at night he had had a number of contrivances arranged to put out or light the gas, or to call for help if needed, for he was an ingenious mechanician. Last Christmas he was taken with a strong bronchitis and a violent attack of what Fred called ' his lightning pines ' (pains), but Fred nursed him through it till the late snow and cold had brought it back. He had been left to sleep one evening, and when Fred and the brother came back in the morning they had found him sleeping still, but he was dead. It was then discovered that during the forty-six years since his wife died, and in spite of growing poverty and difficulties of every kind, he had kept all the things that had belonged to his dead wife, her clothes, garments of the days of crinoline, her jewellery, her ornaments and the furniture of the house where they had lived, stored in a magazine for which he had religiously paid rent, also that he had worn her photograph next to his heart, and they found it on him when they found him dead. A number of his smaller treasures they buried with him in his grave, but the poor old clothes and the furniture in the warehouse will be sold. He had sat all these years under his ' Magnum Opus,' an immense picture in the style of Murillo, representing the Adoration by the Shepherds at Bethlehem, at which Molony used to mock in its unfinished state because the angels, represented as sitting in the clouds, with their harps not having yet been filled in, left the expanded fingers in the grotesque attitude that schoolboys use in ridicule, though this had been altered now and the picture with infinite labour finished. It had been bought of him out of charity by a former friend, Lord Bute, who had been kind to him in many ways, but Lord Bute unfortunately had died, leaving the picture there. Lady Bute was now taking it away to put in her chapel. I asked the faithful Fred what had been done for him. ' He had nothing,' he said, ' to leave me, poor gentleman, but he was generous and good to me. I am by trade a mender of china, I mean to set up in a small business, but I cannot get over the loss. I have been with him seventeen years and never a day off. I do not know now where to turn.' [I took two statuettes of camel riders, which Brown had modelled in his later years, off Fred's hands, they are very perfect of their kind, and had been given him with other odds and ends from the studio by the brother. Fred brought them to me a few days later and left me promising to come again, and I promised I would help him to set up his business, but he never reappeared.]

" 18*th March*.— There has been a debate in Parliament on the military danger from Germany, and Frederic Harrison has a long letter about it in the 'Times.' I agree with him that the danger is a very real one of invasion and ruin within no great number of years, only he does not draw the inference I draw, namely, that we should hasten to divest ourselves of our overgrown overseas Empire and devote our naval and military resources to the defence of our own shores. We shall not do this, and we shall perish, as the Roman Empire perished, by trying to hold too much. I am myself the extremest of all possible Little Englanders and would cheerfully return to the 'spacious' days of Queen Elizabeth when we held not a foot of land outside the kingdom.'

[This is the point at which Harrison and I diverged from what had for twenty-seven years been a common political sympathy about foreign affairs into antagonism, his path being towards war with Germany, mine towards a gradual shedding of our " white man's burden " in Egypt and India.]

" I saw George Wyndham in Park Lane. He is pessimistic about the prospects of a German invasion, and thinks it is certain to happen in a few years. The only thing we can do is to go on building ships. Speaking of the plan revealed to me by Usedom in 1866 of bringing Holland into union with Germany and claiming the Dutch Colonies, he told me he had heard the same a good many years ago from Vitelleschi.

" 19*th March*.— Professor Browne came to luncheon. He has made a wonderful fight of it about Persia, but is beginning to be hopeless, as Russian armed intervention seems imminent. He is losing his influence, too, with the Foreign Office. Grey at first listened to him, but is now less willing. ' Grey,' he said, ' is so ignorant, that he hardly knows the Persian Gulf from the Red Sea.'

" 26*th March*.— Things are going badly both in Persia and the Balkans. As soon as the snow melts, both countries will be occupied, the one by Russia, the other by Austria. Grey has thrown over the Persian Constitutionalists, and has declared that the Russians may do what they like at Teheran.

" 29*th March*.— I have been reading Stead's book about himself and Madame Novikoff, poor stuff as literature, a paste and scissors collection of articles of the last thirty-five years; nevertheless I have managed to extract from it certain historical facts of importance, as also to fix the date of Madame Novikoff's visit to Crabbet. It must have been September or October 1876. She was not at that time a really pretty woman, but was lively and anxious to please, singing Russian songs and making the most of herself. I paid her some attention at first, and wrote a song for her to sing to one of her Russian airs, but she ended by boring us before her week's visit was

out. She was too intent on her own particular politics to be interesting
in any other way. As to these she no doubt began by being an
enthusiast, but she also made a business of it later. Her advocacy of
Ismaïl Pasha's claims in 1885 can hardly have been political. She and
Stead were pretty well matched. I find in the book one important letter
which I wish I had had when I was writing my ' Secret History of
the Occupation of Egypt.' It is from Gladstone, written a few days
after the battle of Tel-el-Kebir, and reveals how entirely that great
moralist had thrown himself into the fury of blood-shedding in that
least just of wars. After thanking his correspondent for her congratulations he says : ' We and the whole country are in a state of
rejoicing, and I hope of thankfulness to Almighty God who has prospered us in what I feel and know to be an honest undertaking. . . .
Whether the England of 1882 deserves to be regarded by some in
Russia with a jealous eye, or whether we, too, have been labouring
in the common interests of justice and civilization a little time will
show. We certainly ought to be in good humour, for we are pleased
with our army, our navy, our admirals, our generals, and our organization ! . . . It is hardly more than seven weeks since we determined
to send some 35,000 men to a distance of say 3,000 miles, and it
has pleased God to give us a quick result.'

" This, be it recollected, in regard to a military adventure undertaken
in the interests of the Stock Exchange, and a battle at which 20,000
of the half-armed peasantry of the Nile had been slaughtered.

" *2nd April.*— There is a telegram in the papers, ' Riots at Cairo,
the garrison under arms on account of new Press Law ' ! I should not
be surprised if what has happened in the Balkans may have had some
connection with it. There Servia has had to accept the terms imposed
on her by Austria — backed as Austria was by Germany — while
Servia failed of her expected backing by Russia, a German triumph
and a corresponding defeat for England. There has long been a connection between Egyptian Nationalists and German policy. It is clear
now that Germany is all-powerful in Europe, and that a great slap
has been given in the face to our Foreign Office, and the King and
Hardinge and Grey, who has played his cards badly. I am only sorry
for the sake of reform prospects in Turkey, which are likely to be
jeopardized.

" *3rd April.*— Rothstein came to see me, and we discussed the whole
state of Europe and Asia, where his views coincide closely with mine.
He looks upon Grey's diplomatic defeat as absolute, and Germany's
position as unassailable in Europe. Grey's (or what is the same thing,
the King's and Hardinge's) attempt to get together a Coalition with
Russia and France against the Central German Powers, he regards as
an immense error of calculation, Grey being unaware first of Russia's

military helplessness, and secondly of France's entire unwillingness to fight. Of this Aerenthal and Bülow have taken full advantage, and have not only gained their end in Servia, but have done it in such a way as to make it clear to all the world that their will is law, and that they care not a brass button for either Russia or England. This cannot but react on Constantinople, and it is probable now that the Turks will have to make terms with Austria, perhaps even an alliance, and leave English influence aside. I confess I do not see what else they are to do. It is clear England cannot and will not give them military help, and they are forced back on Kaiser Wilhelm's good will if they are to preserve Macedonia or even Constantinople. Rothstein, however, assures me that no farther advance will be made by Austria yet, as Germany will not be ready with her navy for some years. Then the war with England will certainly be."

This remarkable forecast of the situation marks the point at which Grey's incredible mistakes in diplomatic dealing with Europe and at Constantinople began to declare themselves. That he should have been ignorant of Russia's impotence and have sacrificed to her alliance all his relations with the East, was a cardinal mistake which led to his subsequent gambler's folly of joining France and Russia in the great war.

"Rothstein had hardly gone when letters came from Farid Bey at Cairo and Malony at Teheran. Malony's account of the Persian revolution is more cheerful than any I have yet read. He considers the whole of Persia to be now on the Constitutional side, even Teheran, where the Shah has a few troops. He does not think the Shah can maintain himself even there. Farid complains of new press laws and laws prohibiting meetings. He urges me to raise my voice once more in the Egyptian cause.

"George and Sibell dined with me and Saleeby and his wife, a fortunate combination, and we had a very pleasant evening.

"11*th April* (*Easter Sunday*).— The news of the day is that Swinburne is dead. 'The greatest lyric poet of the English tongue,' is my judgment of him, and perhaps 'our worst prose writer.' Beyond being a poet, he was almost nothing. He never enjoyed his life, wasting his youth on drink and his old age on Theodore Watts. Mrs. Morris says he never was in love with any respectable woman, but Lady C., who knew him well, says that he was once when quite young. His most respectable connection was probably Ada Menken. It was a poor life as far as action was concerned. As a poet, however, he will live when nearly every other of our age is forgotten, for he was a prince of harmony and rhyme and created an entirely new kind of lyric verse. He was seventy-two last week and died of a rapid pneumonia. He ought certainly to have been Laureate after Tennyson, but the old

Queen refused to appoint him because in one of his poems he had fulminated against the Emperor of Russia, and she said that after that it was impossible he could be in her household service. The last thirty years of his life have been stultified in a suburban villa at Putney with Watts-Dunton, who had used him as an advertisement for his own literary trash.

"Last night Belloc looked in on me very woebegone because he had made a rash vow of total abstinence from liquor during the whole of Holy Week, and it was the last day of his sufferings, which he said were beyond endurance. 'It has its uses, however,' he said, 'if only to make one realize how flat the brain becomes when cut off from wine. There are moments when I find myself thinking and arguing almost like a teetotaler, but I will make it up to-morrow after Mass as soon as ever I have received Communion.' I tried to make him break his vow, but in vain, and he went home sadly. [N.B. He wrote the most amusing of all his books, 'A change in the Cabinet,' during that temperate week.]

"*13th April.*— From Blanche Hozier I get a letter, one of the best she ever wrote. In it she describes her doings at Dieppe, where she has established herself in a home of her own. It also encloses a pretty scrap from Clementine at Blenheim, where she is very happy with Winston. Blanche has a real genius for letter writing, women being far better letter writers than men, they chatter more naturally and are less self-conscious. I am reading 'Pepys's Diary,' the unbowdlerized edition, which is extraordinarily good and has something of both these qualities, but is without grace and is coarsely fibred.

"*14th April.*— There has been a counter revolution at Constantinople, and Abdul Hamid has once more got the upper hand. A mutiny of soldiers against their Young Turk officers, joined in by the less liberal Ulema and a reactionary mob, has upset the Committee of Union and Progress, and has forced Hilmi Pasha, the Vizier, and the Ministry to resign. Constantinople is in full reaction.

"*18th April.*— The Young Turks are marching, it is said, on Salonika from Constantinople.

"*19th April.*— Frederick Ryan, late Editor of the 'Egyptian Standard,' has returned from Cairo, and came to-day with the latest news. He is an intelligent young man of the same Irish type as Malony, good, modest, and sincere. He tells me there is a complete split now between the Khedive and Farid Bey, and the Press Law is directed mainly against the Khedive's opponents. Abbas has lost what little popularity he had with the old-fashioned Ulema by his attempt to misappropriate the Awkaf revenues of the Azhar. The students struck for an increase of their bread money needed by the immense rise of prices. All the Cairo newspapers protested against the Press Law except two.

Ryan complains of the lack of business capacity in the management of the Egyptian newspapers. They are also now without a capable leader. Mustapha Kamel died of cancer in the stomach and suffered tortures.

"*20th April.*— The Young Turks under Enver Bey have again got the upper hand and have marched to Constantinople. There is news to-day, though not certain, that the Sultan has abdicated and fled. This will be a splendid triumph. A revolution to be effective must have a basis of force, force which everybody is afraid of and is bound to acknowledge, otherwise it degenerates into mere chaos. I think they will be well advised to bring Abdul Hamid to open trial; it would be dangerous to leave him at large, or even alive in prison.

"*23rd April.*— Things still unsettled at Constantinople except that the Young Turk Party is in power. It is not yet decided what the Sultan's fate is to be. Enver has declared that Abdul Hamid cannot be allowed any longer to reign, though his life will be respected. I fancy the Kaiser Wilhelm is intervening on his behalf. They may be obliged to consider German wishes. Otherwise in cases of this kind ' stone dead has no fellow.'

"*24th April.*— An order has been given for the occupation of Tabriz by the Russian army, the excuse being that the Shah has broken his promise of allowing food to be supplied to the besieged townspeople. The Russians will now certainly occupy Teheran and Northern Persia and administer it in imitation of our English way in Egypt. Massacres, too, are announced in Armenia and at various places in Asia Minor, which may lead to intervention in Turkey. However, let us hope for the best.

"*Later.*— The Young Turk army has stormed Yildiz, though with what result to the Sultan is not known.

"*29th April.*— Abdul Hamid is at last formally deposed and has been sent as a prisoner to reside at Salonika. Reshad Effendi has been proclaimed Sultan Mohammed V in his stead.

"*30th April.*— Lloyd George has brought in a Budget of a rather Socialistic kind, with a beginning of taxing land values and of things more drastic.

"*1st May.*— To Cambridge, where I am staying with Browne at his villa in Trumpington Road. The garden is large, one of those pleasant suburban gardens which run a long way back, but the house is of the plainest Philistine order — very clean, very handsomely furnished, but everything in it commonplace, Browne being the least æsthetic of men. He has made me, however, extremely comfortable, and is in all things else extremely sympathetic. A nightingale is singing close to us.

"He is writing a history of the revolution in Persia, which will include a life of Seyyid Jemal ed Din, as to whom I have promised to write a monograph.   We had several clever young men at dinner, one of them, Mozley, a young Don, Editor of the 'Cambridge Review,' and Somerset, Editor of the 'Granta,' also Cockerell and his wife, and Angela Mackail; also another interesting young man, Malory, and Haddon, the anthropologist.   Browne is, of course, in despair at the Russian march on Tabriz, and believes the English Government has the idea of partitioning the Ottoman Empire as well as Persia.

" *2nd May.*— Spent the day with Cockerell, going with him to the Fitzwilliam Museum where he showed me Rossetti's MS. of the ' House of Life.'   He has asked me for a MS., if I have got one, of ' Esther.'

" *3rd May.*— Back to Chapel Street.

" *7th May.*— All the past week has been glorious at Newbuildings which is in full Spring beauty.   On looking into the bathroom yesterday I heard a twittering and there were three of the swallows hatched there last year, siting together in last year's nest.   They must have been the same, as they were not frightened at my coming in, and the fact of there being three of them also shows it, for if they had been strangers looking for a place to build there would not have been more of them than a pair.

" Yesterday I watched for an hour the throwing of an oak, one of seven old ones they are cutting at the end of Newbuildings Wood.   I wonder whether oaks have any sense of pain, perhaps a little, but it must be very little, just when the sap is rising.   Woodcraft is the most fascinating of all rural work.

" *14th May.*— I have written a valentine for Nellie Hozier:

AN OUT-OF-DATE VALENTINE

NEW is the morning, child,
  Sunrise for thy heart.
Evening, how near its close,
  Sunset for my heart.
Life in its fulness yours,
  Mine but an ending.
Loyal we yet may be
  Love's cause defending.
I have my wisdom, child,
  You your youth's glory.
Each shall find wealth in each,
  In each a story.
High be our fortune's aim,
  He who would win it
Offerings large must bring
  To Fate each minute.

Zealous is Love for love,
　　Grudge not love's kindness.
Ill 'tis for joy to wait,
　　Light lost is blindness.
Ends life as life began,
　　Heart which would meet heart.
Run we and outstrip Time,
　　Child, be my sweetheart.

"*20th May.*— Meredith is dead after a two days' illness, and there is talk of his being buried in Westminster Abbey. The papers say more about him than they did about Swinburne, though as a poet he was really far inferior to him. With the exception of ' Modern Love ' and ' Love in a Valley,' Meredith wrote no verse that was quite first rate, or even much of it readable, and his novels were not, in my opinion, really great. I never could read quite through any of them. They contained, of course, a number of good things and the style was original and natural to the man, but as stories they had little point, and though he sketched out his characters well at starting he had not the art to give them strong dramatic action, nor had he sufficient knowledge of human nature to make their doings credible. He was without a grain of tragic power, still he had a vast number of readers and I see no reason why he should not be buried in the Abbey. Politically I was for the most part in agreement with him, and we interchanged letters on such subjects more than once. I see in the obituaries that the fact of his having been a tailor's son at Portsmouth is evaded by the paraphrase of his having been ' born in Hampshire.' Only the ' Daily Graphic ' gives a photograph of his birthplace at Portsmouth. According to Meynell the fact of his tailoring parentage was the secret trouble of his life.

" It has been glorious weather all the week, and I never saw the view of the downs from the Hilly Seven Acre field so beautiful. But the ash-trees, checked by the frost of 1st May, are not yet in leaf. Most of them are still quite bare while the oaks are in full plumage. Nightingales are rarer this year than usual, probably because it was so bad a breeding season last Spring.

" I have been reading Rousseau's ' Confessions ' again after forty years and do not find my opinion of them much altered. The early part, before he went to Paris and grew famous, is wonderful as a work of art and justifies itself as a young man's confession, for in spite of its crudities, it is beautiful. But the rest is ugliness unredeemed. I fancy my own memoirs, if they are ever read, will give the same impression, though my youth has been prolonged beyond all measure and his ended very early. It was reading Rousseau's ' Confessions ' about the year 1866 that first determined me to write mine and at the same time to have a more satisfactory life to make record of.

"*21st May*.— Meynell came to dinner and gave me an interesting account of his intimacy with George Meredith and of Meredith's romantic devotion to Mrs. Meynell. It began in this way. Some fifteen years ago Meredith had told a mutual friend of theirs that he was curious to know who ' Autolycus ' was who wrote the literary criticisms in the ' Pall Mall Gazette,' and hearing it was Mrs. Meynell, wrote her a very characteristic letter complimenting her on her style of writing and inviting her and him to pay him a visit. ' You will find,' he said, ' my daughter to receive you, she looks at literature through an eye glass.' It happened soon after that an address was being presented to Meredith by the Society of Authors, and Meynell and his wife joined them and went down from London to Burford Bridge where Meredith met them, and when the presentation was over drove her back with him to his house on Box Hill, while Meynell walked. During the drive Meredith asked her whether she was not the author of a certain book, to which Mrs. Meynell, who has a talent for silence, said simply, ' No,' at which he expressed himself disappointed, and then whether she was not Francis Thompson's sister, to which she again said, ' No,' at which he expressed himself doubly disappointed. Nevertheless they speedily made friends and from that time for two or three years he wrote to her, both letters and verses (these have not been published) and professed a special devotion. It was a great interest for both of them and was continued, as said, for several years. Thus Meynell came to know him well, amongst other things his secret trouble about his parentage, which cast a shadow over the novelist's life. The trouble was that his father had been in trade, in fact a tailor, a fact which in his later years he kept jealously concealed, though his first novel, ' Evan Harrington,' published anonymously, had been founded on that very theme. His father had been the well-known naval outfitter at Portsmouth and his grandfather's name had been Melchisedech, as in the novel. Mention is to be found of him in Marryat's ' Peter Simple,' and again in Hardy's letters to Nelson, where Hardy mentions that he had lodging at Portsmouth with ' the tailor Meredith.' It is curious that having attained to the eminence where he was he should have allowed so small a thing to annoy him. Meredith's life latterly was a very lonely one, though he had many friends he had nobody to be quite devoted to him. He had talked of me to Meynell and had once said, which I am glad to hear, ' Blunt is one of the few honest men we have in public life.' He and I had much sympathy on many matters, and I bear him the reverse of a grudge in that, being Chapman and Hall's literary reader, he was the cause of my first little volume of mixed verse and prose being refused publication. He was entirely right, for the volume, except some of the sonnets, was worthless. That must have been in 1867, Robert Lytton having recommended me to send it to Chapman who was then his publisher. It was a fortunate refusal.

"*29th May.*— Newbuildings. It has been a week of glorious weather, the last of a long drought, but now there have been two days of rain. Our only trouble is that the caterpillar has fallen on the oaks, and half the leaves are devoured. This is always the result of frosts at the time the leaves are first unfolding, for the young grub needs a certain cooking of its food, and the frost does this for it, burning the young leaves. It is the same with the apple blight, which is also upon us. Both apple and oak, however, have a natural regrowth of leaves in July and August, which renews their vigour, giving them a second Spring.

"*30th May (Whit Sunday).*— At Newbuildings. Meynell is here. He has just been for Joan of Arc's canonization to Rome. He saw Monsignor Stonor there, and asked whether he had been to the ceremony. 'No,' said Stonor, 'why should I go? She was a Frenchwoman.' The subject of modernism, he said, is now never mentioned at the Vatican. 'The Pope is a worthy, good man, but his pronouncements are all dictated to him by the Cardinals, and he is allowed no initiative.' I showed him a passage in my diary in 1892 relating to Manning's Modernist sympathies in the last years of his life, and he told me that what I had put down was quite correct, and about his death. Vaughan had been his creature, but latterly the Cardinal had grown to dislike him.

"*2nd June.*— I am at Newstead Abbey, brought here by Beauclerk, who is a country neighbour and friends with Lady Chermside and her sister, who own it. He tells me that his father was once offered Newstead Abbey and a part of the estate for £6,000; then, in 1860, old Webb bought it of Wildman, to whom Byron had sold it. Webb had had two sons, but the elder, a charming young man, had committed suicide while an undergraduate at Cambridge, and the younger had emigrated to Australia at the age of twenty-four. So he left Newstead to his daughters, the eldest, Geraldine, having married Sir Herbert Chermside, a retired General, the same Chermside who was in Egypt and Governor at one time of Suakim. The sisters lived together there, the younger, Ethel, who is unmarried, sharing the ownership of the property in a sort of way, one managing everything indoors, the other everything out of doors. They are both pleasant and conversible, and proud of their family possessions, as they may well be, and of its connection with the poet. They have made me very comfortable in rooms overlooking the garden.

" I forgot to say that Meynell, who dined with me last night in London, narrated to me the true version, as he heard it from Meredith, of Meredith's quarrel with Rossetti. They were at breakfast one morning, and had a dispute about a trifle, and Rossetti, resenting something that Meredith had said, told him that if he said it again he would throw a cup of tea in his face. Meredith thereupon repeated it, and Rossetti threw the tea, and Meredith left the house at once and sent for his effects during the course of the day. I have been reading ' Evan Harrington ' coming here in the train, but as far as I have got, it does not alter my opinion of these novels. I fail to take any interest in the characters. They are cleverly sketched, but act very much at hap-hazard. They are not comic enough to make one laugh, and not tragic enough to make one weep. They bore one before one is half through with their doings. There is a good deal of subtle observation and happy phrasing, but it is strange that anyone should call them great novels. Yet I find people comparing Meredith with Shakespeare and all the heavenly host!

" *3rd June.*— I have spent the day very pleasantly, the morning with Miss Ethel Webb, who, in spite of a rugged exterior, is a nice woman, more conversible, I think, than her sister, though both are good talkers. Having that department under her special charge, she showed me everything outside. Certainly Newstead is a splendid domain, through the abundance of its water and the lie of the land about it. The trees are mostly sycamores, to me a new feature, the soil being unsuited to oaks. The celebrated oak sown by Byron only a hundred years ago, is already dying. I have recommended its being pollarded as the best chance of prolonging its life, but the soil is gravel and sand. Yews grow better than any other tree on it, and the tank, which is overshadowed by them, is one of the most beautiful features of a garden I ever saw. Miss Webb pointed me out the place in the garden wall where there had been a postern gate opening formerly towards the forest. This has been built up, she tells me, for centuries, yet her dogs sometimes scratch at it, recognizing it as a doorway still. We sat in her rock garden in the sun, for the wind was cold, and she told me she had acquired the power of making birds understand her, and that the blackbirds and thrushes give her warning of the approach of strangers when she is there alone, as she often is, not wishing to be disturbed. The outside walls of the Abbey have been much spoiled by restoration, done in Wildman's time, who spent £100,000 on it, so that it is difficult to make out quite what is old and what is new, and the windows have been plate-glassed, and otherwise bedevilled, but it is still a splendid possession, much larger and more important than I had at all imagined, and one can well understand how the sudden inheritance of it by Byron and his mother turned their heads, and helped to give him that

exaggerated pride of birth and position which was his weakness. Inside, too, the house is a noble one, in spite of horrible tampering with
the stonework of the Gothic lower story; all, however, might be made
good with whitewash. The cloisters are less injured, and need nothing
but to be let alone. Upstairs, wicked architectural things have been
done, but the great drawing-room is magnificent, one of the finest
state rooms to be found anywhere, and the long corridors are also fine.
The main front has the advantage of looking south. Byron's own little
bedroom, with its simple furniture, is most interesting, unaltered since
his time, but that has been told in the guide books, so I need not
describe it. Beauclerk has returned from his manœuvring, and we
walked again in the garden. He starts for Central Asia next week,
to remain away a year. He is a very attractive young man, with, I am
sure, an excellent heart. The feeling of the house is strongly against
Lady Byron in the old family quarrel.

" *4th June.*— Back to London early, much pleased with my visit to
Newstead and the good ladies, my entertainers there.

" Sabunji came to dine with me. I had not seen him since 1895, I
think. He has become the type of what he doubtless was till the other
day, a Yildiz Palace spy, a little furtive old man dressed in black with
a black skull cap on his head, a jewel in his shirt front and another
jewel on his finger. He has come to London, I imagine, on some business of intrigue, and to me partly to find out what my opinions are,
partly to get my help in a publishing project he has in hand, a ' History
of all Religions.' I got a deal of useful information from him about
men and events at Constantinople. He tells me he continued to hold his
place at Yildiz and draw his pay or pension till a month ago, but he is
now deprived of it in common with the rest of the Palace employés.
His position with the Sultan Abdul Hamid, which had been originally
that of Reader for him and *précis* writer of the European Press, had
latterly become one of tutor to the young Prince Burhan ed Din, the
Sultan's favourite son, whom he describes as very clever, and knowing
French, English, German, and Italian, besides Turkish, Persian, and a
little Arabic. The fact of his loss of income by the Sultan's deposition
naturally colours Sabunji's views, and he is gloomy about the prospects of Turkey under the new *régime*. I asked him about the revolution of last year, and the counter-revolution of two months ago. As
to the first, he says the Sultan was in complete ignorance till it happened, and this, doubtless, was the fact. The counter-revolution was
got up not by Abdul Hamid or Burhan ed Din, but by an intrigue
between Az ed Din (son of Sultan Abdul Aziz, who is heir to the
present Sultan according to the law of succession), and the Russian
Embassy, the latter being jealous of the influence the English Embassy had acquired under Kiamil Pasha. The German Embassy had

nothing to do with it, nor was it true that the Sultan had distributed
money to the troops to make them revolt against their officers.   The
Sultan had given money for the foundation of a Madrasa (public
school) which had been handed over by the Ulema, who had received
it for the Madrasa, to the troops.   This sounds like an excuse.   What
probably is true is that there was a strong reactionary party at Stam-
boul, which appealed to the soldiers on religious grounds.   Sabunji
declares that this feeling was so strong that it was intended to have a
general massacre of Christians, and that this was only prevented by
the rapidity of the march on Constantinople from Salonika.   Had the
massacre taken place there would have been European intervention and
a partition of Turkey.   He declares that there was a settled plan for
the partition already agreed to, according to which England was to get
Syria as well as Egypt; France, Tripoli; Italy the Albanian coast; Austria, Salonika; and Germany, effective administration of the railway
line from Broussa to Bagdad, with ten kilometers on either side of it,
while Russia was to get the northern part of Asia Minor.   [Compare
text of the secret treaties afterwards discovered at St. Petersburg and
published 1917.]   He says, too, that there was an intrigue between
Izzet Pasha and the Khedive Abbas for getting Abbas acknowledged
Caliph, and that the English Government favoured it, intending to use
the Khedive as a first·step towards an Arabian Caliphate under English
protection.   This, of course, is the old idea which he (Sabunji) with
many others, held in 1881, as shown in my ' Future of Islam.'

"9th June.— Chapel Street.   Met Cunninghame Graham in the Park
and talked with him of Grey's speech at the Imperial Press Conference,
which will need, I think, a manifesto from some of us to the Mohammedan world, for I read it as announcing a definite intention to retain
Egypt.   'English policy,' Grey says, 'is to keep all we have.'

" It is a question now for the Ottoman Empire to make up its mind
whether in the coming conflict it is to side with England or with Germany.   On the whole an alliance with Germany would probably be the
lesser risk of the two, seeing how Egypt and now Persia have been
betrayed by England, and how India is held by us in permanent bondage, also England's power is apparently on the wane, while Germany is
increasing.

" Lady Gregory came to luncheon, and we went after it to the Court
theatre together.   She has just been for three weeks at Venice, staying
there with Lady Layard.   She gave an amusing description of the
arrival one day at luncheon while there of two little ' maids of all
work' rather shabbily dressed, which proved to be Queen Alexandra
and her sister the Empress of Russia, who had arrived together on a
yachting cruise, and had come to call without ceremony.   The Empress,
Lady Gregory says, looks now much the older of the two, for the Queen

is extraordinarily well preserved, whether by nature or art. They
stayed on chattering the little banalities of Court conversation for
half-an-hour with the German accent Lady Gregory imitated well. At
the theatre we found Yeats, who talked to us between the acts. He
told me he had been converted to my use of the Alexandrine metre
for plays in verse, but that he had such a difficulty in finding rhymes
that a rhymed play would take him two years to write. The pieces
we saw given were 'Devorgilla' and the 'Playboy of the Western
World.' The 'Playboy,' I fancy, must have been a bit bowdlerized
from the original version, or else it was not very intelligible to an
English audience, but certainly here in London it seemed a very harmless bit of broad farce which could shock no one. The Irish of it was
such that a good deal of the dialogue was difficult to catch. I found
it immensely amusing and quite admirably acted. The principal girl's
part was done by a sister of Sarah Allgood, who had been engaged to
Synge. Of Sarah Allgood herself I thought less, she was more conventional. The house was half empty, and there was little encouragement given to the actors. Yeats is beginning to get fat and sleek;
he has cut his hair and his cheeks have a pink colour, and he is well
dressed, as a prosperous theatrical manager should be.

"*22nd June.*— George Wyndham came. He is rather out of it just
now in Parliament as he takes no very strong interest in the Budget
dispute, believing the Radical bark to be worse than the bite. I do not
expect the Lords will reject the Budget, as some of the extremists would
have them do. In regard to the land they would be on firm ground,
for the Radical view on the land question is essentially unsound, unless
the full Socialist doctrine be admitted, *la propriété c'est le vol.*

" To the Tate Gallery, which has revived in me many old memories.
The Vernon Collection, which I remember in Marlborough House
when I first came to London in 1856, and used constantly to visit, the
early pre-Raphaelite pictures, most of which I saw about the same time
hung in the Academy, and numbers more. It is wonderful how they
have improved with age, or is it with pictures as it is with a sonnet,
which seems better if one has once known it by heart and half forgotten.

" *24th June.*— Some Persians called on me, introduced by Rothstein,
poor helpless people, knowing hardly a word of any language but their
own and Russian. They had come to London to try and enlist English sympathy for their Constitutional cause.

" *28th June.*—Halil Hálid and Meynell dined with me. Halil has
been with Mukhtar Pasha since his stay of three days in England as
Extraordinary Ambassador, but he had very little to tell me, being
affected with pseudo diplomatic reserve, except that the question of
Egypt was not raised or mentioned by Mukhtar. Cromer, he tells

me, still influences the Foreign Office and was put to sit next to Mukhtar at a dinner given to the Marshal.

"*3rd July*.— We had our Arab sale to-day. Bidders few, but the financial result not unsatisfactory.

"A most important thing has happened in connection with India. Sir Curzon Wyllie has been assassinated by a young Indian at the Imperial Institute. The 'Manchester Guardian' and other Liberal papers are endeavouring to persuade themselves that the assassination is not political; but this is nonsense. It has quite obviously been planned as part of a new departure and almost certainly by Krishnavarna, whose 'Indian Sociologist' of last week contains clear indications of what might be expected. The whole English Press is united in its religious horror at the crime, forgetting how it applauded exactly such crimes in Italy fifty years ago, and in Russia the other day. Krishnavarna's position is precisely the same as Mazzini's then was, whom we all now justify since his plan of assassination led to the liberation of Italy, and if ever people had excuse for means of this kind it is the people of India.

"*8th July*.— Gallifet is dead. I remember him well in Paris in the sixties when he used to play tennis at the court in the Tuileries Gardens, a good looking *sabreur,* with an irresponsible tongue. His wife was one of the pretty women of the second Empire, but he had no respect for her, and I have heard him crack his garrison jokes about her without reticence. She had her lovers, and he his mistresses, but made no concealment of his contempt for her. All the same he was a gallant fellow and has died in deservedly high repute with his fellow-countrymen, for what he was, a true French aristocrat of the old-fashioned fighting and love-making eighteenth century days.

"I went to a party at Button's house at Fulham where his sister Eva was entertaining, a garden party with tea out of doors. Button has made a very beautiful place of it with his marble columns and gateways and well-heads, like a villa at Pompeii. What especially helps the effect is that there are broad walks crossing each other covered with paving stones, the squares enclosed by them being of grass. If I were a millionaire I would certainly buy the whole *en bloc*. Most of the Wyndham clan were there.

"*9th July*.— To an evening party at Stafford House, a really charming entertainment of, perhaps, 200 people, which in those immense rooms looked like a family party, where I met a number of people I had not seen for years, with a few foreign guests, among them Pierre Lôti. The last is a diminutive dapper little Frenchman, very correct in his get up, with scarves and decorations, and a rather aggressive pose. Remembering his joint letter of two years ago written to me,

with Mme. Adam, I got the Duchess to introduce me to him, but found
him less amiable than I had reason to expect. We spoke of Mme.
Adam and Mustapha Kamel, but his tone about them was not enthusiastic, and gave me the impression that there must have come a coolness
between him and Mustapha since the day when they were photographed together. I mentioned having read Mustapha's letters to Mme.
Adam recently published, which are really very pretty, and in which
the photograph is reproduced, but my remark brought no response at
all. Perhaps their publication had displeased him. Then we were
separated by other claimants on his attention. He did not impress me
favourably." There was much else of an amusing nature connected
with this party but which I cannot transcribe here.

"*10th July.*— Good old Lord Ripon died last night at half-past eight
in the evening. One of the few honest men in public life, and the
only Whig who ever showed real sympathy with Eastern liberty.

"I am reminded by having met Pamela Plowden last night of the
beautiful lines Harry Cust once wrote to her, and which I think have
never been published except in an ephemeral 'Book of Beauty.' I
transcribe them here.

> Beautiful face!
> Is your heart broken that you look so sad?
> Is there no heart on earth that once made glad
> Your heart, to hearten yet your flower of grace?
> Is God untender towards you? Or can Man,
> Loving such dear eyes,
> Or, save despairing
> For too much caring,
> Grudge his uncrownedness in the race he ran,
> And squandered life and lived and lost the prize?
> They pay the worthiest cost
> Whose lives for you were lost.

"*13th July.*— Spent the day at Caxtons with Professor Osborne,
head of the Natural History Museum at New York, and his daughter.
He is a highly intelligent man, a pupil of Huxley's and is writing a
book on horse history. He has read my controversy with Professor
Ridgeway on the origin of the Arab horse in Arabia and takes my
side in it, holding the Arab to have been the descendant of a distinct
wild breed in the Peninsula. He wants the United States Government
to start an Arabian breeding stud in some of the dry districts of the
Western States.

"*16th July.*— Late on Tuesday night I got a telegram from Meynell
saying that Father Tyrrell was dying at Storrington, and this morning the 'Times' announces his death. His loss is a great one, both
personally to me and to the world at large, though perhaps for himself

it is a happiness. Miss Petre has very sensibly written to the 'Times' announcing the fact of his having died at her house, and giving the details of the last rites administered. It seems to have been a paralytic stroke, for he had lost the power of speech, and I fear his ecclesiastical enemies will hold this to be a judgment of Heaven upon him, but it will save him at least from the reproach of having 'recanted his errors' in the face of death. I have telegraphed to Miss Petre and shall certainly, if permitted, attend his funeral as an act of sympathy with a persecuted man who was also, I am glad to think, my friend.

"*Later*. I drove over to Mulberry House. Miss Petre had gone out to the monastery, but her sister, Mrs. Powell, took me into the garden house and showed me the poor body. It was laid out in the tiny cell which had been his sleeping place, hardly more than a cupboard, ten feet, perhaps, by five; there was scarcely room to squeeze in between the very narrow bed and the wall. There lay the dead heresiarch, as sad a little shard of humanity as ever my eyes saw. I could not have recognized it as the man I had known so brilliant in his talk, so full of combative life, or indeed, hardly as a man at all. The face was shrunk and the features seemed to have fallen in though he had been only thirty-six hours dead, for he died at nine yesterday morning, and the body with its poor small fingers was more like an accidental handful of shapeless clay than anything that had been alive. Pious hands had clothed him in surplice and stole, as befitted the priest he was, and there were two tapers lighted at his head. I knelt a minute or two beside him and recited a 'De Profundis' and kissed the hem of his garment, or rather the stole, and rose and went out, moved, as one could not help being moved, to tears of pity. It was so utter an ending. I had some talk with Mrs. Powell, a vigorous, unemotional woman of fifty, who gave me the details of his death and of how the Archbishop was raising objections to his being buried as a Catholic with full funeral rights. Her sister was out on this very business at the monastery, but would be back immediately and she urged me to await her. I occupied the half-hour which elapsed in paying a visit to Mrs. Lucas, Meynell's married daughter, who has taken rooms in a farm house, Chantry's, just outside the village. When I came back I found Miss Petre had returned and she received me in her room upstairs. I had been prepared to find her altered by this sudden misfortune, but she met me with her usual cheerful smile and without a trace of sadness on her face. There was no paleness on her cheeks or trace of tears, and she talked at once in her open, straightforward way about all that had happened and was happening. She is a wonderfully wise, courageous woman, for it is certain that Father Tyrrell's death must be a terrible grief to her, and loss in every way. She talked of him simply as a child might talk, but with the wisdom of

a woman, the courage of a man. What she told me is this: Three
months ago there had been some question of Father Tyrrell's health
and he had seen a doctor, some kidney trouble, but the doctor thought
little of it. It was while he was staying at Clapham, nor did he think
much of it himself. He came back to Storrington for his summer
holiday at the end of last month. She thought him overworked, for
he was writing a final apologetic, added to his great daily correspondence. It was not till a week after, that one day he complained of his
head, while at dinner, and rose to leave the table and, as I understand,
fell. Still, for a day, she did not recognize it as serious. ' I am
naturally of a sanguine disposition,' she said, ' and thought he would
recover. He complained of violent pains in the head, and could not
speak plainly, but I did not recognize it for what it was. Then he got
worse. I was with him for forty-eight hours without leaving him
before anyone came to help nurse him. He suffered terrible pain
continuously till he died.' Three doctors have since declared him to
have had Bright's disease and the stroke to have been a consequence,
the breaking of a blood vessel on the brain. She repeated to me what
there was in her ' Times ' letter about his having received the last
sacraments. ' I sent it,' she said, ' because I knew there would be all
sorts of stories told, and I thought it best to let the truth be known
at once.' She was pleased when I told her how wisely, in my opinion,
she had done. ' It was, perhaps, fortunate,' she said, ' that he could
not speak, as it spared him explanations, and enabled his friend Abbé
Brémond, to administer the sacraments and give him absolution, also
it will at least prevent any false account of his having at the last
moment made recantation of his opinions.'

" She went on to speak of their difficulties since with Archbishop
Bourne, and she spoke strongly of the little moral courage existing in
the world, and how all were afraid of undertaking independent responsibility. The Prior of Storrington was anxious to be kind, but
he was without courage, and it seemed as though he would not dare
give a Catholic burial, although he had administered extreme unction.
I suggested that the Crawley monks might be more bold, and it is
settled that we are to apply to them if others fail.

" *17th July.*— The ' Times ' has the following : ' At Mulberry House,
Storrington, the Rev. George Tyrrell, aged 48, fortified by the rights of
the Church. R.I.P.'

" Meynell arrived for the week-end. He has been to the Archbishop's house in Westminster to discuss the case of Tyrrell's burial.
The Archbishop himself is away, having gone abroad to Rheims to
take part in the ceremonials connected with Joan of Arc's canonization,
but he saw Butt the coadjutor. He tells me Miss Petre's letter to the
' Times ' has put them in a terrible fix. Bourne is himself much in

sympathy with the Modernists, and especially with Father Tyrrell. He
had once said, ' I had rather my hand withered than lift it against
Tyrrell '; nor is Butt otherwise than friendly. But the position is
this : Tyrrell, though not technically excommunicated, was cut off from
the sacraments until he would recant three propositions, which he had
not recanted. If nothing at all had been said, the fact of his having
on his death-bed received absolution and extreme unction might have
allowed them to presume a recantation, but Miss Petre's letter makes
this difficult or impossible, and the Archbishop if appealed to must
forbid Catholic burial. To me, however, it seems that in the first
place Miss Petre's letter to the ' Times ' is not authoritative, however
true what it says may be; secondly, burial not being a sacrament while
penance and extreme unction are sacraments, it would be straining at
a gnat to refuse the first, the rest having been swallowed. Meynell
thinks that if the worst comes to the worst it would be best to bury
him at Newbuildings where Abbé Brémond could perform the service,
trusting to a change in ecclesiastical opinion for his subsequent translation to consecrated ground. Meynell cited it as curious that he should
find himself connected with this case as he had been with that of
Mivart. In Mivart's case Meynell had appealed to Cardinal Vaughan,
who left the decision to three of his canons, two of whom decided
against Mivart's being given Catholic burial, so Vaughan forbade it;
but on Vaughan's own death-bed he was troubled at the thought of this
decision. ' I was wrong,' he said, ' in the Mivart case.' And, in fact,
Mivart's body has since been removed (it was done privately at night)
and reburied according to Catholic ritual in consecrated ground. It
is also curious that Bourne should be just now away at Rheims, officiat-
ing at Joan of Arc's canonization; Joan of Arc, who was refused by
the Bishops of her day burial at all, her ashes being scattered to the
winds lest any relic of her should be preserved, and over the place of
whose martyrdom were ecclesiastically inscribed the words ' Heretic
and Sorceress,' yet she is to-day being worshipped on all Catholic
altars. The same might happen, who knows, to Father Tyrrell. The
Archbishop's position is made more difficult because his leanings towards Modernism have delayed the sending a hat to him from Rome.

" The ' Times ' announces the abdication of the Shah Mohammed
Ali and the triumph of the Constitutional régime in Persia, which is
acknowledged by the Russian and English Governments. This is a
victory stolen out of the fire, and Browne may justly claim as his the
whole success. But for him Persia would most certainly have been
annexed by Russia, or rather put under Russian tutelage after the
precedent of Egypt.

" 18*th July*.— After luncheon I drove Meynell to Storrington, where
we found Mrs. Powell. The present situation is that they have got a

telegram from Brentwood, the Petre estate in Essex, to say that the priest there will bury Father Tyrrell; so they consider the matter settled, and Miss Petre has gone to Brentwood to make sure. The funeral will be on Wednesday.

"Mrs. Powell gave us a more detailed account of Father Tyrrell's illness. He had had trouble with the kidneys for some time, but did not pay much attention to it, and his doctor did not consider it very important, though now, since his seizure, all agreed it to have been Bright's disease. He spent the early Spring at Clapham, but when her sister returned from abroad he also returned to Storrington, but had left again for London till the end of June, when he once more came to Mulberry House for the summer. He had been greatly over-worked and felt his quarrel with Rome more deeply than appeared on the surface. He was subject to violent headaches, when he would retire to his own room for twenty-four hours at a time, but in the intervals was cheerful and seemed full of life. His general health had improved latterly.

"*20th July.*— Tyrrell's case seems to have been referred to Rome, and the burial service absolutely forbidden. It is announced to be at Storrington to-morrow, I presume in the parish graveyard, so I go back to Newbuildings to-night. Tyrrell's little book of poems is in print at Elkin Mathews', though not yet published. Meynell took me there and we saw it: 'Versions and Perversions,' with 'To W. S. B.' on the title-page. They gave us a copy of it not yet bound.

"I lunched with Harry Cust and his wife and George Leveson Gower, and Harry's young nephew (Storrs), who has some place in Egypt, a very intelligent youth.

"John Dillon spent an hour with me, and we discussed India and the ethics of assassination. He said he had always been opposed to it, except where there were secret societies, which could not be maintained without it against members who turned traitor. I told him I would send him my 'Canon of Aughrim,' which he said he had never read. He will try and bring forward the case of the Egyptian press persecutions on Thursday, when they have the Foreign Office vote. There may be some chance of getting it discussed now that the Persian question seems in way of settlement. He says, however, that there are not three members in the House that interest themselves about Egypt — and this is true.

"I went down by the last train to Newbuildings, nor do I intend to return to London this summer.

"*21st July.*— The day of Father Tyrrell's funeral. I drove over to Storrington, and arrived at Mulberry House half an hour before the contingent of mourners from London, and had some talk while waiting with Freddy von Hügel, now an old man much grizzled, and the most

distinguished of the lay Modernists in England, and with his daughter,
a devout disciple of Tyrrell's. She was greatly pleased with his lines.
'Two Chambers hath the Heart,' when I recited them to her. The
London friends having arrived, we formed procession some forty or
fifty persons, to the grave, which was in Storrington parish churchyard, a pleasant place under the Down where Tyrrell had been in the
habit of walking and reciting his breviary not twenty yards away from
the Catholic Chapel, just outside the wall, symbolic, so I thought, of
the position into which Tyrrell himself had drifted. Abbé Brémond
read the funeral prayers in English, and then read an address he had
very carefully composed for publication, a moderate and worthy presentment of his poor friend's religious attitude towards either Church,
the English or the Roman. Miss Petre was to me the chief interest
at the grave. She was evidently much moved, and her face showed
signs of weeping, but she stood there valiantly with her sisters and
two little nieces following the prayers out of a book with them and
giving the responses aloud. I shook hands with her when all was over,
and she asked me into the house, but I did not care to face the crowd
there, and drove straight home.

"23rd July.— The Foreign Office vote was taken yesterday, the whole
time allotted to it being occupied discussing the Czar's visit, so that
Dillon could say nothing about Egypt. It is impossible to get any
attention in the House of Commons either about foreign affairs or about
India.

"24th July.— Dingra, the slayer of Sir Curzon Wyllie, has been
condemned to death, having made no defence, beyond a dignified justification of his act as one of political warfare. When the judge, the
Lord Chief Justice, had passed sentence on him that he should be
hanged by the neck until he was dead, 'Thank you, my lord,' Dingra
said. 'I am proud to have the honour to lay down my humble life for
my country.' Also, before the sentence, he had said: 'You can pass
sentence of death on me if you like, it is perfectly illegal. You are
all-powerful and can do what you like, but remember, we shall have our
time.' No Christian martyr ever faced his judges more fearlessly or
with greater dignity. I discussed his case with Kháparde, who is here
for the week-end, his first country visit in England. He is as full of
admiration as I am of Dingra's courage. We agreed that if India
could produce five hundred men as absolutely without fear she would
achieve her freedom. It was recorded in the medical evidence at the
trial that when arrested, Dingra's pulse beat no quicker than was
normal, nor from first to last has he shown any sign of weakening.

"25th July (Sunday).— Kháparde (Mrs. Russell, Miss Cockerell,
and Miss Nussey being here) gave us a most interesting account of
his religious views. He is a Theosophist, having adopted their tenets

as a young man, and he explained, better than I have ever heard it
treated, their teaching of the relation between mind and matter. He
is an admirable expounder, expressing himself slowly in English, but
with extreme clearness and logical exactness, seizing at once the meaning of each question put to him, and evading nothing in reply. By
birth he is a Mahratta Brahmin who has broken his caste. His father
was a Yogi, and he gave us an excellent account of him and the high-
minded simple life he led; how he passed his days sitting for the most
part in the shade of trees in contemplation during his later life, though
earlier he had been in Government service as Deputy Collector, or
something of the sort. His grandfather had been a banker and rich,
but dying his wealth had been lost, and the father had to reconstruct
it and revive the bank. Kháparde himself was brought up in good
circumstances, living on lands of his father's own, with horses to ride,
and a herd of cows. He had made his education in the Government
College in Bombay, and while there had joined the Theosophists. He
is now fifty-six. He reverences Mme. Blavatsky and highly esteems
Mrs. Besant, though the latter, he says, has gone wrong lately on the
political question. Under these ladies' influence he learned to eat meat
and drink wine, but later returned to his vegetarian food. His philosophy is extremely interesting, but it always surprises me that the doctrine of the eternity of the soul renewing itself by passing from body
to body should be so absolutely believed as it is by men so enlightened
in science. In reply to his exposition I set before him my own philosophy of the nothingness of man, a mere scum on the surface of our
little earth. He acknowledges the truth of this, but supposes that in
other worlds of the vast universe a higher kind of animal body exists
into which our souls may transmigrate before they come to perfection.
'Only a few souls, such as Jesus Christ or Buddha,' he said, 'can have
attained to perfection on this Earth.' Arguing on these lines he had
a great success with our house party, his discourse having become a
regular lecture, including Miss Lawrence and Miss Butcher and my
grandchildren, who listened with open eyes fixed on his dark face and
crimson turban. In the course of it his exposition between soul and
body were so closely the same as those I had put into verse fifty years
ago that I recited a stanza of it to him:

> I am but by your union.
>   With either soul or body lost
> All perisheth. Then work ye on
>   Together, friends not corpse and ghost.
> To live and be is my sole boast.
>   Learn this, alone ye nothing can.
> Yet both together ye make Man.

" This he declared to be an inspired verse. Later he displayed great intelligence when I showed him my Arab horses, chestnut with four white feet and a blaze, being, he said, the favourite Indian colour, especially that dark chestnut (Feluka's colour) which he recognized just as Mohammed Abdu had done as *kumeyt*.

" *26th July.*— Belloc tells me that the government is seeking an excuse to treat Dingra as a criminal lunatic instead of hanging him. That traitor Stead had a letter in yesterday's ' Observer ' urging this on the ground that it would punish him more. I have written to Dillon showing how dangerous a precedent it would be, as admitting the right of an English Government to inflict lifelong torture on its political enemies when it finds one brave enough to face death and defy them. Kháparde says that certainly Dingra would prefer death, because he would then at once re-enter life in a higher sphere of being, instead of having to wait twenty or thirty years in prison for it, with the risk of becoming deteriorated by the too long persecution.

" *29th July.*— The papers are full of flying feats, a Frenchman, Blériot, having flown across the Channel. How interested Robert Lytton would have been in this! He always maintained forty years ago that the true solution of the flying problem lay in a machine which should be heavier, not lighter than air.

" *30th July.*— There has been something of a revolution in Spain, caused by an unsuccessful piece of filibustering by the Spanish Government in Morocco. The people at Barcelona and Madrid refused to go on with the War there. It is an excellent symptom of anti-jingo feeling, and will do good everywhere, though it will also work to the profit of Socialism.

" *1st Aug. (Sunday).*— Belloc and Basil Blackwood came to luncheon; Belloc in one of his most talkative moods. He tells me Father John Pollen was with Tyrrell the day before he died. Belloc was at Mulberry House, too, though not inside Tyrrell's room. There has been a great dispute in the papers as to the true facts, but Pollen's visit is mentioned by none of the writers, unless it be as ' the other priest ' who gave him absolution.

" *15th Aug. (Sunday).*— We have Professor Cockerell and his wife here for the week-end with Meynell and again Kháparde. Kháparde, who was born a native of the Berar province of Hyderabad, has told me the story of how the province was finally made over to the Calcutta Government on a perpetual lease in 1903.[1] Kháparde's account is that when Curzon was at Hyderabad in that year he was invited to dine with the Nizam, he being on one side of the Nizam and Lady Curzon on the

---

[1] See my " India under Ripon " for an account of the intrigues by the Indian Foreign Office to get hold of the Berars.

other, they got him to give a verbal promise that a lease should be granted, the Nizam being partly drunk at the time. In the morning he would have backed out of his promise, but Curzon threatened to depose him and forced him to sign the document desired. Thus Lord Ripon's promise that the Berar province should not be taken was evaded by the officials. The Nizam is said to have been so angry at what had been done that he refused to take food for four days. Now there is a new intrigue, which has for its object to get hold of the two other Provinces, Arungabad and Parabhani, they being, after the Berars, the richest of the Nizam's territory. I asked Kháparde his opinion of the Viceroys who succeeded Lord Ripon. Of Dufferin he said he was a diplomatist, who gave fair words but did nothing. On arrival he announced that he intended to carry out Lord Ripon's policy, but he made no step in advance of the Municipal Councils, Lord Ripon's first instalment of self-government. Lords Lansdowne and Elgin also did nothing, letting the officials have their own way. He holds Curzon to have had the ambition to make himself Viceroy for life of India, and to revive the state and splendour of the Mogul Emperors. The great Durbar of 1903 cost £5,000,000 sterling, though only £50,000 figured for it in the budget, the deficit being made up by charges credited to the Public Works Department. This was made easy by the arrangement according to which the provincial budgets are subject to approval and alteration at Calcutta, so that extra expenses can be charged on these if required by the Imperial Government. In Curzon's time all the Councils were officialized, and the management centralized, so as to destroy their independence. He told how the famine accounts had been manipulated in 1900 in Berar and the Hyderabad state. During the famine no accounts were kept by those entrusted with the distribution of relief, the money wanted being drawn from a fund at Hyderabad, which consisted of the surpluses of six or seven years, paid from the Berars and kept there in hand, but when the famine was over those who had administered the relief were called together and were told to write out accounts, so much for one thing, so much for another, so as to make up the sum taken from the Fund; thus there was no real check at all upon the expenditure.

" I asked him about loyalty to the Crown. At this he smiled. There was at one time, he said, a certain feeling towards Queen Victoria, on account of her proclamation of 1858, but all that was long past. The Nizam was bitter about the Berars, and had no love at all for the Imperial Government or for the present King. The Duke of Connaught had good manners with the Indian princes; in this a great contrast with others, but his appointment as viceroy would not alter the situation now. As to the Mohammedans there would be difficulty arising from them in a restoration of self-government, except in the Punjaub, where the feeling between the two communities, Hindoo and Moslem, was still very bitter.

" This afternoon we had quite a garden party, over twenty guests sitting down to tea in the Jubilee Garden. Among them Miss Frances Jennings, who came with one of the Meynell girls. Miss Jennings is a most interesting girl, pretty in the Burne-Jones way, with a rose-leaf complexion, strange blue eyes and flaxen hair. Meynell tells me she is of Welsh origin, but she herself said her father was from Cumberland, her mother from Devonshire. She came up quite young to the Slade School in London, where everybody, girls and boys, fell in love with her, and she having a romantic fancy for Olivia Meynell, became a Catholic, inflicted on herself all kinds of austerities, and wanted to be a nun. In the meantime her drawing at the Slade School became famous, and she went over to Paris to study art there. She was alone, and failed to find a lodging in an inn in the Quartier Latin, and was picked up by a charitable Englishman there, who has ever since wanted to marry her. Then she returned to England, and last Spring was found by her friends sitting outside St. Etheldreda's church in the rain with severe influenza, and she has since been paralysed. I had some talk with her. She has all the look of a Saint, with strange unearthly eyes which seemed as if looking at spirits in the air, and a wonderful ecstatic smile and still more wonderfully sweet voice; her features rather irregular with a wide unshaped mouth, I can imagine her attracting a young man's devotion. Kháparde has talked brilliantly all day.

" *17th August.*— My birthday of 69. They have done me the honour of choosing the day for Dingra's execution, thus making of it an anniversary which will be regarded as one of martyrdom in India for generations.

"Another long talk with Kháparde. He is very angry with the Indian Government, which has just closed five Schools which he had founded in Berar, as seditious. He talked more plainly than he has yet done about the future of India. I asked him whether they could set up a form of Government there which would replace the English, and if so what would be its character? He answered that it could easily be done. First, they would redistribute the provinces, so as to make them coincide with ethnical conditions, each to be governed by a Provincial Council, which in its turn would send delegates to a Central Council. The Provincial Councils would have the management of all provincial affairs, while the Central Council would control the army, the posts and telegraphs, foreign affairs, and other matters called Imperial. Thus, in a way, the old Hindoo Empire and the Empire of Akbar would be refounded. Who should be the head of it would probably be determined by events; it might be a successful soldier, or it might be a President, as in the United States. All would be easy to arrange. He does not give English rule in India more than five to ten, at most twenty, years of survival. A revolution could be accomplished to-morrow if the funds necessary were forthcoming. Five million sterling would be sufficient. As to the army, it was a mere matter of money which side it would take. It was mercenary, and would go where its pay was most secure. It was not loyal for any other reason. As for the native Princes whose loyalty was constantly proclaimed, they hated English rule in their hearts; their loyalty was forced on them by the residents, who ordered all things in their name, by promises held out alternately with threats. One great hold the Residents had over them was this: in former times each independent prince had his treasure house where he stored up his wealth. Now the Residents insisted on their investing it in Government securities, so as to bind their money interests to the existing state of things. I showed him my notes of what Mademoiselle Gaignaud had told me in 1884 about Cordery's threats to the Nizam. He assured me it was true. Since I was at Hyderabad, there had been a plot in Lord Dufferin's time, according to which it had been intended to depose the Nizam, on the plea of unsound mind, and to replace him with a Regency, so as once more to get control of the State Funds; but this had been prevented by the Nizam's appeal to his old minister, the Peshkar, who had him medically examined and pronounced him to be entirely sane before Cordery could get a contrary medical opinion. The plan of Governing by a Regency was a favourite one with our officials, as it threw all power without restraint into the hands of the Resident. As to Scindia, it was the same thing; none of the native princes were really loyal, in spite of their public professions and their subscriptions.

" I asked him whether it would not be better to bring about the coming change peaceably. He said, ' Of course. But it would be impossible; there are too many money interests involved. India, in spite of the great poverty of the people, still had much undeveloped wealth in mines and such like. The Indian Government would always be able to pay a mercenary army for its support, and as long as it could pay its way it would listen to no reason. It would never abdicate its authority while it could buy men to fight. The Government policy was to prevent the growth of wealth in native hands. Nevertheless the present state of things could not be made to last by force for more than twenty years

" Dr. Riza Tewfik. Turkish delegate and member of Parliament for Adrianople, lunched with us in Chapel Street. He is by birth an Albanian Moslem, his mother a Circassian, nor has he till this year been out of Turkey, yet he talks French like a Parisian, and has a great knowledge of French and English literature, and has acquired a very great breadth of ideas. Of Turkey's constitutional prospects he does not speak hopefully; the Empire is so diverse in its languages and nationalities. He believes in ultimate autonomy for the provinces, though at present self-preservation makes administrative union a necessity. He approves my recommendation of allowing the interior of Arabia to govern itself in its own way, holding only the seaports and the pilgrim railway. I asked him about Egypt. 'Egypt,' he said, 'is already independent of the Empire, except in name. We sympathize with their desire for a constitution, but they must look for it to England. We cannot interfere or raise any question likely to make trouble between us and England. England will probably allow the Egyptians some kind of Constitution, as much as they are worthy of. They are a corrupt people without courage. Nevertheless there is no danger of the Ottoman Government selling Egypt to England as the price of financial help. It has been talked about at Constantinople, but will not be entertained.'

"Speaking of the revolution at Constantinople, Dr. Riza Tewfik said that the reactionaries had a certain support from our Embassy through the influence of Fitzmaurice, the Chief Dragoman, our Ambassador, Lowther, being quite ignorant of Turkish affairs. On the whole I find him quite sympathetic, and he urged me to write to him. He returns to Constantinople this week."

I went down in the evening to Clouds, where I spent ten pleasant days.

"18th *Aug.*— Dingra's last dying pronouncement is published in the *Daily News,* all other papers being silent about it. [1] It is a noble declaration of his faith in the destinies of his motherland and in his own. 'My wish,' he says, 'is that I should be born again of the same mother, and that I should die the same death for her again.' No greater fortitude was ever shown by a martyr for any faith. With such men to love her, the Mother India must succeed; but the British public is so besotted with its own self-satisfaction that it refuses to acknowledge in this martyr's death endured so calmly anything but a murderer's wish for notoriety. The day of reckoning, however, cannot be long delayed.

"19th *Aug.*— At Clouds. Lyne Stivens, the doctor, was here today, a vulgar, amusing dog, who told a number of good stories. One of them was how the King received Cromer on his return from Egypt when he went to His Majesty to receive the Order of Merit. 'I am happy,' the King said, 'to bestow this final honour upon you, and all the more so because I hear so good an account of your work in Egypt from my friend Sir Ernest Cassel.' This raised Cromer's bile.

[1] See Appendix III p. 443.

" He told us, too, of how the Duke of Connaught's chauffeur, having been fined by the magistrates of Salisbury for exceeding the legal speed limit in his motor, His Royal Highness had declared his determination never to enter Salisbury again, with more stories of a like high life kind. He had brought with him his wife, a Buenos Aires heiress, whose wealth puts him above the necessities of his profession, much to his fellow-doctors' disgust, who treat him as a quack; but he is a clever fellow, who claps his patients on the back and tells them to ' buck up,' which they do. He talked about the Dingra assassination, which seems to have at last convinced his Royal friends that there is something wrong about the state of India. People talk about poltical assassination as defeating its own end, but that is nonsense; it is just the shock needed to convince selfish rulers that selfishness has its limits of imprudence. It is like that other fiction that England never yields to threats. My experience is that when England has her face well slapped she apologizes, not before.

" *22nd Aug.*— Hugh Wyndham, the younger, arrived last night. He is settled now with his wife near Johannesburg, on a farm eight hours' railway journey from the Natal frontier, where he breeds thoroughbreds for racing. He is a rich man, as his father left each of the younger sons £10,000 a year, and he intends going into the new Cape Town Parliament. He gave me a more intelligent view of the political position that I have yet had. He approves of the Transvaal settlement made after the war, and thinks that in time Boer and Briton will settle down amicably together, though the balance of power will be with the Boer, whose vote on all questions will be given solidly, and who moreover is an increasing population more than is the British. On the negro question he does not think there is any danger of a return to legal slavery. Also it will be impossible to prevent the education of the blacks, or their eventually obtaining the franchise. They are rapidly increasing in numbers and in knowledge of their power. He would like State education for them, so as to direct their intelligence in a right direction. He is opposed to dividing the land into white and black districts, as it would be impossible to enforce the dividing lines. The whole question of the future is whether the white man can be persuaded to do manual labor. If not, South Africa must eventually fall to the blacks, but he thinks the pride of colour will be sacrificed by the whites when they find they cannot live without white labour. He also thinks that the independence of the Basutos and Bechuanas will be respected. His ideas are far more humane than I at all expected.

" *29th Aug. (Sunday).*— I am spending a week-end at St. Giles' with the Shaftesburys, a large and pleasant party with a number of interesting people, George Wyndham amongst them, and we sat up

talking late, Shaftesbury, George and I, when the rest were gone, and
with us De Bary, Shaftesbury's chaplain, once Father Angelo at
Crawley, now doing priestly duty in the Anglican Church. I asked
him what his religious position exactly was, and he told me that, without changing any of his opinions, he had signed the Thirty-nine Articles as expounded to him by Dr. Gore, the Anglican Bishop of Birmingham, and now did duty in the parish church here. He seems
quite happy, and has a very pleasant time of it at St. Giles' and at
Belfast with the Shaftesburys. He is a quiet, serious man, and spends
his time writing books on theology and history, being on the best of
terms with his patrons, making them a very superior chaplain indeed.
George, of course, did most of our talking, and gave us one of his
lectures on Irish politics and the new Land Bill, using arguments which
are precisely the strongest ones for Home Rule. We also discussed
India, and he agreed with my major premise that India was being
ruined by us economically. He does not seem wrapped up in its retention, caring more for the English-speaking colonies. Shaftesbury,
without special brilliancy, is sensible and open-minded, and took full
share in all this.

" 30*th Aug.*— Newbuildings. Kháparde has been telling me some
tales of the great Delhi Durbar of 1903, at which he was present. It
began with a half comic, half ominous incident. All the world was
assembled in the great horseshoe arena waiting for Lord Curzon to
open the proceedings in state, when a fox terrier belonging to a bands-
man in one of the Highland regiments was suddenly seen to mount
the steps of the dais and jump into the throne on which the viceroy was
to sit and began barking, to the amusement of the assembled Princes,
dignitaries of the Empire, and somewhat too to their disgust, till the
dog was driven out. It seemed to some of the Princes to symbolize
the indignity to which they were subjected, and the position of India
as a country with a dog for master. When Lord Curzon arrived, he
took his seat, the Duke of Connaught, representing the King, being
placed at his right on another throne, and the Duke had to rise and
bow to the Viceroy, which gave new offence to the native princes,
while Lady Curzon had to curtsey to the Duchess, each being then
seated behind their respective husbands. A third cause of offence was
when the Begum of Bhopal came forward in public, contrary to all
Indian usage about women, and touched the Viceroy's foot with her
forehead. Lastly, as an ill-omen, three men of the Highland regiments fell down dead with sunstroke. These happenings, which
Kháparde saw with his own eyes, being not more than ten or fifteen
yards from the throne, were the subject of much native talk, though
the incident of the dog was kept out of the newspapers. The chief
offence, however, given to the princes was that, while Curzon returned

none of their visits paid to him in camp, he devoted three hours to newspaper correspondents.

" He told me also some interesting details of the Government's dealings with the rulers of various native States, notably with Scindia, Holkar and the Nizam. Scindia, it seems, had accumulated eighty crores of rupees in specie as a reserve fund in case of actual rebellion and for the payment of an army he kept up of some strength. This immense sum the Imperial Government, taking advantage of there being a Regency (a favourite opportunity), invested in Government securities, and this bound the Gwalior State to loyalty. This was managed under Lansdowne. Under Curzon, the State of Indore, Holkar's, was in like manner manipulated during a Regency.

" 31st Aug.— Newbuildings. Two young Egyptians came to dine and sleep, and consult me about their hopes. They have come to England on behalf of the National Congress to be held at Geneva on the 13th, the anniversary of Tel-el-Kebir. Both young men are courageous in their opinions, and the elder especially of a keen intelligence, reminding me not a little of Mustapha Kamel, but speaking English instead of French. The younger of a purer Egyptian type, the son of a rich man in the Delta, who has been for three years an undergraduate at Oxford. The first was a disciple of Abdu's, and has taken a degree at the University of Lyons, and has been working for some time past among the Delta villages, preaching political sermons in the mosques. He gives a very hopeful account of his progress among them. Both are thoroughgoing in their plans. They came to ask my advice as to the course of action they should take under present conditions. The Khedive, they say, has gone over altogether to the English, but has very little influence, the younger students of the Azhar being now very nearly all Nationalists. What they are afraid of now is lest the Government at Constantinople should sell Egypt to England. On this point I reassured them. I advised them to keep on the best possible terms with the Copts and the European Colonies, so as to conciliate as far as possible the European Powers, and very especially not to quarrel with Constantinople, Egypt's connection with the Ottoman Empire being its real safe-guard against England. We discussed the formation of a secret society on the lines of the Turkish Committee of Union and Progress. One of them has a plan of throwing up his career at Oxford without waiting for a degree, and of going to Constantinople or the United States or Germany to get a military training. He says the Egyptian army is rapidly becoming Nationalist, and they have received assurances that it would join them in case of disturbances. It would not fire on the people, but officers would be wanted when the time came to take the place of the present English officers. He is fired with the ambition of playing

a part like Enver Bey's.   He is a big strong young fellow, rather silent,
but with flashes of enthusiasm and anger.   I much applauded his resolution; also I told them I considered it waste time to try and convert
England to the idea of evacuation.   Englishmen were not open to per-
suasion on that head, but might be convinced if it could be shown that
their hold on Egypt was a trouble and a danger.   I read them my
manifesto, not yet finished, for the Congress, and they will have it
read out at the opening of the proceedings.   It is in French, and they
will have it translated into Arabic as well as English.   We sat up talking till midnight.   These are the sort of young men to make a revolution.
The older Egyptians are useless; they have not the courage.

"*1st September.*— The young men are gone.   Winston Churchill
came down to-day to Carpenters to see his wife, who is staying there
with her mother, and I had tea with them and discussed the Indian
question with him.   I found him sufficiently open-minded to admit that
if it could be proved that India was poorer to-day than a hundred years
ago we ought to leave it.

"*2nd Sept.*— There is a report in the papers to-day that the Grand
Vizier at Constantinople, Hilmi Pasha, has declared his entire approval of the Khedive and of English policy in Egypt; but it is also
rumoured that Hilmi is about to resign.   I have read Gorst's new
White Paper with the text of a new law permitting the deportation of
persons in Egypt without trial.

"*5th Sept. (Sunday).*— Winston and Clementine came to lunch
with me.   Winston is a charming young man, as unconventional as
his father was, and as light in hand.   We lunched in the garden, and
sat there after it till four o'clock, discussing nearly all the great questions of the day, the Budget, the fight with the Lords, South Africa,
Egypt, India, all the tricks of the political game.   He believes the Budget
to be very popular, and that the Government will win on it if it comes
to a General Election; but it will not come to that.   The Lords will
not fight.   Some day there will be a great Constitutional fight, which
he thinks the Commons will win, though, at present, the Lords would
have all the physical force in their hands: army, territorials and Boy
Scouts.   The Lords could be coerced if they refused, after the General Election, a second time to vote the Budget, and the King, if he
refused to swamp them with new peers.

"Talking about public schools he said they were a bad training for
a clever boy.   'I never learned anything at school,' he said, 'and to
be high up at Eton is enough to ruin any boy, and give him a narrow
view of life.'   He likes the universities and military training for a
few years, though the army is a poor profession.   'I got all the fun
of it,' he said, 'for I was on active service nearly all the time in the
Soudan, and afterwards in South Africa, as a newspaper corre-

spondent.' He went on to Kitchener and the Mahdi's head. Kitchener, he said, had behaved like a blackguard in that business. He pretended to have sent the head back to Soudan in a kerosene tin, but the
tin may have contained anything, perhaps ham sandwiches. He kept
the head, and has it still. 'I made a row about that,' he said, 'though
they told me it was bad taste for a young Lieutenant to say anything.
I always hated Kitchener, though I did not know him personally. They
are ashamed of the matter now, but I took pains to remind them of it
two years ago when the case for Mambata's mutilation in Natal was
brought forward. I had to defend the Government. "At any rate,"
I said, "We have an excellent precedent for what was done to the
Zulu Chief in what Lord Kitchener did to the Mahdi when he blew
up the body and kept the head." There was a question raised about
a medal being struck for the campaign amongst the Zulus, and they
sent the sketch of it to me at the Office for approval. I wrote on it:
"Surely the medal ought to have Mambata's head on it, not the King's."
This docket must be still at the War Office.'

"From this we went on to the characters of various personages;
Morley's, which he praised, because he always learned something
from talking with him, though he more or less agreed with me about
him as a poor politician, and the mess he had made about that very
Mahdi's head business. Of Arthur Balfour he narrated how Belloc
had spoiled a dinner-party at Harry Cust's where Arthur and several
others had been. The house had caught fire during the dinner, and
after putting it out they all drank champagne, and Arthur had grown
talkative and confidential, and was just launching into the secret history
of the South African War when Belloc insisted upon giving his own
views and kept on talking all night and Arthur never got in again.
Winston corresponds with Labby, of whom he has a good opinion,
and he admires Chamberlain, 'Old Joe,' because he is unscrupulous
and bold; but he says Labby is an example of failure in that line. He
had the ambition of being in the Cabinet, or else an ambassador, and
he succeeded in neither. About South Africa he told how he had
dined with Moore, the Natal Premier, a little while ago, and how
Moore had said to him, apropos of what was going on in India:
'Well, Churchill, I suppose you'll have to bleed them soon; there's
nothing like it. Next time they have a demonstration ride them down,
and if that isn't enough pour in a volley. You'll bleed a few thousands
of them, but it will be better for them in the long run; there's nothing
like bleeding.' Winston did not talk as much about India as I had
hoped, but he said: 'If they ever unite against us and put us in coventry all round, the game would be up. If they could agree to have
nothing at all to do with us the whole thing would collapse.'

" He went on to Egypt. He said: ' We shall continue to hold it whatever happens; nobody will ever give it up — I won't — except we are driven out of it at the end of a war. It will all depend upon whether we can hold command of the sea; the fate of the war will decide it.' It is something to know from him that this is, in fact, the present Government's policy. It is exactly what I have just written in my Congress Manifesto.

" I talked to him about my prison time in Ireland, and this interested him. ' I am dead against the present system,' he said, ' and if I am ever at the Home Office I will make a clean sweep of it. I promised to send him in a paper on the subject if ever the time should come. He thinks Home Rule will come now very soon. About the suffragettes, he expects them to take to dynamite, he told a story of a man who, talking about their chaining themselves to the railings till they got the vote, said: ' I might as well chain myself to St. Thomas's Hospital and say I would not move till I had had a baby.' Coming indoors he saw the butterflies in cases on the chimney-piece, and told us about those he had found in Uganda. I like him much. He is *aux plus petits soins* with his wife, taking all possible care of her. They are a very happy married pair. Clementine was afraid of wasps, and one settled on her sleeve, and ˜Winston gallantly took the wasp by the wings and thrust it into the ashes of the fire. We had out the stallions for him to look at; Ibn Yashmak being the one he liked best. He is to come again and shoot pheasants here in October. Now he is off to the Prussian Manœuvres and to visit Kaiser Wilhelm.

" Talking about the decay of the House of Commons as a power in the country, he said that if he had his way he would revive the right of adjourning the House once a week to debate any urgent affair of the moment. He is all for the discussion of everything, and is inclined even to adopt my doctrine of no secret diplomacy. He thinks with me that it is monstrous the Government should be able to bind the country by secret treaties for years, while the country knows nothing whatever about them.

" *12th Sept.*— On Tuesday Keir Hardie sent me an urgent message wanting to see me about Egypt at any hour next day that I would name, and I telegraphed that I would give him luncheon in Chapel Street at one; but though I went up to London on purpose he failed to keep his appointment, and it was not till two days later that he wrote to apologize. These M. P.'s have no manners. His reason for wanting to see me was that he was going to the Congress of Geneva with Kettle and two or three other members. I have been hard at work all the week past writing my manifesto for the Egyptian Congress in French, and I have posted it to Geneva.

" *16th Sept.*— De Bary, ex-Father Angelo, came for a couple of

nights. He tells me his father and mother were mystics who looked
for a restoration of a theocracy in Europe under the Pope and a Catholic king in France. They wished all their six children to become
monks and nuns, and all six did so. He himself joined the Capuchins
before he was fifteen, and made his vows without knowing anything, if
I understand him rightly, of the relations of the sexes. For that reason
Father Tyrrell was of opinion that De Bary's vow of chastity did not
bind him, and that he was free to marry if he chose. He showed me
a number of Tyrrell's letters, one of which bore on this point. At
twenty-one he was made to sign a disentailing deed of the family property which he had not read or understood the meaning of. He is
now about forty, and acts as private chaplain to the Shaftesburys at
St. Giles,' where I met him in the summer. I drove him to-day to
Storrington, where we had tea with Miss Petre, and visited Tyrrell's
grave with her. It is kept decked with flowers, and there were two
persons, a man and a woman, kneeling there and praying. This is Miss
Petre's pious work. De Bary and I knelt also. There is yet no
stone placed.

De Bary is an interesting man, and on his own subjects is a good,
though rather vague, talker. He is enthusiastic about the rights of the
weak races of mankind, and is a good Nationalist in Ireland of the
Horace Plunkett school. He was a member of the Roger Bacon Society, which had its meetings at Holmwood, with several other Capuchins.
He has a high opinion of Gibson as entirely devoted to Sinn Fein.
Gibson's wife was sympathetic to a certain point, but, as a Catholic
complained that he adopted 'all the heresies.' Mivart was one of the
most notable of their members. It was Coventry Patmore who started
the idea of the identity of Aphrodite and the Virgin Mary, which Mivart
afterwards brought forward in one of his ' Nineteenth Century ' articles.
Jesus Christ, Mivart said, was first worshipped as identical with Æscu-
lapius. De Bary is a great believer in Bishop Gore and his Christian
Socialism, and he assures me that this section of the English Church is
sound about India and the Zulus and other native questions in the
British Empire. De Bary was a year earning his own living in America,
where he says things are far worse than in England. He has been
fortunate in getting into harbour at St. Giles'.

" *24th Sept.*— Newbuildings. The Geneva Congress has been a success. Osman Ghaleb writes enthusiastically of young Goumah, who
took the lead at the Egyptian meeting, speaking out well in answer
to Keir Hardie (who had made a half-hearted speech), and had carried the Congress with him. They also carried an amendment omitting
the complimentary telegram to the Khedive. It has had its effect here
in England. The Budget debate, however, absorbs all English attention,
and much depends on its issue both for Egypt and for India.

" Bernard Shaw writes to me: 'We are in for a bad time in India I am afraid, but the Indians, like the Egyptians, must work out their own salvation, for we *cannot* let them go on until they break loose, and until defeats and Empire shrinkage in other directions compel us to march out as the Romans marched out of Britain.' Hall Caine, too, writes to me about his new Egyptian novel, ' The White Prophet.' The novel is fantastic, but will do good, as thousands of people will read it. He says in his letter : ' I recall the fact that you kindly sent me " The Wind and the Whirlwind " at the time of its publication. I read your poem again while writing " The White Prophet," and it may possibly occur that certain of my own passages are coloured by yours, etc.' Cromer, he says, has been making efforts to influence the Press against his book, and he wants me to write in praise of it.

"*27th Sept.*— Lady Cardigan's Memoirs have been published, a really audacious book, surpassing everything of the kind that has yet been printed. Most of the stories in it relate to things well known in society, but which have only been talked about in private hitherto. There is very little that is new to me. One thing, however, I may say I know to be untrue, the story of Lord Ward's first marriage, though the versions given of it here I have also heard. What I believe really happened (my informant being Mme. d'Usedom, who told it me forty and more years ago) is this : Miss de Burgh, who was a very pretty girl, had four young men who adored her, and who all had proposed to her. Among them were Lord Mount Charles and Lord Ward (afterwards Lord Dudley). There was another, however, whom she really loved, and finding herself with child to him and him unwilling to marry her, she wrote to the others in turn saying that she was now willing, on the sole condition that the wedding should take place at once. Ward accepted her terms and married her, and for some time remained ignorant of how it was with her, but finding it out at last sent her back to her parents, and a separation, not, I think, a divorce, took place. The wife, however, did not long survive it, and having miscarried badly of her child sent to her husband and begged his forgiveness, and he nursed her with all possible kindness to the end. Mme. d'Usedom said this was the account Ward had given her of the affair, and one that, if I remember rightly, Mount Charles had confirmed. Lady Cardigan's story, a very different one, of Ward's brutality was, however, circulated at the time, Ward being a man of strange idiosyncrasies with women and unpopular with men. She quotes as her authority Lady Duppelin, whose husband was one of the lady's lovers and who doubtless got it through him from the lady — not a very reiable source. The occasion on which I heard my version was when I was staying with Mme. d'Usedom at S. Maurice in Switzerland in 1867, Lord Dudley being at the time on his second honeymoon there.

Through Mme. d'Usedom I made acquaintance with him and his bride, whom I had known as Miss Moncrieff, and formed a high opinion of him in the character of middle-aged husband with a quite young bride. Though it was anything but a love marriage at starting (for she was in love with another man, Lord Tyrone, who had failed to marry her, and took Dudley as a *pisaller*), he was so assiduous and tactful with her that he succeeded in gaining her full devotion, and eventually she bore him sons and daughters not a few, and remained through life attached to him, although he was unfaithful to her. Blanche Hozier confirms my version of the story as being that told her by her mother, Lady Airlie, who knew Miss de Burgh well at the time of her marriage. She says that Dudley died of a too violent passion he indulged in for Sarah Bernhardt. I have a special recollection of a picnic in which we all took part at S. Maurice, and of Dudley's having challenged me to race him a hundred yards down hill, one which, being then young and for a short distance light of limb, I won easily enough to his chagrin and, as I think, to his bride's. She was a lovely girl, tall and framed like a goddess, but with an unlovely voice.

" *1st Oct.*— Belloc was here to-day wanting to buy cord-wood for his winter's firing. He tells me that Gorst is now looked upon at the Foreign Office as a complete failure, and that he himself acknowledges that the whole of his policy has broken down. He wants to leave Egypt for another post, but they cannot find anybody willing to replace him. 'They missed their opportunity,' Belloc said, 'of making a deal about Egypt with Germany.' This was to have been in connection with the Bagdad railway, but the revolution at Constantinople spoilt that. Gorst's policy was what I always said it was, to convert the Egyptians through the Khedive to English ideas, and, of course, it has failed egregiously. Even the wretched old Legislative Council has rebelled, and has addressed a remonstrance against Gorst to Grey for what he said in his last annual report, and claiming a sort of Constitution. Lastly, Ronald Storrs writes from Cairo that he has just been given the succession to Boyle's place at the Agency, another indication of a change of plan there. Boyle has been chief adviser of the Agency for the last twenty years, and has engineered the Cabal against the Nationalists, with the help of the Mokattam newspaper and the Syrians. Storrs has just been at Damascus. He knows Arabic well, and is an extremely clever fellow, and his appointment is significant. It probably means a change of policy, perhaps, a reversion to Cromerism, perhaps, though I don't expect it, something really liberal at last, only all this is dependent upon politics at home and the fate of the General Elections.

" *2nd Oct.*— Our shooting party arrived late last night, Winston and Clementine and Harry Cust and his wife; and we had an exceedingly pleasant evening. Winston was in excellent form, and as he and Harry are old and very intimate friends, the ball of conversation was kept rolling well. Harry described to us Asquith's adventure with the Suffragettes at Lympne. He was there with Asquith and Herbert Gladstone, and the suffragettes assaulted Asquith, striking him on the face with their fists, or rather with their wrists (he gave a demonstration). He, Harry, was Secretary of the Golf Club and intervened, telling the women that whatever their dispute with the Prime Minister might be it was impossible they should be allowed to walk on the grass, as it was against the regulations of the Club. This, he said, impressed them. Asquith defended himself, and caught hold of one of the women and Herbert of another, and eventually got away in a motor. While they were at dinner a stone, a big block of granite, was thrown through the window of their room and fell within a yard of Margot. He says it will come to murder before long. The women were quite mad.

"Winston gave us a very full account of what his policy in the Budget dispute with the Lords would be. He began by saying that his hope and prayer was that they would throw out the Bill, as it would save the Government from a certain defeat if the Elections were put off. The Budget, once it became law, would be immensely unpopular, and everybody would be against it. It was therefore to the interest of the Opposition to let it pass. It seemed, however, likely that the Lords would throw it out. Then there were two courses, either to resign at once or to dissolve. He is for dissolving. Then if the Government came back with a good majority he thinks they could go in for a regular attack on the Lords' veto. He thinks the King would go with them in swamping the House of Lords by a creation of peers, and so would abolish the veto. But, if only with a small majority, they would say the King's Government could not be carried on, and would resign, when Lansdowne would be called on to form an administration; and he also being unable to carry on the King's Government, would have again to dissolve. Thus it would no longer be a question of the Budget but of a quarrel between Lords and Commons, ' and in time we should have all the forces on our side '— except the physical forces. Winston is an admirable and delightful talker; very clear in his ideas and with an extraordinarily ready wit. Harry, though also ready and witty, was nowhere at all with him in the discussion, which he tried to maintain from the Tory side. We had continued our talk after leaving the dining-room and got on the subject of India and George Curzon. Curzon, according to Harry, entirely lost his head in India; and after Broderick became Secretary of State, thought he could do what he liked. St. John, he said, had been George's butt for thirty years. He had always laughed at him and would not treat him ser-

iously. St. John, on the other hand, could not resist the temptation
of having his little revenge on George, when at last he found himself
George's official superior, and was down on him on the first opportunity. As to the quarrel with Kitchener, whom Winston hates, calling him by very hard names, Winston explained how badly Curzon
had played his cards. The quarrel between them he declared to have
been this: when the question of the change in the Commander-in-
Chief's powers was introduced, Curzon agreed to it on condition that
Burrows was appointed, and Kitchener agreed verbally to the appointment. At the same time, however, Kitchener telegraphed privately
to the War Office saying that Burrows was quite unfit. This telegram,
according to the espionage system practised in India, was laid before
the Viceroy. 'Curzon ought then,' said Winston, 'to have called
on Kitchener to explain himself, accused him of being the liar and in-
triguer he was, and reported the whole thing to the India office, when it
would have been Kitchener who would have had to resign. Instead
of this he allowed Kitchener to bring the thing forward as a dispute
about the Commander-in-Chief's powers, where Kitchener was able to
get the best of it. Curzon being Kitchener's superior, ought never to
have allowed this — and it ended in his having himself to resign.' He
lost his temper to such an extent that when Minto came out to relieve
him he refused, contrary to all precedent of etiquette, to attend the
ceremony of handing over his Governor-Generalship to the new-comer,
and remained in his own room.

   "Winston sympathizes much with my ideas about the native question in India, and in general about the enslavement of the coloured
by the white race. But he says he is an Imperialist, and his chief
interest is in the condition and welfare of the poor in England, who, he
says, are far worse off than the poor in any part of the East. 'I
would give my life,' he said, 'to see them placed on a right footing
in regard to their lives and means of living. That is what I am paid
for, and I would really give my life.' I can see all the same that my
arguments have effect on him, just as they used to have with his father;
and I should not be surprised if some day he made the Indian cause his
own. Talking of Kitchener's appointment to Malta he scoffed at
Haldane's pretence that this was destined to be a post of the highest
military importance, comprising the whole of our military communication with India, 'when,' he said, 'we all perfectly well know that our
only road to India in war time is by the Cape.'

   "To-day we shot hedgerows round about Gosbrook and Blinks Wood.
Winston shot very well, though, of course, it was easy shooting. Both
the ladies walked with us. Farid Bey and Osman Ghaleb had announced their arrival, which would have been most inconvenient; but,
fortunately, did not appear, having, I suppose, received my telegram in

time to put them off till Monday. It was a beautiful day, and all went off successfully.

"In the evening we had another great discussion of the fundamentals of politics, each of us holding our own ground. Mine was, of course, that of 'Satan Absolved,' to which Winston opposed one of optimistic Liberal Imperialism where the British Empire was to be maintained, in part by concession, in part by force, and the constant invention of new scientific forces to deal with growing difficulties of Imperial rule. He admitted, however, that India does not pay its expense to us in men or money; and it seems to me that he would be pretty easily persuaded to let it go, were the pressure severe enough. Like most of them, it is the vanity of Empire that affects him more than supposed profit or the necessities of trade, which he repudiates; also, doubtless, his military training counts for much in his Imperialism. He will come round to me in time. Harry Cust, with all his cleverness, was quite outclassed by Winston in the discussion, who has studied all these problems thoroughly, and is wonderfully quick in defending his position. He has just his father's talent of seizing the points of a situation and driving them home in his replies. He fills me with admiration and delight. The two women took little part in the discussion, but sat in rapt attention. Mrs. Cust is a nice woman and her book, 'Gentlemen Errant,' which I have been reading, is a monument of historical research. He, though less attractively brilliant than Churchill, is wonderfully well equipped for talk, having a far greater knowledge of history and literature and a real poetic side, which in Churchill is wanting. His knowledge of poetry is wide, and he has himself written quite excellent verse. Both have wit and quickness of repartee and the power of epigram. It is first-class sword play between them.

"*3rd Oct.* (*Sunday.*)—To-day was rainy and nobody appeared downstairs till noon. But our talk began again at luncheon with new vigour. Then we went out to look at the stallions. I mounted Churchill on Rijim and took him with the others to Worleys to look at the mares, which gave us a fine exhibition of galloping and circling round us. Rijim showed himself nobly, and I promised Churchill he should ride him in the procession there would be one day when he went to open Parliament as the first President of the British Republic.

"Again we sat up till late. Among the many memorable things Churchill said was this: Talking of Dingra, he said that there had been much discussion in the Cabinet about him. Lloyd George had expressed to him his highest admiration of Dingra's attitude as a patriot, in which he (Churchill) shared. He will be remembered 2,000 years hence, as we remember Regulus and Caractacus and Plutarch's heroes, and Churchill quoted with admiration Dingra's last words as the finest ever made in the name of patriotism. All the same, he says that he was strongly in favour of the law taking its course, even to the extent of refusing to give back the body of the hanged man to his friends for their own funeral rites. He quite understood that it would have been an additional torture to have commuted the sentence." [For text of Dingra's speech see Appendix III.]

"Churchill's opinion of Lloyd George is high, but I doubt if he so regards any of his other colleagues in the Cabinet, though he is careful in his words about them. Of Burns he said, 'His attitude is quite excusable. He has been attacked out of jealousy by his fellow Socialists past endurance; but he does not care. He has been three years in office, drawing £2,000 a year salary, of which he only spends £300. He has saved up all the rest. He can afford to snap his fingers at them.' There was much discussion between him and Cust about Asquith's character, and a comparison made by them between him and Arthur Balfour. 'Asquith,' Churchill said, 'is a very simple-minded man, very ingenuous, but he has a wonderful talent for work, and the clearest possible head for business. He will sit up playing bridge and drinking late at night, and yet in the morning he will come to his office or to the House and enter into the most complicated business with his head entirely clear and work on for six or seven hours. He will attend committees and give full attention to every point of discussion, and draft amendments in his perfectly clear handwriting without altering a word clause after clause, and he is far and away the best speaker in the House. That is what gives him his power. He is single-minded and good. Arthur, on the contrary, is in his nature hard; he could be cruel. I call him wicked. He is very courageous, the most courageous man alive. I believe if you held a pistol to his face it would not frighten him. He is not appalled by adverse circumstances, by the number of his enemies. I look on him as my enemy, and I say this of him. The difference between him and Asquith is that Arthur is wicked and moral, Asquith is good and immoral.' This was *à propos* of a question put by Harry as to which of the two it would be pleasantest to spend a week with. According to both of them, Asquith of late years has gone morally downhill. From the Puritan he was, he has adopted the polite frivolities of society. Harry told stories of this, and compared him to Fox and Arthur to Pitt. He had gone all to pieces at one time, but pulled himself together when he became Prime Minister. He had lost his influence with the Radicals by his addiction to fine society. 'But,' said Churchill, 'Lloyd George and I have re-established his credit with our Budget. It has put a stop to his social career.' This evolution of the square-toed Asquith, with his middle-class Puritanical bringing up and his severity of conduct, into the 'gay dog' of London society is to me irresistibly funny. It needs a Balzac to deal with it properly. As to Morley, Churchill is

silent, allowing me to attack him without defending him, and I think
in his heart agreeing with me. We went over the whole history of
Morley's weakness in the Mahdi's head case, and in that of his feeble
opposition to the Boer War and his muddle-headedness about India.
I think Churchill will come round to my views about India, for in all
essentials he is at one with me; and he was fired at the description I
gave him of his father's doings at the India Office and at our formula,
' The Queen and Native India,' against the covenanted Civil Service.

"He is sympathetic, too, about the motor car tyranny, and talks
of children being collected and carried to school so as to escape the
dangers of the road. But he has no scheme of immediate protection
for foot-goers, and says that flying machines will have superseded
motors in ten years' time as an amusement of the rich. He told me
he had a scheme for settling the Somaliland folly on lines precisely
the same as those I proposed five years ago — that is to say, by withdrawing the British troops to the seaports, and providing for the
' friendly ' tribes, if they could not agree with the Mullah, elsewhere.
I told him about the blood money way of settling accounts. Also
he has urged a settlement of the Cyprus trouble by ending the swindle
there in regard to the tribute. All this is excellent, and may lead to
real Imperial reforms.

"*4th Oct.*— They are all gone, much pleased, I think, with their
visit.

"Farid Bey and Osman Bey Ghaleb arrived from Paris to talk
over Egyptian affairs. They intend holding their Congress next year
at Constantinople. I think that a good move. There seems to have
been an intrigue at this year's meeting at Geneva, the Khedive having
got hold of one of their number, Mohammed Fehmi, in the interests of
a rival party, the party of the people. It was only Goumah's courageous speech that turned the tables against these.

"*5th Oct.*—I have received a letter from Arabi after a long silence,
congratulating me on my Congress manifesto. I am glad to get this
from him, for it may be the means of putting him right with the young
Nationalists. Belloc repeats to me that Gorst seems now quite discredited at the Foreign Office. His policy, as he himself admits, having failed, he wishes to be moved to another post, but there is difficulty
in finding any one willing to succeed him.

"*7th Oct.*— Churchill has sent me two secret minutes he had
printed for the Cabinet two years ago about Somaliland and Cyprus.
They are very plain spoken in the sense of our talk. He must have
been Under-Secretary for the Colonies at that time. ' There are
only two secure alternatives,' it says: ' (A) To occupy the country
effectively by holding all the important wells and, in concert with
the Italians, to crush the Mullah, or (B) to withdraw to the coast as

the Italians have done since, and as we did before the rise of the Mullah's power.' Winston recommends the second. Churchill's second minute, that about Cyprus, dated 19th Oct., 1907, recommends the expenditure of the revenue being devoted to the improvement of the island, and that the tribute which goes to the holders of the Turkish loan should be paid by the English Exchequer, which is responsible for the Turkish loan it guarantees.

" 12th Oct.— George Wyndham and Mark Napier have been here to shoot. Last night we discussed the Indian question. George disapproves now of the Japanese alliance, and praises that with Russia. He says that it is quite impossible India should be made self-governing under two hundred years, or that the English democracy will ever consent to a withdrawal. But at the same time he is inclined to agree with me that England would be better without her Indian Empire. In old times, when England was governed by an oligarchy, the administration of India might have been gradually transferred to the natives, and so the country be set adrift, but not now. A Minister proposing to do so could not remain a month in office. This, of course, is true, but it is the same thing as admitting what Gordon said, that no reform was possible in India except by a revolution.

" Conny Lytton and Mrs. Brailsford have been arrested with other suffragettes and mean to starve themselves, and Brailsford telegraphs to me asking me to get George Wyndham to take up their case. George, however, of course would not do this, though he says he is opposed to these violences in prison against women, and we discussed the case of the treatment of political prisoners. He is more enlightened on this point than Mark, who takes a plain lawyer's view. I have written to Brailsford in this sense.

" 15th Oct.— Conny and Mrs. Brailsford have been released by order of the Home Secretary, and Conny has written an extremely able letter to the ' Times ' about her case. It will, I think, force their hand into altering the law about political prisoners.

" 25th Oct.—George Leveson Gower has been here shooting. Talking about the G.O.M. (Mr. Gladstone) whose private secretary George was from 1880 to 1885, he told a good story. At the time of the Kilmainham Treaty he had undertaken to expostulate with his master on the danger he was running by carrying on the negotiation through Mrs. O'Shea. He and Eddy Hamilton (his fellow private secretary) had talked it over together, and Eddy had said he did not dare approach the subject with Mr. Gladstone, but had no objection to George doing so. George opened the matter with what delicacy he could, mentioning Parnell's connection with the lady; but the old man fired up at once, and made him an oration which George repeated to us, imitating exactly the old man's voice and manner : ' You do not

mean,' he said, ' to ask me to believe that it is possible a man should
be so lost to all sense of what is due to his public position, at a moment
like the present, in the very crisis of his country's fortunes, as to
indulge in an illicit connection with the wife of one of his own political
supporters, and to make use of that connection in the way you suggest.'
I asked George whether Mr. Gladstone negotiated the thing personally
with Mrs. O'Shea, and he said, ' Oh, no, not personally; he did not see
her, but it was done through her.' He also told us about Minto, as
Viceroy of India, a mere nonentity in the Government, not even reading the most important documents laid before him. On one occasion
they tested this by gumming the leaves slightly together, which he
returned unopened. A third thing George narrated *à propos* of Lady
Cardigan's memoirs, which have just been published. He went once
to Dene with his father to look at a house, as they were staying in the
neighbourhood at Apthorpe, and while they were being shown round
came to the portrait of Cardigan riding in front of the Balaclava
Charge, when his father nudged him and whispered that it was all
fudge; Cardigan was not in the charge at all, being at the time on board
his yacht, and only arrived on the field of battle as his regiment was
on its way back from the Valley of Death. This sounds incredible,
but George says his father was very positive that the thing was so.

" The chief excitement of the week has been the execution of Ferrar
in Spain for complicity in the Barcelona insurrection. It has roused all
the Socialism of the world to fury, and even in London there have been
demonstrations, in which Cunninghame Graham has taken a leading
part.

" *1st Nov.*— Two events have occurred in the last week; an attack
made on a convoy in Somaliland by the ' Mad Mullah,' in which three
Indian Sepoys have been killed, exactly proves the folly of continuing
to hold the Interior. The second is what is called a ' punitive expedition,' despatched by Gorst to Siwah. There my old friend Haboun has
got into a quarrel with the Egyptian authorities by shooting the Maoun
and two others, who had come to effect a domiciliary visit. A hundred
and fifty men are now being sent from Alexandria to arrest him and
restore order. [This resulted in the capture and hanging of Haboun.]

" *6th Nov.*— Terence Bourke and Basil Blackwood are here.
Terence tells me things are going not so badly in Tunis for the natives;
and there seems to be less violent feeling against the French there than
against us in Egypt. Basil has got an appointment at the Board of
Trade. He is a pleasant fellow, astonishingly like his father in manner
and voice.

" *12th Nov.*— Neville came to dine and sleep. He is much interested
just now in the Steinheil trial at Paris, through his intimacy with
Geoffroy, whose mother was M. Steinheil's sister, and he also knew

the lady herself there in his student days. The Geoffroys had quarrelled with Mme. Steinheil, and Geoffroy's father had even given evidence against her at the trial. As to her connection with President
Faure's death Neville gives me this account of it. She met Faure at
some watering place ' aux Eaux,' and obtained an influence of passion
over him; and it was in her arms that he died. She had been introduced
privately into the Elyseé, and his hand in death was so tightly clutched
in her hair that the hair had to be cut off. This fact and the possibility
of political revelations regarding it seem to have influenced the prosecution into giving her every opportunity of an acquittal; and an acquittal
seems intended.

" 19*th Nov.*— Lord Lansdowne has made the sensational announcement that he will propose an Amendment to the Budget Bill in the
House of Lords to the effect that the Lords are not justified in passing
it without an appeal to the country. This means a General Election in
January. Margot, in a note to me of the 11th writes: ' The Lords
are mad; but I pray that they may help us to a good majority in
January. There will be hot fighting for four weeks and not much
holiday.'

" In Egypt the quarrel over the Suez Canal concession, against which
there has been a strong Nationalist protest, has been solved by the
Canal Company's refusing the terms proposed. I have written to congratulate Farid on what is a victory for his party.

" 22*nd Nov.*— I have been reading the traveller Stanley's autobiography. The description of his early life as a workhouse boy, and
at sea, and as a vagabond in the Southern States of America is extremely interesting; and his wife, whom I used to know before her
marriage, would have been well advised for his fame to have ended her
volume there; for the later record, which is not strictly autobiography,
reveals him as the type of all that is most repulsive in what are called
our ' Empire Builders.' No book ever showed more clearly the demoralizing influence contact with savage life exercises on the average
white man. Stanley, before he went exploring in Africa, though ill-
bred and ill-educated, was a decent working-man with a modest opinion
of himself and a good heart, but the position he found himself in in
Africa filled him with the usual idea of being the representative of a
superior race, with right of command over the people of the country
he was travelling through, and little by little he got into the way of
shooting them if they did not obey his orders, or provide him with
food. All his later writing is an attempt to show that he had a high
motive in excuse for these violences, the cause of Christianity, civilization and the rest, till he became a contemptible humbug. His journal-
ism, too, as he gets to that point of his career, gives him the nauseous
flamboyant style I remember in his lecture at the Albert Hall. He re-

mained to the last the rough lout he began life as, with a veneer of sham romance added, which made his later life so despicable. Nevertheless, as was the case with Burton, his brutality gained him the devotion of a superior woman far too good for him. There are many points of resemblance between the two men revealed in their base countenances, though Stanley's is the more ignoble of the two.

" Morley's Indian reforms are published, poor things in truth, for though an unofficial majority is in name conceded to the Provincial Councils, it is not an Indian majority, the Anglo-Indian non-officials being counted in, so that there remains everywhere an English majority. Also the Government grants itself a power of vetoing the candidature of any Indian; this, with new powers of arbitrary arrest and of seizing newspapers and printing presses, leaves native India in a worse position than when Lord Morley came into office. Nevertheless, his sham reforms are a long step towards real revolution.

" *23rd Nov.*— The Abbé Brémond, Tyrrell's friend, who performed his funeral rights, has recanted his errors publicly and made apology at Rome, so poor Miss Petre is left out in the cold. I did not like the man when I saw him at Storrington.

" *24th Nov.*— Lunched with George and Sibell. They had all been attending the debate in the Lords (about the Budget), the House crowded with peeresses and, George said, the most representative assembly he had ever seen, representing as it did very grade of society from royal princesses down to Rosie Boote, Marchioness of Headfort. George quite approves the fighting attitude of the peers and believes in his party winning at the General Elections. He has been doing a great deal of the fighting himself. George has written an excellent sonnet which he sent me a day or two ago.

" *25th Nov.*— Called on Frank Lascelles. Talking about the Budget quarrel he told me he had a long conversation yesterday with old Joe Chamberlain. Chamberlain is paralysed but quite clear in his mind, though he has a difficulty in speech being unable sometimes to pronounce his words rightly. He assured Frank that the Tories would return to power with a large majority. In England, whatever it might be in Scotland, they would sweep the board. Then to luncheon with Winston and Clemmie. I told him of Joe's prediction, but he declared the Government would remain with a clear majority of sixty after the election, independently of the Irish. About Somaliland he told me things had been arranged according to his wishes. The troops are to be moved to the coast. ' I don't call it evacuation,' he said, ' but concentration, it sounds better.' This is satisfactory. I gave him the first copy of my ' India under Ripon,' which reached me on Monday, and we discussed the whole question of Empire over again and I find him much more favourable to my anti-Imperial views than he was two months ago. Indeed, he is almost converted to the view that the British Empire will eventually ruin England. 'We get no advantage from it,' he said, 'and it's a lot of bother. The only thing one can say for it is it is justified if it is undertaken in an altruistic spirit for the good of the subject races.' I said, 'Yes, but where do we find the altruism?' and I repeated to him a story my hairdresser, Middleton, told me yesterday of how a military customer had come into his shop one day when old Lewis, his former master, was alive, and how he had spent ten minutes expounding to them the glories of the Empire, across the counter. 'Old Mr. Lewis stood there all the time saying nothing, and the customer began to lose patience, "You don't say a word," he exclaimed, "now tell me Lewis, frankly, what your opinion of the Empire really is?" The old man seemed to think awhile and then in his deliberate way replied, "Well sir, you see, I have only been to the Empire twice and I didn't find the entertainment amusing enough to go a third time." He thought, or pretended to think, the talk had been about the Empire theatre. It was a good answer, but we lost our customer, he never came again.'

"Winston was brilliant as usual, and he inspires brilliancy in those about him. I found myself talking in epigrams and we had a merry rattling hour and a half before he was obliged to go back to his office, with intervals of domestic felicity, his baby being brought in with the coffee. There is no more fortunate man than Winston at home or in his political prosperity. He is quite ready, he says, for Irish Home Rule, and I expect him by degrees to adopt the whole of my programme, including my anti-Socialism. He believes in the acquisition of railways by the nation but is not for nationalizing the land, which, he says, will lead to endless jobbery, the nation being the worst of landlords. All this pleases me. He gave me in return for my Indian book a volume he has just published of his speeches.

"*30th Nov.*— Hyndman writes me a long eulogistic letter about my Indian book, 'India under Ripon,' which has just come out, and asks me to help his candidature at the elections; this, of course, I cannot do, though he would be personally an acquisition to the House of Commons. He tells me he is sixty-eight (too old to begin).

"*4th Dec.*— The Lords have thrown out the Budget by a majority of 260 to 75, and the Commons have passed a resolution by a majority of 250, saying the Lords had no right to do it. The Irish did not vote. So here we have war declared, it is pretended to the knife, but I expect it will end in some compromise; there is not stuff enough in the country to make a revolution.

"*5th Dec.*— Belloc and his wife came to dinner. He looks for a 160 majority for the Government, and he expects a great creation of peers, hoping he himself may be one. There was much talk in Belloc's random way about the corrupt practices of Governments and the sale of titles.   Mark Napier was with us and defended Asquith's integrity.

" Belloc has written a very amusing little squib in rhyme which he recited to us, a ballad of which the leading line is ' And Mrs. James will entertain the King.'   If this comes to His Majesty's ears it may stand in the way of his hoped for honour.   I have been reading Belloc's ' Marie Antoinette ' and find it most interesting.

" *17th Dec.*— That scoundrel, King Leopold of Belgium, is dead, the greatest ruffian of all those sitting in the high places of the Earth. I remember once having speech with him as long ago as 1863, when I was an attaché of the Madrid Legation.   It was in the picture gallery in the Retiro where I was copying a Velasquez, and he and an aide-de-camp came behind me and looked over my work and talked to me for a few minutes about matters of art; a tall, black-bearded man, by no means ill-looking; he cannot have been more than thirty then.   It is just a reminiscence and no more.   The history of the Congo State will hand his name down to posterity as that of one of the most infamous among kings.   He has, however, made a pious ending, and has received the sacraments, including absolution of his crimes, so our good Catholics of the Belloc school will doubtless say their prayers to him as to a saint.   His death has disclosed the fact of a secret marriage made by him some years ago with a French girl who has borne him two sons more or less legitimate.   It may give rise to dynastic complications, the papers say.

" *20th Dec.*— The Unwins and Meynell dined with me.   Great talk about the elections.   The King, they say, strongly disapproved of the throwing out of the Budget by the Lords, and will create 300 peers. Redmond has declared in favour of the Liberals in virtue of a not very clear Home Rule pronouncement made by Asquith, but I trust he has got it in writing more clearly from the Cabinet or he runs the risk of being made a fool of should the Liberals return in power enough to do without him.   Their safest policy would be to lower the Liberal majority, and I wrote about it some time ago to Dillon.   If it is true that the King sides with Asquith, it is very important.   Arthur Balfour has chosen the occasion of the elections for one of his influenzas.

" *31st Dec.*— The year 1909 has been a notable one for the world, all that portion of it that most interests me, the deposition of the Sultan, Abdul Hamid, and of the Shah of Persia, with grave events in India. As to my own life I feel that I have come at last to its watershed, and that whatever happens henceforth can only be on the downward slope, not without its little pleasures perhaps, but still with no possibility of again ascending.

CHAPTER VIII

KING EDWARD'S DEATH

" 1st Jan., 1910.— Colonel Louis Gordon came to luncheon, bringing with him several interesting papers of his uncle's. He is the family depositary of these, and is helping me with my proposed new volume, ' Gordon at Khartoum.'

" 16th Jan. (Sunday).— The General Elections began yesterday. George Wyndham is in by an increased majority at Dover, and Belloc keeps his seat at Salford; but Eddy Tennant is out at Salisbury, which means that he will be made a peer. The popular feeling seems not very strong against the Lords, but democracy is a foolish, fickle thing.

" 23rd Jan.— Newbuildings. Belloc was here yesterday, much pleased with having retained his seat, and anxious to know my opinion whether he should accept a place in the Government if they should offer it. I said, ' Of course.' Why, indeed, should he refuse? He is a clever fellow, and wants to get on, and has no particular principle to sacrifice, except his beer.

" On Wednesday two Indian Mohammedans, Saïd Mahmud and Nasir ed Din Hassan, spent the afternoon here, and gave me a deal of information about things in India. They are excellent young men, and are anxious that I should help them to found a society for the Moslems in London, especially the Indian Moslems, which should have nothing to do with Amir Ali and the Government. I agreed to do what I could about it. We might call it the Moslem Patriotic Club or something of the kind, and co-operate with the Hindoos.

" I have written a line to George Wyndham, in which I say: ' I think you have a great policy now to take up. Cannot you come to terms with Redmond by which, in return for Home Rule, he should join you in a Tariff Reform amendment to the Budget? What the elections show more than anything is that England, apart from Scotland and Wales, is an entirely Conservative country. . . . If at the same time you would give Home Rule to Scotland and Wales you would box the compass and remain in office for the next twenty years.'

" 25th Jan.— I have recorded my vote at the election for Winterton, the Tory candidate, his opponent being one Owthwaite, an Australian land nationalizer, a carpet bagger sent down from London.

" 26th Jan.— There is a new assassination in India, this time of a

Mohammedan police officer in the High Court at Calcutta who has been getting up prosecutions for the Government, and Minto announces new measures of coercion. It is the Irish history over again, with Morley playing the part of Buckshot Forster at the Indian Office.

" *1st Feb.*— To London and called on Lady C. We talked about the elections, and she declares that the King will very certainly refuse to create the 400 peers needed to deal with the House of Lords. ' You may take my word for that,' she said. I told her I thought the King would do very wisely to refuse, as there was no really strong feeling against the Lords, and she said : ' I will let him know what you say; he would pay attention to your opinion.' She tells me the King has no ill-will towards me, but my books give offence with the Court people, who cannot understand how I, with my position of an English gentleman and landowner, can go in for revolution in Egypt and India.

" *3rd Feb.*— Spent the afternoon with Rivers Wilson, who told me much that was interesting of his official days in Egypt, and his recollections of General Gordon. [I have embodied most of what he told me in my ' Gordon at Khartoum,' and need not transcribe it here.]

" *4th Feb.*— Called on Clementine Churchill and arranged that I am to lunch with her and Winston on the 10th, just before he attends the Cabinet which will decide the momentous question of the procedure against the House of Lords. So far neither Winston nor any of them knows what Asquith intends about the changes in the Cabinet. We hope Winston may get the Home Office.

" *5th Feb.*— George Wyndham lunched with me. He assures me the Conservative peers have not the least idea of throwing up the sponge about their hereditary right to veto, nor does he at all fear that the King will swamp their House with new creations. He thinks there will be a kind of deadlock in politics, which will prevent legislation of any kind for the next five years. The strength of the Tory position is that they and the King together command the whole material force of the country, besides half its voting strength. They have the money, and the army and the navy and the territorials, all down to the Boy Scouts. Why, then, should they consent to a change in the constitution without fighting?

" *6th Feb.*— Lady Gregory (who is in London trying to raise funds for her Dublin theatre), as well as George Wyndham and Hudson, the naturalist, came to dinner. There is a story about that Lord Percy, who died of pneumonia in a small hotel at Paris six weeks ago, was really shot in a duel there, and, what is quite absurd, that it was by Winston Churchill.

" *10th Feb.*— Lunched, as arranged, with Winston and Clementine. He had just been at the Cabinet in Downing Street, and arrived late, looking rather grave; but he soon cheered up, and began talking about the situation. Nothing has yet been settled about the policy, which depends on two unknown factors, Redmond and the King. The Nationalist alliance with the Liberals is anything but popular in Ireland, and O'Brien's success in getting ten of his men returned may force Redmond's hand. ' Of course,' said Winston, ' if they (the Nationalists) go, we're done for '; but he does not really fear this. The King is the true master of the situation as far as the quarrel with the Lords goes, and they dare not try to force his hand. ' It would never do,' he said, ' to bring the King into the dispute.' What Winston anticipates is a new dissolution, when he thinks they would gain thirty more seats. As to his own position in the Cabinet also nothing is settled. There is to be a ' general post,' but nobody knows who is to get what. He would like the Home Office. He would not take Ireland, unless it were to grant Home Rule. I questioned him as to his understanding to the Home Rule to be given, and he said it would be complete Parliamentary Government of all Irish affairs in Dublin, including finance police, and everything, but not the power of levying Custom duties against England, or altering the land settlement, and, of course, none of levying troops or of treating with foreign Powers. He would have the Irish members still sit at Westminister, but in diminished numbers. He quite admitted the alliance between the Irish and the Liberals was unnatural, and that their natural alliance would be with the Tories. As to Somaliland, he told me that he had managed to get the policy of returning to the sea coast adopted, but the devil of it was that the Mullah would not be quiet. As soon as the outposts were evacuated he came down on the friendly tribes and slaughtered them. The Government had sent a man to propose a money settlement in favour of the tribes with the Mullah, but the Mullah had cut off the man's head. This made an unpleasant situation. He was pleased when I told him I should like to see him Prime Minister. ' I think,' he said, ' you may see me yet carry out your ideas ' (meaning my anti-Imperial ideas). He and Clementine are to come to Newbuildings to hear the nightingales. They are on just the same honeymoon terms as ever.

" On my way home I looked in on Frank Lascelles, who gave me a deal of interesting information about his relations with General Gordon when they were both in Egypt. [But this, too, has been embodied in my ' Gordon at Khartoum.']

" 11*th Feb.*— Lunched at the Reform Club with Fisher Unwin, who had invited Mackarness and Cotton to talk over Egypt and India, both good men who have worked hard in the unpopular cause of liberty and have failed at the elections.

" 13*th Feb.*— John Redmond called on me, and we had a long hour's talk about the situation in England and also in Ireland. I began by giving him my view of the deadlock; the impossibility Asquith was in of getting the King to coerce the Lords, and that I did not think Asquith or Grey or Haldane was really in earnest about Home Rule, though Churchill and Lloyd George were. He said he quite agreed with this view. He believed in Asquith to the extent that he would trust him if he made a promise in so many words, but he had not quite done so about Ireland. What he had promised was full self-government, subject to the control of the Imperial Parliament. Churchill, he believed, was quite sincere. He had a very high opinion of him. Churchill had told him once that it was the ambition of his life to bring in a Home Rule Bill as Chief Secretary. How his own Irish party would vote on the Budget would depend upon whether Asquith kept his pledge of making the House of Lords Veto Bill the first question for the new Parliament. They had no idea of voting the Budget first and waiting for the House of Lords Bill. If that was decided upon in the Cabinet they would move an Amendment and vote against him. He said he did not see there was any good to be got by keeping Asquith in office if he could not give them Home Rule, or anything much to be feared by letting Balfour into office. Unless the Liberal party could abolish the Lords' Veto there was as much to be hoped from the Tories as from them. He told me as a great secret that when Dudley was Lord Lieutenant he had sent for him, Redmond, one day, and had proposed that he should join the Tories on Tariff Reform. Redmond said he was quite willing, but would want Home Rule in exchange. Whereon Dudley had said it was no good going on with the argument. But all the same, he believed the Tory rank and file would make no insuperable difficulty. In Ireland the defeat of the Government would be hailed with delight. 'There will be bonfires lit on every hill in Ireland.' The alliance with the Liberals was very unpopular, and the people wanted a fighting policy again for Home Rule. He also explained to me O'Brien's attitude as largely a personal one. His hatred for Dillon was greater now than if they had never been such close friends. His general attitude was the same as Dunraven's Devolution and Reform; but if it came to a question of real Home Rule they could, of course, count on him. As to the influence of the Clergy it was nothing to what it had been twenty-five years ago; wherever the Clergy had opposed an election the election had been won. He promised to send Dillon to see me. I am sure he has told me the whole of what he thinks.

" 15*th Feb.*— The changes in the Cabinet are announced. Winston gets the Home Office, and I have written to congratulate him and remind him of his promise to reform prison discipline. I shall send him a memorandum of what I think ought to be done.

" 16*th Feb.*— Winston has telegraphed thanking me for my letter, and asking for the memorandum about prison reform.

" Edith Lytton called to-day. Talking of the new Viceroy who is to be named for India, she declared Kitchener to be quite out of the question. His appointment would set all India on fire. It had been found out that he had enrolled spies in Sepoy Regiments to report disaffection, and the Sepoys had been furious. Kitchener was brutal, and had shown himself to be so at Omdurman. I was surprised to hear this from her.

" *17th Feb.*— Victor Lytton came to lunch to talk over the question of prison reform with me. He talked intelligently on the subject, in which he is much interested.

" *18th Feb.*— Redmond seems to be following out the policy we agreed on together, and there is good prospect of the Irish Labour men voting an amendment to the Address, and Asquith having to resign. If Asquith has to resign it will be a fine consummation, and put a final end to what Whig Government we shall see in our time. It has at last been discovered that Asquith had not the King behind him or any promise except that if there was a majority of 500 the King would create peers. As there will be no clear majority at all the King, of course, will do nothing.

" *19th Feb.*— Newbuildings. The political crisis has come to a head, and there is every prospect now of Asquith coming to grief either on the Address or on the Budget. I called on Belloc to-day at Shipley and found him in a great state of excitement, claiming to have caused the revolt of the extreme Radicals by a letter he wrote a week ago to the ' Times.' He showed me an amendment to the Address he intended to move. ' I drafted it,' he said with pride, ' in a pothouse with Maurice Baring, quite in the traditional manner, and I sent it to the " Times," threatening if they did not insert it I would have it in every paper in the North of England. But for me the party would have let Asquith break all his pledges.' Belloc counts now upon breaking up the Whigs and getting office with Lloyd George, Churchill, Loulou Harcourt, and the extreme Radicals, but he will have to wait for that. Asquith may remain in office at present, he thinks, through the support of the Tories.

" *21st Feb.*— Back to London, and was lucky enough to find George Wyndham in Belgrave Square, where we compared notes about the political situation. Everybody, he tells me, has got hold of the idea that a truce has been patched up between Asquith and Redmond, and he was anxious to prove to me that Redmond was a fool to be taken in by Asquith's soft sawder. He has seen the King's speech which is to be read this afternoon; and though he said he had no right to reveal anything, told me it was an absurd document, as I would admit when published. It might mean almost anything. I did not tell him I had seen Redmond, but consoled him in a general way about the Irish vote, which I was sure would not be given to the Government without Asquith's declaration that he had very definite guarantees. He thinks if so that Asquith will be out of office by the end of the week. He would come again in the evening, and give me a full account of everything in the House when it was over. This he did, and unfolded all his secrets. He began by giving a dramatic account of the reading of the King's speech and the debate in the Commons which followed it. The speech is certainly one of the most feeble and obscure and ungrammatical ever composed by the Committee of the Cabinet which draws these speeches up, and reads as if it was the House of Commons, not the Lords, which was to be attacked. He described Arthur Balfour's speech which followed as artistically the best he had heard him make, but too subtle to be understood by the dullards of the House, though leading up to an effective climax, ' a series of lancet wounds,' George said, ' from first to last, ending in a stiletto stab.' Asquith's reply showed courage. He declared he had never intended to imply that he had got any guarantee from the King or even asked for one, only such guarantee as a Bill brought in in Parliament could give. The finance was the first consideration, and then the Veto. His speech was well reasoned, but excited no enthusiasm. Then Redmond got up, and also made an excellent speech, less of an oration than is his usual style, but more effective. He declared roundly that Ireland had no interest in helping the Government to pass their Budget; the Veto was all they cared for, as a preliminary to Home Rule.

" What was most interesting in George's account was his estimate of what next would happen. He became very confidential, and told me Balfour did not intend to take office if Asquith resigned. Certainly he, George, would refuse office, though he knew a high one would be offered him. He thinks there would then be no way out of the deadlock except by Rosebery being invited to form an Administration of a stop-gap kind, which he could do with Milner, Cromer, George Curzon, Hugh Cecil, and Lord Durham. It would be supported by the Tories till after another General Election.

" I asked him about Lord Percy's death, and he told me the story was nonsense of his having died otherwise than of pneumonia. He had known Percy intimately well. He described him as a man who had never had any passionate adventures; who was deeply religious, of his father's Irvingite creed; interested in politics, but only in a pessimistic sense, as he believed all was going hopelessly wrong. His vitality was low, and he easily succumbed. There was no real mystery at all about his death, but the Paris newspapers could not understand how an English lord should be staying at the Gare du Nord Hotel instead of one more fashionable, and so had invented a fanciful explanation, and thus every kind of absurdity had been put about, but there was not a ghost of foundation for any of them. Every public man who fell ill at

Paris was liable to stories about him. It was generally attributed either to delirium tremens or adultery.

"*22nd Feb.*— Boutros Pasha (the Coptic Prime Minister) has been assassinated at Cairo by one Ibrahim Wardani, a young Nationalist, secretary of the Geneva Congress last year. He says he did it to rid Egypt of a minister who was betraying her, as he had already betrayed her on other occasions. It is the first instance of bloodshed by an Egyptian Nationalist. An Egyptian with a letter of recommendation from Arabi lately written, called on me, and when I asked him what he thought of Boutros' death said very simply, 'A good thing. I think it will do good.' Yet he was certainly no fanatic or anything otherwise than a quite harmless sort of professor, wanting to give a lecture on law at the London University. This shows how general anti-English feeling in Egypt has become, and how violent. Rivers Wilson, who asked me to come and see him, had much to tell about Boutros, who had been a friend of his, having helped him on a Commission of Liquidation as long ago as 1879. He had always been an Anglophile, a man of ability but without independence and ready to do what he was told. He was content to be in office and draw his salary, £3,000 a year. This is just what the Nationalists complain of in Boutros. Also they have a special quarrel with him, first, because, as Minister of Foreign Affairs, he had signed the treaty with Cromer which ceded half the sovereignty of the Soudan to England. Secondly, because he connived at the Anglo-French entente about Egypt in 1903; thirdly, because, acting as Minister of Justice, he had presided at the Denshawai trial, and lastly, because, as Prime Minister, he had again played into English hands the other day in the matter of the Suez Canal. It was this last betrayal probably that caused his death.

"*25th Feb.*— The Government have escaped from the Tory Amendment for Tariff Reform by the skin of their teeth, a majority of thirty-one only, the Irish having abstained from voting, as well as Belloc and half-a-dozen other Radicals.

"I have sent in my Prison Memorandum to Churchill. (See Appendix.)

"*26th Feb.*— Mary Wentworth arrived this morning from Teneriffe, very ill, poor girl, and I have put her up in Chapel Street. George Wyndham dined with me, and we both chuckled over the wretched plight of the Whigs. Balfour, he tells me, does not wish them to resign and would be glad to keep them on for another year, as pensioners upon Tory good will. I showed him the prison memorandum I have sent to Winston, which he much approves, also two letters I received this morning, one from Hyndman, about the Chinese in Tibet, the other from Malony, about Persia, both most interesting.

"My old friend, Mme. Arcos, on whom I called to-day, tells me the

Empress Eugénie is delighted with my books about Egypt and about
Cromer, whom she greatly dislikes. The Empress, she tells me, is
wonderful considering her age, neither blind nor deaf, still taking an
interest in everything and entirely up-to-date.

" 1st March.— Asquith has accepted the extremists' lead, it was the
only thing he had to do except resigning, so they are to be helped
through supply by the Irish and the Tories. The Budget is to be put
off till after Easter, and the resolution against the Lords' veto passed
meanwhile.

" 2nd March.— George Wyndham came to luncheon. There will be
dissolution in May or June. Rosebery is to bring in a scheme of reform for the House of Lords at once.

" 3rd March.— Called on Hyndman and had a long talk with him,
mostly on Indian affairs. He believes in a very short date for the
revolution there and that it will come about through the Gurkhas and
the Maharaja of Udaipur. He regards the occupation of Lhassa by the
Chinese as the beginning of a great movement. I don't know how this
may be. Hyndman is a big, burly, bearded fellow, a rough edition of
William Morris, with the same energetic talk on Socialistic topics that
I remember in Morris. He lives in Queen Anne's Gate, which is used
as a Socialist Bureau as well as his residence, and the whole time we
were conversing he was being rung up constantly by a telephone in
his room. 'Hullo! what is it? Yes, thank you, good-bye.' We discussed the prospects of Socialism and how it would affect Imperial questions, and I told him I believed it would be just as bad for the subject
races in Asia under a Socialistic régime in England as now. This he
would not agree to, but he did not convince me I was wrong. 'We are
National too,' he said, 'as well as International and have no wish to
go on preying on the Asiatics. We hold that we could get enough employment for all our millions at home without it, if our energies were
turned in the right direction. He is a strong believer in the intention
of the German Government to attack us, and is for compulsory military
training in England (not military service) in defence of the country,
also for a close union between the democracies of England and of the
Continent, for a Channel tunnel, and for garrisoning Antwerp with
English troops. He says the Belgians are quite ready for this in case
of war. The war itself cannot be prevented as the democracy in Germany is powerless against the Government. Bebel and all the leaders
assure him of this. England from its geographical position, which is
unique in the world, ought to be the centre of the world's industry and
the citadel of democracy. Hyndman, amongst other things, to-day
asked my opinion of Churchill, and I told him there were three things
of value in him, great ability, honesty in politics, and a good heart.
'That,' said he, 'is the first favourable account I have had given me

about him, especially about his heart. They tell me he is rude and brutal with servants.' I assured him it was not so, and he was glad to hear it. He gave me to read the newly published 'History of the Indian Revolution of 1857' [a highly seditious and interesting volume, written by Savarkar, whom afterwards they imprisoned for life].

"*4th March.*— Two more young Indians called, both from Cambridge, Mohammedan Nationalists of advanced opinions and ready to join the Hindoos.

"*7th March.*— Dillon writes: 'I am glad you consider the party has done well. I am extremely well satisfied. I do not think the party ever occupied a stronger position. We have undoubtedly saved the Liberal party from a catastrophe.'

"*8th March.*— There seems a good chance now in Egypt, that the General Assembly will reject the Suez Canal Convention and I see that Prince Husseyn has resigned his presidency of the Assembly. He was the Convention's principal advocate. The new Prime Minister is to be Mohammed Said, a Nationalist of the Saad Zaghloul school, this is a gain. [This is the first mention in my diary of Prince Husseyn, who has since been rewarded for his services to the English party at Cairo by being made Sultan of Egypt.]

"*10th March.*— William O'Brien has sent me an article he has written in the 'Nineteenth Century' in a Union of Hearts sense to which I have answered: 'The older I get the more revolutionist I become about the British Empire, and about Ireland the more Fenian. The Union of Hearts is a long while on its way, and unless it is brought about in some violent form, I hardly hope to see it. I often think of good old Dr. Duggan, whom we loved so much, and who used to wish he was not a Bishop so that he might be in the Portsmouth dockyard blowing up English ships. Perhaps he was right, we English are a very stubborn people to convert.' I have also written to Hyndman about the book he gave me. I find it very interesting but at the same time depressing. One cannot help seeing in the account it gives of the revolution of 1857, that if with all the advantages native India then had of taking us unawares and comparatively defenceless it could not succeed, it has hardly any chance now, nor do I think a rising will be attempted. The break-up of the British Empire will come more likely through a financial collapse and troubles nearer home. India will profit by it but will not initiate it.

"*15th March.*— The Debate on the Reform of the House of Lords began to-day, Rosebery making a great oration. George Wyndham came to tea and stayed on talking. The Tories are angry because the Government have only voted supplies for six weeks with the idea of then resigning and leaving their successors in a financial hole. The only thing then, George thinks, will be to get the Rothschilds and the

City generally to make another advance of thirty millions to carry on
with till the new General Election is over. He thinks Rosebery could
manage this with the Jews. He had just come from the House of
Commons and had heard Churchill announce his scheme of prison reform, which is based closely on my memorandum. George entirely approves the scheme as he did what I had written about it three weeks
ago.

"16th March.— Winston's pronouncement on prison reform reads
better than even George's description of it. It is everything I could
have wished, and I went to Eccleston Square to congratulate, and found
him alone. He is quite thorough about the reforms and said he would
have liked to adopt the whole of my programme only public opinion was
not ready for it yet. However, the Home Secretary will now have full
power to mitigate prison treatment, and, except for crimes of violence,
to put all prisoners with a good character (and that will include political
prisoners) in the first class of misdemeanants.

"With regard to the political situation, Winston said: 'We shall
carry on all right now till the end of April, when the crash will come
either on the Budget or the Lords' veto. If we are beaten on the Budget
we shall resign; but I can't think Redmond will be fool enough to turn
us out, though we don't know what he is going to do. If he votes
against the Budget he will take all the sting out of the attack on the
Lords, and the Irish have no chance of getting Home Rule except by
abolishing the veto.' He is sore with Redmond for making himself a
leader of revolt with the Radicals against the Government. He thinks
his party will win seats at the General Election. If so, they will remain in office, and when the Peers reject the veto will dissolve Parliament.

"Dillon writes showing that he is not for upsetting the Government.
'I cannot quite agree with you about the Liberals. The leaders have
behaved badly, but the rank and file is sounder than at any time since
Rosebery's betrayal of 1895. I do not see why we should break with
the Liberals without reasonable proposals from the Tories. At present the Tories are under the worst possible influences. It is clearly
our policy to support an attack upon the Lords.'

"17th March.— Goumah writes to say that he means to start a
monthly Nationalist paper in England, and asks me for help. [This
was a first suggestion which led to our issue of the monthly paper
'Egypt.']

"24th March.— They have released eight young men in Egypt whom
they had arrested as Wardani's accomplices.

"31st March.— Chapel Street. Dillon spent an hour and a half this
morning with me. He gave me the exact plan he and Redmond have
determined on. The situation is that Grey and Haldane are trying to

get out of a square fight with the Lords, and are manœuvring to persuade the Irish party to support the Budget and let them stay on in
office without bringing the veto question to a positive issue.   This, however, the Irish are determined not to consent to.   Their plan is first
to support the resolutions against the Lords; then when the Government brings in the Budget to vote for it on the second reading, but not
on the third, and to insist that Asquith shall first get guarantees from
the King that he will create a sufficient number of Peers to pass a Veto
Bill.   If the King promises, well and good.   They will then vote the
third reading of the Budget, and help to get the Veto Bill through; but
if, as is almost certain, the King refuses, then they will insist on
Asquith's resigning, or if he will not resign they will vote against the
third reading.   Dillon says they are absolutely determined on this, and
he authorized me to give Churchill a message to that effect.   He cal-
culates that in this way they can force Balfour to take office, which will
lead to a still greater deadlock than ever.   Balfour, he thinks, dares
not pass the Budget, yet cannot carry on the Government without doing
so during the three months needed for a new General Election.

"He told me a number of interesting things about Ireland.   Wyndham's Land Bill has had the effect of changing the whole character of
the peasantry.   Instead of being careless, idle and improvident, they
have become like the French peasantry, industrious and economical,
even penurious.   Marriages are now contracted later, though the limitation of families had not yet begun owing to Catholic influences, and he
repeated to me what he had said about this influence in Australia,
Canada, and the United States.   'It is in this way,' he said, 'that the
non-Catholic civilization will be beaten by the Catholic.   Irish and
Italian are replacing English and Dutch settlers everywhere in America.
Boston, which used to be the home of the Puritans, now always elects
a Catholic mayor.'

"As to the House of Commons, he says: 'The Labour party has
gone altogether to pieces.   They can't collect money enough to keep
themselves going.   The Radicals have no leaders of ability.   They
have been obliged to take us' (Redmond and himself) 'as their leaders.
The Government is weak and divided; it has lost all prestige.'   Dillon
had urged them over and over again to resign directly they found they
could not get the King's help against the Lords, but they clung to office,
and now they are discredited.

"*2nd April.*— A week-end party at Newbuildings.   The Churchills,
the Granville Barkers, and Beauclerk, with great discussions.   Winston
had been to Brighton for the day, and had been entertained by the
Mayor and taken a round of reformatory schools, and had been hissed
and cheered by rival factions at the railway station.   He means business
with his prison reforms, and is making a distinction between political

and common prisoners; but he is obstinate about forcible feeding in spite of all Barker and I could say about torture and the Spanish inquisition, which it closely resembles. Barker has paid much attention to these prison matters, and is a very good talker and a pleasant fellow.

" *3rd April.*— A brilliant day of talk. After breakfast I took Winston into the New Room, and we had the whole question of the Budget out together and the veto and the Irish vote. I gave him Dillon's message, which for a moment rather staggered him, as he was under the impression the Irish would in the end give way and let the Budget pass, and he said that if they persisted in wrecking the Government their blood would be on their own heads. The Liberal party would never support Home Rule again. The policy of wrecking one party after another would only result in the two parties combining to crush them. I explained, however, that they did not want a quarrel, only that they distrusted Asquith, Haldane, and Grey, and did not intend to be humbugged. This made him reasonable again, and he told me what the Government plan is. They are to finish the Veto resolutions by the 13th, and then go straight on to the Budget and carry it right through to the third reading, the Veto resolutions being meanwhile sent up to the Lords. If the Lords refuse, Asquith will at once apply to the King for assurances that a Veto Bill on the same lines as the resolutions shall be forced on the Lords by the creation of Peers or otherwise, but it is not at all likely the Lords will do this at once. They will put it off till after the Budget battle has been fought, and thus it will be impossible to get the guarantees from the King in time to satisfy the Irish. All the same he does not despair of carrying the Budget through its third reading, the Irish vote notwithstanding, by help of the Tories. They will apply to Balfour for his assistance to carry on the King's Government, and if he refuses will resign and leave him to get out of the mess as he can. They mean to stand or fall on this issue. It is extraordinarily even betting, he says, which way it will go.

" We had a great deal of talk about the King, with whom Winston now corresponds, or rather, to whom he writes a daily account of what goes on in Parliament, this duty having been transferred from the Prime Minister to the Home Secretary, and the King now and then writes in reply. He believes he is personally in good favour with the King, though his last speech might get him into trouble, in which he had said that the King and Commons would have to unite against the encroachment of the Lords. Also he had the advantage that the Liberals, when in office, were always more polite to the King than the Tories. The Tories were in the habit of considering they were doing quite enough for the King by being in office and protecting him from the Radicals and Socialists without showing special politeness, while Liberal Ministers showed him the greatest consideration, thus balancing things between the parties. He thinks the King will promise the guarantees. Churchill is already drawing up his list of peers to be created, should it be necessary, and he offered Beauclerk and me to give us each a peerage when the time came on the sole condition of voting the Veto; after which we might do what we liked. 'I can do it for you if you will take it,' he said, and he proposed it again at dinner, and I said I would think it over. He also offered to get Barker a seat at the next General Elections. None of us took it very seriously, though Barker would, I have no doubt, make an excellent M.P. He is a Fabian, and a man of much political intelligence, besides being an excellent fellow and man of the world. At dinner the conversation was more brilliant than ever. We discussed Morley's character, and Kitchener's *à propos* of his possible succession to Minto as Viceroy of India. Churchill hates Kitchener, who, he told us, once prevented his entering the Egyptian Service, and was always rude to him, he does not know with what reason; and we also discussed Curzon. Churchill has a wonderful memory, which extends to scraps of poetry and fragments of speeches of a hundred years ago. He is also a great and very rapid reader of books. He told us he wrote his life of his father mostly in the House of Commons, and while busy with all sorts of other work.

"*4th April.*— Our party broke up this morning, Winston having a Cabinet to attend, where he doubtless will lay before his fellow conspirators what he has learned of the Irish plans from me, and persuade Asquith to make the public declaration of getting guarantees from the King, which he told me Asquith should give.

"*7th April.*— A rumour of our Irish negotiations has got into print through the London correspondent of the 'Irish Times.' It is singularly exact, and would seem to show that Asquith and Churchill have come to terms with Redmond on the basis of Asquith's engaging himself publicly to resign at once if the King refuses guarantees, and not to stay in office over a new General Election. This, I feel pretty sure, will meet the Irish requirements.

"*14th April.*— O'Brien has blurted out that Lloyd George, when they had their Conference, promised to remit all the obnoxious taxes in the Budget as far as Ireland was concerned, and Lloyd George has given him the lie; nevertheless, I have no doubt the thing is true, as Churchill told me almost as much when he was here.

"*15th April.*— We have won a complete victory in Egypt, the Suez Canal Convention having been rejected by the General Assembly, and our Government having withdrawn from it in consequence. At the same time, there has been a new affirmation made by our people of 'England's right to the Soudan' in joint Sovereignty with the Khedive. By the terms of the Convention of 1899 England's right to occupy the Soudan is concurrent with her occupation of Egypt, and lapses when that ends. The Soudan will probably be retained if we evacuate.

"*25th April.*— Asquith has made his declaration in the House of Commons in accordance with the demands formulated through me by Dillon to Churchill. If the King fails to give the guarantees Asquith will resign; if he gives them he will dissolve Parliament. In return for this Redmond has declared publicly that the Irish party will vote the Budget. I am not sorry for the delay in Asquith's resignation, for things are critical in Egypt; and with Balfour in power here and Curzon and Cromer advising him, we risk having a bit of King Stork again. There is a strong demand now at Cairo for a Constitution and with the Radicals and Irish in power here I don't see how the Liberal Government can refuse it, but there is a strong Press agitation beginning here against Gorst. Belloc, who dined here last night, tells me there is talk at the Foreign Office of his being recalled. There is no doubt his policy has failed completely from the Foreign Office point of view. Wardani's trial has begun at Cairo. According to Osman Ghaleb the defence was to be that Boutros was not killed by the bullets fired into him, but by Dr. Milton's surgery in extracting them. It is ingenious, but will hardly save Wardani.

"A young Indian, Savarkar, has been arrested here on a charge of having written letters inciting to murder in India; this on the demand of the Indian Government. The plan, Kháparde tells me, is to get him to India on any plea, true or false, and when once there to deal with him under the Deportation Law. A queer state of things for us to have come to in England, and a good example of how Imperial despotism abroad is ruining National liberty at home. According to Brailsford, young Savarkar is a most excellent and admirable youth, as all the young political murderers seem to be, both in India and Egypt.

"The Egyptian papers have been full of Roosevelt's adventures at Cairo, and the speech he made to University students in praise of British rule. He is a buffoon of the lowest American type, and roused the fury of young Egypt to boiling point, and it is probable that if he had not cleared straight out of the country there would have been mischief. From Egypt he went on to Rome and had a quarrel with the Pope, and he is now at Paris airing his fooleries, and is to go to Berlin, a kind of mad dog roaming the world.

"*27th April.*— Dillon lunched with me to-day in Chapel Street. The Budget of 1909 is at last to have its third reading to-day, and the King is to arrive in London from Biarritz at six. So far, Dillon tells me, they have not the least idea what the King will do about the Veto. He has been written to twice about it, by Winston, I suppose, as he corresponds with His Majesty, but the King has made no reply. Nobody expects him to create the peers or to give any assurance. According to Belloc (and Dillon agrees with him) he will try to have the

General Election put off till January, on the ground that it will be most unpopular, and an immense expense, which it certainly would be. Dillon has no great confidence in Asquith's keeping his promise of resigning at once when the King refuses to give the assurances, but says it will not matter, as they will always be able to turn him out over the Budget of 1910, and will do so if he tries to shirk. Nor does he trust much in the possibility of abolishing the House of Lords, but expects to get Home Rule from the Tories. He would sooner have these in office with a weak majority than the Whigs. I asked him his opinion of the relative merits of Churchill and Lloyd George. He said they were both men of genius and extraordinary eloquence. Lloyd George was a Celt, entirely in sympathy with Ireland and all the causes Irishmen care for. He knows him well, better than Churchill, who as an Englishman is less one of themselves, but he admires and believes in both. As speakers there are only two in the House who can compare with them, Balfour and Asquith. Balfour is not great intellectually, but he is a great Parliamentary speaker, far the best at present; the Tory party are quite unable to do without him, and had to take him back as their leader after the elections of 1906, although he had made every conceivable mistake in office and he did not agree with them on tariff reform. Asquith, too, was a great speaker, with a power of stating a case clearly and powerfully in a few words such as was possessed by nobody else. His influence, however, is gone. He had been ruined by his second marriage to one who was a Tory at heart, and was always advising him to stand out against Lloyd George and Churchill and the mass of the Radical party. Asquith was quite demoralized. Dillon does not trust him. Before his second marriage Asquith was quite different. He was so unused to Society that when Lady Mathew, Dillon's mother-in-law, asked him to dinner, he did not know how to behave according to the usages of the world, and used to give his arm to his first wife to take her in to dinner. He had no pretension then to being anything but what he was, a Nonconformist of the middle-class; now he had adopted all the failings of the aristocracy. Dillon is off now to Ireland for a month, but will be back for the Veto." [The conversations recorded in the present chapter with Dillon and Redmond about their parliamentary affairs have been very much curtailed by me in putting them in print, though nothing of importance is omitted, but a full transcript would take up too much space, and the subject has become unimportant and would weary all but close parliamentary readers.]

"Called on Lady C. Knollys has been lately with her, and she laughed to scorn the idea of the King creating five hundred peers; he was no such fool. Of Lloyd George she spoke with contempt, as a wretched little lawyer, doubtless reflecting the opinion of the Court about him. Churchill was a gentleman, quite a different sort. Kitchener is to go to India as Viceroy, the King being strong for him, though 'of course, the King can't do everything.' Both Kitchener and the King are to arrive from abroad to-night. Later, in the train, as I was going back to Newbuildings, two lawyers got into the carriage, who talked of having just seen the King drive away from the station. He looked very white and flabby, they said.

"*29th April*.— This morning I opened my window at 3.45, and five minutes later a cuckoo began to sing. I counted the number of notes he repeated, beginning when he had done half-a-dozen or so. He must have been sitting in the big oak tree a hundred yards away from the house, and went on and on for some twenty-five minutes while I counted, watch in hand, having got back into bed. He began with a series of 208, when another cuckoo interrupted at a distance, but after some fifteen seconds he went on again with a series of 368 and another of seventy-one, and another of 354 and then fifty-five. In all 1056 notes without a break of more than a quarter of a minute, nor did he change the place he sang from. I noted with the second hand of the watch that he did thirty-eight to forty notes to the minute, though at the beginning he was quicker and more regular. This must be a record performance. I put down the numbers on a card with a pencil while it was going on. It ended at 4.15 a.m.

"*2nd May*.— I have written to the ' Manchester Guardian ' in answer to Gorst's Egyptian Report, just published, advocating evacuation as the sole alternative to a rule of force. The latter is certainly intended. Dillon writes to say so, and there is a telegram in the ' Daily Telegraph ' announcing on the highest authority that ' the Khedive has decided on deportations after the Indian fashion.' This is a return to the régime of Ismail.

"*6th May*.— To London, where I found the world in commotion with the news of the sudden illness of the King, not likely to live through the day, as his heart was attacked. I went to see Lady C., whom I found at home. ' The King,' she said, ' is not likely to get over it.' He is being treated with oxygen and has five official doctors with him, including old Douglas Powell, and also a little doctor of her own discovery, I forget his name. ' The King has for five years had a swelling in his throat which has been sprayed twice a day, and Laking always said it might develop any time into cancer. When the King came home from Biarritz the other day he insisted upon going the very same night to the opera, and has since been to two theatres, and to see the Royal Academy Pictures. He cannot do without excitement. His death,' she said, ' will be a great loss to the world and a great loss to me. He has been a good friend to me, and everything will be changed now. There will be a regular sweep of the people that used to be about the Court, the Jews and the second-rate women that the King preferred to his aristocracy, because they amused him. The Prince of Wales hates all these, and will have nothing to do with them. The King is a Radical, though not a Socialist. He told me once that he had gone to hear Gambetta speak, and that he spoke so well that he had half converted him to be a republican. He is a clever man and a great King. His death will be a great loss.'

"Meynell and Kháparde dined with me. We feel sure that if the King dies the whole question of the Veto will be shelved, at any rate, for a time, as it will upset every calculation. The bulletins this evening are very ominous. When I saw Lady C. to-day she repeated to me that Kitchener was certain to be appointed Governor-General in India, as they were afraid of having him here. She asked me whether I should like to meet him at her house, but I said I would rather not, as I had had a public quarrel with him about the Mahdi's head, and I related the whole story to her. Kháparde thinks it would be a good thing for India if Kitchener went there, as it would bring the revolution to a head.

"Meynell tells me the sale of Thompson's works during the past twelve months has gone to 18,000 volumes. Also that Father Angelo de Bary is engaged to marry Miss Bunston!

"*7th May.*— I was writing this of yesterday in bed at seven in the morning when the milkman brought the news that the King died at midnight. It is a very serious matter for all the world, for internationally Edward VII held a high position, and at home was a guarantee against revolution. Personally, though I had never much to do with him directly, I have regarded him as a friendly influence. Lady C. has always assured me of this. We were pretty nearly contemporaries, and I knew many people he knew. Peace be with him.

"Down to Clouds by the one o'clock train. As I started on my way to Waterloo Station I saw the Royal standard at half mast high on Buckingham Palace, and bells were ringing for the new king, George V.

"Clouds. It is a family party here, and in the middle of dinner George arrived from London full of the news of King George's accession. He and Arthur Balfour had been telegraphed for in the morning to attend a general meeting of the Privy Council, and he gave us the whole story of what had taken place at it. It appears that on the demise of the Crown all authority in the country ceases till the new King is proclaimed, either by Parliament or the law officers or any other body than the Privy Council, whose business it becomes to proclaim the dead King's successor. In theory the King never dies, but until the proclamation it is supposed to be in doubt who the King is, and it is the Council that decides, the Council being the primitive Government of England. At midnight, immediately after King Edward's death (for he died at 11.40), it fell to Winston as Home Secretary to announce the event to the Lord Mayor of London, and from that moment till 4.30 this afternoon there was no Government in England. What authority there is vests in the Lord President of the Council, in this case Crewe, who issues formal notice to each member of the Privy Council to attend a meeting instantly, naming the hour. George showed us his black-edged summons, which I noticed was unsigned by anyone, but sent by hand in an official envelope. He and Arthur had received their summonses in London, having had informal notice by telegraph. On arrival Arthur would not go to the Carlton Club himself, but sent George to find out all about it, and what clothes they were to wear, and they dressed in uniform, with crape sashes round their sleeves, and walked to St. James's Palace, where the meeting was held. There were 150 members of the Council present, more or less, out of 250, the total number, and the Lord Mayor and some Aldermen were there, though these last, not being members, were turned out before the proceedings began. No one sat down except old Lord Cross, who was infirm, and no one shook hands or talked except to exchange a word or two silently. Crewe opened the proceedings, George said, with great dignity. He announced the King's death and the duty of the Council to proclaim his successor briefly and clearly. No one else spoke. Then Prince Christian, as representing the Royal family, went out with the Archbishop of Canterbury and the Lord Chancellor, and presently came back with the Prince of Wales, whom they presented to the Council as King, and the King made a short speech, extremely well expressed and with much feeling, and took his seat, and all those present knelt with the right knee upon a cushion placed upon a stool and kissed his hand and swore allegiance on the Book. Thus was King George V proclaimed. ' A mediæval ceremony,' George said, ' of a most impressive kind, and quite apart from the vulgarities of modern life, there being no reporters or outsiders of any sort, a return to the reality of ancient days, when the King and his Council were the sole legal Government of England, all the rest, the government by Lords and Commons and votes in Parliament and Prime Ministers, being only a modern delegation of authority tolerated, but not strictly legal. At this point old Percy, George's father, woke up from his half sleep into which he had sunk and said he hoped there would be a return to this primitive form of rule in England before long. It was all he said. ' The Jews of the Privy Council,' George went on, ' took their oaths on the Old Testament and the Catholics separately. Amongst these last, to the general surprise, Cassel.'

" George told us next how, on the death of Queen Victoria in 1901, he, as Chief Secretary, had proclaimed the late King Edward at Dublin, and how he had been much impressed by King Edward's good sense when he visited Ireland later, especially in connection with words he had used on landing about the Pope, whose death had been announced the day before. George had gone over from Dublin to meet His Majesty at Holyhead, and all the Dublin officials had been alarmed about what the King might say; but as soon as the King came on board his yacht he sent for the captain and said to him: ' Take Mr. Wyndham to a cabin where he can be alone, and give him a pencil and paper,' and he asked George to draw up a speech for him. This George did. But the King vastly improved the draft, and on landing said exactly the right thing, so that Protestants and Catholics alike were pleased. We all agreed that the late King was a great loss in foreign politics, though George thinks that perhaps his death may bring the Emperor William to the funeral, and so lay the foundation of a peace with Germany. I doubt it. ' The Emperor,' he said, ' is fifty, and has found out that, though he has an immense army, not a single soldier in it has been under fire, and he has no assurance that he would be able to command it in war. For forty years the German army has not fired a shot.' All the same I can see that the prospect of a new and more Conservative King is welcome in this house.

" 11*th May.*— George went away to-day to take the Parliamentary oath to the new king. We have had much talk, both about affairs here in England and also about Egypt. I showed him the proof sheets of my articles on Gorst's report, and he remarked that Egypt would certainly not be evacuated, which, of course, is true. He made me alter a word or two, so as to make it less hostile to Gorst, in whose favour he is interested through his former private secretary, Mark Sykes, who married Gorst's sister. On the main point, however, we are agreed, namely, that the future of Egypt is bound up in the general future of Asia, and especially of the Ottoman Empire. George is inclined to minimize the chances of Asia being able to regenerate herself and hold her own against Europe; while I am strong in my belief in this. He says the Russians are far more bent on recovering their position in Asia than in making any advance westwards. He hears this doubtless from his brother Guy, who is military attaché at Petersburg, but the signs of the times are distinctly of an awakening everywhere of the Asiatic races to a sense of the necessity of self-preservation. Even in China the Emperor has been obliged to summon a kind of Parliament, and the Turks have pretty well tided over their danger of absorption. The real hope for Asia as against Europe lies, in my opinion, in the seeds of social decay so very visible among the Teutonic races and the higher European civilization generally, where these are beginning to commit suicide. My last word to George was in this sense: ' The men will refuse to work and the women will refuse to breed.'

" About the prospects in England, all here seem to think the political crisis indefinitely postponed by the King's death, and that Asquith will be able to potter on now till the end of the year. They tell me the new Court is going to be a very moral one, but they hope it will be saved from dullness by becoming intellectual, but we fear it is not likely to attract many geniuses.

" 13*th May*.— Everybody has gone into black for the King's death, and some enthusiasts talk of going on mourning for a year. It is all very absurd, considering what the poor King was, but the papers are crammed with his praises as if he had been a saint of God. All the week since his death has been one of storms and tempests attributed to a comet so diminutive that nobody has seen it yet, and last night one of the great beech trees was thrown down in the park. I saw it lying uprooted on my way to the station this morning, symbol of the dead King, quite rotten at the root, but one half of it clothed with its spring green.

" Arrived in Chapel Street, I went at once to see Lady C., who had written me asking me to come, as she had things to tell me she could not put on paper. She gave me a graphic account of the King's death as she had heard it from the King's doctors, Laking, Reid, and Dawson. ' The King,' she said, ' has had a swelling in the throat for three or four years past, with latterly a chronic catarrh, but it was not cancer. He had a very bad attack at Paris on his way to Biarritz in the winter, where Reid was with him, treating it with injections recommended by Laking. It was a more or less experimental treatment, and, she says, did him more harm than good. Nevertheless he was very well in his general health when he arrived in London, but the doctors could not keep him quiet. He would not stay at home at night or go to bed early; he must have people with him and go about to theatres and sit up playing cards till two or three in the morning.

" The King had been much worried about the Veto by Asquith and his Ministers. He was written to about it three times while he was at Biarritz, but had evaded it, saying each time that he would attend to it when he returned to England; but on his return they worried him, and he had lost his temper with Asquith, when Asquith pressed him, saying he should resign. Asquith had told him the King ought to send for Lloyd George in his place. This roused the King, who, as a rule, had good command over himself, for they all hate Lloyd George, and the King was quite upset by it. The King rather liked Churchill because he is a gentleman, but Lloyd George he could not stand. Queen Alexandra is furious with Asquith, and said he killed the King. She is going to have Marlborough House probably for her life, but she will not live there, as she is going back to Denmark, where she will keep house with her sister, the Russian Empress. The morn-

ing of Thursday, the day before he was taken ill, he had seen some
of the Ministers who were worrying him about the political crisis, and
he had a bad fit of coughing.   Mrs. Keppel came to tea with him in the
evening with the two Keyser girls.   He had no idea that he was in
danger, and even the day before he died they told him nothing.   He
had people to see him on business in the morning, and again he had
a fit of coughing and choking, which got worse and worse.   They
sent for the Archbishop of Canterbury, but he did not see him, and
he smoked a cigar.   Only once he said : ' If this goes on much longer
I shall be done for,' and soon after became unconscious and never
said another word. . . . He liked the society of women who could
talk, and Jews and people who could amuse him.   He liked also every
sort of public function, and entertainment and theatres and card
playing.   All the same he was a clever man, and knew all about foreign
politics better than any of them, and was a bit of a Radical.   Things
would be very different now.

" Lady C. went on talking about other personages she had known,
the King of Greece, the Emperor William, King Leopold of Belgium,
and the Crown Prince Rudolph, as to whose death she gave me almost
the same account as that I had from Countess Hoyos at Fiume.   She
knew the story from King Edward, and I do not doubt that hers is
the correct one.

" 14th May.— To Newbuildings, where I am entertaining the Rhu-
von Guests, Mark Napier and Shane Leslie.   Leslie, who has recently become a Catholic and a Nationalist, after being by birth an
Ulster Protestant, was run by Redmond at the last elections for a
Nationalist constituency.   His mother, Mrs. Jack Leslie, Lady Randolph Churchill's sister, was a favourite of the late King and a friend
of Mrs. Keppel, and he has heard the story of the King's last days
both from his mother and from Winston.   The first alarm about the
King, he says, was on Monday, the 2nd, when he went to play bridge
with Mrs. Keppel and spend the evening, the same evening, no doubt,
that Lady C. had talked of when the Miss Keysers were there.   But
Mrs. Keppel had got him to go home and to bed early at half-past
ten.   The next day, however, he could not be prevailed upon to stay
in bed, and got up to do business in the morning, and the same on
Wednesday and Thursday, when he had to receive some Colonial people.   He lost his temper because he misunderstood exactly who they
were, and said something *mal à propos*, and this caused a violent attack
of coughing, and the Prince of Wales was telegraphed for and the
Queen.

" 15th May (*Whit Sunday*).— I have had a long talk with Leslie
about Irish affairs and think he may eventually take a lead in them,
as he has had the wit the join the National party.   Young and being

of the landlord class, a tall, good-looking fellow, with much intelligence, heir to a baronetcy, and, Meynell tells me, an excellent speaker, he may even have Redmond's succession some day. It has always astonished me that no great landlord of them all should have come forward long ago in this way even out of mere ambition. Leslie has been at Eton and Oxford, but is nevertheless, as far as I can judge, a quite sound Nationalist. He went away in the evening.

"The Bellocs and Maurice Baring came to dinner.

"*20th May.*— To-day the King was buried, and I hope the country will return to comparative sanity, for at present it is in delirium. The absurdities written in every newspaper about him pass belief. He might have been a Solon and a Francis of Assisi combined if the characters drawn of him were true. In no print has there been the smallest allusion to any of his pleasant little wickednesses, though his was not even in make-believe the life of a saint or in any strict sense a theologically virtuous man. Yet all the bishops and priests, Catholic, Protestant, and Nonconformist, join in giving him a glorious place in heaven, and there were eight miles of his loyal and adoring subjects marching on foot to see him lying in state at Westminster Hall. For myself I think he performed his public duties well. He had a passion for pageantry and ceremonial and dressing up, and he was never tired of putting on uniforms and taking them off, and receiving princes and ambassadors and opening museums and hospitals, and attending cattle shows and military shows and shows of every kind, while every night of his life he was to be seen at theatres and operas and music-halls. Thus he was always before the public and had come to have the popularity of an actor who plays his part in a variety of costumes, and always well. Abroad, too, there is no doubt he had a very great reputation. His little Bohemian tastes made him beloved at Paris, and he had enough of the *grand seigneur* to carry it off. He did not affect to be virtuous, and all sorts of publicans and sinners found their places at his table. The journalists loved him; he did not mind being snap-shotted, and was stand off to nobody. If not witty, he could understand a joke, and if not wise he was sensible. He quarrelled with nobody, and always forgave. He disliked family scandals, and spent much of his time patching up those of the Court and whitening its sepulchres. In this respect he has every right to the title of ' Peacemaker ' given to him.

"It was the same with his peace-making diplomacy. He liked to be well received wherever he went, and to be on good terms with all the world. He was essentially a cosmopolitan, and without racial prejudice, and he cared as much for popularity abroad as at home. This made him anxious to compose international quarrels. He wanted an easy life, and that everybody should be friends with everybody. He sank his English nationality on the Continent, talked French and German in preference to English, and English with a foreign accent. He knew Europe well, and exactly what foreigners thought of England. The knowledge was of use to him and to our Foreign office, especially under such insular Secretaries of State as Arthur Balfour and Edward Grey. He tried hard to win the Irish over to him because he was well aware that the long quarrel with Ireland was a blot on the English name abroad. He had no sympathy with violent measures of coercion. He stopped the Boer War, knowing how upopular it was making England on the Continent and everywhere, and how much we were becoming despised for our childish attempts at subduing this sturdy little people. In Egypt he was shocked at Cromer's brutalities and his unnecessary quarrel with the Khedive and the Sultan. It was entirely due to him that Cromer was recalled. The Anglo-Russian treaty he did off his own bat with Hardinge, Sir Edward Grey looking on. His only notable failure was in the affair of Bosnia, and people in England knew too little of the conditions to understand how great a failure it was. Also, he never succeeded in making friends with his nephew Wilhelm, and I fancy they hated each other to the end. All this doubtless made Edward VII a wiser and a better king than most of ours have been, and he may even rightly share with Solomon the title of ' The Wise.' They each had that knowledge of women which, as we know, is the beginning of wisdom, or at least which teaches tolerance for the unwisdom of others. Of all this the newspaper writers say no word, being professionally what is required of them, virtuous men and fools."

CHAPTER IX

GEORGE V KING

The death of Edward VII was a misfortune for English diplomacy and the peace of Europe. Although in some ways he had launched the Foreign Office on an adventurous course by the two ententes for which he was primarily responsible, that with France about Morocco and that with Russia about Persia, his influence with the Government had been a steadying one, and it is probable that if he had lived another ten years the supreme catastrophe of a European war would have been avoided. He knew what was going on in the various Courts of Europe far better than did our professional diplomatists, and his disappearance from their counsels left the supreme direction of our foreign policy uncontrolled in the hands of Grey, whose ignorance of foreign affairs was really astonishing, knowing as he did no foreign language, and having made hardly so much as a holiday tour in Europe. King Edward's successor, whose life had been that of a sailor, knowing the world only as a sailor sees it at the seaport towns where his ship stops to coal — and seaport towns all the world over are alike — and being without any experience of politics, even those of his own country, was quite unable to supply the directing power his father had exerted at times so successfully. Consequently from this point onward, the year 1910, our English policy on the Continent exhibited a series of blunders of the most dangerous kind, leading by a logical sequence in four years' time to England's entanglement in a war, the result of which was not foreseen, and for which no preparation whatever had been made. How all this came about will, I think, be made clear in the following pages.

" *21st May.*— Newbuildings. Prince Mohammed Ali, the Khedive's brother, who has been representing the Khedive at the King's funeral, arrived here this afternoon with two of his Egyptian friends to see the horses, having an Arab stud of his own at Cairo. While at tea, when he had seen everything, I asked him about the state of affairs in Egypt. He said they had been going very well until about a year ago, but owing to the weakness of the Radical Government here had since gone badly. Too much licence, he said, had been allowed to the Press, so that the Government and everybody connected with it had been attacked, and the Prime Minister, Boutros Pasha, had been mur-

dered, the University students, boys of twelve and thirteen, cheering
the murderer. This was intolerable. I asked him whether he did
not wish to see the British occupation ended, and he said: 'Of course
we all wish to be independent and a great nation, but we are not ready
for it yet. We have not the men to govern.' I asked him why he
did not himself take office. 'What would be the use,' he said, 'without
the power? If you took an agent to manage your estate and forbade
him to climb over a fence how could he succeed?' His idea seems
to be the old one of despotic rule, and doubtless this is the Khedivial
intention if he can get his way. I asked whether he liked Gorst.
'We like him,' he said, 'and you must not believe what the English
newspapers in Egypt write against him. They are angry because in
Cromer's time the English officials did just as they pleased, but now
they have to take a second place.' Mohammed Ali doubtless represents the feeling of the Court party. Gorst has been putting back the
Egyptian Government clock to where it stood in Tewfik's time, who
was allowed to arrest and deport as he pleased so long as he supported
the Occupation. As the Prince was driving away in his motor, he
said, putting his head out of the window: 'We like Gorst anyhow
better than Cromer.'

"*25th May.*— The seven kings assembled for King Edward's funeral
have broken up camp and gone their ways, I fear in peace. I would
rather they had quarrelled, for a peace to which Kaiser Wilhelm is
chief party bodes little good to Asiatics.

"*2nd June.*— That swine, Roosevelt, has made another speech, this
time at the Mansion House, about Egypt, worse than before. I have
written a short answer to it for the 'Westminster Gazette,' but I doubt
if they will publish it. All the Tory papers are in delight at the
speech, and the 'Daily Telegraph' demands the recall of Gorst and the
dragooning of Egypt after the severest Cromerian manner. 'The
Times' is curiously moderate, though Egyptian Unified has fallen to 99.

"*5th June (Sunday).*— Lady Gregory and Yeats came down to
dine and sleep, Yeats in good form, telling a number of excellent stories
at dinner. He said that the three persons he had known who had
most impressed him with their power were William Morris, Henley,
and Madame Blavatsky. He had gone on one occasion with Oscar
Wilde to call on Henley. Oscar did not before know Henley, and
put out all his most brilliant talk to captivate him and succeeded in
doing so, while Henley said nothing. Both professed themselves afterwards much pleased with the other's wit.

"Lady Gregory is bringing out her new three-act play, 'The Image,'
at the Court Theatre. They have also Synge's 'Deirdre' on their
list, but they say it is not successful. Yeats tells me he makes only
about £30 a year by the sale of his poetry. He is an extremely

pleasant fellow, and has a more prosperous look, and is fatter and rosier than formerly. Lady Gregory has been the making of him.

" *7th June.*— One Homer Davenport, a Yankee friend of Roosevelt's, and a breeder of Arab horses, was here to-day. He is an amusing fellow, come over with Roosevelt as newspaper correspondent for the ' New York World.' He tells me he has no very high opinion of Roosevelt's intellect, and treats his pronouncement about Egypt and other things as an overflow of nonsense and high spirits rather than as anything more serious. Roosevelt, he says, is sure to be named President again, as he amuses the American public. I took him the round of our horses here and found him intelligent about them, he having visited the Anazeh tribes once. After going through a number of our small fields surrounded with thick hedgerows he remarked: ' You have the cunningest little paddocks here for breeding that ever I saw.' I sent him back to London with Kháparde, who was also here, an oddly assorted pair.

" *8th June.*— I have written to Dillon and Dr. Rutherford, M.P., advising them that when the question of Egypt comes on in Parliament, the point to urge should be a resumption of the Drummond Wolff negotiations for evacuation. It is no use trying to bolster up Gorst, he is too manifest a failure.

" Belloc has gone to Berlin, news having come that the Emperor William having been stung by an insect in his hand is ill with blood poisoning, and Belloc wanted to be in at the death. Little as I love Wilhelm I should miss him at the present juncture. It would leave the game in the East too entirely in English hands.

" *14th June.*— Chapel Street. Meynell and Everard Meynell dined with me, and we talked much about Egypt. There was a field-day yesterday about it in the House of Commons, Grey solemnly recanting, amid rapturous Tory applause, the whole of his policy of conciliation there, begun three and a half years ago. There is now to be an era of coercion. Nationalism is no longer to be killed with kindness. There will be arrests and deportations, which will go on till one fine day the Khedive is assassinated. Turkey is now Egypt's only chance. Grey's speech shows quite clearly that it was a matter arranged beforehand between him and Roosevelt that Roosevelt should make the speech he did at the Guildhall. It was one of those little perfidies by which Cabinet Ministers sometimes force the hands of their colleagues, and it has been most successful. Without it Grey might have had a difficulty in getting up the agitation about Egypt which was necessary to excuse the change of policy. Cromer will now once more be the Foreign Office adviser, vice Hardinge, promoted as Viceroy to India.

" Hardinge's appointment is probably as good a one as the Government could have made. He is friends with Russia and knows something of the East, and will have the recommendation of having been the late King's right-hand man. Nothing, however, in the shape of new men will much affect the march of Asiatic and Egyptian things. Egypt's future depends on the success of Turkey; India's on the success of China and Japan. One thing Grey's speech will certainly have effected: all Egypt will now become Nationalist and anti-English.

" 15*th June*.— Dr. Rutherford came to lunch with me. In the afternoon I went to Belgrave Square, and on with Madeline and Dorothy to the Court Theatre to see Lady Gregory's play ' The Image,' which disappointed me, being in three acts without much action, and the dialogue being difficult for any but an Irishman to follow. The little farce, ' Hyacinth Halvey,' which followed it, was quite delightful.

" 16*th June*.— I have written to reproach Dillon with his absence and the Irish silence at the Egyptian debate. Dillon, if he had been there, could have led a serious attack on Grey, who once more was able to hypnotize the Radicals below the gangway and obtained a complete success for coercion in Egypt. The Irish were probably afraid of offending Roosevelt. The Irish entertainment of Roosevelt the day after his Guildhall speech was a betrayal of liberty which may cost the Eastern world dear. [The incident of Roosevelt's intervention marks an evil turn in Grey's diplomacy. The American's influence with him was a personal one, due to their common interest in natural history and out of door sports, which with Grey was paramount. I attribute his marked preference for American rather than any other foreign suggestions to the fact that with Americans only he could converse in their own language, being ignorant of French or German.]

" Lady C., on whom I called, told me she had just met M. de Soveral, who had told her the King was certainly killed by his doctors. Soveral was quite broken down by the King's death. As to the new Court, she tells me Knollys was the only one about the old King who was really faithful to him. He was left heir to all the King's papers and correspondence, and knew absolutely everything of the King's secrets, having been entrusted with the keys, while he lived, of every box. Most of these secrets, she said, will die with Knollys. Queen Alexandra has been well provided for, the King having left her £30,000 a year, which will be made up to £100,000 by Parliament. She will go with her sister, the Empress of Russia and her daughter to Copenhagen at the end of July and stay there till Christmas, then to Sandringham, where she will live when in England, her son reserving the shooting. King George is entirely devoted to his mother and will do everything possible for her.

" Kitchener has been recently to see Lady C. She had talked to him about me and he had said I had done a deal of mischief in Egypt; I am glad he thinks so.

"*20th June.*— I have written, at Dillon's suggestion, to Redmond about Grey's speech on Egypt, urging him to take the matter up strongly on the first occasion. Asquith has fooled them after all about the House of Lords, and has gone into conference with Arthur Balfour about the compromise of the quarrel. Unless the Irish get rid of Asquith, Grey and Haldane, they will never gain what they want. They have certainly had bad luck with the King's death, but it was a mistake their allowing the Budget to pass.

"*26th June.*—Newbuildings. D—— G—— was here to-day, just back from the Congo with some friends interested in the rubber trade. It is a sordid and abominable occupation, and D—— has made a fortune out of it, as there has been what is called a rubber boom. He has for some time past had a rubber speculation in the Malay Peninsula and took service under that scoundrel King Leopold to learn the art of the thing, and now, old Leopold being dead, he has returned to Europe. I asked him whether the tales of the atrocities on the Congo were true, and he admitted that they had been so, but said it was all changed now. All the same it is a sorry business for one like D——.

"*28th June.*— Chapel Street. With Beauclerk to the White City to see the Japanese pictures, which are worth looking at, and in the evening with Farid Bey to a Conference at Caxton Hall, where he made a speech about Egypt in French which nobody understood. These meetings are entirely useless, the audience made up mostly of young Indians and enthusiastic middle-aged ladies.

"*29th June*— Dillon and Farid to lunch. We decided that Dillon is to bring on the Egyptian question, if possible, as an Irish party question in connection with the Foreign Office Estimates; otherwise no real debate is possible. The points he is to attack are (1) The financial mismanagement with the spending of twenty-six millions of the Reserve Fund, (2) The new Press and Deportation Laws; (3) The Suez Canal Convention. Dillon recommends that the Legislative Council should sign a public protest against the new coercion laws passed over their heads. I am to write a pamphlet. Farid has his facts well in hand, but, as usual, his inability to speak English stood in his way with Dillon, who speaks no French.

"*10th July (Sunday).*— Newbuildings. Dillon and Kháparde are here for the week-end. Dillon is hopeful about Irish prospects. He says the Sinn Fein movement as far as it was hostile to the Parliamentary party has all but died down. He expects a General Election in January, with a result of even forces between Tories and Radicals; and so the possibility of an arrangement between the two parties favourable to Home Rule. He has seen much of Churchill lately, who is much depressed at the failure of their plans. Dillon will do what he can about Egypt, but it is difficult to keep the Irish members in London, except when it is a case of Irish questions. He understands the Egyptian case thoroughly; the Radical members, however, will give no support; they are too ignorant of foreign affairs, and too much afraid of Grey. Dillon is the pleasantest of companions, and an excellent talker, and we have had a profitable time.

" 11*th July*.— The twenty-seventh anniversary of the bombardment of Alexandria. I am writing my final letter for the ' Westminster Gazette,' disclosing the financial scandals in Egypt, so as to give Dillon a lead on the Foreign Office vote.

" 15*th July*.— Dillon writes that Grey, after saying that the Suez Canal Correspondence would be laid on the table for members to read, has withdrawn these, and there can be no debate about Egypt. Thus the whole attempt to get publicity for the rascalities in Egypt breaks down. My letter was sent in on the 13th, but the Editor says it may be some time before he can print it. Such is the way these things are managed.

"' 16*th July*.— Savarkar, the Indian who was recently extradited and sent to London, has managed to squeeze through his cabin window at Marseilles and swim ashore, but was arrested by a French gendarme and returned to the ship. He had had friends ready with a motor to get him away. Kháparde tells me that Savarkar is the author of ' The Indian Revolution of 1857,' and that is the real reason why they want to get him back to India and punish him.

" 18*th July*.— The Editor of the ' Westminster Gazette ' after keeping it for a week refuses to publish my final letter about Egypt, and as both Dillon and Keir Hardie say there is no chance of Egypt being discussed, I am obliged to leave it there. I cannot fight this battle absolutely alone, the odds against me are too great." [This letter I had printed as a pamphlet under the heading " The Fiasco in Egypt." I am quite sure that it was shown to Grey by the editor, and that in consequence Grey resolved to burk the debate by withdrawing the correspondence.]

" 22*nd July*.— After all, Dillon was able to say a word on the Foreign Office vote, but unsupported by a single member on the Liberal side. It brought Grey out with another still stronger pronouncement about the Government determination to stay on in Egypt. The absolute and entire defection of the Labour members as well as the Liberals is depressing. They have all now adopted Grey's imperialistic doctrine of ' might is right ' in dealing with Orientals. I hold Morley more responsible for this conversion of England to Jingoism than anyone else in the Cabinet. He has surrendered the Indian citadel to the enemy. It does not surprise me, nor do I suppose it will make any difference in the end. Egypt's fate depends on the success of the

Ottoman reformers and on the Kaiser Wilhelm, though I suspect that terms were come to by our Government with Wilhelm about Egypt when he was over here for the King's funeral, otherwise Grey would hardly have been so emphatic. The only thing now for Egypt is to make the closest possible alliance with Turkey and share the fortunes for good and evil of the general Mohammedan world. Gorst is over here.

" Churchill has made a long exposition of his new prison regulations, following very closely the lines of my memorandum. He and Clementine are to spend Sunday week with me here at Newbuildings. Dillon has sent me his speech about Egypt, which is eloquent and well-reasoned, and, he tells me, provoked Grey to great anger, though he did not get into the financial scandals. He met with no sympathy in any quarter of the House, and he is so distressed at this that he would advise the Egyptians to cease their agitation against the Occupation and get what they can from England of self-government. I cannot agree with him in this. The sort of self-government Gorst and Grey would give, a Council without power and without a free Press, would only serve as a disguise for English rule. I have written to him in this sense. France is once more pushing forward in Morocco, and is counting on English help. It would not surprise me if the partition of the Ottoman Empire were in our Foreign Office plan. It is a race between these harpies and the Ottoman army. If this can be reorganized and strengthened in time Islam will be saved and Egypt with it, not otherwise.

" *24th July (Sunday)*.— The Bellocs to dinner. He tells me Dillon's speech about Egypt was really most eloquent but equally ill-received by Radicals as by Tories. It shows that there is no longer the smallest hope of converting England from her imperial ways.

" Goumah writes from Lyons that there is a reign of terror at Cairo, spies everywhere and police arrests. It is a return to the state of things in 1883, a fine comment on the civilizing effect of English Liberal rule after twenty-seven years. I have answered him that I advise closer relations with Constantinople. It is their rightful and legal way, seeing that the Sultan is their Sovereign Lord, and England cannot with any face quarrel with them for their loyalty to him and at the same time pretend to be the friend and protector of Islam. It must now be war between Islam and England, and as the Egyptians have no armed force of their own they must rely on the hope that the Sultan will some day be strong enough to reclaim Egypt as a Province of the Ottoman Empire; it may not be a very good chance but it is the only one they have.

" *28th July*.— There is a new and very ugly development in the world's great affairs. The United States has declared its intention of undertaking the management of Liberia, the black Republic in West Africa, and there is a movement afoot for Christianizing Central Africa in opposition to the spread of Islam, our Jingo paper applauding. I put much of this down to the combination of Roosevelt and Grey.

" *31st July (Sunday)*.— Winston and Clementine came to dine and sleep. He expects now to remain in office, he says, for five years, the General Election to take place in March. I gave him my ' Fiasco in Egypt ' to read, and he tells me that he had precisely the same idea as that I give in it of the Suez Canal Convention. Grey had said that Egypt would be delighted with it, but he, Churchill, had foreseen that it would be quite the contrary. He had written a memorandum for Grey on the subject. He and Clementine start on a yachting tour this week to the Eastern Mediterranean and Constantinople. Their party will be De Forrest and his wife, F. E. Smith and Walter Harris.

" *2nd Aug.*— Newbuildings. The Churchills left yesterday. Ismaïl Pasha Abaza, the most important member of the Egyptian Legislative Council, came to consult me about affairs in Egypt. He had been three days in London, but had found no single person among the M.P.'s and journalists who had the least idea of the state of Egyptian things, nor had Grey received him. He was sore about this and in very low spirits. I have encouraged him to fight on as he has been doing in the Legislative Council, bringing forward especially the iniquities of our financial management, and he has promised me to do so. He is a man of the old-fashioned school with considerable dignity and political intelligence, a sincere patriot of the moderate party, that which has hitherto relied on English promises of self-government and eventual evacuation. His position, he explained to me, is this: he, in common with every other Egyptian patriot, is opposed to the British Occupation, but while he approves the extreme attitude of Farid he thinks it politic to work for reforms in a Constitutional direction, and has clung to the idea that our Liberals in England could be persuaded into granting a Constitution. The demand for evacuation was rightly made by the extremists, but it was right too that there should be certain persons in the party who would try to work with England and attain the end of independence by another and more conciliatory road. I was willing enough to admit this, but have persuaded him that there is not the remotest chance of our ever granting a real Constitution willingly, and made him promise me that he would never in any public way admit England's right to be in Egypt. I asked him about the Khedive, and he assured me that His Highness was at heart a sound patriot, but dared not oppose the British Agency openly. He denied that the Khedive's money speculations were other than honourable ones, or inconsistent with his patriotism. I find this last difficult to believe. On all other points I consider him a trustworthy informant and certainly a far more dignified leader of opinion than Farid or any other of the Nationalist leaders. He is timid, however, as all men in Egypt of his generation are (he must be sixty) and knows little of Europe and nothing of England; nevertheless he has taken the lead, and a bold one, against Gorst in the Council and in the General Assembly, especially on the Suez Canal question. He left with me two copies of the report of the Commission of the Assembly we have been so long trying to get out of Grey. It amply justifies the Assembly for rejecting the Convention, and it contains an important article on our finance, which shows why Grey refused to present it to the House of Commons.

" 14*th Aug.*— Osman Ghaleb writes from Paris that they are to hold the Egyptian Congress there this year, and that there is thought of asking me to be its President.

" 15*th Aug.*— In London and called on Lady C. She talked of Lord Spencer, who has just died. Spencer was a fine fellow, and nobody in England was more respected. He ought to have been Gladstone's successor instead of Rosebery as Prime Minister. I had but slight acquaintance with him, though he was friends with my brother and sister, having gone up the Nile with them in 1863.

" 17*th Aug.*— My birthday of seventy, which I am spending at Clouds, a long and delightful day; also, and on this I pride myself, I was able with my cup and ball to catch it on the point nine times out of twelve, which shows that my eyesight is not failing. In the evening we had the traditional birthday cake with the children, lighting it up with seventy wax matches. Guy's boys amuse me. George, a boy of sixteen, still at Wellington School, but has grown a slight mustache and affects the ways of a young man. He is very good-looking, and spends most of his time with the servants in the pantry and the housekeeper's room, where he talks nonsense to the maids and helps the footmen to clean the knives, smoking a briar pipe with twist tobacco, the most horrible stuff. Upstairs he has a fine assurance with pronounced opinions, as a man of the world. He is to go into the Foreign Office, and seems to have an amusing career before him. Dick, the younger, is of a strict scaramouch type, cleverer but less good-looking. Olivia is an audaciously pretty girl of thirteen, also with a career of pleasure before her, ready for all possible wickedness in a wicked world. They spent the day making a grand picnic with the servants and governesses to Pertwood on the Downs, where they had sack and three legged races and all sorts of boisterous fun, of which Dick, who dined at table, gave us a naïve account.

" 20*th Aug.*— Chapel Street. Meynell and his son Francis dined with me. The young man is clever and agreeable and should make his mark. He is now at Trinity College, Dublin, and is much mixed up with the Sinn Fein movement, being friends especially with the Healy faction.

"*24th Aug.*— Farid has written inviting me to be Honorary President of the Egyptian National Congress to be held at Paris on the 22nd of September, and I have written accepting, though I cannot be there, sending an address to be read at the first meeting.

"*30th Aug.*— The Kaiser Wilhelm has made a speech at Königsberg in which he allowed himself a new outburst about his 'divine right.' I remember just the same thing nearly fifty years ago, when his grandfather came to the throne. His 'Gottes-Gnaden' was a phrase of comic opera mocking in Germany at that time.

"*6th Sept.*— Chapel Street. A Mr. Atkin came to lunch to consult me on Turkish affairs in Arabia. He has been lately at Constantinople and tells me there is a pretty complete *brouille* between the Young Turks and the English Embassy; our ambassador, Lowther, does nothing and knows nothing, and the Germans have it all their own way. There is talk of the Sultan bringing on the Egyptian Question with the support of Germany and Austria. I doubt, however, whether Atkin is a reliable informant.

"*15th Sept.*— Newbuildings. Father John Pollen, S.J., came to lunch from Burton Park and spent the afternoon, he not having been here since 1876, when he went into his Jesuit novitiate. He is a pleasant, good fellow, and we had much talk about old days when the Pollens lived here. Philip Napier and his wife also came, and we had much Egyptian talk. He is living at Sheykh Obeyd now, and has developed good National sympathies, a most unusual thing for an Englishman in Egypt.

"*16th Sept.*— The French Government has forbidden the Congress being held at Paris, and it has had to be transferred to Brussels. According to an account sent me by Goumah, he and Farid had an interview yesterday with the Chef de Cabinet du Premier Ministre, in which he excused the French Government by saying that 'France was so surrounded by enemies that she could not afford to quarrel with her one friend, England.' The forbidding of the Congress is in accordance with an agreement come to with England, that if the French Government will forbid the Congress the English Government will consent to liberate Savarkar. I hope it is so, for the first will be a small misfortune compared with France's surrender of a captured fugitive and her violation of the right of asylum.

"*20th Sept.*— There is a quarrel between the French Government and the Turkish Government over a loan of £6,000,000 arranged by the latter with the Crédit Mobilier, but which the French Government refuses permission to be quoted on the Bourse because it is to be applied to the purchase of war ships in Germany. [The 'Goeben'

was one of these.] The French made a condition that certain protected French subjects in Syria should be given up by the Ottoman
Government, and also a certain oasis on the Tripolitan frontier
evacuated, which, of course, could not be conceded. The answer to
this is a rumoured military convention between Turkey and Roumania,
and the all but certainty that Turkey will now join the Triple Alliance.
This is the best thing that could happen to Egypt, so I rejoice.

"*24th Sept.*— My letter in French to the Egyptian Congress has been
clearly a great success, the London Liberal papers giving extracts
from it, and describing it as a ' sensation,' and the ' Daily News ' giving
it three-quarters of a column under the heading ' Mr. Blunt's Remarkable Prophecy.' I am sure this has been the right way to attack Grey's
position. It is announced now that Cassel has come forward with
an offer of financing the Turkish loan if the French Government refuses to allow the Crédit Mobilier's offer, and that he has support at
Berlin.

"*26th Sept.*— Worth Forest. The news from Brussels is excellent.
Keir Hardie has declared himself at the Congress in unmistakable
terms for evacuation. He has even told the Egyptians they must have
a revolution. The following are the resolutions agreed to :

' (1) The occupation of Egypt by Great Britain being illegal, evacuation must take place immediately.

' (2) The Constitution of 1882 must be restored.

' (3) The Press law must be abolished.

' (4) The deportation law must be repealed.

' (5) Control over the debt must be maintained as long as Egypt is
the debtor of Europe.

' (6) The treaty of 1898 between the Khedive and Great Britain
affecting the Soudan is void.'

" These are exactly the resolutions I should myself have drafted.
I mean now to take a holiday from the whole thing. Clementine
Churchill writes that Winston thinks my advice to the Egyptians very
good advice, but he will never consent to the evacuation. I have
answered that I remembered his saying so last year, and I also remembered how Jules Favre said in 1871 that he would never consent to
the surrender of a stone of France's fortresses.

" *3rd Oct.*— Newbuildings. Riza Bey Tewfik unexpectedly arrived
from London, having found his way on foot from Southwater through
the woods. We had a most interesting talk about Ottoman politics,
and he gave me an exact account of how England had lost her popularity at Constantinople through the stupidity of our Embassy and
the mistake made in giving support to the counter-revolution. At the

time of the first revolution in July, 1908, the English were so popular at Constantinople that Riza, who was one of the two Young Turks whose duty it was to keep order in the capital, had difficulty in preventing the crowds of demonstrators from besieging the British Embassy with their enthusiastic attentions, while there was equal difficulty in preventing Bieberstein, the German Ambassador, from being insulted. Now it is precisely the reverse. Lowther, our ambassador, is a worthy man, Riza says, but quite ignorant of the East, and dependent for his information on his chief dragoman, Fitzmaurice, who has an anti-Islamic twist, and who went in for the so-called Liberal party opposed to the Young Turks. England in consequence has become entirely distrusted, and to such a point that he (Riza), who has all his life been Anglomane, is now for an alliance with the Triplice, England having become anti-Islamic. I told him I held just that view of the position, and that it would be better for Turkey to join the German powers by signing a definite treaty which would guarantee her from danger either from Russia or from France. He promised to repeat my opinion to the Grand Vizier and to Ahmed Riza and the rest of those responsible for Ottoman policy. There is in truth no other course, for England and France and Russia are all now hostile to Islam. They only supported the Young Turks at the outset because they imagined these to be opposed to pan-Islamism. He will also show my memorandum, about the Arabian policy which should be adopted, to those whom it concerns, and we are to correspond. Riza is a very remarkable man.

"I asked him about Abdul Hamid, and he told me the old Sultan was very unhappy, for he is a man of restless energy, and chafes at his position of powerlessness. His temper has become so bad that nearly all his women folk have left him. He lives in a handsome house, almost a palace, at Salonika, where he is kept close prisoner, but he cannot accept his position. After the deposition of Abdul Hamid, Riza saw him twice, though not to speak with personally. He confirms all the stories of the Sultan's dread of assassination, and says that in the room at Yildiz where the Sultan usually slept there were six beds in a row, and no one knew in which he was sleeping, so that if an assassin got into the room in the dark he would not know where to strike. Also there was a secret way of escape under the bed. Sometimes he would eat nothing for days, fearing poison, or he would get some old woman to boil an egg for him in his presence.

"*4th Oct.*— George Wyndham and Beauclerk came to dine and sleep and shoot to-morrow. George is busy with his rectorial address to be delivered at Edinburgh on the 'Springs of Romance.' He and Beauclerk get on well together.

"*8th Oct.*— The last days' newspapers have been full of a revolution in Portugal, the flight of King Manuel, and the proclaiming of a Republic. The movement will probably spread to Spain, and possibly to other countries. Last week there was something like a Socialist rising in Berlin, put down, however, at once with great military violence, in the course of which several English newspaper correspondents got knocked about, the Government offering them no apology. The Savarkar affair with France has been referred to arbitration, thus confirming what Goumah told me three weeks ago.

" *9th Oct.*— Rothstein's book, ' Egypt's Ruin,' is now in print, and ought to be out at the end of next week. I have made myself responsible to Fifield for a first sale of 800 copies, besides advancing him £50. I think, however, the book will be worth it politically. It has given me a deal of trouble, besides writing the introduction.

" *11th Oct.*— To Storrington to call on Miss Petre. She is certainly an attractive woman, attractive by reason of her great simplicity of manner and ready intelligence. She has finished the first volume of her ' Life of Tyrrell,' including his autobiography down to 1885. ' A precious document,' she calls it. She has nobody now living with her at Mulberry House, though one of her sisters lives near her, just outside the village, and they take their meals together. She gave a sprig of myrtle to Dorothy as we went away, and one to Miss Lawrence, and we mean to plant them here in memory of Father Tyrrell.

" *13th Oct.*— France seems to be following Portugal's suit. There is a general railway strike all the country over, and Paris is threatened with starvation. Winston was to have been here this afternoon to shoot, but has telegraphed after attending a Cabinet Council, that circumstances make it quite impossible he should reach us to-night. That sounds serious. The Portugese revolution has completely succeeded, and young King Manuel, after taking refuge at Gibraltar, is to come to live in England at Wood Norton.

" *14th Oct.*— Winston arrived in a motor from London. He was dressed in a little close-fitting fur-collared jacket, tight leggings and gaiters, and a little round hat, which, with his half-mischievous face, made him look, as Miss Lawrence said, ' the exact figure of Puck.' We had already began shooting when he joined us, and talk began at once. It was very brilliant, and, except for the exigencies of the afternoon shooting and dressing for dinner, was kept up on the same high level till near midnight. I had asked Philip Napier to meet him, so as to give him some ideas about Egypt, and Gordon Blunt is also here. We discussed most of the burning questions. Winston is going on energetically about prison reform, and will push it much beyond what he has already announced publicly. He means to arrange matters so that next year there will be 50,000 fewer people sent to prison than this year. He was eloquent about a girl who had had a child and

had put it in the workhouse, and who had been given two months'
hard labour for deserting it, and about abuses he had discovered in a
reformatory. He talked also about public executions. He is in favour
of capital punishment, but, while thinking executions cannot be made
a spectacle for hooligans, will see to it that relations and friends shall
be allowed to be present. This in connection with what I wrote the
other day in the ' Observer.'

" He then got on his travels in the Greek Islands and the Sea of
Marmora, where he has been yachting for the last two months. He
was immensely pleased with the Island of Rhodes and its defensive
works. At Constantinople he had stayed four days, and had been
taken to see the new Sultan, but had found him uninteresting; indeed
gaga. Djavid Pasha had shown him about, and he had talked with
several very intelligent Young Turks; also with Bieberstein, the German Ambassador, of whose ability he had formed a high opinion.
The Germans had got the better of our diplomacy there. He had
brought away a great sympathy with the Young Turks, and was all
for them being encouraged and supported. I told him that I had been
asked to advise the Ottoman Government as to its policy, and inquired
what his advice to them would be. Would he advise them to join
the Triple Alliance? He said: ' I should advise them, while working
up their army and making it efficient, to keep out of all wars for
five years and get their finances in order. As to alliances, I should
advise them to remain in the position of the courted party rather than
of one actually engaged.' I asked: ' Would it not give them a
stronger position to join the Triple Alliance openly? If it is only a
secret understanding they might find themselves betrayed.' He said:
' Perhaps.' I gathered from him that he was well aware of the mistakes made by our diplomacy at Constantinople, but he excused these
by saying that we were hampered by our position in Egypt.

" We then argued the whole Egyptian question, and with Philip's
help, I think we produced considerable effect on him, though still he
declared the impossibility of evacuation. Public opinion in England
would never consent to it. We should hold on to Egypt as we hold on
to India. It was not that it brought us any advantage but it was impossible to go back on what we had undertaken, a necessity of Empire. The fate of Egypt would be decided by the issue of the coming
war with Germany. He used, in fact, all the old arguments; nevertheless, I think, he is shaken about it. Philip staggered him by asserting
that the land of the Delta was being ruined by over watering and that
the rural administration was bad. ' One thing,' he said to me privately,
' I can tell you. There will be no more talk of the Suez Canal Convention.' He asked me what I thought of Gorst, and said they were
going to support him. ' As to the Suez Convention,' he said, ' there

are three people who have always disapproved of it, you and I and
Cassel, each arriving at his view on different grounds.'

" The only subject we avoided was the conference about the Lords,
but I feel sure that they have come to terms with the Irish.   Redmond
has just made a speech in Canada announcing Home Rule all round.
What exactly this may mean is uncertain, but it would hardly have
been made unless some agreement had been come to with the Tories
that the Irish demand was to be conceded.   About the railway strike
in France, he expressed much confidence in Briand.   Besides all this,
a metaphysical argument was started on the old doubt about the existence of matter, and we even got for a moment into theology.   With
Gordon Blunt he discussed military manœuvres, declaring our own
on Salisbury Plain this year to have been absurd.   On every topic he
was good, making from time to time most amusing little House of
Commons speeches and telling anecdotes in illustration.   Nobody could
have been livelier or more witty.   We all agreed, as we went to bed,
that we had had an excellent show.   His last word to me was, ' You
must not quarrel with me if I annex Egypt.'   While at Constantinople
he saw the Khedive whom he described as ' between the devil and
the deep sea,' England and the National Party.

" 16th Oct. (Sunday).— Worth Forest.   I am over in the Forest
for a few days.   On our walk up from Cinder Banks we came upon
four deer, one a white doe, close to the great beech tree.   This was
Percy and Madeline's golden wedding day.

" 19th Oct.— It is announced from Teheran that Grey has threatened
to occupy Southern Persia, a last perfidy which has decided me to write
to Riza Bey and advise the Turkish Government to join the Triple Alliance openly, if they get the offer.   It is the only thing left for any
Moslem state to do.   The Anglo-Franco-Russian Entente intends their
destruction.

" 20th Oct.— Chapel Street.   I have despatched my letter to Riza
Bey, of which I have kept a copy as it is important.   I see there is excitement at Constantinople about the British threat to Persia, which will
certainly make for the proposed alliance.   Riza Bey will show my
letter to the Grand Vizier and it ought to settle the matter.   Our
Foreign Office has been very foolish with its Russian Alliance.   Osman
Ghaleb writes with a full account of the Egyptian Congress at Brussels
and the reception my address to it met with.   He describes this as having been ' profound,' so much so that Baron Max de Wendland, Chamberlain of the King of Bavaria, who was sitting next him, exclaimed,
' There are still honest politicians left in England.'   Copies of my address were sent by him to the Grand Vizier, Hakki Pasha, and to Saad
Zaghoul.   It has been reproduced in full at Cairo and Constantinople,
and it is evident that it came at a most critical moment and has had its

full effect. The Constantinople Press is now violently anti-English, as well as anti-French, and the announcement of intervention in Persia has caused an explosion. It is certain now that Turkey will join the Triple Alliance. There is talk already of sending a Turkish Army Corps to the Persian frontier, and I should not be surprised if war should result. Our Foreign Office game now clearly is to involve Turkey financially, just as Persia has been involved. It all now depends on Germany. When Churchill was here I discussed with him the possibility of an invasion of Egypt, from Syria, by a Turkish army, helped by a German contingent. He seemed to think it impossible, but stranger things have happened.

"*23rd Oct. (Sunday).*— The crisis at Constantinople will have been heightened by a foolish speech made by Hardinge as prospective Viceroy of India, in which he praises the late King's astuteness and his own in making the alliance with Russia. He quotes the saying that Asia is large enough for the two Empires to live at peace in, and applauds the Convention about Persia. This will help to put the dots upon the i's. One must be a fool not to see that a partition of Persia is intended, though official denials are being given in our papers. It is all intensely interesting and can hardly not result in a war, which I may yet live to see, a war for the leadership of the Old World.

"*24th Oct.*— Big headlines announce a demonstration at Constantinople against Russia, England and France, and an appeal to the Kaiser Wilhelm as Defender of Islam. Whether my letter to Riza Tewfik had anything to do with it I do not know. It must have reached Constantinople on the 22nd and the demonstration took place on the 23rd. In any case it follows very closely the lines of my advice.— Rothstein's book, 'Egypt's Ruin,' is out.

"*25th Oct.*— Chapel Street. Mackarness called to talk over the plan of of a new Egyptian Committee, but I foresee it will come to nothing, as he can find nobody in the House of Commons willing to go in for evacuation, and with anything short of that I will have nothing whatever to do. It is ridiculous to go on demanding a Constitution which will never be given, or a resumption of Gorst's futile régime.

"*26th Oct.*— Back to Newbuildings. As I was shooting on Sheppard's Farm an airship passed over us, the first I have yet seen, a sausage-shaped dirigible balloon, drifting along at about 8 miles an hour. The propeller was not working only two little vans which seemed to steer it, keeping its course northward, the wind being south-east. In the brilliant evening sunlight it was rather a pleasing object than otherwise, as it drifted almost directly over Newbuildings at about 500 or 600 feet above us.

"*27th Oct.*— The airship turns out to have been the largest yet launched and to have come from Paris and to have descended at Aldershot. It must have been travelling faster than I thought and at a greater height. On arrival at the garage at Aldershot it got torn and exploded, but the passengers, they say, were unhurt. It seems to have been the first regular passenger ship to cross the Channel.

" *28th Oct.*— I have sent a copy of ' Egypt's Ruin ' to Asquith, with a letter requesting him to read it, and another to Morley. In my letter to Asquith I say, ' Our position in Egypt, taken in conjunction with the general attitude of the Mohammedan world, is a very critical one and may any day need your personal decision in the Cabinet to prevent greater mistakes than those already made at the Foreign Office. It is for this reason that I beg you not to allow things to drift on there as Mr. Gladstone allowed them to drift in 1882, till no issue could be found for them short of a violent one.' In my letter to Morley I have added an allusion to his conscience. I don't suppose either of them will read or answer, but it will at least be on record that I placed the truth before them.

"*2nd Nov.—Jour des Morts,* but whether it will be Persia or Turkey that will die, or the British Empire, depends upon Providence and the Kaiser Wilhelm. I went up to London early, in connection with a Mohammedan meeting to be held about Persia, in the afternoon, and found Syud Mahmud and another young Indian Moslem in Chapel Street, and helped them to draw up a resolution, or rather an amendment to the resolution, which will be proposed there. It is to this effect, 'that in view of the actual presence in Northern Persia of Russian troops and of the recent threat to occupy Southern Persia with British troops, and in view, moreover, of aggressions in the past under closely similar circumstances of ill faith by both Russia and England, this meeting of Mohammedans resident in London, is of opinion that no reliance can be placed on Sir Edward Grey's declarations that Persia's ancient independence will be respected by either of the two occupying Powers and it calls upon His Imperial Majesty, the Sultan, and the Government of Turkey to concert measures with the Persian Government for the speedy ending of a situation which is a menace to both Persia and Turkey, and an intolerable insult to the whole of Islam.' The young men assure me that such a resolution would obtain a large majority of votes. It has been occasioned by the news that British bluejackets have been landed at Lingah on the Persian Gulf ' to protect life and property.'

" Called later on Rivers Wilson, who talked about old times, and especially about the year he spent as private secretary to Disraeli, 1867–1868. Dizzy, he says, was in those days still the *farceur* he had been in his youth, having his tongue in his cheek and not pretending to be serious when behind the scenes. He would sit with him, Rivers, telling stories hour after hour, always amusingly and never pompously. It was not till after the Congress of Berlin, ten years later, that he began to take himself *au grand serieux*. The wonder is that anyone should have been found to take him seriously after such beginnings as his had been. Rivers is indignant with the present Government, and especially with Lloyd George, 'that mountebank of finance.' To his Treasury traditions of economy the present expenditure of £160,000,000 yearly is lunacy ; and so it is, only if people will have an overgrown Empire they must pay for their fun.

" Then on to Horace Rumbold, another relic of the past generation. He, too, is indignant with the Government for having taken up the Young Turks in 1908, and now mismanaged things, so that their joining the Triple Alliance is a certainty. He is hardly consistent, however, I think, as he is strongly in favour of an Anglo-Russian Alliance and against that with Japan. Winston writes that the European situation could not be worse for us. This reassures me about the attitude of Germany, as to which I sometimes fear lest it should be won over from an alliance with Turkey. There is always the danger of the whole of the Great Powers settling their differences by a partition of the Ottoman Empire. It is a risk we have to run, but I am sure the best chance is for Turkey to join the Triplice. We are playing for very high stakes, and this is our weakest card. If William were to die and be succeeded by an unambitious Emperor everything would be lost. All the more reason for hastening on the Alliance now.

" *4th Nov.*— Newbuildings. The Persian meeting turned out to be a poor affair, my young friends having failed to bring forward their amendment, and the original milk and water one is all that the papers publish about it. Mark Napier and Beauclerk came to dine and sleep. Mark, who takes a purely City view of these questions, declares it to be impossible Egypt should ever be evacuated, seeing how many millions of British capital are invested there. ' The British Empire,' he says, ' will muddle through somehow, as it did a hundred years ago in the time of Napoleon.'

" Miss Petre has sent me a copy of a letter she has written to the ' Times.' She has been called upon to sign a declaration that she accepts the Papal Rescript *Pascendi* and the rest, and she has asked in return that she should be informed whether the rescripts are *de fide*. Her position is sound in logic, but the Church can hardly afford to be logical any longer. She proposes to come to luncheon here on Monday and talk it over with me.

" *6th Nov. (Sunday)*.— Last night being Guy Fawkes' day we drank confusion to the British Empire, though, in truth, all present but myself were rank Imperialists. Warburton Pike, Beauclerk's friend, was of the party, and the talk turned mostly on gold mining, in which all of them are interested. Mark told us the history of the Mysore gold mine, of which he is the Director. The mine was discovered some thirty years ago accidentally by two English sportsmen when Mark's father was Governor of Madras, and a company was formed, but it yielded no great result till old Sir Charles Tennant, Margot's father, put £20,000 into it, and became almost sole owner. The thing was treated as a mere gamble, and having nothing reliable to go upon in the way of engineering reports and, nobody knowing where to dig, it was decided that Sir Charles should put his finger at haphazard on the map and that the digging should be begun there, and there exactly the gold was found, several millions' worth of it.'

"Mark gave me to-day also an interesting account of the battle of Majuba Hill, which he got from Sir Ian Hamilton, an old friend of his, and which is as follows: 'General Colley finding himself about to be superseded in the command by a superior officer, was anxious to achieve some notable success before his successor arrived, and with this object he occupied the hill with a few hundred men. The hill dominated the Boer position, and if they could have brought guns with them and entrenched themselves the plan would have succeeded. It was, in fact, near succeeding, for the Boers, finding the hill in possession of the English, were beginning to retire when they thought they might as well first see how strongly it was held. The British army was at that time in a quite undisciplined state, and the men not only refused to drag up the guns but even to entrench themselves when at the top, saying they were too tired for work and lay down to sleep; and Colley, who was a theoretical rather than a practical soldier, had not sufficient personal authority with them to insist, so that the Boer attack found them quite unprepared. The Boers, advancing from below, had the advantage that their heads were comparatively invisible as seen against the rocks, while the English were clear on the skyline, so that the Boers stalked them like deer and got close to the top before they were perceived. Hamilton, as I understand the story, was sent with a detachment to oppose the Boer advance, but being driven in found Colley lying on his back smoking a cigarette, having given up all attempt to cope with the situation. He was alone with only a few men of his staff, but the rank and file had already run in panic down the hill on the side opposite the attack. Hamilton had then returned to the advanced post where he got wounded on the wrist, and once more was driven back by the advancing Boers to the crest of the hill. This time he found all the living and unwounded gone, and Colley lying dead, shot through the head with a pistol in his hand. He had committed suicide. The Boers then rushed over the crest, driving what remained of the advanced guard before them, and Hamilton took to his heels. "I would have jumped over any precipice just then," he said to Mark; as it was he jumped over one twenty feet deep and stunned himself,

remaining unconscious till the next morning, when he found a young
Boer standing over him with his rifle pointed and about to finish him,
but an older Boer stopped the young one, and having stripped him of
everything he possessed, they gave him a kick on the backside and
let him go.'

" All this account is in strict keeping with what Mark's brother Jack
told me many years ago.   According to both accounts it would have
been impossible at that time for the British army to continue the campaign aggressively, as the Orange State would have joined the Trans-
vaalers, and the army was quite disorganized.

" *7th Nov.*— There has been a shifting of places in the Cabinet this
last week.   Morley leaves the India Office to become President of the
Council; Crewe takes Morley's place, and Loulou Harcourt takes
Crewe's place as Colonial Secretary; Beauchamp gets the Board of
Works.   That gives us two of our Crabbet Club men as Secretaries of
State, their chief qualification.

" Beauclerk brings me an important piece of news about Persia.   He
has lately seen Major Sykes, our Consul at Meshed, who is at present
in London, and is chief adviser on South Persian affairs at the Foreign
Office.   Sykes told him that the occupation of Southern Persia on
the same lines as the occupation of Egypt has been decided on, and that
he himself, Sykes, is to be British Agent and Consul General at Kirman, and direct the administration on Cromerian lines.   It has long
been intended but was not expected to take place for five years.   Now,
however, he says, two years will see it accomplished."   [This is an
entry of extreme importance, showing how fully it was intended by
Sir Edward Grey and the British Government to occupy and administer
Southern Persia, notwithstanding all denials.]

" Miss Petre and her sister came to luncheon, and we discussed the
whole question of her quarrel with Rome.   She means to fight it out,
but I doubt if they will give her any answer about the binding character
of the encyclicals.   Her bishop will simply say that if she does not
choose to sign she shall have no sacraments.   To console her I gave her
an account of my own religious experiences of fifty years ago.   I like
her much.

" *9th Nov.*— There has been a meeting at Berlin of the two Emperors, German and Russian, solemnized with an immense slaughter
of Imperial deer, five hundred in the single day's shooting, beasts which
had been penned for the purpose beforehand and let out one by one, as
cockney sportsmen do with their purchased pheasants.   According to
the ' Times' these Emperors and their Ministers have come to an
amicable understanding about Persia.   If so, Persia's fate is sealed.
[Compare Dr. Dillon's book, ' The Eclipse of Russia.']   In the meanwhile, we here in England are entirely engrossed in our local quarrels.

The Conference about the House of Lords has broken down, and there is a strike of miners with fierce riots in Wales.

" 11*th* *Nov.*— The ex-Shah of Persia has suddenly appeared at Vienna, after having disappeared from Odessa, where he was a month ago. This means more than meets the eye, for an Oriental ex-King is a card in the hand of any European Government which wants a footing in an Eastern State. I should not be surprised if this one was taken up by our and the Russian Governments to be restored at Teheran or Kirman, as Tewfik was restored in 1882 at Cairo, with a joint Anglo-Russian occupation indefinitely continued.

" 12*th* *Nov.*— There is an article in the ' Pall Mall,' which is usually well-informed about Foreign Office affairs, lamenting the failure of British policy in the East and announcing as certain that Turkey has joined the Triple Alliance, or rather the Dual Alliance of Germany and Austria, and that an arrangement has been come to between these and Russia for the construction of a railway through Bagdad and Persia to the Indian frontier, which will put India at the mercy of Germany, a death-blow to the British Empire. Redmond has returned from America with £40,000 for the coming electoral campaign.

" 14*th* *Nov.*— To London for the meeting of Parliament, which is to-morrow, and to the Reform Club to concert with Mackarness an opposition to Grey's Eastern policy and the formation of a new Egyptian Committee.

" 15*th* *Nov.*— To the Grafton Gallery to look at what are called the Post-Impressionist pictures sent over from Paris. The exhibition is either an extremely bad joke or a swindle. I am inclined to think the latter, for there is no trace of humour in it. Still less is there a trace of sense or skill or taste, good or bad, or art or cleverness. Nothing but that gross puerility which scrawls indecencies on the walls of a privy. The drawing is on the level of that of an untaught child of seven or eight years old, the sense of colour that of a tea-tray painter, the method that of a schoolboy who wipes his fingers on a slate after spitting on them. There is nothing at all more humorous than that, at all more clever. In all the 300 or 400 pictures there was not one worthy of attention even by its singularity, or appealing to any feeling but of disgust. I am wrong. There was one picture signed Gauguin which at a distance had a pleasing effect of colour. Examined closer I found it to represent three figures of brown people, probably South Sea Islanders, one of them a woman suckling a child, all repulsively ugly, but of a good general dark colouring, such as one sees in old pictures blackened by candle smoke. One of the figures wore a scarlet wrapper, and there was a patch of green sky in the corner of the picture. Seen from across the room the effect of colour was good. Apart from the frames, the whole collection should not be worth £5, and then only for the pleasure of making a bonfire of them. Yet two or three of our art critics have pronounced in their favour. Roger Fry, a critic of taste, has written an introduction to the catalogue, and Desmond MacCarthy acts as secretary to the show. I am old enough to remember the pre-Raphaelite pictures in the Royal Academy exhibitions of 1857 and 1858, and it is pretended now that the present Post-Impression case is a parallel to it, but I find no parallel. The pre-Raphaelite pictures were many of them extremely bad in colour, but all were carefully, laboriously drawn, and followed certain rules of art; but these are not works of art at all, unless throwing a handful of mud against a wall may be called one. They are the works of idleness and impotent stupidity, a pornographic show.

" 16*th Nov.*— Two things of immense importance have happened, though they excite little attention here. At a banquet given to Von der Goltz at Constantinople, Bieberstein has publicly declared the Kaiser Wilhelm's warm interest in Young Turkey and the strengthening of the Ottoman Empire as a military power. Also in Persia the native Press has declared for an alliance with Turkey and Germany.

" Frank Lascelles looked in on me. He admits that Grey has made a terrible hash of his policy abroad, especially at Constantinople. He disapproves of the partition of Persia, where he once was British Minister, and says that the Russians will never leave it. The agreement about the railways will leave everything in the hands of Germany. Even about Egypt he agrees that the position is very bad for us.

" John Dillon came to lunch and stayed till four talking. He says there has never been so complicated a political position as just now. Asquith is absolutely bound to the Irish party by his promise to resign if the King will not give the pledge required, and the Irish party will hold him to his promise. The future rests with the King, and nobody knows which way he will decide. All that he (Dillon) knows is that Knollys, who is acting as go-between for the King with Asquith, is strong for Irish Home Rule and for the Veto; but the King is subjected to other influences, and it is a toss up which side he will take, and on his decision will depend in large measure the fate of the elections. The Irish position has never since Parnell's time been so strong as now. Redmond has got the whole of the American, Canadian, and Australian Irish, with insignificant exceptions, at his back. Their coffers are full, and there is no chance of O'Brien winning more than his half dozen seats at home against them. We also discussed Persia, Constantinople, and Egypt, on which subject Dillon and I are at one. He will help our Egyptian campaign in Parliament, though he will not join the Committee. Dillon gave me a curious instance of the kind of temptations put in the way of the Irish party by the capitalists. In the Spring of the present year he had been approached by representa-

tives of the brewing interest offering him £25,000 for the Irish Parliamentary party fund if they would vote against the Budget. He declined to have anything to do with it, and had told only Redmond and
two or three of the party about it. The Irish party had always refused
contributions coupled with secret conditions. The only instance to the
contrary was Cecil Rhodes' gift of £10,000, but that was publicly acknowledged, and the letters that passed between Rhodes and Parnell
were published. The party accepted contributions from anybody, but
not on conditions. I asked him about Redmond's sale under the Land
Act, and this is what he says: Redmond inherited the family estate
from his uncle, so burdened with incumbrances as to be, in Redmond's
own words, a *damnosa hereditas*. When the Land Act was passed his
tenants had come forward spontaneously offering to buy at terms of
from eighteen to twenty-four years' purchase. Redmond never got a
penny out of the property, as the charges on it covered the whole of
the income. Speaking of the Catholic priesthood's attitude towards
Home Rule, he said they never had the hierarchy more solidly with
them. All the bishops supported them now, except Archbishop Walsh,
Cardinal Logue, and the Bishop of Limerick and one other. He also
says that the national University has turned out a complete success.

"*17th Nov.*— Tolstoy is dead. A few days ago he ran away from
home, tired to death of his wife and children, and announcing his
intention of ending his days in a monastery or as a hermit, or anywhere
out of reach of them. They had made his life a misery to him by their
stupidities, and at the age of eighty-two he at last broke loose. In
Russia, however, it is impossible for anyone to conceal himself, least
of all an old bearded patriarch like Tolstoy, whose photograph was in
every shop window, and his family tracked him down. First a daughter caught him and then the rest. He took to his bed to shut them
out, and as a last resource died at a railway hotel, refusing admittance
to his wife to the end. For Tolstoy as a writer I have the most profound admiration. His two great novels, ' Anna Karenina ' and ' Peace
and War,' are probably the greatest ever written. As a philosopher I
admire him less; as a prophet I do not believe in him at all. Nevertheless he was distinctly the most interesting personality of our generation, the man who commanded the widest following, the man of the
most indisputable genius. Some of his political manifestos are splendid. He had courage to a supreme degree. As a moral teacher his
ideas were sublime, but quite unsound; his religion was absurd. Such
is my brief estimate of him. The world is poorer for his death.

"I have a letter from Miss Petre asking what my religious position
now is. Her own position, Meynell tells me, is considered to be logical
and correct by all the English bishops, except Amigo, her own diocesan.
The Pope's encyclical letters are *not* binding *de fide,* and they all say it

was foolish of Amigo to ask her to sign her approval of them. The demand was quite unprecedented.

"*19th Nov.*— Asquith has declared that Parliament will be dissolved on the 28th. This can hardly not mean that the King has given the guarantees, and if so and Asquith does not cheat, Home Rule is certain. I am not sure of Asquith, but Dillon says he can be relied on.

"*20th Nov. (Sunday).*— More Russian troops are being marched into Persia, and it is telegraphed from Teheran that at a great public meeting there appeal has been made to the Sultan for an alliance and also to the Kaiser. It is the Persians' only chance. Riza Bey writes to me that he has shown my letter to Talaat Bey, the Minister of the Interior, and others, and that my work for them is fully appreciated. He also says that when Churchill was at Constantinople he created an excellent impression.

"*21st Nov.*— A loan of £20,000,000 is announced and put forward with much pomp in 'The Times' for an Anglo-Russian railway to be run through Persia to Baloochistan. It is to pass through Kirman, the intended capital of the British sphere of influence. Belloc is of opinion that Asquith will trick the Irish after all.

"*23rd Nov.*— Chapel Street. Asquith, Birrell, and other Ministers have been mauled by the Suffragettes and their windows broken. They are enraged because Winston will not prosecute them. I entertained my political allies to-day at luncheon, Dillon, Browne, Mackarness. O'Malley and Cunninghame Graham were also to have been of the party, but they did not appear. We got the question, however, of our Egyptian Committee settled on a basis of evacuation, though no action can be taken by it till the new Parliament has met. Keir Hardie is an honest old fellow, with a Scotch terrier's face, rugged and plain spoken. I took much to him. Besides the Committee here in London, we are to get up a proper English paper for Egypt.

"I have been reading a very interesting new book, called 'The Conflict of Colour,' by one Puttenham Weir, but Beauclerk tells me his real name is Robinson, son of an English resident in China, and nephew of Hart, the Director of Customs. His book is an excellent one, and I agree with most of what is said in it.

"*5th Dec.*— Parliament was dissolved on the 28th, and the General Election is in full swing. I have five votes, at Horsham, East Grinstead, Reigate, the New Forest of Hampshire, and Westminster.

"*15th Dec.*— Lunched with Eversley. We talked about Egypt, as to which he is sympathetic. He says there is talk of a reconstruction of the Cabinet, of Loreburn's retirement, and Haldane's appointment as Lord Chancellor, with Birrell at the War Office and Churchill in Ireland. Eversley has the highest opinion of Churchill as a much abler man than his father.

"19*th Dec.*— There are evil rumours in the papers of an entente between England and Germany, which should have for its basis the settlement of their rival commercial ambitions in the near East. This can only be at the expense of the near Eastern populations. [Compare Dr. Dillon's ' Eclipse of Russia.']

"22*nd Dec.*— The Elections are now over, the result being an exact repetition of those of a year ago. The Government claims it as a decisive victory. Though with a majority of 126, Asquith is really in an English minority of fourteen. All once more depends upon the King. If he finds pluck enough to refuse to create 500 peers required to pass the Veto Bill, he will carry general opinion with him. The country cares too little about abolishing the House of Lords to make a revolution for it. Apart from Ireland's chance of Home Rule, which depends upon it, I am personally with the Lords as against the Commons.

"26*th Dec.*— On the 23rd there was an account in the papers of the capture of Kerak (*Crac les Chevaliers*), and this morning a letter has come from Riza Tewfik relating the misdeeds of the party now in power at Constantinople. I am inclined to think he exaggerates these, as he is the leader of the Parliamentary opposition there, but what seems certain is that the Turks have got into a mess in Arabia by trying to coerce the Bedouin tribes. This is a folly I warned them against long ago.

"31*st Dec.*—' The year 1910 has been for me on the whole a happy one.' Politically I still fight on and have accomplished much, but it has been in what looks more and more a losing battle. I doubt if I shall see the accomplishment of any of my dreams. The cause of Eastern liberty is dark at present. In Persia it seems lost and in Turkey to be in no little danger. Without the resuscitation of the Ottoman Empire Egypt will remain in English hands till a stronger robber comes. Still we must fight on, and I have done my best. What will the New Year bring? I dare not prophesy."

CHAPTER X

THE FRENCH INVADE MOROCCO

" *2nd Jan.*, 1911.— The birthday honours list gives Jameson a baronetcy who ought to have had a rope.

" *3rd Jan.*— There has been a battle between the police, helped by sixty men of the Scots Guards on the one hand, and two men on the other, described as anarchists and assassins, who defended themselves in a house in the East End of London for a whole day. Winston in his character of Home Secretary put himself in command of the forces of the Crown, and advanced under fire.

" *12th Jan.*— Farid Bey has returned to Cairo and is to be prosecuted for an introduction he wrote some time ago to one Ghyati's poems. Also Ismaïl Abaza, the only independent member, has been turned out of his place in the General Assembly. All this is disheartening. There is much discussion at Paris, Berlin and Petersburg as to the meaning of the Potsdam arrangement made between Germany and Russia about Persia. It would seem directed against the Anglo-French Entente, but does it not also mean a further division of the spoils in Asia and Egypt? The danger we have to face is a possible Anglo-German Entente. This would be fatal and final—may God forbid it. [Compare Dr. Dillon's 'Eclipse of Russia.']

" *26th Jan.*— Farid has been sentenced at Cairo to six months' imprisonment, a really outrageous sentence, for having written a few words of introduction in a volume of poems, one of which contained praise of Wardani. His defence is that he never read the poems, and being a very busy man it is more than likely that that is the fact. The sentence was, no doubt, dictated by Gorst to the Assize Judge whom he appointed to deal with the case. It is just the same old way of manipulating the law in political cases we used to know in Ireland.

" Dilke is dead. I hardly know what to say of him except that he was in politics, what I most distrust, a Radical Imperialist. The extreme Radicals here had come to look upon him as one of their stalwarts, and only a few days ago Mackarness wrote to me proposing him as Chairman of a new Egyptian Committee, knowing nothing of his past history at the Foreign Office in 1882. Dilke remained very secretive about Egypt, speaking constantly in the House on every other subject but not on this. I advised Mackarness to ask Dilke whether he

repented of his Egyptian sin, and he did so and found him unre-
pentant. Dilke was possessed, as the papers say of him, of 'an almost
encyclopædic knowledge' on foreign affairs especially, but he had long
ceased to be a force in the House of Commons though made use of
now and then. The scandal of his connection with the Crawford
divorce suit stood always in the way of his regaining office, and he had
no wit or personal charm to attract to him a party below the gangway.
Politically and morally he seems to have formed himself on the model
of his friend Gambetta, a republican at home and an Imperial expan-
sionist abroad. It is not for me to cast a stone at him for anything
but his betrayal of Egypt to the Jews in 1882. Peace be with him .

"*27th Jan.*— Cotton, Mackarness, Rutherford and Rothstein came
to tea with me, to arrange about our Egyptian Committee, of which I
am to be Chairman, and our monthly newspaper, 'Egypt.' We are to
publish a first number as soon as possible.

"*28th Jan.*— Lunched in Eccleston Square with Winston and Clementine; Birrell also there, and we renewed acquaintance on the ground
of my former friendship with his father-in-law, Frederick Locker, and
my character as a poet. Birrell has a pleasant reputation in the House
of Commons as a gay trifler, covering his personal appearance of
pedagogue to the extent that his style of wit has been called 'Birrellism,'
and he made play on these lines in conversation during our meal, his
forehead still dotted with sticking-plaster, as sign manual of his adventure with the suffragettes three months ago. I made him give a
narrative of this. He had been walking home alone, he said, and was
crossing the open space by the Duke of York's column when he suddenly found himself in the middle of a group of wild women who
thrust their ugly faces close to his and told him he was a bad, wicked
man for not giving them the vote, and hustled him so that he had to
defend himself with his umbrella, ineffectively, as they caught hold of
his arms and the struggle between them lasted six or seven minutes.
Then a weak knee which he had gave way and he fell down and was
helpless, until Lionel Earle, who happened to be passing in a motor,
stopped and rescued him. He was considerably mauled, and has been
more or less on the sick list ever since. The recollection of it excited
him and he talked of it with resentment, and now he had come to
Churchill for sympathy and to consult how to meet the assaults to be
expected at the opening of Parliament on Monday. I was sworn to
secrecy while they discussed their plans of action. [On account of
my oath I do not transcribe it here.] My contribution to the conversation was that I suggested that instead of being forcibly fed, which
savoured too much of the ways of the Spanish Inquisition, the imprisoned women should have their own meals and their own medical
attendants, and that the Ritz Hotel should be engaged for their accom-

modation, also that if I were a Cabinet Minister I would promise everything and do nothing. Also that if assaulted as Birrell had been I
would go down on my knees and say 'Ladies, have mercy on me, I
am a poor weak man and appeal to your chivalry; spare me in consideration of my sex.'

"From this we went on to Ireland, about which Birrell was sensible
and interesting. He confirmed all that Dillon had told me about the
improved condition of the small farmers and especially of the labourers, for whom cottages had been built. These had given superior ideas
of comfort to all. He also praised the new local administration which
had superseded the old system. It was surprising, he said, how quickly
the small tradesmen in the towns, who now managed it, have picked
up the way of dealing with local matters. The only real difficulty now
in Home Rule was the financial one, caused by the old age pensions.
The English Treasury would have to provide two more millions yearly
for this, and forego all charge for army or navy or interest on the
National Debt. Birrell, however, foresees great difficulty in getting
certain sections of the Liberal party to agree to Home Rule on these
generous lines. Much would depend on how the Irish received the
King on the occasion of his visit to Dublin in the summer. If the
King were not well received it would be difficult to pass a Home Rule
Bill. The whole thing depended for its value to us on our getting the
Irish to join with us in loyalty to the Empire. I pricked up my ears
at this but said nothing. I am sorry to find that Winston is getting
more and more Imperialist. I asked what the King's personal feeling
was about Home Rule, and he said it was favourable. 'It is a common
mistake,' he said, 'to suppose that the late King was more in favour
of it than the present King. The contrary is the case. All King
Edward would listen to was "something in the way of councils,"
whereas this one has quite colonial views about it. He is altogether
colonial about Home Rule and the Empire.' It is useful to know this,
but is of evil omen to that other half of the British Empire where my
interest lies, the coloured half. As I was going away Churchill called
to me, 'What will you say to our making a large increase in the Cairo
garrison and putting the expense of it on Egypt as a result of your
inflammatory pronouncements?' 'You may keep 100,000 men there
if you like,' I said, 'It will make no difference to the result.'

"*30th Jan.*— Called on Weardale at his house in Carlton House
Terrace and asked him to join our Egyptian Committee. Our manifesto he entirely approves, but like all of them, he is afraid of offending
Grey by putting his name to it. He looks upon Grey as an ignorant
commonplace man, quite incapable in foreign affairs, but he, Weardale,
is interested in the question of the Declaration of London, and dares
not quarrel with him on that account.

" *1st Feb.*— We launched the manifesto about our paper ' Egypt ' this morning, with my sole name on it as provisional Chairman, none of my fellow Committeemen being willing to attach their signatures. English Radicals are timorous folk. Parliament met yesterday. The principal incident was a protest made by one Ginnell, an Independent Irish Nationalist, against the system of excluding private members from all opportunity of speech.

" *5th Feb. (Sunday).*— Two young Egyptians, came from Oxford to see me. They described the régime of political terror at Cairo as closely resembling what I remember there in 1883, the city honey-combed with spies, and subject to arrests and imprisonments under the new Press Law. They told me also that two months ago the German Consul General at Cairo, Prince Hatzfeldt, issued an invitation to young Egyptians to go for their education to Berlin. This was published in the ' Mowayyad.'

" Later Dillon looked in. I urged him to bring forward the subject of Egypt in the Debate on the Address to-morrow, but he tells me Redmond would not support any attack on Grey just now, nor will the Irish Party move any amendment. The Labour members cannot be relied on. They are choosing Ramsay Macdonald as their leader. Talking about Ireland he said the King's visit was most unfortunate; he would be badly received in Dublin, but the King had insisted upon going there. Ginnell he described as a clever but quite wild man, who would not conform to the rules of the House of Commons. They had had to carry him out of the House on one occasion by the arms and legs. At one time he had been his, Dillon's, private secretary. Of Birrell he has a high opinion.

" Meynell tells me the Pope has forbidden mixed marriages in Ireland unless solemnized by Catholic rite, and has made the rule retrospective. This will raise trouble, and is contrary to all the formerly received canon law, where the declared consent of the parties followed by consummation was considered to constitute a binding marriage even without any religious ceremony.

" *6th Feb.*— I have been arranging Lytton's letters to me, some two hundred of them, a really wonderful series, from 1865 to 1891, when he died. They are as good as Byron's or Shelley's, and far better than Trelawney's, whose letters to Clare and Mary Shelley I have just been reading. These last are disappointing, being for the most part very badly written; the older ones school-boyish, the later less vigorous than one would have expected from the old buccaneer Trelawney posed as being. Both these women seem to have played with him; Mary certainly did, and it does not appear from the letters that with Clare there was anything more than a single brief passionate episode, never quite realized.

" *9th Feb.*— Rumbold and Lascelles lunched with me.   We discussed
the fortification of Flushing, which is exercising the minds of diplomatists just now.   I told them of Usedom's words about the eventual
union of Holland with Germany which interested them.   As to the
motives that might induce Holland to unite with Germany, they suggested that the danger to the Dutch Colonies from the Naval power of
Japan might be one, as Germany might guarantee these to Holland.
Rumbold has a poor opinion of Grey.   When the revolution happened
at Constantinople he expostulated with Grey on its recognition by England, but Grey told him he did not agree with him.   There is no doubt
Grey entirely misunderstood what was happening, and was likely to
happen.   Lascelles told a story about Kaiser Wilhelm's infatuation for
Lord Lonsdale, whom he regarded as the most reliable of advisers
about English things.   Lonsdale had told the Kaiser once that he,
Lonsdale, was in King Edward's black books on account of his being
unwilling to give up the Kaiser's friendship.   ' I told the King, however,' said Lonsdale, ' that this I would not do.   I was ready to lay
down my life for the Crown as my ancestors had done, but not to betray
my friends.'   This is considered a good joke.

" *13th Feb.*— To London to interview Miss Howsin, whom I have
engaged at five pounds a month to edit our paper ' Egypt ' under my
direction.   She is an intelligent young woman of about thirty-five.

" *15th Feb.*— To see Maud Allan dance, a great performance, in the
Palace Theatre.   It was finer than anything of the kind I have ever
seen, especially the Mænad prancing, which one cannot doubt is a true
reproduction of the old Greek way.   She is a very beautiful woman.

" *17th Feb.*— Lunched in Downing Street.   [I had so far avoided
going there though often asked.]   A large casual luncheon party of
unexpected guests, for luncheon is an occasion for Margot's friends to
drop in.   I found myself next to Julia McGuire, with Asquith beyond
her, who came in rather late, and chattered gaily during the meal.   I
had not seen him to speak to since he became Prime Minister.

" Phil Burne-Jones dined with me and Meynell and his daughter
Viola.   George Wyndham came in immediately after in uniform from
the Speaker's banquet.   He was in one of his most loquacious moods,
and entertained us with theories of Post-Impressionism and art in
literature.   He out-stayed the rest and sat on with me well into the
night, explaining to me the troubles of his Conservative Party, which
is at sixes and sevens, Balfour away and no two of the others of the
same opinion how to act on the Veto Bill.   ' In the House of Commons,' George said, ' there is an absolute dearth of ability.   The Leadership in Balfour's absence is disputed by Walter Long and Austen
Chamberlain, a choice of mediocrities.   Both look to Arthur's succession, and Arthur is tired of politics and affects to be unwell, though he

has nothing at all the matter with him, and has taken a holiday exactly
at the crisis.   Walter is ambitious without ability; Austen plodding and
industrious; neither has any imagination.   He, George, is the only one
with brains, and he is standing aside, as he does not care to give up his
literature and social amusements for the mere chance of being some
day Prime Minister.   Still, it lies within his reach, he says, if he wishes
it, and he wants my advice.   If he goes in for it, it will mean ten
hours' work daily, taking on three or four Secretaries, spending all his
money and abandoning romance and friendship.   What is he to do?
If it was a question of saving the Empire from ruin, he would, of
course, do it.   But can the Empire be saved?   His plan would be, when
Asquith faces them with the Veto Bill to dare him to do his worst, to
say ' You threaten us with a revolution, we threaten you with a counter-
revolution; create the five hundred peers if you can, we refuse to have
the constitution destroyed.'   If Arthur would call a meeting in St.
James's Hall and declare war in this way he would carry the country
with him, only Arthur won't.   Arthur is not sufficiently interested in
the issue.   He is disgusted with the way things have gone, he does not
want to fight.   He takes too scientific a view of politics.   He knows
that there was once an ice age, and that there will some day be an ice age
again.   This makes him indifferent.'   My advice to George was that
if he cared about it enough to make a real revolution on these lines it
would be worth doing, but that otherwise he had better enjoy himself.

" 19*th Feb.* (*Sunday*).— Yesterday I stayed in all day writing.   I
have done three articles for ' Egypt,' the leading article, ' Secrecy in
Foreign Affairs,' and ' The Bagdad Railway,' besides most of the rest
of the first number.   I never had such work."   [The article on " Secrecy in Foreign Affairs " was the reproduction of an old protest against
the ways of the Foreign Office which I had first made as long ago as
1885 at a meeting at Islington Hall presided over by Frederic Harrison,
and was at that time a novelty in politics.]

" To-day Dillon came to luncheon and stayed three hours talking.
He approves of all I have written, especially about the Bagdad railway
(see ' Egypt,' No. 1), and will get the new labour leader, Ramsay Mac-
Donald, to bring our Egyptian questions forward in Parliament.   About
home politics, he told me the Opposition was all at sixes and sevens;
they had no leader.   He did not believe in the Lords throwing out the
Veto Bill; the threat of creating the peers would be enough.   The
King would write a letter to Asquith promising the necessary number,
and the Lords would give in.   Still it all depends upon the King.   I
told him what I have often told George — that the obstinacy of the
Tory party about Ireland was like the obstinacy of Pharaoh.   They
had been refusing for the last thirty years to let the Irish go, and had
sacrificed first the House of Commons, now the House of Lords, and

to-morrow very likely would sacrifice the Monarchy, and all for nothing. This pleased him. We talked about Asquith, whose intellectual power he greatly admires, though he says his range of interest is too narrow to govern an Empire. For myself I consider that Asquith has always been a wet Home Ruler, if one at all. Asquith is above all things a lawyer, and knows how to talk both ways.

"*21st Feb.*—With Phil Burne-Jones to his studio. He has done several nice little portraits on a very modest scale, the best being one of his father. It is not great art, but respectable and good. He is a pleasant, good fellow.

"Neville took me in the evening to a prize fight, where four or five thousand persons had collected to see a battle in gloves between a black man and a white man. It was very interesting, indeed exciting, as it involved a question of race superiority. The white man (Lang) was an English Australian, six feet and an inch high, with an immense width of shoulders, and limbs which looked as if they could smash everything; while the black man (Langford) was short, only five foot six, Neville said, but astonishingly well put together head to heel, lithe and strong. The contrast in build was great, but that of *morale* was still more remarkable, contradicting all my expectations. Lang was nervous, and though he had never been beaten was manifestly afraid of his enemy, who from the beginning took the offensive with a quiet, persistent attack which demoralized the other, and a rapidity of striking power which left him no chance. At the end of the fifth round Lang was smashed flat, so that I thought him killed, and though he got up pluckily his face was a mask of blood, and he staggered like a drunken man. The end of the fight was disappointing. Lang, to save himself more punishment, hit a foul blow. The black man, while pommelling him, happened to slip down on one knee, and Lang struck him while down. This disqualified him and ended the fight. It was a great triumph for the black, and I was pleased to see that the feeling of the spectators was mostly on his side, which was right, for he fought not only fairly, but with a certain generosity, while the other showed poor courage. Neville tells me the blacks as fighters have far better nerve than the whites, and are much more dogged. A fight between two blacks generally goes over forty rounds." [The result of this fight was a surprise to me. I had expected to see a gigantic black man subdued by the scientific persistence and higher *morale* of his smaller white opponent, a triumph of white mind over black matter, but it turned out absolutely the reverse. It was the black man that wore the white down by superior science and superior courage.]

"*25th Feb.*—We have got our first number of 'Egypt' into print, every word of it written by myself, except a review of Rothstein's book by Sir Henry Cotton. Miss Howsin, though enthusiastic and painstaking, is, I fear, useless as editor, as she has had no literary experience.

" Savarkar's case has given in favour of the English demand, which refuses to send him back to France. I am sorry for the poor young man, whose real crime in Anglo-Indian official eyes has been his authorship of the ' History of the Indian Revolution.'

" *26th Feb. (Sunday)*.— Newbuildings. Belloc to dine. Very cock-a-hoop about the success of his ' Party System,' which has come very opportunely. It is most amusing, though, unlike his books, is written seriously. He tells me he gets constant letters about it and invitations to lecture at £20 a night. We discussed, among other things, the fortification of Flushing, which he declares the French Government would make a *casus belli*, but I doubt the French fighting for it.

" *28th Feb*.— Chapel Street. Beauclerk brought Lord Ronaldshay to luncheon, a pleasant young man of thirty-five, who has travelled much in Asia, and is now in Parliament, with aspirations of being some day Viceroy of India. He was A.D.C. to Curzon for a year, and regards him with much admiration, though understanding the weak points of his character. My view of Imperial matters was entirely new to him, as it is to most people, though it is really forty years old. He, like everybody else, confuses the meaning of the word Empire, which has only quite recently been applied to our white colonial system, which is no more imperial than was the Greek colonial system in the days of Pericles. Empire properly means what the Roman Empire was, the subjugation of a number of races by a single race or a single man. This is the Imperialism I repudiate, not the other.

" *1st March*.— Called in Park Lane and found George Wyndham working up a speech on the Veto Bill. He told me the party had made up its mind to fight. The Lords would not pass the Bill, whatever threat of creating peers might be used.

" *2nd March*.— There is a new Ministry at Paris, Monis, Prime Minister ; Delcassé, Marine ; and Cruppi, Foreign Affairs.

" Mrs. Harrison told me of a luncheon at which her husband had been present at Morley's, there being Alfred Lyall also there and Chirol. Morley had put to them three questions. (1) Was the entente with France less cordial than when it was made? (2) Was it possible to improve it? (3) How could it be improved? All but Morley agreed that it had ceased to be effective; that the French were disappointed at the results, and that the only thing that could make it effective would be the introduction of some form of conscription in England which would enable us to place an army at the service of France in the case of a war with Germany. Also that it is impossible we should raise such an army. The Entente is pretty nearly dead.

"*3rd March.*— The first number of 'Egypt' was distributed this morning, sixteen hundred copies. It happened to be the bicentenary to a day of the first issue of Addison's 'Spectator.'

"*5th March (Sunday).*— Newbuildings. Belloc to dinner. He assures me Haldane has not got 50,000 men to send to Egypt if they want to do so. He thinks it more likely that the condominium will be re-established there, with a joint French and English garrison.

"Eddy Tennant has been made a peer (yet another member of the Crabbet Club arrived at high honours). He is also made Lord Commissioner of the Church of Scotland.

"*7th March.*— There was a pronouncement yesterday in all the papers from Berlin and from Constantinople, in which it was clearly declared that England will not be allowed to meddle with the Bagdad railway, a final blow to Grey and the Foreign Office in exact confirmation of what I had just written about Grey's blundering. Happening to meet Belloc, I asked if he had noticed it, and what would be the result. He said: 'The danger is that Grey may make a *coup de tête* and rush into a war with Germany.'

"*9th March.*— There has been a debate on the Bagdad Railway. Dillon writes excusing himself for not having taken part in it, but he has arranged with Ramsay MacDonald that they are to act together.

"*10th March.*— With Beauclerk to the National Gallery, where we looked at the Lansdowne Rembrandt. This, though a good landscape, is not at all worth the £100,000 Lansdowne has been offered for it, nor, I think, 100,000 pence. It is ridiculous giving long prices of this kind for small unimportant pictures, however good, and here we have nothing very wonderful. The new rooms at the Gallery do not display the pictures to such advantage as the old ones, and the walls are decorated too much like a railway restaurant.

"*12th March (Sunday).*— Chapel Street. Dillon came to lunch, and we had another long talk about the Bagdad Railway, Persia, and Egypt. As to Ireland, he thinks Home Rule will be come to by agreement, the younger Tories seeing now that their party has been ruined by its obstinacy in opposing it. He gave an interesting account of the Irish debate on Thursday, an all night sitting, where, Asquith having been called away, Churchill was for the first time left Leader of the House. A band of young Tories, Hugh Cecil, Winterton, Castlereagh, and one or two others, took the occasion to rag Winston, and succeeded in making him lose his temper by continual noise and calling out 'Rats!' so that he was driven to a standstill. It is strange to see him thus hoist with his father's petard.

" 14*th March.*— My cousin, Percy Wyndham, George's father, is dead. Here is a good photograph of him. It gives all his best qualities of honour and benignity. I know of no one who in these had his equal. His death leaves me without anyone now with a right to lecture or reprove me, for he was my elder by over five years, and had the position with me through life of an elder brother. George was with him when he died.

" 15*th March.*— The papers have been full of the Bagdad Railway all the week, while Grey's climb-down seems to have satisfied the German Government, and now he has made another speech about disarmament. Both speeches are very able, and Dillon tells me that the first about the railway was admirable in style. Grey has a fine House of Commons manner, which imposes on his hearers. Indeed, he seems to fulfil the ideal of British statesmanship as it is described by Wells in his ' New Macchiavelli,' a dignified attitude which is always ready under pressure ' proudly and quite firmly to take the second place.' The ' Temps,' however, calls his disarmament speech childish, which is also true, inasmuch as it does not deal with the reality, that in order to economize in war preparations you must have a peace policy abroad. It is impossible to run high Imperialism on the cheap.

" As to Bagdad, I see Curzon has given notice of a motion in the House of Lords to move for papers. This ought to clear the atmosphere and bring to light at last the text of his secret treaty with Mubarak at Koweit in 1899. I have been looking through my diaries of 1898, and find that at the time of Curzon's going to India the young Tories, of whom he was the leader on foreign affairs, looked to a partition of the Ottoman Empire between England, Russia, and Germany, England to have the Arabic speaking provinces. Curzon's intrigue with Mubarak was one of his first moves in preparation for it. My chief fear now is least the German Government may after all weaken in its Bagdad policy and come to terms with England for an immediate division of the Ottoman spoils. There was a little paragraph the other day in the papers saying that Frank Lascelles, who has been passing through Berlin on his way back from Sweden, dined with the Emperor. May he not have been used by the Foreign Office to negotiate this?

" 19*th March (Sunday).*— Newbuildings. Belloc came to dinner. He says of Grey's arbitration alliance with America that such an alliance will certainly bring about a rapprochement between France and Germany, and the uniting of all Europe against us. He also says, speaking of the threatened quarrel between America and Mexico, that the United States have not a strong enough army to coerce the Mexicans.

" 20*th March.*— Beauclerk went up to London with me, and we went to his rooms in Mount Street, where we met a certain Fielding, a mining engineer, whom he had made acquaintance with in Persia. Beauclerk explained the position of the Russians with a map on the Chinese frontier. The Russians have two strong military stations on the frontier, the one at Tashkend, the other at Kiahta, threatening Kulja and Urga respectively. The Russian colonists cannot in any way compete with the Chinese, and it is difficult to see what they want with extending their Empire in the Chinese direction, except that just over the frontier towards Kulja there is a valuable coal mine, which they covet.

"*21st March.*— Browne came to luncheon and brought with him Mirza Abdul Ghaffar, of the Persian Legation, an intelligent man, with whom we discussed the Persian and other Eastern questions for full three hours.

"*22nd March.*— To the House of Lords to hear the debate on Bagdad. It was a disappointing affair. Curzon made a long, dry, and pompous exposition of the case, carefully avoiding, however, the point of real interest, namely, his own intrigue with Mubarak Ibn Sbaa at Koweit. He just mentioned that place, mispronouncing it Ko-ite (as one might say 'go right') instead of Quate, but only to say that it need not be discussed. His whole speech was a shirking of the real matters in dispute, and Morley, who followed him, in reply, was only too glad to leave it so. I never saw anything feebler or less imposing than Morley showed himself on this occasion, unless it was the same Morley twelve years ago dealing with Kitchener at Omdurman in the House of Commons. He seemed ashamed of himself there in the House of Lords, a little old senile vestryman fumbling with his papers, ignorant of the whole case he had to state, timid in addressing his brother peers, contradicting himself and saying the wrong thing, at times quite inaudible. It seemed absurd that he and Curzon between them had had the whole fortunes of the British Empire in the East in their hands for the last dozen years, and that the Empire should have survived it. The debate ended in the *non sequitur* of Curzon withdrawing his demand for papers.

"Beauclerk on Sunday repeated to me the account of Major Sykes having fortified his house at Meshed. When Beauclerk stayed with him there three years ago, Sykes had 200 Indian Sepoys as his Consular guard, and he used to drill them daily to rifle practice. Also he had dug a mine from his garden 100 yards long, passing under the street to that of the Governor of the town, and had even undermined the Governor's house. He learned this from Sykes himself. [A pleasant instance of what diplomatists call 'peaceful penetration.']

"*24th March.*— Bain, the author of the 'Digit of the Moon,' dined with me. He is less interesting than his books, a typical Anglo-Indian with more knowledge than sympathy in Indian things, and no sympathy at all with modern India.

" 25th March.— Dillon lunched with me to concert measures about 'Egypt,' which seems to have been put on the official black list at Cairo. I am off now to Newbuildings till after Easter.

" 26th March (Sunday).— Newbuildings. Belloc came to dinner with Maurice Baring. Baring is intelligent and pleasant, but showed no extraordinary brilliancy in talk.

" 11th April.— Moberley Bell's and Alfred Lyall's deaths are announced to-day. Bell I never knew personally, but Lyall was for many years my friend. He died suddenly of *angina pectoris* at Farringford, where he was staying, apparently in good health, at the age of seventy-six. He had a successful Anglo-Indian official life, and twenty years ago was much cherished in London society; but, as old people are obliged to do, had dropped out of it laterly, and we had not met for the last eight or nine years. Without being a poet, he wrote some good verse, and had much knowledge of the East with as great sympathy for it as an Indian official dared to show.

" 12th April.— Laid the foundation stone of my new Manor House in Worth Forest.

" 18th April.— George Howard Lord Carlisle is dead. He was one of the best of men, as well as one of the most domestically tried.

" 19th April.— Newbuildings. One Duse Mohammed, who has written a good book on Egypt, cribbed, nearly all of it, from me and Rothstein, came to see me. He is an odd creature, an Egyptian mulatto, he says, but knowing no word of Arabic; a Mohammedan, but unable to recite the formula of the faith; an Egyptian historian with almost no knowledge of Egypt. He tells me he was circumcised a Mohammedan, that his name is properly Mohammed Ali Ibn Abd El Salaam, but was taken to England by a Frenchman named Ducey when he was ten years old, and has only once been in Egypt since, namely from May 1882 till February 1883, when he returned to England. There he went on the stage, and later in America, lecturing on Shakespeare and writing for the Press. To test him I tried whether he could recite the Fatha, but he was unable to so much as repeat the words after me. It reminds one of the Tichborne claimant, who, asserting that he had been brought up a Catholic, was unable to repeat the ' Hail Mary.' He has married an English woman and goes sometimes to church, but has always refused, he tells me, to be baptized.

" 22nd April.— The French Government seems drifting into an invasion of Morocco, just as Gladstone drifted into invading Egypt in 1882. Our fine Liberals here are all applauding out of ' loyalty to France '; this is their thieves' honour.

" 25th April.— Rothstein is furious about Duse Mohammed's appropriation of his work, which is more flagrant than I thought. Also, I fear, we may have trouble about the management of our paper, as Keir Hardie wants to run it his own way. Dillon advises me to get rid of the Committee.

"*28th April.*— It has been decided by the Committee that 'Egypt' is to remain under my sole political and financial direction with no other interference than the advice of an Executive Committee, consisting of myself, Ryan as Editor, Miss Howsin as Sub-Editor, Dr. Rutherford and El Alaili. Ryan and Miss Howsin will be paid by me. This leaves me in sole control.

"*1st May.*— Newbuildings. Belloc dined with us last night. He has been in Germany and has come back more than ever certain that in the next war the French will beat the Germans. His new paper is to be called 'The Witness,' with £2,000 to start it, and much promised help.

"*6th May.*— The event of the past week has been the invasion of Morocco by the French, a scandalous affair, exactly on the same lines of financial speculation and Colonial and Imperial intrigue which were followed by us in Egypt thirty years ago. Belloc tells me that the French Government has this time defied the German Government. He has information that a few days ago Delcassé (who manages French Foreign Policy, though not Minister of Foreign Affairs) had the German Ambassador at Paris invited, a very unusual thing, to attend a Cabinet meeting convened to discuss the Moroccan question, and that, on the Ambassador's observing that the Algeciras Convention would have to be respected and that the German Government's information about Fez was that there was no danger for Europeans there, Delcassé told him roundly that France was determined to march on Fez, and this time would do so whether Germany liked it or no. Belloc declares the French army to be better than the German, and that Germany will not dare to go to war.

"*7th May (Sunday).*— Chapel Street. Dillon and the Persian Consul, Ghaffar Khan, came to luncheon, and we had a long talk on Eastern affairs. Ghaffar would like England and Germany to compose their differences and unite in an alliance with Turkey and Persia, Turkey abandoning Egypt to England, a fanciful idea, which would only mean an end of all things for Islam in Turkey as well as elsewhere. There is but one chance for Islam, and that is Germany's friendship, not, of course, a disinterested one, but still one that would protect them from the other European Powers until Islam is strong enough to stand alone. I explained the same thing to an intelligent young Egyptian from Oxford, Abd el Ghaffar, who came to consult me. He is of St. John's College. He tells me there are about eighty young Egyptians in London, who are here studying.

The German Crown Prince

" Yesterday, while at Newbuildings, three aeroplanes passed over at a great height, racing from Brooklands to Shoreham. We first heard shouts of boys and then the rattle of the machines. They were near enough for us to be able to make out with a glass that there was some-body in each. The leading one was a monoplane, a much more work-manlike machine than the others and extremely like a bird. Machinery, however, does not interest me, and I have not the smallest wish to take a flight in one.

" 11*th May.*— Worth Forest. Gorst's Egyptian Report is published, a lame affair, which will do him little credit. It justifies all I have writ-ten about him and the advice I have given to the Egyptians. He admits that there was never anything at all serious in his Constitutional re-forms. There is no chance whatever for Egypt, and has not been since 1904, except in the revival of Turkey's military power and the interven-tion of Europe.

" 14*th May* (*Sunday*).— Newbuildings. Meynell is here, with his nephew, Captain Butler, of the Royal Irish Fusiliers, Sir William's son, an exceedingly nice young fellow, of thirty, with all his father's anti-imperial ideas, an unusual phenomenon in a soldier; clever, original, a Home Ruler and a pious Catholic, who would like to fight for the Pope. I asked him how he managed to get on with his fellow-officers, having such ideas. He answered, ' They do not think, and I play polo.' He is just back from India where he saw a good deal of the German Crown Prince, who was travelling there during the winter. He confirms Philip Napier's account of his unconventional ways. The Crown Prince would not pay attention to the official big-wigs or be bored with German deputations, but he made great friends with the English officers, ' messing with them like a subaltern and playing polo. We all liked him much.' At Cairo, according to Napier, he gave great offence, refusing to wear uniform on solemn occasions or keep tire-some engagements. When he was to visit the Khedive on one occasion he was not ready, being occupied with a lady, and sent his Aide-de-camp on in the Khedivial carriage intended for him, arriving too late himself in a taxicab (with the lady) in a suit of overalls. Butler un-derstands horses and took an intelligent interest in everything here.

" 17*th May.*— Ryan enters on his duties as editor of ' Egypt ' from the 15th. I like him much.

" 19*th May.*— A great fuss is being made in London about the Kaiser Wilhelm's visit, and a gala representation of that ancient play ' Money ' is being given in his honour. I only hope this visit to London is not to be another Reval meeting, with some ' plot of peace ' involv-ing the ruin of some Eastern nation. That is always the danger on these gala occasions. It is easy for robbers to make friends over a corpse, and Morocco is there ready to their hands.

" *22nd May*.— The French Prime Minister, Monis, and the War Minister, Marceaux, have been, the one killed, the other seriously hurt by an aeroplane which they were watching the start of in an air race from Paris to Madrid yesterday. This may make a difference in the political world, and just possibly save Morocco from being invaded by the French. May God confound them! I fear it is as Belloc told me, the German Government have either given in or come to an arrangement about Morocco, for the occupation of Fez is no longer concealed, the price perhaps of France's and Russia's withdrawal of their opposition to the Bagdad railway. [Compare Dr. Dillon's ' Eclipse of Russia.']

" *24th May*.— The French have entered Fez, it is said, without opposition, the whole story of Europeans whose lives were reported to be in danger having proved to be a fable of the same kind as that invented about Johannesburg at the time of the Jameson raid (N.B.— Jameson has just been made a knight by our Liberal Government), and now the same course of lying is to be pursued by the French about remaining there as we pursued in Egypt.

" *26th May*.— There has been a report of a threat issued by the Russian Government to Turkey in regard to Montenegro, but to-day it is announced that its arrogant tone is apologized for. Germany once more has intervened.

" *28th May (Sunday)*.— Newbuildings. Shane Leslie, Patrick Butler, Francis Meynell, and Ryan were here for the week end, and yesterday Mallock. Young Meynell is clever and interesting, and Butler a good young man, with no little wisdom too. With Belloc and his wife who came to dinner, an entirely Catholic party.

" *1st June*.— The foolish Lords have passed the Veto Bill, and so have committed suicide without a division and without glory. Never was a position so frittered away. Arthur Balfour is principally responsible for this, acting on the advice of the two Whig deserters, Rosebery and Lansdowne. If he had stood firm two years ago and risked a civil war he would have had all the physical force of the country with him, and popular opinion, at least in England, too. There would have been no civil war, and he would have come back to office and stayed there for twenty years. It was the Whig obstinacy about Home Rule in Ireland that prevented it, and has caused their ruin.

" *6th June*.— A young Copt, Louis Aknoukh Fanous, came to consult me as to how to bring about a reconciliation between the Copts and Moslems in Egypt, in which I was very ready to help on two conditions — that the Copts should declare themselves (1) honestly for evacuation and (2) for the maintenance of the connection with the Ottoman Empire. He told me that the younger generation of Copts were quite ready for this. They did not want foreign rule, or to be separated from the Empire, where they were more at home than they would be in any European hands. Only they insisted that in their schools they should not be forced to learn to read out of the Koran, and that they should have Sunday as their holiday in the public offices, and should have a share in the provincial administration. I promised to speak to the Nationalist leaders about this. The young man is extremely intelligent, speaks English perfectly, and took a degree in Oxford three or four years ago. His father is one of the richest and most influential Christians in Upper Egypt.

" 11*th June (Sunday)*— There is more trouble brewing in Albania, the Catholic Mirdites having joined the Rebellion, and the Austrian Government having issued a warning of a moderating kind to Turkey. It would alarm me more if there was not news from Berlin which seems to show that the Turks are still backed by Germany. Goltz has publicly expressed his entire confidence in the Ottoman army, and the Emperor William is to receive a deputation from the Ottoman Parliament. But for this I should say the situation was very serious. The Bellocs dined with us and Cecil Chesterton, with whom he is collaborating his paper, 'The Witness.' They have asked me for some verse, and I have given them my 'Coronation Ode.' Belloc is delighted with it, and will print it on the first page of his paper.

" 14*th June.*— There is a new complication in Morocco, the Spanish Government having sent troops into the country in exact imitation of the French.

" 15*th June.*— Newbuildings. Yusuf Bey el Moelhi and a friend, Doctor Rashad, arrived to consult me in Egyptian affairs. He is all for alliance with Constantinople and Berlin, and is starting for Berlin to-morrow. He complains of the inefficiency of Hatzfeldt, the German Consul-General at Cairo, and of the little pains taken by him to strengthen German influence. Yusuf Bey is intelligent and patriotic, but, like most of them, looks to money as the main object in life. It is only the younger generation which has larger ideas. He has my 'Secret History' translated at his own cost, but doubts whether it will not be seized under the new Press laws.

" 17*th June.*— The Albanian quarrel seems arranged, and the Sultan recited the prayer yesterday at the tomb of Sultan Mourad at Kossovo, 80,000 Albanian clansmen praying with him.

" 19*th June.*— Dr. Rifaat, a Nationalist exile, arrived from Paris; he, too, to consult me. He is an extremist in his views, very hostile to the Khedive, and without much confidence from any quarter in the future. He looks upon the Ottoman connection as the best chance for Egypt, but is gloomy about the Ottoman Empire. The Egyptians are easily cast down, just as they are too ready to shout victory.

" 20*th June.*— Drove over to Greatham to call on Meynell at his new home there, a most beautiful site. He has just secured between Parham Park and the Amberly Marshes eighty acres of waste land, where he intends to found a family colony, wild heath, overgrown with fern, for which he has paid no more than £20 an acre. We found him in high delight at his sudden good fortune as a landed proprietor, a good fortune he deserves, and made our picnic under a clump of hollies, discussing the sites of cottages he intends to build.

" Belloc's paper is published under the title ' The Eye Witness,' with my ' Coronation Ode ' occupying the most prominent position.

" *21st June.*— Old Riaz Pasha is dead, the last of the old Pasha gang in Egypt. He began life as a dancing boy of Jewish origin at the Court of Abbas I, and has ended in high consideration and respect, though his subservience to English policy had lost him latterly the popularity he enjoyed twenty years ago, a patriot according to his lights, but these were never clear. I liked him personally much. *Allah kerim.*

" *22nd June.*— Coronation Day. We drank the King's health and the Queen's and all the Royal Family's, not, I fear, very devoutly.

" *28th June.*— Hassan Bey Sabri, an old disciple of Abdu's, came to see me. He belongs, if anybody in Egypt does, to the English party, expecting to be one of the nominated members of the Legislative Council, and is a follower of Saad Zaghloul. He thinks there is some new Liberal policy being planned for Egypt. Gorst, poor fellow, is dying, and his successor is to be Arthur Hardinge, and if the Nationalists will only be quiet, and not oppose English policy, something in the way of a Constitution will be given them. Personally I always liked Gorst, and used to find him more amenable to my ideas than Cromer, but he has proved a bad friend to Egypt, because, knowing her better than Cromer, he was better able to betray. Arthur Hardinge is a man of the same school, both having been Cromer's pupils, Hardinge probably the cleverer of the two. The Legislative Council will be allowed to pass laws, and even to control finance, as far as these relate to internal affairs. I asked him what his ultimate plan was, and he said he wanted evacuation, but not yet. I found him an honest man but timid, and as such in favour of half measures. Talking about Mohammed Abdu's death and in answer to my question whether he thought the Mufti had been poisoned, he said he was sure of it. He had been with Abdu at Alexandria on the 13th of June (Abdu died on 11th July) and he had suspicions then which have since been confirmed. He believed the same plan had been pursued with Abdu as with Seyyid Jemal ed Din, cancer had been communicated by means of a poisoned toothpick.

" *2nd July (Sunday).*— There is a sensational announcement in the ' Observer ' of the landing of German troops in Morocco. Belloc, who dined with us, declared the French Government will not fight. The French Government are in the throes of the reconstruction of their Cabinet, Monis having resigned, and the moment has been well chosen by the Germans for their coup.

"*5th July.*— The 'Daily Telegraph' has a paragraph saying that Kitchener is to have Gorst's place at Cairo.

"*7th July.*— The position in Morocco is very serious. I have been talking it over with Belloc. He is sure there has been an understanding between the German and French Governments about Agadir, and that the quarrel will be settled at our English expense. Agadir, he says, is of great importance to Germany, as the only possible seaport on the Moroccan Atlantic coast, and is of no importance to France in any hostile sense. The hostility is all towards us. Also he says that the French and Germans are too much afraid of each other to go to war, and that France will not join us in any attempt to expel Germany from its African position (at Agadir) unless we can guarantee her the support of a hundred and fifty thousand men landed on her frontier in France, a force we are unable to provide. We shall have therefore to make up our minds either to submit to the German seizure of Agadir or to go to war with Germany alone or find her compensation elsewhere. Where can we find such? Our Government seems aware of the position, for Asquith made a declaration yesterday in Parliament that England had interests of her own in Morocco separate from those entailed on her by her engagements to France. The question may possibly lead to war, though more likely to Germany's keeping Agadir."

[This shows, as an early link, the connection between France's invasion of Morocco in 1911 and the great war of 1914, with the part we played in it as France's ally, supplying a contingent in a land campaign against Germany.]

"*9th July (Sunday).*— Lady Gregory is here. She has been very successful this year with her plays, having cleared £500 by her theatrical visit to London, and got £3,000 of subscriptions, while Yeats has received a Government pension of £150. The King and Queen are in Ireland, where they are having a loyal reception carefully prepared for them, though the Dublin Corporation has refused to vote a penny or authorize an address.

"Belloc dined with us. His view that the occupation of Agadir was arranged beforehand between the French and German Governments seems the correct one. They seem to be on excellent terms with each other, and it is we that are to be left out in the cold. There is sufficient danger of war to have made me write to my bankers about it.

"*11th July.*— Newbuildings. The anniversary of the Bombardment of Alexandria. Miss Howsin came from King's Mead, where

she is staying with Mrs. Mackarness, to talk over the affairs of
'Egypt.' I hear from Osman Ghaleb that the Khedive is making
overtures of reconciliation to the Nationalist Party, being angry at the
idea of Kitchener being re-imposed on him to succeed Gorst. When
one remembers their quarrel in 1893, and how Kitchener, being in
the Khedive's service as Commander-in-Chief of his army, left Egypt
for South Africa without having so much as the politeness to take
leave at the Palace, one wonders at his having been sent back to Cairo
by the Foreign Office. I have drawn up a resolution to be issued
by the Egyptian Committee protesting against Kitchener's appointment.

" 12*th July.*—Caffin (my land agent, who is also a miller,) tells me
that war is an absolute impossibility for this country at the present
moment as we have no supply of food whatever in store, and even a
belief in war would be ruin. ' We are all,' he says, ' living literally
from hand to mouth. I have large contracts to supply flour at given
dates, and last week was within twenty-four hours of shutting down
my mill because it was impossible to buy wheat anywhere. I could not
get a hundred sacks at Chichester for love or money, Chichester being
the centre of our Sussex wheat supply, where in my grandfather's
time a thousand sacks were always to be had. England would starve
in a fortnight; war is impossible.'

" 13*th July.*— Everybody believes Kitchener's appointment to Egypt
certain. If it is so, it can only mean that Grey has taken the bit
between his teeth and means some form of Protectorate there. The
Khedive is furious at the idea.

" 14*th July.*— Chapel Street. The ' Pall Mall Gazette ' announces
Kitchener's appointment, not only as Consul General in Egypt, but also
to command the army of Occupation and all the forces on the Nile,
with a great flourish about some form of Protectorate. I cannot
get the Egyptian Committee to make any vigorous protest.

" To Hugh Lane's house in Chelsea where Lady Gregory is staying, for a tea party in connection with the Abbey Theatre. It is a
nice house in Cheyne Walk, which is being redecorated for him by
John, and contains two or three good pictures with others less good.
Lane is Lady Gregory's nephew, a young Irishman who began with
nothing but his wits. She apprenticed him to Colnaghi at a hundred
a year, where he learnt his business of picture dealing. He began
his fortune, she tells me, by an accident. He happened to hear of a picture which was for sale in some remote country place, and travelled
down to look at it, but, having no money to buy, although there was
almost no bidding, was obliged to let it go for a very small price.
When the sale was over, the bidders, who were all professional dealers,
went to a public house, and he with them, and then it turned out
that they had been standing in together not to bid, and they held a

private sale of the picture amongst themselves, dividing the price realized between them, and as Lane was known to belong to Colnaghi's he was included in it, and got £160 as his share. This started him, and he has now made a fortune and been knighted for presenting a collection of pictures to the Dublin Gallery. Also being a good-looking youth with much pleasant audacity, he has become a man of fashion in London. Among other fine ladies at his tea party to-day I found the Duchess of Sutherland, Lane playing his part of host nobly.

" Meynell dined with me, and we went on together to Stafford House, an amusing evening, as evenings there always are, and where I met a number of ancient friends, ex-beauties, and others who seemed pleased to see me. Among them Lady Desborough, who reminded me of the Sunday we spent together, hard on thirty years ago when she was Etty Fane, at Brocket. She was a beautiful girl then, not yet out, and is now probably forty-seven, and has seen much racket in the world, and there was Lady Randolph and Mrs. Jack Leslie and Lady Horner and a number more of that generation. The girls of the present generation have the disadvantage of the grotesque fashion now prevailing in dress in which no woman can look otherwise than a bundle, but there was no lack of amusement. At a certain stage in the evening, after much loud comic singing, the guests sat down in a circle on the ground, and certain performers from Paris danced the *Danse des Apaches,* which is the same which used to be called the *Can-can,* with other gymnastic eccentricities formerly confined to the Jardin Mabille, for our amusement; an astonishing display, which would have shocked us, I think, even at Mabille, in the days of the Second Empire and would certainly have been impossible in London in my young days at a public dancing hall, let alone in a drawing-room, but which now delighted us all without a suspicion of indecorum, young men and maidens applauding unrestrainedly, for such is our new kingdom of Heaven. It is not for me to find fault, and I suppose we enjoy our lives more.

" *16th July (Sunday).*— Newbuildings. Belloc dined with us. He says that Cromer is very angry at Kitchener's appointment, declaring him to be a thief, which was, I believe, Mohammed Abdu's opinion too. Cromer and Kitchener were never fond of each other, and it is certainly a preposterous choice to have been made if they have no design of annexation up their sleeves. According to Belloc there was a great effort made to obtain the place for Sir Charles Eliot, but it failed through the refusal of Lord Lansdowne to agree to it, Lansdowne had recalled Eliot from Uganda, and would not consent to his being employed again by the Foreign Office, for these things are arranged now by the two front benches in private agreement.

" *17th July.*— A telegram from Gros Bois to tell me of the death of my dear old friend Wagram. It was signed by Alexandre and the two girls.

" 18*th July.*— Grey has declared, in answer to a question in Parliament, suggested by me, that Kitchener's instructions, which he declines to produce, 'will involve no change in the general policy of his Majesty's Government.' He said the same thing when Gorst succeeded Cromer. What he probably means is that, with the same pretence of preparing Egypt for self-government, the military occupation, which is all they really care about, will be maintained. There will, however, most certainly be a change of tactics, the entente with the Khedive will give place to an entente with the Khedive's enemies, and there is already sign of it in a telegram from Cairo saying that the Nationalists are pleased with Kitchener personally. Osman Ghaleb writes from Paris sending me a message dictated to him by the Khedive. In this letter Abbas declares himself quite ready to grant a Constitution, and says that it was in reality he who caused the Suez Convention to be rejected by the General Assembly last year. Osman Ghaleb adds a private P.S. saying that Abbas talks of abdicating; but that would only mean the substitution of his son with a Regency giving complete power to Kitchener.

" 20*th July.*— Worth Forest. Things are happening fast in Europe, and it seems pretty certain now that Germany has made terms not only with France but with Russia, in order to break up their entente with us. The 'Conversations' which have been held at Berlin between Von Kiderlin Waechter and Cambon (Jules) are announced to have resulted in a claim made by Germany of the French Congo as a set off for Morocco, and at the same time the Spaniards are pressing things on at Alcazar and a French Consul has been insulted there. This means that the Germans are determined on having their naval station on the Atlantic whether we choose or not. The 'Times' has a warlike article to-day reminding Asquith of his bold words of a fortnight ago, and pressing him to make them good. I don't suppose he will, for he is entirely occupied with his quarrel with the House of Lords, which has reached its crisis, while the Dock Strike continues, making the shortage of wheat in the country so great that Caffin tells me even a well-founded rumour of war would bring about a collapse. People don't believe in war as a possible thing concerning England.

" The ex-Shah of Persia has landed at a Caspian port, and is raiing an army obviously with the consent of the Russian Government. The Turkish quarrel with Albania has developed too, and almost anything may happen in that direction. It is impossible things can settle down without great changes and shiftings to the detriment of Mohammedan lands, and this makes me unhappy.

" Osman Ghaleb has written again, and I have sent a letter in reply, which I intend him to forward to the Khedive as my advice. It is that His Highness should write a formal letter to our King George, protesting against Kitchener, and asking for an *homme d'état* to be sent to Egypt in Gorst's place, one who shall work with him to set the Government of Egypt on a Constitutional basis. Such a letter, if published, will at least serve to reconcile the Khedive with the Nationalists.

"Dillon writes: 'I have read your poem, the "Coronation Ode"; it is a fine powerful denunciation, rather too hard on your own country and your own people. If I were an Englishman I do not think I could so utterly have condemned England, much as I detest Grey's policy. The Rosebery gang and the Tories have undoubtedly led England through the mire, as far as foreign policy is concerned, but in spite of all England remains the freest country in the world, and that is something.' This may be true, but it is precisely the position taken by the Primrose League with its motto '*Imperium et Libertas,* Empire Abroad, Liberty at Home.'

"The Bearwood Estate, belonging to the Walter family, was put up for sale a few days ago, with a reserve of £150,000, but no bidding. Meynell tells me that the Walters have come to complete ruin, a wonderful event when one thinks of their career of glory as proprietors of the 'Times' and the power they wielded in the world, wielded and abused to the ruin of how many weak nations. The 'Times' was the source of their wealth, and it no longer pays its expenses and has passed into other hands.

"*23rd July (Sunday)*.— Ryan came and also El Abd, president of the Egyptian Society of London, which has written to the Khedive demanding of him a Constitution for Egypt, but he declares the Khedive is not to be trusted.

"To dinner came Belloc and with him a French Jesuit, Father Courvois, who is the director of a kind of Catholic Socialism — an intelligent and agreeable man, who speaks excellent English.

"*24th July*.— Osman Ghaleb writes from Paris, saying he has sent on my message to the Khedive, but he is unlikely to take my advice. On leaving for Italy the Khedive had told him that he had had a letter from Kitchener announcing his appointment, and saying that he hoped they would work together for the regeneration of Egypt.

"*25th July*.— To London for a great luncheon given by the Eastern Association to the two delegates of the Ottoman Parliament, Bostani Effendi, senator, and Riza Tewfik, Deputy, a heavy affair with long-winded speeches by Admiral Fremantle and other ancient bores, and by the delegates, who spoke in very creditable English, but were afraid of saying anything precise about the actual situation. I had, however, a private talk with Riza Tewfik, who takes a gloomy view of the situation in Albania, and thinks that the war will extend to the other Balkan States, and perhaps to intervention by Austria. I asked him whether Germany would not prevent this, and he said: ' Germany will give us advice and her moral support, but nothing more than that, as she has always done.' He condemns the present Government at Constantinople in the strongest terms, he being the leader of the Opposition in the Chamber. He told me that the letter I sent him last October warning them of the folly of campaigning in Arabia, had been shown by him to Talaat Pasha and others, but they had paid no attention to it, though my advice had since been entirely justified. ' For instance,' he said, 'what you said about paying the Arabs rather than fighting them. The whole quarrel with the Druses could have been settled for £200, and it cost us £600,000, beside the bloodshed.' Riza's fellow delegate, Bostani, is a learned Arabic scholar, member for Beyrout, who was made Senator last year. His speech was lengthy and terribly dull, but I found him pleasant to talk to.

"In the evening, just before dinner, I looked in at 44 Belgrave Square and found George Wyndham there with F. E. Smith and Bendor, all three much excited. ' Here you see the conspirators,' said George. For some time past George has been organizing a revolt against Lansdowne and Arthur Balfour's management of the Tory party in the matter of the Veto Bill, and yesterday they brought matters to a head by making a violent scene in the House of Commons, and refusing to let Asquith speak. Hugh Cecil and F. E. Smith are the leaders of the revolt with George. Bendor has turned Grosvenor House into an office, where they hold their meetings, and they are to give a banquet to old Halsbury to-morrow as the saviour of the Constitution. They are all in the highest possible spirits at the commotion they have caused and consider that they have forced Balfour's hand. ' You ought to have done it,' I said, ' two years ago, and you would have had the whole country with you, Army, Navy, Territorials, and all down to the Boy Scouts.' The two others did not stay many minutes, and when they were gone George talked it over with me, promising an absolutely full account of it when the crisis should be over, but he had given his word of honour not to reveal certain things at present. Nevertheless, I gather from him that they suspect Arthur Balfour of having been all through in secret collusion with Asquith, and that perhaps now Arthur is in secret collusion against Asquith with them. It appears that just before the last election in January Asquith got the King to promise to create a sufficient number of peers to pass the Veto Bill, which the King promised, thinking the elections would go more against Asquith than they did. The King does not at all want to create the peers, neither does Asquith, though the King is in favour of Home Rule for Ireland. They hope that the peers will give in

without that necessity, and have been looking all along for a compromise, but the extremists on both sides will have none of it, and now
George says the country is in revolt, meaning the Tories in the constituencies. 'If we had given in without a fight there would have
been an end of the Tory Party.' George thinks they have saved that
at least. They are ready for actual armed resistance, or rather, they
would like that. They have chosen old Halsbury for their nominal
leader because of his great age (eighty-eight), otherwise there would
have been jealousies. All the best men of their party are with them,
including Austen Chamberlain, whom they did not expect. The only
one who has disappointed them has been George Curzon. 'He is a
fool,' said George, 'for he might have been next Prime Minister.'
However, I am to hear *all* as soon as the crisis is over. George thinks
war with Germany quite possible, and he wants it.

"*26th July.*— To Shaw's new play, 'Fanny's First Play,' last night,
at The Little Theatre, with Meynell and Miss Montgomerie, an American beauty. The play was screamingly amusing, and I laughed till
the tears ran down my cheeks. Mrs. Granville Barker, who was acting the principal character, sent me a message when it was over, and
I went into her room and congratulated her, which I was glad to do,
as she had heard that I did not like her in 'The Witch.'

"To Lady C., who tells me Kitchener called on her yesterday, and
quite contrary to his custom, spoke in high terms of me. This seems
to show that he is trying to play the diplomat, and wants to conciliate
his enemies, for he knows that I am a friend of hers and that she will
repeat it. I asked her what he had told her about his mission to Egypt,
and she said, 'Oh, he did not want to go there, he wanted to stay at
the War Office, and says he is getting old and Egypt will be his last
post, but he is to organize everything, the army and all, and make a big
thing of it.' She tells me that she knew Kitchener when he was quite
a young man. 'I knew Horatio,' she said, 'forty years ago, when
he had just left the French Army. He was in a very poor way then,
so low that he had accepted an offer from Toole to go on the stage at
£2 a week. Talking about his never having married, she said, ' he
had no time to trouble himself with ladies.' He wouldn't marry because he was determined to succeed in his profession, and he could
not drag a wife about after him, and he had to be careful not to make
scandals because of his men. I told her that I was afraid I should
have to bring up the Mahdi's Head against him, and, in fact, I had
just been writing as strong an article as I could find words for about
it, this very morning, for our next number of 'Egypt.'

"I forgot to say that talking to George yesterday, he told me that
once in talking to the late King about Ireland when he was Chief
Secretary, the King had said: 'We must either govern Ireland like

an English county, or give them complete Home Rule; there is no middle course.' This, I know, is George's own view, yet in public he is always saying Home Rule is impossible and so is the other.

"*27th July.*— George's revolt is not likely to succeed. They held their public dinner to Halsbury last night, and were only able to muster some forty peers at it, while Balfour and Lansdowne have produced a list of 250, and these have threatened to vote for the Bill rather than have peers created to swamp them. The fact is the revolt is all too late.

"Dillon lunched with me and described the scene in the House of Commons on Monday, and Hugh Cecil's behaviour. The *mot d'ordre* for the Irish party had been that they were to sit absolutely silent during the row, which they knew was intended, but at the height of it, some of the Irish grew excited and began to shout, while Redmond turned on them and said in the hearing of the Tories, who sit with them on the Opposition benches, ' If these damned Englishmen choose to make bloody fools of themselves, it is no reason for us not to behave.' The sentiment was approved by some of the Tories, and one of them said to Redmond, ' Though you did call us damned Englishmen I agree with every word.'

"Down to Worth Forest in the afternoon. Quite late a messenger from Glyn's Bank made his appearance, having wandered all over the woods at Newbuildings, and on here, carrying £500 in gold for me, my provision for war. He, poor man, was nearly dead with his exertions in the heat, and I made him stay and dine with me and found him good company, with his reminiscences of the Bank and City affairs. He has been twenty years at Glyn's. I gave him a full meal and plenty of wine, and sent him away happy somewhere about midnight!"

[This adventure, unique in the good man's experience, has become a legend now in Lombard Street.]

"*28th July.*— Asquith has given in about Agadir, pretending that he did not mean that the Germans were not to have a naval station on the North Atlantic coast. Rothstein, whom I saw three days ago in London, tells me that before Lloyd George's war speech at the Banker's dinner was made, a Cabinet was held, at which it was decided, with only one dissentient, Loreburn, the Lord Chancellor, that Germany should be defied about Agadir at the risk of war. Loreburn, however, went to the London Editor of the ' Manchester Guardian,' and told him about it, and got him to write in a pacific sense. The ' Daily News ' had been notified by the Government in a contrary sense, and orders had been issued to the Northern Squadron. Their swagger, however, did not frighten the Germans, only made them angry, and as the French have not the least notion of going to war about Agadir to please us,

Asquith has thought better of it, and now makes this explanation. War for this country is an economical impossibility, the Germans will have their naval station at Agadir or wherever else they choose.

"*29th July*.— In the early morning we buried our box of gold in the middle of a fir wood under a sycamore tree, the only one there.

"Dillon has sent me the Hansard account of the debate on Thursday on Egypt, in which he took part. Grey made in it some valuable admissions, declaring that anything like a reactionary policy in Egypt was unthinkable. It will make it very difficult for Kitchener to play the tyrant. He will try to play the lapdog first.

"*30th July (Sunday)*.— Having been away for two nights, on our return to-day to the Forest, we went to look whether our hiding-place had been disturbed, and to our astonishment found a toad seated on the box that contained the gold, a curious circumstance, like what one reads of in the middle ages." [The box had been buried only a few inches below the surface, and the toad had made his way down to it. It will save future treasure hunters trouble to be told that the box and its contents have long left the forest precincts and been returned to Glyn.]

"*1st Aug*.— Our annual Arab Sale, a smaller attendance than at any previous one.

"*3rd Aug*.—Newbuildings. Ismaïl Pasha Abaza came with Surur Bey to consult me about what line should be taken at Cairo towards Kitchener, whether to oppose him or make the best of him. I advised opposing him. He gave me a long account of the Khedive's troubles, being in his confidence. He explained that His Highness was as much opposed as anybody to the Occupation, but had not means of resisting. He had tried it many years ago, but had found himself without support, and had been obliged to yield. At present he was without a friend in Europe, and was on bad terms with the Government at Constantinople, and if he brought things to a quarrel with the Cairo Agency, he could not count on support anywhere. If he refused to sign the decrees forced on him they would govern the country without him; they would declare a Regency. I do not believe this, or that if he chose his occasion of quarrel wisely they would dare any such violent measures against him, but it would be no good to quarrel about trifles. I asked him about the Khedive's relations with Gorst. He said that except at the beginning, when they had been really friends, Gorst had obliged him to do this and that just the same as Lord Cromer did, only politely instead of brutally. I recited to Abaza the old fable of the Wind and the Sun, which was new to him and amused him much. He declares the Khedive had been ready to grant a constitution two years ago, but Gorst would not hear of it, the Khedive had said as much to the Editor of the 'Temps.' I said that was not the right way of doing things. The Khedive ought to issue a proclamation to his people and show himself their leader. It is clear, however, that Abbas has no stomach for strong measures. In Egypt they are all dreadfully afraid of personal loss. If they are patriotic, the Nile water would be cut off from their estates, and other material injuries be inflicted on them. Abaza had had a personal quarrel with Gorst, and it was Gorst who had intrigued against his election for the Legislative Council. Abaza is pessimistic, but he reassured me on two points:

" (1) There is no party anywhere in Egypt favourable to the Occupation, unless it be with the foreigners and some of the Copts.

" (2) The Porte will never consent to make over Egypt to England in any legal way, nor in his opinion with Europe. It is against the Khedive personally that the anger is, and the danger of the Porte's playing into English hands. Gorst was never in earnest about reforms, and was never really friendly to Egypt. I asked him whether the Khedive had not sufficient patriotism to disregard his material advantage, but all he could say was that if the Khedive could be sure that it would profit the country he would make the sacrifice, but at present he was convinced that nothing he could do would change the situation. It is this lack of real patriotism that stands in their way. These rich men hate the English Occupation, but will run no risks to get rid of it.

"*7th Aug. (Sunday)*.—To Storrington to call on Miss Gordon, General Gordon's niece, who is the acknowledged authority on all Gordon matters. She had read my account of the digging up of the Mahdi's body in 1899, as published at the time, and said it was quite correct, except that the Mahdi's head was really buried again in the desert. Two officers, she said, took it out with them when the trouble about it had been made in Parliament and buried it by night in the open desert, some miles away; they themselves did not know exactly where, so they could not have found it again if they had tried. She said this in so positive a manner that I feel sure her brother (Bill Gordon) must have been one of the two. All the rest of the story she confirmed in every particular. Bill had been specially employed by Kitchener to do the work of destroying the dome by blowing it up after it had been shelled, but he had had nothing to do with the digging up of the body, which was a piece of rowdyism done at night by some of the young officers. These kept the head, and gave it to Kitchener, who entrusted it to Bill to take down with him to Cairo when he returned there, where it was deposited, she believes, at a bank, Kitchener's intention being to present it to a Museum, at least so it was supposed. Bill was immensely disgusted at the whole business. She talked with great enthusiasm about her brother, almost with tears, and anger at the way he had been treated and made use of by them, and in the end worked to death. She lives at Hove, but is staying with her sister (Mrs. Jones), who has a house called the Manor House, at Storrington.

"To-morrow the great debate begins in the House of Lords, which is to seal its fate, old Halsbury leading the Opposition to Lansdowne, who has gone over to the Government, and is supporting the Bill which is to abolish the power of the Lords. It is a great occasion inadequately dealt with.

"*11th Aug.*— Newbuildings. The Lords have voted their own death by a majority of seventeen, great numbers abstaining, a pitiful ending for an institution of such antiquity. They have played their game with inconceivable stupidity, making miscalculation after miscalculation. When the quarrel began they had the game in their hands. They might have declared for Irish Home Rule and defied the House of Commons, which was at that time quite discredited. They might have rejected or amended the budget as they chose, asserting their own necessary position in the Constitution, and effecting a *coup d'état* which would have restored the Tories to power for another generation. But they idiotically referred the decision to a General Election. Then they counted on the King to help them, and they went in for a second election, having first abandoned the hereditary position of the House, which was the essence of its being. The revolt from all this absurd blundering came too late, and now they are laid out dead as door nails. Belloc maintains that the whole thing has been arranged from the beginning between Balfour and Asquith, and it looks like it. Irish Home Rule has now also, he says, been agreed upon between them.

"*22nd Aug.*— Spent the day with George Wyndham in Worth Forest. George gave me a gloomy account of his campaign in the Lords, which, however, he says, he was very near winning. They did not count on so many traitors being found to vote their own destruction as the thirty-one who voted with the Government. They are especially angry against Curzon. It was all snobbishness, George said, on Curzon's part. He could not bear to have his Order contaminated with the new creations. They are going to boycott him. I asked if he had really quarrelled with Arthur, and he said, ' Yes, politically, but not privately.' The peer he thinks most of is Willoughby de Broke, who when reproached with deserting his leader, Lansdowne, said : ' As master of hounds, I don't like killing a fox without my huntsmen, but it is better than losing my hounds.'

"*23rd Aug.*— The Russo-German agreement about Persia is published in full text. It is clearly directed against England, but does not make the situation worse for Persia than it already was. [Compare Dr. Dillon's ' Eclipse of Russia.']

" *1st Sept.*— The world is much disturbed just now here in England with our strikes, in France with bread riots, and in Germany with warlike talk about Morocco. If there is no war between England and Germany it will be because we cannot fight economically, and because Germany is not ready for a naval war with us. I still think the Germans will remain at Agadir, and a full settlement of the Morocco disputes will be adjourned.

" *8th Sept.*— The ex-Shah's army has been defeated at Teheran and its leader executed. The complicity of the Russian Government in the attempt at counter-revolution is proved. The Morocco quarrel still goes on.

" *17th Sept. (Sunday).*— Stolypin, the Russian Prime Minister, has been assassinated at Kief in presence of the Emperor while at the opera. This may lead to serious consequences. Stolypin had been the head and front of the reaction in Russia, a tyrant of the worst kind, affecting liberal ideas, and at the same time ruling by spies and secret police and arrests and hangings and deportations to Siberia. His example has been followed by Morley in India, by Grey in Egypt. These modern Liberals are worse than any of the old-fashioned reactionaries. Stolypin's assassin turns out to be a Jew, one of his own secret police, and the man specially entrusted with his personal safeguard. The outlook for liberty in the East is a bad one. If Germany agrees to a French protectorate in Morocco it will lead to England claiming a protectorate in Egypt, and to Italy claiming a protectorate in Tripoli. The situation seems to be that the German Government is not quite ready yet for war with France and England, while France, though unwilling to fight, is aware of this. Neither is likely to give in in any formal way, and the quarrel will be left open to be taken up again in two or three years' time. An accident, however, might precipitate matters. The outlook for Egypt is bad any way things go, for I imagine that at the outbreak of war England would annex Egypt, or declare a protectorate as an excuse for governing by martial law and treating all patriotism as rebellion. [N.B. Compare this with what actually happened in December 1914.]

" *22nd Sept.*— News has come of Arabi's death, and the morning papers give obituary notices founded on Cromer's 'Modern Egypt' and Milner's 'England and Egypt,' official and untrue. I have written to Ali Bey Kamel, urging that some public recognition of the old National leader should be made by the new Nationalists on the occasion of the fortieth day, seeing that it is already too late to give him a public funeral, but most of them are too dull-witted to see how great an opportunity it is. At Cairo the death seems to have been kept unknown until the funeral was over.

" *24th Sept. (Sunday).*— There is ominous news to-day of a threatened invasion of Tripoli by the Italians. This taken together with a settlement of the Morocco quarrel between France and Germany which seems now to be pretty certain, has a very ugly look.

"*25th Sept.*— My kinsman, Gordon Blunt, was here yesterday to say good-bye on his starting for Malta, where he is to be in command of the mechanical transport.

"*26th Sept.*— Things look uglier than ever in regard to Tripoli. I feel certain it is part of a general agreement, come to very likely as long ago as last year, for the dismemberment of what remains of the Islamic States of North Africa, and probably brought to a head by the disclosure of the fact that Germany is not prepared for a war with France. The Italian Fleet has already put to sea, and Tripoli or Benghazi, or both, will be bombarded and a landing attempted. Turkey must fight, though at the immense disadvantage of the Italians holding the sea, and so cutting her communications with Constantinople. Germany is said to be persuading the Turkish Government to yield half the Sultan's sovereign rights to Italy, but this they cannot do. It is a still more lawless affair than the French raid on Tunis of thirty years ago, and with less pretence of right. Indeed, no pretence is being made except that Italy needs compensation for France's raid on Morocco. It can hardly not lead to a general dismemberment of the Ottoman Empire. It is a thoroughly black outlook.

"*28th Sept.*— Chapel Street. Halil Hálid was here in the afternoon. He tells me the Turks will certainly fight, but they have only 10,000 men in Tripoli, and no commander of ability. They have been betrayed there by the Freemasons belonging to the Committee of Union and Progress, who playing into the Italian hands, have neglected sending reinforcements. If this is so, and he says the Freemasons have it all their own way in Salonika, Turkey's case has become hopeless. He says also that the Turkish Ambassador here has applied to Grey to intervene, but Grey has refused categorically.

"*30th Sept.*— War is declared, and the Italians have landed troops at Tripoli, Benghazi, and in Albania. Also, and this is the worst feature of the case, there is a change of Government at Constantinople. Hakki Pasha has resigned, and is succeeded by Said and Kiamil, a combination sure to be in English interests as to Egypt, while Shefket, the fighting head of the Army, is no longer Minister of War. This means, I fear, a tame surrender, though the Tripoli Arabs will not accept Christian rule without fierce fighting.

"To 'Man and Superman' with Dorothy in the afternoon. A good play, like all of Shaw's, but less amusing than 'Fanny's First Play,' or 'Arms and the Man,' or 'John Bull's Other Island.' These three are the most amusing plays ever written in any language.

"*1st Oct. (Sunday).*— With Meynell to call on old William

Rossetti beyond Regent's Park. He lives with his two daughters in a villa well filled with family mementos. Among the many drawings by Gabriel Rossetti I noticed two water colours by William Rossetti's wife, who was a daughter of Madox Brown, which seemed to me gems, worth all the rest. It pleased him much when I told the old man so. He is hale and hearty, though eighty years old, with a clear, healthy complexion, somewhat bronzed and showing his Italian origin. His manner precise, with considerable dignity. He spoke of the Italian raid on Tripoli, and I was glad to find his sympathies were with the Turks. He had read my ' Secret History,' and approved all my ideas. We talked, however, most of the past, his brother Gabriel, Burne-Jones, Morris, and Watts, and he was interested to find my recollection of Watts going back four years further even than his own.

" *3rd Oct.*— I am sick of Eastern politics and intend to take no more part in them when this Tripoli business is over. It cannot end otherwise than in the partition of the Ottoman Empire, a little sooner or a little later. There are too many hungry wolves in Europe to be satisfied with less, and it is thirty years since I began the battle. I feel inclined to say with Pitt: ' Roll up the map of Islam.'

" *4th Oct.*— To London for a Mohammedan meeting to protest against the attack on Tripoli. Lamington, in the Chair, made an unmeaning speech, excusing the Italians and excusing Grey, and exhorting all men to moderation, till the meeting rose against him. Two M.P.'s, Cox and Mason, made strong speeches, but Browne had been engaged beforehand for moderation. Then I was called for and rose, Lamington trying to stop me, but I persisted, and pointed out the uselessness of relying upon mediation and the German Emperor, and that if the war was to be stopped it must be by England alone. The English Mediterranean Fleet should be sent to Tripoli. Finally Farid Bey, just arrived from Paris, spoke amid much applause. They all came back to supper with me in Chapel Street, and we sat on talking till midnight. Meetings of this sort, unless they are indignation meetings, do less than no good. It was absurd to hold this one under a man like Lamington, a mere wet blanket.

" *5th Oct.*— Tripoli was bombarded on Tuesday, 3rd, but it is still doubtful whether the Italians have landed troops. At Constantinople Saïd Pasha has formed a Ministry, but without Kiamil. Mabmur Shefket continues Minister of War. These absolutely refuse to give up Tripoli on any terms, and the war is to continue. It will be a fight between a whale and an elephant, and may go on interminably.

" Meynell brought Padraic Colum to dine with me. He is a modest and at the same time intelligent young man with no little good Irish wit and much feeling about poetry and knowledge of the poets. He recites well, and is what is called a genius, that is to say, one out of the common, altogether sympathetic, but with hands which crush one's fingers with a grip of iron, all the more unexpected because he is a diminutive personality. Irish hand-shakings are a terrible experience.

"*9th Oct.*— The newspaper news from Constantinople is very contradictory, as also from Rome. Halil Hálid told me last Thursday that the withdrawal of the Turkish garrison from Tripoli and the undefended state of the town was due to treachery on the part of the Freemasons at Constantinople, who were in secret agreement with Italian Freemasonry. All the Ottoman troops but 10,000 regulars were withdrawn a year ago and sent to Yemen. They hold Hakki Pasha responsible for this.

"*13th Oct.*— Newbuildings. I have been pleased by an affectionate letter written me by George Curzon, a letter in which he recalled the 'immortal wassail' of the Crabbet Club. It was to thank me for a small donation I had made toward the rebuilding of the Royal Geographical Society's rooms. It had given him all the more pleasure 'because I know it to spring from personal affection which I most heartily and eternally reciprocate. In this respect we remain for ever young.' Mark Napier and George Wyndham came to shoot, and Belloc dined with us, keeping it up till one o'clock in brilliant talk.

George told us all the secrets of the intrigue of the 'Die Hards.' What started the rebellion against Balfour was a letter, or the draft of a letter, he wrote agreeing to the creation of 160 peers to pass the Parliament Bill. This George Curzon, when he read it, dramatically tore up, exclaiming 'That won't do'; and this made the support he later gave Balfour all the more unaccountable, and hence the anger of the secessionists against him. Now George declares that, with the exception of Curzon and Long, they have all the Tory party with them of those that count and nine-tenths of the rest, still 'Arthur will not resign.' Mark and I think it is rather a dispute about nothing, as there is no chance of the Tory party getting back into office at any nameable date, though Belloc says they have a chance if they will attack the Insurance Bill boldly. This George says they intend to do.

"We had a grand discussion later about Morocco and Tripoli, and the chances of a European war. George's view of the situation is this. He says that it is absolutely known to him through his former connection with the War Office that it was part of the Entente with France that, in case of war with Germany, an English contingent of 160,000 men should be placed on the Continent in support of the French Army. It was intended that this should operate at Antwerp, but later the plan was changed, and now the extreme north-west of the French line from Calais would be the scene of the English operations. The German plan of campaign, which he has also been shown, is to have a very extended line of attack, which should include southwards Western Switzerland, the main attack on France being intended from the southern end of the line. This the addition of the English contingent would enable the French army to meet. George declares he has seen the plans of military railroads already made in Switzerland in accordance with an arrangement concluded some years ago with the Swiss Government. We asked him what inducement had been offered to Switzerland for this, and he said that the Swiss Government was to be rewarded on the Italian frontier with those portions of the Italian Kingdom which ran up into the Swiss Cantons, and parts of Savoy. Italy had for some time past been dropping out of the Triple Alliance, and Germany no longer counts on her.

"I asked George whether in the late crisis about Agadir troops would have been landed in France, and he said that orders had been given for an expedition, though it was no longer possible to send more than 80,000 men instead of 160,000. These would have been placed under the nominal command of General French, though the man they really relied on at the War Office was another General (I forget his name) in whom George himself has full confidence. He says that when the Emperor William was here for the Queen's Memorial, he, Wilhelm, expostulated with King George for interfering between Germany and France, and used the words 'We wish to be friends with England, but if you force us, beware. Remember that Germany's sword is sharp.'

"We three shot Buzland's and Sheppard's beats, and got nineteen wild pheasants, with 166 rabbits. George and all of us shot extremely well, notwithstanding our overnight discussions, the day hot as summer.

"*15th Oct.* (*Sunday*).— George went away early to London, being busy with his leadership of the 'Die Hards' and the Constitution of the new Halsbury Club. Mark and I have talked over George's political prospects which we agree might yet be retrieved in his party if he could only be less self-indulgent. He is the imaginative brain of them all, having engineered the whole revolt against Balfour, and might have the Leadership if he would amuse himself less. As it is, he is likely to have to play second to dull men like Austen Chamberlain, and whipper-snappers like F. E. Smith. We have both spoken seriously to George about it, and I lectured Mark about his own imperialistic doctrines, arguing that after all honesty would be the best policy in foreign politics if they would only believe it. He is to spend a week at Glen with Grey, and I am anxious he should represent a more respectable view of Egyptian and other Eastern questions in the talks they are sure to have together. The Glen influence is a bad one for Grey. I

asked Mark what his opinion of Grey was.   He said he had seen much
of him formerly on political platforms, and that he used to be a stupid
fellow and a dull speaker, but had ' greatly improved,' he was ignorant
and a second-rate man, though personally charming and most distinguished.

" *16th Oct.*— The most important news of the last few days has
been the revolution in China.   It seems to be much on the lines of the
Tai Ping rebellion which Gordon suppressed fifty years ago, a rising
of the true Chinese against their Manchu rulers, only the present movement is led by a highly civilized and Europeanized young man, the
same who was not long ago arrested and held captive at the Chinese
Embassy in London and liberated in deference to English protests.
The revolt has already affected a third of the Empire, with all the
Central part, including Hankau.

" *17th Oct.*— Worth Forest.   Terence was here this afternoon.
Talking of Tripoli he tells me that there is little prospect of any determined opposition being made to the Italians by the native Tripolitans.
The Turks were so unpopular that they would have welcomed strangers
against these only they would rather it had been any other than the
Italians.   Fanaticism, he says, is dead in North Africa, it being recognized that resistance to Christendom is useless.   The Senussia may
show some fight in the desert but not the people of Fezzan, who are
traders and care little for anything except money.   The Italians are
less liked than any other of the Europeans.   Terence is more likely to
know about these things than any Englishman I know, and he is probably right.   If so the case is a very hopeless one.   Terence does not
believe in the rumoured intention of our Government annexing Egypt.
Annexation is not in the English programme, as it is found much more
advantageous to govern Mohammedan lands indirectly through a Moslem prince.   It is not any scruple of morality that prevents annexation,
only a calculation of interest.   My book, ' Gordon at Khartoum,' is
being well reviewed.

" *19th Oct.*— There is a scare at Berlin and Vienna that Egypt was
to be annexed, but it is denied officially here and seems really to have
had no foundation.   I had a letter from Winston yesterday saying
that he wanted to come here for a night and have a talk.   He says in
it, ' I am glad to find that my belonging to a Government wicked enough
to send Lord Kitchener to Egypt has not altered our relations.'

" People in Egypt are subscribing to the war in Tripoli, and the Indian Mohammedans have taken it up.

" *23rd Oct.*— Ryan came, and with him Malony, fresh from Persia.
Malony is engaged to marry a daughter of Sir Francis Elliot, our
Minister at Athens.   About Persia he is very hopeless, not on account
of the Persians themselves, but because of Grey, who has sold them

to Russia. The Russian Government is determined they shall not recover financially or politically, and Barclay, our English Minister at Teheran, is instructed by the Foreign Office to play into their hands, though he personally would help them. The British Government is reinforcing the Legation guard at Teheran with 200 troops from India, which will be a new pretext with the Russians for increasing their garrisons. Malony has been seeing much of my old friend the Bakhtiari Chief, Ali Kuli Khan, now holding the title of Sardar Assad, who Malony says often talks of me, and is a man of great ability. [He travelled with us for three weeks from Haïl to Bagdad in 1879. See 'A Pilgrimage to Nejd.']

" *25th Oct.*— Cabinet changes are announced. Winston goes to the Admiralty, which will be an advantage to him as helping him out of infinite hot water he is in at the Home Office. I am writing to congratulate him, and have expressed a hope that if he bombards a town it will be Naples or Messina, rather than Constantinople or Jeddah. The Turks and Arabs have been fighting the Italians well at Benghazi, and at Tripoli the Turkish army has followed the same programme as Arabi's did at Alexandria. It has retired out of reach of the ships' guns, and is harassing the Italians on shore. At Constantinople the Parliament has met, and is for continuing the war. The Italians have committed atrocities in the way of drumhead court martials just as Beresford did in 1882.

" *27th Oct.*— Winston answers me from the Admiralty through Eddy Marsh, his private secretary. 'Winston wishes me to thank you and to say that he is very busy settling down here, but hopes to come and see you as soon as he can. Your wishes as to bombardments have been noted in the Department, and every care will be taken to prevent mistakes.' I fear Winston is still on the best of terms with Grey, as I see in the papers that Grey stood godfather with F. E. Smith to Winston's son and heir, the new Randolph, yesterday.

" *31st Oct.*— The atrocities committed by the Italians at Tripoli have passed all that have ever been heard of for a century. On the pretext that the Arab inhabitants of the palm groves behind the town joined the Turkish army in its attack on the Italian troops, the whole of the native population, men, women, and children have been exterminated, to the number, it is reported, of 4,000 persons. This is absolutely against the laws of war, and puts the Italians in a position of piracy which Europe will hardly tolerate. They seem to have been pretty soundly beaten in the fighting and have been obliged to retire inside the town. The Italians are a cowardly people, utterly vicious and corrupt, and this cruelty is a part of their nature. It will deprive them of any right to pose as the champions of civilization in this war or of Christianity, while it will unite all the Moslem world against them and against

England and France, who are supporting them. I ought to say, perhaps, the English and French Governments, for public opinion both here and in Paris condemns them. The Catholic bishops in Italy have declared themselves in favour of the war as a crusade, and it is said the Pope supports it, though Patrick Butler, who is staying with me, strenuously denies this. If true, I can only say what I have never in my life said, or thought to say, ' To Hell with the Pope.'

" These abominable doings have been overshadowed by a still more important event in the world, a revolution in China, which is being entirely successful on the lines of the Turkish revolution of 1908.

" *3rd Nov.*— Poor Lady Colin Campbell is dead.

" *4th Nov.*— The news from Tripoli is sickening. A young English officer serving with the Turkish army as volunteer has telegraphed how he and another Englishman, a correspondent of the ' Daily Mirror,' were with the Turkish troops when they reoccupied the oasis outside Tripoli, and how they found hundreds of women's corpses mutilated in the mosque with children's corpses, the work of these cowardly Italian ruffians. It is the most hideous story ever told about any war, and must I think force our infamous Foreign Office to intervene, although Grey and Asquith have both been excusing the Italian Government in Parliament, and refusing all information. The Turks now have reoccupied the outer forts of Tripoli, and are summoning the Italians to surrender. The Italian fleet has sailed away, it is said, to do new murder in the Ægean, but I cannot think that this will be allowed. Good may yet come out of this monstrous evil, for there will be a revulsion of feeling, and the world will see how hideous Christianity has become divorced from its beliefs, a mere religion of rapine.

" Stead has written again asking me to attend a meeting he is getting up at Whitehead's Tabernacle against the Italians. The November number of ' Egypt ' is out, and will probably be suppressed at Cairo. I have promised Stead to get him a handsome subscription if he adopts my programme of coercing Italy, but I do not trust the man. One never knows whether there may not be some Russian intrigue at the back of his philanthropic agitations.

" *8th Nov.*— The Italian horror gets worse and worse as more news comes in. Grey, in order to distract attention from Tripoli has come forward with a statement in explanation of our relations with Germany, and the newspapers are away after this new hare. It is an old trick he has played more than once, for though an ignoramus in foreign politics he knows exactly how to deal with the House of Commons. I am preparing my letter to Stead as a pamphlet, and shall call it ' The Italian Horror.'

" *9th Nov.*— Half-a-dozen foolish Major Generals have written to the ' Pall Mall Gazette,' outraged at my ' Gordon at Khartoum,' saying they are going to memorialize the Lord Chancellor with a view to my being deprived of my functions as Justice of the Peace in the County of Sussex. These wise men have not stopped to enquire whether I have any such function to be deprived of, their anger being caused by a passage which they consider vilifies the British Army. I shall let them run on and make fools of themselves for awhile.

" 12th Nov. (Sunday).— Beauclerk just returned from his gold digging in Alaska. He and Belloc dined with us. The sensation of the moment is that the Tory Party has decided to elect as its leader, in succession to Arthur Balfour, who resigned last week, one Bonar Law. It appears that the old Tories would not stand Austen Chamberlain for the place, and the Tariff Reformers would not stand Walter Long, and this Law is a compromise.

" 13th Nov.— Worth Forest. The Ottoman Government has remonstrated to the European Powers about the Italian atrocities as a breach of the rules of war, but these have answered that they are ' unable to take action.' It is certain that the Tripoli raid was arranged beforehand with France and England at the time of the Agadir business. I am less sure about Germany. [It is now known that the German Government did not approve of the raid. The French had agreed to it with Italy as a ' compensation' to Italy for their own misdeeds in Morocco. Our Foreign Office approved, seeing in it a means of detaching Italy from the Triple Alliance. A scoundrel affair as ever was perpetrated.]

" 15th Nov.— Worth Forest. There was a debate yesterday in the House of Commons about my book, ' Gordon at Khartoum,' in which Colonel Seely, representing the War Office, used strong language, and undertook to approach the Lord Chancellor with a view to having me removed from the Commission of the Peace and from my position as Deputy Lieutenant of the County, neither of which dignities has ever been mine. It is all very absurd, and now I shall answer. I had just sat down to write one when a young man named Duckworth arrived, much bedraggled by the rain, after a long wandering to find me in the Forest, and asked for an interview on the subject for the ' Daily News.' I gave him tea, but no information.

" 17th Nov.— My reply to Seely is printed in the ' Daily News,' ' Daily Mail,' and other morning papers. The gallant Generals are more angry than ever at having made fools of themselves, and there is talk of their getting the law strengthened, so as to prevent criticism of the Army.

" 18th Nov.— The post has brought me a number of anonymous abusive letters, with others of congratulation on my reply to Seely.

" I have just finished reading the first volume of Count Paul Hoensbroech's ' Fourteen Years a Jesuit,' which interests me enormously, though his attitude of antagonism to the Society is not mine. Still I know enough of Jesuitism to recognize his narrative as in the main true. For instance, I remember well a terrible 'retreat' given at Stonyhurst, in which the physical horrors of hell were emphasized in detail just as he describes them, and there are a hundred small points of discipline I recognize as exact, while also the general spiritual atmosphere of the place is vividly reproduced. The Jesuit novitiate is the most mentally crushing process ever invented, and I remember well meeting William Kerr on the first day of his release from I forget how many years of absolute seclusion. It was at some function of the Redemptorist Convent at Clapham, and I walked back with him from it across the Common, I think to Putney, and he told me something of his life as a novice. He was like an owl that had wandered out into the daylight, an absolutely different man from what I had known him before his experience. This must have been somewhere in the seventies.

"*22nd Nov.*— George Curzon made an excellent speech the other day at a Persian dinner, and I have written to him, urging him to take up the Mohammedan cause as champion of Islam.

"*25th Nov.*— Newbuildings. The recent attacks on me and my book are causing it to sell well, and we are printing an extra 200 copies. Meynell arrived for the week end with Housman, author of 'The Shropshire Lad,' and we had a poetical evening, Meynell reading us 'Modern Love' with a running commentary, an excellent entertainment, as good as the best of lectures.

"*26th Nov. (Sunday)*.— I took Housman for a walk and asked him how he had come to write his early verses and whether there was any episode in his life which suggested their gruesome character, but he assured me it was not so. He had lived as a boy in Worcestershire, not in Shropshire, though within sight of the Shropshire hills, and there was nothing gruesome to record. He shows no trace now of anything romantic, being a typical Cambridge Don, prim in his manner, silent and rather shy, conventional in dress and manner, learned, accurate, and well-informed. He is professor there of Latin, talking fairly well, but not brilliantly or with any originality, depressed in tone, and difficult to rouse to any strong expression of opinion. Nevertheless, I like him, and with Meynell's help we got him to discuss his own poems, though he refused absolutely to read them out. He read instead one of mine, in response to my having read one of his, the one I like best, 'Is My Team Ploughing?' I have a great admiration for his 'Shropshire Lad,' on account of its ballad qualities and the wonderful certainty in his choice of exactly the right word. We had much pleasant talk all day, and sat up again till twelve at night telling ghost stories.

He takes an interest in these. Housman's personal appearance is one of depression and indifferent health. He does not smoke, drinks little, and would, I think, be quite silent if he were allowed to be.

" *28th Nov*.— Grey has made his promised declaration on foreign affairs, avoiding, as I thought he would, all dealing with the Tripoli atrocities, or explanation as to whether he knew of the intended raid. All he said was that the attitude of the Government was one of neutrality and non-intervention, and that he had no ' *official* ' information of the barbarities committed on either side.

" *29th Nov*.— Russia has sent a new ultimatum to Persia demanding the dismissal of Schuster [an American who had for two years been working successfully to reorganize Persian finance, too successfully to please the Russian Government], complete control at Teheran, and an indemnity. This means the conquest of Persia, and already Russian troops have marched. The old Shah will probably be restored, and North Persia Cromerised after the fashion of Egypt. It is an infamy for which Grey is responsible.

" *2nd Dec*.— The Persian Government has refused the Russian ultimatum, denouncing at the same time the perfidy of England. This is the only dignified way to take it, and though it sounds desperate, the best chance for the Persians of saving their national life. It is just possible there may be a revulsion of feeling in this country which may upset Grey, though it is unlikely, and a new policy substituted favourable to Islam.

" *5th Dec*.— The Russians are invading Persia. McCullgan, the war correspondent in Tripoli for the ' New York World ' and ' The Westminster Gazette,' an excellent Irishman from Tyrone, came to see me. He has arranged to give a course of lectures in the principal towns in England on the Italian barbarities. I offered to help him financially, but he said his lectures were to be well paid by a business firm, which had undertaken it at £10 a night.

" *6th Dec*.— The royal tent set up for the Durbar has been burnt at Delhi, which looks like the beginning of demonstrations against the King, who has just landed at Bombay.

" *7th Dec*.— Pierre Lôti has written an excellent letter condemning the Italian raid on Tripoli, in reply to an Italian editor, asking his opinion on their glorious campaign. George Curzon has made another admirable speech in the Lords about Persia and has drawn from Morley something like a repudiation of Grey's outrageous approval of the Russian ultimatum. It is a great thing to have secured a man of his calibre on our side.

" *10th Dec. (Sunday)*.— A letter from Margot which amuses me. I had asked whether I should send her pheasants. She says she loves game, hares and pheasants, or even turkeys; all are of real use to her vast family, living in Downing Street and entertaining sixty to eighty people a week in the season, and thirty to fifty just now, is too much to expect of a Prime Minister with seven children, on £5,000 a year, etc. There is something comic in the idea of my contributing to the support of Downing Street just at present, and acting the part of Whiteley to the Prime Ministerial family.

" 13*th Dec.*— The newspapers print news of a proclamation at Delhi, removing the seat of the Viceregal Government there from Calcutta, restoring also the unity of Bengal.   This is a notable event.

" 15*th Dec.*— Grey has made another long speech in the House of Commons about his Persian policy, in which he approves all the Russians are doing.   What he is really aiming at is to Cromerise Persia, preserving the form of its independence while destroying the substance.   Russia is to do this in Persia as we do it in Egypt, and Italy, perhaps, in Tripoli, and France in Morocco.   They would do it in Turkey, too, if the Turks had no army.   It is the modern way of devouring the Eastern nations.   The Russian army is advancing on Teheran, where the Mejliss refuses to comply with the ultimatum, and we shall see a second edition there of Tripoli.

" 16*th Dec.*— I have written a Ballade of resignation for Margot, which I intend to send her with a peacock for her Xmas dinner.

" I have been reading a volume of Scotch ballads, the only poetry now that gives me any pleasure.   They rouse me from my gloom, especially that best of all, ' Sir Patrick Spens.'   I am troubled at the scramble for Asia which is going on.   The Russian army, with Grey's approval, is advancing on Teheran, where the Mejliss refuses to comply with their ultimatum, and we shall see a second edition there of Tripoli. There is talk of joint European intervention in China, and the year 1912 will see a partition of the Ottoman Empire.   As for Egypt I no longer see any hope.   Its chance of independence is bound up with that of Turkey, and will not survive the destruction of the other.   Winston, I heard, has written to Seely, scolding him for his rudeness to me.

" 20*th Dec.*— Browne has written to me in despair about Persia, where the Mejliss is standing to its guns.   I think the Mejliss quite right.   To accept the ultimatum would be to abandon all hope, and it is better to die fighting than to be swallowed slowly by the Russian boa constrictor and digested at leisure.   Theirs is a council of despair, but even despair has chances.

" 26*th Dec.*— There has been an abominable massacre by the Russians at Tabriz, 500 persons, men, women, and children, killed, women raped, and every imaginable abomination perpetrated.   This is Grey's doing as distinctly as if he had given the order, yet almost no protest is made in our press, nor is there chance of an indignation meeting. It is hopeless my going on fighting under these conditions, a single voice against the world's, and I am weary of a useless struggle. Belloc dined with me last night, but I could not get him to take much interest in anything but the parochical politics of the Insurance Bill. He asked me who I thought ought to be Poet Laureate after Austin. I said Gilbert Murray. [Because he had written no original verse.]

"*29th Dec.*— Went to see McCullagh at a nursing home in John Street, where he has been for an operation. The Tripoli atrocities are all condoned now by English public opinion as will be the Russian atrocities at Tabriz. Grey has invented a formula about these things. He has ' no official knowledge,' which means that the Consuls have not reported them as having themselves witnessed what has been done. They have had orders to hold their tongues.

"Meynell dined with me to-night, and we discussed the future of civilization. Meynell declares that the world will eventually come round to my opinions and acknowledge me as a forerunner. I wish I could believe it, but I see no sign of any such conversion. On the contrary I fear I am a belated survival of an age which has almost disappeared. The best chance the world has is perhaps the possible resurgence of China, which yesterday proclaimed itself a republic, and chose Sun Yat Sen, a Christian, its first President. But will not Europe intervene to wreck its chances as it has intervened in Turkey and Persia? It is all a question of material strength, and Asia, in order to survive, is obliged to remodel itself according to European standards, although in so doing it sacrifices half the value of its traditional ideas.

"*31st Dec. (Sunday)*.— To-day a sad year ends, the worst politically I can remember since the eighties, bloodshed, massacre, and destruction everywhere, and all accepted here in England with cynical approval, our Foreign Office being accomplice with the evildoers, and Grey their apologist. It has been a losing battle in which I have fought long, but with no result of good. I am old, and weary, and discouraged, and would if I could slink out of the fight. I am useless in face of an entirely hostile world.

"In the afternoon I went to see Mrs. Morris at her daughter's house in Hammersmith Terrace, and found her lying alone, quite invalided in a chair. She had come up to London for her teeth, and other ailments, but was glad to see me. We were, however, interrupted in our talk by de Morgan and his wife, who looked in. He is a lugubrious little man with a certain caustic wit battling with senility, his wife a busy little woman, with a more cheerful manner. I remember having met her at Kelmscott House when she was tending Morris, which she did with great devotion during his last illness. Then I went on to Walker's, who lives next door, who showed me some of his book treasures, amongst them a complete set of the Kelmscott Press works in vellum. He is a good and modest man, who began as a plain workman and has now an assured position at the head of the printing trade, at least of that branch of it which deals with illustrated books. Morris, he told me, had once offered him partnership in the Kelmscott Press, ' But I had too good a sense of proportion,' he said, ' to accept.' And so the year 1911 has slipped away."

CHAPTER XI

GENERAL TROUBLE IN EASTERN EUROPE

" 4th Jan., 1912.— Chapel Street. Rothstein called and told me much about affairs in Europe. He says true reason the German Government would not fight this year was not any doubt of the superiority of its army, which is infinitely more powerful than the French, but because it had not the mass of the people with it. These did not think Morocco worth a war. He says, however, that Germany is of one mind to fight England on the first occasion, as they were very angry with us, far more so than with the French. All now are for war, except the Socialists, and even these are not all of them against it. He is sure the German Government was not privy to the Italian raid on Tripoli. On the contrary they are very angry with the Italians on account of it, so much so that they would join England in putting a stop to it. As to Persia, Rothstein assured me the Russian army was not formidable, the officers being just as corrupt and ineffective as before the Japanese war. If there was a quarrel with England about Persia the Japanese would advance on Siberia. They would also very likely intervene in China to replace the Manchus in power. Rothstein's opinion on all these things is the best in London." [N.B. Rothstein, whose opinions are constantly quoted in my diary, owed his wonderful knowledge of the European situation to the fact that he was London correspondent to nearly all the Socialist newspapers on the Continent. He was by birth a Russian subject, born at Kief, who had made his studies at the Odessa University, and having become involved there with the authorities about twenty years ago had made his escape to Western Europe, and had taken up his residence in London. He was on the Staff of more than one of our newspapers, but often complained to me that the Editors would not listen to him on subjects of European importance. To me he always spoke frankly, and I never found him mistaken in the information he gave me, as will be shown in the sequel.]

" 5th Jan.— Irene Noel dined with me. I had not seen her for nearly two years, during which she has been flirting with the Crown Prince of Greece, and trying to get up with him what she calls a Balkan Federation which is to include the Greeks, and even perhaps the Turks. She is a clever girl, and has a talent for political intrigue.

376

" 10*th Jan.*— The Russian Government has declared its intention of taking possession of Mongolia.   Grey seems to have committed us to an approval of this as well as of the Persian robbery.

" 17*th Jan.*— Labouchere is dead at the age of eighty, universally esteemed after a life which began in disrepute.   I remember old Paddy Green, of Evans' music hall, with whose son I had been at school at Stonyhurst, talking of him in pitying tones as ' Loboucheer, Loboucheer, poor young man!   He was always his own worst enemy.'   This was somewhere in 1861, when Labby was still looked upon as something of a greenhorn.   My first acquaintance with him was of this date, when he was living at Homburg entirely in the society of whores and croupiers.   He had belonged to the Frankfort Legation, where I had succeeded him, and was nominally attached to the Embassy at St. Petersburgh, but had not proceeded there (pretending he was too poor to pay his railway fare).   At Frankfort he was considered too disreputable for admission into society, and I have a caricature I drew of him walking with Madame d'Usedom, the Olympia of Bismarck's memoirs, who on one occasion had given him her countenance.   It is labelled ' The Deformed transformed,' and was a very good likeness of him as he then was (a chubby young man with little slant eyes and pink cheeks).   Later, I remember him at St. James' Club, the house in James Street that had once been Crockford's, boasting to all who would listen how he had bribed his way into parliament as member for Windsor.   It was a short lived glory as he was at once unseated.   In after years I saw much of him at his house in Queen Anne's Gate, where I often lunched with him and his wife in the eighties and nineties, and liked him greatly.   He had become one of the very few quite honest M.P.'s, who always told the truth, and was always amusing.

" 21*st Jan. (Sunday)*.— Newbuildings.   Belloc dined with us, and gave us some good talk.   The Italians have seized two French ships as carrying contraband of war, which is making a commotion in France, and may possibly lead to a stopping of the war in Tripoli.   Grey has been apologizing to his constituents in the North for his Foreign policy so piteously that Belloc thinks he will resign.   If so I imagine the Foreign Office would be given to Haldane as the only member of the Cabinet who knows French and German.   In Ireland Carson is campaigning on the Orange platform, threatening fire and flame if Winston is allowed to speak at Belfast: ' Ulster will fight, and Ulster will be right.'

" 30*th Jan.*— Chapel Street.   Lunched with Winston and Clementine. He was in excellent form, and I had an interesting conversation with him about Eastern politics, his private secretary, Masterman Smith, being also there.   About the Turco-Italian war I asked him which way his sympathies lay.   He said, ' I have my official sympathies, and **and** those are strictly neutral.' His private sympathies are clearly not Italian. ' The Italians,' he said, remind me of the story of the giant who went to cleave an oak in two with his sword, and who caught his hand in the cleft and was held by it, till he was eaten alive by the wild beasts in the forest. They cannot get further, and they cannot get away. They are spending a quarter of a million daily, and will be ruined before they have done. As to the Turks, it is their own fault if they come to grief. They ought to have made friends with us instead of running after Germany, which will not help them. I said, ' They could not afford to quarrel with Germany which could have destroyed them in Roumelia, also you wanted too much.' *He.* ' They ought to have let us reorganize the police with English officers over them, all we wanted of them was our commercial share in the Bagdad railway.' *I.* ' Yes, and to stay on in Egypt.' *He.* ' We shall never clear out of that till the Empire breaks up.' As he seemed inclined to listen, I propounded my alternative scheme of policy, to make alliance with Turkey against Italy and Russia. Italy could easily be dealt with by the Fleet, while Turkey would willingly help to turn the Russians out of Persia. ' I thought,' he said, ' The Turks had made friends with Russia about it.' Returning to Egypt I gave him my solution there, the English garrison to be replaced by a regiment of Turks at Cairo, and another at Alexandria, to keep order, things otherwise to go on just the same. On this basis an alliance with Turkey could be arranged. It is clear, however, from his talk that he is bitten with Grey's anti-German policy. He said of the Germans, ' I never could learn their beastly language, nor will I till the Emperor William comes over here with his army.' Nevertheless Winston strikes me as being open to conversion on all these matters. Clementine talked about an act of rudeness shown to her and Winston the other day by Cambon, the French Ambassador, a trifle of no importance, except as showing that Winston also, like Grey, does not know French. We talked also about the Belfast meeting as to which I advised Clementine not to go with her husband, though the chief danger is over now as the meeting is no longer to be held in the Ulster Hall, but under a marquee in a meadow, which it would be difficult to blow up. Talking about Italy, Winston said chuckling, ' The Italians tell us now that if Turkey won't make peace, they will have to declare war again.'

" Browne came and gave me an account of the dinner given to Schuster yesterday, in which he had explained his doings in Persia. He has the highest opinion of Schuster, who made an admirable speech. Poor Browne is in terrible despair at it all.

" *1st Feb.*— Meynell dined with me, and I have read him Margaret Sackville's ' Wooing of Dionysos,' which he agreed with me in pronouncing a very first-rate poem. We also had a great discussion about

Ward's 'Life of Newman,' which is just out. Meynell has taken up the cudgels for Manning in the 'Tablet,' which has moved the Duke of Norfolk to anger.

"*6th Feb.*— Sat with Rivers Wilson at his house in Berkeley Square. He has been reading my Gordon book and also 'Egypt's Ruin.' He says both are very accurate, and that I have converted him on many points regarding Egypt. He told me some interesting things. First as to the origin of the famous Joint Note of 1881. [The Joint Note signed by the English and French Governments promising help to the Khedive Tewfik against Arabi and the Parliament. It was that that caused the war of 1882 and the English Occupation.] Wilson told me that it was he who suggested the idea of it to Gambetta, assuring him that the English Government would go with him. Though he did not take part in drafting the note, Gambetta sat down to draft it before he left the room, where they had been discussing it. It was to be a dead secret between the two, but Wilson told Nubar of it, who highly approved, and Nubar let it out to Blowitz, and it thus got talked of in the 'Times.' Gambetta was very angry with Wilson on account of it. Also he told me a number of tales about Omar Lutfi, Shahin Pasha, and others, and what scoundrels they had been, with other stories nearer home.

"*9th Feb.*— Haldane has been sent on a secret mission to Berlin, well advertised in all the papers. There seems to be a real attempt at a rapprochement with Germany. If it comes to anything they will probably shift Haldane to the Foreign Office in Grey's place. Anything will be better than Grey, though I don't trust the other.

"*11th Feb. (Sunday).*— A young man, Borthwick, appeared with a letter of introduction from Stead. He has been in the 10th Hussars for three years in India, and since in Algeria and Morocco. He wished to consult me about a wild cat scheme he has of going to Ghadamès raising the Senussia against Italy, and driving the Italian army into the sea. I had him up to talk to me, but did not much encourage him, as I think the thing impossible of success, though of course desirable. The right strategy for the Arabs is to harass the Italians and prevent their moving inland, and not to attempt to retake the sea coast towns where the Italian army is protected by the Fleet. Belloc dined with me. He says he hears that Kitchener is considered at the F. O. to be overdoing his part at Cairo.

"*12th Feb.*— I am reading Ward's 'Life of Newman,' a rather dreary work, though it interests me from the many mentions it makes of persons I used to know, nor do I think the book does any good service either to Newman or the Catholic cause. The truth is, a religious life is at least as unsatisfactory as any other, and seen near at hand there is much in Newman's which would have been better forgotten. Great men and holy men are very like other men, and there are just as many petty interests served in the Government of the Church as in other Governments. One had imagined Newman leading a life of prayer and self-sacrifice. He is shown by Ward dissatisfied with obscurity and running from one journalistic scheme to another, neither successfully nor with dignity. Human nature is human nature, whether in a convent or a palace. Newman was a great man notwithstanding, a great controversialist, and a master of English prose.

" 18*th Feb. (Sunday)*.— I have been a whole week in bed with influenza, and in great desolation of soul, the subject of my delirium being Grey and the Garter he had just been given, and this worried me for two days and nights. I am better to-day, and begin to see things sanely.

" *23rd Feb.*— Parliament has met in London, and Grey's Garter has provoked speculation as to coming changes in the Cabinet. They say Loreburn is to retire and let Asquith be Lord Chancellor in his place, which would secure him £10,000 a year for life; Grey to be his successor as Prime Minister, giving up the Foreign Office, for which he is incompetent, in favour of Haldane. What they want now is to pacify Germany, and Haldane is Germanophil.

" *1st March.*— Things have gone badly. The coal strike has monopolized attention, and Grey has been allowed to carry on his detestable policy in Persia and Tripoli, almost unrebuked. The latest diplomatic development is an attempted combination of the European Powers to coerce Turkey into ceding Tripoli to Italy, and so making peace. So far the Turks are standing firm.

" Monsignor Stonor is dead at Rome, where he has lived all his life. I remember assisting at his first mass at Oscott how many years ago. May he rest in peace, good man : they ought to have made him a Cardinal.

" I have been nearly three weeks in bed.

" *8th March.*— Chapel Street. Bendor came to see me. He has been in Egypt this winter, and brought to show me an *antika* he had picked up there of the hawk-headed God or Goddess, which by some odd accident had been fashioned into the exact image in caricature of our good Queen Victoria. It amused him much. He is a kindly, good-humoured fellow, like a great Newfoundland puppy, much given to riotous amusements and sports, with horses, motors, and ladies. The fast life clearly suits him, for he looks a model of health and strength. He was at Sheykh Obeyd, and saw the Stud there, which he appreciates.

" 10*th March (Sunday)*.— Syud Mahmud called. He is going back to India in May, very much in earnest about getting his fellow-Mussulmans to oppose the Government if it refuses to take up the defence of Islam, but I fear that like all the rest his courage will ooze out of him under the influence of his native air.

"Dillon came to lunch, and stayed on talking for two hours. Home Rule he hopes to see carried through both Houses of Parliament in two years' time (it cannot well take less), and there are many accidents that may still further delay it. If the coal strike should go on over Easter it will hang up the Home Rule Bill over the present session, and there are the suffragettes who have threatened to wreck it, or there might be a war or a revolution; otherwise all would be plain sailing now. There was no difference at all between them and the Government as to the details of the Bill.

"Then he went back to past events, and gave me a full history of Parnell's connection with Mrs. O'Shea. Parnell, he said, as a young man, was no paragon of virtue, but his loves had not before been with married women, nor had they been serious. He met Mrs. O'Shea first at Thomas's Hotel in Berkeley Square at a party given by the O'Gorman Mahon to some of his political friends. Justin McCarthy, who knew the O'Sheas, had introduced Parnell to her there. She was a sister of Sir Evelyn Wood. She, like her sisters, was attractive, and O'Shea took advantage of it. There is no doubt that he got money from Parnell, and that Parnell kept the establishment at Eltham going. The lady, however, was really in love with Parnell, who was a very good-looking fellow, and she gradually acquired complete dominion over him. I was quite right, Dillon told me, in supposing that she not only made him neglect his parliamentary work, but was a force hostile to his patriotism, especially to that part of it which concerned the land movement. She also encouraged him in his pride, and made mischief between him and his colleagues in the House of Commons. Hers was a disastrous influence. It ended in ruining his career, and it was she who prevented him from accepting any compromise about the Chairmanship of the party after the great scandal when he (Dillon) and O'Brien had met Parnell to talk matters over with him at Boulogne. Every day they thought they had persuaded him to agree to a temporary retirement of six months, and every evening Parnell crossed the Channel back to spend the night at Eltham and return in the morning more obstinate than ever. 'I repeatedly promised Parnell,' Dillon said, 'that I would resign the Chairmanship back to him at the end of six months, indeed, I would only act as Vice-Chairman for him during his retirement, and it was he that each time he came back from Mrs. O'Shea refused all compromise.' [*Note.*— I am informed by Mrs. O'Shea's niece, Mrs. Steele, that I was misinformed as to Parnell's ownership of the house they lived in. Eltham Lodge was an old family residence of the Woods.]

"15th *March.*— George Wyndham came to lunch with me. He com-

plained of being tired of politics, but says that he cannot break loose
from them. His ambition now is to be some day Father of the House
of Commons, one he is not unlikely to achieve, for he has been twenty-
three years member for Dover, and there are only four or five men
with a better record, and he is still young. About his private plans
he says he does not mean to have a London House, and would live
entirely at Clouds. In these days all will have to live well within their
incomes. Rich men are shutting up their large houses, amongst others,
Plymouth, who is shutting up Hewell, and means to live all the year
through at St. Fagans.

" 16*th March.*— This morning Margot brought her daughter Elizabeth to see me. The child is sixteen, attractive and clever, with a soft,
sympathetic hand, which will help her to be loved. I had not seen
Elizabeth since the day when she recited ' Maître Corbeau ' to Coquelin
ainé. She is just the nicest age now, and I am glad to have seen her
before she begins going out in society.

" Later came Nellie Hozier and her mother for our midday meal, and
Nellie took me to see the Futurist pictures. These, as art, are mere
nonsense, the sort of things a child might make by pasting strips of coloured paper together as patchwork. They have neither design nor
drawing, nor other colouring than a haphazard one, chiefly reds and
yellows. One cannot assign a meaning to any of them, or even the
suggestion of a meaning. Degeneracy cannot go further than this, and
it is mere stupidity to talk of it as art. But we found the little rooms
in Sackville Street crowded with visitors, who each had paid his shilling, while critics have been found sufficiently uncritical to treat the
exhibition seriously.

" 18*th March.*— Abd el Ghaffar came to see me, back from Egypt
ten days ago. He gives a bad report of things; the National party
without a capable leader and split into factions, each with its separate
newspaper. Farid has lost his political credit. The Hesb el Ahali,
or Party of the People, is now beginning to take the National Party's
place. Its principle is to trust to England to give some sort of a Constitution and make Egypt entirely independent of the Porte. If England could be trusted to do this, and Egypt could become strong enough
to defend herself against other European aggression, the policy might
be a good one, but such trust and such hope are mere delusions. The
connection between Egypt and the Ottoman Empire is the only possible chance Egypt has of escaping permanent subjection to Europe, and,
slender though that chance is, I will not abandon it for the other, which
is no chance at all. Abd el Ghaffar tells me that he has learned on the
authority of Rushdi Pasha, Minister for Foreign Affairs at Cairo, that
there have been negotiations between the English Government and the
Porte for a cession of the Cyrenaica to the Khedivial possessions.

" *21st March.*— There is talk of further troubles in Europe, possible war between France and Spain about Morocco, and a reported secret treaty between Italy and Russia against Turkey. [Compare Dr. Dillon's ' Eclipse of Russia.']

" The coal strike is in a worse state than ever, as Asquith's proposed legislation has been repudiated by the Labour Party, and Arthur Balfour is to lead the Tory Party against it. There is a probability of a prolonged crisis.

" Two young Indian Mohammedans lunched with me, Syud Mahmud (as before) and Syud Hussein, the latter the grandson of my old friend Nawab Abdul Latif, of Calcutta. There has come about a split among the Mohammedans of India owing to recent events. The Agha Khan has resigned the presidency of the All India Moslem League, a body of timid folk loyal to the British connection, and has declared himself for common action with the Hindoo Progressives. The principal cause of this is the connivance of our Government with the Italians and Russians in Tripoli and Persia, and Syud Mahmud tells me our little paper ' Egypt ' has helped in effecting this. They are beginning to see that it is only the pressure that can be put on the Government by India that can change Grey's treacherous policy. The Indian Mohammedans in London, numbering 250, intend to make a demonstration in this sense, and they will do well. Ameer Ali has lost what little influence among them remained to him.

" *23rd March.*— Browne and his wife lunched with me, and Desmond MacCarthy. Browne very despondent about the East, as he is right in being.

" *24th March (Sunday).*— Dillon came to lunch. He says that during the last few days the Asquith Cabinet has been on the verge of a break up over the coal strike, and that the country is menaced with revolution. There is to be a new conference between miners and mine owners to-morrow. If it fails there will be a general industrial collapse. The miners demand a minimum wage, but if the Government embody this in their Bill it will open the door to a system of minimum wages for every class of labour, and to this Dillon is strongly opposed as an extreme form of Socialism, while a continuance of the strike will so delay things in Parliament that it will be impossible to get the Home Rule Bill through this session. He thinks all the same that a settlement will be reached to-morrow. Should it be otherwise and should Ireland by this accident lose her opportunity, I must say that it will in some measure serve Redmond and the Irish Parliamentary Party right. Ever since they made their compact with Asquith two years ago the Irish in Parliament have identified their fortunes with the English Whigs, abetting them in all their Imperial misdeeds, and treating Grey's alliances with the French in Morocco, the Russians in Persia, and the

Italians in Tripoli, as pleasing to Irish ideas. It has been a disgraceful betrayal of the cause of liberty, and it will be no more than justice if in aiding our diplomatic jugglery abroad they lose their own chance of freedom at home. Dillon alone of all the Irish members has so far preserved his integrity, but even he has come to regard the retention of Egypt as a necessary part of British interests, and I have been unable to get him to ask questions involving an attack on Kitchener, who he thinks will be recalled some day, when the revolution at home has been followed by a reaction, to play the part here of military dictator.

"*26th March.*— The Conference with the miners has failed, and anything now may happen, from a general breakdown of trade to a revolution. The trains are ceasing many of them to run and I am going back to Newbuildings, where we can better stand a siege than here.

"*27th March.*— Lunched at the Duchess of St. Albans', where I found a large party, her son-in-law Lord Richard Cavendish, Lord Grey, young Baird, M.P., who is Bonar Law's private secretary, Garvin, and others — an extreme Tory assemblage, discussing their plans, of which Garvin is just now the inventor and chief prophet. Garvin began as an Irish Fenian writer on the ' United Ireland,' but has gravitated to the position he now occupies of ultra anti-Home Rule Editor of the ' Pall Mall Gazette ' and the ' Observer.' He asked me what my view was of the situation. I said, ' I take my views every afternoon from the " Pall Mall Gazette," and every Sunday morning from the " Observer." '

" They have rushed a Miners' Wages Bill in twenty-four hours through both Houses.

"*29th March.*— Kaiser Wilhelm seems to have stopped the nonsense of Russia's joint action with Italy against Turkey. He met the King of Italy at Venice two days ago and probably told him not to be such an ass.

"*31st March.*— Belloc and Chesterton dined with me, Belloc complaining terribly of the fast from liquor he has been maintaining during Lent and to-day is Palm Sunday. ' Ah,' he said, ' if you want to see a really happy man you should come to me on Easter Monday afternoon.' He consoled himself at dinner with a sad lemonade, but talked all the more brilliantly for it. He admits now that he made a mistake about the coal strike in predicting the miners would win. Asquith, he says, has been too astute for them. He amused them by his Miners' Minimum Wage Act, over which they lost their time and spent their money, and now he has them in his hands.

"*6th April.*— Newbuildings. Belloc tells me the miners are very angry with their leaders, especially in the north of England, and thinks there will be riots. Fortunately these things do not affect us here in Sussex (where we have not a single mine or factory).

" I have been reading Eversley's ' Gladstone in Ireland '—a good and useful book which gives the public facts fairly. But history written as this is under the House of Commons restrictions of suppressing private conversations and refraining from assigning private motives for public action cannot be satisfactory. How futile to go on representing Parnell's neglect of his public duties to ill-health instead of to its true cause, Mrs. O'Shea, or Hartington's implacable opposition to Home Rule to anything but his brother's assassination. Yet there is no hint of either of these veracities in Eversley's book. All the same the book is a good one, and its writer was a good friend to me at the time of my trial at Portumna, the only man in Parliament with a front bench position who had the courage to support me there.

" 13*th April.*— Farid writes from Constantinople, whither he has fled from Cairo to avoid arrest and perhaps four years imprisonment for a speech made at a general meeting of the National Party. I think he is quite right to have made this *hegira,* as he can be of more use at Constantinople, and the present régime at Cairo against which it is useless to struggle until the Ottoman Empire is in a position to insist. It appears that Saad Zaghloul has resigned at Cairo, having refused to prosecute Farid.

" 14*th April (Sunday).*— Young Borthwick came again to talk about his scheme of joining the Turks in Tripoli. It has developed now into the idea of fitting up an old man-of-war with which to land artillery somewhere on the coast. Of this the Turkish Embassy in London approves. He has an old connection with Turkey through his father, who was in the Ottoman service, and went through the campaign of Plevna, and he himself was born at Constantinople. He is also nephew to the Borthwick of the ' Morning Post,' a good looking, active young fellow, who knows Arabic, having lived, he tells me, for a year in a village in Oran, and having accompanied the French expedition to Fez. He gave me a detailed account of the rogueries that go on officially in Algeria from the Governor-General downwards. Borthwick's business in Algeria was to buy land for an English company, and thus he became acquainted with the way in which things are done there. The French officials in charge of large districts get only 200 francs a month pay, and are allowed to make what money they can out of the Arabs; the taxes are farmed out, and the officials make a profit by lending money on usury to the Arab landowners to enable them to pay the rates imposed (£4 a year is the rate for each plough), and then to foreclose, and get possession of the land. It is a settled policy of the French Government to get rid of the native population, and replace it with

Europeans. The officials all go away more or less rich, and the Governors-General amass fortunes. Borthwick is of opinion that if the Turks can get artillery enough to do it, they may drive the Italians into the sea at Tripoli, and that then the whole of native North Africa will rise in Tunis and Algeria as well as in Morocco. The plan is an adventurous one, and he is aware that he is running a great risk. He has been three years in India serving in a cavalry regiment and left it four years ago. I advised him as a first step to go to Constantinople, and see what help he could get there. He came to me from Stead, who had suggested to him that I might help him to get the money necessary.

" 16*th April.*— There has been an astonishing disaster at sea, the *Titanic,* the largest vessel ever built, wrecked in mid Atlantic by collision with an iceberg. It was her first voyage, and she was carrying over 1,000 passengers to New York, many of them millionaires. Most of the women and children seem to have been put in boats and picked up by a passing steamer, but the rest have perished, over 1,000 souls, including the ship's company. Among them is Stead, about whom I was talking to Borthwick last Sunday, the very day of the wreck. He was on his way on some newspaper business, and was to have written a sensational account of the voyage. I cannot say I ever liked or respected Stead, he was too much of a *charlatan.* It is impossible that a man who has made himself the agent of the Russian autocracy, who has intrigued for the restoration of the ex-Khedive Ismaïl, and who has been named by Cecil Rhodes executor of his will, all the while calling himself a friend of liberty, can have been quite honest. The Irish always refused to trust him, and they were right. Still one cannot help feeling a pang at so appalling an end. One thing is consoling in these great disasters, the proof given that Nature is not quite yet the slave of Man, but is able to rise even now in her wrath and destroy him. Also if any large number of human beings could be better spared than another it would be just these American millionaires with their wealth and insolence.

" 20*th April.*— Newbuildings. There has been a demonstration of bombarding the Dardanelles by the Italians, a childish and cowardly proceeding, the ships opening fire at 8,000 yards, and firing 342 shots without any result whatever.

" 21*st April (Sunday).*— I have been reading Davitt's book, the ' Fall of Feudalism,' an interesting bit of Irish history, though a stupid title, also Barry O'Brien's ' Life of Parnell.' The Turco-Italian war drags on, but is beginning to get on the English commercial nerves, the passage of mercantile ships having been blocked through the Dardanelles by the Italian attack. Nearly all our newspapers now lay the blame of the war on Italy, even those which have hitherto been most in Italy's favour.

" *30th April*.— Miss Frances Jennings appeared here this morning with her donkey and van in which she has been travelling since the beginning of the month, and I have established her and them in the goat field. Hers is a forlorn and uncomfortable existence, though being entirely out of doors she is happy, and though she is still partly paralyzed, and unable to walk or stand up except on crutches, she manages to harness her donkey, and lift herself into the cart, and she travels absolutely alone. She is naturally of a very fair complexion, and she is much sunburnt, going bare-headed and wearing her hair in long plaits. Her dress is of coarse green woollen stuff, her legs cased in huge pilot boots. She has no mattress to lie on, or other bed than some sheep skins, and a bit of eider-down quilt, but she says she can sleep all night and more, twelve hours at a stretch. It is difficult to say whether she is in her right mind or not. One would say not, except that her talk, though strange, is quite reasonable; it ripples perpetually on in a very sweet voice, broken with little waves of laughter, describing things she has seen and the small adventures of her life. We had our tea with her in the meadow, and have lent her books, for she has none with her. She lies all day on the ground, or sits in her van, which is very small and low, with an oil cloth hood. For her meals she crawls about gathering sticks to make a fire and hang a little pot for cocoa, but she cooks nothing in the way of meat, eating bread and herbs, docks, and nettles, which she finds close by. Hers is an entirely defenceless life, except for her power of talk and her appearance of utter guilelessness, but she is only twenty-six, and sufficiently attractive I should say to run some risk at the hands of drunken roughs. Her chief fear, however, she tells us is of slugs, and possible snakes crawling over her at night. I have advised her, since she intends to travel all through the summer, to go north to Holywell, and bathe at St. Winifred's shrine, but she says she has too little faith, though she became a Catholic some few years ago, but I have told her that faith is not necessary there for a cure, witness my own.[1]

" *2nd May*.— Drove with Miss Lawrence to Reigate Priory, where we lunched with the Somersets. Lady Katherine is pleasant and very like her brother Osborne Beauclerk, with just his way of talking and asking questions. (I had not seen them since they came to see us at Sheykh Obeyd on their honeymoon tour.) I like both of them, and found the house most interesting, with gardens, and grounds, the prettiest in Surrey.

" *3rd May*.— The ' Times ' announces that our paper ' Egypt,' has been forbidden entrance circulation and sale at Cairo, its articles ' disturbing public order.' This is doubtless Kitchener's doing. I have protested in a letter to the ' Times,' and am also writing to Grey.

[1] See Appendix VII, p. 458.

Dillon is unfortunately away in Dublin, and the other Irish members are too closely pinned to the Government to help us much in Parliament. The Italians have seized Rhodes.

" Miss Jennings, who is still here, tells me she spent two years in a room entirely occupied in watching the fire, and that she kept a diary of what she saw there. Then another year watching the sea, now her diary is about the people she meets on her country wanderings. Those she likes best on the roads are the blacksmiths. She tells me they are always kind. We had her in to a dinner of roast beef, which she enjoyed, having been carried indoors by one of the stable helps, and is now sitting by the fire. She is to go on to-morrow in the direction of St. Winifred's well.

" *7th May.*— Syud Mahmud came down to wish me good-bye before going back to India, a most excellent young man, the very best Moslem in London — what will become of him?

" *9th May.*— Chapel Street. Dillon is back for the second reading of the Home Rule Bill to-night. He expects no difficulty about its becoming law in two years, barring accidents. There are three rocks ahead of the Government — Welsh Disestablishment, the Insurance Act, and I forget the third (War?). Else all is plain sailing. He thinks Grey contemplates a great coup in Egypt, certainly the abolition of the Capitulations.

" *12th May (Sunday).*—Newbuildings. Baron Marschall von Bieberstein has arrived as German Ambassador in London.

" *14th May.*— Old May Day. Caffin calls it St. May, a name for it I never heard before.

" *19th May (Sunday).*— Dillon has put a whole sheaf of questions about the prohibition of ' Egypt,' and has got from Grey that he accepts the responsibility of it. He has ' personally satisfied himself as to the contents of the paper, and that though it may not contain any direct incitement to disturbance, he is of opinion that it might cause disturbance, that Kitchener has written to him on the subject, in fine, that he will not give us his protection, and declines to lay papers.'

" The Turkish garrison in Rhodes has had to surrender. Two thousand three hundred regulars, through lack apparently of food, for there has been no fighting. There is prospect now of a European Congress which is certain to be hostile to the Ottoman Empire and Mohammedan interests.

" *20th May.*— I have been reading Crispi's Memoirs, dull stuff, most of it, but there is a chapter at the end giving important documents which show that as long ago as 1890 Lord Salisbury made a secret engagement with the Italian Government, allowing its seizure of Tripoli as a counterpoise to French naval power in the Mediterranean, also that at that date the Italians had begun to intrigue with Hassuna Karamanli, and that he had assured them he could command the hill tribes of Jebel Gharian, who were tired of their connection with Turkey, and would welcome an Italian Occupation. This explains much that has been doubtful, though of course I long ago suspected it.

" *26th May (Whit-Sunday)*.— Newbuildings. Abdul Ghaffar is here, a very excellent young fellow, serious, and without any nonsense or exaggeration, accurate, and well-informed. He has been three years at St. John's College, Oxford, and talked about Oxford affairs well with Belloc. His father is a large fellah proprietor at Tola, in the Delta, and he is an excellent specimen of his race, quite unspoiled by his English education.

" Kitchener is clamouring for reinforcements at Cairo, and for the stationing of the British man-of-war at Alexandria. He is to meet Asquith and Winston at Malta to discuss Mediterranean matters. It looks very much as if he were meditating a *coup* of some kind in Egypt, and I remember Winston's words to me last year, ' You must not quarrel with me if I annex Egypt.'

" *31st May*.— The newspapers are full of the meeting at Malta to which Winston and Clementine have gone with Nellie Hozier in the Admiralty yacht to meet Kitchener, Asquith too."

[It was on this occasion that our people came to the decision of getting the French Navy to police the Mediterranean, while the English Navy should keep to North Sea and English Channel for the French in the event of a war with Germany, thus enabling them to make a definite promise to the French Government of help by land in a war with Germany. It was on this occasion, too, that Winston, abandoning his long feud with Kitchener, made friends with him to Egypt's detriment.]

" The war in the Mediterranean drags on, the Italian Fleet making a round of the Ægean and seizing the islands. The Arabs of Southern Morocco have at last risen against the French. They are stalwart men, but quite unorganized as soldiers. They have proclaimed a new Sultan in place of Mulai Hafiz, abdicated, and may give the French trouble.

" *2nd June (Sunday)*.— I hear from Paris that there are several Orientals recently arrived there from India with a plot to assassinate Grey, as also Kitchener, but it is not likely to come to anything. Things in the Mediterranean are more mixed than ever. The Italian Fleet has occupied most of the Turkish islands, the idea being to get Europe to force the Turks to make peace.

" Kitchener's meeting with Asquith and Churchill at Malta is really an important one, as they will have to settle between them what is to be our Mediterranean policy. Some want an alliance offensive and defensive with France, others peace with Germany. It will end in the Mediterranean being left to the Mediterranean Powers. Then we shall leave Egypt, holding on only to the Soudan, but this will not take place yet for some years.

" McCullagh has written a quite admirable book, ' Italy's War for a Desert.' I am reviewing it in ' Egypt.'

" *23rd June (Sunday).*— Dillon is here for the week-end, and we have been talking over past Irish history.' [All very interesting, but I have given most of it in my ' Land War in Ireland.'] I drove him this afternoon to the top of Chanclebury with my Arab team. We came back from the Ring by Dial Post in an hour and thirty-five minutes, having driven there by Broomer's Corner in a little over two hours, good going.

" *24th June.*— The Bellocs came to dinner last night. Belloc and Dillon had much talk, but they proved not very sympathetic, the one being essentially serious, the other as essentially unserious.

" With Dillon I had a talk before he went away, he giving me an account of the Kilmainham treaty, and Parnell's dealings with Gladstone in connection with the Phœnix Park assassinations [matters which I need not repeat here, as they have been fully dealt with elsewhere].

" *4th July.*— Reuter announces the discovery of a plot to assassinate Kitchener, the Khedive, and the Prime Minister, Mohammed Saïd. Four Nationalists arrested.

" *5th July.*— A young Egyptian, Abdul Halim Alaili (brother to the other Alaili), professed partisan of the Khedive, was here to-day, whose apologist he made himself, defending him from the charge of unpatriotic action in the war of which Egypt had accused him. ' In stead,' he said, ' of joining Kitchener against the Ottoman Government, Abbas has secretly helped to facilitate the passage of Turkish officers through Egypt on their way to the Tripolitan frontier, as well as the introduction of arms into the Cyrenaica, nobody in reality was so patriotic or hated Kitchener more. Abbas would willingly abdicate, but who was there to take his place? In four years his son would be of age, then Abbas would retire. The Khedive was quite ready, he said, to grant a Constitution, but Kitchener would not allow it. Abdul Halim gave us an account of the Khedive's visit to Windsor. According to this the Khedive represented to King George the danger to Egypt involved in the seizure of the Ægean Islands, and that the English Government ought to intervene in favour of Turkey, but the King said that ever since the revolution at Constantinople, the Turks had refused to follow English advice. They could not intervene now without a quarrel with Italy. This is just what Churchill told me, so doubtless it is true. The Khedive, Abdul Hamid says, was received with honour this year in Constantinople, and had had some sort of mission, when he came to England, to bring about a *rapprochement* between the two Governments. Belloc, who is very anti-Turk, declares that he knows it to be true, that the German, Austrian, and Russian Governments have come to an agreement for partitioning the Ottoman Empire.

"There has always been a danger of this sort, but I doubt its being nearer now than a year ago, anyhow England could not prevent it, and her friendship for Turkey would not amount to much more than preventing Arabia from being meddled with by the European Powers, and making herself protector of the Caliphate.

"I asked the young Egyptians about the reported plot at Cairo. They consider it probable as against Kitchener. Indeed, how could it be otherwise. He has played the despot there and governed by despotic methods, but they knew no details.

"10th *July.*—Two Spanish Americans were here to-day to see the horses, the one Pereira from Buenos Aires, the other from Uraguay. I was interested to find them both very pious Catholics, who had been quite lately at Rome, and had had private audience of the Pope, of whom they gave exactly the same description as I have heard from others, declaring him to be a Saint who works miracles. His Holiness had been seen by one of his suite in a state of ecstasy, floating some feet above the ground, and they told the tale of a North American, a Protestant, who coming with his Catholic wife and daughter to Rome, had been converted. The daughter (she was still a child) had been afflicted with an eruption on her face, which disfigured her to the extent that her eyes were hardly visible, and when she went out of doors she had constantly to wear a veil. She had insisted with her parents upon being taken to Rome, where she said the Pope would cure her. They had obtained an audience, a public one, with many others, the child attending it veiled, and the father had besought the Pope to bless her, and the Pope had put his hand upon her head, promising she should be cured. When the audience was over the father had pulled off the veil, and behold, the child's face was whole. Whereupon the father, as was the way with North Americans, had purchased the largest photographic portrait he could find of the Pope, and had had it framed in silver. When they left Rome he had taken four places in the train, the fourth seat being occupied by the portrait, which he declared he would travel with through the world, proclaiming the miracle.

"11th *July.*—Anniversary of the Bombardment of Alexandria, thirty years ago to-day, and there is no sign of repentance in this country. I am the only person left who remembers that abominable event and still protests. Margot had chosen to-day for her garden party in Downing Street, and a card of invitation had been sent to me, but, of course, I did not go.   Precautions have to be taken against the Suffragettes, who come on these occasions to knock Asquith about.

"*12th July.*— Bad news from Constantinople. Shefket Pasha has resigned the Grand Viziership, and there is talk of Kiamil succeeding him as Grand Vizier and making a disgraceful peace with Italy.

"*19th July.*— There is a general change of Ministry at Constantinople.   Kiamil is to be made Minister of Foreign Affairs under Tewfik Pasha as Grand Vizier.   If true it will mean a triumph for English intrigue and a disaster for Turkey.   Kiamil would betray Egypt to England, and probably agree to base terms of peace with Italy.   There has been a new Italian attack on the Dardanelles, this time by torpedo boats, two of which are said to have been sunk.

"*21st July (Sunday).*— Drove Belloc to Steyning, where we had tea with Mackarness.   We found Gokhale there, who exhorted me to use my influence with Indian Mohammedans to get them to join the Hindoos in working for self-government.   I have, of course, been doing this for a long time.   I reminded Gokhale of my advice to him four years ago to put a couple of bombs in his pocket when he went to see Morley at the India Office.   The reminiscence shocked him, for he is a timid man, and terribly afraid of being thought an extremist, especially in presence of Mackarness and his fellow judge, Lord Coleridge, and his language in answer was very demure.   He is in favour of a Trans-Persian railway, he told us, because it would put the Indian Moslems in close touch with their co-religionists in Afghanistan and Persia, and give them more progressive ideas perhaps; but it will be a danger for India some day, and I exhorted him to waste no time in bringing Indian self-government forward in view of the coming collapse of the British Empire.   He did not seem to realize this as a thing to be provided against, though it is the real chief factor of the situation.   My last word to Gokhale on going away was: 'Above all don't be too moderate.'

"*23rd July.*— Winston has made his expected speech, a regular Imperialist manifesto, which will delight the Tories and accentuate the quarrel with Germany.

"*24th July.*— Newbuildings.   An important *communiqué* by Grey has been published in the 'Westminster Gazette,' taking for its text some words of mine.   It denies categorically that Grey either consented to or approved of the Italian raid on Tripoli."

[Nevertheless it is quite certain that our Foreign Office did approve of the raid, though probably not in any written form.   Its complicity after the fact, at any rate, is proveable in two ways. (1) by the fact that Rennell Rodd, our Ambassador at Rome, though according to official accounts he knew nothing of the raid until it had taken place, an ignorance and neglect of duty which must have brought on him

official blame, so far from being punished was rewarded and confirmed in his post at Rome, where he is still Ambassador; and (2)
Kitchener, who at Cairo had helped the Italian Government in Egypt,
with the complicity of the Foreign Office, by preventing the passage
of Ottoman troops through the Nile Valley, was entertained on his
return home through Italy at a complimentary dinner, where he was
hailed as Italy's best friend and ally. The truth is that Italy was
allowed to invade Tripoli without our disapproval at the Foreign Office
as part of Grey's policy of detaching Italy from the German alliance
in favour of the Ententes, which were gradually becoming a coalition.
In this he succeeded four years later.]

" *27th July.*— George Wyndham writes that in consequence of Winston's Mediterranean speech, which he ' admires and respects,' he is
quite willing to meet him at my house (a meeting he has hitherto refused), and proposes October 18th for a shooting visit.

"*28th July (Sunday).*—My letter headed ' Grey and Tripoli' is in
yesterday's ' Westminster.'

" To Meynell's at Greatham, where I met young Padraic Colum
honeymooning with his bride, Molly Maguire, a red-haired Celtic girl,
whom he married last week. Colum is an intelligent, eager little man,
with much simplicity of character, mixed with practical good sense.
I like them both.

" *30th July.*— I have given up my house in Chapel Street.

" *1st Aug.*— Newbuildings. Padraic Colum and his bride spent the
day here. They intend to live at Dublin, where he has journalistic
work.

" *7th Aug.*— Called on Lady C., who told me curious details about
Kitchener's private life. She tells me that the plot against him at
Cairo was a very serious one. A great deal, she says, is talked of
his popularity in Egypt. He is really disliked, and seems to think
that his position there is insecure.

" Cockerell dined with me. He is very busy just now looking after
a bequest made to his Fitz-william Museum by an old millionaire, Mar-
lay, who died the other day. This will be our last dinner in Chapel
Street." [I had sold my house, or what they call selling it, paying £100
to resign the remainder of the lease, as part of my resolve to retire
altogether from the world for my hermitage in Sussex. I have never
since been in London, even for the day.]

" *9th Aug.*— Philip Napier came to luncheon, just back from Egypt.
He is not enthusiastic about Kitchener. Thinks him more feared
than loved. Also Goumah writes pessimistically from Cairo.

" *13th Aug.* —Newbuildings. Old Evershed, my former tenant here,
is dying, and I went to see him at his cottage on Dragon's Green. He
is eighty-six years old, as fine a type as could be found of the old-

fashioned West Sussex farmer, one more distinguished than one sees in East Sussex. He held this farm of me forty years ago (and moved afterwards to Baker's over the way) ; an excellent farmer and a hard worker, but hampered with the misfortune of a mad wife, whom he was too kind to send to a hospital, and kept for many years at home, and thus was unable to save money, and now in old age finds himself too poor to carry on his business. He would not borrow money, and for the last half dozen years has retired into a little cottage of mine, his wife being at last dead, and is looked after by a girl. I found him very tidy there in a clean shirt lying in bed, complaining of nothing, but perplexed at small money troubles. A curious episode in his life is that as a young man he was tempted away to Australia to dig gold at the time of the gold fever there, but he made nothing of it, and came back to his Sussex farming quite unchanged by his experience, a good and honourable man, of a finer breed than can easily be found.

"*17th Aug.*— I entered my seventy-third year to-day.

"*23rd Aug.*— Patrick Butler, who is here, tells me that everybody in India among the military men is aghast at the plan of a Trans-Persian railway from the Caspian; also that the transfer of the new capital to Delhi is disapproved. They have no great opinion of Hardinge as Governor-General. Butler has been quite unexpectedly ordered home from India to the depôt in Ireland. They are in want of Catholic officers there in view of the threatened rebellion in Ulster. Most of the officers of the garrison at the Curragh would sympathize too much with the rebel Ulstermen.

"*2nd Sept.*— We have just finished reading Balzac's great series of romances, 'Illusions Perdus,' 'Splendeurs et Misères,' and 'Vautrin.' They are the most wonderful of all his work, and show him the Shakespeare of novelists without any real competitor worthy of even a second place. In it he runs through the whole gamut of civilized human nature from the highest to the lowest note, and his women are equal to his men. That is what distinguishes him from our own novel writers with whom we compare him, from Scott and Thackeray, who was his special imitator, down to Meredith.

"*14th Sept.*— My 'Land War in Ireland' is published. The moment is very opportune as the anti-Home Rule campaign is once more in full swing. The Government has lost the Midlothian seat, and people are beginning to talk after all of the Bill not going through. Belloc declares it will be abandoned, and Churchill has made a speech at Dundee forecasting a multiplicity of Parliaments in the United Kingdom. I have been reading a most amusing book, 'The Red Hand of Ulster,' which has done more than anything yet written to popu-larize Protestant Ireland. It has made the Orangemen interesting — even to me. I must say it will serve Redmond right if the Bill collapses, seeing the cowardice he and his party have shown, Dillon only excepted, in abandoning the cause of India, Persia, and Egypt, and backing up Grey and the Whigs in all their iniquitous doings abroad in payment for Irish Home Rule. It will serve them right if they are choused out of their thirty pieces of silver after all. As far as the larger world of Asia is concerned it will be no great misfortune, seeing that the Irish Parliamentary Party has gone over soul and body to our execrable Whig Government and richly deserves its discomfiture. It is time I should cease to worry myself with the world's ways and the ways of the British Empire and the ways of Ireland.

"*15th Sept.*— George Wyndham writes a long letter from Clouds, describing a visit he has just paid to Cockermouth Castle. It reminds me of by-gone times when Francis and I stayed there some fifty years ago with Percy and Madeline, George's parents, when they first married. My recollection of it is of an ancient stone fortress, rough and unfurnished, without covering to the stone walls, and with curious mediæval conveniences still in use, amongst others one projecting from the castle wall, which had a clear drop of perhaps a hundred feet down into the Derwent river below. I remember, too, how one day being out shooting in a covert below the castle, a cock pheasant which had been winged and had fallen beyond the river, which is there very wide and swift, deliberately took to the water and swam across the river back to its own side. We went once or twice to shoot grouse on Skiddaw, but there was more walking than sport. George, in his letters, talks of himself as being now a country squire, with the prospect of ' conceivably being Minister of War, when his side comes into power again.'

"*20th Sept.*— The papers announce a visit to be paid to the King at Balmoral by the Russian Minister of Foreign affairs, Sazanoff, Grey, and Kitchener, a black combination. Belloc declares positively that the Home Rule Bill is to be abandoned and it really looks like it. My ' Land War ' has so far been very well received, and yesterday there was a laudatory review of it in the ' Nation.' It is probably the last prose work I shall publish, though there may be more than one posthumous volume of my diaries.

"*22nd Sept. (Sunday).*— Dr. Renner, a quite black West African from Sierra Leone, is here for the week-end, having been brought by Miss Howsin, an M.D. who is interested in the future of his race, and looks to Islam as the best means to its salvation in Africa, though not himself a Mohammedan. He talks no native language, and his mastery of English is very imperfect, though he is a well-educated man. His name, he tells us, in the Fanti tongue is Aouna. He gets £550 a year a chief of the Native Medical Staff at Sierra Leone, but complains that Englishmen are now being appointed to supersede the native doctors.

"*25th Sept.*— General Marschall von Bieberstein is dead, a great misfortune for Turkey, whose sincere friend he was. The shadows are darkening over the East.

"*29th Sept.* (*Sunday*).— The Bellocs to dinner and Somers Cocks, the latter just back from Berlin, where he says the Emperor William directs all his own diplomacy himself.

"*3rd Oct.*— Another very lovely day. In the afternoon we made a round, gathering crab apples and choke pears, of which there is an immense abundance this year such as never before seen. The pears are excellent, stewed with blackberries and clotted cream, better than garden pears, and the crabs do well for the goats. The hips and haws this year are astonishing, and every kind of berry. We filled the American cart with our spoils — a real pleasure.

"*4th Oct.*— It is all over I fear with Turkey and the Mohammedan world. The long intrigue against it seems to have prevailed, and the papers to-day announce that peace is made with Italy on the Italian terms. The way in which the end has been obtained has been through stirring up the Balkan States to the point of war. Until yesterday I still hoped that the Turkish Government would elect to fight against these rather than yield to threats, but the Ottoman citadel has already been betrayed, and the Jew, Kiamil Pasha, has played into the joint hands of the English and Russian Foreign Offices, and the disgraceful terms have been agreed to. Nothing can now save Islam from its doom of subjection to the will of Christendom and its ultimate destruction. Egypt's cause too is lost, with that of the Ottoman Empire. I shall trouble myself with Oriental futures no further, being impotent either to advise or control, I ' roll up the map of Islam.'

"*8th Oct.*— Montenegro has declared war on Turkey. [This was the first act of the Balkan War.]

"*10th Oct.*— The war news is confirmed and fighting has begun in Albania. There seems no doubt now that Bulgaria and Servia will join in the fray, though the Austrian Government is trying to stop it. I am somewhat consoled by it, for though it may be the beginning of the end for Turkey in Europe, it will be better for Islam that the Empire should die sword in hand than that it should be cheated out of existence by our diplomacy. War gives at least a chance. Not that I have much hope of a victorious ending, for the concert of Europe will prevent that; still a chance there is. Abdul Ghaffar agrees with me in this. He also announces an intention by our Government to give a Constitutional Government to Egypt, a sham one, of course, but it is to be called a *Mejliss el Nawab*. Abdul Ghaffar is an excellent fellow, with a closer understanding of English ideas than I have found in any Egyptian, yet without loss to his patriotism.

" 13*th Oct.* (*Sunday*).— Newbuildings. Terence arrived here from Pekes with his friend Percy Fielding. He tells me it is quite certain that the German Government intended to buy Tobruk, on the Tripolitan coast, from the Sultan, and that that had been the cause of the sudden decision of the Italian Government to seize Tripoli. It has been said often, and often denied, but he tells me it is quite true. As to present affairs in the Cyrenaica, he says that if the Turks conclude a peace with Italy, Enver Bey will proclaim himself Sultan, and will be acknowledged as such by the Senussia, but the Ottoman Sultan Caliphate will lose all prestige in Africa. The Italians are hated in Tunis both by Arabs and French, and the war has made France almost popular. The Italians might have conciliated the Tripolitans but for the massacres. Now they are hated and despised, hated because they are known to have intended to dispossess the Arabs of their lands, despised because they are cowards, and also because they are willing to work for less wages than the Arabs will take. They are of the dregs of Europe.

" 16*th Oct.*— Peace has been signed at Ouchy between Italy and Turkey on disgraceful terms to Turkey. What will now happen I imagine is that, the Italian end being gained, England and Russia will put pressure on the Sultan to agree also to the loss of Macedonia. Without some extraordinary manifestation by the Turks of military power, of which so far there is no sign, the Ottoman Empire is ruined. This preys upon my mind. Egypt will now be permanently enslaved to Europe.

" 17*th Oct.*— Worth Forest. We drove here in the afternoon to get ready for our *ouverture de la chasse* on Saturday, when George Wyndham, Mark Napier, Winston Churchill, and perhaps Beauclerk are up to celebrate with me the completion of the new Manor House, with a deer drive in the Upper Forest. The bucks are beginning to bell, and we heard them in the night, which was clear with a half moon. When we were here last week young Henry Blunt, who had been here to see me, and was bicycling back, was confronted with a buck in one of the forest paths, which disputed the way with him. This frightened him so that he did not get back till half-past nine. He will have to do better than that with the lions and rhinoceroses of Uganda, whither he is about to emigrate.

" 18*th Oct.*— George arrived in the afternoon, and we spent a pleasant evening together talking about Ireland and my book, the ' Land War.' He told me that it was certainly true that if things had gone a little differently at the 1885 elections, Lord Salisbury would have given some form of Home Rule, also that there was no choice now but either to treat Ireland exactly as so many English counties, or give Home Rule on the model of Canada.

" *19th Oct.*— This has been a great day. Mark arrived at ten in glorious sunshine, and we made a long beat for deer in the upper Forest without result, however, as far as getting a buck was concerned, though we flushed several woodcocks. Clementine joined us at one, and walked with us in the afternoon's shooting, but Winston not till tea-time. Then he at once began a political discussion with George which was both amusing and enlightening, and went on with occasional breaks through dinner and till midnight. It was a fine night, and we dined in the bungalow, dressed in gorgeous Oriental garments, Clementine in a suit of embroidered silk, purchased last year in Smyrna, Winston in one of my Bagdad robes, George in a blue dressing gown, and I in my Bedouin clothes, Mark adorned only with his wit, but that was of the best. It recalled the most glorious night's entertainments of the Crabbet Club, a true feast of reason and flow of bowl. The secrets of the Cabinet were gloriously divulged, and those of the Opposition front benches no less, from Home Rule to a reconstruction of the House of Lords by common accord after George Curzon and Asquith had been got rid of, while George Wyndham declared with great oaths that he would rather go to hell than see the British Constitution made ridiculous by single Chamber Government, at which point I left them for my bed. Winston was very brilliant in all this, as though he kept on at the Madeira he also kept his head, and played with George's wild rushes like a skilled fencer with a greatly superior fence. He is certainly an astonishing young man, and has gained immensely within the last two years in character and intellectual grip; also he is in more vigorous health now that he has left the Home Office for the Admiralty, where he is able to spend most of his time on board the *Enchantress,* the Admiralty 3,000 ton yacht, which he makes his home.

" Among the many things discussed was that of the coming European war and the chances of a German invasion. This, Winston declared, could be easily effected on the east coast where it would certainly be the German game to land 20,000 men so as to make a diversion and prevent our helping the French with an English contingent. He said the idea of the Fleet being a sufficient safeguard was entirely out of date, and without a strong army there was no safety. He also believed in the coming of a war in which we shall be involved in order to prevent France being overpowered by Germany, and forced into an alliance against us. He has a great belief in submarine warfare as the weapon of the future and is pushing that branch of the service on all he can. He is to go on Monday to Sheerness to witness trials of artillery and he described the prodigious effect of the new explosives. He is enthusiastic about his naval work, but I know too little about military affairs, either by sea or land, to appreciate the whole of his talk, and I was tired with the shooting and so cannot do justice to the wonderful evening it has been.

" *20th Oct. (Sunday).*— Another day of excellent talk. Cockerell came for luncheon and to spend the afternoon, and Winston told us admirable stories of his experience as Home Secretary and of how it had become a nightmare to him the having to exercise his power of life and death in the case of condemned criminals, on an average of one case a fortnight. Nearly all of the cases of murder are a combination of love and drink, young fellows who on a sudden impulse kill their sweethearts, sometimes in the most barbarous fashion yet with the excuse of temporary rage amounting to madness. He described the power of the Home Secretary as absolute, either to quash the sentence or to confirm it. The Home Secretary can go into any prison and on his sole authority can order a release, which if once notified to a prisoner cannot be changed afterwards by any power in England. He had several times done this, and just before leaving the Office he had ordered a number of remissions of sentences, notwithstanding the protests of the judges in the cases. He spoke of these cases with emotion, and giving us all particulars.

" About the war in Turkey I told him that it was his fault, or rather Grey's, that it had broken out, that the outbreak could have been stopped a year ago by ordering the British fleet to the Mediterranean and notifying the Italian Government that their raid on Tripoli would not be tolerated. He said, ' Yes, it was so, but we could not afford to make for ourselves yet another enemy in Italy.' Talking of the Italians I remarked that they were contemptible as fighting men, they have been beaten always by every other people by sea and land since Lepanto. He said, ' That is interesting, if true, but how about Garibaldi?' ' Garibaldi,' I said, ' was an Italian fighting against Italians. He and his men never beat a foreign enemy.' Winston, however, will not hear of Grey as being other than a splendid specimen of an Englishman, the best of the type, and they are evidently close friends, indeed Grey is Winston's son's godfather.

" Winston is also a strong eugenist. He told us he had himself drafted the Bill which is to give power of shutting up people of weak intellect and so prevent their breeding. He thought it might be arranged to sterilize them. It was possible by the use of Röntgen rays, both for men and women, though for women some operation might also be necessary. He thought that if shut up with no prospect of release without it many would ask to be sterilized as a condition of having their liberty restored. He went on to say that the mentally deficient were as much more prolific than those normally constituted as eight to five. Without something of the sort the race must decay. It was rapidly decaying, but would be stopped by some such means.

" After lunch I drove Clementine with my team round by Turner's Hill and Caxtons, and we overtook my grandchildren coming up to tea.

" Another long evening's talk followed.

" *21st Oct.*— The party is over and all are gone their several ways, Winston to Sheerness with Clementine, George to London, and Mark to Puttenden, and I am left in a state almost of collapse alone. We had a last try for a buck to-day, but again without success, though three were seen, and we got a score of pheasants.

" I am the more depressed because of the evil news from Turkey, where the five armies of the Balkan States and Greece have invaded Ottoman territory, and so far successfully. The only chance for the Turks seemed to lie in a vigourous offensive, and it is clear they lack initiative now that Shefket has left their War Office. They are being betrayed by Kiamil and English advice and will end in their dismemberment. I judge of things being at their worst in regard to any hope of help here from Winston's talk. He has become most truculent about international affairs, being engrossed in preparations for war with Germany and ready with Grey for any betrayal of weak nations needed for the game of alliances. Talking of Somaliland, where there has been fighting between the Mullah and the ' friendly ' tribes, he said he would like to make a present of it to Germany and of other places as coaling stations which would be so many hostages to fortune. They (meaning our Government) would be obliged to take some action against the Mullah, not an expedition, which was too expensive an affair, but they would send aeroplanes to drop bombs into the Arab camps. He gave us a graphic description of his experiences at Omdurman in the charge of the 21st Lancers, and of how he had seen these spearing the wounded and leaning with their whole weight on their lances after the charge to get the points through the thick clothes the wounded Dervishes wore as they lay on the ground. As the points went in the Derwishes would kick up their feet and hands. One trooper had boasted of his kind-heartedness because he had only put four inches of steel into his man. ' He ought to be thankful,' he had said, ' to find himself in the hands of a good-natured chap like me.' Winston is quite changed on these matters from what he was two years ago when I had hopes of encouraging him to better things. How like his father! He and George had been talking these two days in absolute accord on army and navy affairs and the coming war with Germany. Hearing them talk, one might be excused for thinking what is commonly said by the Tories, that Winston will one day return to the Tory fold. His old connection with the army and now with the navy has turned his mind back into an ultra Imperialist groove. This, I think, will be a stronger temptation for him than any mere intrigue of ambition. Talking yesterday about his career, he said, 'I have never joined in any intrigue, everything I have got I have worked for and have been more hated than anybody.' He speaks highly of both Lloyd George and Edward Grey, both of whom stand probably in the way of his becoming Liberal Prime Minister, while he would certainly lead the Tory party were he one of them again. He avows a great contempt for Bonar Law. Arthur Balfour, George declares, really means to be out of politics, and George himself, clever though he is, is a mere child in argument compared with Winston.

"*23rd Oct.*— Cockerell has written, thanking me enthusiastically for his share in Sunday's party. It was certainly very brilliant, though it has left me with the remorseful feeling an orgy always leaves, and I think, I will not indulge in another.

"*25th Oct.*— A great battle is going on around Adrianople, and the Turks are evidently getting the worst of it. The papers try to make out that it is part of a strategical plan on the Turkish side, but I do not believe it. The only chance the Sultan had was to overwhelm his enemies at once by marching on Sofia, and here they are being invaded and retreating. I fear there is little hope. Abdul Ghaffar, who is a good young man and a good Moslem, writes quaintly and pathetically from Oxford, 'After all God is there, and we may in the last resort rely on him. . . . Do not give up hope yet, you will live to see Turkey strong. God grant you the fulfilment of your wishes. . . . Keep up heart and rely on God. Those who take refuge in God he helps; anyhow this is all we can do now.' I wish I could have his trust, but I feel ashamed of having had that uproarious time with Winston and George, two outrageous political gamblers just now at this tragic time when we ought to be in sackcloth and ashes.

"*26th Oct.*— The St. Martin's summer is over and heavy rain has set in. I feel like Napoleon at Moscow, and that we have outstayed the season here in the Forest. Clementine has written her 'Collins' from the 'Enchantress,' and Winston keeps on telegraphing about an overcoat left behind, I believe his chauffeur's, and taken by George's man.

"*27th Oct. (Sunday).*— The Ottoman cause seems lost in Europe, and with it all I have been fighting for for so many years, and the collapse is a personal collapse for me, which I feel at every turn, day and night. Egypt now will never get out of the grip of Europe — I do not say of England, because the British Empire will not long survive in the Mediterranean, but of whatever other Empire takes its place. I shall not live to see this ultimate change, but others will, and Islam's chance is gone."

From this point onwards, the autumn of 1912, the close of my practical activities in Eastern affairs may be dated. I had given up my house in London, and at the end of the year I took my name off my Clubs, cutting myself off from all temptations to continue these activities, such as I could not have avoided had I continued to frequent my many London friends; nor have I from that date so much as visited Piccadilly, even for the day. All my subsequent life has been spent in Sussex, either at Newbuildings, or from time to time in Worth Forest, leading the life there of a country squire to which I was born, and which is naturally mine. Nevertheless I continued to take an onlooker's interest in the great drama of European politics, which was shaping itself into the supreme tragedy of 1914. A few friends came from time to time to see me in my hermitage, and these for a while gave me news of the diplomatic doings which were leading on to war, and I had at my hand a neighbour and constant ally in Hilaire Belloc, than whom no one was better acquainted with the intrigues and rivalries of our political leaders in Parliament, besides being always an instructive and amusing companion. Thus I did not wholly lose touch for another year with public affairs, and my diary, though less important in its entries, continues to be a record of the chief events which preluded Armageddon. They will show how little truth there is in the current story that in the quarrel our Foreign Office was wholly innocent, more especially in that with the Ottoman Empire.

"31st Oct.— The news from Constantinople is rather less hopeless to-day in regard to the battle being fought east of Adrianople, but I feel no revival of confidence in the ultimate result. Even if Nazim Pasha, should manage to beat off the Bulgarian army, and save the Eastern Province, it would not restore the Ottoman prestige as a military power, or safeguard the Empire from dismemberment. It is an ugly feature of the case that Mukhtar Ghazi has resigned the Vizierate and Kiamil Pasha remains on now in supreme authority. That means that a disgraceful peace will be made through European, in other words, Anglo-Russian intervention, and the Sultan will be reduced to the position of England's servant and the Czar's. The dream of a regenerated Caliphate, strong, and reformed, is at an end. Egypt will be England's bakshish for the service rendered, and Russia's will be the opening of the Dardanelles. This is what has all along been aimed at by our Foreign Office.

"I have written to resign my chairmanship of the Egyptian Committee, and to say that I cannot carry on our paper 'Egypt,' beyond the end of the year. In the afternoon I shot with Victor Lytton, who has been here to consult me about the Life of his grandfather, the novelist, which he has been writing, and after dinner we had a long talk on religion and philosophy as well as my remembrances of the grand-

father and of Victor's father. I like Victor much. Though far less
brilliant than Neville, he has good solid qualities, and a much wider
range of interests. He has a good heart and a logical mind. What he
told me of his boyish devotion to his father in the year after his
father's death was very interesting as a spiritual experience. He is
himself devoted now to his own children.

"*1st Nov.*— A great Turkish defeat is admitted, and it is only a
question whether the Bulgarians will march on to Constantinople or
forestall European intervention by making a separate peace with the
Sultan, which shall include the cession of the whole of European Turkey west of the fortified line between the Black Sea and the sea of
Marmora. This is the more likely result of the two.

"Victor has gone back to Knebworth, and his place here is taken
by Beauclerk just returned from his gold-mining adventure in Alaska,
and bringing with his fresh ideas as well as a huge nugget of copper
for me.

"*13th Nov.*— My recent sadness has been deepened by reading
Miss Petre's 'Life of Father Tyrrell,' which at last is out. It is a
record of failure, though intensely interesting — indeed the auto-
biographical part is comparable in its ways to Rousseau's, a real self-
dissection. His failure at Rome is very like mine with Cairo or Constantinople, attempts both of them to make silk purses out of sow's
ears, and reading it has filled me with a double gloom. Up to the
present moment it had been possible for me to feel that I had played
a useful and successful part in the regeneration of Islam. Now I can
no longer feel this. It is too patent to me that Islam will never be regenerated, and that my work of thirty years has been absolutely thrown
away. The Mohammedan religion will of course survive the present
shock for many years, perhaps for many generations. But Islam, as
a political institution and power in the world, has had its death blow,
from which it will not recover. The Ottoman Caliphate will drag out
a crippled existence in Asia, but it will be under European, probably
Russian tutelage, and will be used as an instrument for enslaving what
were once the Ottoman provinces, and will have fallen into Christian
hands. Islam's sole chance now as an independent social existence
will be in the deserts whence it originally sprang, Arabia and North
Africa, and the chance is a poor one at best. At any rate it must be
on lines other than those I have pursued, or of which I can hope even
to see the beginnings.

"*14th Nov.*— I have written to Miss Petre congratulating her upon
her book, an admirable piece of work. Tyrrell's case and my own, as
I said yesterday, have a certain analogy. Not that in either case the
ideals we pursued are false, but rather that the men in whose hands
the issues lay were unworthy and unwise. Thus I have read the

book with a fuller sympathy to-day than would have been the case
two years ago. Apart from this, Tyrrell's account of the Jesuit
system is certainly the most convincing that has been published, and
this was the chief theme of my letter to Miss Petre.

" *17th Nov. (Sunday)*.— I have talked over ' Egypt ' with Ryan, and
persist in my intention to resign my chairmanship of the Committee
and future connection with the paper. Not that the paper has not
been a success on its own lines. On the contrary, it has exercised a
wide influence in Mohammedan lands, if little here. But it is clear that
under the new conditions brought about by the collapse of the Ottoman
Empire, Egyptian patriotism must take a new direction, and I am too
old to begin with a fresh policy. Others may do so without inconsis-
tency; I cannot.

" Belloc dined with us. The Turkish army is still fighting in defence
of the Chatalja lines. But the result of the war will be the same —
the loss of all the European provinces.

" *20th Nov*.— My resignation of the Chairmanship has been notified
to the Egyptian Committee in London, and Rutherford will, I hope,
succeed me. In some ways they will get on better without me, as
my anti-Imperialism is so notorious that it frightens moderate English
Nationalists, and prevents all help being given us in the House of
Commons, even among the Irish. Indeed the Irish parliamentarians
have become more Imperialistic than our own. It is the Fenians and
Sinn Feiners that are pleased with me now, not the men with whom
I worked in 1887; all these have been converted to English Liberalism.
Thus I find myself left a solitary figure, pleading an absolutely lost
cause among Englishmen, that of Conservative Nationalism. All the
rest have gone their ways as Whig Unionists, or Socialistic Interna-
tionalists. I console myself as I can by repeating the line, *Causa
deis placuit victrix sed victa Catoni,* but it does not help me far.

" *22nd Nov.*— I have been reading George Meredith's letters, just
published. They give one the impression of a tender-hearted man
and playful companion, rather than the profound thinker his extreme
admirers would have him to be. His style, jerky and obscure though
it is, is I think the best feature of his prose. His knowledge of
human nature as shown by his novels is quite superficial, a theory of
what life ought to be, not of what life is. His only one great work
is in verse, his ' Modern Love,' and this he drew as a young man
from his own personal experience. The fine ladies in his novels,
with their odd characters, are entirely fanciful. They do not exist
in English, or any other feminine life, yet they have had a considerable
influence on our modern ladies — who like to think themselves as he
represents them. He has certainly had a great deal to do with their
present sex emancipation. Such women, however, as he describes in

his novels are not those who will ever really rule the world, rather the
weak ones. They will never attract the men, and in the marriage
competition will be edged out, pussies who run about continually, but
fail to find corners. To me they are wearisome to read of, because
unreal. These letters show well the narrow limits of Meredith's personal experience. His knowledge of life was three parts of it acquired
at second hand. I am sorry all the same not to have known him better
than I did, for he was clearly one of the best of companions and of
friends.

"*23rd Nov.*— Rothstein and Ryan are here winding up the affairs
of ' Egypt.' The Bulgarian advance on Constantinople seems at a standstill, and it looks very much as if the war had been arranged beforehand with the Powers. . . . I suspect Kiamil Pasha of having pur-
posely left the army in Macedonia unprepared for fighting, so as to
serve English and Russian plans of dismemberment, on a promise of
retaining Constantinople. He is just the man to entertain the idea
of putting the Sultan in the same position of English dependence that
the Khedive had been reduced to at Cairo. It would not suit either
English or Russian plans to have so strong a fighting State as Bulgaria
in possession of the Dardanelles. What Russia principally wants is
to get free passage to the Mediterranean, and what Grey wants is to
please Russia. With a Sultan Caliph in leading strings on the Bosphorus, they would both be able to work their will, Cairo would be
held on a perpetual lease by us, and our Protectorate of the Persian
Gulf be acknowledged."

This, I believe, is exactly what the position was at Constantinople
between our diplomacy there and Kiamil. It was certainly due to him
that the Ottoman army in Macedonia was left only half mobolized
until too late to escape defeat.

"*24th Nov. (Sunday).*— Belloc dined in the evening alone with
me and Ryan, and was most agreeable. I like him better thus than
when he is showing off before a number of people, with noise and fire-
works, which is his usual form in a mixed company. He has just
brought out a new book called ' A Servile State,' whose principles
he expounded to us at the latest counterblast to State Socialism. Rothstein had just given us the socialist side of the democratic case, but
I have given up trying to solve the domestic conundrum of the European future. Things as they are will last my time, and beyond that
who can tell?

"*3rd Dec.*— Our armistice has been agreed to before Constantinople, and the war with Bulgaria is probably over. It is said that the
Sultan is to keep Adrianople, as well as the Marmora coast and the
Dardanelles. If so, things will have been put back exactly to where
they were placed by the treaty of San Stefano in 1878, and it is just

conceivable that the Ottoman Empire may some day recover strength. The best thing about the terms of peace is that there is a prospect now of a Bulgaro-Turkish Alliance, a solution which long ago seemed to me the right one, and which I have more than once discussed with Irene Noel as 'a general Balkan alliance, which should include Turkey.'" [Miss Noel's interest in Balkan politics rested on her intimacy with the King and Queen of Greece, whose views she was well acquainted with. King George of Greece at that time was anxious to form an alliance of all the Balkan States against Austria and Russia, and it was thought might include Turkey.]

"*18th Dec.*— Our final number of 'Egypt' is out. It appears at an opportune moment, for the Peace Conference met in London two days ago, by a strange irony, under Grey's Presidency, the principal causer of the war.

"*24th Dec.*— There is talk to-day of a renewal of the war, and of Shefket Pasha being the Generalissimo (a word which shows that 'Egypt' has been read at Constantinople), also Poincaré at Paris has talked publicly of asserting French rights of intervention in Syria. The chief news, however, is that Hardinge has been wounded by a bomb, dropped into the howdah of his state elephant while he was riding in Viceregal procession to proclaim the new Indian capital at Delhi. This is an event of supreme significance, and ought to be a warning to our people against their alliance with despotic Russia in Asia, but they will not take it so.

"*31st Dec.*— The last day of 1912, a sad year for me, as it has seen the downfall of my larger hopes in the East without bringing any new absorbing interest, also I am growing older and more infirm.

"*10th Jan, 1913.*— The peace negotiations between the Turks and the Bulgarians are hung up, as they will not agree to a frontier line, and there is some chance of the Roumanians intervening. This of course means indirect pressure put on King Ferdinand from Vienna, counteracting the pressure put on the Turks by Grey and the rogues he is allied with at Petersburg and Paris. It is really an all-important point, because if the Bulgarians are to have access to the Sea of Marmora, the Sultan's position at Constantinople will have been turned. The Bulgarians could build a fleet on it and have it at their mercy, so the Turks are right in standing out. It will probably end in their keeping Adrianople and the whole Marmora Coast, in spite of our Foreign Office's bluster. We hope now that 'Egypt' may be continued, if only for the Indian Moslem's sake. Syud Mahmud has written me a most encouraging letter about the influence the paper is having with them.

"*16th Jan.*— The deadlock continues at Constantinople, the Turks refusing to abandon Adrianople, and the Bulgarians being backed up by our Foreign Office and the French and Russian. McCullagh has returned from the war, and gives a bad report of the Turkish military position. It is a case for them, he says, of the devil or the deep sea, of being driven finally out of Europe, or of remaining at Constantinople on terms of slavery to Christendom. They may well prefer to fight, even with every chance against them, but I dare not advise.

"*21st Jan.*— There is a violent attack in last night's ' Pall Mall ' on the Gaekwar of Baroda, insisting on his ' disloyalty to his Sovereign ' at the great Durbar last year — quite true I dare say, as why should it be otherwise? From India I continue to receive messages from Moslems in admiration of ' Egypt ' and praise of my services to Islam in telling them the truth. I wish the paper could be continued for their sake.

"*22nd Jan.*— Lord Ashburnham is dead, a good Sussex nobleman, and long my friend. A year ago his little daughter, whom he had brought up a Catholic, and who was all he had to love, went into a Convent, and with that his life ended. He is succeeded by a childless brother, settled somewhere in the colonies, and, though another branch of the Ashburnhams exists in Sussex, the peerage and the connection of the family with the Stuart fortunes is closed. Ashburnham became a Catholic some thirty years ago through political sentiment, as connecting him more closely with the Stuarts. Through this cause, too, he affected an allegiance to Queen Mary, the Stuart representative, and maintained close relations with Don Carlos and other exiled dynasties, also on that account he was an Irish Nationalist.

"*23rd Jan.*— It is announced from Constantinople that the Grand Council of the Empire has agreed to the cession of Adrianople, as the price of peace and being allowed to live. If this includes a cession of the Marmora coast the Ottoman Caliphate is at an end. Europe will hold it in vassalage to do its Christian bidding, that is to say, the bidding of cosmopolitan finance. I have a letter to-day from John Dillon, lamenting this.

"*24th Jan.*— Great news! There has been another revolution at Constantinople. The traitor Kiamil has resigned, and Mahmud Shefket is named Grand Vizier, with the avowed determination to refuse submission about Adrianople, and, if necessary, renew the war. This is better than I could have hoped, and I have telegraphed to Ryan to come, and we will bring out a special number of ' Egypt.' Our London papers are furious, and, no doubt, Grey will be very angry. It is a rude slap in the face to his diplomacy, and there is talk of all sorts of coercive measures to be taken by the Powers. I rejoice, if only that the Turks have once again recovered their dignity. It will be better for them to lose Constantinople, if that should happen, than to to yield to Grey. Yesterday the posters were, 'Turks yield. Place themselves in the hands of Europe.' To-day it is, 'No surrender, Young Turks in power.' This is the cheerfulest announcement we have had for six months.

"*25th Jan.*— Yet more from Constantinople. Nazim Pasha has been shot while resisting the Revolutionists. He deserved his fate, as he was one of those who brought about the military revolt of last year, which placed Kiamil in power while his conduct of the campaign has been inept. I have telegraphed to Shefket 'Félicitations. Votre heureux retour au pouvoir. Allah Yénsurak!'

"*26th Jan. (Sunday).*—-It turns out that Enver Bey took the lead in bringing about the fall of Kiamil, going himself to the Porte, where one of his aides-de-camp shot Nazim dead in the scuffle, and afterwards to the Palace where he insisted on Shefket's appointment as Vizier. Enver is just the man for the situation, with his experience of the war in Tripoli, and jointly with Shefket may yet renew the campaign at Chatalja. My belief, however, is that pressure will now be put on Bulgaria to yield the point of Adrianople and that things will be settled without more fighting between Turks and Bulgarians. Grey will be angry, but that does not matter. Just now English attention is engrossed with Woman Suffrage and can spare very little for the male affairs of Islam. I have written to Loulou Harcourt, who has been making fun in the House of Grey and Lloyd George on this question, congratulating him and saying, 'I rejoice to see that the principles of the Crabbet Club still live.' [This probably marks the date of the Agreement between Germany and Turkey and the eventual alliance.]

"*1st Feb.*— George Wyndham, writes from London, envying me my happy life away from politics, but why does he grind on? He wants me to come up and stay with him at Belgrave Square. It is stated in the 'National Zeitung' that an agreement had been come to between England and Turkey that Egypt should be given autonomy under English protection. The fall of Kiamil must have put an end to this plan.

"*7th Feb.*— The war has been renewed by the Balkan States and is being well responded to by Mahmud Shefket and Enver Bey who are giving it a frankly religious character. The Mullahs are preaching in the Mosques at Constantinople.

"*9th Feb. (Sunday).*— A violent attack by the Bulgarians is reported at Gallipoli, and a bombardment of Adrianople. If Gallipoli were taken by the Allies it would end the war, for Constantinople would then be at the mercy of any fleet that might choose to threaten a bombardment, but the thing is not done yet.

"*14th Feb.*— A letter from Beauclerk dated 31st January. In it he says 'Bouchier has been this morning with Sir Edward Grey and

Benckendorf and he thinks that war will begin on Monday evening.
. . . The Great Powers want the Allies to exhaust themselves before
stepping in. Germany is sincere in her desire to avert a war and
has her eye on Asia Minor. We will remain on in Egypt and attempt
to annex it. . . . The Turks have been getting in guns and money
recently from Germany.'

"18*th Feb.*— A letter from George Wyndham, four sheets long,
telling of his son Percy's engagement to Ribblesdale's daughter, Diana
Lister. He is much excited about it.

"21*st Feb.*— A black melancholy is on me caused by a sense of my
failure every where in life. My poetry, my Eastern politics, my Arab
horse breeding, were strings to my bow and they have one after another snapped, and to-day looking through my memoirs I perceive how
slackly they are written and how unworthy they are of survival. Yet
the diaries are full of things too important for me to destroy and they
overwhelm me with despair.

"22*nd Feb.*— Syud Mahmud writes from Benares telling me that
the whole Moslem community in India has now adopted my views in
connection with the Turco-Bulgarian War and the complicity of our
Government in the intrigue with Russia against Islam, and I see in
the Reuter's telegrams of to-day that the ferment is beginning to alarm
the Government of India. Syud Mahmud ends thus, ' Your most kind
and pathetic letter has touched me very much and I actually wept.
Your sentence " my long advocacy of Islam has been a complete failure," is most touching as coming from one who has spent the best
years of his life in fighting for Moslems and then this is the conclusion
he arrives at. . . . You say your advocacy has ceased to exercise any
influence even on Mohammedans. I say it has just begun. They now
realize the true meaning of what you told them years ago, because they
are shaking off a bit of their slavishness, developed since the mutiny
of 1857. Your articles in ' Egypt ' are widely read here. They are
translated and reproduced in the vernacular papers. If possible, please
write a long article, a sort of appeal to the Mussulmans, telling them
what they should do in the future. It will greatly influence them.'
This is an unexpected encouragement.

"23*rd Feb.*— Belloc's friend, Cecil Chesterton, is to be prosecuted
for criminal libel in the ' Eye Witness ' by the Samuel family, and
Belloc is a bit uneasy for himself too. He declares that there will
be war this year between France and Germany, in consequence of
Germany's increasing armaments which force the French to call out
one man in three as compared to the German one man in four, and
the French will not stand being conscripted to that amount, they prefer
fighting.

"1*st March.*— Gertrude, Lady Kenmare, is dead, once a considerable

figure in my life, being one of the coterie of ladies, friends of my sister
Alice who were my friends for her sake. I can remember her being
married fifty-two years ago, a beautiful girl, daughter of Lord Charles
Thynne, in 1858. She must have been exactly my own age and had
been at the Roehampton Convent School with Alice. Then, as Lady
Castlerosse, she became one of the beauties of the day, the very first
Englishwoman to dress herself well, indeed extravagantly, at Paris,
and there is much about her in my diaries, then and later, as Lady
Kenmare, but it is many years since I last saw her.

"13th Mar.— Peace seems likely now to be made between Turkey
and her enemies, leaving her Constantinople with a fairly defensible
position for the future, a frontier drawn from the Black Sea to the
Ægean, the whole Marmora coast remaining to Turkey. This is what
I have been contending for. Adrianople itself is of less consequence
and will probably be dismantled as a fortress while ceded to Bulgaria.
If these comparatively good terms have been obtained it has been due
to German intervention, and the restoration of German influence with
Shefket Pasha's return to power at Constantinople. Grey is now on
his knees to Berlin and there are signs that the triple Entente is breaking up. Our Government has probably made up its mind that it will
not, because it cannot, help France in a war with Germany. This
will put off, for a while at least, the Anglo-Russian plan of partitioning
the Ottoman Empire in Asia and annexing Egypt, which may God
forbid !

"19th March.— King George of Greece has been assassinated at
Salonika, fortunately not by a Turk but by one of his own subjects.

"26th March.— Lady Dorothy Neville is dead, a worthy old dame,
at the age of eighty-six, also Lady Cowper and Lord Wolseley. Lady
Dorothy I knew pretty well thirty years ago, a sprightly little lady with
much pleasant Primrose League talk and knowledge of our local Sussex
things ; Lady Cowper, less well, though she was one of the early 'Soul'
group and a friend of all my friends. Lady Dorothy kept her social
flag flying to the last.

"27th March.— Adrianople has at last surrendered to the Bulgarians,
after a five months' siege. The city could not have been kept, but its
resistance has probably saved Constantinople to the Sultan. The Turks
have little to boast of in this campaign.

"2nd April.— Ryan has come down to make up a final number of
'Egypt' to end the series, after which if we get sufficient support we
may continue it as 'The Voice of Islam.' After tea we drove to
Belloc's and found him in high spirits over the cross-examination of
Rufus Isaacs and Lloyd George before the Marconi Committee which
has disclosed the irregularities and equivocations of these two members
of the Government, laid bare mainly by Belloc and Chesterton. They

had gone in for a Stock Exchange gamble a year ago and denied it flatly last summer in the House of Commons and now it turns out to be true."

" *3rd April*.— The terms of peace are at last come to between Turks and Bulgarians with the Enos Midia line of frontier, this saves the situation for the Sultan as it keeps the enemy out of the Sea of Marmora, an essential condition.

" Poor Ryan was taken ill last night, and we had to send for a Horsham doctor, who pronounced it a case of appendicitis and talks of an operation."

I omit my diary of the next days which were wholly occupied for us in the tragedy of poor Ryan's illness, operation, and death, which took place the morning of 7th April, at 8 o'clock. I was with him to the last and he was buried in the Crawley Monastery churchyard on the 9th. On that day I write:

" *9th April*.— All is over. The funeral left our door at half-past one. . . . One thing is certain, it is useless continuing our paper in any form without Ryan, so I have written to Syud Mahmud begging him to stop all subscriptions for the paper, we cannot attempt it.

" The following is a sonnet acrostic I have written to one of the purest of Irish patriotic souls:

' TO FREDERICK RYAN

' Fabric of clay, poor, impotent child's face,
 Ransomed from thought, its load of life laid down !
Earth of all earth, disrobed and passionless,
 Dead mask of a man's brow, which once could frown,
Eyes which could smile, lips which could hold their own
Relentless against wrong in eloquent stress
Indignant at our English ill crop sown,
Curse of the World, its tares of bitterness !
 — Kind Irish soul, free labourer in a field
Rich with rebellion's mint from age to age,
Young ever in revolt, and child-like still !
Are these thy wages then of sword and shield,
Naked to lie and never take thy fill
Of human pleasure, to the end thus sage ? '

" *20th April (Sunday)*.— Rothstein is here for the week end and a Frenchman, Maurice Bourgeois, who holds a travelling fellowship at the Sorbonne, and is getting up as a subject the Irish literary movement, an intelligent young man of the serious University kind, very academical, somewhat priggish, but a good fellow. He and Rothstein have got on very well together, talking Socialism and Continental politics. Belloc came to dinner, and we had a most pleasant evening.

"A woodcock's nest, the first for many years at Newbuildings, was found to-day in Marlpost Wood, the young just flown.

"*30th April.*— George Wyndham was here to-day. Talking of Winston's recent outburst on the Marconi business, he thinks he (Winston) will be Prime Minister one of these days. Grey, however, will have a first claim before him, being by birth a traditional Whig, though very inferior to Winston in ability. We had much talk, too, on family affairs.

"*12th May.*— Winston writes from the train while on his way to join the Admiralty yacht, the *Enchantress,* with his wife and Margot and Asquith and Eddy Marsh at Venice. They are all to cruise together in the Mediterranean during the Whitsuntide holidays.

"*18th May (Sunday).*— Farid Bey has written from Geneva asking me to join his society, *Le Progrès de l'Islam,* and I have taken advantage of it to write a final letter to be read at the Egyptian Congress about to be held there. I think we, with our paper ' Egypt,' may claim to have converted Grey, or at any rate Asquith's Cabinet, from its active hostility to Islam by encouraging the Islam Moslems to show their teeth on the subject. Certain it is that the Foreign Office policy has undergone a change in the last two months. Grey is now working with the German Government for the re-establishment of the Sultan's Asiatic Empire — the project of annexing or proclaiming a Protectorate over Egypt is abandoned, and every attempt is being made to pacify Mohammedan feeling. As a clear sign of this new policy, Sir Gerald Lowther has been recalled from Constantinople, where he had intrigued for the past three years against the Young Turks. I have embodied this in writing to the Society.

"I have been reading Lady Gregory's new Irish comedies. They are altogether excellent. The dialogue has qualities which remind me of ' The Assemblies of Hariri.'

"*23rd May.*— The news from European Turkey is all of quarrels between Bulgarians and Greeks and Servians over a division of the spoils, but in this I take small interest, or in the fate of Albania, where the Moslems have earned their misfortunes. Theirs is a lost cause. At Constantinople an understanding has been come to between Germany and our Government to keep Russia out of the Bosphorus and the Sultan in authority there under a kind of joint control. Anything is better than Grey's policy of the Entente with Russia. It means another twenty or thirty years' life for the Ottoman Empire. In consideration of this Grey has been allowed a Protectorate of the Persian Gulf, and the last news is that Ibn Saoud has occupied El Katíf, and that the Turkish garrison there has been shipped back to Busrah."

This last piece of my Constantinople news, though it unfortunately proved to be less than true, indicates, I believe, ideas then current at the Foreign Office connected with an undoubted attempt being made at that time to smooth down things with the Berlin Government. It seems to have failed through the opposition of the Russian Government to the recognition by England of the full German claim of extending their interest in the Bagdad railway to the Persian Gulf.

"31st May.— Both Farid Bey and Abdul Ghaffar write from Cairo in gratitude for my services to Egypt.

"2nd June.— A good letter from Syud Mahmud at Benares. I have been drafting a letter of advice according to his request to the Indian Moslems, which will also be a farewell message to my Mohammedan friends everywhere. I am glad to see that Kiamil Pasha has been refused permission to remain at Constantinople. It is a great slap in the face for Grey, whose special *protégé* he was, and for Cromer and Kitchener, and all the Cairo gang.

"4th June.— There is news from Constantinople that a treaty has been concluded between England and the Porte guaranteeing the integrity of the Sultan's remaining dominions for forty years. That is still 1953. It sounds improbable, but there is certainly a great effort being made just now at the Foreign Office to regain the friendship of the Moslem world."

All this, alas! proved untrue news, though it doubtless represents a phase in Grey's diplomacy when a better thought for a while prevailed with him, as here suggested, of regaining the friendship of the Moslem world, and at the same time of Germany. But his unfortunate Ententes with France and Russia always prevented an honest understanding. Egypt especially stood in the path of a settlement, and Russia's unwillingness that her partner in Persia should agree to any extension of German influence in Mesopotamia. The peace of the world was practically sacrificed by Grey at this time through his obstinate weakness about Egypt and his bondage at Bagdad to the Czar.

A more terrible tragedy than poor Ryan's death and one which, even more absolutely than that determined me on my retirement from all active work in the great world, was the sudden and entirely unlooked-for death of my dear cousin, George Wyndham, so long the link which bound me closest to it. It was a blow which struck me to the inmost fibres of my heart, bewildering in its unexpectedness, and touching me on every side of my existence.

His last letter, written a few weeks before, had given no hint of any failure of health or of anything but his usual delight in life and his especial joy in his son Percy's marriage. It had been written in acknowledgment of a trifling wedding present I had sent, chosen expressly because I knew that it would be appreciated by George rather than for any other reason. It was a fine old edition of "Ronsard," a folio of 1609, a thing of all others I knew that George would delight in. It is thus he had written: "Your wedding present to Percy is, in fact, a most priceless gift to me. I know and love that 'Ronsard.' Percy has been soldiering with his General all over the south-west of England, so we only met to-day on the eve of his marriage. He had, as I had not, opened the parcel, and will thank you. He proposes to put the 'Ronsard' in my library. . . . These days have been tense. Rosebery, I don't know why, asked me to dinner yesterday week, the 8th April. He felt then that unless the Emperor of Russia could squash the King of Montenegro there might be a mobilization here before Percy's wedding. But those clouds are dispersed, so we have enjoyed the preliminaries of Percy's nuptials. We had a display of gifts at Ribblesdale's house this afternoon, and a dinner of both families at Grosvenor House this evening. We all feel that politics are a bore, and should be quitted by honest men, and that soldiers are menaced. So, as you won't come to Clouds, *we* (by which I mean Percy, Diana, and myself) hope in the interval of peace to invade you at Newbuildings in the course of the summer. I would like you to see Percy and Diana in the prime of their mating. It is just possible that they have hit off an alliance of heroic love, combined with matrimony. If this should prove to be so they are lucky. In any case they are happy to exorbitance for the moment. For the moment they are lovers, and they ought to visit your shrine and lay a wreath at the feet of Proteus. As a rule, people do not know how to love; as an exception, they love now here, now there; as a rarity, almighty lovers find each other after both are married. It is extravagant to suppose that Percy and Diana are going to be lovers and also husband and wife, but it is pleasant to contemplate the hypothesis. In any case I ought to take them in their youth and delight to see you. Your affectionate, G. W."

It is impossible for me to tell here all that George was to me and what I lost by his death. He was my nearest male relation, and very much my nearest friend. I had looked upon him as the inheritor after me of our family traditions, and in some measure of my family possessions as trustee and knowing all. No thought had ever crossed my mind that I could have the misfortune to survive him. Although on politics we were a whole world apart, on all things else we were in perfect unison of thought and taste and literary sympathy. I find this in my diary:

"10*th June.*— I have thought of nothing else to-day but George. Only yesterday, before I knew of his death, I had taken down from its shelf his little book on Ronsard, and had begun reading it again. The preface is one of the most brilliant pieces of writing I know and the

translations in verse are admirable. His poetry belonged to his hidden
life, of which I knew more than the rest of his friends.   In nearly his
last letter to me, when writing to announce his son Percy's marriage,
he says: 'I write at once to you because you and one other are near
to me in all that really touches my life.   I am determined to be your
guest with luck when the birds are in chorus, and in any case when the
wild roses bloom. You are fortunate. To select and print poetry
seems to me — after influenza in a dark drizzle damned to the hell
of politics — an inconceivable extravagance of joy.   Now if this world
was made for joy (if it was not made our revolt should be for joy),
you are accomplishing the design of the great artificer; or else (if he
never was) helping to fill the gap of his non-existence; but I, good
lack! am a member of Parliament! I mean, however, to escape and
to get you to London to see pictures and plays, or to go to you to
hear the birds and see the blossoms.' And here is June and he is
dead!"

CHAPTER XII

THE WAR WITH GERMANY DECLARED

From this point my diary contains little that is of historical importance till the breaking out, a year later, of the Great War of 1914. With George Wyndham's death my most intimate connection with the parliamentary world ceased, and my mind busied itself more and more with its local surroundings and with that refuge from sadness, verse, which has always been its consolation. I therefore end my transcriptions in their integrity here, and add only to the present volume such few extracts as may suffice to carry my record of public events to the verge of the final catastrophe, reserving a full account of the war itself to yet a third part, still perhaps to come.

To complete my record of the crisis which decided Turkish patriotism to take definite part with Germany rather than with the Entente Powers in the coming struggle I will continue to tell it in as few words as possible.

My latest entries of 1913 show that about the time of George Wyndham's death I had satisfied myself that Grey was beginning to see the danger of his coalition policy against the Central Powers, and was beginning to look round him for a means of conciliating its War Lord, Kaiser Wilhelm, in whom the maintenance of peace chiefly lay. These were the days of Lichnowsky's Embassy in London a mission which undoubtedly was intended at Berlin to smooth the diplomatic wheels with us. Lichnowsky was a quite honourable man and personally friendly to England, but I notice that in all our English appreciations of him as such he is invariably claimed as an exception among *Germans* for this or that good quality, an enemy witness giving testimony in our favour. This is to exaggerate and mistake the case. Prince Lichnowsky, a Polish nobleman of ancient family, though in the German diplomatic service, was no German either by birth or sentiment, and his friendly feeling for England was that common to all the Polish aristocracy, and it was for that reason, as also to conciliate his fellow Poles, that the Kaiser Wilhelm sent him to London on a friendly mission which he undertook *con amore*. I see no reason for doubting that Wilhelm, at that moment, was sincere in wishing to keep on terms with England. In 1913 he had made up his mind to bring matters to an issue with France on the very next opportunity rather than submit to any new rebuff, such as he had sustained at Agadir, but it was certainly no part of his plan to have England on his hands again as well as France and Russia. It is altogether improbable that he was seeking a quarrel just then with us, whatever he might dream as to an eventual trial of strength with us at sea.

It is, I believe, quite a mistake to suppose Kaiser Wilhelm otherwise than personally well inclined to England. He liked English society, and his summer visits to Cowes more than anything he could find on the Continent, and he enjoyed being adulated by our aristocracy. He had far rather have had England with him than against him; but he resented our Foreign Office having allied itself with his two most dangerous enemies, Russia on his eastern, France on his western, frontier. Nor, in my opinion, was the resentment unjustified. Our policy of helping the Russian Czar financially after his defeat by the Japanese, and so enabling the Czar to renew his military strength, seemed to Wilhelm a gratuitous menace as obliging him to increase his own army on that side, while our Entente about Persia seemed a menace to the development of his commercial plans connected with the Bagdad railway. Nor, doubtless, was it unknown to him that part of our plan was that Russia should be put in possession of Constantinople, and thus permanently block for Germany her trade route eastwards. All this added to our support of France in Morocco, was resented at Berlin, and as I have said, not without reasonable cause.

This, however, is not the same thing as saying that a war between England and Germany was inevitable sooner or later through the Kaiser Wilhelm's designs against us. I am convinced that even so late as June 1913 not only our own peace, but the peace of Europe might have been saved for an undefined period had we then found a statesman at the Foreign Office possessed as Grey was of the ear of the House of Commons, but with better knowledge of Europe and of the true needs of our Eastern Empire, and with the courage of acting on his knowledge. Such a one might have insisted on a withdrawal from the false position we had taken in Egypt and at Constantinople through our ill-omened Ententes with France and Russia, chief enemies, both of them, of Germany, and also of that Mohammedan world with which we were so closely connected in India, and so have averted all that happened to ourselves and others. The gain, if it had only been of a few years longer peace between France and Germany, would have given time for the socialistic forces in either country to gather strength, and if it had been openly known that England would take no part in it, France certainly would not have invited war for Alsace-Lorraine or given that excuse to Germany by making Russia's quarrel with Austria her own over so small a wrong as Servia's.

For, be it understood, the Great War which has destroyed all Europe and half destroyed ourselves, was essentially in its origin an Eastern, not a Western War, and the inclusion in it of Turkey to its immense prolongation was due to our blundering diplomacy at Constantinople. Had England been reasonably ambassadored there and free in her dealings with the Porte from the evil counsels of her sad confederate the Czar, it is impossible she should have failed to retain the Ottoman goodwill, once so strong for her and even as lately as the days of the revolution of 1908. But Egypt always had forbidden. The obstinacy of remaining on in occupation there in spite of right and law and promises, and now the Russian partnership, which regarded the dispute in the Balkans with Russian eyes and the dismemberment of Turkey as a crusade — these were the true obstacles to peace. That Grey was beginning in the early summer of 1913, as I have said, to suspect the danger of general war to which his policy of Entente was leading in the East there are several indications, and I give here a single entry from my diary, the last of importance of that year:

"11*th June.*— H. arrived, bringing the ill news of Shefket Pasha's assassination at Constantinople. This is, doubtless, the result of the Russian intrigue there, Shefket being head of the Young Turk Party, and the most capable military leader of the Independent Ottoman policy allied with Germany. How far our diplomacy is responsible for the deed I cannot say. Grey seems of late to have withdrawn from his Russian Alliance, but Fitzmaurice's influence is probably still supreme at our Embassy, and one cannot help remembering that the intrigue of a year ago which caused Shefket's resignation of the Ministry of War and replaced Kiamil in power, was an Anglo-Russian intrigue, also that it closely preluded the Balkan war. I connect the present assassination with Kiamil's return the other day to Constantinople. Kiamil arrived there suddenly, and though allowed to land, was kept by Shefket, a prisoner in his own house, till he could be shipped back to Smyrna, whence he had come. This new *coup d'état* would seem to synchronize with the re-opening of the war in the Balkans, Russia's object being, as always, to prevent any settlement of the Turkish question which should keep her fleet permanently out of the Mediterranean. This may be the first move in it. H —, who has just come from Paris, declares that people there all believe in the imminence for them of an European War."

The assassination of Shefket Pasha here recorded proved a great misfortune for the chances of that peaceful period which I was hoping for for the Caliphate, in order to give the Young Turk's régime at Constantinople time to consolidate its administration and effect its reforms on a basis of Liberal pan-Islamism, which I had come to see was the only possible one for an Empire so divided in race and speech as was the Ottoman, and where the bond of nationality had for so many centuries been replaced by those of religion, the largest section of the population being Mohammedan. Religion was the only strong sentiment, at any rate, which could re-establish Turkey as a virile community able to defend itself against its many enemies, and everything else was secondary to that. It was the true reason why, when it came to a choice between alliance with Kaiser Wilhelm and trust in English goodwill, Young Turkey necessarily chose the first. Grey, with Russia prompting him, had nothing better to propose than disarmament and economy in an emasculated State sterilized of all religious ardour. This the Young Turks saw could only prove slow death to them, while alliance with Germany, a military Power which offered to reconstruct their army for them and restock their arsenals, gave them at least a chance of new national life. All the patriotic Turks whom I came in contact with gave me this account of it. The German Government, they said, does not seek our dismemberment, it wishes us to be strong. What it wants of us is not political but commercial advantage, whereas Russia wants political possession of our provinces, while you at the English Embassy, so far as you wish us good, wish it for the Christian section of our people only. And this was true. Our Embassy at Constantinople in Lowther's day had been, and still was in 1913, under the influence of Fitzmaurice, the Embassy chief dragoman who saw things through the spectacles of the Christian Missionary Societies, as did such of our Radicals in Parliament as took an interest in Turkey. Grey's Eastern policy, the Young Turks perfectly understood, was before all else an anti-Islamic policy, and this struck at their one surviving element of strength. They preferred to trust Kaiser Wilhelm's pagan attitude, and his promise of protecting Islam, made on his Syrian tour, and more than once renewed. What was a special misfortune in Shefket's death was that he, unlike Talaat Pasha, who succeeded him as Vizier, was a sincere Moslem of the Liberal school which understood the necessity of uniting all the Ottoman forces in a common pan-Islamic patriotism. He was their most capable soldier, too, and his loss universally ascribed to the Anglo-Russian party acting under Kiamil, England's *protégé,* though it did not result in Kiamil's recapture of the Vizierate, placed sole power with those who by their racial arrogance had driven Arabia into rebellion against the Sultan. I do not, of course, suppose that our Embassy was cognizant of the design to assassinate Shefket. Crimes of this sort are outside the range of English diplomatic activities. But the plot to restore Kiamil was probably known, while a much larger responsibility may have lain with the Russian Embassy. The curse of Grey's policy of Entente with the Czar in Asiatic affairs is, that it involved us in practices of violence foreign to our English traditions.

Moreover Grey, as recorded in my Diary, was at that time becoming aware of the danger, and was seeking to relax his solidarity with Russia's action in the East, and to get on less hostile terms with Berlin in the West. These were the days when an attempt was being made to settle the Bagdad railway quarrel with Germany. It failed through this very cause, the objection of Russia to our recognizing any extension of German rights in that direction as likely to prejudice extensions of her own 'sphere of influence' in Persia — this and, in our dealings with the Porte, our insistence on remaining in Egypt.

My Diary contains nothing more of importance during that year. I continued to receive letters from India, telling me of Moslem gratitude for my work in placing the true nature of Grey's anti-Islamic policy before them, and assuring me of its success in counteracting the officially inspired utterances of the Agha-Khan on the subject, and asking me for advice as to the attitude they should assume, and this led me to write a long letter to one of them, the concluding paragraphs of which, as it had a wide circulation in the Mussulman community, I may print here. My concluding words were as follows, dated 28th July, 1913:

"The duty of the Mohammedan community of India, therefore, under the circumstances, seems to me to be pretty clearly marked out. As regards Persia, Afghanistan, and the still independent provinces of the Ottoman Caliphate menaced by Christendom, a courageous public attitude should be adopted, which should let our Government clearly understand that Indian sympathy with these is so strong that it will not permit any further participation by England in attacks made on them, and that none such can be indulged in without the certainty of incurring the dangerous resentment of every Moslem subject of the King. Let there, when complicity in these attacks is suspected, be no hesitation in denouncing it. Let there be no such milk-and-water appeals to the Government's better feeling as allowed Sir Edward Grey two years ago to treat the All India Moslem League with contempt when he made himself the accomplice of France and Italy in their invasions of Morocco and Tripoli, but plain language of the most indignant kind, worthy of the force of 80,000,000 Moslems behind it, and which it represents. In this way only can their duty to their co-religionists outside India be performed effectively.

"Besides this, they have another duty to themselves within the borders of the Indian Empire, taking an active part in that of preparing for the great changes which are most surely coming there, as throughout all Asia. You know that from the very beginning of the Congress movement in 1884, I urged on the Indian Moslems that they should take part in it with the Hindoos, and I am therefore rejoiced to-day to learn that it has at last been decided that the policy of abstention recommended in opposition to my advice by the late Seyd Ahmed of Aligarh, and so long followed, should cease. Much ground has been lost, I fear, by this long period of inaction, but it is ground that can be recovered, and I trust now to see the Mohammedan body taking its full share in the movement for self-government. What it is necessary to insist on is the danger of delay. Time needs to be taken by the forelock, lest while you are waiting the British Empire should collapse prematurely, and find the machinery of a native administration which is to replace it not yet ready for its work. This would be a great misfortune. Indeed, I will go so far as to say that in Mohammedan interests the imperial connection between England and India should be prolonged rather than shortened, and in this sense the Moslem subjects of King George may well continue to display their loyalty. It is another thing, however, to be what is called loyal to the existing régime of the Anglo-Indian Civil Service. The servile attitude of helping this alien body to maintain itself in place and power against all native effort at self-government is neither dignified nor profitable, and will not in reality serve the interests even of the Empire, for nothing is more certain than that the only way in which the English connection with India can be placed on a basis of any permanence is, by obtaining the consent of the Indian peoples, and their active zeal in administering their country under its imperial shield. As self-governing Colonies the provinces of British India might survive many a shock under which the Indian Empire, as now administered, must certainly succumb.

"My present motto, therefore, for Indian patriotism, Mohammedan and Hindoo alike, would be 'Loyalty to the Imperial Crown but insistence on self-government under it.' And these are, in all probability, the last words of advice on Eastern matters I shall presume to utter in any public form. If you should think them worthy of a wider consideration than that of just yourself or your personal friends, you are at liberty to publish them, but that point I leave to yourselves to judge. And so may God prosper you and hasten the day of Islamic and Asiatic independence."

This letter, part of which was published in India, was instrumental, to a large measure, in causing the resignation which took place in November, of the Agha Khan, my principal opponent, of his position in the All Moslem League of India, an event which synchronized with an apology made at home by Grey on the shortcomings of his Eastern diplomacy. A short entry of that date, says: "The truth is, no foreign policy ever more completely failed. My work has been to put all the dots upon the i's in a way that has convinced Mohammedan India that the Agha Khan and Ameer Ali, who have been preaching loyalty to the British Empire, are blind guides leading to an impotent result."

Again, two months later, I find myself writing to the "Westminster Gazette," warning our English peace lovers of the futility of their trust in the so-called " Concert of Europe," armed to the teeth, under Grey's un-armed leadership, in preventing the coming European war. It was my last appearance in print, and I have remained silent since, notwithstanding solicitations to speak not a few times during these astonishing five years of fighting folly, and white man's suicide, knowing I should be powerless while the war fever lasted, to obtain a hearing for a word of truth in a world of illusion befooled, but happy in its patriotic blindness.

The year 1913 closes with this personal lament: " I am alone just now here and in this dark world I am overwhelmed with woe. I see myself as one sees the dead, a thing finished which has lost all its importance, whatever it once had in the world. I realize how little I have accomplished, how little I have affected the thought of my generation in spite, as I am still convinced, of the soundness of my view of things, and of some skill and courage in expounding it. I have made almost no converts in Europe, and am without a single disciple at home to continue my teaching after I am dead. Even in the East, though my ideas are bearing fruit and will one day be justified in act, I have founded no personal school where my name has authority. The consciousness that it is so wounds me with a sense of failure and I despise myself the more for feeling it as strongly as I do. Why should I mind? I ask myself, and I find no answer. Perhaps the immediate cause of my gloom has been a life of Gobineau which has been sent me by a Dr. Schemann. Gobineau was in some ways like myself, a man of ideas opposed to those of his own people and his own generation, and who, though his talent was recognized as a writer, failed to find disciples in France. He was an aristocrat in a democratic age, an orientalist, out of harmony with received orientalist ideas, a poet who was never popular, and an artist who was never more than an amateur. It has been reserved for this little group of Germans to discover his value twenty and more years after his death, a discovery due mainly to the devotion of a single disciple, this good Schemann who has sent his book to me. Gobineau, like me, had his romantic side. There are many pieces of poetry inserted in their original French in it, of one of which I made a translation this morning. It is called " Don Juan's Good Night," a pleasant piece of cynical French wit which deserves to live, perhaps, when the rest is forgotten.

The Spring of the year 1914 found me, like the rest of our English world, thinking more of Ireland than of the coming Armageddon. Some of the vicissitudes of the Irish case are noted in my diary:

" *28th March,* 1914.— There has been an astonishing crisis in Parliament over the Ulster business. What has happened is this. Winston and Seely, at the Admiralty and War Office respectively, seem to have made up their minds to deal drastically with the Ulster Volunteers, and arranged a combined movement of sea and land forces to put them down. Of course, it ought to have been done a year ago, but Redmond persuaded Birrell that the Ulster movement was all bounce and it was allowed to go on. Now it has got beyond them and has been taken up on a large scale by English Unionists, and worked up by the London press and in the army by old Lord Roberts, and at last they got King George to approve, so it came to pass that the garrison at the Curragh refused to move when ordered to Belfast without a guarantee that they should not be used against the Orange volunteers. This frightened the two Ministers. Seely patched up things by giving the assurance wanted, and Winston counter-ordered the warships he was sending to Belfast, whereupon a hullabaloo in the House of Commons and a Cabinet crisis with the usual lying and denying, which ended in Seely's offering to resign as scape-goat for the rest, and Asquith refusing to accept his resignation, a little comedy played on much the same lines as that used in the Marconi crisis, Seely admitting an error of judgment and Winston using swear words to cover their retreat.

" 31st March.— Asquith appoints himself War Minister in Seely's place.

" 5th April.— Belloc was here to dinner. Baker, one of Asquith's private secretaries, has just explained to him the recent Ulster crisis. The resolution to send troops in force to Belfast was agreed to by the whole Cabinet, who also agreed to the letter which was to be written to General Gough, and they had just dispersed, leaving Seely behind them with Morley, when Gough's letter arrived. Seely saw at once that it meant that something more than the draft agreed to would be needed to get Gough's assent, and he added some words, pledging the Government not to employ the troops actively against Ulster, and Morley only half understanding what it was all about, agreed to the addition. All then would have gone well but for Gough's boasting of having coerced the Government. Belloc's view is that Asquith allowed the arming in Ulster to go on as a way of putting pressure on Redmond to give in politically and allow a separate Ulster while for the same reason he won't allow Catholic Ireland to be armed.

" 7th April.— The Irish Home Rule Bill has passed its second and final reading by a majority of eighty. This is due to Redmond's insistence, for Asquith, Grey, Haldane and the rest of the Whigs in the Cabinet have been quite ready to throw the Bill over in favour of some scheme of all-round Devolution, any time since they came into office.

" 26th April (Sunday).— I am writing a letter in answer to one sent me from Dublin by Mrs. Colum, asking me to say a word in favour of a plan of arming Catholic Ireland as a counter demonstration against

the arming of Protestant Ulster, and as a precaution against a possible
betrayal of Home Rule by Asquith.

"It is announced that the United States Fleet has landed troops at
Vera Cruz in Mexico, President Wilson at the same time declaring,
in imitation of Gladstone when he sent troops to Egypt, that he is not
making war with the Mexican Republic, but with a person named
Huerta, who calls himself President of Mexico. Rothstein, whom I
saw yesterday, attributes this to Wilson's *naïveté,* which believes it
possible to reconcile moral principles of Government with the rascalities
of financial politics.

"*30th April.*— My answer to Mrs. Colum is this:

"'Thank you for the Volunteer Manifesto. You know I have always been a Fenian in my sympathies, and, though it is twenty-five
years since I was in Ireland and I am living now quite away from
politics, I confess it rouses me to hear talk again of physical force. I
never believed much in the Union of Hearts without a reserve of the
other, and a long experience of British Imperial ways has taught me
(if I may be allowed the bull) that in dealing with British Governments, the best sort of moral force is always material force. Our people cannot be trusted to go straight without two strong incentives, money
in front of them (like the carrot in front of ·an ass) and a big stick
behind. The Irish National Volunteers must be the big stick.

"'I am not sure whether it will not prove a useful reminder to
your own parliamentary people. Some of them have been talking a
deal of Imperial nonsense lately, and it is time they should remember
that until the Irish Parliament is actually open in College Green, the
British Empire is still *the enemy.* I send you £10 for your Defence
of Ireland Fund, as a small token of my sympathy and a proof that I
remain true to the old motto, "Ireland a nation and as much and
well armed a nation as you can make it.'"

"*14th May.*— Sir Roger Casement came to lunch and to talk over the
Volunteer movement in Ireland, of which he is one of the chief organizers. He had seen my letter to Mrs. Colum, which it appears was
published in a Dublin newspaper, and wished to consult me. He is an
interesting man of the same Irish type as was Michael Davitt, only
much bigger and better looking, still very like him; an Ulsterman, he
tells me, and a Protestant, but his mother was a Catholic, and he now
is of no religious complexion, only a strong Nationalist. He is not in
favour with Redmond, who considers him a dangerous revolutionist,
being anti-imperialist, and opposed to the Parliamentary alliance with
the English Radicals. He holds Dillon greatly responsible for this,
and and that it is demoralizing Irish patriotism. Hence his zeal for
the Volunteer movement. He considers that unless the rest of Ireland
arms itself as the north-west of Ulster is arming it will be cheated out

of Home Rule. There are two difficulties in their way, the first is a lack of money; they have no rich men to help, and secondly, a lack of officers. Of men there are plenty, ex-soldiers of the British Army, but they are unarmed, and the question is how to get the arms. He believes if they could obtain only 5,000 rifles they would be in a position to coerce the Government. He is working in conjunction with Professor McNeill and has to be back in Dublin on Saturday. He told us also a good deal about his Congo experiences and in South America, and described a talk he had had with King Leopold of Belgium, who had tried to get hold of him when he was first appointed Consul on the Congo, and of how old Leopold had managed even to shock Rhodes by the crudity of his ideas of native exploitation. In describing his interview with Leopold he told how the old king in tempting him had watched him the the whole time through his fingers, shading his face with his hand. On the whole, Casement's statement of the Irish case does not sound to me very encouraging. The want of funds will prevent any great effect being given to the Volunteer movement in the South, where they have nobody like Lord Londonderry in the north to subscribe the thousands needed, nor will the American-Irish help. These take their view of Irish affairs entirely from Redmond and the Parliamentary party, and until these last declare themselves in favour of it, money will not be subscribed. Also, and this seems to me the most serious side of it, the movement is more one of the towns than of the country. All the same I wish it well, and if anyone can manage it, Casement seems to be the man. He is well bred, well educated, altogether vigorous, and a good talker."

It is worth noting that in this entry of my conversation with Casement there is no mention of anything connected with Berlin or European politics, nor I am sure, was there anything suggesting that his mind was in that direction. During the following few weeks I received three letters from him (see Appendix VI) which treat entirely of Irish affairs. The only thing omitted in the diary that I can recollect was that we discussed Mrs. O'Shea's revelations just then being printed in one of the London papers. Casement's remark about it was that if the revelations had been made two years ago there would have been no statue of Parnell to-day in the streets of Dublin.

" 16th May.— Patrick Butler came for the day, being on leave from Clonmel. We talked about the National Volunteer movement, with which he is entirely in sympathy. Butler, however, is alone in his opinion at the Curragh among the officers there, and says that the army will not act against the Ulstermen, while it will certainly act against the National Volunteers. He also says that the three Protestant counties of Ulster would accept the Emperor William as their king rather than obey the Dublin Parliament. He is for giving them a separate status, with a Parliament and an executive of their own, 'like the Isle of Man,' I suggested. That perhaps would be best. In the meanwhile he was emphatic on the evil being done to the Catholic Irish by the English garrison. He says that it is no longer the case that the women refuse to have to do with the English soldiers. On the contrary, it is becoming as bad in Ireland and worse than in English garrison towns, *corruptio optimi pessima,* the whole country is being demoralized, especially by the cheap English papers, with their indecent illustrations. These the country girls get hold of, for they are sold at every railway station, and read in secret, sitting under hedges, in spite of the prohibition of the priests, and so go the way of prostitution. He says it is worse in Dublin far than in London, girls beginning there at fifteen and sixteen in the streets. Drink and gambling are destroying the country side. We talked about the O'Shea revelations. Everybody is reading them all over Ireland.

" *17th May (Sunday).*— Belloc to dinner. He tells me it is now certain that Asquith connived all through at the arming of the Ulster Protestants in order to get out of his agreement with Redmond for National Home Rule. Asquith has always been in favour of Federal Devolution for Scotland and Wales as well as Ireland. Now he will deprive the Home Rule Bill of what little autonomy it gives by an amending Bill voted in conjunction with the Tories.

" *22nd May.*— Dillon writes asking my opinion of Mrs. O'Shea's book. He says about the situation in Ireland: 'I am strongly in favour of the Volunteer movement, but it is playing with fire, and unless it is kept under reliable control it might at any moment utterly ruin the national movement and repeat the disasters of 1798. We are getting a very exciting, strenuous time here (the House of Commons), but I think we shall pull through successfully. The forces against us are terrible, and a Radical Government is always weak and timorous.'

" *26th May.*— The Irish Home Rule Bill has passed its final reading in the House of Commons by a majority of seventy-seven, but without enthusiasm, as it is threatened with an amending Bill depriving it of its entire efficacy by giving a full status to the Protestant counties of Ulster, and so nobody is pleased.

" *28th May.*— Mrs. Padriac Colum writes me a long letter about the Volunteer movement in Ireland and upon the great effect my letter has had on it. Casement also writes at great length, and the movement, according to both, is assuming large dimensions.

" *11th June.*— About the Volunteer business, which has taken a prodigious start since I first heard of it a month ago, Dillon says: ' The Volunteer business is a VERY serious one. Sir Roger Casement is, I have no doubt, an excellent and able man, but he knows no more of Irish politics than I do of the Congo, and Irish politics are no more safe for amateur idealists to play about in than a powder magazine for children.'

" *20th June.*— Dillon arrived for the week end, and we sat up till past midnight talking. He told me many interesting things. He and Redmond were in great alarm at the Curragh fiasco, which he says was grossly mismanaged through the fault principally of General Paget. Dillon believes that if the men at the Curragh had been simply ordered to Belfast to preserve order without any explanation or inquiry whether they were willing they would have obeyed, but the thing was terribly bungled. He was surprised at what I told him of Butler being the only officer at the Curragh who was not disaffected to the Government. It was the Curragh incident that convinced him that the National Volunteers should be openly supported, for it was beginning to be thought that nobody in Ireland cared any longer for Home Rule. Indeed, the vehemence of the feeling in connection with the volunteering had surprised him. Now the Parliamentary party have regained all their authority both in Ireland and America. All the same it was a dangerous game they were playing — arming the whole country.

" *21st June (Sunday).*— Drove with Dillon to Judge Mackarness's at Steyning, where we found Sir Henry Cotton, Lajpat Rai and Gupta, all these being friendly to Home Rule. Dillon gave us his views at length. I had a long talk with him later about Ireland. He does not think the Volunteer movement will lead to civil war, though there is always danger of local riots. On the contrary, he thinks that both sides being armed will inspire mutual respect. We talked, too, about religion, *à propos* of his son's education. His eldest boy, who is eighteen, has just left Downside, and he is sending him to the new Catholic University at Dublin. The boy had learned nothing at Downside except to write good English, and he was unhappy there, being an ardent Home Ruler with all the other boys opposed to him. Politics was all he cared about. Dillon has always been against clerical interference with politics, especially Vatican interference, and succeeded in getting the new University put under lay management. This has made the Jesuits very hostile to him, and they spare no occasion of doing him an ill-turn. He is convinced they are the ruin of every political cause they favour, and have always been blunderers in public affairs.

" *25th June.*— A new expedition is projected in Somaliland. A force is to be raised at Nairobi to start at the end of the summer. It is to pass from Nairobi through Abyssinia, or Italian territory, and another expedition at the same time from Berbera, a punitive affair to avenge the death of one Corfield, killed last winter by a band of Somalis in Abyssinia."

At last we come to the first premonitory thunderclap of the European storm.

"*30th June.*— There has been another assassination, this time of the heir of the Austrian Emperor. I do not quite know how it affects the political situation.

"*20th July.*— The 'Times' to-day announces that the King has invited eight leading politicians to a conference on Ireland — Asquith, Lloyd George, Lansdowne, Bonar Law, Redmond, Dillon, Carson, and Craig. This is a quite new departure, a move probably of the King in conjunction with the Whig section of the Cabinet — Grey, Haldane, and Winston — and agreed to by Asquith. I do not expect any great result from it one way or other, as neither the Nationalists nor the Ulster people are prepared to give in.

"*22nd July.*— Margaret Sackville came down unexpectedly, bringing with her Ramsay Macdonald, leader of the Labour Party in Parliament, who had expressed a wish to make my acquaintance. I found him intelligent and reasonable, with many ideas in common with mine, especially on India, which he has just been perambulating as member of the Commission of Inquiry into the Civil Service, and sufficiently anti-Imperialist. He is a man of forty-five or fifty, and talks with a slight Scotch accent. He told us some amusing stories of his Indian tour. I had a thorough talk with him about the situation in Ireland, and gave him as my advice to have nothing to do with the attempt to compromise on the Ulster question —'Let the Ulstermen do their damnedest and get the Government to arm the National Volunteers.' He said he believed that if the Conference at the Palace broke down, which it probably will, the Government would enrol the Volunteers as a Government force, and arm them and use them to keep order if the Ulstermen broke it. He told me he had been approached about having an invitation as Leader of the Labour Party to the Conference, but had not encouraged the idea. He does not think the King will refuse his consent to the Home Rule Bill if the Amendment Bill is thrown out. If there is a dissolution in October the Liberals will fail to get a majority. He has no high opinion of Grey's intelligence, but considers him sure of Asquith's succession, as he has a great hold over Liberals in the House of Commons. If Grey were to leave the Government on the Ulster question, the Liberal party would be split in two, while it would not matter if Winston resigned; Grey was indispensable. Of Lloyd George he has a mean opinion, a very high one of Dillon. I asked him whether if the democracy really got into power in England the Labour party and the Socialists would continue to be anti-Imperialist. He said: 'I think they would, but I understand your doubt.'

"*24th July.*— The Conference at Buckingham Palace has failed.

A much more important matter is an ultimatum addressed by the Austrian Government to Servia, which may very likely lead to real war between Austria and Russia.

"26th July (Sunday).— The quarrel between Austria and Servia seems certain now to result in war, and war with Russia. Belloc dined with us. He says Germany is afraid of war, but I am inclined to think it is pushing it on, the occasion being a convenient one, especially in view of our Irish difficulties.

"27th July.— To-day's papers are sensational. War seems to have begun on the Danube, and there has been rioting in Dublin, with firing on the mob and a bayonet charge, with two or three people killed and many wounded. This will bring things to a head and oblige Asquith to allow the arming of the National Volunteers if he does not throw up his cards and resign. This is an astonishing show of weakness and mismanagement. I see the Labour members are threatening a revolt from Asquith and a hundred Liberals as well if he does not withdraw the Amendment Bill and keep the Army in order.

"28th July.— The riot in Dublin has, I think, improved Home Rule prospects, showing that there is at least as much danger of trouble in disappointing the National hopes as in displeasing the Ulstermen.

"As to the larger matter of war abroad Grey has come forward amid a flourish of trumpets in the press to offer his little remedy of a conference of Ambassadors in London. But it is not likely to be more effective than his interventions of a year and two years ago. It will only make our diplomacy still more ridiculous. Belloc, however, thinks Germany is afraid of fighting, being unprepared for war. My view is that it is Russia that is unprepared, and that the fatal year 1913 having passed by, Kaiser Wilhelm thinks he may try his luck at last, and means to stand his ground with Austria against the Franco-Russian Entente, England being practically negligible just now."

[This allusion to the fatal year 1913 refers to the prediction made in 1871 to Kaiser Wilhelm's grandfather, Wilhelm, the first Emperor, that in 1913 would see the downfall of the Hohenzollerns. It was made to him by a gipsy, but, unlike such gipsy predictions, was based upon the mathematical calculation in which the letters of the Emperor's name were represented by figures which worked out very exactly at 1913. I remember hearing several years before the war that Kaiser Wilhelm was so deeply impressed by it that he would not dare fight with France till the date was over.]

"29th July.— It is announced that Austria has declared formal war on Servia; the question is now whether Russia will join in. There is every probability she will, as it is a question of predominance in the Balkans between the two Empires and the two religions, Catholic and Orthodox, and this will bring in Germany, and Germany will bring in France. There is wild excitement in London, and people are beginning to talk of England's fulfilling her promises to France, but I do not believe in this, or in there being any definite promises. It would be too stupid even for Grey.

" *30th July.*— The crisis is worse than ever, with panic on all the Stock Exchanges of Europe and our own. Advantage is being taken of it to defer any settlement of the Irish question on the ground that all parties are of one patriotic mind, Irish as well as English, towards events abroad. This is of course absurd, but so long as the King puts his signature to the Home Rule Bill, the rest will not matter. The first shots have been fired in Servia.

" *31st July.*— The ' Times ' to-day has a special article in largest print recommending England to go to war in aid of France against Germany, but I do not believe in any such folly. Belgrade has been bombarded, and it is all but certain now there will be general European war, but not for us. Belloc and I differ in this. He is convinced that France is stronger than Germany. I am not. He talks of Germany as calling out to our Foreign Office to mediate. I believe Germany means war, and is rejecting Grey's foolish intervention.

" *1st Aug.*— There is a general panic, the London Stock Exchange closed, and the Bank rate raised to 8 per cent. Germany has sent ultimatums both to Russia and to France; general war is certain, but the ' Times ' has a letter from Norman Angell in large print to-day contradictory of its yesterday's article. The ' Nation ' and all the Liberal papers denounce the idea of war, and I cannot believe we shall be such fools as to take part in it if we are not attacked. Italy is proclaiming neutrality; we shall do the same.

" *2nd Aug. (Sunday).*—Belloc dined with us again to-night, and we had another great argument, whether to join in the war or not. Belloc is for it, I against. He looks upon Prussia as a ' nation of atheists,' who, if they beat the French, will destroy Christianity, whereas if the French beat them, ' Prussia would be hamstrung.' Russia, he thinks, will never be a danger to Western Europe. If we do not side with France now we shall be left without a friend. England will cease to be a great Power. My view is a very simple one. It seems to me that having no army of any value it would be ridiculous to fight, and would only hasten our discomfiture. Between France and Germany one seems to me as atheistical as the other, and Russia worse than either. England is in no condition to fight any but a naval war, and France does not need us at sea. Grey might have stopped all the trouble three years ago by forbidding Italy its raid on Tripoli. It would have been a cheap display of strength. He will hardly be fool enough now to send a twopenny-halfpenny Army Corps to the Continent where he can effect nothing. No. Asquith will announce neutrality to-morrow, not perhaps a very *beau rôle,* but less absurd than the other.

" *3rd Aug.*— Things are marching fast. The Germans have begun their campaign against France by seizing Luxembourg, and seem to be already in Belgium. The news of this they say reached the Cabinet while it was sitting last evening (the second in the day, and that Sunday), and united all the Ministers to resolve, it is not said what. The naval reserves are being called out.

" *4th Aug.*— Grey's declaration turns out to be not quite what the evening papers said. It is evidently a compromise between the two opinions in the Cabinet. It denies the obligation to assist France against Germany, except to the extent of preventing bombardment by sea of the French seaboard in the Channel, but it affirms the duty of defending Belgian neutrality, and will lead us farther than the peace division think, for it must be remembered that all the action will be left in Grey's hands at the Foreign Office, and in Winston's at the Admiralty, and it will be easy for them to manipulate accidents into a case of necessity for despatching a land force to Antwerp. So we are not out of the wood yet. On the contrary, the British Army has been formally mobilised, and the reservists called to the colours. Our local policeman called to-day to inquire how many horses I could put up in my barns. Both Burrell and Leconfield have had a number of horses ear-marked for service, Leconfield as many as forty. I said I could put up twenty under cover, but everything connected with soldiering is hateful to me. There is talk of a British ultimatum to Germany, demanding an answer about the neutrality of Belgium being respected.

" *5th Aug.*— The thing has been decided faster than we imagined. Yesterday Asquith announced in the Commons that Grey had sent his ultimatum to Berlin about Belgian neutrality, and had received an unsatisfactory answer, and to-day the morning papers publish ' British Declaration of War against Germany."

With this last entry I close the present volume, reserving my Diary of the War itself for a posthumous occasion, if it should seem worth transcribing to those I may name literary executors of my last Will and Testament, for I am entering on my eightieth year this month, August, 1919, and shall make no further venturings in my lifetime with publicity. Suffice it here to say that my attitude during the four years the war lasted was from the first day one of severest abstention. I called it " unarmed neutrality." I knew enough of our Foreign Office ways and past doings to be quite certain that the reasons put forward by Grey and Asquith for their declaration of war were not and could not be the real reasons, and I refused to follow the pacific herd in its shameless *volte-face* from Opposition to support of the war, or find excuses for its weaknesses in the absurd false doctrine of " My country, right or wrong." I knew, especially, that the plea put forward by Asquith of " a necessity of honour " obliging us to fight for Belgium, was a false plea, good at most as a forensic argument, but quite untrue in fact, for there was not a word in any of the Neutrality treaties affecting Belgium which entailed an obligation on England, or any other Power, collectively or individually, to go to war for a breach of it.

The neutrality of Belgium was indeed already a by-word in the European Chancelleries for obsolete ineffectiveness as long ago as when I was myself in diplomacy (and I left it in 1870) — nor would any one then have been much shocked at the treaties concerning it being spoken of as " scraps of paper," which in fact they were as far as entailing any *obligation* of war on any of the signatories to maintain it went. To suppose the contrary would be to have entailed the impossible condition of a single Power being called upon in honour to fight the other four Powers had these combined to partition Belgium between them, an extremity of logic amounting on the principle of *qui nimium probat nihil probat* to initial disproof. The plea might be good enough for the occasion as a lawyer's argument addressed to an ignorant Parliament, but could not be the real one. The real cause of the quarrel with Germany, I well knew was no more honourable a one than that of our dread of a too powerful commercial rival and the fear of Kaiser Wilhelm's forcing France, if we stood aside, into commercial alliance with him against us in the markets of the world — that and a gambler's venture almost desperate, seeing that we were without an army fit to take the field abroad, and were dependent on the thousand and one chances of the sea for our daily bread at home. In this madness I would take no part. That these were the true causes of the war, and not the pretended altruistic ones I have since acquired a certain knowledge from one of its chief promoters.

The obligation of fighting in alliance with France in case of a war with Germany concerned the honour of three members only of Asquith's Cabinet, who alone were aware of the exact promises that had been made. These, though given verbally and with reservations as to the consent of Parliament, bound the three as a matter of personal honour and were understood at the Quai d'Orsay as binding the British Nation. Neither Asquith nor his two companions in this inner Cabinet could have retained office had they gone back from their word in spirit or in letter. It would also doubtless have entailed a serious quarrel with the French Government had they failed to make it good. So clearly was the promise understood at Paris to be binding that President Poincaré, when the crisis came, had written to King George reminding him of it as an engagement made between the two Nations which he counted on His Majesty to keep. Thus faced, the case was laid before the Cabinet, but was found to fail as a convincing argument for war. It was then that Asquith, with his lawyer's instinct, at a second Cabinet brought forward the neutrality of Belgium as a better plea than the other to lay before a British jury, and by representing the neutrality treaties of 1831 and 1839 as entailing an obligation on England to fight (of which the text of the treaties contained no word) obtained the Cabinet's consent and war was declared. This, I have full reason to know, was the true history of this astonishing venture entered on by Asquith through a miscalculation of the military value of Russia, and saved only from supreme disaster by the fighting tenacity of our ignorant boy soldiers, who believed what they were told, and throughout the war pretended, that it was one for liberty waged in the defence of weak nations, and to set the whole world free.

I write out here, as my last word to-day, George Wyndham's pathetic verses, repeated to me more than once by him, and which have rung ever since in my ears. I read them as prophetic of the world's doom, a doom, alas, which he, by a strange contradiction of his better nature, was nevertheless among the most active to bring about:

> The waves climb to the cliff and the cliff repels them,
>   So the waves sing their long desire of the land.
> The winds ask their way of the night, but she never tells them,
>   Complaining still of a sorrow she cannot understand.
>
> The conquered Nations of Earth have lost their birthright,
>   They sing of the long ago when their rulers were kings,
> All their value that rose once proud to set the Earth right
>   Sinks in a sob of sorrow and sobbing sings.
>
> Woe for the kings who conquer, their pride, their glory!
>   The wage of victory see, new battles to be fought —
> Those who adventuring lose, sing their souls in story
>   In the voice of wind and waves whose endeavour is nought.
>
> The music heard afar in the void's unanswering blindness
>   Is only of love poured out and lost in space.
> All songs are children of love and the loved's unkindness
>   Sad with rain that implores the beloved's face.
>
> These are the voices of God to the lost souls' anguish,
>   Wounded souls that complain when they cannot climb,
> Souls that aspire to heaven yet only languish,
>   Captives of life in pain and the bonds of Time.

APPENDICES

APPENDIX I

THE GRAND MUFTI OF EGYPT TO COUNT LEO TOLSTOI

AIN SHEMS, NEAR CAIRO, *April 8th,* 1904.

To THE ILLUSTRIOUS LEO TOLSTOY,

Although I have not the pleasure of being personally acquainted with you, I am not without knowledge of your spirit; the light of your thoughts has shone upon us, and in our skies the suns of your ideas have risen, making a bond of friendship between the minds of the intelligent here and your mind.

God has guided you to the knowledge of the mystery of that inborn essential nature according to which He formed men, and He has shown you the end towards which He has directed the human race. And you have grasped this, that man has been planted in this present existence that he may be watered by knowledge and that he may bear fruit by labour, which may be a weariness of body bringing repose to his mind, and a lasting effort through which his race may be elevated.

You have perceived the misery which has befallen men when they have turned away from the law of their nature and have employed those powers given to them to obtain happiness in a way which has disturbed their repose and has destroyed their peace.

You have cast a glance on religion which has dispelled the illusions of distorted traditions, and by this glance you have arrived at the fundamental truth of Divine Unity.

You have raised your voice calling men to that whereto God has guided you, and have gone before them in practice. And as by your words you have guided their intellects, so by your deeds you have stirred up in them firm resolves and great aims. As your ideas were a light to bring back those who had gone astray, so was your example in action a model to be imitated by searchers for truth.

And as your existence has been a reprimand from God to the rich, so has it been a succour held out by Him to the poor.

Verily the highest glory you have reached, the most sublime reward you have received for your labours in advice and teaching is what they have called excommunication and interdict. It was nothing — what you incurred from the heads of religion — nothing but a confession declaring to the world that you were not among those men who had gone astray.

Give praise to God that they have cut themselves off from you as you also had abandoned them in their creeds and in their deeds.

This, and verily our hearts are in expectant desire of what shall come anew from your pen in the future days of your life — may God prolong its extent and preserve your strength and may He open the doors of men's hearts to understand what you say, and may He urge men's souls to imitate you in what you do.   And salutations.

MOHAMMED ABDU.

APPENDIX II

THE AKABAH QUARREL

MR. BLUNT TO SIR EDWARD GREY, 9TH MAY, 1906

SIR,

" The demand made on the Ottoman Government within the limit of ten days to evacuate Tabah and other points in the neighbourhood of Akabah is so serious a matter that, as one acquainted with the district in dispute and interested for thirty years in Egyptian affairs, I feel it my duty to lay before you my reasons for thinking that the demand is an excessive one and due to a serious mistake as to facts.

" I am, of course, ignorant of the secret reasons which may possibly be impelling His Majesty's Government at the present moment to force on a quarrel with the Sultan, and if there are such what I have to say will necessarily pass unheeded. I notice that the chief organs of the Liberal press seem to regard the quarrel somewhat in the light of a crusade. But I am unwilling to believe that any such thought inspires the attitude taken by the Government, and am inclined rather to the view that they would be glad to avoid a violent issue. I therefore venture to make the following observations :

" (1) His Majesty's Government, believing their case to be a just one, probably calculate that, inasmuch as the Sultan has on several occasions yielded to pressure vigorously applied by European Powers, the same result will now be obtained. It is possible that it may be so, but the chances, I think, are otherwise. In the cases of Dulcigno, Smyrna, and Crete, to take typical examples, it was the rights and interests of Christians that were in question, and the Ottoman Government has always acknowledged a certain moral, if not legal, right in Christendom to intervene for their protection. In the present instance, however, there is no question of Christians being oppressed. It is a matter purely domestic and purely Mohammedan, and one in which the Sultan doubtless feels that the whole moral right no less than the legal right is his. The positions occupied in the neighbourhood of Akabah are closely connected with the pilgrim road and the facilities of pilgrimage to Mecca, and in Mohammedan eyes it is the Sultan's right and duty to guard them. If, therefore, the dispute with England should lead to hostilities the Sultan knows that he will be enthusiastically backed by the all but universal approbation of his co-religionists. It is almost impossible, indeed, without abandoning his whole religious claim to leadership, that he should yield to Christian menace without fighting.

" (2) I believe from an examination of printed documents and from

439

matters within my personal knowledge that the case of His Majesty's Government is technically less strong than they perhaps understand it. The delay in publishing recent correspondence prevents me, of course, from knowing what has passed lately between the Foreign Office and the Otto-man Government, but, taking the older documents as they stand with the statement made by you yesterday in the House of Commons, I think it not difficult to show that the position taken up by Lord Cromer in 1892 was founded on a double error both as to these and as to the local facts.

"Lord Cromer's contention originally was that the Sinai Peninsula, in which he seems to have included not only the geographical triangle known as Tor Sina, but the desert lands north of the pilgrim road between the Suez Canal and the Syrian frontier, was part of the old Pashalik of Egypt, and he made appeal to its "ancient boundaries." But a closer examination of historical documents has shown that this was an error, and I observe that the reference to ancient boundaries has been abandoned by His Majesty's Government in favour of another hardly better founded.

"The contention now is that the district in question has been adminis-tered by the successive Viceroys since Mohammed Ali's time in such a way as to constitute a territorial right. This I believe to be a wholly untenable view, in accordance neither with the facts of the case nor with a right interpretation of the political situation. With regard to the facts, my recollection of the district as it was in the time of Ismail Pasha and later in that of Tewfik is clear. My first visit to it was made in the spring of 1876, and I have continued ever since in touch with the Arab tribes who are its almost sole inhabitants. At that date there certainly existed nothing in the way of civil administration, and military authority was only represented by a score of soldiers holding the small isolated fort of Nakhl, seventy miles eastward from Suez on the pilgrim road, whose sole duty it was to prevent Bedouin interference with the highway for the protection of travellers. Civil authority there was none. No taxes were collected, no justice was dispensed, no conscription was enforced. I believe I am right in saying that no part of the Peninsula was included in any Egyptian mudirieh. With the exception of the monks in the Mount Sinai convent and a few persons, principally Greeks, at the port of Tor, connected with it, there was absolutely no settled population. The few Bedouin tribes, grouped principally in the south, governed themselves pre-cisely as in Arabia, according to tribal custom — and so long as they did not interfere with the pilgrim road or molest travellers they were free to all Government interference. There was not a soldier or policeman except at Nakhl.

"As to the Gulf of Akabah, I travelled up its western shore from Mount Sinai to the fort of Akabah, a distance of some seventy miles, and found not a living soul on my way, except one naked Arab, who had his home under a tussock of rough grass and was living on shellfish. I can testify, if necessary on oath, that neither the island of Faraoun nor the well of Tabah possessed a single inhabitant. It was only at the head of the Gulf, in the Wady Akabah, that I found any Bedouins. The eastern half of the Peninsula is without camel pasturage, and the Sinai Bedouins do not frequent it. The talk, therefore, of this shore as having been at any time administered has really no meaning. The commandant of the fort of Akabah would no doubt have dealt with any disturbance at the head of the Gulf threatening the pilgrim road either at Tabah or elsewhere, but the disturbance would not have come from the Peninsula, but from the Bedouin tribes north and east. There was no military force westwards nearer than Nakhl, eighty miles away. The contention, therefore, of the Ottoman Government that Tabah, within seven miles of the fort, is included in the military radius of Akabah is perfectly correct.

"The same year, 1876, I went on from Akabah north-westwards to the neighbourhood of El Arish, Rafeh, and Gaza. The few tribes I met on the road, Azazimeh, Teaha, and Terrabin, belonged to Syria, if to any settled Government. In the year 1881 I again visited this Northern district, which was then almost unknown, travelling eastward from Ismailia across the sand-dunes to the hills of Magara, Hellal, Yellak, and the rest. I found Jebel Magara, which lies west of Wady Arish, occupied by the Aiaide tribe, a section of which is to be found in Egypt, and so having a certain connection with the Nile valley, but beyond the Wady, which, it may be mentioned, is held to be identical with the river of Egypt mentioned in the Bible as the boundary of ancient Egypt, the tribes owned no such connection. Jebel Hellal, almost due south of El Arish, was certainly considered by the Bedouins as within the district of Palestine. They lived, it is true, under their tribal law, and were at chronic war with each other, but taxes had at times been levied on their casual crops by the Turkish Caimakam of Gaza, and the Sheikhs of two of the tribes had been recently imprisoned by him at Jerusalem. Jebel Hellal, it may be noted, was a long way west of a line drawn from Akabah to El Arish, and still more of one to Rafeh. Certainly no part of the district had ever been administered from Egypt.

"It seems to me, therefore, that when the Sultan withdrew Akabah in 1892 from the military garrisoning by the Khedive he logically withdrew also the military control, and with it all territorial right to its uninhabited neighbourhood. The truth is that the garrisoning of Forts Akabah and Nakhl had no administrative character in a territorial sense, and had been merely entrusted to the Viceroys of Egypt in connection with the pilgrim-age, and that the land pilgrimage having now been abandoned, the *raison d'être* of the garrison at either place had ceased. I am quite sure that if you will make further inquiries you will find this to be the case.

"I am convinced also that it is a mistake to suppose ill-faith in the present instance on the Sultan's part. The Sultan is doubtless a master of diplomatic craft, and I have never been his apologist or admirer; my sympathies having always been, on the contrary, with liberal as opposed to reactionary Islam. But I am sincerely of opinion that he has been guilty here of no trick. He is deeply interested in all matters connected with the pilgrimage, and I do not for an instant believe that his recent occupation of Tabah had any other motive than to secure the anchorage of Akabah from the possible occupation of a hostile Christian Power. He considers, doubtless, and rightly so, that the present Government of Egypt is no longer a Mohammedan but a European Government, and one therefore unfit to discharge any duty connected with the pilgrimage conflicting with the freedom of the pilgrim highway. At the same time it is wholly improbable that he should have any design of menacing either Egypt or the Suez Canal from so remote a point as Akabah, seeing that a much nearer road of invasion is already in his hands by way of the comparatively well-watered road passing through Arish, the traditional road of all invaders of Egypt. I think His Majesty's Government is quite needlessly alarmed on this head and unduly suspicious of the Sultan's honesty. If there has been sharp practice in these negotiations as far as they have as yet been published, it seems to me, if I may say it without offence, to be rather on the other side. The Grand Vizier's telegram declaring that ' in the Peninsula of Tor Sina the *status quo* is maintained, and that it will be administered by the Khedivate in the same manner in which it has been administered in the time of Ismail Pasha and Tewfik Pasha ' cannot under the true circumstances of the case have been meant as a cession of territorial rights, at least in these uninhabited districts of Akabah. Still less can it have meant a cession of such rights in the districts north of the pilgrim road, which have never been geographically or administratively part of the Peninsula. Yet Lord Cromer twisted the phrase into an admission of such cession, and His Majesty's Government seems now determined to hold the Sultan to his fanciful interpretation. It has, I fear, been decided that the Sultan should be coerced into an acceptance of a line of boundary never heard of in history and arbitrarily drawn ' from a point a short distance to the east of El Arish to the head of the Gulf of Akabah.' I need hardly point out that the fact of the English Consul-General at Cairo having communicated his interpretation of the telegram to a Minister of the Khedive at Cairo has no legal value whatever as between England and the Sultan, nor has it been asserted in any official way that the Sultan endorsed the interpretation. Lord Cromer's logic is of a kind which no doubt is often used in dealing diplomatically with Asiatic States. But a civilized Government loses much, by resorting to it, of its moral standing when the logic leads to a quarrel. It is inconceivable that it would be supported or the case given in our favour were it submitted to arbitration.

" Under the circumstances, then, is it not unwise to press this extreme claim of the Arish-Akabah boundary and the evacuation of Tabah on the Sultan as a preliminary to all negotiations? A fair settlement would probably be to leave to the Sultan the almost uninhabited region east of Wady el Arish, the ancient Biblical boundary between Egypt and Palestine. The Sultan would doubtless be satisfied with this, as would, I am sure, be all Egyptians, who have no practical interest in the far-away region except that of the Mecca pilgrimage. To press the matter to a violent issue, when the ground of right is so very doubtful, by a formal ultimatum, which will probably be disregarded, is to run the certain risk of a religious quarrel of indefinite magnitude with the whole body of Mohammedan believers. I am, etc.,

"WILFRID SCAWEN BLUNT."

APPENDIX III

DHINGRA'S DYING SPEECH AND EXECUTION

As Reported by the "Daily News," 18th August, 1909

Dhingra, the Hindoo murderer of Sir Curzon Wyllie and Dr. Lalcaca, was executed yesterday morning at Pentonville.

A copy has been placed in our hands of the statement which he drew up before the murder, intending it to be read as if it had been subsequently drawn up. To this document the prisoner referred in the course of the trial, but it was not given to the public. We may add that a copy has been for some time in the possession of certain of Dhingra's compatriots. The statement is as follows:

"I admit the other day I attempted to shed English blood as an humble revenge for the inhuman hangings and deportations of patriotic Indian youths. In this attempt I have consulted none but my own conscience. I have conspired with none but my own duty.

"I believe that a nation held down by foreign bayonet is in a perpetual state of war, since open battle is rendered impossible to a disarmed race. I attacked by surprise; since guns were denied me I drew forth my pistol and fired.

"As an Hindoo I felt that wrong to my country is an insult to God. Her cause is the cause of Shri Ram, her service is the service of Shri Krishna. Poor in wealth and intellect, a son like myself has nothing else to offer to the Mother but his own blood, and so I have sacrificed the same on her altar.

"The only lesson required in India at present is to learn how to die, and the only way to teach it is by dying ourselves. Therefore I die, and glory in my martyrdom.

"This war will continue so long as the Hindoo and English races last (if this present unnatural relation does not cease).

"My only prayer to God is may I be reborn of the same Mother, and may I re-die in the same sacred cause till the cause is successful, and she stands free for the good of humanity and to the glory of God.—Bande Mataram."

At the police court, it will be remembered, Dhingra claimed his right to commit the deed as a patriot, and at the Old Bailey he denied the Lord Chief Justice's power to pass sentence upon him. After one of the shortest trials of a capital charge on record, lasting hardly an hour, he was found guilty by the jury, and listened to the passing of the dread sentence without a tremor of his features.

Some little time before the execution took place a large crowd gathered outside the approach to the prison, but it was noticeable that there were very few Indian students among those present. Shortly after nine o'clock the Under-Sheriff left the prison, and in reply to a question as to how the execution passed off, said that everything had been in order, and that death had been instantaneous. Pierpont was the executioner. An application for leave to have the body cremated was refused, and it will be buried, in accordance with the usual custom, within the walls of the prison.

At the inquest at the prison, Mr. J. S. Master, representing the " Parsee," Bombay, was the only Indian admitted to the inquest. The jury found that the sentence of the law was duly executed.

Mr. Master applied to the Deputy Under-Sheriff for admission to the prison, but was refused. He was referred to the Home Office, where, after waiting an hour and a half, he received an intimation to the following effect:

" The Under-Secretary of State is directed by the Secretary of State to say that he regrets that Mr. Master's request to be allowed to visit the prisoner Dhingra cannot be complied with."

APPENDIX IV

MR. BLUNT'S MEMORANDUM ON PRISON REFORM, ESPECI-
ALLY AS TO THE TREATMENT OF POLITICAL PRISONERS

Forwarded to the Home Secretary, Mr. Winston Churchill, M.P.,
25th Feb. 1910

As the question of prison reform has become one of urgency in connection with the suffragette movement and the many women who have recently undergone detention for offences, more or less political, I offer these remarks founded on an experience of some years ago, which I think may be of use.

In the early months of 1888 I served a sentence under the Crimes Act in Ireland, of two months in Galway and Kilmainham gaols. My treatment was that of an ordinary prisoner with hard labour, though hard labour was not named in the sentence — that is to say, I was made to wear prison dress, sleep on a plank bed, pick oakum and perform the other duties assigned to hard labour prisoners. I was forbidden to receive visits or write letters, or to have any books to read but a Bible and a Prayer Book, except during the last week of my confinement, which was strictly silent and separate during the whole two months. With the exception of the plank bed, which prevented sleep for more than a very short portion of the long winter nights passed in darkness, I found little to complain of in the way of physical hardship. The cells were clean and fairly well aired, the food sufficient, and the exercise, a dull round in the prison yard, more than I needed. The oakum picking was so little a trouble to me that I came to be glad to secrete a piece of the tarred rope on Saturday nights so as to have it to pick on Sundays. It gave an occupation to the hands and slightly to the brain of the kind that knitting gives. It was pleasant to the sense of smell and to the eye. The life under these physical heads was hardly worse than one has to put up with on a sea voyage and may pass without special comment. The suffering inflicted on prisoners under the present system I found to be of a different kind, moral, not physical. But this was severe.

The silent and separate system in the treatment of prisoners was, I believe, introduced as a humanitarian reform with the idea of preventing the less depraved among these from contamination with companions wholly vicious. Some reform of this sort no doubt was needed. But I doubt if those who devised it either understood its full effects or intended that it should be pushed as far as has been the case. Carried out as we see it under the present regulations it is a punishment in addition to the

445

loss of liberty which I do not think society has any right to inflict for less than the most serious crimes, while its effect on the sufferers is wholly evil. Judges who pass long sentences on comparatively innocent breakers of the law, and visiting justices who go the rounds of cells periodically and find all neat and clean, do not understand the severity of the suffering inflicted by leaving the minds of prisoners for long periods of months and years deprived of any spiritual sustenance whatever. It is starvation of a kind quite as real as the cutting off of meat and drink and more enduringly pernicious.

Perhaps I am the better qualified to speak on this head because my experience in the two gaols, Galway and Kilmainham, is diverse in regard to it. Galways gaol was an old-fashioned, rambling place, with cells of various sizes, and the one I was given was well-lighted, showing a good patch of sky and the windows of a building opposite, so that there was some pleasure to be got from watching the sea-gulls as they hovered overhead, and the jackdaws and sparrows, to which it was even possible to throw bread crumbs. The discipline was lax and the warders, most of them Nationalists, were entirely friendly. I was allowed to do many small things contrary to strict regulation, such as to sit on my blanket on the floor, instead of perched on a stool, to have a Bible with good print instead of the hardly readable regulation Bible, and even to scribble verses on its fly leaves. These small infractions of the prison code were connived at, if not permitted, and they mitigated the rigour of the cast-iron laws which rule gaol life, and so made it tolerable. The warders always stopped on their rounds for a few minutes to chat with me; they were polite and kind; the Governor of the gaol paid me a daily visit of a quarter of an hour; the chaplain brought me little packets of snuff besides his spiritual consolation. I was not unhappy. In the first fortnight I read the whole of the historical books of the Old Testament, which for a political prisoner and for one who, as in my case, was acquainted with the East are most consolatory reading from their description of free life in the desert and the trust they inspire in a final justice for the oppressed and the promises they hold out of vengeance on the wicked. " Thou shalt bring my soul out of trouble, and in Thy mercy Thou shalt destroy my enemies." Thus Galway gaol was for me a house of penance rather than of punishment, and my time in it, for the first fortnight, a kind of spiritual retreat. I still look back on it with affection as a softening influence in my life.

A change, however, came with the visit of the Official Inspector of Prisons from Dublin. He happened to be a connection of my own, Charlie Bourke, a brother of the late Lord Mayo, and being a violent Unionist, he made it his business to put a stop to the irregularities he detected in the treatment accorded me. My quarto Bible was taken from me and a regulation one with small print, which hurt my eyes, was substituted. The friendly warders were reprimanded and eventually dismissed, not nominally on my account but later on, as occasion offered, on charges of drunkenness (all prison warders in Ireland at that time were addicted to drink, and so easily dismissable) and the small amenities of my life were stopped. Nevertheless, as long as I remained at Galway, things went fairly well.

It was only on my removal to Kilmainham that I was subjected to the full rigours of prison discipline and came to understand the extent of its demoralizing influence and the hatred it excites against society and what is called the " law and order " which maintains it.

Kilmainham was a gaol of the scientific modern type, with cells all of one pattern set in a circle round an enclosed central hall in such a way as to enable the chief warder to have his eye on each one of them and so to prevent any irregularity on the part of his subordinates. The discipline was thus perfectly preserved and to the prisoners a cause of constant irritation as to spying. Here, no kind of familiarity was permitted nor the least show of kindness between warder and the men under his charge. All was gloom and severity. At Galway there had been a pleasant feeling, or what was near it, between them, at least when the Governor and Chief Warder were out of sight, the warders and prisoners being much of the same class, peasants born, with the same natural ideas, virtues, vices, and weaknesses. The Galway prisoners were none of them in gaol for serious crime, the most criminal among them being a man who had got drunk and stabbed a sheep at a fair. The most of them were very pious Catholics, as their demeanour in the prison chapel testified, and I suspect that their moral lives were at least as good as the warders' and better than my own.

At Kilmainham, on the contrary, our inmates were thieves and pickpockets, the rif-raf of the Dublin streets, and a stricter rule was doubtless excusable. But, excusable or not, the effect was of the most deadening kind, deadening and at the same time exasperating. It is not good for any man to be treated for weeks and months only with contempt, and prisoners shut off in separate cells from their fellow creatures and subjected to ignominious treatment from callous masters (for such their warders were) lose all their self-respect as men, and acquire the ways of slaves. Silence and solitude when prolonged beyond a certain point of time have a physical effect upon the nerves and brain allied to mental disease and play havoc with the imagination. The sense of proportion in things is destroyed and the mind revolves upon the axis of its own imaginings to its spiritual hurt. I myself, though I had nothing really to reproach myself with, for all my crime had been to call a meeting in a proclaimed district at which I had not been given time to finish so much as a single sentence, felt myself drawn into sympathy with the Dublin criminals, my fellow sufferers, and into a revolt with them against the barbarities of civilization. How much more must it have been with these poor wretches condemned to long terms of an iron system of repression for deeds of which they were really in their hearts ashamed. Everything was done in Kilmainham to shut us out of the poor natural pleasures of light, air and sunshine, which the least beast, bird or insect can enjoy. The windows of our cells, high up and out of reach, were glazed with ground glass to prevent us from seeing the smallest patch of sky. All our actions were regulated as by machinery, and no word was spoken to us but of command. The prison chaplain was a man with a smug, false face, chosen for his subservience to the Castle, a weigher of his words and an economizer of his sympathies. The doctor was much such another, and the Governor, a worthy man I believe, at heart, was officially reserved in his brief visits to our cells. The silence of the place was a systematized oppression worse to my mind than the noisy discomfort of the rude prisons I had seen in the East, where men, perhaps in chains. are at least permitted to sit together in the sun and talk, if it is only of their sufferings. How willingly would I not have exchanged the cleanliness of my Kilmainham cell for the dirty prison yard at Aleppo where I had seen murderers and honest men placed cheek by jowl on a common footing of humanity. Here there was no humanity; it was forbidden by the rules and regulations of the Prison Board.

I left Kilmainham at the end of my two months in a spirit of revolt against all Society — a feeling which I am certain is the predominant one in every released prisoner at its gates — I left it without a smile with the eightpence halfpenny in my hand which I had earned by my good conduct — without a smile, though the worthy governor of the gaol had been good enough to tell me mine had been exemplary, and had added (good man) that instead of the customary advice given to prisoners on their discharge he would inform me of a pleasant piece of news — his wife had been brought to bed two days before, and it had been decided by him and her to name their child after me.

Such is an imperfect record of my experience of twenty-two years ago in a gaol managed on the silent and separate system. Certain alleviations in the treatment have, I understand, been since introduced, but the silence and the separation still continue without practical change in all English prisons. It is this part of prison discipline that I would see modified — I do not say abolished, for seclusion has its uses — but humanized and made less absolute.

Apart from crimes of violence which need to be treated penally — and for my part I should be quite prepared to see corporal punishment of the severest kind inflicted in cases of rape, wife-beating, cruelty to children, and the like, with capital punishment still for murder — I do not see any advantage in severity of treatment for crime unattended by violence, more than is necessary to keep loafers out of our gaols. The loss of liberty is in itself sufficient penalty to deter all but the most hardened, and for these hard labour is probably the only cure. Yet, even with the habitual thief, though he should be made to dig till he sweats and be put to labour of the least lenient kind, I see no reason that his taskmaster, the prison warder, should deny him a cheerful word, or look upon him sourly. Nor do I understand that the prison dress which he is forced to wear should be made the obvious garb of infamy it is. The Spanish Inquisition in its day clothed the heretics it burned in fantastic robes with the object of robbing its victims of all human sympathy. Our twentieth century prisons should make an end of this barbarity. It is an infamy to clothe a grown man, used to decent dress, in a boy's jacket and knickerbockers and deny him skirt enough to cover his loins. I felt the indignity of this so strongly at the outset of my prison life that I rebelled (it was my only rebellion) and made appeal to the visiting justices, and with the result that a skirted coat was ordered me, as may be seen in the annexed photograph. Why

undertake the executive duty. It is clear that none of them are willing, and, that being so, it is all but hopeless to expect them to act in concert. In my own opinion, I have no hesitation in saying that the duty of intervention is rightly England's own. England is, in the first place, by far the strongest power at sea, and this is essentially a naval affair. Secondly, England is far more free than the rest to act. Were the German Powers to intervene, there would always be the risk of a combination against them of Italy with France and England. Were France to act, there would always be danger of such a combination with the German Powers. England's island position and her entente with France leaves her free. Lastly, England is in reality the Power more than any other responsible for the partition of North Africa, the cause of the present trouble and Italy's excuse for aggression. I need not argue this point — our position in Egypt, our agreement with France seven years ago about Morocco, are sufficient proof, even without the all but certainty we have that Sir Edward Grey was secretly cognizant this summer of the intended raid on Tripoli, and consented to and approved it. It is, therefore, England's duty, one of reparation, more than the duty of any other Power, seeing what inhuman results have followed from Sir Edward Grey's connivance, to intervene now and bid Italy go no further.

I will not do Sir Edward Grey the injustice of supposing that he foresaw, when he consented to the raid on Tripoli, that it would be carried out by the Italians as a war of extermination against the Arab population. Sir Edward Grey is a worthy English country gentleman of old-fashioned Whig opinions, and he cannot have foreseen the massacres that have resulted, the lust of slaughter, the murder by hundreds of women and children. Sir Edward is neither brutal by nature nor callous, but he is singularly ignorant of any country but his own, and he is entirely without imagination, and woefully ill-advised by his subordinates. He probably had been told that the Arabs, because they do not love the Turks, would greet the Italians with joy as deliverers. And he gave consent on this understanding in England's name. The raid was, of course, immoral in itself, but not more immoral than many an English raid which he and statesmen of his Whig type of Imperialism have schooled themselves into regarding as necessities of civilisation. He foresaw nothing except, perhaps, a little bloodshed of the ordinary military type. All the same, he has made one of the most ghastly mistakes ever an English Foreign Secretary committed this country to. If you want to do any good with your agitation, you should therefore begin with Sir Edward Grey and our own Foreign Office. You should insist on his making a clean breast of the whole affair. If he says he knew nothing of it, tell him he ought as Foreign Secretary to have known. The result has been criminal, his ignorance in itself was criminal. If he admits his knowledge and consent, then insist on his resignation, as the admission involves a double criminality. Above all, insist on reparation at once being done and the murderous work being put an end to; insist on a cessation of hostilities.

Sir Edward, when closely pressed, will probably plead that England cannot withdraw from her plighted word to Italy; that England has declared neutrality; that she cannot now resort to force or to anything more than expostulation. These are idle words. It is a maxim in law that an immoral agreement canont be enforced; it is not binding either in law or equity. It is null and void. Neither is a dishonourable agreement binding in honour. Insist, with Mr. Asquith's Government, that the language his Foreign Secretary shall use to Italy shall be this: " When we agreed that you should take possession of Tripoli, we thought that the Sultan, its legal owner, would be willing to part with a province, useless to him, for money; we thought that the Sultan's subjects there would be glad to transfer their allegiance from him to you; we thought that things would go easily, that it would be a walk over for you; above all, we thought that you would behave like a civilized people, not like wild beasts, in your conduct of the war. We see we were mistaken, that you are without honour, without civilization, without Christian decency. We will have no farther part in this affair. We will not continue to be your accomplice; we summon you to recall your fleet and evacuate the ports you have seized. We insist that this war shall cease." This, translated into the polite phraseology of diplomacy, would suffice; Italy would give in. If she does not give in, insist that England shall make common cause with Turkey and mobilize the British Fleet. We have no right to remain neutral. There is a saying of the late Lord Salisbury which I was reading only yesterday in Mr. Holland's " Life of the Duke of Devonshire," and which applies well to the case: " Those," said Lord Salisbury, " who have the absolute power of preventing lamentable events, and, knowing what is taking place, refuse to exercise that power, are responsible for what happens."

As you were good enough to ask my opinion, this is what I send you, believing it to be the right and reasonable way, and I shall esteem it a favour if you will read my letter in its entirety to the meeting and invite a decision on it. Also I shall be glad to help you in any way I can to carry on an agitation on the lines suggested, including a subscription towards expenses. I believe I could raise a very handsome sum from among my Mohammedan friends.

Believe me, very truly yours,

WILFRID SCAWEN BLUNT.

APPENDIX VI

SIR ROGER CASEMENT'S LETTERS TO MR. BLUNT

I

50 EBURY STREET, S.W., 12 *May* 1914.

DEAR MR. BLUNT,

My name may be known to you — either as a friend of Mrs. Dryhurst and the late " Egypt "— or perhaps in connection with Congo and later Amazon rubber crimes. Now I am only out to end the Irish crime — and I write you on that account.

Your letter to the Women's meeting in Dublin was very welcome to us all — particularly the reference to the " Stick behind." I came over from Dublin with Professor Mac Neill of the N. University on a Volunteer mission (we are both among its chief organizers). He had to go back to Dublin on Saturday night much regretting he could not see you. I thought you were still in Chapel Street where Mrs. Dryhurst told me you used to be — only to-day I got your address in the country. Professor Mac Neill said the last time he saw you was in convict's clothes at the Four Courts (I think) where he used to work. He would very much have liked to see you — so too should I. Your " Land War in Ireland " I have often rejoiced over.

If you would care to see a wild Irishman (something of the type possibly of your old Irish Bishop who wanted the dynamite!) I would come down for an hour. There are things I would like to say to you, and hear from you before I go back to Ireland very soon. If, then, you feel disposed to have a wholly Irish talk for an hour or two with one somewhat in need of advice I should be very glad to come and see you. I go back probably Saturday to Ireland.   Yours very truly,

ROGER CASEMENT.

II

50 EBURY STREET, S.W., 14 *May* 1914.

DEAR MR. BLUNT,

I want to thank you very warmly for the delightful day and kind welcome you gave me. The copy of your book I shall treasure. Were it for nothing else but that noble preface I should treasure it.

Please God we *shall* have the Harp without the Crown some day. I may have some writings of my own — on Ireland — out before long and if so I shall so gladly send you a copy. They do not omit the " Empire " and the other " lost causes," India, Egypt, &c.— I feel always they are links with ours and we must help them. Meantime I send you a " leaflet " on the Irish language — for I see in your book that you realized how the language, too, had been marked out for destruction. So very few Englishmen, even friends of Ireland politically, ever knew or dreamed there was such a thing as an Irish language! This leaflet I wrote some years ago (1905) for propagandist purposes in the North of Ireland — and it went broadcast over National Ulster and is still going. When the momentary collusion of English Whig and Tory has passed away, and a resurgent and free Ireland emerges, with a Volunteer Army to guard and keep its liberty, rest assured that army of a recovered Ireland will *not* be used " as a new weapon of offence in English hands against the freedom of the world elsewhere." Wherever I go to-day in Ireland (and I go widely) I say that we stand in the forefront of human freedom — fighting a battle that is world-wide — and that altho' we fight it to-day with unarmed hands we shall see the day when we'll fight it with armed manhood.

I came over to London only about the Irish Volunteers, and now I return to Ireland, glad to have seen you and talked with you. When I get back to Malahide I will send you a letter I recently wrote to the Irish press on that very point — in which I cite Egypt and India. Meantime I hope the *flamboyant* appeal in this leaflet for the old tongue of Ireland will not shock you. It was written for popular gatherings — in a style they like — and it is always something to get them, in Ireland, to read at all.
                                            Yours sincerely,
                                            ROGER CASEMENT.

III

City of Dublin Steam Packet Co.'s
R.M.S. Ulster,
May 16, 1914.

DEAR MR. BLUNT,

The inclosed article from to-day's " New Statesman " may interest you. I have not any idea of the identity of the writer — but he, or she, is fairly right in the line of criticism. Whoever it is has read the Dublin papers because they only, I think, had your letter; and they only, I know, had the quotation I have marked with double lines which is from a speech of mine at Tullamore on the 19th April, to a great Volunteer gathering. I am now returning to Ireland and shall go to Ulster very soon, and try to get the Ulster Nationalists — Protestant and Catholic — pledged to fight against Exclusion and any " clean cut."

I am taking over an air gun — to shoot pellets — in the sure and certain hope it will be seized by the Customs at Kingston on arrival. The people who cannot prevent 20,000 (or 50,000) rifles with 3,500,000 cartridges from being imported by special vessel into Ulster are powerful elsewhere! The grave and unprecedented outrage in Ulster goes unchecked, unchallenged, and unpunished — and I'd wager 5 to 1 my boy's air gun, this evening, will be triumphantly confiscated and the packet of pellets too.

I am more and more convinced that Asquith and Co. mean to betray Home Rule after they have got their Parliamentary Act put to the test, by successfully passing a bare and empty formula. The " Amending

Bill" will kill Home Rule. If we had 10,000 rifles in the rest of Ireland we'd kill the British Empire. The young men in the Volunteers are out for one thing only — to revive the Fenian spirit, and please God will do it.

I had often thought of you and wanted to meet you — years ago when I read of your championing the cause of Egypt — and wondered how any Englishman could be brave enough and unselfish enough to attack the British Holy of Holies — their right to exploit weaker peoples.

Now that I have met you I am glad — and if I never see you again I shall carry with me always the memory. I wish you were young and able to come and help us in Ireland as you did in the Land War, now thirty years ago. We have so few to lead in the brave direction — and there are none of those old Bishops left. We must get some rifles in for the Volunteers. If only we could arm Irishmen again the question of Irish freedom would be settled then and there, I believe — for the British Empire can grow fat and rich but it dare not fight. A free Ireland will mean a free India — and a free Egypt in the end. I send you a most treasonable pamphlet called the "Elsewhere Empire." Read it if you are not shocked, for it is not polite literature but a crude appeal to nationality versus Imperialism. It is an instance, a poor one perhaps, of the new Ireland — an Ireland reverting to '48 and '98 — when Irishmen preached not freedom for themselves alone but freedom for all others.

Forgive a hurried line on the boat going over and believe in the very sincere regard and esteem of an Irishman who puts national life and realization wherever it may struggle in the forefront of human causes.

> Yours sincerely,
> ROGER CASEMENT.

I cannot find the pamphlet on board, I'll get it at Malahide and send it to you. R.C.

IV

> MALAHIDE, CO. DUBLIN, IRELAND,
> *22 May* 1914.

DEAR MR. BLUNT,

I came across the review of your "Land War" from a small Irish paper ("Sinn Fein") to-day in looking thro' Home papers and thought it might interest you. The writer is the Editor — Mr. Arthur Griffiths.

The Irish Volunteers are swelling daily! The whole countryside is pouring in — and if we had rifles we could get 100,000 men inside a month — and in six months they'd be one of the best forces in Europe — for the young men take to drill like a duck to water.

> Yours sincerely,
> ROGER CASEMENT.

APPENDIX VII

Miss Frances Jennings to Miss Elizabeth Lawrence

Your long letter did put some spirit into me. So few say to me *"go on"* to St. Winefreds Well; — they all say " stay," " stop," " you can't." I am feeling my way in that direction, but just now I am not moving fast. I've discovered a splendid way of getting through the mid-winter, I am travelling from farm to farm, making my houses of great barns. Outside I hear the storms raving, but my great beams don't even creak. They are such beautiful houses, great oak beams, with the scales of the bark in their hollows, and with beautiful curves in their bodies, and I see the barn-cats run and sit along the beams; and spots of sun, and often in the same house with me are milky calves and wooden chests of meal and gold straw and cider casks that bubble like a spring, or as if a mouse jumped under the water. And heaps of red apple must, which they use to bank up their fires with, the same as with peat. Then in the same house are many little mice, and big rats; and in the Spring they say they are full of singing wild birds making their nests above. I am in the cider country now (Herefordshire). As soon as I crossed the border I heard the talk of cider, and beautiful apple dumplings and apple cake. They say the farm hands here know of nothing but cider; it is their whole world. They rise to drink it, and they would not work without the cider. They think of cider alone! What a simplicity of thought! They are cider, body and soul, so they are a queer people. I drank mulled cider (warmed in a copper cup like a dunce's cap, to push deep inside the fire) with spoons of honey in it and a lump of butter out of a lustre basin.

The man here tells me: "Apples for sleeplessness — apples clear the brain, apples for the brain — juice of apple dabbed in the eye makes you see beautiful — apples give you appetite. Cider makes you eat — cider makes you hearty," etc.

My small cart is put inside the barns, they usually have three bays, and I have a cask (an " apple-pot " they call it here) turned up for a table, and a bundle of straw for a seat — most often I am on the stone threshing floor of the barns or on an earthern floor.

I am not feeling the cold at all and now have friends by the hundreds in the country I have passed across; but few as yet in front.

I have stayed with shepherds, cowmen, blacksmiths, bakers, a poet, a barber, a cobbler, at the village shop, applemen, nurses, basket makers, waggoners.

I am going to move now from Hereford to Aberystwith, then around the coast to Holywell, and to see a certain mountain they tell me is shaped like a pyramid; and is not a mountain but is a God!

I want to reach the sea and hear talk of the sea. The man here (above Stoke Edith) tells me that the hawkers and gypsies many of them used to make turf huts on the common above. They dug a hollow in the ground and piled a wall around of turf, and gradually made it round, and had a little hole in the top for their smoke to escape, and the grass grew all over the top and cast off the rain, and they had a little fire in a corner inside. Now they are driven away. I want to try and sleep a night in a manger and put up in a kiln some days and nights. I find it is a long way I have set out into.

My journey so far has been alongside the wall of the Sussex Hills. The northern border of the New Forest, across Salisbury Plain, into the Cotswold and now into what might be called Apple-land; of what is coming I am in ignorance. Lately I've slept some nights on people's hearths and nursed the fire asleep (*i. e.,* into darkness). In one village they called me, " Princess," but usually I am " The Tramp-woman," " The poor woman."

I hear some queer tales of men whose loud singing can be heard miles, of a shepherd called Basil, more than six feet tall, who, going down a steep hill, fell, standing on his head — of people so fat that they are mountains — and so old that they never die, and so strong. And at each farm I am told their milk is the richest and sweetest, and that their clay makes the best apples, and each woman tells me how she is beautiful more than all the rest; and it's all truth.

The woman I am staying with at present wears a strange sea-green glass snake at her neck, it is black and white, and sea-green, and seems Egyptian in a way. Another one I stayed with, dressed in black, wore at her neck a great silver Bee, with wings as beaten petals and scales.

This farm is called " Hazel," and many springs of water burst out about it, and the master of it has the blackest brows above his eyes, and a grand lot of words. I feel you are my friends and remember the smallest details of your kindness to me. I hope I shall see you again and hear of you.

FRANCES JENNINGS.

Received *February* 13, 1913.

APPENDIX VIII

CHRONOLOGY OF EVENTS

LEADING TO THE GREAT WAR OF 1914 AND ESPECIALLY TO ENGLAND'S QUARREL AND WAR WITH TURKEY

1875   Ismaïl, Khedive of Egypt, having involved his country in a heavy foreign debt, Disraeli (English Prime Minister) purchases his Suez Canal shares, Rothschild advancing the necessary four millions.

1876   Servia and the other Christian Provinces of European Turkey, aided by volunteers from Russia, revolt against the Sultan. They are repressed with great severity by the Turkish irregular forces. Agitation in England is roused by Gladstone's " Bulgarian Atrocities " campaign.

1877   Czar Alexander threatens war on Turkey as a crusade in their support.

A revolution breaks out at Constantinople under Midhat Pasha, leader of the Liberal party. Sultan Abdul Aziz is dethroned. A Constitution is proclaimed under the Sultan's next heir, Murad, who, being found insane, gives place to Abdul Hamid, and a Parliament assembles amid a general rejoicing of all religious sects of the Empire. War is declared by Russia.

1878   A Russian Army, having forced the Balkans at Plevna, imposes on the Sultan the Peace of San Stefano under the walls of Constantinople.

Disraeli, objecting to the Treaty as a violation of the International Peace of Paris of 1856, orders a British fleet into the Sea of Marmora and Indian troops to Malta. Derby resigns the Foreign Office and is succeeded by Salisbury.

A Congress is summoned by Bismarck to meet at Berlin to deal with the Ottoman case.

While the Congress is assembling Salisbury concludes two secret Agreements regarding Ottoman affairs, the one with Russia about Turkey in Asia, the other with the Sultan, known as the Cyprus Convention, whereby Cyprus is leased to England, with rights of supervision in Asia Minor, in return for an English guarantee of the Sultan's Asiatic dominions and promised reforms.

Salisbury denies in Parliament the existence of any convention. He accompanies Beaconsfield to Berlin, and at the first sitting of the Congress, 13th June, declares in common with the rest of the Ambassadors that he enters the Congress free of all secret Agreements regarding Turkey. The next day, 14th June, the full text of the

1878 Agreement with Russia is betrayed to the London press, and the Cyprus Convention also becomes known at Berlin.

Waddington, the French Ambassador, threatens to leave the Congress, but is pacified by Bismarck, Salisbury promising Waddington that in return for Cyprus the French Government shall be allowed (1) to take possession at its convenience of Tunis, (2) to be given an equal share with England in the financial control of Egypt, and (3) that the French claim to protect Latin Christians in Syria shall be acknowledged by England.

A new treaty, in place of that of San Stefano, is signed at Berlin regulating European Turkey, the Peace of Berlin.

Beaconsfield and Salisbury return to London announcing "Peace with Honour," and are banqueted at the Mansion House. England takes military possession of Cyprus, and appoints perambulating Consuls in Asia Minor, as arranged by the Convention.

The Anglo-French control established in Egypt. Rivers Wilson appointed Finance Minister, Baring Controller and Blignières French Minister of Public Works, Nubar Pasha (an Armenian) Prime Minister. Rothschild finances the new régime with a loan, raising the total debt to £68,000,000.

1879 Financial Reforms are introduced by the new Control in the interest of the Bondholders rather than of the people. These increase the misery of the fellahin and bring the foreign Control into discredit.

Wilson and Nubar, with the Khedive Ismaïl's complicity, are mobbed in the streets. The Khedive dismisses both, and decrees a Constitutional Government in native hands.

Rise of the first National Egyptian Movement.

Bismarck makes alliance with Austria against Russia.

Wilson, returning to Europe, appeals to Rothschild for help. The English and French Governments being unwilling, Bismarck intervenes.

The Sultan is invited to depose Ismaïl. His son Tewfik is named by the Sultan in his place with limited rights of borrowing.

The Dual Financial Control restored under Tewfik with a new Law of Liquidation, moderating the excessive claims of the bondholders.

An Egyptian Ministry is appointed by England and France conjointly.

1880 Gladstone succeeds Beaconsfield. Granville at the Foreign Office.

Granville threatens to bombard Dulcigno in company with the French fleet in order to enforce on Turkey a rectification of the Greek frontier.

Sultan Abdul Hamid suppresses the Ottoman Constitution at Constantinople. Much religious unrest in the Mohammedan world.

1881 The French, under St. Hilaire, on the pretext of punishing a tribe on the Tunisian frontier of Algeria, send a French army, which crosses the frontier, marches unopposed to Tunis, and forces the Bey to sign the Treaty of Bardo accepting a French Protectorate.

1881   The Sultan, as suzerain of Tunis, protests, but the *fait accompli* is accepted by Granville, Salisbury in opposition maintaining silence.

General rising in the Tunisian Regency against the French.

Sfax is bombarded by the French fleet and given up to pillage.

The Mohammedan rising spreads through North Africa and affects Algeria.   The Mahdi first heard of in Kardofan.

In Egypt it strengthens the hands of the National Movement, and is joined by the army. Arabi, being in command of the Cairo garrison, is recognized as National Leader.

An attempt having been made to arrest Arabi, he heads a popular demonstration before Abdin Palace, and demands the summoning of a Chamber of Notables. This, contrary to the English Financial Controller's advice, is promised by the Khedive Tewfik, and the Notables are summoned.   Great popular rejoicings.

Gambetta, alarmed at the violence of feeling in North Africa, persuades Granville to issue a Joint Note with the purpose of detaching Tewfik from the Egyptian Nationalists and promising him support against them. The Joint Note is published, causing extreme popular anger at Cairo.

1882   1st Jan.— The first Nationalist Programme is published in the " Times."

The Notables having met, insist on Constitutional Government with power, vested in a Legislative Chamber, of voting the annual budget, except that half of it affecting the interest of the National Debt.

The Controllers refuse to allow Financial Control of any kind to the Chamber.

The Notables insisting, the Ministers resign, and are succeeded by a Nationalist Cabinet, with Arabi as War Minister.

7th Feb.— A Constitution is decreed by Tewfik.

Preparations are made by Gambetta at Toulon for sending French troops to Egypt to put down the Constitution, England to send ships to Alexandria, but this is prevented by Gambetta's defeat on a question of home policy, and his retirement from office.

He is replaced by Freycinet, who adopts a friendly attitude towards the Constitution, Granville remaining hostile. Blignières, the French Controller, is withdrawn by Freycinet.

The Egyptian Parliament meets at Cairo and announces a programme of reforms. Order is maintained throughout the country. Nevertheless, under financial pressure in England, and through false reports of disorder in Egypt, Granville insists with Gladstone on intervention by force.

British and French men-of-war sent to Alexandria under Beauchamp Seymour.

The Sultan is once more invited by Granville to exert his authority as Suzerain in Egypt.

He sends a Turkish Commissioner, Dervish Pasha, with instructions

1882 to arrest Arabi and place himself in command of the Egyptian Army and restore order.

Dervish fails to intimidate the Nationalists, and confines himself to making peace betweeen the Khedive and Arabi, on whom he confers a high decoration from the Sultan, with the title of *Ferik* (Field Marshal).

The British fleet continuing at Alexandria, great popular excitement ensues.

11th June.— Riots occur with loss of life, and the English Consul at Alexandria is mobbed.

11th July.— The Europeans having been withdrawn from Cairo on board ship, Admiral Seymour bombards Alexandria, the French Admiral having refused to join in it.

The city being on fire, Arabi withdraws his forces to a defencible position inland, and Alexandria is burnt and given up to pillage.

Dervish Pasha escapes in his yacht to Constantinople, and Tewfik places himself under the protection of the British fleet.

A Grand Council assembles at Cairo, and declaring the Khedive to have deserted to the enemy, assumes supreme authority, order being well maintained. It entrusts Arabi with the defence of the country.

A conference meanwhile of Ambassadors assembles at Constantinople, the lead being taken by Dufferin to decide on a course of action.

The Ambassadors sign a protocol of disinterestedness in any new Egyptian settlement on behalf of their Governments.

The Sultan is once more invited to restore order, but while he hesitates to send troops, Gladstone despatches an army of 34,000 men to Egypt, the French Government refusing as before to take part in it, so also does the Italian Government, invited by Granville.

The British Army under Wolseley occupies the Suez Canal in spite of French protests, proclaiming that it has come, not to take possession, but to re-establish the authority of the Khedive and maintain the Sultan's suzerain rights. A similar declaration had been previously made by Seymour at Alexandria.

13th Sept.— Wolsey, marching on Cairo defeats Arabi at Tel-el-Kebir with the slaughter of 20,000 Egyptians, most of them unarmed peasants. Arabi surrenders to General Drury Lowe.

Cairo is occupied and the Khedive replaced in authority. An intention is announced of hanging Arabi, but is prevented by feeling in England. Many thousands of the Nationalists are arrested and imprisoned, and a reign of political terror prevails.

Liberal opinion in England, shocked at these extremities of repression, expostulates with Gladstone, and Dufferin is sent as High Commissioner to Cairo to make a settlement on Liberal and Constitutional lines.

Arabi, induced by a private agreement with Dufferin to plead

1882 guilty to rebellion, all other charges being withdrawn, he is condemned to death, but his sentence is at once commuted to one of honourable exile. A general amnesty is proclaimed.

Riaz Pasha resigns office, and Sherif Pasha is appointed to succeed him.

1883 The Joint Financial Control is abolished in favour of a single English Adviser, with full financial power.

Dufferin, in an eloquent despatch, while ignoring the existing Constitution of 1882, sketches a future of freedom, happiness and self-government for the Egyptians under free institutions. It is hailed as a charter of Egypt's liberty. The English Army of Occupation is to be withdrawn as soon as order can be made secure.

Dufferin's new institutions for Egypt are to consist of a Consultative Chamber without power of naming Ministers, and a General Assembly vested with the sole right of vetoing new taxation.

The French Government, resenting its exclusion from the Financial Control of Egypt, and prompted by Bismarck, turns its attention to Colonial matters. It takes possession of Madagascar.

Baring returns to Cairo as Consul-General, with special mission to set the finances on a sound footing and carry out Dufferin's recommendations as to self-government.

He announces that the British garrison shall be withdrawn from Cairo by the end of the year, leaving only " a Corporal's Guard " at Alexandria.

Bismarck's " Three Emperor " League.

A large Egyptian Army, under an English General, Hicks, is defeated by the Mahdi, who advances on Khartoum. A military police force, under General Valentine Baker, is sent to Suakim to act against the Mahdists. Baker is defeated, and Suakim is beleaguered by Osman Digna.

The Egyptian Government, being left without an army, Baring insists on the Khedive abandoning the Soudan.

1884 This being refused by the Khedive, Cromer dismisses Sherif, and takes the Government into his own hands. He reappoints Nubar Pasha Prime Minister. The withdrawal of the British garrison is postponed *sine die.*

King Leopold of Belgium is entrusted by the Powers with the founding of the " Congo Free State " in the " interests of humanity," and as a bar to Mahdist progress in Central Africa.

Gordon is sent to Khartoum to withdraw the Egyptian troops from the Soudan. He is defeated by the Mahdi and is besieged in Khartoum.

1885 Granville, to create a diversion, encourages the Italians to take possession of Massowah on the Red Sea and the French of Zeila, both being possessions of the Khedivate. The Sultan protests, but is disregarded.

An English army is sent up the Nile under Wolseley to relieve

1885 Gordon. It arrives too late, Khartoum having fallen to the Mahdi and Gordon having been slain.

Wolseley's army is ordered home. The Soudan is abandoned south of Wady Halfa.

Gladstone resigns office, and is succeeded by Salisbury.

Salisbury sends Drummond Wolff to Constantinople to arrange terms with the Sultan for evacuating Egypt.

News of the Mahdi's death.

1886 *Feb.*— Gladstone returns to power. He continues the occupation of Egypt. The Drummond Wolff Mission makes no progress.

1887 Salisbury, once more in office, renews negotiations for evacuating Egypt.

22nd May.— The Drummond Wolff Convention is signed. It provides that the British troops are to be withdrawn from Egypt at the end of three years, unless prevented by external or internal danger: on ratification the Powers to be invited to recognize and guarantee Egypt's territorial inviolability; the Ottoman Government reserves a right to occupy Egypt in above said cases of danger, but failing to restore order, England may reoccupy.

A Turkish Commissioner is appointed to reside permanently at Cairo, representing the Sultan's authority.

France, supported by Russia, threatens the Sultan with hostility if he should ratify the Convention, and at the last moment he refuses his signature, although Queen Victoria had already signed.

Salisbury, regarding the Sultan's refusal as an insult to her Majesty, resolves to remain in Egypt, with or without legal warrant.

Cromer's policy of the Veiled Protectorate.

The Franco-Russian Alliance dates from this incident.

Stanley's Expedition up the Congo.

1888 Italy joins Germany and Austria in the Triple Alliance.

Kaiser Wilhelm II succeeds his father as Emperor.

1890 Treaty of Madrid assigning joint powers of Protection to the Great Powers, including Germany, over Morocco.

Bismarck is dismissed by Kaiser Wilhelm II.

France fortifies Bizerta contrary to agreement, and talks of annexing Tunis.

Crispi complains of this in London as menacing the balance of power in the Mediterranean. His agent, Catalani, is assured by Salisbury that England would be willing, but advises " Not yet." " Sportsmen," he says to Catalani, " do not fire until the stag is within range."

Crispi thereupon commences an intrigue against the Sultan in Tripoli with Hassouna Caramanli, representative of the former Deys of Tripoli, but Italy having sustained a defeat in Abyssinia, Crispi is driven from office and the project of Tripoli is for the ·time abandoned.

1891 The French, defeated in Tonkin, moderate their Colonial policy.

1891 The fortifications at Bizerta are stopped and the policy of a war of revenge for Alsace Lorraine is practically abandoned.

Comparative quiet in Egypt, the Government is continued on lines of strict despotism and financial economy. No attempt made to carry out Dufferin's "Institutions." Egypt's material prosperity is pushed forward as an excuse for continuing the Occupation.

1892 *7th Jan.*— Death of the Khedive Tewfik. Accession of his son, Abbas II.

Cromer treats the young Khedive with scant consideration.

Resurrection of the Egyptian National Party, headed by Abbas, who acquires great popularity.

Cromer, fearing lest after the General Election Gladstone should return to power, has Milner appointed to a place in the Egyptian Finance Office, his duty being to organize the press and popularize the policy of retaining Egypt.

Milner's book, "England in Egypt," is published. It effects its purpose with the English Radicals.

Gladstone returns to power in July. He appoints Rosebery to the Foreign Office, who makes condition that Egypt should not be evacuated. Grey appointed his Under-Secretary.

1893 The young Khedive attempts to assert his authority in the matter of appointing Ministers, but is opposed by Cromer, who is supported by Rosebery.

More than one serious crisis at Cairo.

The new Nationalists demand their promised Constitution. A strong feeling prevails aaginst the Occupation.

French diplomacy alternately encourages and disappoints the Khedive, a "policy of pin pricks."

Kitchener appointed Sirdar of the Egyptian Army. Though in the Khedive's pay he takes his orders from Cromer, and a quarrel ensues.

Cromer threatens the Khedive with violent measures, and, supported by Rosebery, reduces him to obedience.

1894 Rosebery succeeds Gladstone as Prime Minister in March. Sir Edward Grey at the Foreign Office.

Riaz Pasha resigns office, and Cromer appoints Mustafa Fehmy as dummy Prime Minister in his place. English officials multiplied in Egypt.

In Turkey the Armenians, encouraged by English sympathy, form a National Committee, with the design of an independent Armenia. They ally themselves with Katkoff and the Russian Nihilists. They refuse taxes at Samsun, and are massacred by the Turkish Governor.

Japan makes war on China and obtains rights in Corea.

Death of Czar Alexander of Russia.

The French under Joffre occupy Timbuctoo.

1895 Rosebery proposes to France and Russia that they should join in intervention for the Armenians. These, believing Rosebery to be willing to dismember the Ottoman Empire, agree.

Rosebery out of office. Salisbury Prime Minister.

In Russia Giers dies and is succeeded by Lobanov. Lobanov, see-

1895 ing Salisbury unwilling to dismember Turkey, and being opposed to the creation of a buffer Armenia as likely to prevent further designs in Asia Minor, backs out of joint action with England.

The Sultan is privately counselled by Lobanov to initiate against the Armenians the severities used in Russia against the Jews and Catholic Poles.

Salisbury reverses Rosebery's policy, but having inserted a phrase in the King's Speech favourable to Armenia, makes a show of going on with it alone.

The Armenian agitation is continued in England by Gladstone, who makes his Armenian speech at Chester.

The British fleet is ordered to the Dardanelles. Armenian risings ensue at Constantinople and are suppressed by methods of massacre. But Salisbury goes no further. Salisbury commences with Chamberlain a forward Colonial policy.

Dispute with America about Venezuela.

Ashanti expedition.

Chartered company formed by Rhodes in East Africa.

Matabele War.

Rage of African speculation in England.

1896 The Jameson Raid.

Kaiser Wilhelm congratulates Kruger on the defeat and capture of Jameson.

Jameson, released by Kruger, is treated as a hero in London.

Zanzibar is bombarded by a British man-of-war.

Heligoland is given by Salisbury to Germany in exchange for the Zanzibar Hinterland.

Matabele War ended.

The Italians, renewing their attempts on Abyssinia, are totally defeated by Menelik, and find themselves in peril at Kassala.

The King of Italy appeals privately for help to Kaiser Wilhelm, who induces Salisbury to order an Egyptian advance up the Nile on Dongola. The advance is made contrary to Cromer's advice and without consulting the Khedive.

1897 Trouble between Moslems and Christians having occurred in Crete, Greece declares war on Turkey and invades Thessaly, but is totally defeated by Shefket Pasha. The Powers intervene to stop the Turkish march on Athens. The Sultan assumes the title of Ghazi (conqueror), and his prestige is increased throughout the Mohammedan world.

Kitchener, with an Egyptian army, occupies Dongola, and constructs a railway from Wady Halfa to Korosko.

Marchand starts on a secret expedition to the Upper Nile.

The Dreyfus Case occupies all attention in France, to the exclusion of foreign politics.

1898 The road having been prepared by the Egyptian army, British troops are sent to reinforce Kitchener, who advances against the Khalifa.

1898   Battle of Omdurman, with immense slaughter of Dervishes.

The Mahdi's tomb is violated by Kitchener's order, his body dug up and thrown into the Nile, he himself retaining the head as a trophy.

A solemn service is held at Khartoum of thanksgiving for " Gordon avenged." The English flag is hoisted with the Egyptian flag, and the Soudan is declared to be under the Joint Sovereignty of the Queen of England and the Khedive.

Marchand is discovered in possession of Fashoda. War nearly ensues between France and England. Marchand is recalled.

War with France having been narrowly avoided, a treaty is signed at Cairo between Cromer and the Coptic Minister, Boutros, on the terms of Joint Sovereignty of the Soudan already proclaimed, the Sultan's rights being ignored.

Russia occupies Port Arthur.

Kaiser Wilhelm visits Syria and declares himself the friend of Islam.

Paul Cambon arrives as Ambassador in London on a mission of reconciliation.

Milner is sent to Cape Town to carry out a policy of reannexing the Transvaal.

America makes war with Spain. She annexes Cuba and Philippine Islands.

Much imperialist talk in England of a coming war for the overlordship of the world.

1899   Curzon appointed Viceroy of India.

He enters into negotiations through Colonel Mead with the Sheykhs of the Arabian shore of the Persian Gulf against the Ottoman Sultan, and promises British Protection to the Sheykh of Koweït.

Milner picks a quarrel with Kruger on the pretext of a refusal of the franchise to Outlanders in the Transvaal. This pretext obtains the approval of Morley and other Liberals.

Milner delivers an ultimatum to Kruger.

The Queen of Holland writes to Queen Victoria, praying her intervention in the cause of peace. War is nevertheless declared.

Buller is sent with a large army in October. It expects no resistance, but is defeated repeatedly by the Boers.

1900   The Boers having invaded Cape Colony, Roberts is sent with Kitchener to relieve Buller in South Africa.

Kruger meets with general sympathy in Europe.

The Boers are defeated at Paardeberg, and Roberts occupies Pretoria.

The War being considered over, Roberts returns to England, leaving Kitchener to finish with the Boers' resistance. He adopts severities (recommended by Kaiser Wilhelm) of burning farms and constructing concentration camps for the Boer women, but the Boers still hold the field.

Belgian atrocities on the Congo denounced by Casement.

Stock Exchange scare of a " Yellow Peril."

1900   The foreign Ambassadors falsely reported to have been murdered at Pekin, a Joint English, French, German, and Italian force is sent to Pekin. Kaiser William announces it as a divine mission entrusted to him by God.

Pekin is stormed, and great atrocities are committed, especially by the German troops.

The King of Italy assassinated.

Death of the Emir Mohammed Ibn Rashid, chief ruler of Nejd.

Central Arabia revolts against his successor, who is defeated by Ibn Saoud.

The Hedjaz railway is built by the Sultan, connecting Damascus with Medina, subscribed for throughout Islam.

The Americans having made peace with Spain, continue to make war with the Philippine natives.

The Boer War continues under Botha, to the general scandal of Europe.

1901   Death of Queen Victoria.

The Emperor William attends Queen Victoria's funeral.

Arabi is pardoned by King Edward's intervention and returns to Egypt.

Intrigues in the Arabian Peninsula; guns secretly supplied to Koweit and Nejd from India.

1902   Methuen is defeated and taken prisoner by Delarey.

Peace of Pretoria.

July.— Lord Salisbury resigns. He is succeeded by Balfour.

A defensive alliance signed between England and Japan.

1903   The King assumes personal influence in foreign affairs. Hardinge his chief adviser.

Joan of Arc canonized.

War in Somaliland.

The Khedive visits the King at Newmarket, and is entertained by Cassel in London.

Pope Leo dies. Is succeeded by Pope Pius X.

1904   War between Russia and Japan.

Great financial speculations in Egypt.

Gorst's quarrel with Cromer. He leaves Egypt.

Anglo-French Convention assigning Morocco as her sphere of interest to France, Egypt to England. It is signed by Balfour and Lansdowne with Cambon, it being understood that nothing is to be changed in Egypt's political status.

Somaliland and Thibet evacuated.

Oct.— The Dogger Bank incident.

Cromer, confident of his popularity in Egypt, offers to withdraw the Army of Occupation to Alexandria, but this is refused at the War Office.

1905   Germany protests against the Anglo-French Agreement about Morocco, and demands a European Conference.

Kaiser Wilhelm lands at Tangier. He promises his protection to

1905 the Sultan of Morocco. Anger in France. Delcassé forced to resign.

The Conference meets at Algeciras (England, France, Germany, and Spain represented), to settle the Moroccan quarrel.

The Act of Algeciras, signed by all four Powers, proclaims the integrity and independence of Morocco, assigning spheres of commercial influence to each Power. The help of Austria is acknowledged by Kaiser Wilhelm in a telegram promising to help in return. It leads later to the combination against Germany and Austria.

Fall of Port Arthur. Peace of Portsmouth, U.S.A., between Russia and Japan.

Attempted revolution in Russia.

Financial help given to the Czar in England, which enables him to suppress the revolution.

Balfour resigns. He is succeeded by Campbell Bannerman. Grey at the Foreign Office.

1906 General Election in England with large Radical majority. Campbell Bannerman confirmed as Prime Minister, with Grey at the Foreign Office. Morley at the India Office.

Cromer's quarrel with the Sultan about Akabah. He is supported by Grey, who mobilizes the Mediterranean Fleet, and delivers an ultimatum to Turkey.

Cromer invites the Khedive to join him in pressing his claim about Akabah against the Sultan, but the Khedive refuses, the claim being ill-founded.

Cromer upon this, and finding native Egypt on the Sultan's side and the Egyptian army not to be relied on, calls for additional English troops, which are sent him.

Grey mobilizes the Mediterranean Fleet, and delivers an ultimatum which the Sultan, on failing of support from the Kaiser, yields to.

Much excitement in Egypt.

An English regiment promenading in the Delta, a conflict occurs with villagers (the affair of Denshawai).

Cromer orders severe punishment to be inflicted on the villagers and leaves Egypt for London.

The villagers, tried before a packed tribunal, are sentenced, four to death, four to penal servitude for life, others to fifty lashes.

The sentences are executed under circumstances of extreme barbarity.

Cromer receives the Order of Merit.

The whole world shocked at the occurrence.

Mustapha Kamel takes the lead of the National Party in Egypt demanding Cromer's recall.

Cromer returns to Egypt in the autumn.

He expresses an intention of administrative reforms, and appoints Saad Zaghloul, a leading Nationalist, Minister of Public Instruction.

Meeting of the first Duma in Russia.

The Shah of Persia, Muzaffar ud Din, grants a Constitution. The Mejliss meets at Teheran.

1906   France begins her pacific penetration of Morocco, French troops being sent to occupy Ujda.

1907   The Shah of Persia, Muzaffar ud Din, dies. He is succeeded by his son, Mohammed Ali, who swears fidelity to the Constitution.

A new quarrel having taken place between Cromer and the Khedive, Cromer threatens to resign unless Abbas is deposed. This being refused by the King, Cromer resigns.

Repeated lynchings of negroes in America, with growth there of radical intolerance.

Cromer receives a grant of £50,000 for his public services.

Gorst succeeds him at Cairo with a programme of friendly relations with Abbas.

The General Assembly is convened at Cairo.

Grey signs a Convention with Russia, partitioning Persia into two spheres, a Russian in the North and English in the South. This is resented by the Persian Mejliss.

Bombardment of Casa Blanca in Morocco by the French.

The Hague Convention laying down the rules of warfare, including the rights and duties of neutrals.

Riots at Lahore. Morley adopts " firm measures." Arrests without trial. Severe Press Laws.

A new era of naval activity begins in Germany. England proposes a limitation of armaments. Kaiser Wilhelm's letter to Tweedmouth.

1908   The King of Portugal, having assumed extra Constitutional powers is assassinated.

He is succeeded by King Manuel.

Mustapha Kamel dying, his funeral is attended by 50,000 persons at Cairo.

Farid Bey succeeds him, but the Nationalists are much disorganized.

Nicholas O'Conor dies. He is succeeded by Lowther as Ambassador at Constantinople. As he is ignorant of Eastern affairs the Embassy dragoman, Fitzmaurice, directs the policy in an anti-Islamic sense.

A rising in Southern Morocco. Sultan Mulai Hafiz deposed in favour of Sultan Abdul Aziz.

April.— Campbell Bannerman retires.

Asquith Prime Minister. Grey allowed full liberty at the Foreign Office. Morley at the India Office.

The Italian Government, on a trifling pretext connected with the Post Office, quarrels with the Sultan and prepares to invade Tripoli. The Italian Fleet mobilized. This is prevented by the Emperor William, who persuades the Sultan to yield the point, and the sailing of the Italian Fleet is countermanded.

Farid Bey visits London. Grey refuses to see him.

June.— King Edward accompanied by Hardinge, meets the Czar at Reval. The dismemberment of European Turkey agreed to.

Coup d'Etat at Teheran. The Shah, supported by Liakhoff and his Cossacks, dissolves the Mejliss.

1908   The Foreign Office policy in full reaction against Liberal institutions in the East.

Revolution at Constantinople.

The Sultan is forced to summon a Parliament under the Constitution of 1877.

Liberal sympathy in England expressed for the Young Turks, believing them to be anti-Islamic.

For the same reason the King telegraphs to the Sultan to congratulate him, especially on his appointing Kiamil Pasha his Grand Vizier.

England's influence for the moment becomes supreme at Constantinople, Germany's credit falling to a low point.

The Egyptians ask, as a province of the Empire, to be represented in the Ottoman Parliament.

Grey declares that this cannot be granted as Egypt has a Constitution of her own.

The Bulgarian Government seizes the Orient railroad.

Austria, with the approval of Germany, annexes Bosnia and Herzegovina.

Albania declares its independence and Crete annexes itself to Greece.

1909   *April.*— Counter-revolution at Constantinople.

Abdul Hamid once more gets the upper hand.

The Ottoman Parliament dismissed.

Many arrests of Young Turks made.

The British Embassy sides with the Sultan, the German Embassy with the Constitution.

The Young Turks, under Enver Bey, march from Salonika on Constantinople, the German Embassy providing funds.

They force the Sultan to abdicate and restore the Constitution.

Abdul Hamid's next heir, Reshad, is proclaimed Sultan Mohammed V.

Riots at Cairo against new Press Laws. From this point England loses all popularity at Constantinople.

July.— Teheran being threatened with a Russian occupation, the Bakhtiaris march there and depose Mohammed Ali and restore the Constitution. His son Ahmed, a boy of twelve, is recognized as Shah.

Grey approves the Russian policy in Persia.

Tabriz is occupied by Russia.

Great atrocities committed.

Deportation Law decreed in Egypt.

Great popular resentment.

The young Indian Dingra assassinates Sir Curzon Wyllie in London.

The extreme Turkish Party at Constantinople raise up trouble in the Arabic speaking provinces of the Empire by insisting on centralizing their power.

King Leopold of Belgium dies, leaving enormous wealth.

1910   Boutros Pasha is assassinated at Cairo.

1910 Roosevelt, passing through Cairo, rouses Nationalist anger by his violent speeches.

May 7.— King Edward's death.   George V proclaimed King.

Roosevelt, going on to London, counsels Grey to violent action in Egypt.

In complicity with Grey he makes a speech in that sense at the Mansion House, responding to which, in the House of Commons, Grey recants his policy of conciliation in Egypt, and announces an era of coercion there and in Persia.   This is accepted by his Radical following in Parliament.

The Egyptian National Congress, announced to be held at Paris, is forbidden there in deference to English representations, but meets at Brussels.

Discussion in the General Assembly at Cairo about the Suez Canal, in which Abaza Pasha opposes the Suez Canal extension arranged by Gorst and Boutros.   The Convention has to be withdrawn, to English official displeasure.

Revolution in Portugal.   A Republic declared.

At a banquet given to Von der Golst at Constantinople Bieberstein declares the Kaiser Wilhelm's warm interest in Young Turkey, and in the strengthening of the Ottoman Empire as a military Power.

The native press in Persia declares for an alliance with Turkey and Germany.

Kaiser Wilhelm entertains the Czar at Potsdam, with great slaughter of deer.

An understanding come to by the two Emperors about Persia.

The project of a railway is announced through Persia to the Indian frontier.

Kaiser Wilhelm's warlike speech to his officers at Koenigsberg asserting his " Divine Right."

1911 Farid Bey is sentenced to six months' imprisonment for having published a few words of introduction to a volume of poems, and Saad Zaghloul having refused to act with Gorst in this matter resigns office.

The question of the Bagdad railway causes much friction with Germany.

Debate in the Lords about it and the Persian Gulf, brought on by Curzon.

The French on the pretext, proved to be false, of danger to Europeans, send an army to occupy Fez.

The German Ambassador at Paris protesting that the Algeciras Convention would have to be respected, he is told by Delcassé that the French march on Fez would be continued whether Germany like it or not.

The French propose to withdraw their opposition to Germany on the question of the Bagdad railway.

The Emperor William visits London and is received with much official empressement.

1911 The Catholic Mirdites in Albania join the Albanian rebellion. Goltz publicly expresses confidence in the Ottoman army.

The Ottoman Parliament sends a deputation to the Emperor William.

The Russo-German Agreement about the Bagdad railway.

Sir Eldon Gorst dying, Kitchener is appointed to Cairo.

A German man-of-war is sent to Agadir on the Atlantic coast south of Morocco. Great official anger at this in England, objection being raised to Germany's acquiring a naval station on the northern Atlantic.

Asquith's Cabinet with one dissentient voice, Loreburn's, decides to defy Germany about Agadir.

Lloyd George makes a warlike speech against Germany at the Bankers' dinner.

France is invited to join England on the question and a land force of 160,000 men is secretly promised in case of a war with Germany; Antwerp to be occupied.

The French Government, however, not being ready for war, does not agree to this, and Grey compromises the matter with Germany by offering Germany compensation in West Africa.

England insisting, the German man-of-war *Panther* is recalled from Agadir. Great indignation in Germany against England, the Crown Prince taking the lead. Kaiser Wilhelm abandons his policy of peace in Europe, and prepares for war rather than submit to another rebuff.

Stolypin is assassinated at Kief in presence of the Czar.

The Italian raid on Tripoli, consented to by France and connived at by Grey, but disapproved at Berlin.

The Italians commit atrocities on landing at Tripoli, massacring several thousand Arab peasants with women and children.

The Turkish Ambassador appeals to Grey on the strength of international treaties to intervene, which Grey refuses, informing him that England's attitude is one of neutrality.

He denies in Parliament that he has " official information."

The Sultan, having appealed in vain to England and to The Hague, declares war on Italy.

An Italian fleet parades the Eastern Mediterranean bombarding Ottoman coast towns.

Churchill appointed to the Admiralty works up the navy in preparation for war.

Kitchener is instructed, contrary to the terms of the Sultan's firman appointing the Khedive, to declare Egypt's neutrality and to refuse the passage of Ottoman troops by land to Tripoli. This causes great dissatisfaction in Egypt where large subscriptions are raised to help the Sultan in the war.

Revolution in China against the Manchu dynasty.

The Russians insist by an ultimatum to Persia on the dismissal of the American, Schuster, charged with restoring the Persian finances. To this, notwithstanding Schuster's ability and honesty, Grey consents.

The Russians invade northern Persia.

1911 They occupy Tabriz and advance on Teheran, where they deliver an ultimatum to the Mejliss, which refuses to comply.

Grey publicly approves the Russian action.

Great massacre at Tabriz by the Russians, with public executions under revolting circumstances.

It is announced that the seat of Government in India is to be moved to Delhi.

China declares itself a Republic.

1912 Haldane is sent on a secret mission to Berlin with a view to allaying Liberal apprehension of a coming war and appeasing Mohammedan anger in India.

Grey receives the Garter.

Kitchener deals autocratically with Egypt, favouring the Italians in the war.

The Italians occupy Rhodes and the Ægean Islands. They blockade the Dardanelles, causing great inconvenience to neutral shipping.

Kitchener demands English reinforcements at Cairo.

Asquith, Churchill, and Kitchener meet at Malta where they concert measures in case of a war with Germany.

An agreement is come to with France that in case of war with Germany the French fleet shall police the Mediterranean, the English fleet guarding the North Seas.

Southern Morocco rises against the French, Mulai Hafiz abdicates.

A reported plot to assassinate Grey and Kitchener.

Sazonoff, the Russian Ambassador, Grey, and Kitchener meet King George at Balmoral.

8th Oct.— Montenegro declares war on Turkey and is followed by the other Balkan states.

Turkey makes peace with Italy at Ouchy, ceding the province of Tripoli.

Servia and Bulgaria join with Greece in an attack on Turkey.

The Turkish army relying on asurances given to Kiamil, the Vizier, by Lowther, that the prosecution of war will be prevented by the Powers delays mobilization, and, taken unprepared, is defeated by the Bulgarians outside Adrianople, its able commander, Shevket Pasha, having been replaced by Nazim Pasha.

The Bulgarians threaten the Chatalja lines in front of Constantinople.

Grey invites a Peace Conference of Ambassadors.

Poincaré speaks publicly at Paris of asserting French rights of intervention in Syria.

A bomb is dropped on the Viceregal procession at Delhi injuring Hardinge, the new Viceroy.

The Palace of Peace opened at the Hague.

1913 *1st Jan.*— Acting under advice given by the English and Russian Embassies, Kiamil summons a Grand Council of the Empire, which agrees to cede Adrianople to Bulgaria, but the Turkish army refuses

1913 to evacuate the place and Enver Pasha carrying their refusal to the Porte, Nazim Pasha is shot by Enver's aide-de-camp. Enver then proceeds to the palace and forces the Sultan to dismiss Kiamil as a traitor and to name Shevket Vizier in his place.

War is then renewed with Bulgaria.

Much popular resentment in France against the increased conscription and talk of war with Germany rather than submit to it.

The Bulgarians threaten Gallipoli.

King George of Greece is assassinated.

Adrianople surrenders to Bulgaria in March.

Germany intervenes to bring about peace between Bulgaria and Turkey.

A quarrel breaks out in May between the Bulgarians, Greeks, and Servians over a division of the Ottoman spoils in Europe.

The Bulgarians, beaten by the Servians, come to terms with Turkey.

Adrianople is restored to Turkey, and peace is made.

Grey disturbed at the failure of his joint policy with Russia at Constantinople and the growing influence of the Central Powers, recalls Lowther from Constantinople and attempts a policy of conciliation with the Turkish Government.

He attempts to arrange the question of the Bagdad railway with Germany, but fails through the unwillingness of his ally Russia, jealous of German expansion in the direction of Persia.

His obstinacy, too, about Egypt prevents a real accommodation with Turkey.

Kiamil, encouraged by Russia, attempts to regain power at Constantinople.

Shevket Pasha, the Vizier, is assassinated.

The death of Shevket a severe blow to the Young Turks, he being their ablest commander, a man of high character and an enlightened Moslem, is attributed to the Anglo-Russian intrigue with Kiamil and is a final blow to English influence at Constantinople. From that point his successors, seeing nothing to hope from the conjunction of England, France, and Russia, decide to throw in their lot with Germany as the least of the two perils threatening Islam and the Ottoman Empire.

INDEX TO VOL. II

477